REFUGEES IN AMERICA

Sponsored by the American Christian Committee for Refugees, the American Friends Service Committee, the Catholic Committee for Refugees, the National Refugee Service, and the United States Committee for the Care of European Children. (National Refugee Service was consolidated with the National Service to Foreign Born of the National Council of Jewish Women on August 1, 1946, to form United Service for New Americans, Inc.)

REFUGEES
IN AMERICA

*Report of the Committee for the Study
of Recent Immigration from Europe*

By

MAURICE R. DAVIE
Yale University

WITH THE COLLABORATION OF SARAH W. COHN, BETTY DRURY,
SAMUEL KOENIG, DOROTHY FOOTE TATE, CAROLYN ZELENY

HARPER & BROTHERS PUBLISHERS
New York   *London*

THE LIBRARY
COLBY JUNIOR COLLEGE
NEW LONDON, N. H.

REFUGEES IN AMERICA

Copyright, 1947, by Harper & Brothers

PRINTED IN THE UNITED STATES OF AMERICA

All rights in this book are reserved.
No part of the book may be reproduced in any
manner whatsoever without written permission
except in the case of brief quotations embodied
in critical articles and reviews. For information
address Harper & Brothers

FIRST EDITION

B-W

D
809
.45
C6
27881
1947

Committee for the Study of Recent Immigration From Europe

ALVIN JOHNSON, *Chairman*

HENRY BRUERE, *Treasurer*

RALPH ASTROFSKY, *Secretary*

JOSEPH P. CHAMBERLAIN

STEPHEN DUGGAN

DOROTHY CANFIELD FISHER

DIETRICH VON HILDEBRAND

SIDNEY HOLLANDER

AGNES KING INGLIS

RUFUS M. JONES

MAX JORDAN

ALMON R. PEPPER

CLARENCE E. PICKETT

CHARLES A. RIEGELMAN

LELAND REX ROBINSON

WILLIAM ROSENWALD

WOLFGANG S. SCHWABACHER

GEORGE N. SHUSTER

ALFRED F. WHITMAN

D. ROBERT YARNALL

Staff

MAURICE R. DAVIE, *Director*

Research Staff

SARAH W. COHN

BETTY DRURY

SAMUEL KOENIG

CAROLYN ZELENY

Statistical Staff

DOROTHY FOOTE TATE, *Director*

ROSALIND HEIDENHEIM

HELEN S. MEISTER

Clerical Staff

JEAN SHOSTAK, *Secretary*

FLORA BOR

REGINA FREUDENTHAL

LUISE HAESSLER

FAY KOSS

IDA LIEBERMAN

BETTY LOHNES

ELIZABETH BICKNELL VAN WYCK

Sponsors Committee

C. A. Dykstra, Los Angeles, *Chairman*
William Rosenwald, Greenwich, Conn.,
   Vice-Chairman
George ·N. Shuster, New York, *Vice-Chairman*
Edith Abbott, Chicago
Theodore Abel, New York
Louis Adamic, Milford, N. J.
James R. Angell, New Haven
Lady Margaret Armstrong, New York
Sholem Asch, Stamford, Conn.
Frank Aydelotte, Princeton
Hon. Joseph H. Ball, Minnesota
Hon. William A. Barrett, Pennsylvania
Bishop Bruce R. Baxter, Portland, Ore.
Charles A. Beard, New Milford, Conn.
Mrs. Richard J. Bernhard, New York
Bruce Bliven, New York
Clarence M. Bookman, Cincinnati
Henry Bruère, New York
Mark Brunswick, New York
Ernest W. Burgess, Chicago
Allen T. Burns, New York
Fred M. Butzel, Detroit
Henry J. Cadbury, Cambridge
Henry Seidel Canby, New York
Joseph P. Chamberlain, New York
Harry Woodburn Chase, New York
Ben M. Cherrington, Denver
Morris R. Cohen, Washington, D. C.
Alfred E. Cohn, New York
Richard K. Conant, Boston
Hon. Edward F. Corsi, New York
Gardner Cowles, Jr., Des Moines
Virginius Dabney, Richmond
Hon. Joseph E. Davies, Washington, D. C.
Hon. Samuel Dickstein, New York
Marshall E. Dimock, Evanston, Ill.
Harold W. Dodds, Princeton
David Dubinsky, New York

Stephen Duggan, New York
Clark M. Eichelberger, New York
Milton S. Eisenhower, Manhattan, Kan.
Frederick M. Eliot, Boston
Edwin R. Embree, Chicago
Henry Pratt Fairchild, New York
Dorothy Canfield Fisher, Arlington, Vt.
Very Rev. Vincent J. Flynn, St. Paul
Guy Stanton Ford, Washington, D. C.
Rev. Harry Emerson Fosdick, New York
Dr. Hugo A. Freund, Detroit
Carl J. Friedrich, Cambridge
Very Rev. Robert I. Gannon, S.J., New York
Seth T. Gano, Boston
Harry Gideonse, Brooklyn
Lester Granger, New York
William Green, Washington, D. C.
William Haber, Washington, D. C.
Gordon Hamilton, New York
Henry I. Harriman, Boston
Rufus C. Harris, New Orleans
Hon. Earl G. Harrison, Philadelphia
Shelby M. Harrison, New York
Hon. E. H. Hedrick, West Virginia
Adolph Held, New York
Christian A. Herter, Washington, D. C.
Dietrich von Hildebrand, New York
Sidney Hollander, Baltimore
Quincy Howe, New York
B. W. Huebsch, New York
Frederick M. Hunter, Eugene, Ore.
Mary E. Hurlbutt, New York
Agnes King Inglis, Washington, D. C.
Hon. Stanley M. Isaacs, New York
Alvin Johnson, New York
Charles S. Johnson, Nashville
Rufus M. Jones, Haverford
Max Jordan, New York
Samuel Joseph, New York
Hon. B. W. Kearney, New York

Frank Kingdon, New York
Freda Kirchwey, New York
Rufus B. von Kleinsmid, Los Angeles
Hertha Kraus, Bryn Mawr
Monte M. Lemann, New Orleans
Katharine F. Lenroot, Washington, D. C.
Hon. John Lesinski, Michigan
Samuel M. Levitas, New York
Isidor Loeb, St. Louis
Rev. Sidney Lovett, New Haven
Robert S. Lynd, New York
Henry N. MacCracken, Poughkeepsie
Robert M. MacIver, New York
Thomas Mann, Pacific Palisades, Calif.
Hon. James G. McDonald, Bronxville, N. Y.
Carey McWilliams, Los Angeles
Leonard W. Mayo, Cleveland
Eliot G. Mears, Stanford University
Hon. George P. Miller, California
Robert A. Millikan, Pasadena
Felix Morley, Haverford
Hon. Newbold Morris, New York
Thomas F. Mulholland, New York
Paul Muni, Hollywood
Philip Murray, Washington, D. C.
John W. Nason, Swarthmore
* William A. Neilson, Falls Village, Conn.
Brig. Gen. Henry Clay Newcomer, U. S. A. (Ret.)
Rt. Rev. Msgr. Patrick A. O'Boyle, New York
Howard W. Odum, Chapel Hill, N. C.
William Fielding Ogburn, Chicago
Bishop G. Bromley Oxnam, Boston
Frederick D. Patterson, Tuskegee, Ala.
James George Patton, Denver
Mrs. Malcolm E. Peabody, Syracuse
Rev. Almon R. Pepper, New York
Ralph Barton Perry, Cambridge
Walter W. Pettit, New York
Clarence E. Pickett, Philadelphia
* Hon. Gifford Pinchot, Milford, Pa.
Hon. Justine Wise Polier, New York
Arthur Upham Pope, New York
Kenneth L. M. Pray, Philadelphia
* Deceased.

Hon. Joseph M. Proskauer, New York
A. Philip Randolph, New York
Aurelia H. Reinhardt, Oakland, Calif.
Wilfred Reynolds, Chicago
Charles A. Riegelman, New York
Leland Rex Robinson, New York
Mrs. Franklin D. Roosevelt
Most Rev. Joseph F. Rummel, S.T.D., New Orleans
Richard B. Scandrett, Jr., New York
Rt. Rev. William Scarlett, St. Louis
Arthur M. Schlesinger, Cambridge
Wolfgang S. Schwabacher, New York
Murray Seasongood, Cincinnati
Charles Seymour, New Haven
Harlow Shapley, Cambridge
Rev. Guy Emery Shipler, New York
James T. Shotwell, New York
William J. Shroder, Cincinnati
Lee P. Sieg, Seattle
Rabbi Abba Hillel Silver, Cleveland
William F. Sollmann, Wallingford, Pa.
Rev. Russell H. Stafford, Cambridge
Rt. Rev. W. Bertrand Stevens, Los Angeles
Hon. John W. Studebaker, Washington, D. C.
Linton B. Swift, New York
Raymond Swing, Washington, D. C.
Ordway Tead, New York
John J. Tigert, Gainesville, Fla.
Channing Tobias, New York
D. Elton Trueblood, Stanford University
Hon. Robert F. Wagner, New York
Bruno Walter, New York
Constance Warren, Bronxville, N. Y.
Robert J. Watt, Washington, D. C.
Max Weinreich, New York
Mrs. Joseph M. Welt, Detroit
William L. White, Emporia
Alfred F. Whitman, Boston
Ray Lyman Wilbur, Stanford University
Mary E. Woolley, Westport, N. Y.
D. Robert Yarnall, Philadelphia
Adm. Harry E. Yarnell, U. S. N. (Ret.)
Owen D. Young, New York

CONTENTS

INTRODUCTION: Purpose and Method of the Study   xi
    I. CONDITIONS CAUSING FLIGHT   1
   II. EXTENT AND CHARACTERISTICS OF THE REFUGEE MOVE-
       MENT   15
  III. WHAT THE REFUGEES THINK OF AMERICA   47
   IV. THE DISTRIBUTION OF REFUGEES IN THE UNITED STATES   77
    V. PROBLEMS ON ARRIVAL   84
   VI. ASSISTING THE REFUGEE   93
  VII. THE PROBLEM OF ECONOMIC ADJUSTMENT   119
 VIII. OCCUPATIONAL ADJUSTMENT OF THE REFUGEES   128
   IX. FACTORS IN THEIR SOCIAL ADJUSTMENT   143
    X. THEIR SOCIAL AND CULTURAL ADJUSTMENT   156
   XI. ORGANIZED LIFE OF THE REFUGEES   171
  XII. THE REFUGEES AS CITIZENS   189
 XIII. YOUNG REFUGEES   204
 XIV. BUSINESSMEN AND MANUFACTURERS   233
  XV. PHYSICIANS   257
 XVI. LAWYERS   287
XVII. PROFESSORS AND SCIENTISTS   300
XVIII. ARTISTS AND WRITERS   324
 XIX. OTHER PROFESSIONS   345
  XX. WHAT AMERICANS THINK OF THE REFUGEES   369
 XXI. SOLUTION OF THE REFUGEE PROBLEM AND ITS INTERNA-
       TIONAL ASPECTS   391

APPENDICES
    A. National and local agencies participating in the Study   405
       Questionnaire returns by states and number of communities   413
    B. Study forms   414
    C. Nobel Prize Winners   432
       Refugees listed in *Who's Who in America*   432
       Refugees listed in *American Men of Science*   435
INDEX   441

PURPOSE AND METHOD OF THE STUDY

The recent refugee movement to the United States has aroused unusual interest because of its dramatic character, the type of people it involved, and the international unrest characterizing the period when it occurred. Composed primarily of middle- and upper-class persons, it contrasted sharply with earlier immigration movements and attracted the interest and sometimes the opposition of American professional and business people who hitherto had seldom if ever been directly concerned with immigrant arrivals as associates or as competitors. Since a majority of the refugees were either Jews by confession or "non-Aryans," that is, Jews by descent only, the movement provided a basis for anti-Semitic agitation, which was intensified by German propaganda. The refugees became the object of widespread discussion. On the one hand, they were hailed as a superior group greatly enriching American cultural and economic life and, on the other hand, as a destructive and subversive element in our society.

What are the facts? How many of our recent immigrants have been refugees? To what nationalities and religious groups do they belong? How have our immigration laws functioned during this period, and how have they been administered? Where have the refugees settled? How have they adjusted themselves to American life? What do they think of Americans? What do Americans think of them? What is their attitude toward assimilation? Do they intend to remain or to return? What effect have they had on American society? What contributions have they made to our culture and economy? In short, have they been an asset or a liability to this country?

It was in the attempt to answer these and similar questions in an objective and impartial way that this Study was undertaken. It is essentially a fact-finding investigation. As one refugee commented in his reply to our questionnaire, "I don't think one can solve the so-called refugee problem by putting up another statistic. However, it's worth trying."

Though on a much smaller scale, the present Study is perhaps most comparable to the investigation conducted by the United States Immigration Commission appointed under the Congressional Act of February 20, 1907, in being a nation-wide study of a contemporary immigration movement, comprehensive in scope, and involving field surveys and the collection of firsthand materials.

The committee was able to make a truly nation-wide study only because it had the co-operation of over 200 agencies or committees, some of them state-wide, located in 41 states and the District of Columbia. As a result of their combined efforts, replies to the questionnaire were received from recent immigrants in 638 communities in 43 states and the District of Columbia. If the returns from the physicians' questionnaire should be included, the coverage would be increased by the addition of one state and 234 more communities. These data are given in detail in Appendix A.

The organizational plan adopted for the purpose of collecting original data was twofold: one for New York City and another for the rest of the country. In regard to the latter, the organization of the work was arranged in the following manner. The initial step consisted in securing the participation of the branches of local co-operating agencies of the national refugee service organizations sponsoring the Study. These organizations invited their member agencies to take part in the Study, explained its purpose and method by letter and bulletin, and in several instances—notably by the National Refugee Service* and the American Christian Committee for Refugees—sent field representatives to various communities to follow up with further explanation and to help organize the local survey. The director of the Study also met with representatives of the local agencies and committees in a number of cities in the East and the Middle West, and attended several regional conferences, in which the proposed questionnaire and methodology of the Study were discussed.

The Study Committee then secured the co-operation of national organizations in the field of general immigrant welfare. Among them were the American Federation of International Institutes, the National Council of Jewish Women, the Hebrew Sheltering and Immigrant Aid Society (HIAS), the Jewish Agricultural Society, and the National Board of the Young Women's Christian Association. These organizations co-operated in the Study both through their national offices and their branches or member agencies throughout the country.

The several hundred national and local agencies participating in the Study are listed by state and locality in Appendix A. They include both sectarian and nonsectarian organizations. In numerous localities the Study Committee had the co-operation of several agencies. These either set up a special interdenominational or co-ordinating committee or they worked closely together while maintaining their separate identities. Some communities, like Philadelphia, already had a local co-ordinating committee for agencies serving the foreign-born, while others engaged in a joint

---

* The National Refugee Service has since merged with the Section of Service to Foreign Born of the National Council of Jewish Women, to form United Service for New Americans, Inc.

enterprise for the first time. In some instances, such as in New Haven and Detroit, the local Council of Social Agencies served as the sponsoring and co-ordinating agency. The widest coverage so far as nationality and religion among the recent immigrants are concerned came from the International Institutes.

The local co-operating committees often had the assistance of family welfare societies and other social and civic agencies, both public and private. In some instances graduate students in local colleges and universities helped in the distribution of questionnaires, in obtaining life stories, and in securing data on community backgrounds and attitudes. Of outstanding importance was the co-operation of the recent immigrants themselves. Both individually and through their organizations they assisted the local co-operating committees throughout the country in a number of ways, such as explaining the purpose of the Study at meetings of their group, building up a list of names of refugee immigrants in the community, and distributing questionnaires. In many communities this co-operation between American agencies and immigrant organizations was a new adventure.

The local co-operating committees drew up master lists or made estimates of the number of refugees in their communities, assisted the Study Committee in compiling a file of refugee physicians and dentists, distributed the general questionnaire and in numerous instances the special questionnaires on business enterprise and on refugee organizations, interviewed refugees for life stories, reported on community backgrounds and attitudes, and investigated special problems.

In the case of New York City, a modified plan of operation was adopted because of the size of the community and of the refugee population. Since New York was the headquarters of the Study, the Study Committee itself assumed direct responsibility for the collection of data from that area. In this endeavor it had the co-operation of its sponsors, the national refugee service organizations, the other national organizations co-operating in the Study whose headquarters were also in New York City, numerous local immigrant-aid and social and civic agencies, and the organizations established by refugees which were especially numerous in that city. Some of them, like Selfhelp of Emigres from Central Europe, Inc., had a national membership to whom questionnaires were sent. In the case of the special study of business enterprises established by refugees, the Study Committee had the co-operation of the American Federation of Jews from Central Europe, Inc., a refugee organization also with a membership extending beyond the city of New York. For the investigation of special groups of refugees such as children, scholars, and physicians, the Study Committee was aided by the United States Committee for the Care of European Children, the European Jewish Children's Aid, Inc., the Emergency Committee in Aid of Displaced Foreign Scholars, the National Committee for

Resettlement of Foreign Physicians, and other committees serving special groups.

The method adopted in studying the adjustment of the refugees and their effect on American society consisted of two main procedures: (1) the analysis of existing materials and (2) the collection of new data. In the first instance, published materials dealing with refugees—books, magazine articles, pamphlets, and newspapers, including both the English-language and the foreign-language, and especially the refugee press—were analyzed. Also the available records of official and private agencies were consulted. The Immigration and Naturalization Service not only provided its regular statistical material but made special tabulations as well. The files of the Emergency Committee in Aid of Displaced Foreign Scholars and those of the Lawyer Retraining Program of the American Committee for the Guidance of Professional Personnel were turned over to the Study Committee. The research staff also consulted the files of the Committee on Refugee Musicians, the Committee on Refugee Jewish Ministers, the Committee on Refugee Librarians, and the National Committee for Resettlement of Foreign Physicians. It analyzed thousands of case records of the refugee service organizations aiding children in particular or refugees in general.

For the collection of original data bearing directly on the questions to be studied, various methods were used, including general and special questionnaires, case studies, life history documents, community surveys, interviews, the use of informants, and participant observation. The effort was made to gather qualitative as well as quantitative material so as not to lose sight of the individual. The Study also undertook to focus on the community in order to observe the individual in his community setting and the reaction of the community to him.

The largest body of firsthand data collected consists of the replies to the general questionnaire. This questionnaire was designed for the individual immigrant 16 years of age or over. Care was taken to have it as self-explanatory as possible so as to avoid the need of interviews and to obtain the maximum number of returns. The questionnaire was tested in several preliminary trials before being printed in final form. A copy of the questionnaire is reproduced in Appendix B.

The problem then arose of how to reach a representative sample of the refugee population. No national file of such individuals exists. The closest approximation to such a register would be the records of the Alien Registration Division of the United States Immigration and Naturalization Service established in 1940 in compliance with the Alien Registration Act. All recent immigrants except those who had become citizens by 1940 would be included. Only a small proportion, however, of the five million aliens thus registered are recent immigrants, and a still smaller proportion are ref-

ugees. Since the records are not filed by year of arrival, it would be necessary to sort the entire file in order to segregate that group with which the
Study is concerned. This was not deemed advisable since, during the years
the United States was at war, recent immigrants, like native Americans,
moved about the country a great deal, with the result that a considerable
proportion of the addresses in the file were not up to date. A special tabulation of the registrants by year of arrival and state of residence in 1940 was
useful, however, in giving some idea of their numbers and geographic
distribution, which was a guide in building up our list of co-operating
agencies throughout the country.

To secure an adequate sample of recent immigrants to approach for
questionnaire purposes the Study Committee thus had to resort to the files
of the refugee organizations—the largest list of such names and addresses
in existence—and to methods of extending these lists by the addition of
non-agency cases. The agency lists, it should be noted, included not simply
those refugees who had received financial assistance but also those who
came to the agency for placement, resettlement, advice on immigration
matters, and other technical services. The following sources were used
in the various communities in establishing a list of recent immigrants not
known to the refugee service agencies: the enrollment records of English
and citizenship classes; the membership lists of International Institutes,
social settlements, young people's associations, and similar organizations;
the membership lists of societies established by and for refugees; the faculty
lists of colleges and universities; and the cases of individuals known personally to board members, social workers, and refugees assisting in the
Study. Frequently a refugee not on the list of a social agency sent in the
names of similar persons in his circle of acquaintances. Other cases were
brought to our attention through notices about the Study that appeared in
agency bulletins, professional journals, the general press, and the foreign-
language newspapers. The Foreign Language Press Division of the Common Council for American Unity was most helpful in publicizing the
Study in the foreign-language press, and some of the refugee newspapers,
like *Aufbau*, carried editorials as well as news stories. As a result, many
refugees wrote in for questionnaires or sent in life stories.

The questionnaires were distributed either in person or through the mail.
In the latter case a covering letter from the co-operating committee always
accompanied it, and a return addressed envelope was enclosed. The questionnaires were returned either to the local committee or directly to the
Study headquarters. The questionnaire called for no signature. A few co-
operating committees made the mistake of numbering the questionnaire or
the return envelopes. Though done solely with the purpose of checking on
the number of returns and of being able to follow up those not heard from,
it was interpreted by many of the recipients as being a means of identifi-

cation, and the number was cut or blotted out or no return was made. With the assistance of refugee leaders the wrong impression made was somewhat rectified.

The original plan had been to distribute some five to ten thousand questionnaires on a sampling basis ranging from complete coverage in communities with fewer than 100 recent immigrants to 10 per cent of the estimated refugee population of the largest cities. Most of the co-operating agencies, however, preferred to circularize the entire list, with the result that some 50,000 questionnaires were sent out. A large number were returned unclaimed because of change of address, amounting in some of the large mailings to one-third of the total.

When the books were closed 11,233 questionnaire returns had been received, which were sufficiently complete to be used. Only 126 had to be discarded because essential information, such as date of arrival or country of origin, was lacking. The proportion discarded is remarkably small for an investigation of this size. Both the number and the rate of returns were highly gratifying. Europeans are not accustomed to giving information other than police identification; they are not used to questionnaires, especially anonymous ones, inquiring about personal and business matters. Moreover, many of the refugees were still affected by the fear under which they had lived in Europe and suspicious of the effect an inquiry might have on themselves or their relatives who were still living under Nazi terror. In fact, it was an extraordinary undertaking to utilize questionnaires in a study of recent immigrants. It was feasible only because of the unique characteristics of the present-day group which consists so largely of individuals with sufficient education and willingness to co-operate in responding to a complex questionnaire. The intelligence of the group is further evidenced by the accuracy and completeness with which they filled out the forms. It is significant, further, that, although the group is composed of recent arrivals, they were competent to use a questionnaire in English. Only in the case of New York, Chicago, and Philadelphia, containing the largest concentrations of recent immigrants, was it necessary to provide a questionnaire in German, and even there it was required by only a small proportion of the refugee group, mostly elderly people. It is also noteworthy that, although the questionnaire was designed to be anonymous, a large proportion of the respondents signed their names.

The 11,233 questionnaire replies, received from 638 communities in 43 states and the District of Columbia, constitute in themselves a goodly body of data. More important, they constitute a representative sample of the total body of refugee immigrants, estimated to be between 250,000 and 300,000. Since no such separate classification as refugees exists under our laws, but only immigrants admitted for permanent residence and nonimmigrants for temporary stay, there are no official figures on the number of refugees admitted. Resort must be had to estimates, which are given in Chapter II. As to year of arrival, the cases included in our sample practically coincide with the total group, as is seen in the following graph.

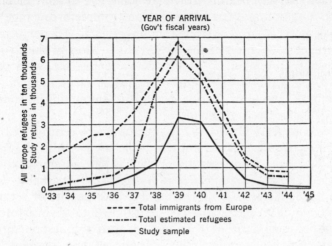

YEAR OF ARRIVAL
(Gov't fiscal years)

----- Total immigrants from Europe
--·--·-- Total estimated refugees
——— Study sample

As regards nationalities represented, they show a similar ranking so far as the major groups are concerned, with the exception of a higher representation of the Germans and Austrians, and a lower representation of the Poles and French. As is mentioned in Chapter II, only a small proportion of the Italian immigrants fall into the refugee category, so that their numerical ranking is much closer to the percentage in the sample study than in the estimated number of refugees according to immigration statistics.

The official immigration statistics do not include data on religion. Up to the end of 1943, however, the Immigration Service reported on the number of Hebrew arrivals, under the caption "race or people." Jews thus constitute from one-half to two-thirds of the estimated number of refugees. Our sample, however, plus other aspects of our Study, indicate that the proportion is probably closer to four-fifths. Protestants constitute about 9 per cent, and Catholics 6 per cent, and the balance consists of a small proportion of persons of no religious affiliation or cases where affiliation was not designated.

As to occupational distribution, our sample follows practically the same rank order as the total estimates, with some over-representation of professional and business classes, and considerable under-representation of the unskilled labor group. The Study sample, however, being based on known refugees, is more accurate than the estimate based on over-all statistics of immigrants from certain countries (see Chapter II). Although comparable data concerning the whole group are lacking, the sample is probably somewhat biased as to educational background, since the more educated and articulate are more likely to respond to questionnaires.

PER CENT DISTRIBUTION OF REFUGEE IMMIGRANTS BY COUNTRY OF BIRTH

Country of Birth	Total Estimated Refugees*	Study Sample
Total	*100.0*	*100.0*
Germany, incl. Austria	53.1	82.3
Poland	11.1	5.2
Italy	8.9	1.0
Czechoslovakia	5.0	4.1
Soviet Russia	3.4	2.0
France	2.7	.6
Hungary	2.2	1.7
Netherlands	1.6	.6
Yugoslavia	1.5	.4
Greece	1.5	.1
Belgium	1.3	.1
Rumania	1.2	.3
Spain	1.2	**
Norway	1.1	**
Finland	.9	**
Lithuania	.8	.2
Denmark	.7	**
Latvia	.4	.1
Bulgaria	.2	.1
Estonia	.1	**
Other European countries of refugee emigration	1.1	1.2

* Estimates based on official immigration statistics by selected races or peoples, provided by the Immigration and Naturalization Service.
** Less than one-tenth of 1 per cent.

PER CENT DISTRIBUTION OF REFUGEE IMMIGRANTS BY OCCUPATIONAL BACKGROUND

Occupation	Total Estimated Refugees*	Study Sample
Total	*100.0*	*100.0*
Professional persons	8.5	17.8
Proprietors, managers and officials	13.0	29.7
Clerks and kindred workers	5.8	10.8
Skilled workers	6.3	1.6
Semiskilled workers	3.3	1.6
Unskilled workers	9.4	0.7
No occupation	53.7	37.8

* Based on official immigration statistics by selected races or peoples, provided by the Immigration and Naturalization Service.

With regard to sex distribution the sample is somewhat biased on the male side, with 56 per cent males as compared with 49 per cent in the case of the total estimated refugee group. The distribution as to age is closely comparable, as is seen in the following table.

Per Cent Distribution of Refugee Immigrants Over 16 Years Old, by Age on Arrival

Age	Total Estimated Refugees*			Study Sample		
	Total	Male	Female	Total	Male	Female
16–45 years	73.7	73.8	73.5	65.2	61.9	69.6
Over 45 years	26.3	26.2	26.5	34.8	38.1	30.4

* Based on official immigration statistics by selected races or peoples, provided by the Immigration and Naturalization Service.

Regarding geographical distribution by states, the only comparable material, however inadequate, is that of all aliens registered in 1940 who entered the United States during the period of the calendar years 1933 through 1940. While these figures include perhaps a majority of the refugee immigrants, they also include a great number of non-refugees. The distribution of our sample cases corresponds very closely to that of the total alien group, which is probably due to the fact that immigrants in general have tended to concentrate in certain states. Compared, for example, with 1940 census data on the total foreign-born white population, our sample cases show practically the same distribution (see Chapter IV).

Checked by these sources and by the results of other types of investigation carried on by the Study, we feel confident that the general questionnaire returns constitute an adequate and representative sample.

A special questionnaire was drawn up for refugee physicians and dentists, in which the Committee had the invaluable assistance of American physicians conversant with the field and of refugee physicians themselves. It was mailed to 4,774 individuals whose names and addresses were complied in an effort to create a master list. The basis of the list was the file of the National Committee for Resettlement of Foreign Physicians. To this were added the names furnished by the local co-operating committees throughout the country and by refugee physicians and dentists themselves. The list was very adequate as measured by the following facts. According to the official immigration statistics, the total number of physicians admitted to the United States during the entire period 1933 to 1944 from all countries was 6,426. The number of these admitted from countries of refugee emigration was 4,657, according to the statistics by country of last permanent residence, or 5,480, according to the statistics by race or people. (Figures on occupation are not given by country of birth.) On the generous assumption that all physicians and dentists admitted from these sources during this entire period were refugees, then the number would be not far from 5,000.

At the time the tabulations were started some 1,600 replies had been received. Only 23 had to be discarded because of insufficient information. Fifty-three questionnaires were returned too late to be included, but they would not have altered the general findings. Replies were thus received from 33.5 per cent of the questionnaires sent out. They constitute a 40 per cent return if the number of questionnaires that failed to reach their destination because of incorrect addresses (709) is subtracted from the total original mailing (4,774). This is a remarkably high rate of return, especially since the questionnaire required the respondent to give his name and address. A copy of the questionnaire is included in Appendix B. The replies constitute a 30 per cent sample of the larger of the estimated number of refugee physicians (5,480), and even a 25 per cent sample of all physicians admitted from all countries (6,426) during this period. In either case, it is clearly adequate in size, and as compared with the characteristics of the physicians as recorded in the file of the National Committee for Resettlement of Foreign Physicians it is very representative.[1]

Other questionnaires used in the Study include one asking for information on the purpose, membership, and activities of organizations of recent immigrants, to be filled out by the secretary or other officer, and one on business enterprises established by recent immigrants, to be answered by the individual in question. Both forms are reproduced in Appendix B. The Study Committee received 74 replies to the questionnaire on organizations and 271 replies to the business questionnaire. The information was supplemented in both instances by numerous interviews and by examination of the literature on the subject. In the study of business enterprises, the Committee also collected data on the type of business and nationality of the entrepreneur in several thousand instances and analyzed the several hundred unpublished case records collected in 1939 by the National Coordinating Committee which were made available to it.

Another important body of firsthand material collected consists of our 200 life stories of recent immigrants and essays on their impressions of America. Some of the life stories were autobiographical. Others were based on interviews by trained workers, to whom was supplied a Guide to Interviewers and Suggested Topics for the Interview, a copy of which appears in Appendix B. Cases in the body of the report are given in the original form, so the reader can judge the validity of the inferences made. The life stories are representative of the major occupational, religious, and nationality groups and also of the various age groups and both sexes.

A schedule was prepared for a Report on Community Backgrounds and Attitudes, which the local co-operating committees filled out. The data were obtained from the United States Census and various local statistical sources, from interviews with government officials, businessmen, civic leaders, social workers, and representatives of the recent immigrant group, and from the experience and observation of those working in the field of immigrant adjustment. A copy of the form is reproduced in the Appendix.

[1] Central Index of Refugee Physicians, Dentists and Medical Scientists, and Tabulation as of July, 1944, Division of Statistics, National Refugee Service (mimeographed).

Over fifty of these community survey reports were obtained. They came from all sections of the country except the Northwest, where the number of recent immigrants is negligible.

Finally, the method of interviewing was extensively used. Valuable information was thus obtained from persons, both native Americans and recent immigrants, who were representative of various groups and callings and possessive of special knowledge and experience bearing on the adjustment of refugees and their effect in various spheres of American society. Among the persons thus seen were businessmen, representatives of the various professions, college presidents and deans, school principals and teachers, labor leaders, foreign consuls, newspaper editors, the officers of refugee societies and organizations, social workers, social scientists and other special students of the problem, and refugees in all walks of life. Many of the latter either furnished personal data about themselves or served as informants regarding their particular nationality or occupational group. In addition, members of the research staff attended numerous meetings of refugee organizations and private social gatherings, visited their neighborhoods and places of recreation, and otherwise engaged in participant observation.

To the great number of people throughout the nation who took direct part in the Study or furnished information or provided counsel and guidance, the Committee owes a great debt of gratitude. It keenly regrets that they are too numerous to mention.

REFUGEES IN AMERICA

CHAPTER I

CONDITIONS CAUSING FLIGHT

The phenomenon of individuals fleeing from their homelands to escape oppression or persecution is not new in human history. The uniqueness in the present-day mass flight of human beings is to be found in the magnitude of the movement and its compulsory character. Never before were so many countries involved either as sources of refugee emigration or as places of refuge. Also unprecedented is the fact that people were forced to leave their homelands on account of their descent or "race." The individual was thus left with no choice, for while it is possible to change one's faith or political views, one cannot change one's ancestry. Similarly without parallel was the new doctrine of nationalism which resulted in the deification of the State and the exclusion of all conflicting loyalties, whether political, social, or religious. This extreme nationalism led to depriving the nonconformist of the rights of citizenship, leaving him unprotected by any government.

The recent refugee movement has also been marked by (1) the extremely cruel treatment of the victims of political, religious, and "racial" persecution; (2) by the difficulty which these victims encountered in escaping and in finding a secure refuge as Nazism spread to ever larger areas; (3) by the reluctance of the countries not immediately affected to admit them because of the deep economic depression and later because of the war; and (4) by the breaking up of families on a scale previously unknown. Such has been the refugee movement which began with the rise of Hitler to power in 1933.

A refugee remarks: "It often strikes me that refugees have a new way of counting time: pre-Hilter—post-Hitler . . . For a whole generation of Europeans that name has become a terrible signpost marking the break of a century."[1]

Groups fleeing from persecution and establishing themselves in other countries have frequently become great assets to those countries. As far as America is concerned, it may be claimed with a good deal of justification that the foundations of this nation were laid by people escaping oppression. The Puritans, the Huguenots, the Quakers, the Scotch-Irish, and the Spanish-Portuguese Jews were all refugees.

[1] Gertrude Kummer, "Is There an Answer?" *Survey Graphic*, August, 1944, p. 360.

Although the term "refugee" appears to be simple to define, in reality many obstacles are encountered in any attempt to do so. Legally, as far as the United States is concerned, there are no refugees. All aliens admitted to the United States are either immigrants, if admitted for permanent residence, or "nonimmigrants" or visitors, if admitted for temporary stay. Since the vast majority of refugees belong to the first-named category they are simply immigrants. This view, however, does not take into account the fact that the immigrants of the past decade have been of a special kind, presenting a special problem, and hence of unusual interest.

On the other hand, the popular view of refugees as simply people in flight is not discriminating enough to be of much practical use, since according to this view any displaced person, such as one fleeing from an invading enemy, would be called a refugee. A more accurate definition of a refugee is "one who has left his country of residence on account of threat to life or liberty growing out of race, religion, or political belief."[2] According to the Institut de Droit International, perhaps the best authority on international law in Europe, "The term refugee means any individual who, as a result of political events which have occurred in the territory of the state from which he derived, has left that territory, either voluntarily or involuntarily, or dwelt away from it, who has acquired no new nationality and does not enjoy the diplomatic protection of any other state."[3] According to this view, the fact that he does not enjoy the protection of the government of his country of origin seems to be the decisive factor. In many cases, he has also lost his nationality or citizenship and has become stateless. Even in cases where the refugee retains his nationality he usually does not enjoy *de facto* the protection of the state to which he nominally belongs, which is akin to being stateless. Statelessness is not the essential quality of a refugee, though many refugees are in fact stateless people.

This legal definition, while accurate at the time it was formulated, does not include a large number of people who have since come to be regarded as refugees, on account of the war and of political events. These are displaced persons who have, at least nominally, the protection of the government of their country of origin, but who for various reasons are unable or unwilling to return to their native land. The term "refugee" must therefore be expanded to include this group as well as those who have been deprived of national protection in law or in fact.

The typical refugee leaves his place of residence not voluntarily but is forced to flee because of actual or threatened persecution on account of his race, religion, or political convictions. Economic factors, of primary importance in the case of the regular immigrant, are practically absent in the

---

[2] Patrick M. Malin, "The Work of the Intergovernmental Committee on Refugees," *Interpreter Releases*, Vol. XXI, No. 25, June 27, 1944, p. 211.

[3] *Annuaire de l'Institut de Droit International*, Vol. II (1936), p. 294.

case of the refugee. The time he leaves and often the place of destination are also not of his choosing. Consequently, the refugee, unlike the ordinary immigrant, finds it usually difficult, if not impossible, to settle his financial affairs and to take along his possessions. Being often a stateless person he has difficulty in finding a haven, and being a sort of outcast he may be looked upon with suspicion even by the country receiving him. Because of all this, the refugee often finds adjustment extremely difficult.

STATELESSNESS

The problem of statelessness, which looms so large in the case of the present-day refugee, is a recent phenomenon. It did not arise as a serious problem until after World War I when, as a consequence of the Russian revolution, the revision of national boundaries in the Balkans and elsewhere, and large-scale persecution of Armenians and Assyrians in Turkey, virtually millions of individuals found themselves stateless and without the protection of the government to which they formerly belonged. Although most of these refugees were eventually settled in various countries (in some instances by exchange of populations, as between Greece and Turkey), large numbers remained stateless, especially the Russians, constituting a problem of international proportions. These people without nationality lacked the legal protection of any state, and, moreover, were deprived of all identification papers, which hampered their freedom of movement.

It was this situation, which became aggravated as time went on, that the League of Nations sought to solve. Under the leadership of its first high commissioner, Fridtjof Nansen, an international identity document which came to be known as the "Nansen passport" was devised. The issuance of such a document was agreed upon and authorized by 51 nations at a conference in July, 1922, and thereupon an international certificate, the first of its kind ever issued, began to be granted to stateless individuals, thus facilitating their travel and giving them advantages heretofore reserved only for those in possession of a national passport. At first this kind of document was issued only to the Russian exiles but later it was extended to Armenian, Saarlander, and other refugees. While the Nansen passport was valid only for a period of one year and denied the right of the person holding it to return to the country of issue, unless that right was expressly granted, and thus was inferior to a national passport, it ushered in a new phase in international responsibility and general humanitarianism.

The Nansen passport did much toward alleviating the lot of the stateless refugees, especially by the subsequent extension of the period of validity of the certificate and the obligation the League of Nations assumed of helping the refugees in various countries by co-ordinating the activities of governments and private organizations. Being designed, however, merely to help temporarily the most distressed of the refugees and being handicapped by the apathy of the governments, this noble effort fell short of solving the problem. As late as 1939, twenty years after the conclusion of World War I, Judge Hansson, retiring president of the Nansen Office for Refugees, which was at that time combined with the office of the High Commissioner for Refugees of the League of Nations, stated that over 600,000 refugees were still under the care of his office.

Although after World War I, as noted above, certain groups of people were rendered stateless, the deliberate and systematic denationalization and denaturalization of large masses of people began with the rise of Fascism. Both the scale on which this was done and the grounds, which were based primarily upon race or ancestry, were unprecedented. The main victims were German Jews. By the end of 1941, according to an estimate by the American Jewish Joint Distribution Committee, there were some 335,000 stateless Jews in Europe outside of Russia, and in August, 1944, according to the Intergovernmental Committee on Refugees, there were between 1,000,000 and 2,000,000 stateless individuals of all origins in the world.

THE PRESENT REFUGEE MOVEMENT

The rise of Fascism in Italy marked the beginning of a new refugee movement which was destined to become the largest and most far-reaching in modern history. Thus, the first to flee from the scourge of Fascism were those opposed to Mussolini's doctrines and practices. These first victims, drawn from among the most gifted and accomplished in the population, were few in number. Following the civil war and the victory of Franco in Spain, however, an immense stream of refugee migration was started. After the fall of Barcelona about a half million Spaniards poured into France. Approximately half of these soon returned to their native land, leaving about a quarter of a million Spaniards as refugees. About 100,000 of these emigrated overseas, mainly to Mexico, and the rest stayed chiefly in France. In 1940 France reported that about 140,000 Spanish refugees were still within her borders, and tens of thousands still remained there after the end of the war. With the rise and spread of Nazism, flight became an almost universal phenomenon in Europe, involving a constantly increasing number of individuals and continuing as long as any avenue of escape remained open.

No sooner did Nazism step into power than the suppression of all opposition to it began. Although individuals from among all religious and national groups were affected, the Jews were the first and chief victims. The elimination of the Jews as a factor in the social and economic life of the German nation was one of the main items on the Nazi program. The reasons given for singling out the Jews as a group was the allegation that they had been at the root of all Germany's troubles and that their elimination was essential to the welfare of the German nation. Nazism subsequently went farther than that and directed its attack against the Jews in general, aiming at their extermination in every country that came under its domination or influence.

The refugees from Nazism, it should be emphasized, were not by any means the Jews alone, even though, as intimated above, they were the first and chief victims. Nazism right from the beginning turned against all those who would not conform to its philosophy and dictates, as well as those whose political past made them "undesirables."

The non-Jewish refugees may be divided into two categories: (1) "non-Aryan" Christians, that is, baptized Jews and those who were partly of Jewish origin, all of whom were treated as Jews by the German racial laws; (2) Christians who were not of Jewish origin but who left Germany or had to flee on account of their religious or political convictions. Included among the latter were pacifists, members of political parties in the German Republic which were proscribed by the National Socialist regime, Protestants and Catholics who protested against certain pagan tendencies which their consciences forbade them to accept, and trade-union leaders and intellectuals who were opposed to the totalitarian state. Moreover, there were some who left Germany not because they were persecuted, but because they refused to take part in the persecution or even bear indirect responsibility for it—men like Hermann Rauschning, president of the Danzig Senate, who preferred exile rather than, at Hitler's command, inaugurate the persecution of Jews and Christians in Danzig, proscribe political opponents, and follow similar practices of the Nazi party; and Thomas Mann, Nobel Prize laureate and world-famous author, who chose self-exile rather than play the role of a cultural signboard of Nazi barbarism. The main point of difference between the Christian and Jewish refugees was that the Christians were persecuted as individuals, while the Jews were proscribed as a group. This largely accounts for the much higher proportion of Jews among the refugees.

Since by Nazi decree all Christian Germans descended from Jews even to the extent of having one Jewish grandparent were considered Jews, the proscribed group was much larger than the actual Jewish community in Germany. An elaborate classification was evolved creating such categories as "confessional," "racial," "hybrids" (*Mischlinge*) of first class, that is, those with two Jewish grandparents, and second class, that is, those with one Jewish grandparent, all of whom subsequently were accorded the same treatment.

Early in the Nazi regime, a German professor wrote to an American colleague regarding a scholar who was a Jew only by decree of Hitler:

I have a letter received from a friend of mine, Professor K. of the University of M. He is of non-Aryan stock, which I presume means Jewish, although he had never impressed me as being a Jew, and for two generations the family has been Protestant. His family has been in Germany for three hundred years, and his father was a professor in Göttingen. He was himself for several years at Heidelberg, and for the last five years at Münster. His wife is of pure German stock. He has a wide reputation in the field of classical archaeology and would be a valuable addition to any university staff in this country. Nevertheless the Hitlerites have turned him out.

THE ASSAULT ON THE JEWS OF GERMANY

According to the German census of 1933, the year the Nazis assumed power, there were 502,799 confessional Jews in Germany proper (*altes Reichsgebiet*), or less than 1 per cent of the general population. It is interesting to note that, although actually increasing, the Jews, owing to their lower birth rate, had constituted, since 1880, a progressively smaller proportion of the total population of Germany. The Jews in Germany were predominantly urban and concentrated in the larger cities. Over four-fifths of them lived in cities of more than 100,000 and over 70 per cent in the twelve German cities with more than 500,000 population. Berlin alone, with 160,600 in 1933, contained almost one-third of the total Jewish population in Germany. Nevertheless, no German city had as large a Jewish population as such cities as Warsaw, Lodz, Moscow, Budapest, or London in Europe, and New York, Chicago, or Philadelphia in the United States. Even in Berlin the Jews constituted only 3.8 per cent of the total number of inhabitants. Their geographic concentration, however, had the effect of making them highly visible—despite their small proportion in the population—and a most convenient target.

Another characteristic of the German Jews was their occupational concentration. This, too, the Nazis deliberately magnified and exploited for their own purpose. A few figures will show that the influence of this minority could easily be exaggerated. According to the 1933 German census, 61.3 per cent of all gainfully occupied Jews were engaged in trade and commerce in contrast to 18.4 per cent among the total population, but altogether they constituted only 2.5 per cent of all engaged in these fields in Germany. Similarly in the professions, only 2.3 per cent of the total were Jews. Only in law and medicine, traditional Jewish professions, did they make up comparatively large proportions, 16.3 per cent and 10.9 per cent, respectively. On the other hand, only 2.6 per cent of the university professors and 0.5 per cent of the elementary and high school teachers were Jews. Jews constituted only 0.4 per cent of all engaged in industry and handicrafts.

The Jews of Germany had contributed to every aspect of German life and culture out of proportion to their numbers. They helped substantially in the unification of the German states and in extending the country's influence both economically and culturally. Much of Germany's fame in the realms of science, scholarship, and letters was due to them. Of the forty-four Germans to whom the Nobel Prize had been awarded, no fewer than eight were of Jewish origin. It is, indeed, one of the great ironies of history that a country that owed so much of its greatness to its Jewish citizens should have become their most relentless enemy, seeking actually their complete physical extermination.

The German Jews, moreover, were regarded as the most assimilated branch of European Jewry. They considered themselves as an integral part of the nation and were Germans first and Jews second. They also enjoyed the universal respect of other Jews, to whom they often served as a model. They had lived in Germany for centuries and considered the country their *Vaterland*—and with as much right as any other section of the population.

Against this minority the fury of the Nazis was turned loose. Within two months after gaining full power, they began to organize their campaign of extermination of the Jews in Germany, and, as history proved, eventually of the Jews in Europe. Since the Nazis defined as Jews Christians with even one Jewish grandparent, it meant that a large group of so-called "non-Aryans" was also involved. The story of how the Nazis went about realizing their inhuman plan is by now quite well known.

The attack started on April 1, 1933, with the staging of a nation-wide boycott against Jewish-owned shops. This was soon followed by steps calculated to eliminate gradually the Jews and "non-Aryans" from the economic and social life of the nation. The ousting of Jews from public offices began a week later, on April 7. In May "the destruction of the Jewish spirit" was celebrated by public burnings of the literary and scientific works of Jews, and on July 6 a decree restricted the attendance of Jewish students in the secondary schools to 1.5 per cent of the total enrollment.

Although the Nazi aim was definite and unequivocal from the very beginning, the plan called for a staggered procedure, partly because this method was to result in the greatest benefits to the Nazis and partly because of sadism. Political reasons undoubtedly also played a part. Thus, in the first period all Jews naturalized since 1919 were deprived of their citizenship, and all other Jews excluded from official state and local positions. Jews were also eliminated from the film industry, newspapers, and literary and scientific institutions. Jewish businessmen were forced to "Aryanize" their businesses, that is, sell them at ruinous prices to "Aryans." This was accomplished within the two-year period from 1933 to 1935.

On September 15, 1935, the Nuremberg laws were passed which inaugurated a new phase in the persecution of the Jewish minority in Germany. All German Jews were deprived of their citizenship and reduced to subjects without any rights. They were gradually removed from all economic and professional activity, except serving their own people, and even that to a very limited extent. Marriage and all sex relations between Jews and "Aryans" were forbidden. Among other regulations were the stamping of the letter "J" on all identification papers of Jews, the compulsory wearing of the yellow badge, the exclusion of all Jewish children from schools attended by "Aryan" children, the abolition of all rights enjoyed by Jewish communal bodies. The Jews were forbidden to reside and even to be found in any but the streets and sections of the city designated to them, thus being confined to a ghetto where practically all amenities of civilized society were lacking.

The laws and regulations designed to strangle the Jews economically and socially were accompanied by acts of physical abuse including murder. Although physical violence marked Nazism right from the beginning, it found its most monstrous expression in the later phases and primarily during the war period. Inaugurating this phase of violence were the pogroms of November 10 and 11, 1938, instigated under the pretense of popular retaliation for the assassination of an official of the German embassy in Paris by a Jewish youth. In scores of German and Austrian cities Jews were assaulted or shot in the streets and thousands were dragged into concentration camps, where many were beaten to death. Jewish stores were looted, about 500 synagogues were burned, and all remaining Jewish businesses were "Aryanized" or liquidated. In addition, a fine of a billion marks was imposed upon the impoverished Jewish population of Germany. It was at this time that President Roosevelt, who had previously denounced the persecution, the regimentation, and the barbarism of the Nazi creed, protested to the Nazi government and recalled the American ambassador.

The months immediately preceding Germany's launching of war were also marked by the beginning of a policy of mass deportation of Jews, which was later pursued on an ever-larger scale and turned into mass slaughter in the huge concentration camps in Poland. The first victims were the German Jews of Polish origin. In a single night in November, 1938, some 12,000 Jews, including little children who according to their passports were still Polish citizens, were dragged from their beds and forced to leave in freight cars for the Polish frontier.

THE EXODUS

The flow of refugees from Germany was at first slow and somewhat hesitant, for many thought that Nazism was only a passing phase and even some Jews believed that the Nazis would not actually put into effect their announced intention of making Germany free of Jews. During the first two years of the Nazi regime, 1933–1935, it is estimated that about 75,000 persons, including about 9,000 non-Jews, left Germany. Moreover, during this period most of the victims of Nazism sought refuge in other European countries. They did this partly because of failure to recognize the full implications of Nazism and the extent of its eventual spread and partly because of the greater accessibility of these countries and the difficulty of gaining admittance to overseas countries, particularly in the Americas, which were the most coveted. It is interesting to note that until 1937 Palestine surpassed by far all overseas countries as a haven for refugee Jews from Europe. We have no accurate knowledge concerning the number of Christians who left Germany because of oppression by the National Socialist government, but Mr. James G. McDonald, the former High Commissioner for Refugees of the League of Nations, estimated in 1935 that they comprised 15 to 20 per cent of the total number of refugees from that country.

The enactment of the Nuremberg laws in September, 1935, ushered in a new phase in the Nazi drive against the Jews. The added restrictions and increased brutality of treatment precipitated a new wave of emigrants, the climax of which was reached following the massacres of November 10–11, 1938. By the end of 1937 an estimated 150,000 Jews had left Germany. With the occupation of Austria in March, 1938, another substantial number of Jews, about 200,000, had been added to Hitler's victims. The treatment of the Austrian Jews exceeded in brutality that of their German coreligionists. What took the Nazis years to accomplish in Germany was accomplished in a few months in Austria. Thousands of Jews were rounded up and put into concentration camps or forced to leave. Within a year, the Jewish population of Austria decreased by 110,775, representing a loss of 56.8 per cent. Altogether about 140,000 left Greater Germany in 1938 alone. As far as the Sudetenland is concerned, by 1939 about 93 per cent of the approximately 25,000 Jews had left the region. The exodus of Jews from Germany proceeded at an ever-accelerated pace until the outbreak of the war. During the first four months of 1939, 30,000 emigrants were assisted in leaving Germany, while an unknown number were able to leave without outside aid.

Despite this large-scale exodus of Jews and their desperate attempts to leave the country, about 330,000 "racial" Jews remained in Greater Germany, especially in Austria, at the time war broke out.[4] This was because of the tremendous obstacles put by the Nazis in the path of their victims to prevent them from leaving the country, but, much more important, because of the greater difficulty of finding a country willing to admit refugees.

In April 1939, after a desperate struggle [writes a Jewish woman], we emigrated to Belgium . . . When Hitler invaded Belgium in May 1940, we were all arrested at 7 o'clock in the morning. All women and children were sent home in the afternoon, the men were shipped to the French concentration camp. After two days we heard that the Germans approached. I decided to abandon everything and to flee. In my opinion everything was better than to meet the Nazis again, even to be machine-gunned or blown to bits on the roads crowded with refugees. We left our apartment with furniture and linen and silver and took only what we could carry by hand. It was like a terrible nightmare. After 5 days, we arrived in Southern France near the Spanish Frontier. From then on

[4] Clarence B. Odell and Robert H. Billigmeier, "Jews in Germany, 1933–1939," *Department of State Bulletin*, Vol. XII, No. 309 (May 27, 1945), p. 971.

for two years we lived in eternal fear, persecuted, chased around, traveling from one place to another.

I had hopes [writes a German Jewish lawyer] of joining my sister who had emigrated to the United States two years before, but since the necessary papers could not be secured I managed to get passage on the steamer "St. Louis" hoping to go to Cuba and from there to the United States. Unfortunately for me and for a great many other refugees whose plight was similar to mine, we were not allowed to land in Cuba and the steamer "St. Louis" was forced to return with us to Antwerp. . . . With the outbreak of the war there seemed no possibility of leaving and I remained in Belgium for a whole year, and then before the invasion of Belgium I went to France. It would be humanly impossible for me to describe the terror and the suffering entailed in the period until 1942 when I was finally fortunate enough to leave for the United States. Even now it is too painful an experience to recall all the agony I lived through, first in a concentration camp and later when the necessary papers were received it seemed unbelievable that rescue was at hand. Need I mention with what joy I looked forward to the new life in America? I was prepared to work very hard and asked for nothing more than an opportunity to live once again as a free human being.

Thousands of immigrants were tossed back and forth endlessly by the frontier guards of Germany and its neighboring countries. Many countries admitted refugees only to expel them soon afterward.

Escape from Germany became also more difficult as time went on because the victims were stripped of practically all their means. Whereas in the beginning of the Nazi regime it was possible for the emigrants to take out a good part of their capital, later it became increasingly difficult for them to salvage any part of their possessions, the opportunity to do so finally disappearing altogether. Moreover, the extension of outside help was also made more and more difficult, if not impossible. All efforts to effect an organized removal of the Jews from Germany broke down soon after they were started. Thus, masses of innocent people were forced to leave a country while being denied the means of doing so.

The months preceding Germany's invasion of Poland on September 1, 1939, saw most desperate attempts on the part of the Nazi victims in Germany to escape. Moreover, many of those who had fled from Germany into neighboring countries were hard pressed and often forced to seek again a refuge elsewhere. Overseas countries, particularly those in the Americas, seemed to provide the safest havens. Hence efforts were redoubled by the victims to escape across the ocean. But the difficulties were tremendous, and only comparatively few could save themselves, millions being left to face starvation, torture, or death. Despair drove many to resort to illegal ways of entering overseas countries, but often individuals acquired visas and passports which, although supposed to be bona fide documents, turned out to be invalid. Thus, thousands of individuals with invalid visas were refused admittance and forced to return to the country of their persecution. The case of the 907 refugees sailing from Germany to Cuba on the

SS *St. Louis* on May 15, 1939, and being denied entry because of their invalid visas, was typical of many others.

While the goals of most Nazi victims were countries in the Americas, particularly the United States, permission was sought from any country willing to admit them. The territorial spread of refugees thus became world-wide, indeed. These unfortunates found their way even to far-off Japan, China (particularly Shanghai), Siam, Burma, the Dutch East Indies, Australia, the Fiji Islands, East Africa, Mauritius, the Belgian Congo, North Africa, Iran, and numerous countries of the Western Hemisphere. As the situation became more desperate the victims were no longer concerned with what opportunities for a livelihood or other possibilities different countries offered. The only thing that mattered was to escape from the Nazi inferno.

Many countries enacted discriminatory measures designed to obstruct the entry of these desperate people. Argentina ordered its consuls in Europe to delay, under every possible pretext, issuing visas even to those Jews who met all the requirements for obtaining entry. Brazil instructed its representatives in Europe to require baptismal certificates of all prospective immigrants, which meant the automatic exclusion of Jews unless they apostatized. Bolivia decreed that any person with "Jewish blood" was ineligible for entry. At one time the Australian law forbidding entry to Asiatics was taken to mean that, since Palestine was in Asia, all Jews were to be refused admission to Australia.[5] Other countries, because of the depression and wartime regulations or out of anti-Semitism, adopted restrictive policies with the result that millions of lives were lost.

It should not be inferred, however, that strenuous efforts were not made by various democratic countries and private and semiprivate agencies in those countries to assist in every possible way the victims of Nazism. These efforts, often undertaken by individuals at the risk of their very lives, form the only bright chapter in the dark book of Nazi persecution.

EFFORTS AT RESCUE AND RELIEF

The activities of the League of Nations and the agencies connected with it have already been mentioned. In July, 1938, under the leadership of the United States, there took place what has come to be known as the Evian Conference, in which over thirty countries participated, the object of which was to secure concerted action with regard to the refugee problem. As an outgrowth of this conference the Intergovernmental Committee on Refugees was established. The committee started negotiations with the German government for the purpose of effecting an orderly migration of those forced to leave that country. These efforts brought no conclusive results because of the insurmountable obstructions on the part of the German

[5] American Jewish Committee, *To the Counsellors of Peace*, 1945, pp. 64–65.

government. With the outbreak of the war all negotiations had to be dropped. Meantime, efforts continued, with the assistance of voluntary organizations, to find permanent homes for many persons forced to migrate. But the United States and the British Empire showed no inclination to receive a still larger number of refugees, and their admission to Palestine was severely restricted for political reasons. This was the true reason, along with the outbreak of war, for the failure of the Evian Conference. In 1943 the Intergovernmental Committee on Refugees was reorganized and its scope widened. Since the end of the war it has been concerned with the problem of persons who cannot be repatriated.

Another very important step taken in helping the refugees was the establishment by executive order of the President, on January 22, 1944, of the War Refugee Board of the United States. This board, consisting of the Secretary of State, the Secretary of the Treasury, and the Secretary of War, was charged with the responsibility of taking "all measures within its power to rescue the victims of enemy oppression who are in imminent danger of death, and otherwise to afford such victims all possible relief and assistance consistent with the successful prosecution of the war."[6] The functions of the board included the development of plans and measures for (a) the rescue, transportation, maintenance, and relief of the victims of oppression and (b) the establishment of havens of temporary asylum for such victims. Under the latter program, a haven was established at Fort Ontario, New York, as is discussed elsewhere.

The creation of the War Refugee Board enabled all organizations engaged in rescue and relief of refugees to deal with a single United States government agency and greatly increased the effectiveness of such work. The board stationed special representatives, who were accorded diplomatic status, in strategic neutral countries such as Switzerland, Sweden, and Turkey, and with the aid of these countries, the Vatican, the International Red Cross, and other international organizations, it made insistent demands on behalf of refugees which even the Germans could not wholly disregard. "The main obstacle which faced the Board was the adamant attitude of the enemy. The Nazis were determined to wipe out innocent minorities and did not regard them as being protected by any law, national or international."[7] Since evacuation from German-controlled territory for specially marked victims was not possible on an official and open basis, the board and the co-operating private agencies sent trusted agents into enemy areas to hide refugees from the Nazis, maintain them, and transport them through underground channels to safety. Tens of thousands were rescued from the Nazis by these clandestine means. Measures were also taken to

[6] War Refugee Board, *Final Summary Report*, Sept. 15, 1945, p. 1; cf. Blair Bolles, "Millions to Rescue," *Survey Graphic*, September, 1944.
[7] War Refugee Board, *Final Summary Report*, Sept. 15, 1945, p. 16.

safeguard those victims who could not escape from enemy territory. For example, approximately 8,000 orphaned Jewish children were kept alive in France by means of American funds sent from Switzerland. These children were hidden in convents, schools, and private homes by compassionate Christian families. In various countries both clergy and laity saved and protected many thousands, both children and adults. Among other accomplishments of the board was the restraining, with the assistance of other governments, of the Nazi puppet regime of Hungary from proceeding with its plans of deporting Jews to the murder camps in Poland. Besides the tens of thousands rescued through activities organized by the board, hundreds of thousands continued to live and resist as a result of its unremitting efforts, until the Allied armies finally saved them and the millions of others who survived the Nazi terror.

Besides these government agencies, numerous private organizations, as already noted, have been performing various services for refugees. There is hardly a major religious, nationality, or welfare group that has not come to the aid of the victims of Hitlerism. While some have concentrated their efforts in assisting the refugees in Europe, others have specialized in helping them after arrival in this country or other countries of refuge. Outstanding among the agencies that have aided the refugees abroad are the American Jewish Joint Distribution Committee, the World Jewish Congress, the American Friends Service Committee, the Unitarian Service Committee, the War Relief Services of the National Catholic Welfare Conference, the Emergency Rescue Committee, now the International Rescue and Relief Committee, the Hebrew Sheltering and Immigrant Aid Society, Hadassah, the Jewish Labor Committee, various Zionist organizations, the National Refugee Service, and other refugee service committees. Hundreds of thousands of individuals owe their lives to these and scores of other organizations.

As Nazism spread through conquest and domination over the European continent, millions were added to its victims. The aim to extirpate all Jews in Europe, proclaimed by the Nazis, came now within the range of possibility and, as later events proved, came close to being realized, since of the approximately 6,000,000 Jews living in Europe outside of the Soviet Union, about 4,000,000, it is estimated, have been exterminated, and the total number of Jews annihilated on the Continent has been estimated as 6,200,000. Instead of hundreds of thousands, millions of human beings were now seeking to escape torture and death.

How many anti-Nazi Christians were killed is unknown, but the number was small compared to the Jews who were the main victims.

The Nazi invasion of Poland in 1939 practically amounted to a pronouncement of a death sentence upon the three million Jews living there. Massacres, executions, deliberate starvation and torture became the order of the day. Later, with the invasion of the Russian territory, additional millions came to share this lot. Ghettos were established in many large cities and "reservations," such as the one in the area of Lublin, were set aside for the Jews, aiming not only to separate them from the rest of the population, but actually to exterminate them gradually by various scientifically calculated means. The 600,000 Jews of Warsaw were herded together within a small walled area and exposed to conditions which meant their gradual elimination. When, by April, 1943, the majority of this ghetto population had perished, the Nazis decided to liquidate the rest, which they did but only after a 42-day struggle with the desperate victims. Dozens of huge extermination camps were established in various parts of Poland and Germany where human beings in the hundreds of thousands were killed by gas, live cremation, and other means. With the spread of Nazi conquest, many thousands of Jews and Christians in Belgium, Holland, Denmark, Norway, France, and other countries were subjected to a similar treatment. Many of them were transported by the Nazis to the slaughterhouses of Poland to be disposed of there. Those fortunate enough to escape spread all over the world in quest of refuge.

Some countries, such as France, afforded a temporary haven, and others, especially Switzerland and Sweden, a more lasting place of refuge. Estimates of the number of refugees, Jewish and non-Jewish, admitted into countries other than the United States vary widely. The following may be taken as rough guesses of the number admitted, at one time or another, into the most important refugee-receiving areas. These figures do not represent the existing situation and may involve some duplications: France (including North Africa), 800,000; Palestine, 150,000; Great Britain, 140,000; Latin America, 125,000; Italy, 116,000; East African colonies, 90,000; Switzerland, 80,000; Sweden, 44,000; Shanghai, 20,000; Spain, 18,000; and Canada, 6,000. How many refugees were admitted to the United States will be discussed in the following chapter.

CHAPTER II

EXTENT AND CHARACTERISTICS OF THE REFUGEE MOVEMENT

How many refugees came to the United States? The answer to this question is basic to any discussion of the so-called refugee problem. Although there is official recording of all arrivals to the United States, the number of refugees admitted cannot be determined with exactitude, since there is no such separate classification under our immigration laws. While their numbers are not definitely known, it is possible nevertheless to make fairly accurate estimates and to define closely the limits within which the exact number must fall. The methods employed and the results obtained are given below. Before presenting them, however, it is necessary to consider first our general immigration laws and procedures, for these determine the qualifications and the number of aliens admissible, no matter what their motive for emigrating to the United States may be.

The United States Immigration Laws and Procedure

Basic to our system of regulating immigration is the question of quality. No alien is admissible if he fails to meet certain physical, mental, moral, and financial requirements. Furthermore, his admission is conditional, in that he may be deported if found to be undesirable. The main legislation imposing such selective requirements is the Immigration Act of 1917.

Superimposed on this basic system of selection is a system of restriction or numerical limitation set forth in the Immigration Act of 1924. For the purpose of such quantitative control the world is divided into three zones, which may be termed the unrestricted area, the barred zone, and the quota countries.

The unrestricted area includes the independent countries of the Western Hemisphere in North, South, and Central America and the West Indies. Eligible native-born citizens from these countries may enter without limitation on their number.

The barred zone includes Asia and the Pacific islands not owned by the United States. From this area no immigrants are admissible, as being ineligible to citizenship. Exceptions have been made in the case of the Filipinos, who were granted an annual quota of 50 under the Philippines

Independence Act of 1934, and the Chinese, who were given an annual quota of 105 when the Chinese Exclusion Acts were repealed in 1943. Nonimmigrants, such as government officials and visitors, are, however, free to enter for temporary stay.

The quota countries include all other sections of the world—mainly Europe, the Near East, Africa, Australia, and New Zealand. Of these, Europe is by far the most important, since 85 per cent of all immigrants who have ever been admitted to the United States have come from this region. According to the Immigration Act of 1924, a total annual quota of 150,000 is set for the area to which the act applies. This is apportioned among the separate countries according to their relative contribution to the American population as enumerated in 1920, with the proviso that the minimum annual quota of any country shall be 100. The quotas are counted or controlled through the issuance of quota visas by American consuls in the countries to which the act applies. The total annual quota since 1943 has been 153,879.

Certain classes of immigrants are exempt from the quota restrictions. These nonquota immigrants include the wives, unmarried children under 21 years of age, and husbands by marriages occurring before July 1, 1932, of citizens of the United States; ministers, professors, their wives and unmarried children under 18 years of age; students entering solely for the purpose of study at an accredited institution; American women who have lost their citizenship; and aliens previously lawfully admitted who are returning from a temporary visit abroad.

The above provisions apply to all immigrants, that is, to aliens admitted for permanent residence. In addition, there is the class of aliens known as "nonimmigrants" according to the Immigration Act of 1924. These include:

1. Government officials, their families, servants, and employees.
2. Temporary visitors for business or pleasure.
3. Aliens in continuous transit through the United States.
4. Resident aliens who go from one part of the United States to another through foreign contiguous territory.
5. Seamen entering temporarily in pursuit of their calling.
6. "Treaty aliens" entering to carry on trade under and in pursuance of the provisions of existing treaties of commerce and navigation, their wives and unmarried children under 21 years of age.

There is no restriction on the number of such nonimmigrant aliens who may enter from any country. They are all temporary sojourners.

All aliens, whether immigrants or nonimmigrants, must have a visa issued by a United States consul. Persons coming for permanent residence must secure immigrant visas; those coming for a temporary stay, visitors' visas; those who desire to pass through the country en route to another country, transit visas. The granting of visas is under the jurisdiction of the Department of State. Persons arriving on visitors' visas are under the law permitted to remain a temporary period, taken to mean not over one year. Those arriving as transients are limited to 60 days. If the privilege is not extended, the person is supposed to leave the United States or be deported. The extension of privilege and the steps looking to departure or deportation are under the jurisdiction of the Department of Justice.

To obtain an immigration visa every quota and nonquota immigrant must present certain documents in connection with his application. These include passport, birth certificate, marriage certificate (if applicant is married), divorce or death certificates if husband or wife has been previously married, police certificate, military certificate, photographs, and evidence of assets (proof of employment or proof of support). The visa fee is $10.[1]

Sketched in broad outline, these are the requirements or conditions under which refugees fleeing from Fascism in Europe could be admitted to the United States. Actually, the situation was even more stringent, since the immigration of refugees occurred at a time when the administration of our laws was made much stricter because of the economic depression and the war. It was thus the refugees' added misfortune to be forced to leave their homelands during a period when this country, like all others, was less able to receive the normal flow of immigrants despite the tremendous urgency of the situation. One of the administrative measures which greatly reduced the volume of immigration was the presidential order, in effect since September, 1930, instructing the consular officers to apply rigidly the clause in the Immigration Act of 1917 excluding persons likely to become a public charge. The consuls were ordered not to issue an immigration visa to an applicant who did not have sufficient resources to maintain himself for an indefinite period without employment or else satisfactory assurances of support from relatives or friends which would make it unlikely that he would become a burden on the community.

The outbreak of war led to new administrative measures resulting in further reduction of immigration. Following the closing of American consulates in Nazi- and Fascist-dominated countries, the control of visa issuance was vested in the Visa Division of the Department of State as of July 1, 1941. New regulations were adopted to ensure the public security and interests of the United States. Steps were taken to exclude persons who might be sent into the United States as foreign agents in the guise of refugees. Applications for admission were considered by an Interdepartmental Visa Committee composed of one representative each of the Department of State, the Immigration and Naturalization Service, the Federal Bureau of Investigation, Military Intelligence, and Naval Intelligence.

---

[1] *Immigration and Nationality Laws and Regulations as of March 1, 1944.* Washington, U.S. Government Printing Office, 1944.

Should an unfavorable decision be reached by the committee or should the alien be classified under the regulations as an alien of enemy nationality, each case was given further consideration by an Interdepartmental Visa Review Committee. Aliens of enemy nationality, in which classification most of the refugees then fell, had to file special forms; and their applications, even if approved by the two bodies mentioned above, had also to be considered by a Board of Appeals consisting of two members appointed by the President. The board approved such visa applications in meritorious cases. With regard to the admission of enemy aliens it stated in its Report to the President in 1942:

> Manifestly natives, citizens and denizens of hostile nations are as a group more likely to be dangerous to the United States than are other persons. Yet it seems obvious that a person who has been deprived of his citizenship and of his property by Germany, and who faces punishment and perhaps death if he returns to Germany, will not in all probability be friendly to the Nazi regime, even though he may be technically classified as an enemy alien.

To determine whether it was to the interest of the United States to admit an alien during a period of national emergency, the wartime regulations listed the classes of aliens whose entry was deemed to be prejudicial to the public interest. Among the categories listed was the group of aliens having close relatives in Axis or occupied territory. It was deemed likely that such an alien might have pressure brought upon him to engage in hostile acts against our country to protect his relatives. Other factors besides this "hostage angle" were considered, however, and decisions were affected by the intelligence reports received, not only about the applicant but frequently about the sponsors and the sponsors' references. Following our entry into the war, greater emphasis was placed on the probability of benefit to the United States if the applicant were admitted. Approval was granted to persons whose skills and training made them desirable as residents of this country. Approval was also frequently granted to applicants who had fireside relatives in this country and those who were closely related to members of our armed forces.[2]

The wartime regulations served to prevent the entry into this country of many agents who might otherwise have got here. At the same time they made it more difficult for all immigrants, including refugees, to enter. These restrictions plus the disruption of transportation facilities, including the practically complete disappearance of neutral shipping, reduced the number of immigrants admitted to a point that was one of the lowest in the history of immigration to this country. These new regulations were

[2] Graham H. Stuart, "Wartime Visa-Control Procedure," *Department of State Bulletin*, Sept. 10, 1944, pp. 271–278.

time-consuming, with the result that not infrequently individuals were unable to leave in time to save their lives.

The wartime visa procedure was discontinued effective July 1, 1945, and the final authority to grant or refuse visas was restored to American consular officers. Except in unusual cases, advisory approval by the Secre-

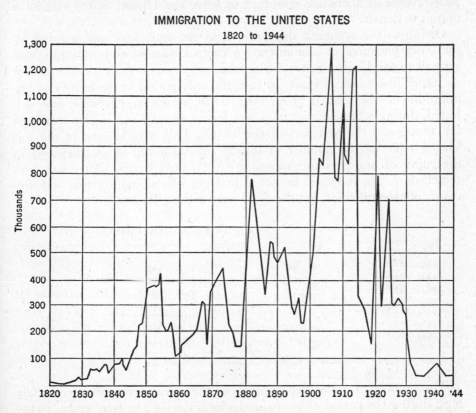

IMMIGRATION TO THE UNITED STATES
1820 to 1944

tary of State is no longer required. The revised regulations, however, continue to exclude aliens whose entry would be prejudicial to the interests of the United States. To them a new category has been added: "any alien found to be, or charged with being, a war criminal by the appropriate authorities of the United States or one of its cobelligerents, or an alien who has been guilty of, or who has advocated or acquiesced in activities or conduct contrary to civilization and human decency on behalf of the Axis countries during the present world war."[8]

Similarly, the strict wartime control over the departure of aliens from the United States has been relaxed. These regulations, pursuant to the

[8] *Federal Register*, Vol. 10, No. 145, Publication No. 1709, Department of State, July 21, 1945.

President's Proclamation of November 14, 1941, prohibited the departure of any alien from the United States unless he had received an exit permit, for which application must be made on special forms. Very few, if any, aliens of enemy nationality were granted exit permits, even those who had entered the United States on visitors' visas before the outbreak of war. Most classes of aliens are now free to leave the United States without a permit to depart.

Owing to the economic depression and the war, and implemented by the strict measures of administrative control, the number of immigrant arrivals to the United States during the period 1931–1944 was the lowest on record in a hundred years. In fact, the only period in the history of immigration to the United States since 1820, when records were first collected, during which immigration was less in amount was in the decade of the 1820's and the first part of the 1830's. This may be seen in the following table on the number of immigrants admitted by decades and in the curve of annual immigration to the United States 1820–1944 presented on p. 19. It should be noted that our official immigration statistics cover, not the calendar, but the fiscal year ending June 30.

IMMIGRATION TO THE UNITED STATES, 1820–1944*

Period	Number	Period	Number
1820–1830	151,824	1891–1900	3,687,564
1831–1840	599,125	1901–1910	8,795,386
1841–1850	1,713,251	1911–1920	5,735,811
1851–1860	2,598,214	1921–1930	4,107,209
1861–1870	2,314,824	1931–1940	528,431
1871–1880	2,812,191	1941–1944	132,833
1881–1890	5,246,613	Total 1820–1944	38,423,276

* Annual Report of the Immigration and Naturalization Service, for the Year Ended June 30, 1944, p. 46.

The number of aliens departing from the country was proportionately high during the period 1931–1944. Indeed, during the four years, 1932–1935 inclusive, the number of departures exceeded the number of arrivals. This was the first time since 1908, when the recording of departures began, that this country had experienced a net loss of immigrants.

That the period 1931–1944, which includes the period of the refugee movement in which we are especially interested, was one of very limited immigration is further attested by the small percentage of the quota that was used. During this period the quota fulfillment ranged from a low of 5.3 per cent in 1933 to a high of 40.6 in 1939, with an average for the entire period of 17.5 per cent. In other words, the total number of quota immigrants admitted 1931–1944 was 377,597 out of a possible permissible number under the immigration law of 2,154,306. The following graph reveals the per cent of immigration quotas fulfilled, in the case of all

Admissions and Departures of Immigrants 1931–1944*

Year	Immigrant Aliens Admitted	Emigrant Aliens Departed	Net Entries
1931	97,139	61,882	35,257
1932	35,576	103,295	−67,719
1933	23,068	80,081	−57,013
1934	29,470	39,771	−10,301
1935	34,956	38,834	−3,878
1936	36,329	35,817	512
1937	50,244	26,736	23,508
1938	67,895	25,210	42,685
1939	82,998	26,651	56,347
1940	70,756	21,461	49,295
1941	51,776	17,115	34,661
1942	28,781	7,363	21,418
1943	23,725	5,107	18,618
1944	28,551	5,669	22,882
Total	661,264	494,992	166,272

* *Annual Reports of the Immigration and Naturalization Service*, for the appropriate years.

countries and of Europe, for the period from 1925, the first full year the Immigration Act of 1924 was in effect, to 1944. The quota situation since 1931 stands in sharp contrast to that of earlier years.

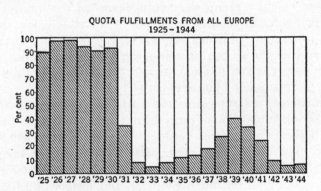

QUOTA FULFILLMENTS FROM ALL EUROPE
1925–1944

Per cent

'25 '26 '27 '28 '29 '30 '31 '32 '33 '34 '35 '36 '37 '38 '39 '40 '41 '42 '43 '44

Estimated Number of Refugees Admitted to the United States

The passage of the Immigration Act of 1924, designed as a permanent system of quota restriction, marked the beginning of a new phase of immigration to the United States. The economic depression and the war reduced the volume of immigration to the lowest recorded point in a hundred years. Within this framework of legislative restrictions and the limitations imposed by outside conditions, the immigration of refugees to the United States occurred. The number must of necessity have been comparatively small. Since refugees are not designated as such in our official immigration records, resort must be had to an estimate of their number. The accepted procedure is to base this estimate on the number of arrivals, both "immigrant" and "nonimmigrant," during certain years from Axis-occupied or Axis-dominated countries.

The list of such countries varies according to the different estimates that have been made. For our estimate we have included the maximum possible, namely, every country in Europe with the exception of Great Britain and Northern Ireland, Eire, Portugal, Sweden, and Switzerland. As compared with the estimate made by the Immigration and Naturalization Service, for example, we include the following countries which they omit: Albania, Finland, Soviet Russia, and Spain. Immigration from Albania, which was invaded by Fascist Italy, has been negligible. We have included Finland because she was for a period, at least, a satellite of Germany. Russia was included because part of the country was once Axis-occupied and because many Russians by birth who were living as emigres in other countries came here as refugees. Spain was added to the list because it has been a totalitarian country since 1936, and a source of refugee movement. Perhaps a better term than Axis-occupied or Axis-dominated countries would be countries of refugee emigration.

On the assumption that all immigrants admitted during the fiscal years 1933–1944 from all the countries listed as sources of refugee emigration from Nazi or Fascist tyranny were refugees, then the number would be 318,235. The figures by country are given in the table below. It might be noted that, while most estimates begin with the fiscal year 1934, we have "leaned over backwards" by including the year 1933, which covers the period from July 1, 1932, to June 30, 1933, though Hitler did not attain to power in Germany until January 30, 1933.

This estimate of 318,235 places the maximum possible or upper limit of the number of refugee immigrants admitted to the United States. Since, however, all these countries of refugee emigration were not Axis dominated or occupied during the entire period 1933–1944, a more accurate estimate would be one that is based on the period since 1933 for Germany but on a later period for the other countries. The history of refugee emigration may be divided into two broad phases: the developments in Germany after the Nazis rose to power, and the conditions in other countries that came under Nazi control as the German empire expanded. The year 1938 has been selected as marking the period when German aggression began and it became clear that there was no escape from Axis domination. It was the peak year of immigration to the United States in the case of eleven of the countries listed as sources of refugee emigration. In the case of six countries the peak occurred in 1939, in the case of two countries (Hungary and the Netherlands) in 1940, and in the case of two other countries (Belgium and France) in 1941.

United States immigration figures for the fiscal years 1938–1944 for all these countries except Germany appear, therefore, as being a more accurate measurement of the refugee movement to this country. A further refinement may be made in the case of Spain. Since the rebellion that doomed Spain's third republic and brought Franco to power was launched on July 18, 1936, we have taken the fiscal year July 1, 1936, to June 30, 1937, as the starting point for estimating refugee immigration from that country.

On the assumption, then, that all immigrants admitted to this country from Germany since 1933, from Spain since 1937, and from the other European countries since 1938 were refugees, the total number of refugee immigrants admitted to the United States through 1944 was 243,862. Even this is a generous estimate, as evidence cited below indicates.

IMMIGRANT ALIENS ADMITTED, BY COUNTRY OF BIRTH,
FROM COUNTRIES OF REFUGEE EMIGRATION

Country	Gross Estimate	Refined Estimate
Germany, incl. Austria	132,012	129,582
Italy	50,638	21,672
Poland	37,597	27,158
Czechoslovakia	17,418	12,016
Soviet Russia	11,212	8,223
France	9,057	6,535
Hungary	8,069	5,461
Greece	7,086	3,629
Yugoslavia	5,790	3,641
Netherlands	5,310	3,989
Rumania	5,195	3,018
Norway	4,382	2,740
Spain	4,198	2,826
Belgium	4,038	3,109
Lithuania	3,079	1,914
Finland	2,896	2,039
Denmark	2,568	1,671
Latvia	1,459	1,063
Bulgaria	785	504
Estonia	618	413
Other European countries of refugee emigration	4,828	2,659
	318,235	243,862

Theoretically, a further refinement should be made by subtracting from the number of immigrants admitted from these countries during the given periods the number of such immigrants who departed from the United States. Though figures on net immigration are available, data are lacking which would make it possible to distinguish the refugees from other emigrant aliens departing from this country. It clearly appears, however, from other evidence gathered by the Study that the number of refugee immigrants who have left the United States has been very small. On the other hand, in the case of the nonimmigrant group, the number of departures, as will be seen later, has been large.

The above computations indicate that the number of immigrants seeking refuge from Nazi and Fascist oppression who were admitted to the United States up to June 30, 1944, was roughly somewhere between 240,000 and 320,000, and most likely closer to the lower estimate than to the higher. If the larger estimate is taken, then refugee immigrants constituted 60 per cent of total number of immigrants admitted to the United States 1933–1944 and 87 per cent of the immigrants admitted from Europe. On the basis of the smaller estimate, refugee immigrants comprised 46 per cent of the total number of immigrants and 66 per cent of the European immigrants admitted during the same period. The accompanying table presents the figures of arrivals by years.

IMMIGRANT ARRIVALS IN THE UNITED STATES, 1933–1944

	From all Countries	From Europe	Number of Refugees Gross Estimate	Number of Refugees Refined Estimate
1933	23,068	14,400	11,869	1,919
1934	29,470	19,559	16,323	4,241
1935	34,956	25,346	21,915	5,436
1936	36,329	26,295	22,875	6,538
1937	50,244	35,812	31,537	12,012
1938	67,895	50,574	44,848	44,848
1939	82,998	68,198	61,882	61,882
1940	70,756	56,254	50,581	50,581
1941	51,776	36,989	30,808	30,808
1942	28,781	14,881	12,620	12,620
1943	23,725	8,953	6,629	6,629
1944	28,551	8,694	6,348	6,348
Total	528,549	365,955	318,235	243,862

In addition to the refugees, estimated above, who were admitted to the United States as immigrants on permanent visas, some refugees were included among the nonimmigrants admitted on temporary visas during the same period. The admission of these aliens has much less significance and effect on American society than that of immigrant aliens, since they are admitted only for a temporary period, which may range from a few days to one year. Upon application to the Immigration Service, the permit may be extended for a further period. This is the regular and long-established procedure. Our immigration laws place no limitation on the number of persons who may enter the United States temporarily. Under the administrative regulations in force during the period of the depression and the war, however, relatively few aliens were granted permission to come to the United States, temporarily or otherwise.

In estimating the number of nonimmigrant refugees admitted to the United States, the total figures on nonimmigrant aliens should be corrected by excluding those for two classes, viz., government officials and returning residents, who are obviously outside the refugee category. In the period under discussion the number of returning residents, that is, aliens previously admitted who were returning from a temporary visit abroad, decreased from 62,485 in 1933 to 4,745 in 1944, reflecting in part the in-

Non-Immigrant Aliens (Exclusive of Government Officials and Returning Resident Aliens) Admitted, by Country of Birth, from Countries of Refugee Emigration

Country	Gross Estimate	Refined Estimate
Germany, incl. Austria	92,407	88,716
France	34,405	14,911
Italy	21,228	8,426
Spain	19,759	14,139
Netherlands	18,594	10,564
Poland	18,321	11,425
Norway	16,234	9,638
Soviet Russia	15,383	8,221
Denmark	10,140	5,542
Belgium	8,088	4,040
Czechoslovakia	7,445	3,440
Hungary	6,295	3,335
Rumania	5,692	2,662
Greece	4,227	2,632
Finland	4,143	2,203
Yugoslavia	3,578	1,836
Lithuania	2,141	1,082
Latvia	1,122	610
Bulgaria	645	369
Estonia	511	297
Other European countries of refugee emigration	3,618	2,344
	293,976	196,432

creasing difficulty of travel as the war developed. Government officials, on the other hand, increased from 4,053 in 1933 to 23,630 in 1944, an increase to be expected in view of the international conferences held in this country and the collaboration with our Allies in furthering the war effort.

Exclusive of returning residents and government officials, the number of nonimmigrant aliens admitted 1933–1944 who were born in Europe totaled 583,029. In estimating the number of refugees among them, we may follow the two procedures used above in the case of the immigrant arrivals. On the assumption that all those admitted during this entire period who were born in countries of refugee emigration were refugees, then the number of nonimmigrant refugees was 293,976. If the second method of computation is employed and it is assumed that all nonimmigrants coming from Germany since 1933, from Spain since 1937, and from the other designated countries since 1938 were refugees, then the number of nonimmigrant refugees admitted would be 196,432.

In considering the statistics of nonimmigrant arrivals, especially over a period of years, it should be borne in mind that they include many duplications. More accurately, they refer to "entries" rather than persons. The same person might have entered the United States as a visitor on more than one occasion. In fact, many individuals who were born in Nazi or Fascist countries came to the United States at least once a year on visitor visas for business purposes. During the anxious years of 1938–1939, hundreds of people from Germany and Austria came on temporary tourist visas, remained here for a few weeks in order to explore the opportunities for settling in the United States, left this country, and later returned on permanent visas. Figures showing these duplications are not available. Nor are figures available on the number of persons who entered as visitors, left for Canada, Cuba, or other neighboring country, and re-entered on permanent visas. These cases of change of status are of course included in the figures of immigrant arrivals, but cause double counting when the figures of immigrant and nonimmigrant arrivals are considered together. It should further be noted that a large number of the persons included in the figures of nonimmigrant arrivals from the countries listed were not, strictly speaking, refugees at all, but professional and business people and tourists who came to this country for business or for pleasure, many of them for the World's Fair, and were caught here by the outbreak of war in Europe in 1939 and unable to return.[4]

Another significant factor to be considered in interpreting these statistics is that a large majority of the nonimmigrants admitted during the period covered by the table have already left the United States. For instance, during the period 1933–1944 the total number of nonimmigrant aliens admitted from all countries was 1,628,459, while the number of nonemigrant aliens departing was 1,594,422. The net entries therefore were only 34,037.

Tabulations made by the Immigration and Naturalization Service and published in their annual reports for the fiscal years of 1943 and 1944 show that nearly 15,000 aliens admitted on temporary visas since July 1, 1938, were still here in 1944 on extended permits. In view of the unusual length of stay of most of them we may safely assume that the great majority are refugees who have been unable to return to their homelands.

If we now combine the estimates of both immigrant and nonimmigrant refugees, we may conclude that the United States has offered permanent refuge since 1933 to between 240,000 and 320,000 individuals and temporary refuge to between 200,000 and 300,000. The weight of evidence

[4] Common Council for American Unity, *Interpreter Releases*, Vol. XXI, No. 9 (Feb. 28, 1941), p. 66.

inclines toward the smaller and more refined of these estimates. It therefore seems reasonable to conclude (1) that approximately 250,000 refugees had been admitted up to June 30, 1944, for permanent residence, (2) that approximately 200,000 refugees were admitted for temporary stay, and (3) that of the latter approximately 15,000 were still here at the close of the fiscal year 1944. The remainder of the group admitted on temporary visas have either left the country and returned on permanent visas, thus being included in the number admitted for permanent residence, or have departed for their homelands or for other countries. Aside from the decrease occasioned by death, the number of refugees in the United States in 1944 was probably 265,000 (250,000 on permanent visas and 15,000 on temporary visas). To this estimate we should add 1,000 more, to include the special group of refugees interned at Oswego, New York, who were brought here outside of the regular immigration procedure for temporary shelter until conditions in Europe would permit their return. This group will be discussed below.

Our estimates compare favorably with those made by others on the basis of official records. For example, the Immigration and Naturalization Service has estimated the number of refugees admitted during the fiscal years ended June 30, 1934–1943, to be 279,091 immigrants and 228,068 nonimmigrants. The basis used was the number of arrivals during the entire period from European countries which in 1944 were Axis occupied or Axis dominated.[5] How much lower a refined estimate would be was indicated by Earl G. Harrison, then commissioner, Immigration and Naturalization Service, who estimated the number of refugees actually admitted to the United States during the ten years of the Nazi regime, 1934–1943, to be somewhere between 200,000 and 300,000.[6] The Common Council for American Unity, using a slightly different list of countries, arrived at the figure of 279,649 refugee immigrants for the same period, 1934–1943.[7] The National Refugee Service, using immigration data for the period from January 1, 1933, to June 30, 1943, arrived at a maximum estimate of 270,919 refugee arrivals, including both immigrant and nonimmigrant. These figures include all Jewish arrivals during the entire period and non-Jewish for Germany since 1933, Austria since 1938, Czechoslovakia since 1939, and other European countries since 1940.[8]

[5] Immigration and Naturalization Service, *Monthly Review*, Vol. 1, No. 8 (February, 1944), pp. 3–4.

[6] Address delivered at a dinner of the Refugee Relief Trustees, Inc., Town Hall Club, Feb. 18, 1944, published in Common Council for American Unity, *Interpreter Releases*, Vol. XXI, No. 10 (Feb. 28, 1944), pp. 80–84.

[7] *Interpreter Releases*, Vol. XXI, No. 9 (Feb. 28, 1944), p. 73.

[8] National Refugee Service, *Reports and Agenda, Annual Meeting of the Members and Board of Directors*, Jan. 15–16, 1944, p. 28.

These careful estimates, based on official immigration records, definitely refute the notion advanced in certain quarters that a million or more refugees had been admitted. Some of the more irresponsible statements given to the public have spoken of "millions of refugees flooding the country"—and this during a period when the total immigration from all countries was only 528,549!

Some of the public misconception on the subject has been due to the confusion between immigrants in general and immigrants who are refugees. Further misunderstanding has arisen because of the confusion between the records of immigration visas issued and of persons actually admitted to the United States. The former are the concern of the State Department, while the latter are kept by the Immigration and Naturalization Service in the Department of Justice. For example, in testifying on November 26, 1943, before a Congressional committee which was considering the number of refugees admitted into the United States during the past decade, Assistant Secretary of State Breckinridge Long stated that we had taken into this country about 580,000 victims of persecution by the Hitler regime. A correct statement, as he himself later acknowledged, would have been that we had authorized and issued some 580,000 visas for such persons. Actually less than half of the total visas issued were used for admission to the United States. The large number of visas authorized may well be regarded as a token of the good will of the United States toward the victims of Nazi oppression, but many who received them were unable to reach this country. Finally, other misconceptions concerning the number of refugees in the United States have had their origin in sensational stories appearing in newspapers and magazines, some of which contain such fantastic exaggerations and ill-disposed allegations that a reasonable person would conclude that they constitute deliberate misrepresentations.

Among other allegations that have been made is that the immigration laws have been changed or set aside in favor of the refugees. The facts are that there was no new legislation affecting the number of immigrants admissible or altering our immigration system in any way during the entire period 1933–1944, except for the granting of an annual quota of 50 to the Philippine Islands in 1934 and an annual quota of 105 to the Chinese in 1943. The European quotas were not only maintained intact, but for the entire period 1933–1944 only 16.8 per cent of Europe's quota was used. As regards the countries of refugee emigration, only 42.1 per cent of their quotas were used. Nor were the quotas permitted to be exceeded by any country of refugee emigration. In the case of Germany, the most important of such countries, only in 1939 and 1940 was practically all of the German quota exhausted. In no instance was the legal limit of issuance of visas exceeded. In the entire period 1933–1944 less than two-

Per Cent of Immigration Quotas Fulfilled by Countries of Refugee Emigration, 1933-1944[*]

Country	Annual Quota	Per Cent of Quota Fulfilled												Average 1933-44
		1933	1934	1935	1936	1937	1938	1939	1940	1941	1942	1943	1944	
Belgium	1,304	4.6	8.1	13.4	14.6	16.5	21.4	23.5	34.0	89.9	31.9	15.6	9.8	23.6
Bulgaria	100	11.0	17.0	52.0	63.0	57.0	100.0	100.0	92.0	100.0	14.0	8.0	20.0	52.8
Czechoslovakia	2,874	5.9	13.5	21.2	26.7	52.9	99.3	94.5	68.9	62.2	19.8	12.6	11.2	40.7
Denmark	1,181	10.4	8.6	12.4	11.4	16.3	27.4	23.9	21.6	26.9	9.1	11.2	9.0	15.7
Estonia	116	14.7	31.0	24.1	29.3	25.9	34.5	92.2	84.5	54.3	23.3	15.5	23.3	37.7
Finland	569	12.7	20.0	18.5	12.7	37.8	87.2	81.0	49.6	62.4	10.2	17.4	11.1	35.0
France	3,086	8.5	10.5	14.0	15.9	18.8	24.3	27.5	25.0	60.2	35.1	16.3	7.1	21.9
Germany-Austria	27,370	5.3	13.7	20.2	24.3	42.1	65.3	100.0	95.3	47.7	17.4	4.7	4.8	36.7
Greece	307	35.2	65.1	100.0	100.0	100.0	100.0	100.0	100.0	75.6	64.8	98.0	93.5	86.0
Hungary	869	21.5	24.1	45.9	59.3	85.0	100.0	100.0	100.0	67.2	32.7	18.8	24.4	56.6
Italy	5,802	19.1	23.5	36.7	42.6	50.1	59.2	71.7	68.4	11.9	1.0	1.2	2.8	32.4
Latvia	236	12.3	20.3	20.8	25.4	48.3	65.3	94.5	78.0	72.5	44.5	26.3	26.3	44.5
Lithuania	386	24.9	32.1	49.2	39.1	57.3	100.0	94.6	76.2	60.1	32.6	30.3	24.1	49.7
Netherlands	3,153	4.2	4.5	8.2	8.3	12.0	11.6	21.2	36.2	37.3	7.5	7.0	8.2	13.8
Norway	2,377	5.9	6.5	8.8	8.3	13.9	21.8	19.6	19.2	18.8	4.2	4.3	7.4	11.6
Poland	6,524	14.7	17.4	25.8	19.2	28.4	64.7	99.8	66.7	67.5	33.8	23.5	20.5	40.2
Rumania	377	80.0	52.8	78.2	74.8	98.4	100.0	100.0	100.0	75.9	74.8	58.4	61.0	79.5
Soviet Russia	2,712	11.8	15.7	13.6	15.1	21.8	34.7	65.3	60.7	59.4	27.0	15.7	14.3	29.6
Spain	252	65.1	90.5	100.0	99.2	96.8	100.0	100.0	89.3	100.0	69.4	100.0	95.6	92.1
Yugoslavia	845	12.4	13.0	25.4	34.4	62.4	100.0	100.0	77.0	28.2	12.7	10.7	19.8	41.3
Total, average by years		19.0	24.4	34.4	36.1	47.1	65.8	75.4	67.1	58.9	28.3	24.8	24.7	42.1

[*] Data provided by the Immigration and Naturalization Service. Cf. Gertrude Krichefsky, "Quota Immigration, 1925-1944," Immigration and Naturalization Service, Monthly Review, Vol. II, No. 12 (June, 1945), pp. 156-159.

fifths of the German-Austrian quota was used. As the accompanying table discloses, the full quota was utilized during the period 1933–1944 more frequently by Greece and Spain, countries with small quota allotments.

Groundless also is the impression held in certain quarters that European refugees used Canada, Cuba, and other countries of the Western Hemisphere, natives of which are exempt from quota restrictions, as a "springboard" for emigration to the United States. It is true that many refugees migrated to such countries, but residence or domicile there, or even naturalization, confers no privileges under our immigration laws. Immigration quotas are based on country of birth, and no matter how long an immigrant alien has been away from his native country and no matter what country he may be residing in, he is counted against the quota of the country of his birth. Moreover, like immigrants coming directly from their country of birth, they must be in possession of an immigrant visa issued by an American consular officer after careful scrutiny of their record and in the majority of cases upon an advisory opinion from the State Department.[9]

In times of peace an immigrant's country of birth is usually also his country of last permanent residence. In recent years, however, this has been far from true, owing to the displacement of population as a result of oppression and war. A large proportion of the refugees admitted to the United States came, not directly from their country of birth, but from other countries in which they sought immediate haven. This tendency was furthered by the urgency of escape, on the one hand, and the United States quota limitation and the time required to secure an immigration visa, on the other hand. In addition to the countries of the Western Hemisphere, as mentioned above, a number of European countries thus served as places of temporary asylum, notably France, Great Britain, Switzerland, Belgium, and the Netherlands.

A number of measures designed to increase the number of refugees admitted were introduced in Congress, but none was passed. Even the proposal to admit 20,000 refugee children from Germany (the Wagner-Rogers bill, introduced in the 1938–1939 session of Congress) failed of enactment. While there was no new legislation in favor of refugees, their entry into the United States was somewhat facilitated by certain administrative measures, all operating within the quota requirements.

The admission of refugee children unaccompanied by their parents was facilitated by the use of a corporate affidavit in lieu of the usual personal affidavit. This guarantee of support was furnished by the United States Committee for the Care of European Children and the European-Jewish Children's Aid, Inc., and these children were placed in foster homes under the supervision of approved child-caring agencies. About 1,000 refugee

[9] Immigration and Naturalization Service, *Monthly Review*, Vol. I, No. 10 (April, 1944), pp. 12–13.

children were admitted within the quota under this special arrangement during 1934–1944. In the case of refugee immigrants over 16 years of age, it might be noted parenthetically, private individuals and groups did much to aid their admission under the laws. For example, a program initiated in 1938 by Harvard University and adopted by some 200 other colleges secured the admission and maintenance of several hundred refugee students who were selected by the International Student Service. By executive order the visitors' visas of refugees were extended to enable them to stay in this country until it was safe for them to return to their homelands.

It will be recalled that every prospective immigrant must present certain documents in connection with his application for a visa. Since refugees from political or religious persecution would have difficulty in obtaining the required documents from their governments, the Department of State issued instructions permitting consuls to waive the requirement with reference to documents not available, where personal risk or acute embarrassment might ensue in an attempt to obtain them. At the same time it was made clear that no relaxation of the law was contemplated. Also, as was provided by earlier consular regulations, if no regular passport could be obtained a Nansen passport or a travel document issued by another state would be accepted.

Another administrative measure, designed to facilitate the entry of political refugees, was the procedure known as "unblocking the quotas." Quotas are normally arranged in a priority list according to date of application. By "unblocking" is meant that if a person whose application was made earlier was unable to leave the country, the next person on the list who had travel documents and an exit permit and could use the visa would be granted a visa without delay. Under former practice the name at the top of the list stayed there even though the applicant could not use the visa, and those below him on the list were blocked. The unblocking procedure was adopted late in 1940 to meet the emergency created by the collapse of France and to rescue the political refugees who had fled there from Germany and other countries.

For the specific and emergency task of aiding the immigration to the United States of this class of refugees, the President's Advisory Committee on Political Refugees was created in July, 1940. It made arrangements with the State Department to unblock the quotas and give preference to those in special danger. With the aid of private agencies here and abroad it compiled a list of about 4,000 such persons, secured documentary proof of the bona fides of the applicants as political refugees, and recommended that they be granted visas. For this purpose visitors' visas were used as being quicker to obtain and involving no numerical limitation, but they were soon recognized as a special category of emergency visas to be renewed for as long as necessary. Later, many of the political refugees came in on permanent visas. Approximately 2,000 such political refugees—including famous political figures, former high government officials, lawyers, judges, editors, university professors, and internationally known writers and authors—arrived during the 12-month period the Committee functioned. It ceased its operation in July, 1941, when, under the wartime regulations, the issuance of visas was centralized in the State Department.[10]

Aside from the refugees who entered this country under our immigration laws, 982 refugees were admitted in 1944 outside of the regular immigration procedure and placed in an emergency refugee shelter established at Fort Ontario, near Oswego, New York, under the authority of the War Refugee Board, where they remained until 1946. This group was made up of persons of 18 different nationalities, but primarily Yugoslavs and Austrians, who had fled from their homelands to southern Italy. To relieve the refugee problem in that area and, more important, to indicate to our allies that the United States was ready to share the burden of caring for refugees during the war, they were brought here on government transport to be given temporary haven until conditions in their native lands should enable them to return. This group was in a different category from all other refugees admitted to the United States. They were not immigrants admitted for permanent residence nor nonimmigrants admitted as visitors, though they were eligible for admission under the immigration law and places were available under the quota. Their status was rather that of guests, albeit restricted guests, of the government.[11]

While the War Refugee Board, consisting of the Secretaries of State, War, and the Treasury, was charged with the over-all responsibility for this project, the Army was responsible for seeing that these refugees remained in the camp and the War Relocation Authority for the actual administration of the camp.[12] All expenses in connection with the project were borne by the United States government except that the costs of certain supplementary services were defrayed by private sources. The group in the refugee camp at Oswego were in a sense interned; they were restricted to the Oswego area, they could not work in the town, they could not have overnight leaves. They might, however, receive visitors.

The end of the war raised the question of their future status. A few,

[10] Interviews with George L. Warren, Adviser on Refugee and Displaced Persons, President's Advisory Committee on Political Refugees; Ruth Larned, Associate International Director, International Migration Service; Sheba Strunsky, Executive Secretary, International Rescue and Relief Committee; Henry E. Muller, Executive Secretary, Unitarian Service Committee. Cf. Arieh Tartakower and Kurt R. Grossmann, *The Jewish Refugee*, pp. 90–92; Common Council for American Unity, *Interpreter Releases*, Vol. XX, No. 41 (Nov. 9, 1943), pp. 362–363; Robert M. W. Kempner, "Who Is Expatriated by Hitler?" *University of Pennsylvania Law Review*, Vol. 90, No. 7 (May, 1942).

[11] War Refugee Board, *Final Summary Report*, September, 1945, pp. 64–65, 69.

[12] When the War Refugee Board was terminated in 1945, over-all responsibility for the Oswego project was transferred to the Department of the Interior.

mainly Yugoslavs, had already returned to their homelands, but the majority, finding it impossible or undesirable to return, wanted to remain in America and become citizens. A number of these had relatives living in the United States, including persons who served in our armed forces. Educators praised the work done by refugee students attending Oswego schools, and other Oswego citizens testified to the superior quality of the refugee group and their contribution to the social life of the community.[13] If they should leave the country they would be eligible to apply for admittance as permanent residents, and there were sufficient unused quotas to take care of them. In view of these facts, President Truman ordered on December 22, 1945, that their immigration status be adjusted so that those who wished to remain here might do so. By February, 1946, the entire group had been admitted on permanent or temporary visas in accordance with our immigration laws, and the refugee shelter had been closed.

It might be mentioned parenthetically that, besides the Oswego refugee group, the only other aliens admitted to the United States outside the regular immigration procedure were the prisoners of war who were brought here and the civilian internees from Latin-American countries sent here for custody during the war. The return of these alien enemies to their countries of allegiance was under way by the fall of 1945.

Proportion of Jews among the Refugees

A notion widely held is that practically all recent immigrants are Jews. Another popular notion, which is a little more discerning, is that practically all those recent immigrants who are refugees are Jews. Actually, Jews constitute a minority of all recent immigrants to the United States but a majority of the refugees.

The Immigration and Naturalization Service keeps no record of the religious affiliation of aliens admitted to the United States, but in its report on immigrants "by races or peoples" it included up to 1943 the rubric "Hebrew," which may be taken as an index of the Jews admitted. On November 8, 1943, the Immigration and Naturalization Service issued an instruction to the effect that Jews shall no longer be classified as such in the immigration records. The student of immigration, while agreeing that the system of classification "by races or peoples" is very faulty, nevertheless deplores the omission of a group as important as the Jews. This basis of classification was adopted in 1899, in the prescientific era so far as the study of race is concerned. It includes a conglomeration of items, a few of which are racial designations scientifically speaking, while the rest con-

---

[13] Common Council for American Unity, *Interpreter Releases*, Vol. XXI, No. 28 (July 18, 1944), pp. 231–232; Vol. XXII, No. 19 (May 14, 1945), p. 116; Vol. XXII, No. 45 (November 7, 1945), pp. 285–292; *PM*, Feb. 25, Feb. 26, and May 17, 1945; *New York Post*, May 17 and June 6, 1945; *New York Times*, June 3 and June 27, 1945.

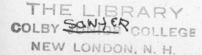
THE LIBRARY
COLBY SAWYER COLLEGE
NEW LONDON, N. H.

27881

sist of a number of geographic terms, one religious designation (Hebrew), and a majority of labels that refer to nationalities. A new classification that will indicate the broad racial divisions and designate clearly the cultural or ethnic groups, preferably with the additional notation of religious affiliation, among the immigrants is greatly needed.[14]

Taking the immigration statistics of "Hebrews" as a measurement of the number of Jews, we find that during the fiscal years ended June 30, 1933 to 1943, a total of 168,128 Jewish immigrants were admitted on permanent visas from all countries. They constituted 33.6 per cent of the total immigration (499,998) during that period. The great majority of them, 160,718, were born in Europe and comprised 44.9 per cent of all European immigrants (357,261) admitted during those years. In addition, 43,944 Jews, exclusive of government officials and returning residents, were admitted on temporary visas from all countries, constituting 4.4 per cent of all such admissions. Assuming even that all these Jewish immigrants and nonimmigrants were refugees, which is unlikely, the total number would be 212,072.

On the other hand, taking the larger estimate of the total number of refugees from Europe 1933–1944, given in the table on p. 23, and correcting it to cover the period 1933–1943, which would be 311,887, and assuming that all Jews from Europe were refugees, we find that the Jews would constitute 51.5 per cent of the total estimated number of refugees. If, however, the smaller estimate is taken, namely, 237,514 for the period 1933–1943, they would constitute, at most, 67.6 per cent of the total.

On the other hand, if, instead of including all the Jews born in Europe, the Jews were to be treated in the estimates the same way that non-Jews were treated, that is, by including only those coming from selected countries for selected years, the percentage of Jews among the refugees would be somewhat smaller (50.4 per cent and 61.0 per cent, respectively, according to the gross or the refined estimate). The assumption, however, that a higher proportion of the Jews than of the non-Jews coming here in the period 1933 to 1943 were refugees seems entirely tenable in view of the singular fate of the European Jews since the rise of Nazism. In fact, the great majority of the Jewish arrivals, regardless of what European country they originally came from, were fleeing from threatened or feared, if not actual, persecution. The number of Jewish immigrants admitted during the period 1933–1943 from the countries listed as sources of refugee emigration, namely 157,473, was almost equal to the total number of Jewish immigrants admitted from all European countries (160,718).

The following table represents the total number of Jewish immigrants admitted to the United States from all countries during the period 1933–

[14] Cf. Max Weinreich, ed., *The Classification of Jewish Immigrants and Its Implications, a Survey of Opinions*, 1945.

Hebrew Immigrants Admitted to the United States, Fiscal Years Ended June 30, 1933 to 1943, by Country of Birth and by Country of Last Permanent Residence*

Country of Birth	Number	Per Cent	Country of Last Permanent Residence	Number	Per Cent
Total	168,128	100.0	Total	168,128	100.0
Europe	160,718	95.6	Europe	141,873	84.4
Belgium	1,477	0.9	Belgium	3,878	2.3
Czechoslovakia	7,113	4.2	Czechoslovakia	4,064	2.4
Denmark	55	**	France	10,627	6.3
Finland	39	**	Germany (incl. Austria)	82,014	48.8
France	2,103	1.3	Great Britain	11,160	6.6
Germany (incl. Austria)	97,374	57.9	Greece	112	0.1
Great Britain	2,023	1.2	Hungary	4,050	2.4
Greece	118	0.1	Ireland (Eire)	35	**
Hungary	4,195	2.5	Italy	1,925	1.2
Ireland (Eire)	27	**	Netherlands	3,466	2.1
Italy	956	0.6	Norway	49	**
Lithuania	1,754	1.1	Poland	9,282	5.5
Netherlands	1,491	0.9	Portugal	983	0.6
Norway	31	**	Rumania	1,526	0.9
Poland	28,989	17.2	Spain	274	0.2
Portugal	59	**	Sweden	528	0.3
Rumania	2,907	1.7	Switzerland	2,859	1.7
Soviet Russia	6,648	4.0	Yugoslavia	447	0.3
Spain	39	**	Other Europe	4,594	2.7
Sweden	67	**	Canada	9,959	5.9
Switzerland	841	0.5	Mexico	1,275	0.8
Yugoslavia	455	0.3	West Indies	5,659	3.4
Other Europe	1,957	1.2	Other America	2,730	1.6
Canada	4,542	2.7	Asia	5,457	3.2
Newfoundland	17	**	Other countries	1,175	0.7
Mexico	172	0.1			
West Indies	275	0.2			
Central America	82	**			
South America	172	0.1			
Asia	1,693	1.0			
Africa	391	0.2			
Other countries	66	**			

* Data compiled from *Annual Reports* of the Immigration and Naturalization Service.
** Less than one-tenth of one per cent.

1943, first by their country of birth and then by their country of last permanent residence (i.e., for one year or longer). A comparison of the two reveals in cold figures the tragic flight of this group, especially from Germany, Austria, Czechoslovakia, Poland, and Rumania, to countries of temporary refuge throughout the world—in Europe, particularly Belgium, France, Great Britain, Italy, Netherlands, Portugal, Sweden, and Switzerland; in Asia; and in the Western Hemisphere, especially Canada, Mexico, and the West Indies—before reaching permanent haven here. Certainly not all but just as certainly the great majority of these immigrants may be termed refugees.

The more closely the refugee group can be distinguished from other immigrants, the higher the proportion of Jews among them becomes. Thus, according to the estimates based on official immigration statistics given above, the proportion rises from approximately one-half to about two-thirds as more refined methods are used. The Study Committee, by gathering data directly from the individuals themselves, was able to differentiate clearly the refugee group. Its findings lend support to the conclusion that the higher of the above percentages is the more accurate. In fact, they suggest that the proportion of Jews among the refugees may be even higher, falling somewhat within the upper limit of 80 per cent. This coincides with the estimate made by the High Commissioner of the League of Nations with reference to the refugees in general from Germany, the largest source of refugee emigration.[15] The questionnaire returns showed a proportion of 83 per cent, but they contain a slight bias, arising from the fact that the Jewish group was better organized and hence the coverage was more complete. Among the non-Jewish refugees there are more Protestants than Catholics, the ratio being approximately three to two. In a number of instances, the Christian refugees were married to Jews or were persons with one or more Jewish grandparents.

According to the questionnaire returns, the proportion of Jews was especially high among the Polish and Rumanian refugees, followed by the German, Lithuanian, and Dutch. Jews were in a minority in the case of Italians, Yugoslavs, Bulgarians, Greeks, and Norwegians. Catholics outnumbered Protestants appreciably among the refugees from Poland, Czechoslovakia, Italy, and Yugoslavia; they were the only religious group represented among the Greek and Spanish refugees. Protestants were relatively more numerous in the case of the German, Dutch, and French refugees; they were the only religious group in the case of the Norwegians. Among the Austrians, Hungarians, and Belgians, the proportions of Catholics and Protestants were about equal.

The percentage of Jews among recent immigrants is comparable to the percentage of leading nationalities in immigration movements of earlier years, such as the Irish during 1847–1854, the Germans during 1846–1854 and 1866–1873, and the Italians during 1901–1914. In actual numbers, Jewish immigration to the United States in the period 1933–1943 was small compared to earlier Jewish movements, averaging only 15,284 a year. It was only half as great as the number of Jewish immigrants admitted during the 1920's and only one-eighth of the number admitted in

---

[15] *Letter of Resignation of James G. McDonald, High Commissioner for Refugees (Jewish and Other) Coming from Germany, addressed to the Secretary General of the League of Nations,* London, 1935, p. 34.

the 10-year period preceding World War I. Thus both absolutely and relatively the United States was far from being flooded with Jewish or any other immigrants during the period 1933–1943, despite the fact that these were the most fateful years in the life of European Jewry. During this period Palestine played a large role in absorbing Jewish immigrants. Until the enactment of the Immigration Act of 1924 the United States held first place among the countries receiving Jewish immigrants. Since then its role has been dwindling and that of Palestine increasing.[16]

Characteristics of the Refugee Immigrants

As regards the proportional representation of the various nationalities among the refugees, the findings of the Study Committee agree in general with the estimates of nationality given in the table on p. 23, which is based on official immigration statistics by country of birth. In some cases, however, these findings suggest certain modifications. For example, only a small minority of the Italian immigrants were actually refugees, probably not many more than 4,000. The Italian refugees, therefore, should rank numerically much lower. Similarly, the ranking of the Greeks, Norwegians, Finns, and Danes seems too high for the same reason. The Germans and Austrians rank first among the refugees, followed by the Poles, Czechoslovaks, Russians, French, and Hungarians. Prominent among the smaller representations are the Italians, Hollanders, Belgians, Yugoslavs, Rumanians, and Lithuanians. It is noteworthy that the great majority of the refugees were native-born citizens of the countries from which they fled, this being especially the case with the Germans, Italians, Russians, and Yugoslavs. It was least true of the refugees who came from France, many of whom had been born elsewhere, chiefly Germany and Russia, but had acquired French citizenship. In the case of the Jews, who showed the greatest variety of nationality background, their mother tongue was characteristically the national language of their country of birth or citizenship; only in the case of the Polish Jews, and to a much lesser extent the Russian, was Yiddish an important language.

The Immigration and Naturalization Service has long reported on the composition of the immigrant group by age, sex, marital status, and occupation. With the cessation of mass immigration, effected by the adoption of the policy of restriction, especially by the enactment of the Immigration Act of 1924, changes have occurred in the distribution of these characteristics. In the days of mass immigration the typical immigrant was an unattached young male of the laborer, artisan, or servant class. Recent immigrants, as compared with earlier arrivals, show a more even distribution of the sexes, a larger proportion of persons over 45 years of age, a

[16] Jacob Lestchinsky, *Jewish Migration for the Past Hundred Years*, Yiddish Scientific Institute—YIVO, 1944.

larger proportion of married persons and consequently of family groups, and a larger proportion of professional, commercial, and skilled workers and of persons with no occupation. The refugees, so far as they can be distinguished in the immigration statistics, resemble in general other recent immigrants and in some respects exhibit the above-mentioned trend in a more marked degree.

Since 1820, when the collection of official immigration statistics began, the over-all sex ratio of the immigrants admitted has been 150 males to 100 females. However, this preponderance of male-immigrant arrivals has been offset to some extent by the higher rate of return of male immigrants to their native lands, so that the ratio of net immigrant arrivals is something less than 150 males to 100 females.[17] The ratio has been steadily declining, especially since 1921, and since 1930 it has fallen to less than 100 males per 100 females. In the following table, showing the per cent sex distribution of immigrant arrivals by decades since 1911, the declining proportion of males and the increasing proportion of females are evident.

PER CENT SEX DISTRIBUTION OF IMMIGRANT ALIENS ADMITTED TO THE UNITED STATES, FISCAL YEARS ENDED JUNE 30, 1911–1944.

Years	Per cent Male	Per cent Female
1911–1920	63.5	36.5
1921–1930	55.6	44.4
1931–1940	43.4	56.6
1941–1944	42.7	57.3

What is the situation among immigrants admitted from countries of refugee emigration? The Immigration and Naturalization Service does not report sex distribution and other demographic characteristics by country of birth, but by "races or peoples" and by country of last permanent residence. These data it made available to us in special tabulations which distinguish, so far as is possible, refugees from other immigrants. The statistics by races or peoples lent themselves to refinement by the same procedure as used above in estimating the total number of refugees by country of birth.

In regard to sex distribution, the special tabulations show females to be in the majority but not to quite the same extent as in the general statistics given above. By selected European races, the percentages are 47.4 per cent male, 52.6 per cent female; by Europe as place of last permanent residence, 45.8 per cent male, 54.2 per cent female. The refined estimate by selected races is 48.6 per cent male and 51.4 per cent female.

The most striking trend in the age distribution of immigrant arrivals

[17] Ernest Rubin and Reuben Speiser, "Immigration and the Sex Ratio," Immigration and Naturalization Service, *Monthly Review*, Vol. II, No. 11 (May, 1945), p. 143.

since 1924 has been the decreasing proportion in the age group 16 to 44 years and the increasing proportion 45 years of age and over. The refugee group exhibits this trend to a marked degree, as indicated both in the general immigration statistics (1935–1944) and in the special tabulations.

PER CENT OF DISTRIBUTION BY AGE GROUPS OF IMMIGRANT ALIENS ADMITTED TO THE UNITED STATES, FISCAL YEARS ENDED JUNE 30, 1925–1944[']

Age group	From all countries				By selected European races 1933–1944		By Europe as last permanent residence 1933–1944
	1925–1929	1930–1934	1935–1939	1940–1944	Gross	Refined	
Under 16 years	16.3	17.4	16.3	14.0	16.1	14.8	16.8
16 to 44 years	74.7	70.5	66.5	62.4	63.2	62.8	61.4
45 years and over	9.0	12.1	17.1	23.6	20.7	22.4	21.8

As might be expected from their age distribution, a majority of recent immigrants, including the refugees, are or have been married. The percentage is practically the same in all calculations, viz., 55 per cent on the basis of all immigrant arrivals 1933–1944, 56 per cent by selected European races, and 54 per cent by Europe as place of last permanent residence. The effect of the immigration quota act, with the preferences it gives to close relatives of citizens or aliens resident here, has been to make recent immigration more of the family type, at least in the way of uniting family groups. The effect of persecution has been similar. Moreover, since it has hit whole families and not just individual members of a family unit, refugee immigration has been largely a family type of movement. At the same time, as we shall see later, there are many separated families among the refugees; that is, certain members of the immediate family were unable to escape or to escape to the same country.

Perhaps the most striking difference between recent immigrants, especially the refugees, and other earlier immigrants is to be found in the kinds of jobs they held before coming to this country. An unusually large proportion of the refugees were engaged in professional and commercial occupations, while the proportion of unskilled laborers and servants was far below average. Most striking is the high proportion of persons, well over one-half, reporting as having no gainful occupation. This latter group is composed of women, children, and older persons with no regular occupation. These facts are of considerable significance, as we shall later see, with regard to the extent and nature of the economic competition offered by the refugees. The following table, with comparative figures for earlier years, shows the trend in occupational distribution and the extent to which that trend has been intensified by the coming of the refugees. This is seen most readily by contrasting the occupational distribution since 1931 with that of earlier periods.

PER CENT DISTRIBUTION BY OCCUPATION OF IMMIGRANT ALIENS ADMITTED TO THE UNITED STATES, FOR FIVE-YEAR PERIODS, FISCAL YEARS ENDED JUNE 30, 1911 TO 1944*

Occupation	1911–1915	1916–1920	1921–1925	1926–1930	1931–1935	1936–1940	1941–1944	By selected European races 1933–1944	By Europe as last permanent residence 1933–1944
Total	100.0	100.0	100.0	100.0	100.0	100.0	100.0	100.0	100.0
Professional	1.4	3.2	2.9	3.6	6.1	8.5	11.2	7.7	7.4
Commercial	1.6	2.7	2.2	1.8	3.2	9.9	9.0	11.6	11.0
Skilled	14.9	16.7	18.6	18.7	11.7	12.2	13.6	12.5	11.3
Farmers	1.2	2.6	2.9	3.1	2.0	1.6	0.9	1.4	1.3
Servants	12.3	8.8	10.5	10.3	6.2	6.1	2.8	4.3	5.3
Laborers	39.9	23.1	20.2	18.7	6.1	3.5	2.5	3.6	3.4
Miscellaneous	1.5	4.8	4.0	3.5	3.3	2.5	3.2	2.6	2.7
No occupation (women & children)	27.2	38.1	38.7	40.3	61.4	55.7	56.8	56.3	57.6

* The system of classification is that employed by the Immigration and Naturalization Service. Clerks, for example, are included under skilled workers. Percentages in the case of total immigration were computed from its annual reports, in the case of the estimated refugee group from data especially provided.

In actual numbers, skilled workers in various fields and clerks make up the largest single group of workers among the refugees, but the number engaged in commercial pursuits is nearly as large and is closely followed by that of the professional workers. From the special tabulations mentioned above, it is possible to give a fairly accurate estimate of the number of refugees in certain specific professional and commercial pursuits. Since these figures cover the entire period 1933–1944, they represent a gross estimate and therefore set the upper limit of the possible number of refugees in the various callings. These figures; given on p. 41, will be referred to later when discussing the refugee businessman and professional worker.

The extraordinarily large proportion of the refugee arrivals who were skilled workers, professional persons, and businessmen is further emphasized by comparing the occupational structure of the refugees with that of the American labor force as reported in the 1940 census. Although the system of classification used by the Immigration and Naturalization Service is different from that employed by the Bureau of the Census, sufficient details have been provided to make it possible to classify the data in roughly the same manner. The percentages in this case are based on just the group gainfully employed, omitting those with no gainful occupation. (See p. 42)

While the statistics below with reference to the refugee group should not be taken too literally, they provide strong evidence that the incidence of professional persons, who present little difficulty of classification, is several times as large among the refugees as among the general American population gainfully employed. Some persons included under "dealers, proprietors, etc." may more properly belong, if full information were available, under "clerks and kindred workers," but there is no doubt that

Estimated Number of Refugee Immigrants Admitted to the United States, Fiscal Years Ended June 30, 1933–1944, Who had Followed Certain Professional or Commercial Occupations*

Occupation	Estimate based on arrivals by selected European races or peoples	Estimate based on arrivals from Europe as place of last residence
Professional pursuits		
Actor	767	836
Architect	402	380
Chemist	507	432
Clergyman	2,489	2,273
Editor	457	440
Engineer (technical)	2,818	2,471
Lawyer	1,989	1,819
Musician	1,501	1,281
Nurse	707	609
Physician	5,516	4,684
Professor and teacher	3,569	3,415
Scientist and literary person	1,900	1,907
Sculptor, artist	702	717
Other professional	2,211	1,578
	25,535	22,842
Commercial pursuits		
Accountant	253	200
Agent	6,045	5,441
Banker	805	808
Manufacturer	2,115	1,792
Merchant and dealer	30,000	26,196

* Based on data provided by the Immigration and Naturalization Service.

the former of these groups, which may be termed businessmen, is proportionally unusually large among the refugees. The classification as between skilled and semiskilled workers presents numerous difficulties, but the impression is clear, and it is supported by the evidence of our questionnaire study, that among the refugees skilled artisans predominate among the manual workers. It should be recalled that the estimates of the occupational distribution of the refugee arrivals are not refined and that they include a great many non-refugees, especially it would seem among the unskilled workers. Prominent among the skilled workers are tailors, dressmakers, furriers, textile workers, butchers, bakers, barbers, carpenters, painters, and mechanics. In our questionnaire returns, the largest occupational group is composed of dealers, proprietors, managers; followed in turn by professional persons, clerks and kindred workers, and skilled and semiskilled workers. Though these returns are biased with reference to "head" workers as contrasted with "hand" workers, they present a reliable

PER CENT DISTRIBUTION, BY SOCIAL-ECONOMIC GROUPS, OF THE ESTIMATED REFUGEE ARRIVALS, FISCAL YEARS ENDED JUNE 30, 1933–1944, WHO HAD GAINFUL OCCUPATIONS, COMPARED WITH THAT OF PERSONS IN THE LABOR FORCE IN THE UNITED STATES IN 1940

	Per Cent Distribution		
Group	U.S. Labor Force	Refugee arrivals estimated by selected European races	Refugee arrivals estimated by Europe as last place of permanent residence
	1940*	1933–1944	1933–1944
		Gross *Refined*	
Total	100.0	100.0 100.0	100.0
Professional persons	6.5	17.5 18.3	17.5
Farm owners and tenants	10.1	3.3 3.5	3.1
Dealers, proprietors, managers and officials	7.6	22.2 24.7	21.7
Clerks and kindred workers	17.2	11.5 12.4	11.5
Skilled workers and foremen	11.7	21.4 13.7	19.3
Semiskilled workers	21.0	6.0 7.1	6.4
Unskilled workers	25.9	18.1 20.3	20.5

* *Statistical Abstract of the United States*, 1943, p. 133.

picture since they all came from known refugees. Considered by religious background, the returns show that a larger proportion of the Christian than of the Jewish refugees were professional workers. Persons in this occupational category ranked first among the Christians, followed by proprietors, managers, and officials. Among the Jewish refugees, this order was reversed. This generalization holds true of all nationality groups.

The refugees were thus primarily a middle-class group of professional and business people and artisans, with a considerable minority of persons who were economically independent and well situated. They brought with them more money per capita than is ordinarily brought or shown to immigration officers upon arrival. From our questionnaire returns and life histories, as will be seen later, they had commonly lived in rather comfortable economic conditions and were in a position to enjoy the cultural advantages of their homelands.

Unlike most earlier immigrants they did not come here to better their material lot. Some two-thirds (67.5 per cent) of them emigrated to escape actual persecution, this being twice as frequently the case among Jews, especially the Austrian and German, as among Christians. In addition, 21 per cent left to avoid anticipated persecution. This was more commonly the case with the Christian refugees. Twenty-seven per cent of the latter, as compared with 1.5 per cent of the Jews, were political refugees, that is, persons whose main or sole reason for leaving was opposition to the political regime. This was especially characteristic of the Polish, German, Russian, French, Yugoslav, and Austrian Christian refugees in that order. All told, political refugees numbered about 5 per cent of the total. The remainder, about 7 per cent, came here primarily to join their families, to improve their economic or social position, or for temporary stay.

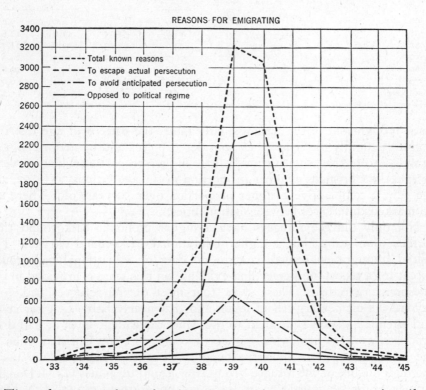

REASONS FOR EMIGRATING

Total known reasons
To escape actual persecution
To avoid anticipated persecution
Opposed to political regime

The refugees, as shown by the questionnaire returns, were primarily a middle-aged group. The questionnaire, it will be recalled, was designed for persons 16 years old and over. For an estimate of the number and proportion under 16, we have to rely on immigration statistics regarding age on arrival. A refinement of such data shows the percentage of persons among the estimated refugee group under 16 years of age to be 14.8 per cent. On this basis, there were about 35,000 refugee children (under 16) admitted to this country, boys being slightly more numerous than girls.

A large proportion of them have since become over 16 years old, and, as is brought out in the special chapter on children and youth, have served in the armed forces; some have married. The present age distribution of the refugees 16 years old and over shows the modal group to be in their forties, closely followed by those in their thirties or fifties.

PER CENT DISTRIBUTION BY PRESENT AGE (1945) OF REFUGEES 16 YEARS OLD AND OVER

Present age	Total	Male	Female	Jewish	Christian	No religion or unknown
Total	100.0	100.0	100.0	100.0	100.0	100.0
16–20	4.3	3.8	4.9	4.4	4.0	3.2
21–30	11.5	9.7	13.8	11.5	11.6	12.8
31–40	21.0	18.9	23.6	20.3	24.7	21.2
41–50	27.5	28.2	26.7	27.2	29.3	29.2
51–60	21.2	23.1	18.8	21.5	19.5	20.8
61–70	11.4	12.9	9.4	11.8	9.2	9.6
71 and over	3.1	3.4	2.8	3.3	1.7	3.2

As is brought out in the accompanying table, the pattern of age distribution is essentially the same when considered by sex and by major religious groups, except that women show a little higher proportion under 40 years of age, the Christians a higher proportion in the age groups 30 to 50, and the Jews a comparatively higher proportion over 50 years old. There are no marked differences between nationalities.

Not only did the refugees have a higher economic background than former immigrants, but a higher educational background as well. The official immigration records contain no data on educational background except for a report on literacy, but evidence on this score is provided in our questionnaire returns. These show that most of the refugees had gone beyond the elementary school level, and that nearly half (44.3 per cent) had attended schools equivalent to the American college level or had done graduate work. A somewhat higher percentage of the Christian than of the Jewish group were university people. All other evidence also points to the high quality of the refugee group. For example, James G. McDonald, former High Commissioner of Refugees under the League of Nations, described the exiles from Germany as being among "the political and intellectual leaders under the German Republic—Democrats, moderate Socialists, pacifists, liberal professors, journalists, Catholic priests, and Protestant pastors." So selective was the emigration that Hitler's Germany, Mussolini's Italy, and Franco's Spain became practically intellectual deserts. As a further indication of the outstanding quality of the group, it should be noted that twelve were Nobel Prize winners and that at least

103 of them have attained the distinction of being listed in *Who's Who in America* and 220 in *American Men of Science,* despite the short time they have been here. The number so listed is twice as large as would be expected if the same ratio to general population characteristic of Americans were to be applied to them.

The refugees were primarily an urban group with a cosmopolitan outlook, many of them having come from the largest cities of the Continent. A not inconsiderable number of them had traveled widely and knew languages other than their own, including English. All of these characteristics of the refugee group have an important bearing on the question of their adjustment and assimilability. This may be illustrated, and the background traits mentioned above may be summarized, as follows:

REFUGEE IMMIGRANTS COMPARED WITH EARLIER IMMIGRANTS

Refugee Immigrants	*Earlier Immigrants*
1. Came primarily to escape persecution.	1. Came primarily for economic reasons.
2. Few planned to return to homeland.	2. Many intended to return.
3. High proportion of women and young children.	3. High proportion of unattached males.
4. Mainly middle- and upper-class movement.	4. Mainly lower- and middle-class movement.
5. Primarily business, professional, and white-collar groups; unusually large number of intellectuals.	5. Primarily peasants, laborers, and artisans; few intellectuals.
6. Majority had education above elementary school level; many college and professional school graduates.	6. Majority had elementary school education or less; few college and professional school graduates.
7. Came chiefly from cities, especially large ones.	7. Came chiefly from rural areas and small towns.
8. Had cosmopolitan outlook; traveled widely; familiar with languages other than their own.	8. Had limited horizon; had seldom traveled beyond their region or country; were unfamiliar with other languages.
9. Occasionally came with means.	9. Rarely came with means.
10. Widely distributed in different sections of the community.	10. Tended to concentrate in colonies.
11. High standard of living; reluctant to work for low wages.	11. Low standard of living; were willing to work for low wages.
12. Sought the more desirable types of jobs.	12. Accepted less desirable jobs.
13. Competed on the "higher" occupational levels; aroused the opposition of American business and professional groups.	13. Competed on the "lower" occupational levels; aroused the opposition of American wage-earners.

Refugee Immigrants	*Earlier Immigrants*
14. Aspired to equal successful native Americans in these fields.	14. Primarily concerned with making a living.
15. Located business and professional offices in general business districts; served general community.	15. Located usually in immigrant colonies; served primarily immigrant community.
16. Learned English rapidly and dissatisfied with superficial knowledge of it.	16. Acquired English slowly; did not seek to master it.
17. Placed great stress on education of their children.	17. Placed little stress on education of their children.
18. Tended to join American organizations and to get into main stream of American life.	18. Tended to join immigrant organizations and to remain apart from American life.
19. Made contributions on intellectual level right from the beginning.	19. Made contributions at first mostly in brawn.
20. Became naturalized rapidly and in high proportion.	20. Tended to delay naturalization; considerable proportion remained aliens.

The broad contrasts between refugees and earlier immigrants given above indicate that the background traits of the former favor a more rapid assimilation. Refugees, to be sure, face some special problems of adjustment and encounter certain kinds of opposition which the earlier immigrants largely escaped, as will become abundantly clear in the ensuing chapters. But, so far as the process of Americanization is concerned, they start off with an advantage over their predecessors.

CHAPTER III

WHAT THE REFUGEES THINK OF AMERICA

The essential fact in any immigration movement is the transference of a group of people from one country to another. There are thus brought into contact peoples—natives and newcomers—of different cultural heritages, that is, with different languages, ideals and traditions, concepts of government, standards of living, customs, and sets of values. The attitudes of the two groups toward each other become an important factor in intergroup relations. In a later chapter the reactions of the American community to the refugees will be considered. Here we are concerned with the attitudes of the refugees: their impressions of America, what customs they found strange and difficult to understand, what aspects of American culture they like and what they dislike, how they reacted to their reception here, whether they intend to remain or return to their homelands. These psychological factors have considerable bearing on the adjustment of newcomers and their assimilability.

The reactions of newcomers are also significant as revealing their own cultural traits. Statements by members of one culture group regarding the characteristics of another group not only hold the mirror up to the latter but reveal the traits of the former. Thus the cases cited below may well be regarded as further material on the characteristics and background of the refugees themselves. As one refugee, a former businessman in Germany, remarked: "I am very happy to be co-operating with this survey and would point out that nothing like this could happen in Germany in spite of the German love of statistics. There, they might make a precise catalogue of dates of birth, schooling, employment, etc., backed up by elaborate verifications, but there would never be any interest in people's attitudes or social adjustment." The material given below is typical of the great body of data obtained from interviews, life stories, and replies to the questionnaire. It may be recalled that the last page of the questionnaire provided for comments on the experience and reaction of the individual. In a few instances, the citations are from books and articles written by refugees, in which cases the bibliographical reference is given.

NOTIONS ABOUT AMERICA BEFORE ARRIVAL

The refugees were asked, among other questions, what notions they held about America before coming here. In a number of instances, their views were generally correct, as they discovered upon arrival. These are cases of persons who had had business connections with this country, had previously visited the United States (one respondent, a wealthy dealer in Oriental antiques, had visited here nine times before he came to live here permanently), had relatives here who wrote to them or visited them abroad, or had specially studied American history. More commonly, however, the refugees held inaccurate or distorted notions about America. This appears to be the usual situation in regard to the conceptions a given people has of the inhabitants and conditions in foreign lands. Numerous refugees, for example, had the previous notion that music and the fine arts were undeveloped here; that America was all business and haste; that it was highly mechanized, with wonderful inventions, "where potatoes are delivered peeled at your doorstep"; that it was fabulously wealthy and that nothing but money mattered; that gangsters and racketeers dominated the big cities; that there was little countryside, few small towns, but only huge cities of skyscrapers; and that the amount of freedom was unlimited. For example, a German Protestant research engineer writes:

"I am not ashamed to admit that my ideas about the USA were as screwy and silly as they could possibly be. This is the more remarkable as I was, for many years prior to 1933, genuinely interested in this country. Two close friends, of my graduating class, had immigrated in 1925, and urged me continuously to come over also. It was not until Nazism had attained disproportionate dimensions (to put it as mildly as it can possibly be said) that these ideas became a reality. In the years between, America was for me the country of rugged individualism in the extreme, with little regard to safety, security and interest for anything besides the dollar. How utterly false was this picture! I didn't trust my eyes when I read, in the subway in New York, that spitting is fined $500, or half a year in prison, or both! When I saw the museums, the libraries (which are open in the evening!), heard the good music on the radio, I felt nearly ashamed . . . I cannot but love and admire the people here in their magnanimity and their wholesome constructiveness."

Adolph Lowe, formerly professor of economic theory and sociology, Kiel University, and now a member of the graduate faculty of the New School for Social Research, has stressed the importance in international relations of the knowledge and impressions each nation has of other nations, and the need for investigating the sources of these notions and their effect. To judge from the experience of this Study, impressions are frequently derived from motion pictures, tourists, books, and official propaganda, and they are often ill-founded, incorrect, or greatly exaggerated.

From the impression they gained from seeing American movies, many refugees expected to see the Indians in full regalia, orange trees bearing fruit for the picking along every roadside, and continuous sunshine in California. A German Jewish student writes: "In school I had been taught quite properly about American geography, etc., but in my head there was a curious mixture of skyscrapers, kidnappers, horses, Indians, guns, Broadway and Hollywood." A Spanish Catholic woman, now a teacher in Philadelphia, states:

"I do not think that most Europeans know much of anything about America. I have to admit that many of my ideas of America had come from the movies. I'm afraid that when I left Spain I once said to my husband that I was going to be afraid of the gangsters. Yet since I have come here I have a greater sense of security than I ever had in Europe. I leave everything open around the house and never think of its safety."

Even persons connected with the motion-picture industry may be misled, for one refugee, formerly manager of Pathé abroad, observed that his whole picture of American life was pretty largely what he gained from the movies.

American tourists sometimes give Europeans a false impression of this country and its people. A doctor in law and economics from Czechoslovakia states that prior to coming to the United States she did not think there were any cultured Americans. Her ideas were gleaned through observing tourists, most of whom impressed her as being a noisy, flamboyantly dressed group who spent money freely and vulgarly. In her circle the American tourist was an object of derision. Since she has been in this country she has drastically changed her opinion about Americans in general, having met many cultivated people. Since most American tourists are wealthy, Europeans frequently assume that the majority of the American population enjoy a similar status and that "money lies on the street."

Notions about the United States gained from reading, while less gross and distorted than those obtained from observing American movies and tourists, are nevertheless often vague and biased. Even university graduates may lack clear conceptions of conditions here, just as educated Americans may be far from cognizant of life in European countries. Of American authors read by our refugee respondents, the two most frequently mentioned are Upton Sinclair and Sinclair Lewis, the former by the labor group and the latter by the bourgeoisie. Upton Sinclair has had a larger sale in Europe than over here, and has deeply influenced the thinking about America. A Hungarian machinist states that before his arrival he thought the United States was a republic in name only, that American society was divided into the two extremes of the very rich and the very poor, and that the condition of the latter resulted from impositions of powerful monopolies, as exemplified in Upton Sinclair's books. A number of workers and labor leaders from Central Europe, believing that conditions in the meat-packing industry were the same as Sinclair described them in *The Jungle* (1906), were at first afraid to eat canned meats. Another American author extensively read by this group is Jack London. The writer most frequently mentioned by the professional and business group is Sinclair Lewis, and of his books reference is made chiefly to *Babbitt* and *Main Street*. Among other authors mentioned by this group are Thomas Wolfe, John Dos Passos, Sholem Asch, and Ernest Hemingway.

In some instances the opinions held about America were influenced by government propaganda. Thus both German and Italian refugees report that they had been led to believe that Americans were suffering great hardships, that food was scarce, and that since America was a democracy there was no discipline, order, or unity here. A former German steel manufacturer states:

"Before I came to this country I had the impression that American production was junk and humbug . . . I don't think that all Germans really felt in their hearts that American production was junk. That was what we were taught to believe. Actually, we saw a few American cars, American machines in Germany, saw they ran well and were a good product, but we could not accept the idea that they were real."

IMPRESSIONS OF AMERICAN LIFE

After having lived for years in the severe blackout of Europe, many refugees on arrival were amazed and frightened by all the lights. Entering, as most of them did, the port of New York, they were deeply impressed by the skyline of New York City and its symbolism as a land where they could start life anew in freedom and self-respect. "Why didn't they tell us in Europe that New York is the most wonderful city in the world?" On the other hand, the huge buildings, the traffic, the noise, the hustle and bustle were overwhelming. Coming from countries suffering from a depressed economy because of war conditions, the refugees were struck by the economic abundance, greater conveniences and luxuries of the United States. They viewed with amazement "the lavish display in the grocery store windows," the quantities and varieties of fruits and vegetables. "We were spellbound. We could not believe that we saw real meat, real eggs, cans of vegetables and fruit, and milk and bread." A former Austrian salesman and his wife found ice cream to be the greatest treat. "We could only spend one nickel for one cone, so we both took turns eating the cone in the park. When we changed turns, we were ashamed to have anyone see us." A German of Jewish extraction had heard about American chewing gum, so the first thing he did was to try to buy some.

"I went into a little store but I couldn't speak very well so I kept making motions and saying, 'rubber, rubber.' You know, it was very funny, he gave me rubber but he didn't give me chewing gum. He gave me a box of rubber bands. Finally I cleared the matter up and I got my chewing gum."

To the thrifty European the waste here was appalling. "Americans throw everything away. There is bread in the streets, paper in them. In Germany the poor people would sell that paper, even before the war." Another German comments:

"The first thing that impressed me when I came to this country was the abundance of food and the variety. The waste shocked me. Garbage, when it was collected, contained not only surplus food, tabs of butter, rolls, and what not, but furniture and radios were left on the street to be collected by the garbage collector. I read in the paper how the farmers spilled their milk in a strike. I didn't realize there was a gap between production and distribution. It was shocking. At the same time I saw store windows filled with oysters, lobsters, available to almost anybody at any time; strawberries in January, a variety in fruits and vegetables, fish, quantities of food that was available. It was not possible for any middle-class person to have that in Germany. In Germany during the winter they eat meat and all kinds of cabbage as there is no other vegetable."

The apartment houses with all modern conveniences, the kitchen facilities and appliances in the home, the delivery service, refrigeration, even soap that floats, all these available even to lower paid workers, were things to be remarked about. "The commonplace in America is luxury in Europe." And so many automobiles! "In Austria only the top few hundred had cars, and most cars on the streets were taxis." Here even the workers have cars. "The parking lot [at a factory] could rival that of the Munich opera on the eve of a gala performance."

Having lived, especially the Germans, under authoritarian regimes and in fear of the Gestapo, the refugees were impressed with the freedom and security they found here. To the question "What aspects of American life do you regard as most satisfying?" one refugee replied, "That nobody bothers you. If somebody is knocking at the door, you have not to be afraid. It's the laundry man and not the Gestapo." Another typical response: "Going to bed and not being afraid that any Gestapo murderer can break the doors, penetrate my house at two o'clock in the morning and under the pretext of searching for weapons, steal away every valuable belonging. . . . Only a person who has lost freedom can realize what it means to enjoy it again, and appreciate it accordingly." The refugees are impressed that "the man in the streets is not nervous at all," that even children speak up without fear, and that everybody feels free to express his opinion about the government. In such an atmosphere, "it is amazing what a short time it took us to get over the horrors we had lived through and to feel like healthy normal human beings once more." They wonder if Americans, never having experienced anything else, fully appreciate the freedom they possess.

The new arrivals were also impressed by the lack of regimentation here and the absence of *Verboten* signs. They were amazed that people were allowed to walk on the grass in the public parks, and many of them found a symbolic thrill in exercising this right. Breathlessly they watched the traffic roll by with but a minimum of police control. "Woe to the German who had crossed a street at the red light even if there was no car in sight. The hand of the law came down upon him immediately. Here people could risk their own lives as they chose." To be able to work without a license, to walk around without identification papers, and to move without reporting to the police were new and welcome experiences. So were the absence of signs: "For Jews Forbidden," "Jews Unwanted." The feeling of independence and the democratic way of life were "as a gift from heaven." The familiar and the beautiful things about European life were missed, but all of these "don't mean a thing compared to the intangible things that everyone enjoys in this country—the Bill of Rights, the standards of equality and justice."

The refugees were amazed to discover that government officials are public servants instead of petty tyrants to be feared and distrusted. "In Europe," writes an Austrian tailor, "a teacher is feared and a policeman is a threat, whereas here they are friends and public servants." A Czech businessman states: "A small governmental official in Southeastern Europe never takes the attitude of being a public servant as we are accustomed to find it in the United States, but he personifies in himself the supreme state authority." A German housewife, surprised to find that American customs officials and other men in uniform were human beings, remarks:

"In Germany anyone in uniform represents a threat and is to be treated with great deference; the policeman on the street, the janitor of a building, the ticket agent, each one represents a high position and is not to be taken lightly. Here in America I am spoken to in a very friendly and warm manner."

A German businessman, now plant foreman in Little Rock, Arkansas, relates the following incident:

"My mother-in-law, a German and on a visit here, had to register as an enemy alien, and my wife went with her to the post office. My mother-in-law was somewhat frightened due to the fact that she is an enemy alien and was about to see government officials. Waiting in the hall to be admitted to the registration room and standing next door to the postmaster's office, she read the word "Postmaster." The German uniform-clad *Postmeister* came into her mind as a high official who would hardly speak to an insignificant woman, as she deemed herself to be. Humbleness and submissiveness is the general attitude of a German subject to officials like a postmaster.

"These were her thoughts when the assistant postmaster stepped out of the office. Seeing the group he asked if he could be of some service. My wife told him they were waiting to be admitted to the registration room. But he politely invited them to wait in his office and arranged seats for them. My mother-in-law was perplexed. A high official who in her native country she would hardly dare address, treated her, the enemy alien, on equal terms. And more than that, he was concerned with her comfort and showed the distinguished manners of a gentleman. No longer could she control her pent-up emotions. Tears came in her eyes and in her heart she experienced in this moment religion in action and a part of our American way of life, unknown to her as a German."

Losing the feeling of fear and of inferiority so far as authority is concerned represents a change in attitude commonly experienced by Jew and Christian alike. It was also a new experience to find that the government exists for the people and not the people for the government. The participation by citizens in governmental and civic affairs was a novel practice. The Germans particularly were not accustomed to such voluntary group action. It is interesting to note that in translating our questionnaire into German we could find no equivalent for "civic or community organizations," and were forced into rendering it as *Buergervereinigung*, literally a union or association of citizens.

Some of our customs the refugees found strange and hard to adjust themselves to because they involved numerous changes in commonplace matters to which they were long habituated. An elderly housewife stated in an interview that the refugees found it necessary to relearn their table manners, their simple everyday practices, the things that are taken so much for granted. They wanted to relearn them because they wanted to be like the Americans. She pointed out that in this country a man walking along the street with a lady walks on the outside, which is different from the custom in Germany. Simple things like a mailbox, a window, and a door, all open differently from what she was accustomed to. These present no problem to her children, but cause her to stop and think each time she encounters them. American cuts of meat are different, the units of weight and measurement are different, and the Fahrenheit thermometer is unfamiliar. Since there are no self-service stores in Germany, a refugee had the mistaken notion that people being checked out at the counter of an A & P Super-Market were being investigated for theft. A surprising sight to a German woman was the inside of barbershops:

"In Europe we regard barber shops as mysterious. Even in a hairdresser shop, every booth was strictly closed and full of secrets. In America the idea is just the opposite. Here we see every manipulation, in fact, we can't help seeing it . . . Seeing these acts was very amusing to me. It looked really funny. Little by little I understood that open view of such manipulations is rather characteristic of American people. Nobody has to hide anything. Nobody has to fear anything. People are free in every way. The doors are always open."

While admiring the independent and natural behavior of American women and girls, some refugees are critical of the amount of freedom allowed young girls; their seeming preoccupation with "dates," clothes, and light entertainment; and the amount of make-up both women and girls use. "In Germany we did not know any make-up except on the stage." American women of the business and professional class are regarded as better informed and less restricted in social life than their counterparts in Europe. The lot of the American housewife is idyllic in comparison. The European middle-class home lacks the conveniences of the average American house and the laborsaving appliances. The hardworking *Hausfrau* does not exist here. Writes a German Protestant woman:

"The German wife saw it as a 'sacred' duty to be tired and overwhelmed by housework and to do it in as difficult (*umständlich*, detailed or troublesome) a way as possible. It would have been a 'sin' to go in a drug store for a snack, and 'drug stores' with restaurants (fountains) such as here did not exist! The wife who would send her husband to a restaurant during the 'wash-days' ('wash'—a terrible institution, full of horrid overwork) was soon known in the neighborhood as 'not a good housewife!' Especially in the smaller towns, but also in big cities like Berlin . . . the housewife was always busy. It is only here that many European women see a different way of living and therefore so many are in the typical 'U.S.A. rapture.'"

One of the most interesting aspects of American life to the newcomers is the lack of rigid class lines and the non-existence of a military caste. Typical comments are:

"People of all strata mingle freely here." (German store manager)

"A rich man and a poor man may sit at the same counter and eat lunch and neither of them would feel embarrassed." (German salesman)

"Here manual labor does not prevent a person as it did in Germany from taking part in social activities." (German lawyer)

"No one is ashamed to go out and sweep the sidewalks or do other seemingly menial tasks when the occasion requires it." (Polish store owner)

"If I walk about town in a pair of overalls I am not looked down upon." (Italian business manager)

"You can work in a cannery or at a university, and nobody thinks more or less of you because you do one or the other." (Austrian housewife)

"I appreciate that nobody asks my wife or me what kind of work we are doing, the main thing is that we work and make our living in a decent and lawful way. This is the reason that we do not feel the difference in our pecuniary situation." (Wealthy Jewish manufacturer abroad, wife never before employed)

To immigrants from Europe where social background, family connections, and religious affiliations are all-important, the American ideal of judging a person solely on his own merit and making him constantly prove himself anew comes as a revelation. According to a refugee philosopher, the profound sense of the dignity of the common man is one of America's most admirable traits.[1]

Many refugees have found it difficult to get used to the informal, democratic relationship between employer and employee. In Europe, "the employee takes off his hat and is very formal whenever the boss appears." In

[1] Jacques Maritain, "En quittant l' Amérique," *La République Française,* May, 1945, p. 6.

Germany, "one could *hear* without seeing whether a person was talking to a *Vorgesetzte* [superior] or to somebody of his own rank or to one below his rank. Here the janitor speaks to the director just as the director speaks to the janitor." "It took us a while," writes a German couple, "to forget that a boss has to be bowed to and addressed formally with all signs of devotion." Another surprise is that domestic workers are treated here as employees, not as servants. Some refugees think there is no laboring class here in the sense that it exists in Europe, since there is always an opportunity to shift from job to job and from one income group to another. In Europe a change of occupation is not looked upon favorably, and only rarely are people given a chance to work themselves up to higher positions.

The educational opportunities available here have aroused great admiration on the part of the refugees. They are amazed to find almost every type of school, and libraries and museums as well, open to all the people and not only to those with means. This is in contrast to European custom according to which opportunity for education is measured in terms of money. The European is accustomed to pay for access to schools, libraries, museums, and public recreational facilities. "Even the public parks in Europe are not playgrounds as they are here, trespassing on the lawns is forbidden under penalty and a toll is extracted even for occupying some of the benches." The newcomers are also impressed by the variety of classes made available in our system of public education—for adults as well as children, in the evening as well as during the day, in technical subjects as well as academic, and ranging from the elementary to the university level. They express great appreciation of American generosity in opening these facilities to them and of the helpfulness and understanding of the schoolteachers and principals. They observe with great satisfaction that their children liked to go to school, that they were treated as individuals, not automatons, and encouraged rather than punished. A German lawyer comments:

"Here children grow up without fear. I believe that the German school discipline is the cause of most of the evil in Germany and that the love of freedom, self-reliance, and respect for the right of the other fellow are the natural results of American education."

On the other hand, the refugees do not think so highly of American music and art. Knowledge of these subjects, they believe, is not so deeply rooted here as in Europe. One refugee, German-Jewish in origin, a concert pianist here as he was abroad, thinks that music has not developed well in this country because it is considered as business rather than art. Another refugee musician and music teacher is convinced that enthusiasm for the loftiest musical standards can be aroused in American youth by the right approach, and to that end he has composed a series of operas designed to appeal to the youthful mind. Two German schoolteachers, settling in Detroit, were surprised to find that in a city of that size there was no regular opera and complained that the few operas played there were of a standard to be found in small German towns lacking in cultural tradition. Some refugees like modern American painting, but the artists among them believe that it is impossible here to live by professional work alone. The American theater, they think, is good, but the interest in movies is excessive. The movies, to their mind, follow a narrow pattern and are uncritical, although they exhibit a high level of performance.

With regard to religious organizations in this country, some of the Christian refugees think the churches have a more liberal standard and are closer to the needs of the people; others think they are not so idealistic as in Europe. Active participation in church affairs is a novel experience to the refugee. In Europe the church was supported by taxes. "Here," comments a German Protestant, "unless you support the church, spiritually, physically, financially, it goes to pieces. Hence, it becomes your church, and you become vitally interested in all its phases of work." A Hungarian states:

"I am impressed by the fact that in America there is freedom of worship and people are not forced into the churches. While in the old country we see small houses and high churches, in America it is the opposite. There are higher buildings and smaller churches. In many European countries religion is forced upon people and if you could not pay the taxes you were disowned, or at least disgraced."

As regards the Jews, the emphasis in Europe was on the community; here it is on the congregation (see also Chap. XI).

In the eyes of the refugees, the American people are distinguished by certain traits, of which generosity, friendliness, and helpfulness are outstanding. Time and again the refugees express their profound gratitude to America for accepting them and giving them an opportunity to begin life anew. "It was hard to believe," writes a German Jew, "that so much generosity was still alive." An Austrian Protestant states, "What impressed us most in the United States was the fact that private persons who had no personal interest in refugees should help perfect strangers to adjust themselves." A middle-aged woman remarks that everybody has been kind to her, even the streetcar conductors. "Americans can be proud of the manner in which they accepted the refugees," comments a former movie producer from Germany. A Jewish artist, now living in San Francisco, says, "Much of the hardship of our Nazi experiences, the sadness of leaving our home and our once beloved, now deteriorated and corrupted Fatherland, has been smoothed over by the liberal and human approach of my newly-won American friends." And an Austrian Jewish businessman in Youngstown, Ohio, states:

"The hospitality and good will of many people in this town, without distinction of color and creed, has surely helped us a lot to overcome the deep moral depression caused through the atrocities and deprivations upon our own people. I have the feeling that the warm reception and the understanding support which many of the victims of the Nazis received upon arriving here, and the security they got, will spur them on to their utmost in putting all their abilities in the service of this country."

The friendliness and cordiality of Americans greatly impressed the newcomers. "The people here," comments a Spanish refugee, "seem to be more openhearted and kind. In Europe you have very good friends but on first acquaintance people take precautions against getting too friendly with a stranger. Here they trust you even though you are a foreigner." A German Jewish woman states, "I found that people were not only friendly but without exception insisted to go out of their way to be of help to me. Such willingness to help is not found in any other country that I know of." A German Christian woman likewise reports, "The Americans are so friendly. They ask you to their home and show affection. In England it takes years for a friend to ask you to her home. I have had more invitations here in one year than I had in five years in England." Another German, a salesman, is particularly impressed by the friendly attitude of fellow workers, who are "always ready to explain, to show how it is done. In Europe, your fellow workers would never take the time nor show such interest." A student is struck by the fact that "here you can sit down in the streetcar, turn to your neighbor and say 'good morning,' and usually get an answer."

At the same time, the newcomers found it disconcerting at first when Americans said, "You must come and see us," and then issued no formal invitation. A German Christian woman remarks, "Americans are nice and friendly people, but sometimes it is hard to know what they mean. They ask you to their house, and after you have been there tell you, 'Oh, I'm so glad you have come, and please come again.' You don't know whether they mean that, and being a foreigner, you don't like to take them up on something they don't mean." Another states, "In Germany people were perhaps more rude and straightforward, but at the same time if they asked you to dinner you knew they meant it." A German Jewish businessman used to take seriously the parting words of a friend who would say, "See you soon," or the woman who graciously said, "You must come over to our home and have dinner with us some evening"; and he found it difficult to get used to disregarding "the easy promises" that people made. A banker states, "Here people you have never seen before call you by your first name and ask you to come over to see them, when they really don't mean it." In the beginning he took this seriously, but now he regards it as "empty talk" and "typically American." Some newcomers feel that Americans are only superficially friendly and that their politeness is not to be taken at its face value; others think that in their desire to help, Americans are apt to make promises which they are unable to keep; while still others realize that there is involved here simply a manner of expression. "To save the newcomer some disappointment," advises one respondent, "instruct him that 'How do you do?' means

'Hello,' and that 'You must come and see us someday' is not usually an invitation." Another language folkway which is strange, especially to the German immigrant, is the American's lack of definiteness in his answers. "It is hard to distinguish between a straightforward yes, a noncommital remark, and a polite refusal." "Americans are not used to clear, strong, positive statements." "The American is always polite and does not wish to hurt your feelings, so he is not apt to tell you if he thinks differently, quite contrary to the German habit." Newcomers should be instructed, advises a recent arrival from Germany, not to say "Yes" or "No," but to say instead, "I think so" or "I do not believe so."

Some of the refugees find it difficult to get accustomed to the informality of Americans, the lack of distinctions in forms of address, and the free use of first names. It is a jolt to the Herr Doktor Professor to be called "Doc." On the other hand, once they are used to it, the refugees like the easygoing, informal manner of Americans, the common bond of the universal "you" instead of the formal "Sie" and informal "du" of the Germans. In response to the question as to what had changed most in his way of life, a German states, "From the very formal, very bourgeois businessman, Herr K., to the hardworking war worker, 'Fred'—and I like it."

The refugees also find it remarkable that Americans are not tense and that they are not always worrying about the future or their *Seelenleben* (inner or spiritual life). One states that it is difficult to integrate German idealism and skepticism into American pragmatism and optimism. Many like the American lightheartedness, which is in such contrast to the German "heavy touch." Others think that Americans are not sufficiently serious, especially about political and cultural matters, and that they are provincial in their outlook. This is a view frequently expressed by refugee students concerning American youth. Some newcomers think there is little expression of individuality among Americans, that the daily pattern of life is highly standardized. Another trait frequently commented upon is the habitual hurry, often by people who have no place to go but are most intent upon getting there as rapidly as possible. "America," says a bewildered new arrival, "is a huge factory made up of human machines in perpetual motion." "My life here," states an artist, "has changed from *Vita contemplativa* to *Vita activa*." Even in their recreation, comments a German couple, the Americans never stay put. "We newcomers were puzzled as to what it was that always lured them [the Americans] from one place to another. But then we could not have explained to them what had made us sit in the same café or beerhall all our leisure hours. The European likes to be anchored to one spot in the swiftly turning universe, whereas the American wants to be moving with it. There will never be an approachment of the continents in this matter." A businesswoman from Germany cannot understand why Americans feel little or no need for the European siesta period between noon and 2:00 P.M. Numerous business and industrial workers state that they prefer the European slowness and thoroughness to the American speed and superficiality. They are astonished at American technical ability and the widespread familiarity with machines. Says a German mechanic, "Americans do not have five senses, they have six. The sixth is technical ideas and understanding." Others observe here a materialistic philosophy, with over-emphasis on the principle of efficiency, and a dominating role that money plays.

The following document, based on an interview with a cultured refugee, the wife of an eminent German professor, contains excellent observations on American life as contrasted with European.

IMPRESSIONS OF AMERICA

By Ise Gropius

There are five things in particular, each of them more or less related to one another, that strike a European living in America. I was first of all impressed by your general fearlessness. Children are not afraid of their parents, students are not afraid of their teachers, men of their bosses. Women don't seem to be afraid of anything or anybody.

Eloquent of this fearlessness is your "open door and no fence" policy. Nobody closes doors here, or erects fences and walls that might serve as a hostile or discriminating gesture. Even your houses look inviting. The New England architecture, which is the kind I know best, stems from the English, but where the English houses by their appearance ask you to stay out, American houses ask you to come in. People keep their shades up for everybody to look in and nobody seems disturbed by the fact that his privacy can be violated at any time on the slightest pretext.

The fact that everything in America is public at first impresses a European as rather indiscreet. This is especially true of your newspapers. Even your most famous, most important men must share their private lives with their fellow Americans. They are under a magnifying glass all the time. The public knows how many socks and ties they own and how they live in general. Heroes are at the mercy of everybody, and either such personages live their private lives publicly or else under suspicion.

It is hard for a European to understand this publicizing of a man's private life. While the Germans aren't as baffled by it as the people in England, where they still consider the telephone a violation of their privacy, yet they are far more self-conscious than Americans and feel reluctant to have their private affairs exposed to public curiosity. And yet, this open door custom of Americans is very appealing to Europeans, once they realize that it aims at banishing all barriers. It's tantamount to saying "You're welcome to drop in." We feel it is a desire to keep things democratic by having them open to investigation.

The second thing that strikes a European in America is what I call "action preferred." In the U.S. dreams are made to come true. The gap between dream and reality is narrow, and while Europeans are often unwilling to bridge it because they feel the result might not live up to their expectations, Americans seem to know no such hesitancy. Sometimes they prefer action even to reason. An idea strikes them today and tomorrow they are already busy realizing it. Whereas Europeans are often frustrated and hampered by conditions and traditions in their overcrowded countries, Americans still find elbow room to carry out the most fantastic schemes. Practical activity is usually preferred to contemplation, and with this impulsiveness anything can happen and usually does. Because of this belief in action every able immigrant is sooner or later given his chance to participate and work, a thing they all need so badly to integrate them into their adopted country.

Sometimes the American impatience for the "good life" takes on quite surprising forms. A New York paper once announced that New York needn't worry about the heat next summer because the World's Fair would provide Christmas festivities three times during the summer in their Swiss village with snow and all the trimmings. Or when the wish to show that America is the land of dreams come true prompted somebody to present Mr. Maeterlinck with a live bluebird on his arrival in this country.

One thing we have been puzzled about in this country is the emphasis put on the knowledge of facts. The amassing of a stupendous amount of information, as is, for instance, demonstrated in the various quiz programs has baffled us like everybody else. We feel it may mislead people into believing that the aim of education is to acquire a vast collection of uncorrelated facts instead of learning a method to coordinate and integrate the things that come our way.

Again, if you make a mistake in America your life isn't ruined. You have tremendous reserves and tremendous room. Innovations are commonplace. Americans will greet a new idea or experiment with "why not try it?" and, strange to say, it does not kill them. To a friend who wrote me from England, worrying about the race riots, I replied: "You forget the margin for error here is so wide. These symptoms aren't as threatening as they appear to be. They may look wild and woolly and the papers play them up, but things settle back into place soon again and there is luckily time and space to work gradually toward an improved balance."

In Europe on the contrary every mistake strikes back at you tomorrow, and that was particularly true of postwar Germany. We always had to make final and irrevocable decisions. Germany has no room, no reserves. Whatever she does is bound to have more threatening consequences. So many things are inched up along with it. Her geographical location alone narrows down this margin for error as she has little natural frontier protection. Every historical mistake she makes is therefore fatal. This is the same for France, who lost an empire in a few months, whereas England is still intact because the sea separates her from Europe.

As another result of the wide margin for error in America I find no one here as serious minded about money as the Europeans are. For the Americans, making money is a kind of game, something you win or lose. You never seem to take it seriously in the first place. If you lose you are just unlucky but you can always say: "I shall send the family to my great-aunt who has a farm in Vermont" and you can start all over again. But in Europe it's a different story. If you lose your money it is considered as a serious character defect. It proves that you are either extravagant or stupid, and it is hard, if at all possible, to make a comeback.

The same holds true of jobs. If a European is forced to change his job he is apt to call himself a failure. But in America most curricula vitae of outstanding citizens show that they have had lots of different jobs in their life, all varied. They change easily and without regret to take on what proves most promising at the moment. They are in business with their hats on, as it were. This all presupposes versatility and flexibility, but also the great opportunity one finds here to earn a living no matter how.

The fourth thing that impresses me about this country is the great influence your women wield. This doesn't mean that we don't have outstanding women abroad, but they rarely find such large audiences as for instance Mrs. Roosevelt, Dorothy Thompson, and others. I find American women in general far more alert and progressive than European women. For instance, I regard the League of Women Voters as an excellent idea. Those women often make more sense than some of the senators. When we arrived in this country we were surprised that it was the women's college that asked my husband to lecture about modern architecture, and that it is the women who direct the trends in home building and furnishing.

What really amazes the foreigner, however, is the way American men have been domesticated. Much as they compete with each other in business, at home they seem to be more or less content to leave the management of their private lives to their wives. In relegating almost the whole field of culture and relaxation to the women, the American men all but kill themselves in their efforts to earn money. True, they play that as a game, like a boy who takes his hockey seriously while remembering that it is a game. But it leaves them little time for leisure, play, friendship. When they do relax, they are apt to mix business with pleasure and go off playing golf with their business associates. Go to any social function and you will see the women having most of the fun. Their husbands have to be coaxed along and arrive too tired and nervous to enjoy themselves. They are merely a backdrop for the real show. I remember, when I first came to America how amused I was at a newspaper item describing a social event. It stated that Mrs. So-and-so arrived in her so-and-so gown, and, after a detailed description of what she wore, wound up at the very end, "She was accompanied by her husband."

A lot has been said and written by Europeans about "love in America," but I have found it easier to be witty about it than it is to be reasonable. The misunderstandings between different nations about their respective morals and habits are as numerous as they are ludicrous, and trying to measure other people's problems with your own native yardstick seems a hopeless job. Continental and English views on this subject are very different and things in the U.S.A. are certainly based on the English pattern. So I won't even pretend to be able to form accurate opinions about it.

I find all the above views pointing up my fifth and final impression, i.e., respect for the individual—the pursuit of happiness. Indeed, this is acknowledged as a worthy aim and has become a leading principle of this nation. A German would be suspicious of that. German education is a formidable ordeal of school and parental discipline. The German is brought up on the duty principle, serious study and thoroughness, and he can immerse himself so deeply in an idea (whether good or bad, and Nazism proved to be the latter) that he may kill all life and living in its pursuit. He is taught that an objective ideal is bigger than he is. Not that he doesn't strive for personal happiness, but he is so used to a training that makes the object of his work and study seem so much more important than his own person that he tends to forget all about it. Moral discipline and severity are contagious, and in Germany have superseded all immediate and personal goals. The Germans are highly individualistic, but en masse they can be hypnotized into sacrificing themselves for an abstract idea. This quality is at once one of their most arresting and most dangerous characteristics. It explains why they excel in any work that demands unusual devotion and it explains at the same time why they were a pushover for Hitler.

In contrast to this, even though you Americans will conform en masse, you can never be talked into forgetting your own comfort and happiness and the human side of things. You will even put up with a certain degree of incompetence and sometimes corruption if you can keep the individual functioning happily. And you are just as ready to drop an idea if the individual doesn't function happily in it.

But instead of mentioning only the differences between Germany and the U.S.A., I should like to point out one great thing they have in common. They are both nations who live with the accent on the future and once the vicious spell that has been cast over the German nation by their present government has been lifted they will therefore probably look to America first for inspiration.

The Study Committee received 8,217 replies (4,659 from men and 3,558 from women) in the general questionnaire to the question "What aspects of American life do you regard as most satisfying?" They are summarized and their frequency indicated in the following table.

ASPECTS OF AMERICAN LIFE REGARDED AS MOST SATISFYING

	Per cent distribution	
	Men	Women
Democracy or political equality	26.9	23.7
Freedom	26.4	26.7
Opportunities	12.1	11.5
High standard of living	8.3	9.6
Friendliness	6.2	6.5
Good, inexpensive education	5.4	9.3
Social equality	5.6	4.1
Fairness	3.2	2.2
Informality	2.4	2.5
Optimism	1.5	1.5
Libraries	1.4	2.0
Privacy	0.6	0.4
	100.0	100.0

There are other aspects of American life which the refugees regard unfavorably. They disapprove of "the exaggerated value of money as a measure of social prestige" and "the poor taste to talk constantly about money and the cost of articles." Some think that the sanctity of private property is carried further here than abroad and that the social concept of property is less developed. "The only thing we dislike," comments a German manufacturer, "is the American newspaper. We find the newspapers hard to understand, particularly the headlines, and we do not like the way they publish scandals." Another German businessman finds it hard "to penetrate the fog of ballyhoo and exaggeration in headlines," especially during political campaigns. Still another dislikes the way Americans conduct themselves in times of election.

The language used in speeches and newspapers is dangerous. Even the people of America are good-natured and able to forgive and forget, but foreign people, foreign nations and their newspapers will be able to say, "See, America is asking us to go their way of democracy, but they themselves condemn their leaders as being corrupt and unable to govern their own people." I know from the bottom of my heart that this is not true. What I want is to give, especially at election times, the whole world a true picture of the American way, of which I am proud.

Certain aspects of our economic life are a disappointment to the refugees. Being accustomed to learning a trade or preparing for a job as a career, they deplore the attitude of American workers expressed in the sayings "It's just a job" or "I just work here," which seem to indicate that "you merely work for a living, that it does not seem to matter what you do." The constant shifting of jobs they find disconcerting, and they do not think the worker should feel free to quit on a moment's notice. This further reflects, some state, a lack of thoroughness and a disregard of craftsmanship. Others complain about the instability of employment: "You are either working overtime or else laid off because there is no work." Frequently the refugees are deeply concerned about the economic insecurity here—the lack of health insurance and the comparatively inadequate coverage of other types of social insurance. Having been a deeply rooted people in a relatively static society, they not only feel a loss of moorings as a result of their forced migration, but believe that American society is too fluid and economic conditions too unstable to provide an adequate sense of security.

Many of the refugees were shocked at the amount of race prejudice they observed here, particularly at the treatment accorded to the Negro. This was a situation with which they had previously had no experience. They find it hard to reconcile such practices and attitudes with the principles of democracy. They not only feel sorry for the Negroes, but some of them want to champion their cause, like the refugee student who declined an offer of membership in a national honorary agricultural fraternity because of its restriction to white students only (*New York Times*, April 7, 1940). Both Christians and Jews among the refugees are appalled at the amount of anti-Semitism in this country and at the organized propaganda, of whose existence they had previously been unaware. A German Catholic engineer stated in an interview that he thought he was in a position to evaluate the anti-Semitic sentiment, which had been openly expressed to him. Among his fellow workers he has frequently heard derogatory remarks made about the Jewish employees. He feels that the latter are often not given advancement primarily on the basis of their religion. People with education, he thought, were more subtle about expressing their feelings. He was concerned about religious propaganda by certain newspaper columnists and felt that steps should be taken to have them stopped. Prejudices, he believed, were as intense here as they had been in Germany before Hitler, and he was quite concerned as to the effect this might have after the war. The French philosopher Jacques Maritain[2] wrote just before he returned to Europe: "It is possible that in years to come this country may have to defend itself against the spiritual wave of destruction of human values which has submerged Europe at the present time, and which can arrive at the other shore of the Atlantic under forms now unforeseeable as under forms already active, such as anti-Semitic propaganda." A number of German Jews express their fear that the seeds sown by the Nazis have taken root here. A Hungarian Jew comments that the freedom permitted to those who propagate anti-Semitism is a mistaken one. An Austrian Protestant sees a hopeful sign in the openness with which prejudices like anti-Semitism are being fought here and in the number of political parties, churches, universities, and civic organizations that have taken a stand against prejudice wherever encountered. He contrasts this situation with that in Austria where the Social Democratic party carried the fight practically alone. A German Jewish teacher hopes "that the counteractions are strong enough to prevent growth of this movement so that our brothers and sisters in the armed forces won't have died in vain."

The extent of anti-Semitism in this country comes as a great and deplorable surprise to refugees from countries like the Netherlands and Italy, which traditionally have been much more tolerant than the United States. A forthright statement by a Netherlander is cited below. An Italian Jewish banker believes there is much more anti-Semitism in America than in Italy, and remarks, "I am a little afraid to be known as a Jew in America." Refugees from a variety of countries point out differences in practice here as compared with Europe. Some think the pattern of religious segregation is more highly developed in this country. They are surprised to find social welfare, civic, and other activities often dividing along religious lines, and to discover the extent to which such cleavages permeate the organized life of the various nationality groups. It is asserted, for instance, that it was not until they reached this country that the Polish immigrants became conscious of the necessity for separating into religious groups so far as membership in professional and other societies is concerned. In Europe, the Jews had been among the most ardent Polish nationals; in this country, they were frequently more nationalistic than Polish Catholics. Nevertheless, there is a tendency among the latter group in the United States to consider as Poles only those with what they call Polish background. The Jews, no matter how many generations their families may have lived in Poland, they regard not as Polish nationals but as Jewish nationals, which is a bitter pill for many of the Jews to swallow.

It is further stated that in pre-Hitler Europe Christians and Jews mingled more freely or generally than they do here. Especially was there more

[2] *Op. cit.,* p. 7.

social intercourse among cultured people of both groups. Friends and associates were chosen more on the basis of intellectual and cultural affinity than on religious affiliation. "In Europe," comments a concert pianist, "Judaism is a religion, which one can change and then find complete acceptance in Christian society [as witness his cousin who became a cardinal]. In the United States, being a Jew is something one can't change. Conversion doesn't eliminate the prejudice; it's something a Jew lives with and dies with." Many refugees also affirm that the practice of restricting neighborhoods, hotels, and schools is more widespread here than in Europe. This came as a great shock to them. They deprecate particularly the quota rule of colleges which, they hold, should be taking the lead in educating people toward tolerance and democracy. It would appear that these various restrictions were less frequent in Europe, especially so far as the educated and wealthy Jews were concerned, and certainly less obvious. It would appear also that in the more static and stratified European society custom played a greater role than it does in America where social mobility is marked and the ideal of democracy proclaimed. A Protestant refugee remarks: "I had never before seen signs indicating that only Gentiles would be welcome. Discrimination on the basis of color or religion was quite foreign to my way of thinking, and it was a real disappointment to find it in a country that professes to be democratic. I feel that there is not yet real democracy in America."

An American-born Christian woman from the Netherlands has written the following frank statement on religious divisions and anti-Semitism in the United States:

AMERICA NEEDS MORE TOLERANCE

I am an American by birth, and come from a Protestant family. My husband is Dutch and my children were raised in Europe. We returned here in 1939 after a stay for more than ten years in France and Holland. Here are some observations on the experiences of recent immigrants and some of my impressions of American life.

We belong to a large group of European artists and intellectuals to whom considerations of race, religion, color, and even nationality are secondary. In Paris and Amsterdam we weren't in the least concerned with whether our friends were or were not Jewish, or even whether they were or were not "colored." In Holland, for instance, the blackest Surinamer is accepted freely by his white colleagues and neighbors. So much by way of introduction: Now for some brief reports from members of this group now in America.

A blond, young Dutchwoman, a writer and student who has traveled the length and breadth of Europe, went into a travel bureau in New York to inquire about summer hotels. The first question she was asked made her so angry she left the place at once. It was: "Are you a Gentile?" She is, actually, but the idea that she would "naturally" want a hotel patronized only by Gentiles, or that a "free" country like America should make such discriminations was very upsetting to her. This disappointed and disillusioned her about this country.

A friend of mine, a Dutch Jewess, reports that in this country for the first time in her life she has felt discrimination; she has been "made to feel Jewish." She found that her Jewish relatives who had lived in America for some years were much more clannish and unassimilated than her family and friends in Holland. I have talked this over with many Jews, both European and American. It is a fact which distresses all of them, and embarrasses them. We have never come to a conclusion which would be of any practical value. Why did the Jews in France and Holland seem so much better assimilated? Have we, in the U.S., forced them, with our discrimination, back among themselves, and put them on the defensive? As matters now stand, we seem to be caught in a vicious circle. We see on every side bad manners toward Jews and bad-mannered Jews.

We were once invited to visit European Jewish friends at their rented summer home near New York. A swimming party was proposed at a small lake, which, they had heard, had been arranged by the community for the community. When we arrived, all in our bathing suits, we were told we couldn't swim. We were not "members." Our host asked if he could join and was told he would have to see the manager, who was not there . . . So we turned around and went home. Then I knew just how it must feel to be a Jew in America!

We know a fine young boy of fifteen. He was born in Vienna, raised in Paris, and is now on the way to becoming American. His family is Jewish, by race not religion. He, himself, has become interested in an Episcopalian church. His neighborhood was largely Catholic, and he became very good friends with a Catholic child . . . until the Catholic discovered that he ate meat on Fridays! That was the end of the friendship!

My own observations have been made in the course of watching children—my own and other people's—here in the West Bronx. We find that we have settled (in all innocence) between a large group of "fighting Irish" and a large group of "clannish Jews;" lower middle class, I would call them. When we first came here, relations between the groups were strained, and now they have reached the point of actual riots, at least among the children. My children first went to the public school, which is about two-thirds Jewish. The children my son brought home were nice, intelligent lads, but no close friendships were formed. I tried to be active in the Parents' Association, but always felt completely "foreign." The Jewish women, quite a number of them recently from Europe, were energetic, friendly and full of good ideas about the school, but they formed such a closed community, with their own language, customs, food, and holidays, that I found it impossible to get anywhere with them.

As I said above, we had never been a churchgoing family. Nor had we ever felt the necessity of going to church for social reasons. It remained for my son, aged nine at the time, to come to the conclusion that it was practically necessary to belong to a church group in this country. There had been a long spell of Jewish holidays at school, which meant that two-thirds of the children were absent, and the rest marking time. Then came a day when the teacher (Catholic, that year) said that the Catholic children might take the following day off. Johnny raised his hand, "Please, Teacher, I'm not Jewish and I'm not Catholic, when do I get *my* holiday?" After that, the only other Protestant child in the class took him to an Episcopalian church where there were many activities for boys, and he has been going there ever since. Also, the only intimate friends he has made have been from that church.

Now, although I have only praise for what the church has done for John in ethics, music, scouting and friendship, I still feel that this community is being pulled to pieces by its various religious groups. The only thing that makes one person different from the next is his religion, and the more emphasis that is placed on these differences the worse for the total community. Naturally, each one has the "right" to his fish-on-Friday, or what-have-you. It is the implication behind that "right" that bothers me. In exercising his right, he is reminding himself and everyone else that he belongs to a group. It is natural to suppose that he belongs to that group *because he believes it to be superior* to other groups. In spite of all protestations to the contrary, the "holier-than-thou" attitude is there.

We do not have freedom of religion in this country because we do not have the freedom to accept or reject formal religion. Both in Holland and in France one can be perfectly "respectable," can have plenty of friends, and can find groups with whom to work and play without being attached to any church. I am perfectly sure that, if the pressure from parents and "grownups" were not so great, young people would soon do away with many of these symbols and attitudes which divide communities.

I would like to add a word about the school problem. In this matter we stand pretty much with the college professors and others whose intellectual standards and ideals for their children are high, while their funds are low. The quality of public school teaching here in the city certainly leaves much to be desired. If one manages by scholarships and sacrifices to send the children to private schools, where the teaching is certainly more thorough, one runs into the "social problem." The children make friends from much wealthier homes and often become unhappy because of our relatively shabby manner of living. In Europe this educational-social problem was much simpler: (1) the public school education was more thorough; (2) there was less display of wealth; (3) artists and professors were more appreciated for their own merits. The yardstick of success was not financial.

It may seem trivial to mention these little things, when we remember what is going on in Europe at present. Therefore I want to make it clear that my remarks are not intended as complaints, rather as observations and warnings. We in America cannot afford to be complacent because we have "saved" a number of refugees. If we want to recommend ourselves and our so-called democratic system as an example to certain misguided European countries we have simply got to put our house in order first.

So far as their personal experience goes, as reported on the questionnaire returns the Study Committee received, nearly one out of every four refugees has encountered some type of discrimination since his arrival in the United States. Of the 11,233 respondents, 806, or 7.2 per cent, did not answer the question on discrimination, 7,822, or 69.6 per cent, stated that they had experienced no discrimination, and 2,605, or 23.2 per cent, replied that they had experienced discrimination of one form or another. The discrimination may have been on account of religion or nationality background or cultural differences. For example, some Jews report that when applying for a position they have been frankly told that Jews would not be hired. Other refugees have encountered discrimination in trying to find a place to live because they were foreigners, whether Jews or not. A German Protestant woman, reporting on the difficulty her husband had in getting them an apartment, states, "People would say No, because he is Jewish; No, because he is Italian; No, because his wife is a German." A German Protestant man, formerly employed by the American embassy in Germany relates:

"We have not suffered too much prejudice because of our nationality. Only once, in Denver, an incident occurred which we can't forget. I was talking to my children in German on the street when a woman spit at us and called us names. My wife felt badly and cried. I have found it difficult to get a job because of being an alien."

Another German Protestant remarks:

"Yes, I have experienced discrimination and prejudice here. There is, in my opinion, just as much (if not more) prejudice in America as we had in normal times in Germany. I found out about all this in a very peculiar way. From the very beginning I avoided to be classified as a 'refugee' because I knew how the average American felt toward these unfortunate beings. Therefore, I was passed on as a Nazi. It seems to the average American that every recent immigrant is either a 'Jewish refugee'—they have become acquainted with the word 'Aryan' and don't accept anybody as a 'Christian refugee'—or he is a Nazi. In both cases they are resenting him: they dislike the Jews and, thank God, they have no use for the Nazis. However, many Americans are Nazis without belonging to the party. By that I mean that there are an awful lot of people over here too who go around and preach hatred against the Jews, or against the Catholics and, of course, against the Negroes."

Others report that the newly arrived immigrant in the United States is looked upon as uneducated, without manners, and not fit to associate with native Americans.

In the replies to the questionnaire, it is interesting to note that the percentage of Christian refugees who stated that they had experienced discrimination (23.1 per cent) was practically identical with the percentage of Jews so reporting (23.0 per cent). The percentage was higher (30.1 per cent) in the case of those relatively few individuals who had no religious affiliation or who neglected to indicate it. When the situation is examined by type of discrimination experienced, it appears that the Jewish refugees, as compared with the Christian, have experienced more discrimination while at work and in finding a place to live, and that the Christian refugees have encountered it more in getting a job, in social relations, and in aiding in the war effort.

When the cases of discrimination experienced are broken down by size of community where the refugees in question reside, it appears that in general the situation is more unfavorable in the larger-sized communities in all respects except in social relations, aiding the war effort, and at school. The smaller-sized communities exhibit relatively less discrimination in economic matters but more in the social realm, while the larger-sized communities exhibit the reverse. This difference may be explained in part as arising from the relatively small number of both refugees and earlier immigrants in the smaller-sized communities.

A further analysis of the cases where discrimination or prejudice was experienced in getting a job reveals a variation according to occupational groups. A higher proportion of the professionals than any other groups reported having experienced discrimination in getting a job. They were followed by clerks and kindred workers, proprietors, managers, and officials, and those who had been students abroad. Less discrimination was reported by manual workers and by women who had been housewives in Europe. A smaller proportion of Germans, Poles, Russians, and Netherlanders report such discrimination than do Austrians, Czechs, Hungarians, Italians, and Frenchmen. It further appears that the refugees who arrived before 1940 experienced more discrimination than did those who arrived subsequently. This difference may be accounted for by the contrast between the depressed economic conditions prevailing during the 1930's and the wartime prosperity of the 1940's.

INTENTION TO RETURN

The vast majority of the refugees in the United States have no intention of returning to Europe or settling in any other part of the world. They are content to remain here and are grateful for the freedom and opportunity that this country provides. Their hopes, especially for their children, are now centered here. A large proportion of them are already citizens. The break with the past is definite and final. This was the reaction of 96.5 per cent of those who replied to the questionnaire. This extraordinarily high indication of permanency is characteristic of the refugee type of immigration. Throughout our history immigrants who came here to escape persecution and oppression have remained to a much greater extent than have immigrants whose motive in coming was to improve their economic condition.

Among the small minority of 3.5 per cent of the refugees who intend to return, professional workers—especially writers, architects, artists, professors and teachers—are proportionately more numerous among the occupational groups, and Christians—especially Catholics—among the religious groups. Only an insignificant percentage of the Jewish refugees intend to return. A considerable variation is shown by nationality groups. Practically no Germans intend to go back and relatively few Austrians, Czechs, Poles, and Hungarians. On the other hand, an appreciable proportion of the French, Russian, Italian, Rumanian, Netherlander, and Norwegian refugees signified their intention of returning to their homelands.

These findings are corroborated by reports concerning refugees in other countries. A British refugee service society indicates the same variation by nationality in the intention to return as that noted above.[3] Reports from

[3] Society for the Protection of Science and Learning, Cambridge, England, March, 1945.

Switzerland state that the German refugees there are overwhelmingly opposed to returning to Germany.[4] Austrian Jews in Palestine at a general meeting expressed themselves against returning to Austria.[5] The American Joint Distribution Committee, reporting on the situation among the Jews in Europe, states that the vast majority of them do not want to go back to or remain in their former homelands.[6] The Report to the President by Earl G. Harrison on Conditions Among Refugees in Western Europe[7] affirms that most of the Jews who have been liberated in Germany and Austria want to leave those countries as soon as possible. Among the nationalities represented, very few Polish or Baltic Jews wish to return to their homelands; higher percentages of the Hungarian and Rumanian groups want to return, although some hasten to add that it may be only temporarily, in order to look for relatives. Some of the German Jews, especially those who have intermarried, prefer to stay in Germany. The great majority of all nationalities, however, want to be evacuated, preferably to Palestine.

The attitude of the refugees regarding the question whether they intend to remain in the United States or to return to Europe may be illustrated by citations from comments they made in the life history documents which the Study Committee gathered. These will be considered by nationality groups, beginning with the Germans. A few German Christians have expressed themselves as not wanting to return, but most of the comments are by German Jews who are unanimous and emphatic about not wishing ever to live in Germany again. A former businessman states:

"It is a very silly question whether or not I will go back to Germany after the war. Go back to what? To no business? Go back to an anti-Semitic people? For whatever people here may think, the people of Germany are going to be anti-Semitic after the war, whether Hitler is there or not. And they're going to be Nazi too, whether Hitler is killed or not. People don't get over those things quite so quickly as they seem to think here. No, we certainly have no desire ever to go back to Europe even for a visit."

A banker abroad, now a social work executive here, comments:

"We have lived, or tried for more than eight years now to live, and think and feel as Americans. Our children are Americans all through, and to return to Germany would be as much an uprooting for them now as it was for us when we left there, and it would also be a difficult breaking-up for us also. Naturally, we do not feel as deeply rooted in this country as we were in Germany, but we have tried from the very first to forget our former life, because that seemed to be the only way to be at home and happy here, and it would be a tremendous change for us also. Besides that, I am convinced that anyone who thinks he can go back is only fooling himself. There is no such thing as

[4] New York Times, June 19, 1945.
[5] Jewish Way, June 17, 1945.
[6] Aufbau, June 29, 1945; New York Times, June 18, 1945.
[7] Text reprinted in New York Times, Sept. 30, 1945.

a return to our former life, because things can never be the same again in Germany; no one could erase those last twelve years and their influence on the German people, and the memories to which some of the older people would like to go back can never come to life again."

Some German refugees state that they would return only to help the American government in the rehabilitation program, while others affirm their unwillingness to return even under these conditions. One of the latter gave as a reason his conviction that the Germans as a people are beyond rehabilitation. He illustrated it in the following manner: When he was about to leave Italy, where he lived from 1933 to 1939, the heads of the German insurance companies which he represented there were so concerned about his welfare that each individually approached him with offers of assistance and sympathy. Individually, he said, they were ten good German gentlemen, but he was convinced that had they been called together as a unit and asked whether he should be condemned to death as a Jew they would have agreed to it. He believes that the mass psychology of the Germans has made them brutes. If he were to be called upon for service in Europe, he would prefer to serve in Italy. Others feel that Germany is a lost nation, that she exhibits little sense of guilt or remorse, that she has lost her soul, and that the German attitude toward the Jews has so completely degenerated it will take a generation or more to eradicate the Nazi poison. Comments a middle-aged business manager, "To uproot Nazism at least two generations in Germany will have to die out and by that time I shall have no more worries in this respect." Besides the deep infection by the virus of anti-Semitism, of which a spiritually bankrupt Germany will not purge itself quickly, there are economic reasons why the lot of the Jews may continue to be unfavorable. Many Christians, not only in Germany but in other Nazi-dominated countries as well, have willingly or unwillingly benefited from the confiscation of Jewish property and expropriation of Jewish economic positions. Though the United Nations plan to return the Nazi loot to its rightful owners, in many instances it will be impossible to do so or even to trace ownership through forged records and repeated sales. For selfish reasons those who hold property or positions formerly Jewish-held will seek to perpetuate policies of Hitlerite anti-Semitism.

Among other comments by German Jewish refugees are the following:

"I think that assimilation is highly desirable. I would never return to Germany to live and there could not be any inducement whatsoever to influence me to do it." (A former judge, now a salesman in Detroit)

"We feel that our whole future is in this country. If I could get back all the money the Nazis took from us I would not spend a night in Germany; not for everything I had would I sleep in a bed made up by a German chambermaid or eat one meal in a restaurant where I had to be waited on by a German waiter." (A formerly very wealthy German woman, now in San Francisco, whose husband owned a large factory abroad.)

"I have no desire ever to return to Germany, even under the most ideal conditions. All our hopes are centered on remaining here and making a good life for ourselves and our child, as well as contributing toward the good of our adopted country." (Polish businessman expelled from Germany, now an office clerk in Columbus, Ohio)

"Because of our total loss of possessions in Europe, our advanced age, and many other factors, we do not have any desire to return to our former homeland. We have only one future plan, and that is to keep well fit, keep on working, and remain independent." (A 70-year-old man who was a manufacturer abroad and is now a gardener in Los Angeles)

"I am too old now to make anything different of my life. But even though I have little, I have something that is more precious than money, and that is freedom. It is wonderful living in a free country like ours. . . . I would never want to return to Germany." (Owner of a toy manufacturing concern abroad, a shipping clerk here, in Dayton, Ohio)

"I have no thought of ever returning to Germany. I am happier here than I have ever been in my life and have no worries about the future." (A 60-year-old man, formerly well-to-do businessman abroad, a successful salesman here, in Philadelphia, who has bought $2,400 worth of war bonds and feels as secure as one of his age and position could expect)

"I am very happy to be in the United States and would under no condition return to Germany although I was happy there before the Hitler regime. I feel that no one who was treated as we were would ever want to return, irrespective of any possible material advantage. I have met with no personal experience of anti-Semitism here." (Formerly an upper middle-class housewife, now a semiskilled factory worker in Milwaukee)

"Although when we first came to this country we thought it might only be for a temporary period of time, I would not under any condition want to return to Germany, even if it were safe for Jews. I have become adjusted to the American way of life and want to remain here not only because I am satisfied, but because my children feel that this is their country." (A wealthy housewife abroad, a business manager here in New York)

An interesting and significant statement, corroborating the evidence cited above, has been made by a rabbi, now in Springfield, Missouri, who was formerly head of a congregation of 1,200 in Augsburg, Germany. He corresponds with some six hundred members of his former congregation, who are now scattered in 28 countries, on six continents. He writes:

"Never in my entire correspondence has one of the Augsburg people expressed the desire to return. . . . The break between them and Germany is definite and final. And this despite all that these refugees have left behind in material possessions, despite the fact that most of them are at present living on a much lower social and economic level than they knew in their German past, and despite the fact that, with few exceptions, they had been 100 per cent assimilated Jews and fervent German patriots. They have only one wish, and that is to become useful and loyal citizens of their new home-lands."[8]

Like the German refugees, few Austrians desire to return to their former homeland. The Jewish group particularly feels that there is nothing to return to; the Austrian Jewish community has disappeared through extermination or exile. Despite their formerly favorable position, especially in Vienna, the Austrian Jews were among the worst sufferers from the ravages of political anti-Semitism. Both Mr. and Mrs. K., who managed to escape from Austria, want to forget the past. They are enthusiastic about California and wish to remain there the rest of their lives. "In Austria," writes a former salesman, "my family was well off. But I would not go back even if conditions were normal because freedom is so important." Although his first impressions of the United States were not too favorable, comments a university graduate and businessman, he does not plan to leave this country and return to Austria. He is convinced that this land offers freedom and opportunity to his children that would not be open to them any place else. An Austrian Protestant woman and her husband, here on temporary visas, plan to go to England and return later to make their permanent home here. Their two children will remain; the girl has married a native American, and the boy after discharge from the Army wants to settle down here as a farmer.

While the majority of the Czech refugees intend to remain in this country, a higher percentage of them plan to return than is true of the Germans and Austrians. Many, especially among the scholars and professional people, feel it is a national duty to return and help rebuild the country. Those who have put down roots here and have intermarried with native Americans will remain.

The return movement of the Poles is highly dependent on the development of political events in Poland. If the new Poland is dominated by Russia, the intellectuals and the anti-communistic groups generally are not likely to return. Even the labor group feels that it would suffer under a policy of sovietization. Polish Jews, here as well as elsewhere, have little inclination to return. Their lot was far from favorable under the somewhat feudalistic conditions existing in Poland before the German invasion, and now there is almost no Jewish community to go back to. To return to Poland now would be like going to a cemetery. Many of the Polish nationalists are worrying about the reception they may expect if they return, since those here have lived and worked under far more favorable conditions than those who carried on the struggle at home.[9] Others say they feel like renegades by de-

[8] Rabbi Ernest I. Jacob, "The Refugees Won't Go Home," *National Jewish Monthly*, October, 1944, p. 50.
[9] Jan Karski, "The Emigres and Those Over There," *New Europe*, September, 1944, p. 16.

ciding not to return but to remain here out of consideration of personal safety and the welfare of their children. As one comments, "For the sake of my children, who are of high school age, I want to stay in the United States. Here we feel as human beings, and are not persecuted. Here we can speak our own language if we want, read our Polish newspapers, visit our friends, and go about our business."

Hungarian refugees state that their decision as to whether or not to return to Europe depends upon postwar conditions in Hungary, the attitude of the Allied governments toward the role Hungarians may play in the reconstruction of the Continent, and the influence of Russia. Businessmen among them will be reluctant to return unless capitalism is dominant. If they should return, some are planning to introduce American products, such as refrigerators and soft drinks. Some of the physicians would be willing to go back if their services are needed. Most of the Hungarian refugees, however, have taken a liking to this country, are fairly well settled, and plan to remain. Especially is this the case where they have young children.

The return movement to Italy will very likely be larger than that to the countries already reviewed. As in other instances, it will depend on the factor of time and on conditions in the homeland. It may amount to 15 to 20 per cent of the refugee group. Physicians may be inclined to return since they could make a better living in Italy. If stable economic conditions develop in the postwar period, some Italian businessmen also may return. A number of refugee professors, diplomats, and other officials have received official notification requesting their return. The attitude of the Italian Jewish refugees is likely to be more favorable to returning than is true of the German, Austrian, Polish, Czech, and Hungarian Jews. This is because of the long favored position of the Jews in Italy, who were very few in numbers and so well accepted and assimilated that they were hardly distinguishable from other Italians. Despite Mussolini's decrees and rantings, anti-Semitism never made much headway with the great masses of Italians. The Jews, even after Hitler forced the Nuremberg laws on Italy, escaped the more virulent forms of anti-Semitism. In this they were aided by the Catholic and Protestant clergy, who hid the hunted. Moreover, the war was more than half over before Italian Jews were sent to concentration camps, and thus a large proportion survived. The loss in numbers was less than in any other nation engulfed by war; of the 40,000 to 45,000 Jews in Italy in 1938, approximately 35,000 remain. Even after the camps were established, the policy was one of studied neglect rather than of active torture, and while the Italians were in charge there was sufficient leniency for many to escape. The Jewish community in Italy will thus soon be restored, and this will influence the return of the Jewish refugees. On the other hand, many of the Italian Jewish refugees recall that there was no organized protest against anti-Semitism in Italy, feel that the country is morally bankrupt, and believe that it is to their best interest to remain here.

The view of the Spanish refugees in the United States, most of whom are intellectuals, may be summarized by saying that most of them would like to return to Spain; they cannot, however, return until their personal liberty is secure; and this will not come to pass until Franco is expelled.

The following nationalities among the refugees show a greater tendency to return to their homelands than those already mentioned, though the majority of them plan to remain in the United States. Quite a number of the French refugees have either left or have made plans to leave. This appears to be especially true of the artistic, motion-picture, and scholarly groups. Some of these have held the intention to return from the start and have not wanted to learn English or otherwise establish roots in this country. One states, "I am too much of a Parisian to want to stay in New York indefinitely." However, many of them are appreciative of the hospitality and opportunities extended to them here, and would like to maintain the contacts they have made, some planning to divide their time between France and America. A number of Russians who had lived in France as emigres plan to return there as soon as conditions permit. The French Jews, however, are not so anxious to return. The dead hand of Nazi propaganda is still felt among the returned prisoners of war and other repatriates, and the Frenchmen who occupy confiscated Jewish apartments or business offices have frequently refused to give them up.

Although the seed of anti-Semitism sown in Belgium and Holland by systematic German propaganda has produced an awareness of a Jewish problem hitherto negligible in those countries, the Jews remaining there will not suffer discrimination, and Jewish refugees from these countries will likely return in considerable numbers. Both countries, and particularly the Netherlands, have a long tradition of religious and racial tolerance. Even when under Nazi control, the citizens took a stand against anti-Semitism. When the Nazis put into effect the law requiring Jews to wear the Star of David, many Christians, following the suggestion of their pastors, wore the star in order to confuse the invaders and help to defeat the purpose of the ruling.[10] The same thing happened in Belgium. Both clergy and laity hid hundreds of Jews from the Nazis and helped to keep them alive during the occupation. The first death sentence imposed by a special Netherlands war crimes tribunal was on a man charged with betraying a number of Jews to the Germans.[11] While the attitude of the Netherlands and Belgium thus appears favorable, both countries suffered greatly as a result of the war, and

[10] Henry Smith Leiper, "Effects of Occupation on Morals and Morale," *New Europe*, January, 1943, p. 3.
[11] Associated Press dispatch, Sept. 4, 1945.

economic conditions compare unfavorably with those in the United States. This may lead many of their nationals to decide to remain here. From interviews and life stories the impression is gained that, although many Belgians and Netherlanders had no intention, when they came here, of becoming citizens and remaining, they have changed their mind, and that as time goes on fewer and fewer will actually return.

Like the Low Countries, Norway and Denmark have strong liberal traditions which the citizenry refused to compromise at the behest of the Nazi overlords.[12] The number of refugees from these countries to the United States was very small, and the proportion of Jews among them tiny, as is the situation in the homelands. Most of them will very likely return as soon as conditions permit. This may take some time in the case of Norway, which suffered much destruction and dislocation under Nazi occupation.

[12] Henry Smith Leiper, *op. cit.*; Hans Bendix, "Denmark," *Life,* March 5, 1945, p. 60.

CHAPTER IV

THE DISTRIBUTION OF REFUGEES IN THE UNITED STATES

The geographic distribution of any group of immigrants—regionally, by states, and by local communities—has an important bearing on their economic and social adjustment, their rapidity of assimilation, and the reaction of the native group to them. A high degree of concentration draws undue attention to a group, like the Japanese in California and the Jews in New York, often retards assimilation, and sometimes gives rise to fear, dislike, and other unfavorable reactions. A wide distribution, on the other hand, frequently facilitates the incorporation of immigrants into American society and lessens the strain on intergroup relations. This situation is also a function of numbers: a relatively large number of immigrants in any region or locality obviously presents more difficulties than a relatively small number. The refugees, as we have seen, present no over-all problem on account of numbers, since they constitute but a minute proportion of the nation. Even if they were all settled in New York City they would comprise little more than 3 per cent of the population of that metropolis. Their distribution, however, though widespread, is uneven as compared to that of the native population, and they have had a greater effect on American life than their mere numbers might indicate.

The distribution of refugees in the United States parallels that of the total foreign-born white population, showing a concentration in the East, especially in New York, Pennsylvania, New Jersey, and Massachusetts; in the Middle West, especially in Ohio, Illinois, and Michigan; and in the Far West, especially in California. These eight states outrank all others both in the number of refugees and in the total number of foreign-born. While they contain an almost identical proportion of both groups, approximately three-fourths, the ranking order is not the same. New York has by far the largest proportion of both groups, but the refugees, as contrasted with the total foreign-born white population, have shown a greater tendency to go to California and Ohio, and a lesser tendency to settle in Illinois, New Jersey, and Michigan, as the following table reveals.

Refugees have settled all over the United States. Questionnaire returns were received from 44 states and the District of Columbia. The only states not represented were the sparsely populated ones of Idaho, Montana, Nevada, and Wyoming. This wide distribution has occurred despite the fact that nearly nine-tenths of the refugees entered the country by the port of New York. A higher proportion of the Jewish refugees (78.6 per cent)

PER CENT DISTRIBUTION OF REFUGEES AND OF FOREIGN-BORN WHITE POPULATION, 1940, IN THE HIGHEST RANKING STATES

| Refugees* | | Foreign-born whites† | |
State	Per cent	State	Per cent
New York	24.5	New York	24.8
Pennsylvania	10.6	Pennsylvania	8.5
California	10.2	Illinois	8.4
Ohio	9.2	California	7.6
Massachusetts	6.2	Massachusetts	7.4
Illinois	5.6	New Jersey	6.1
New Jersey	5.0	Michigan	5.9
Michigan	3.0	Ohio	4.5
	74.3		73.2

* Based on questionnaire returns.
† *Statistical Abstract of the United States*, 1943, p. 20.

than of the Christian (69.5 per cent) left the New York area. Dispersal from New York was especially marked in the case of Italian and Yugoslav Christians, and Italian, Hungarian, German, and French Jews. The tendency to remain in New York has characterized especially the Russian, Hungarian, Austrian, and Polish Christians and the Netherland, Russian, and Czechoslovakian Jews. Considered by their occupational background, refugees in professional service have tended to remain in the New York area, while other occupational groups, especially manual workers and students, have shown a greater tendency to leave. Of the professional persons, writers, physicians and dentists, and clergymen, among the men, and writers, physicians and nurses, among the women, are outstanding in the inclination to stay in New York.

The refugees have settled in communities of all sizes, ranging from rural areas and villages to the largest cities. Three and three-tenths per cent of the total refugee group are living on farms or in rural communities of less than 2,500 population, 13.8 per cent in cities of 2,500 to 100,000 population, and 82.9 per cent in cities of 100,000 or more population, including 18.6 per cent in New York City, the largest single center of refugee settlement.

The tendency to settle in rural communities, while characteristic of only a small proportion of the total group, is twice as pronounced among the Christians as among the Jews. The Christian refugees have also settled in medium-sized cities to a greater extent. This is especially true of the Germans, Poles, and Czechs. With the exception of New York City, where a larger proportion of the Christian refugees may be found, the Jews have located to a higher degree than the Christians in large cities of 100,000 or more population.

Viewed from the standpoint of occupation, professional persons among the refugees are noteworthy for their higher rate of settlement in rural

Per Cent Distribution of Refugees by Size of Community Where now Residing

Size of Community	Total	Jews	Christians
Total	100.0	100.0	100.0
Under 2,500	3.3	2.9	5.9
2,500 to 9,999	3.3	2.9	3.6
10,000 to 24,999	2.2	1.8	3.8
25,000 to 99,999	8.3	7.7	11.4
100,000 to 499,999	27.6	29.1	20.1
500,000 to 999,999	17.1	17.6	15.4
1,000,000 and over	19.6	20.9	12.7
New York City	18.6	17.1	25.1

communities, small cities, and New York City, a situation largely influenced by the physicians among them. The proprietors and managers show a distribution closely paralleling that of the total refugee group, with the exception of a higher proportion in small towns and rural areas, representing mainly the farmer element. Clerical and other white-collar employees, skilled and semiskilled workers exhibit the greatest tendency to locate in cities of 100,000 or more population, exclusive of New York. The concentration in New York is especially characteristic of professional persons, as already mentioned, unskilled and home workers, and those having no occupation (women, retired workers, and the wealthy). When the distribution of the refugees is considered by the date of their arrival in this country, it appears that the more recent arrivals tend to concentrate in New York and other large cities to a greater extent than those who have been here longer.

In actual numbers, how many refugees are there in New York and other cities? The impression is current, fostered by rumors and sensational articles, that our largest cities are swarming with refugees, though actually the total refugee group is so small that it comprises but a tiny percentage of the population of any of these cities. On the basis of the Study Committee's questionnaire returns and community surveys, and checked by the data on internal migration gathered by the U.S. Bureau of the Census, the number of refugees residing in large population centers may be estimated as follows. The internal migration figures cited consist of "immigrants" enumerated in the respective cities in 1940 who reported that their place of residence in 1935 was in an outlying territory or possession of the United States or in a foreign country. The term includes United States citizens as well as aliens.

ESTIMATED NUMBER OF REFUGEES IN CITIES WITH LARGEST REFUGEE POPULATIONS

City	"Immi-grants"* 1940	"Immi-grants"† Estimated 1945	Refugees‡ 1945	Total Population 1940	Per cent of refugees in total city population
New York	98,845	137,394	70,000	7,454,995	0.9
Chicago	11,234	15,615	12,000	3,396,808	0.35
Los Angeles	12,060	16,763	6,000	1,504,277	0.4
Philadelphia	3,872	5,382	5,000	1,931,334	0.3
Boston	3,058	4,250	3,500	770,816	0.4
San Francisco	6,785	9,431	3,500	634,536	0.55
Detroit	8,227	11,435	2,000	1,623,452	0.1
Baltimore	2,248	3,124	2,000	859,100	0.2
Cleveland	2,215	3,078	2,000	878,336	0.2
Oakland	1,448	2,012	1,500	302,163	0.5
Newark	1,966	2,732	1,500	429,760	0.3
St. Louis	1,205	1,675	1,200	816,048	0.1
Milwaukee	1,097	1,524	1,000	587,472	0.2
Washington, D.C.	4,044	5,621	1,000	663,091	0.15
Cincinnati	1,074	1,492	1,000	455,610	0.2
Seattle	3,954	5,496	800	368,302	0.2
Pittsburgh	1,374	1,909	800	671,659	0.1
Kansas City, Mo.	652	906	700	399,178	0.2
Buffalo	1,736	2,413	600	575,901	0.1
Paterson	386	536	500	139,656	0.35

* U.S. Bureau of the Census, *Population, Internal Migration 1935 to 1940.*
† Estimated by adding 39 per cent to the enumeration of 1940, since total immigration 1941-45 was in that ratio to immigration 1935-1940. Based on the assumption that the later arrivals distributed themselves in the same way as the earlier arrivals.
‡ Based on questionnaire returns and community surveys.

Cities with an estimated refugee population of 100 to 500 are as follows:

Bridgeport, Denver, Portland (Ore.), Rochester	400
Atlanta, Houston, Indianapolis, Louisville, New Haven, New Orleans, Providence	300
Hartford, Richmond, Toledo, Vineland (N.J.)	250
Elizabeth, Omaha, San Antonio	200
Columbus (Ohio), Minneapolis	175
Albany, Dallas, Jersey City, Passaic, Springfield (Mass.), St. Paul, Syracuse, Trenton, Wilmington	150
Camden, Memphis, Nashville, Scranton, South Bend	100

The case of New York City calls for special comment, since it is unquestionably the largest center of refugee population and since the impression is widespread that most of the refugees, said to number several hundred thousand, have settled there. It is unfortunate that official data are lacking, but from the evidence on hand the conclusion can definitely be made that the number of refugees in New York City is well under 100,000.

The distribution of refugees in communities throughout the country has been determined largely by the location of their relatives and friends, job or school opportunities, and the resettlement program of the various refugee service agencies. The location of their affiants, or sponsors who guaranteed that they would not become public charges, has also been a factor. Commonly the affiants were relatives or friends. A special study of refugee heads of families in Philadelphia, conducted in connection with the Study Committee's survey, suggests the relative importance of the various factors.

REASONS FOR SETTLING IN PHILADELPHIA

Reason	Number	Per cent
Relatives live there	164	52.7
Job offered there	45	14.5
Seemed to offer opportunity	28	9.0
Resettled there by committee	27	8.7
Sponsors live there	21	6.8
Friends live there	11	3.5
No special reason, mainly chance	10	3.2
School located there	3	1.0
Foster home or guardian's home there	2	0.6
	311	100.0

Additional factors, which operated in the case of other communities, were the selection of a place because of its location or climate, e.g., the Middle West, California, or the character of its population, e.g., a large number of people of the refugee's nationality. It is also noteworthy that an appreciable proportion of the refugees lived in other communities before deciding on their present place of residence, and that they shared in the rather extensive internal migration that characterized the American population during the war years. Judging from the letters returned unclaimed in large mailings of the Study questionnaire in a number of cities, based on the complete list of active and closed cases of refugee service agencies, about one-third of the refugees had changed their address since arrival in this country. This is the same proportion that the Alien Registration Division of the Department of Justice found in checks on its data, originally gathered in 1940, which were made for selected cities in 1944.[1]

The resettlement of refugees through the efforts of refugee service committees was mainly a matter of moving them from New York City where nine-tenths of them landed. The logic behind the program was to prevent the concentration of refugees in a few metropolitan areas, to place refugees in communities where job opportunities were better and more in line with their past occupational experience, and to promote their assimilation by increasing their contacts with native Americans. The wishes of the individuals concerned were taken into consideration in the selection of communities, though in some instances pressure was used and the refugees resisted being

---

[1] Interview with Donald R. Perry, director of the Alien Registration Division, and E. P. Hutchinson, supervisor, General Research Unit, Immigration and Naturalization Service, 1944.

moved. Much care was exercised in gathering information about communities and work opportunities and in setting up organizations for receiving the newcomers and assisting them in adjustment. Nothing comparable to this program had ever been done before during earlier immigration movements, with the exception of the efforts of certain Jewish societies a generation ago, and its benefits have been clearly demonstrated. About 15,000 refugees were resettled through the assistance of various refugee service agencies. In some instances the individuals later returned to New York or resettled themselves elsewhere.

The following comments are typical of the reaction of refugees who were resettled from New York in other communities.

"I feel as a matter of fact that I am living only one year in America. I discount the five years I had been in New York because that is not living in America. There is too great a tendency to live with other foreigners and I think it is a great mistake. When people ask me how long I am living in this country I say one year—five years in New York and one year in this country." (Manufacturer in Fairfield, Conn.)

"Committees should intensify the call that 'New York is not America.' " (Farmer, near Vineland, N.J.)

"My stay in New York City for more than two years after my arrival in the United States did not bring me in close enough contact with the American life. Only after I had left New York City and gone to smaller cities, I was able to more or less assimilate myself." (Businessman in Newton, Mass.)

"We thought we would not fit in with the proverbial 'American tempo,' which was one of our main reasons to go to a smaller city, besides the idea that adjustment might be easier. We found out that we fit very well." (Manager of family's factory abroad, machine operator now in Fort Wayne, Ind.)

"Luckily New York is not America." (A teacher who did poorly in New York but made an excellent adjustment in Haverford, Pa.)

"We were offered several choices and we accepted a midwestern city which had industries which were full of opportunities for my profession." (Engineer and designer in Cincinnati, Ohio)

"Detroit is not a very good place for a textile expert and I should have gone to North Carolina, for instance. In this respect I was not well advised." (Store salesman in Detroit)

"Told that we would have to leave New York, we resisted this at first, dreading the unknown, but eventually chose to come to Milwaukee because we knew it was a German community, which we felt would minimize our language handicap." (Former businessman, now factory worker)

"Immigrants should certainly be helped to get out of New York. In New York people aren't friendly. It is not till an immigrant gets to a small community that he discovers Americans are nice." (Teacher, still looking for a suitable job; Philadelphia)

"We are very glad we moved to Kansas City. In New York they stick too much together and speak too much German. For the first year in the United States I did not speak English. When I came here I made mistakes, but talked anyway." (Housewife)

"This little country town in Pennsylvania has been our home for three years. It is here that we made the best progress in getting Americanized, more rapidly than we would have done had we stayed in New York and spent our time with relatives and fellow-refugees, bemoaning our misfortune and reveling in memories of bygone days. Here, there are no relatives and no refugees. We were eager to meet the people, share their way of life and probe into their minds. Many of them were easily accessible, ready to befriend us." (Part-time farmer and factory worker)

The following statement was written by an Austrian political refugee, graduate of the Technical University of Vienna, resettled from New York:

"After my arrival in the midwestern city I made the acquaintance of the members of the committee that had made resettlement possible, and learned that we were the first refugee couple they helped. We felt a heavy responsibility since the fate of other refugees depended on us. After a week, through recommendation of the chairman of the committee, I was hired as a draftsman in one of the then defense plants and I have held this position for more than five years.

"In addition to this I suggested and worked out several courses in mathematics and mechanical subjects for the war-training program of the local university. I have taught those courses of which three have been offered for the first time for the last six terms. I have donated so far ten pints of blood to the Red Cross and my wife has donated three times. We were tremendously pleased to receive our American citizenship papers shortly after our five years' stay in this country. The difficulties in continuing her profession as a kindergarten teacher, especially her accent, proved insurmountable to my wife. Therefore she decided to take up tailoring, which she had learned before embarking on her career as a kindergarten teacher. After working as a power machine operator she was able to utilize her knowledge of tailoring by conducting a vocational class in women's tailoring at one of the city's evening high schools. She now works during the day as a sewing supervisor for a war relief organization.

"I have learned to appreciate and understand democracy in the United States better than ever before in my life. What impressed us most in the United States was the fact that individuals who had no personal interest in refugees helped perfect strangers to adjust themselves. In European countries, in Austria particularly, when refugees came in from Germany hardly anybody, except particular sectarian organizations, had any interest in their welfare."

CHAPTER V

PROBLEMS ON ARRIVAL

Immigrants coming to this or any other country inevitably face difficult problems of adjustment. They have left behind all that is familiar and must establish themselves in a strange environment, find a job, learn a new language, and gain an understanding of a new set of customs and values. Deprived of former friends and recreational outlets, they must try to find a place in an alien community whose attitudes and standards they little understand.

In many ways the process of adjustment to life in the United States has been more difficult for the refugee than for the usual immigrant. This has resulted both from the peculiar circumstances of refugee immigration and the types of individuals it comprised.

The refugee, whose migration was forced by outside pressures and effected with comparative suddenness, was not so well prepared for life in this country as the usual immigrant whose migration was voluntary and the result of long planning. Plans for his future in this country had to be made in most cases after arrival, and his attitudes had to go through a gradual process of adaptation.

The fact, moreover, that most of the refugees arrived here after tragic experiences militated against an easy adjustment. All had been subjected to persecution and had spent years in anxiety lest they be deported or interned in a concentration camp. Many had suffered humiliation and physical abuse, or had lived for a period in refugee camps under conditions of severe hardship. Others had been in flight for years from one country to another before they reached the United States, in some cases effecting an escape under extremely perilous circumstances. As a result of these upsetting experiences the refugees often arrived here in a state of physical and nervous exhaustion. This state of tension was prolonged for an indefinite period by worry over family members, relatives, and friends they had been forced to leave behind in Europe, and by efforts to bring them to safety before it was too late. In addition, especially in the case of those living in refugee communities, new arrivals from Europe, showing the effects of physical and mental abuse, kept alive their harassing memories.

It was difficult for the refugees who had lived so long in the shadow of fear to rid themselves of its terror. They showed themselves to be tense and apprehensive in many situations, in interviews with social agencies and in general relations with people. The refugees themselves, in their life stories, have stressed the struggle they faced in overcoming fear. As one woman expressed it:

"When a person has lived under a regime like Hitler's, with restrictions, surrounded by hate, afraid to answer the ring of the doorbell, waiting if a brother would come home alive, not knowing what terror the next day would bring, when a person has lived like that for five years and comes into a country where all such things do not exist, this person is full of fear. He can not make use of all the privileges poured upon him. One has to learn slowly the ways of using them. I was weary and tired, still under the dominating strain of German laws."

Another declared:

"You can understand that when you have been through these horrible experiences and have lived for months with this terrible fear, it is hard to shake it off. We wanted to be sure to live in a country where we would not have to be afraid, but even in this country it takes time to lose this fear. Recently I was talking to an Austrian friend who talked rather loud in German. A man came up and said, 'Oh, I see you are German.' I shook like a leaf for hours. I don't trust any German Gentiles and never will again."

In addition to the difficulties created by his tension and insecurity, the state of mind of the refugee served to isolate him from the American community. He was preoccupied with the problems of the Europe he had so recently left and found it hard to concentrate on the issues of everyday life in America. He felt at first little in common with the pleasant, busy, polite American community which seemed little concerned with the war-torn world of which he still felt very much a part. He worried constantly over the fate of friends and relatives left behind in Europe and was absorbed in efforts to help them escape before it was too late. The average American, on the other hand, was too busy with his own affairs to attempt to fathom the mental state of the refugee and to recognize the degree to which it handicapped his adjustment. The barrier created between refugees and other Americans by this difference of interest is often referred to by refugees in their life stories. For example:

It was hard for the S's at first to understand how people could be as happy, as gay as they were here, when there was so much unhappiness and misfortune and fear of the future everywhere else.

The emotional adjustment of many refugees and their integration into American community life were handicapped, moreover, by the fact that members of the immediate family had been killed or left behind in Europe. Normal home life was difficult to achieve when the mother or father, wife or husband had not succeeded in coming to the United States. In many cases the husband had been incarcerated in a concentration camp before the wife left home either alone or with the children. Family separation under such circumstances involved great emotional strain. In other cases families were separated in flight; the wife or husband either was trapped in Europe or forced to flee to the East or some other part of the world while the rest of the family continued their journey to this country. Some individuals came here alone, the only members of their family to succeed in migrating, and were forced to live in isolation from all those dear to them. Many women were forced to earn a living for themselves and children, to carry the whole responsibility of raising the family, and at the same time to bear the emotional strain of separation from and worry over their husbands.

The task of becoming oriented to American culture, always arduous, was especially difficult for the refugee because of the circumstances of his migration. He had to begin to learn the language and customs of the new land and to understand its attitudes and values when he was in a condition of physical exhaustion and confusion. As one refugee describes it:[2]

> The immigrant must learn anew how to stand, walk, eat, sleep. You are at once dead-tired and excited. Only a few grasp that so tremendous a readjustment resembles a state of physical illness. Ignorance of the simplest customs and formalities, the difficulties of communication, uncertainty as to your own situation and worry about those for whom you are responsible—all these only serve to heighten your state of confusion.

There is, moreover, no short-cut method of learning the more subtle elements of a culture which mold personality and behavior. Mistaking characteristics based on cultural differences for those resulting from personal reactions, Americans have frequently misunderstood and misjudged the refugee. Few Americans fully comprehend the difficulties involved in learning even the simple elements of a different culture. Moreover, the refugee frequently tried to find his place at once in the American community rather than joining an immigrant colony, as other immigrants had done, and gradually learning American ways. To attain a status in line with his background he had to become assimilated quickly. When he tried to mingle at once with native Americans, his European manners and ideas were all the more conspicuous, with the result that he attracted undue attention, much of it unfavorable.

The problem of finding a job also was particularly difficult for the refugee. The bulk of previous immigration had been comprised of skilled and unskilled laborers and agricultural workers who were readily absorbed into the then expanding economy of the country. Refugee immigration, on the other hand, contained a substantial proportion of businessmen and professionals who could not hope to find suitable work until a certain proficiency

---

[2] Martin Gumpert, "Immigrants by Conviction," *Survey Graphic*, Vol. XXX, (Sept. 1941), p. 487; cf. Martin Gumpert, *First Papers*, 1941, chap. 3.

in the English language and a certain degree of general assimilation had been achieved. The fact that the earlier period of refugee immigration coincided with a nation-wide depression and that during the later period restrictions against enemy aliens were in force increased their difficulties.

The majority of the refugees arrived here, moreover, without financial resources. By 1937 the increasingly strict restrictions upon the property allowed to be taken out of the Reich had reduced the sum to 10 marks, or about $4. All those coming after this time, except for the few with international investments, arrived here practically destitute. They were forced to find some kind of work immediately upon arrival, to rely on relatives or friends, or to find means of support from some other source.

There is no doubt that relatives already living in the United States did much to aid the immediate adjustment of the refugees. Refugees often settled in the communities where their relatives lived, were sheltered by them for a time, and assisted in finding a job and establishing a home. Relatives were not always so helpful, however. Refugees often tell of the disappointments they suffered when they turned to relatives for aid or advice. Some relatives appeared to resent the arrival of the newcomers and treated them rather coolly. The following amusing account written by a young woman tells of the reception given her and her husband by one of her husband's cousins when they called at his home:

Then the cousin came, a nice-looking, middle-aged gentleman. "So you're Arthur's son. How long are you going to stay in this country?"—as if he had never heard of a guy named Hitler and people trying to get away from him. We pointed out modestly that we had come to stay if he did not mind. "But there are ten million out of work here already"—evidently he wanted to encourage us in his own way. . . . However, the cousin did not entirely lack a family conscience. Some weeks later we received a postcard. It sagely advised us to go and try the New York office of a big shirt company, for which Fred had worked in Europe. Not that he could recommend us to them, it was just an idea. We had had that splendid idea weeks before, but to no avail.

In the same way, although many refugees placed high hopes on the references to important people in this country which they brought with them, there were not many cases where these were of any real value. As the wife of a German-Jewish businessman says:

"We went through the same experience as most of our friends, namely, that connections and recommendations to influential people are of little value and mostly stop at a lunch invitation. Everybody has to find his way himself."

The first year or two of life in America were usually the most difficult. Many refugees were obliged to accept menial positions or jobs requiring physical labor for which they were often ill equipped, or to live on a small stipend from a refugee agency. They were forced to live in crowded, unattractive quarters which were a great contrast to the comfortable surroundings to which they had been accustomed in Europe. Tension and family friction were often created by the cramped living accommodations several generations of one family were forced to share. The hardship and insecurity of the first years of life in this country are brought out by many life stories in such descriptions as the following:

"If somebody had told me how bad that first year would be I don't know whether I would have had the strength to go through it. We had a tiny room near Broadway over a sea food restaurant which made it a very odorous place in summer. The gas stove leaked and the place always had an awful smell. And we had plenty of cockroaches too. This wasn't so bad, but the trouble was that we were really pioneers. We were among the first people to come over, in our family anyway, and there was no one to give us any advice and tell us how to get along. . . . It got my wife down more than it did me, but I remember one morning when we both felt at the end of the world. My wife was so sick and weak that morning that she couldn't get up, but I had to go out and work anyway. We knew nobody would come in and see her all the day, and we just sat down and cried."

The refugees also encountered at times an unfriendly attitude. The form of anti-Semitism existing in this country, with its patterns of segregation for Jews and non-Jews, was a surprise and a shock to them, as has been mentioned in an earlier chapter. Feeling against Jews and against other refugees was fanned, moreover, by subtle Nazi propaganda in this country. With the approach of the entry of the United States into the war, developing anti-alien feeling often failed to distinguish the refugee victims of Nazi theories from other "enemy aliens." Considerable animosity developed, moreover, in some communities toward the refugees themselves because they were considered an economic threat.

Interesting light is thrown upon the relative importance of the various difficulties faced by the refugees by the weighting they themselves have given them. In the questionnaire distributed among refugees by the Study Committee was included a question: "What do you regard as the greatest difficulties or problems which you personally have faced in adjusting to American life?" Replies to this question were received from more than 6,000 individuals. They have been summarized in the following table which shows the frequency with which a given type of difficulty was mentioned.

Especially significant is the outstanding place refugees have given to language as being their chief difficulty. It is a matter of wide general knowledge that the refugees have made unusually rapid and successful progress in learning English as compared to other immigrants. The fact that most refugees consider that language has presented their greatest difficulty indicates how much struggle was involved for the individual in this achievement. The special pressures which led the refugees to make this outstanding effort in the field of language were of various sorts. In the first place, a fairly good knowledge of English was necessary for an adequate occupational adjustment for those in the business and professional fields. Public opinion has, moreover, exerted strong pressure against the use of German on streets and in other public places. More important, the aspirations of the refugees themselves drove them to strive for language facility which

REPLIES TO THE QUESTION: "WHAT DO YOU REGARD AS THE GREATEST DIFFICULTIES OR PROBLEMS WHICH YOU PERSONALLY HAVE FACED IN ADJUSTING TO AMERICAN LIFE?"

Difficulties or Problems	Males		Females	
	Number	Per Cent	Number	Per Cent
Total	3,958	100.0	2,802	100.0
Language	1,694	42.8	1,381	49.3
None	419	10.6	359	12.8
Different customs and values	417	10.5	322	11.5
Finding suitable job	348	8.8	119	4.3
Making friends with Americans	216	5.4	200	7.1
Unsympathetic or hostile attitude of Americans	148	3.7	76	2.7
Age	145	3.7	55	2.0
Different business methods	128	3.2	29	1.0
Social isolation	124	3.1	118	4.2
Change of occupation	99	2.5	34	1.2
"Enemy alien" status	63	1.6	26	0.9
Difference between European and American education	56	1.4	20	0.7
Anti-Semitism	54	1.4	44	1.6
Unfriendly attitude of earlier immigrants	30	0.8	14	0.3
Miscellaneous	20	0.5	5	0.2

was prerequisite to building up associations with Americans of their own status and to taking part in the general community life. They have not been content with a superficial knowledge of the English language, but have been anxious to master it and use it like educated native Americans. The apparent contradiction between the general success achieved by the refugees in the field of language and the outstanding place they give it among their difficulties is understandable in the light of these factors.

The strain resulting from the language problem was somewhat less severe for those living in refugee colonies where they could continue the use of their mother tongue than for those living in native-American communities. This is shown by the fact that in New York only 36.7 per cent of the replies cited language as a special difficulty as compared to 45.5 per cent for the country as a whole. A slightly larger percentage of women than of men considered language their chief problem. This is probably due to the fact that a larger proportion of the men considered their chief difficulties to lie in the job-finding or economic sphere.

It is easy to see how the language problem, permeating every aspect of the life of most refugees, has assumed an overwhelming importance among their many difficulties. For those with no previous knowledge of English the first period of life in this country was painful and complicated. Even the simplest needs could not be met or the most general directions understood before a few words were mastered. The sort of trials the newcomer suffers because of his ignorance of English is suggested by an anecdote told in refugee circles:

A refugee knowing no English asked a compatriot who arrived earlier what is a typical American dish to order for lunch. He was told pea soup. He learned the word and ordered pea soup daily for some time. Growing tired of it, he looked up his friend to find out some other favorite American food. He was told ham sandwich. Next day he ordered ham sandwich, but when he was asked "white or rye?" which he didn't understand, he fell back on pea soup.

Among the special difficulties cited by refugees in regard to language, "colloquialisms," "conversational language," and "slang expressions" recur most frequently. As one refugee expressed it, his greatest problem was in "learning the 'slanguage' in addition to the language." Some blamed their lack of knowledge of idiomatic language upon the fact that they had little opportunity to mix with Americans, and that their knowledge of English had been gained largely from reading. Refugees who had studied English previous to coming to this country particularly stressed the difficulties presented by the peculiarities of American pronunciation and slang, the change from "English English" to "American English," and from an academic knowledge of a language to conversational application of it.

Accent is likewise another source of difficulty frequently cited. Some individuals resent the fact that they are easily identified with the refugee group because of their accent, and consider this a disadvantage. On the other hand, a number of refugees declare that they have found their accents to be an asset rather than a liability. For instance, a man who is now a Fuller Brush salesman declares:

"My wife and I have spoken about getting rid of our accent completely. Still we don't know whether to do this or not because we've found that the foreign accent is really an asset in our business. People like to hear it. It seems a little funny to them. Of course at first in New York there used to be a few people who would look at you as if they would kill you and say, 'To hell with you. My husband is an American citizen, and he's been six years unemployed. You can't speak English and you have a job.' But you don't get that any more."

Certain occupational groups such as actors, writers, and teachers, whose work is tied to language, have faced particularly severe problems in this area, as is discussed in later chapters of this book. "If I had known the tremendous ordeal ahead of me in learning English adequately," a Czech actor who has successfully established himself in the theater declared, "I believe I would rather have stayed in Europe and faced Hitler."

As an aid to the refugees in learning English, special classes have been established for them by various organizations and in various communities, which have taken into consideration their particular interest in the language and their particular needs as a group of highly educated immigrants. Existing language and citizenship classes have also been adapted to their needs. Other aids which the refugees mention as having been particularly helpful in learning the language have been the radio, the movies, and the English-language press.

Next to those refugees who cited language as their chief difficulty, the largest group replying to the question, answers to which are tabulated above, declared that they had experienced no particular difficulties in adjusting to American life. Many such replies came from young refugees, particularly from those who arrived here before the age of 20, but refugees in the older age brackets were not unrepresented. Some gave their reply a positive turn by declaring that they had had no difficulties in this country because of the help given them by relatives ("God bless them!") and by the sympathetic and co-operative attitude of the American people.

Other replies regarding their chief difficulties fall under the general headings of problems created by cultural adjustment, by economic adjustment, by social adjustment, and those resulting from the unfriendly attitudes of Americans. Problems in the field of cultural adjustment were more frequently cited than those in any other field. Next to language, which overshadowed all other sources of difficulty, different customs and standards of American culture rank highest, in the estimation of the refugees, as an obstacle to adjustment. Together they account for 53.3 per cent of the replies from males and 60.8 per cent of the replies from females.

Difficulties rooting in the different customs and values of American culture were, according to the answers to this question, of two main types: first, the difficulty involved in learning American customs—"ways of dressing, eating, thinking, and acting"—or the general process of cultural assimilation; second, the difficulty created by specific conflicts between American and European standards and attitudes. Examples of the second type of answer point back to the general reaction of the refugees to America and American culture, which has been discussed in a previous chapter.

Difficulties in economic adjustment are indicated by the replies that finding a suitable job, change of occupation, different business methods in this country, and differences between American and European systems of education have proved to be the chief problems. Such difficulties in economic adjustment are cited by 14.5 per cent of the males and 6.5 per cent of the females. The fact that language had an important bearing on economic adjustment should, however, be kept in mind in any true evaluation of the weightings given by refugees to their difficulties in the various fields.

Difficulties in social adjustment were considered by males as secondary in importance to those in economic adjustment, but by females as of greater importance. The difficulties experienced by refugees not only in making friends with Americans but in making friends of any sort or in developing adequate social and recreational outlets (termed in the chart "social isolation") are considered in detail in later chapters on social adjustment.

Related to both economic and social adjustment, but not clearly to be considered under either category, are several groups of answers which indicate that the greatest difficulties in adjustment have been presented by the attitudes of Americans, a subject that is considered in detail in another chapter. The largest grouping in this category have found a major obstacle presented by the lack of understanding of the situation of the refugees or by antagonistic attitudes toward them on the part of Americans. A number of replies coming from doctors, teachers, and other professionals cite professional hostility as the chief obstacle to their adjustment to life in America. This topic is developed in later chapters. In a special grouping are those answers which declared that the attitudes of earlier immigrants groups, especially among the Jews, had been particularly unfriendly. The general problem of anti-Semitism was cited as the greatest obstacle by 1.4 per cent of the males and 1.6 per cent of the females. Such answers often included unfavorable reactions to the various types of anti-racial feeling existing in this country.

Other answers to this question cited age, enemy-alien status, change of visa status, climate, and finding adequate housing as the major problems in their adjustment to American life.

CHAPTER VI

ASSISTING THE REFUGEE

The special problems of adjustment presented by the refugee immigrants led to the development of a program of refugee service. This in turn contributed substantially toward the successful adjustment of the total group of refugees in the United States. Integrated with the world-wide organizational network of refugee aid, this program was made possible through the support given the refugees as victims of Fascist oppression by humanitarian, liberal, and religious groups in this country. It was a collaborative enterprise shared by a large number and wide variety of agencies, both those existing previously for more general purposes and those established especially for the aid of refugees. The total program at the height of its development offered a large number of different services, including financial relief for those in need, assistance in job finding or in becoming established in business and professional life, special services for particular professional and occupational groups, retraining for new occupations, aid in cultural and social adjustment, and planned resettlement in communities outside of New York.

RELATION TO PREVIOUS PROGRAM OF IMMIGRANT AID

This broad program of refugee service constituted a new chapter in the history of immigrant aid in this country. Although the United States has been one of the chief immigrant-receiving nations of the world, the government has never sponsored an extensive official program to aid the adjustment and assimilation of immigrants. The activities of the U.S. Immigration and Naturalization Service in this field have consisted primarily of encouraging local agencies to provide citizenship classes and of preparing textbook material for the use of naturalization candidates attending public schools. A few states, such as Massachusetts, Delaware, and California, have supported public agencies to assist the foreign-born, especially in citizenship education. But most of the agencies promoting immigrant welfare have been privately organized and supported.

These existing immigrant-aid organizations extended their services to the refugee immigrants and made efforts to adapt them to the needs of the new group. Particularly extensive was the work of the Jewish organizations, such as the Hebrew Sheltering and Immigrant Aid Society (HIAS), which gave temporary shelter to thousands of refugees each month at the peak of refugee immigration, and the National Council of Jewish Women, whose aid to unaccompanied women and naturalization work were integrated into the refugee service program. Services offered by immigrant-aid organizations in the field of migration work and naturalization procedures became part of the refugee service pattern. But the limited aims of these organizations failed to meet the basic problems of refugee adjustment, and the refugee service program which developed transcended the bounds of the previous immigrant-aid program.

The refugee service program depended heavily, for one thing, upon family service agencies and the use of case-work techniques. Many of the refugees arrived here penniless and in need of temporary relief. Since they were ineligible for public relief they were referred to private social agencies throughout the country. In addition, the personal and family problems resulting from refugee experience and family separation, which frequently retarded adjustment, were best treated by social case-work procedure. To be sure, earlier immigrants had been cared for by private social agencies, but never before had an organized social service program of guidance and financial support for an immigrant group been sponsored.

Another basic element of the refugee service program sprang from the special problems of economic adjustment resulting from the substantial proportion of refugees in business and professional fields. Special techniques to aid economic adjustment, such as loans to help refugees establish themselves in business and professional practice, and special agencies to aid the adjustment of particular professional groups formed an important part of the total program of refugee service.

Distinctive likewise was the integrated nation-wide organization of services to the new group of immigrants. Local refugee committees and social work agencies serving refugees co-operated with national organizations and served under their leadership. The refugee service program was at once more comprehensive and more scientifically planned and co-ordinated than previous services to immigrants. Finally the refugee service program, while specialized in certain aspects, has made a substantial contribution to the development of a more adequate permanent program of immigrant aid.

GENERAL ORGANIZATIONAL HISTORY OF REFUGEE SERVICE PROGRAM

The total program of refugee service which had emerged by 1939 at the peak of refugee immigration was the result of a process of growth and experimentation. Existing agencies attempted to deal with the general problem until it was obvious that new measures should be taken. The heaviest load fell upon private social work agencies, especially those in such areas of refugee concentration as New York. Such agencies proved to be unprepared organizationally or financially to meet the peculiar and pressing problems of the refugees, and new agencies or new financial resources had to be made available. Other new agencies were created as special needs of the refugee group became apparent.

The organizational pattern of the refugee-service program reflects the many different groups rallying to the support of the refugee. The incentive to aid refugees in making an adjustment was found among a variety of groups and for a variety of reasons. Jewish philanthropy made the largest single contribution to the work. In addition to being prompted by a humanitarian urge and a sense of group solidarity, the Jews considered it essential to the well-being of the whole Jewish group in this country and to the continued success of their efforts to bring more of their stricken people to this country, that Jewish newcomers be aided to make an easy and rapid adjustment. The usual concern of the Quakers for all those in distress led them from purely humanitarian-religious reasons to make important contributions to the program of refugee aid in this country as well as in Europe. Other Christian church groups, notably the Unitarians, have considered it a Christian responsibility to help aid both the Jewish and non-Jewish victims of Nazism. Nearly every denomination of the Protestant Church established committees to help furnish affidavits and transportation funds for individuals in danger in Europe. Moreover, agencies to aid Catholics and Protestants, both "Aryan" and "non-Aryan," were set up by the Catholic and Protestant churches respectively.

In addition to the support of denominational organizations, the special interests of other groups led them to sponsor projects to aid the refugee. Liberal and progressive groups were particularly interested in aiding anti-Fascists or political refugees, and set up agencies or committees to help in their rescue. The interest of professional groups in this country in extending aid to fellow professionals from Europe and their recognition of the potential contributions of the newcomers led to the establishment of a number of special committees to aid different groups of professionals. The concern of child-welfare workers and other American citizens over the fate of European refugee children similarly led to the formation of agencies to bring children to this country and make arrangements for their care.

Agencies to aid refugees fall under two general classifications: first, general refugee-service agencies offering a variety of services and, second, special agencies established for the aid of particular groups of refugees. Although in point of time agencies of the second type, such as those set up to aid scholars, physicians, or children, were among the first to appear, a dominant role was played in the whole program by the large general refugee-service organizations.

Some notion of how these agencies came into being as a response to the needs of the refugees can best be gained by a brief summary of the development of the National Refugee Service, the largest refugee-service agency in the United States, an organization which, though nonsectarian by the terms of its incorporation, has been supported by Jewish funds. The development of this organization is one of the chief threads of refugee-service history in this country and illustrates the manner in which special refugee-service agencies evolved from existing agencies as the need arose. It shows also how important a role was played by the social-service agency throughout the country.

When the first refugees came to the United States following the rise of Hitler to power in 1933, aid was given to them largely on an emergency basis. Organizations and individuals extended whatever help they could to meet the needs that happened to come to their attention. Both immigrant-aid and social-service agencies shared in the work. Jewish refugees, moreover, tended to apply to the synagogues, Jewish centers, and other resources of the Jewish community, as well as to the Jewish social-service agencies. Because of the resulting confusion and the inadequacy of financial resources and personnel of existing organizations to cope with the mounting problem, the National Co-ordinating Committee for Aid to German Refugees (later called simply the National Co-ordinating Committee to indicate its general inclusiveness) was established. This was a nonsectarian committee, financed by Jewish fund-raising organizations, which functioned to integrate the activities of agencies giving aid to Jewish and non-Jewish refugees and to provide a clearinghouse of information about them.

On a nation-wide scale the National Co-ordinating Committee served to give financial aid and leadership to the numerous local committees and Jewish social-service agencies aiding refugees. An important part of the national program was the resettlement plan by which local communities throughout the country co-operated in helping to divert a portion of the stream of refugees away from such centers of concentration as New York to other sections of the country. Subcommittees organized on a state-wide and regional basis followed the geographic organizational pattern of member agencies and made use of their personnel to carry on the work of the national committee.

From the very outset the Co-ordinating Committee was much more than its name would indicate. Although it was not intended to supplant the organizations affiliated with it, its central body grew constantly in size and strength and became the central agency for Jewish refugees. To cope with the refugee problem in the New York area a Greater New York Co-ordinating Committee was established to serve under the National Co-ordinating Committee. This committee co-ordinated the activities of the Jewish social-service agencies which were caring for refugees in New York and Brooklyn (the New York and Brooklyn sections of the National Council of Jewish Women, the Jewish Social Service Association of New York, and the Jewish Family Welfare Society of Brooklyn). These individual agencies were subsidized for their refugee clients by the Co-ordinating Committee and given guidance in refugee care, although they remained autonomous organizations. In 1936 the New York committee engaged a co-ordinator to study the situation and make recommendations for improved services.

The system of caring for refugees through the Co-ordinating Committee and its affiliated organizations proved inadequate to the stresses of the peak years of refugee immigration. An investigation in 1938–1939 showed that refugees often had to wait days and weeks for an appointment with the individual social-service agencies and that considerable overlapping of services existed between member organizations. For these reasons the National Refugee Service was established in 1939 as a single multiple-function agency to carry on the work handled previously by the federation of independent agencies under the Co-ordinating Committee. This represented a further step in the centralization and integration of services. The National Refugee Service established its own social-service department to take over the work of financial relief and family service formerly carried on in the New York area by the various private social-service agencies. In addition to the Service and Relief Department, it maintained a Migration Department, a department to give aid in naturalization and citizenship, a department giving loans for self-support in business and professional enterprise, a retraining and a resettlement division, and a division for social and cultural adjustment. Included in its over-all structure were a number of independently organized agencies such as the European-Jewish Children's Aid and the Emergency Committee in Aid of Displaced Foreign Physicians, which were subsidized by and housed with the National Refugee Service, as well as a number of committees serving special groups, such as rabbis and musicians. On a nation-wide scale the National Refugee Service took over the network of local co-operating committees and extended them into new areas until more than 900 local community committees were co-operating in its refugee-aid program.

Other general refugee-service agencies were organized by Christian groups. In 1934 a special committee—the American Committee for Christian German Refugees—was sct up by the Protestant denominations, financed at first by Jewish as well as Christian funds, to offer to "Aryan" and "non-Aryan" Christians the types of services being given by the National Co-ordinating Committee. Later it changed its name to the American Christian Committee for Refugees, Inc. In 1936 a Catholic Committee for Refugees was likewise set up, an organization which offered a variety of services to Catholic refugees, including help with religious adjustment.

The American Friends Service Committee established a special Refugee

Division in 1938, which in addition to sponsoring extensive overseas activities, set up offices to aid refugees in various cities in the United States. Through these offices the Quakers extended the usual types of aid and advice to refugees of all creeds, but did not provide financial relief. In addition to their general services the American Friends Service Committee specialized in programs directed toward the particular orientation needs of teachers, scholars, and other professional people, which are described later in this chapter.

The volume of work done by the three Christian general-service agencies mentioned above was much less than that carried on by the National Refugee Service. Whereas the expenditures of the National Refugee Service exceeded two million dollars each year between 1939 and 1942, and reached a peak of $3,500,000 in 1940, the combined expenditures of the three Christian organizations for refugees totaled only between $300,000 and $400,000 a year in this period.

In addition to these general agencies, a number of agencies and committees were established by denominations of the Christian Church. Of these the most extensive was the Unitarian Service Committee, which was active in refugee work both in Europe and in this country, concentrating especially on aid to political refugees. Among church organizations assisting refugees here were the Episcopal Committee for European Refugees, the Congregational Christian Committee for War Victims and Services, the National Lutheran Council, the Federal Council of Churches of Christ in America, the Greater New York Federation of Churches, and the Board of Missions of the Presbyterian Church. Most of these agencies, while they sponsored special types of aid, referred refugees of their faith to the American Christian Committee for Refugees for general types of service.

In addition to the services organized for refugees by Americans, the refugees themselves set up programs for aiding members of their own group through self-help activities, described more fully in the chapter on refugee organizations.

PROCEDURE AND GENERAL TYPES OF SERVICE

Refugees often applied to a refugee-service agency within a few days after their arrival in New York, the chief port of entry. Those who arrived without funds and who had no relatives or friends to give them assistance applied usually in great haste. Refugees had heard of these agencies through various means. Oftentimes the application at an American refugee-service agency was the last of a long chain of services which had reached from the home town of the refugee in Europe to the shores of America. In these cases the name of the American agency had been given to the refugee by the European agencies which had previously served him. In other cases the name and address of the American agency had been written on a scrap of paper by a friend or adviser at some point along his wanderings, and on arrival in New York the refugee had made his way through a strange city of people speaking an alien tongue to the destination it indicated. Thousands of other refugees met at the docks and sheltered during their first days here by the HIAS organization or the National Council of Jewish Women were referred to the general refugee-service agencies. A number of other refugees were referred by relatives or friends in this country. Although the specific services they were seeking varied, there was a common pattern to what they asked for. "The client . . . in diverse individual ways and with varying significance to himself says, 'I am new in America—I have suffered—I have to start all over again. How can you help me?'"[1]

Refugees were first interviewed by reception workers or members of the intake departments of the various agencies, most of whom were conversant with several languages. Through these interviews sufficient information was gathered about the applicant to be able to refer him to the department or departments from which he needed aid. Interestingly enough many refugees who came to the agencies did not want service of any kind. They simply wished to have their names on file somewhere, to have someone to whom to turn if need arose.

1. *Relief and Adjustment Services.* Refugees like other immigrants were deprived of public relief during their first five years in this country because of the clause in our immigration law providing for deportation of aliens who become public charges within that period. But since many arrived in this country without financial resources it was necessary to provide means of support for them until they had established themselves here and found work. Financial relief was extended to refugees through the relief and family service departments of the various national refugee-service agencies and through private social-service agencies in communities throughout the country. Before being granted relief their eligibility was carefully investigated. The agencies made contact with any existing relatives and with the affiants (those who had signed their affidavits) to see whether any help could be extended by them to the newcomers. Although the affidavits contained pledges of the affiants to care for the immigrants, neither the agency nor the immigration authorities have exerted legal pressure in this direction. If the affiants could not afford to give financial help the agencies took over this responsibility.

Giving relief was a major function of all the general service agencies, and a substantial proportion of their budget was devoted to it. From 1939 to 1945 the National Refugee Service alone gave financial assistance to more than 35,000 individuals. In 1940 the relief load of this organization

[1] Mary Siegel, "Case Work with Refugees," *Proceedings of the National Conference of Jewish Welfare*, 1941, p. 165.

reached a peak averaging 3,162 family cases, and between 7,000 and 8,000 individuals per month, but after 1941 improved economic conditions led to a rapid decline in numbers receiving relief. By 1944 the cases remaining on relief averaged only about 300 a month. A similar drop in numbers on relief was experienced by other refugee-service agencies.

Most refugee families received relief for only a short period, especially during the early years of the refugee-service agencies. These agencies were set up as short-term contact agencies to assist refugees in their initial adjustment to American life and they gave strong emphasis, during the years of heavy immigration, upon achieving a rapid economic adjustment. However, the difficulties of and penalties for making such a rapid, and sometimes only temporarily adequate, adjustment were increasingly realized, and a more solid basis for adjustment was attempted. The average duration of relief to refugee families in such an organization as the National Refugee Service increased from an average of from five to eight months in 1939 to an average of twelve months in January, 1941. This rise in the average duration of relief was not only the result of a change in policy in regard to the type of adjustment to be desired, but also of the growing proportions of the old and the sick left on the relief rolls as the younger and more able-bodied among the refugees were absorbed into our expanding war economy.

In addition to the financial relief given by refugee-service and social-service agencies, financial aid was granted in a small way by national benevolent societies, consular offices, and self-help groups. This usually took the form of grants to meet special emergencies, such as medical and dental care, for such organizations did not have the financial resources to maintain a program of general relief for refugee families.

The success of the organization of financial services for refugees through private funds is indicated by the fact that there is no known instance of a refugee having been deported as a public charge. At the end of five years in this country immigrants may legitimately apply for public aid, but agencies, especially the Jewish, have tended to avoid referring clients to public service agencies even after the allotted five-year period, because they fear that if this practice were to become common it might result in an unfortunate reaction in the general attitude towards refugees.

In addition to giving financial relief, local family welfare agencies and the relief and family service departments of national refugee-service agencies rendered a variety of other services. Health services were an important part of the work, for many refugees were in need of such aid when they arrived. Refugees requiring medical attention or dental care were given medical consultations and referred to private doctors and clinics and given financial aid to meet this cost if they needed it. Through the agencies the refugees received other types of services such as advice on how to budget to live on their low relief allotments and help in finding lodgings.

The aid given to refugees on problems of personal or family adjustment, whether by general social service agencies or by special refugee service organizations, was especially significant. In either case, the social case-work techniques, based on the individual aspects of each problem against a common background of refugee experience, were utilized to good advantage. Problems of personal and family adjustment were related to many aspects of the refugee situation. Separation of families between the New and the Old World left many families without a father or mother and created a variety of domestic problems. Another important source of maladjustment was the difficulty in securing suitable work. Some refugees accepted work unsuited to their ability and suffered both physically and psychologically as a result. Some grew bitter or depressed by their difficulties in securing work and their feelings further impeded them in their efforts to obtain jobs. Some felt humiliated by the low wages offered them and others developed feelings of inferiority and defeat as they repeatedly faced rejection. In such situations case workers tried to help offset the refugee's feeling of failure by recognizing his potentialities, offering services of a supporting, reassuring nature, and giving him an insight into the difficulty presented by his own emotional reactions to the situation.

Traumatic experiences precipitating exile were likewise a source of emotional maladjustment for refugees. Some individuals who had passed with courage and resourcefulness through the most difficult experiences of refugee flight seemed to lose energy and motivation once they had reached a haven of safety. Their last ounce of strength had been exhausted in making the escape. Such individuals had to be helped through a period of adjustment and rehabilitation until they reached the stage where they could work realistically toward solving the problem of making a new start.

Case workers felt that in most instances refugees could make good use of the case work treatment they were offered in overcoming these difficulties. Most of the emotional disturbances of the refugees proved to be situational rather than rooted in deep-seated personality difficulties. The larger number of refugees who at one time faced emotional difficulties proved themselves to be "adequate" people and were able to adjust fairly successfully to life in the new country.

Social workers, however, were handicapped in their relations with refugee clients owing to certain difficulties arising out of the Old World background and attitude of the newcomers. In the first place, the refugees were not familiar with the American type of social work and tended to feel humiliated by their relationship with a social agency. In the countries of Europe from which they had come, social insurance was the form of aid to which they were accustomed; the more personal form of aid they received from agencies here tended to make them feel that they were receiving charity and they reacted strongly against it. The degree of direction of their personal affairs exerted by the agency was also sometimes hard to accept, and cultural differences in the status of women in Europe tended to make many men resent having a woman social worker give them help and advice.

To the refugee, unused to the process, the personal interview at the agency office in which problems as to his future course were discussed often proved to be an arduous and painful experience. One refugee writer described it in the following way:

> The problem is almost exhausted and so are we. We are panting from the exertion of discussing it, of seeking its solution. Charity, it seems, is as debilitating for "him that gives" as for "him that takes."[2]

The overly sensitive refugee, moreover, found the recital for the case worker's records of the intimate facts of his life, and of his hopes and dreams for the future, an excruciating experience.

2. *Aid in Job Finding and Self-support.* Another pivotal area of aid in the whole refugee-service program was employment service. The most pressing problem of the majority of refugees when they reached this country was to find some means of self-support, and to meet this need a variety of services were set up. Existing American employment agencies were too busy with the problems of unemployed Americans at the time when the refugees began to arrive to be able to devote much attention to their problems. Moreover, the language limitations of the refugees, the difference between European trade and professional techniques, and the prejudice in some areas against "alien labor" created the need for special treatment of their problem. Special committees or agencies were formed to help certain groups of professionals, such as scholars and physicians, to become established in their own field, which are described elsewhere in this chapter. Employment services of a less specialized type were likewise set up through general service and other refugee agencies. In many communities throughout the country committees were formed by interested citizens to help find employment opportunities for refugees.

In the early years of refugee immigration the problem of finding jobs was a particularly knotty one owing to the unfavorable employment situation. Because many Americans were unemployed, a special effort was made by refugee-service agencies to find jobs for refugees which would not place them in competition with American job seekers. In the early years many refugees were placed in domestic service and other positions below the level of their capabilities in order to speed their economic inde-

[2] Hans Natonek, *In Search of Myself*, 1943, p. 52.

pendence. As time went on and the general employment field offered more opportunities, an increasing effort was made to place them in fields offering a more permanent adjustment. The advanced age level of refugees arriving in later years, the effects on them of long periods of inactivity in transit countries, and the increasing anti-alien sentiment complicated the process of job finding. In 1941, however, with the country moving toward the mobilization of labor for defense and ultimately for war, employment divisions were able to find jobs for many refugees, including long-unemployed older men, although the declaration of war in December caused a growth in anti-alien sentiment which for a time retarded placement of refugees in certain fields. In 1942 and 1943 the mounting needs for manpower and the demonstrated loyalty and reliability of refugees gave hundreds of other refugees, many of whom had formerly been considered unemployable for reasons of age and health, an opportunity to become self-supporting. As a result of these favorable conditions a large number of placements were made and the relief loads of refugee-service agencies were decreased during these years to an irreducible minimum of the aged and incapacitated.

3. *Retraining*. Special problems in the economic adjustment of refugees led to the development of a program of retraining them for new occupations. The notion back of the American retraining program had its roots in the work of European organizations, several of which instituted programs of retraining refugees for agricultural and industrial enterprise during the period while they were waiting for emigration. The possibilities in retraining in the United States were explored rather late in the period of refugee aid, beginning about 1940. The program was developed as a solution for refugees who, due to the different standards and techniques required in American mercantile and professional fields, had not been able to achieve an adequate adjustment. Retraining aimed either (1) to utilize the previous skills of the refugee in some related field where job opportunities existed or (2) to train refugees for employment in fields experiencing a shortage of labor.

Retraining divisions were established within the employment service departments of a number of refugee-aid organizations. Through this division refugees were either enrolled in classes run by the organization itself or were enrolled and subsidized for courses offered by trade schools and other institutions.

The American ORT Federation, a branch of an international organization which gives training courses for Jews in many countries (ORT stands for *Organization* for *Rehabilitation* through *Training*), has been especially prominent in the field of retraining. This organization set up two trade schools in New York City in 1939–1940, which have since given free training to more than two thousand refugees. ORT declares that all its former students are now employed. An investigation made by the National Refugee Service of individuals retrained in 1941 revealed that at the time of the inquiry, several months later, seven out of every ten were working in the field for which they were retrained or had got a start in new occupations by having worked for some time in the retrained field.

4. *Loans for Self-support.* Another form of economic assistance that was widely adopted was the granting of loans to refugees who wished to establish business or agricultural enterprises or to set themselves up in professional practice. Divisions for making these loans were established in a number of refugee-service agencies. Applications for loans were carefully investigated as to both the need of the individual involved and his qualifications for the proposed field of endeavor. The majority of the refugees receiving loans have been those in the over-40 age group for whom employment opportunities are often limited and self-employment the answer.

The extension of loans to refugees for self-support is sometimes cited as one that has fitted particularly well into the tradition and psychology of the refugee group, because it has aided them in using their own initiative to make a new start. When they are sufficiently well established, refugees usually repay these loans on an installment basis.

5. *Resettlement.* Another important aspect of the general refugee-service program was the resettlement plan. The object of this plan was to prevent too great a concentration of refugees in the New York area, which would place undue emphasis on the refugee problem and lead to false conclusions regarding its size. It was believed, moreover, that resettlement would be a beneficial policy for the refugees because dispersal into smaller communities would help speed their social and cultural adjustment and would open up to them new fields of economic opportunity.

The National Refugee Service, which inaugurated the resettlement plan, placed great emphasis on its importance in the total refugee-service program. In developing this service it established contacts with the existing sectarian agencies throughout the United States, who were asked to participate in the program of settling the newcomers in their own communities. In sections of the country where there were no established agencies, refugee committees were set up on a local basis. As the program developed, a quota system was instituted by which each community pledged itself to be responsible for a certain number of refugees who met the specific qualifications which they desired. A regional plan of organization was later adopted. Instead of the national agency dealing directly with each community in a given geographic area, refugees were sent to central regional distribution points which effected an equitable distribution among the several communities involved. Through the regional organizations smaller communities were enabled to use the professional field workers of the regional offices, and an interchange of experiences and techniques was promoted. In the communities themselves refugee committees of lay citizens were set up which received the refugees, offered them various forms of hospitality, and helped them to find work.

Following the same general plan, such general refugee-service agencies as the American Christian Committee for Refugees, the Catholic Committee for Refugees, and the American Friends Service Committee likewise used their branch offices and local co-operating agencies to advance a program of resettlement. The last-mentioned of these committees settled refugees into midwestern communities after an intensive Americanization course in Quaker hostels.

In all, approximately 15,000 refugees were relocated in interior cities and towns through the resettlement plan, in addition to those refugees who on their own initiative left the port of entry to join relatives and find work in other communities. The National Refugee Service during the entire period resettled some 13,500 individuals, the American Christian Committee about 200, and other agencies about 1,000 together.

It was generally accepted that only the better qualified and more adaptable members of the refugee group were suitable material for the resettlement program. Health, language, personality, occupational background, age, adaptability, and individual talents of applicants were all basic factors in guiding the selection of candidates for the plan. In the placement of individuals the economic, cultural, and social opportunities of the specific communities were likewise taken into consideration.

The most difficult problem concerning the resettlement program revolved around the amount of pressure an organization should exert on refugees to make them co-operate in the plan. Many refugees showed much resistance to leaving New York to settle in other unknown communities in the United States. Refugee-service organizations attempted to create interest in other sections of the United States through lectures, pamphlets, and motion pictures. Through such means the refugees helped select and became familiar with the community to which they were sent. In actual practice a fairly high degree of pressure seems to have been exerted, early in the program, to secure refugee co-operation in the plan. When refugees were interviewed, those who were considered to be material for resettlement were often denied relief or other forms of aid unless they agreed to accept the agency plan for resettlement. This method of exerting pressure met with considerable criticism, and came to be considered inadvisable. It was demonstrated that real willingness on the part of the refugee was an essential part of the success of the resettlement plan for any individual or family. Pressure methods were therefore supplanted by an approach depending on education and persuasion.

6. *Social and Cultural Adjustment.* Refugee-service agencies likewise

made an effort to aid the refugees in their problems of social and cultural adjustment. The various agencies active in the field tried by various means to help the refugees to develop social and recreational outlets, and to achieve a degree of cultural and social integration into their new communities.

In the first place, these organizations acted as referral agencies, providing information to the newcomers about community resources such as libraries, museums, the Y's, community centers, language and citizenship classes, and recreational facilities.

Such an organization as the National Refugee Service used its Social Adjustment Division to refer refugees not only to the resources of the American community but also to established refugee organizations, especially those in New York City. These refugee organizations, described in a later chapter, did much to help break down the social isolation of the newcomer upon arrival in this country.

Other work in the field of social adjustment was directed to building up social relations between refugees and Americans, as well as to speeding the cultural assimilation of the newcomers. Especially noteworthy were the hostel projects in the Middle West sponsored by the American Friends Service Committee, where refugees of all faiths lived and worked on a co-operative basis with an American staff. These hostels served as temporary refuges and centers of orientation in American ways and customs. When the individual or wage earner of the family was considered ready to leave the hostel, a position was sought with the aid of the hostel vocational counselor, and many of the refugees were resettled in midwestern communities.

In addition to these hostels for refugees of various occupational backgrounds, the social and cultural adjustment of European intellectuals was advanced by seminars established by the Quakers at Wolfsboro, New Hampshire, in the summer of 1940, at Plymouth, New Hampshire, in the summer of 1941, and in connection with the Universities of Maine and New Hampshire in the summer of 1942. The Cooperative College Workshop at Haverford, Pennsylvania, was a similar project covering the school years 1940–41 and 1941–42. In these projects European scholars studied and participated in round-table discussions under the direction of American teachers and graduate students in order to learn the techniques of American pedagogy. Like the Quaker hostels these were experiments in co-operative living in which none was too learned to help perform everyday chores. A vacation hostel, Sky Island at Nyack, New York, also was adapted especially to the needs of refugee intellectuals.

In addition to these interesting group-living projects through which refugees were given an intensive exposure to American people and ideas, a number of different efforts aimed to promote social relations between refugees and Americans through community houses and similar programs. The American Friends Service Committee established Powell House in New York City in September, 1943, in response to the desire expressed by many refugees to meet more Americans. In Philadelphia the Friends likewise sponsored "Friendship Parties" or monthly teas attended by refugees and Americans in about equal numbers.

In New York City, another community house, called Friendship House, was established in 1939 under the auspices of the Greater New York Federation of Churches, with the co-operation of the American Christian Committee for Refugees and the Immigrants Conference of 1939, to help the refugees feel more at home in a strange city. Congress House, run by the American Jewish Congress, likewise served to bring together Americans and refugees of various nationalities in a social, recreational program. Such groups as the Fireside Group for New Americans sponsored by the International Center of the Y.W.C.A. in New York City, which offered opportunities for social intercourse and orientation to the American community through an informal social hour, lectures and discussions, had similar aims.

The Ethical Culture Society likewise sponsored a broad program of social and cultural orientation in New York City, including a series of "Lectures for Newcomers," followed by "socials," English classes, and various types of general services. The Good Neighbor Committee (on the Emigre and the Community) organized under its auspices played an active role in persuading neighborhoods to take in the refugees and in bringing native Americans and refugees together.

The parent-teacher associations of the New York City Schools tried to help integrate the refugees into the various communities of that city. Refugee parents were visited by parents who were older residents in an effort to make them feel more at home, and they were invited to participate in the parent-teacher gatherings.

The National Council of Jewish Women extended hospitality to refugee women in communities throughout the country. Members of the council opened their homes to the newcomers for social gatherings which helped to develop understanding and friendly relations between the new and old groups in the Jewish community.

Special refugee committees in widespread communities also served to spur the native population to a recognition of their responsibility in easing the social adjustment of the newcomers. Much effort was also devoted specifically to cultural adjustment. Refugee-service agencies referred refugees to English classes offered by boards of education, the WPA, and various colleges and universities. In New York City a special committee, the Committee on Refugee Education, was formed through the joint action of the New York Adult Education Council, the American Christian Committee for Refugees, the Young Women's Christian Association, and the New York Section of the National Council of Jewish Women. Courses taught by volunteers aimed not only to teach English to the refugees, but also to aid their total adjustment by familiarizing them with American history, customs and ideas.

The various organized efforts to help the refugees to become better adjusted in the social and cultural spheres drew the attention and interest particularly of refugees in the middle-aged or late middle-aged group. Young refugees, through their school or work connections, appear to have been able to achieve an adequate adjustment in these fields without the need of special services.

7. *Migration and Allied Services.* Aid and advice with regard to migration procedures were offered by most of the refugee-service agencies as well as by such organizations as the International Migration Service and the International Institutes. The broadest service, and quantitatively the largest part of the job, was performed by the National Refugee Service which, in fact, may be said to have created migration service in its present form. Its services in this area included liaison with government offices in Washington and Philadelphia on individual cases, interpretation of immigration laws and regulations, technical services in regard to such matters as the corporate affidavit, cases of persons admitted on bond, and the immigration status of refugees at the Oswego Emergency Shelter, assistance to local communities on migration problems, and a variety of other activities.

The migration departments of the various agencies also aided from this side in the rescue work abroad. People in America who were trying to bring friends or relatives here to safety were advised as to the correct procedure, aided in corresponding with organizations in Europe active in rescue and emigration work, and given help in making actual applications for visas. Although visas could never be obtained for hundreds of cases receiving the attention of these agencies, many thousand intended victims were successfully rescued from the European death centers by their work.

During the period when refugees were technically classified as enemy aliens, refugee-service agencies supplied information to refugees regarding enemy-alien specifications and restrictions and helped to work out with them some of the resulting problems.

The liberation of Europe through successive victories of the United Nations led to increasing demands from refugees and others to secure information about the fate of relatives and friends in Europe. Were they still alive? Did they manage to escape? If so, where were they now? How could they be located? A flood of inquiries poured in. In order to handle them efficiently and to avoid overlapping and confusion, a Central Location Index was set up in 1944 by various agencies as a clearinghouse to centralize all efforts to obtain such fateful information.

8. *Educational Work in the Field of Attitudes.* Several agencies, such as the Refugee Committee of the National Board of the Y.W.C.A. and the National Refugee Service, were actively concerned with educating the American public toward an understanding of the refugee and his problems. Special bulletins and other publications, distributed through their nation-wide organization, gave the facts concerning the refugee and dispelled common errors concerning his situation. Other organizations already active in the general field of combating anti-Semitism and prejudice against minority groups, such as the Common Council for American Unity, the American Committee for Protection of the Foreign-Born, the National Conference of Christians and Jews, the American Jewish Committee, and the Anti-Defamation League of B'nai B'rith, made an effort to prevent the development of unfavorable attitudes toward refugees.

AID TO SPECIAL GROUPS

In addition to the general program of aid to refugees an important and distinctive feature of the total refugee-service program was the establishment of special agencies or special services for particular groups of refugees. The development of most of these special services was a response to the rather intricate problems of adjustment presented by the professional groups among the refugees. In many cases the initiative for the establishment of such services was supplied by American professional groups who showed sympathy toward the newcomers and a cordial desire to see their abilities recognized. Other special organizations were formed to help rescue political refugees, and to bring over and supervise the care of refugee children.

1. *Scholars and Intellectuals.* Refugee scholars and intellectuals were among the first groups to need help. Barred from their positions in European universities or put on indefinite leaves of absence, some of the leading intellects of Germany (and later of other countries) were deprived of institutional connections by the Nazi attacks on intellectual freedom. The immigration of many of this group to United States, their placement in American colleges and universities, and their general adjustment to American life were aided by the collaborative effort of individuals and groups in this country interested in their welfare, not only by the work of the agencies established for the purpose, but also by the co-operation of colleges, universities, and research institutions.

Efforts to aid this class of refugees were started shortly after the beginning of Hitler's regime. One noteworthy project was the University in Exile of the New School for Social Research, backed by Dr. Alvin Johnson, a great friend of refugee scholars. Through the establishment of this

University in Exile, the faculty of which was made up entirely of Europeans, a number of refugees were brought to this country and given an opportunity to work in their field.

Other agencies devoted to the interest of refugee scholars served to find teaching and research positions for them in institutions throughout the United States. Chief among these was the Emergency Committee in Aid of Displaced Foreign Scholars (originally called the Emergency Committee in Aid of Displaced German Scholars). This committee, established in 1933 and active until June of 1945, was supported by funds from both Jewish and non-Jewish foundations and fund-raising organizations. Universities and colleges which were interested in having a European scholar temporarily join their teaching staff were extended grants ranging from $450 to $2,000 to use as a partial payment of the individual's salary. By June, 1945, the committee had assisted a total of 335 scholars, some 153 of whom were considered to have received permanent places in their colleges and universities and were being paid solely through the budget of those institutions. Although it remained an autonomous agency, the committee was integrated into the over-all structure of the National Coordinating Committee and the National Refugee Service as a co-operating organization.

The Oberlaender Trust of Philadelphia assisted approximately 330 refugee scholars from Germany and Austria to find suitable positions. It made grants either directly to individuals or to institutions to supplement their salaries. Moreover, refugee writers have received sympathetic understanding, hospitality and assistance from the American Center of P.E.N., a world association of writers.

The special nature of the problems of the scholar was likewise recognized by general service agencies. In 1943 the American Christian Committee for Refugees set up the Refugee Scholar Fund, which it financed itself. In 1945 it created the American Committee for Emigre Scholars, Writers and Artists, which was supported also by the National Refugee Service, to carry on in a more limited way the work formerly done by the Emergency Committee in Aid of Displaced Foreign Scholars. In carrying out the programs of these committees, helpful working relationships were established with representatives of the Institute of International Education, the New School for Social Research, the American Friends Service Committee, and various social agencies. The American Friends Service Committee from 1939 through 1945 placed approximately 200 refugees in teaching, research, or apprentice teaching positions.

All these committees in addition to aiding refugee scholars to find positions in this country helped by giving them advice and information concerning American customs and academic practices. Especially noteworthy, as we have seen, were the community-living projects and seminars con-

ducted by the American Friends Service Committee to help introduce the
refugee scholar to American ways of living and thinking. Special intern-
ships for European intellectuals in American colleges and universities also
were sponsored by this committee. Moreover, it co-operated with the "experiments in international living" at Goddard College, Vermont; Stillwater, Minnesota; and Hidden Valley Ranch, California, which were
instituted to bring Americans to study under eminent Europeans and to
lead to a merging of the cultural interests of the two groups.

2. *Physicians.* The refugee physicians constitute another group whose
adjustment in this country presented a particularly intricate problem, and
whose potential contribution to our society led to the formation of special
agencies for their aid. The first of the two main committees aiding this
group was established in 1933 as the Emergency Committee in Aid of
Displaced Foreign Physicians. In its first years this committee gathered
information regarding displaced foreign physicians who were in need of
assistance and made it available to universities, medical schools, hospitals,
research laboratories, and other institutions. After the establishment in
1939 of the National Committee for Resettlement of Foreign Physicians,
the earlier committee changed its name to the Emergency Committee in
Aid of Displaced Foreign Medical Scientists and devoted its funds to
granting stipends for full-time research positions to a limited number of
specially qualified physicians, while the new committee sponsored a broader
program. The two committees worked closely together, and the funds for
medical scientists were allocated through the new committee.

The National Committee for Resettlement of Foreign Physicians was
formed under the auspices of the National Refugee Service with the aid
of a group of American doctors who wished to help their European colleagues become established in this country in such a way that their services
would be most valuable. This committee strove to place refugee doctors in
sections of the United States where medical care was inadequate or completely lacking. The eligibility of refugee physicians to practice medicine
in the United States was carefully evaluated by the committee's advisory
board of American doctors. Those found competent were aided in preparing for examinations and for American Medical Association requirements before their resettlement was planned. During its existence the
committee has placed more than 1,700 doctors in laboratories, in hospitals,
in private practice, in research, or in teaching positions.

3. *Lawyers.* The adjustment of European lawyers was especially difficult because of the difference between European and American legal
practices. Even though agencies were established to help them with their
problems, only a small proportion were able to continue in their chosen
profession. The chief agency giving them aid was the American Committee
for the Guidance of Professional Personnel, which was formed through

the efforts of a group of prominent men in the field of law who believed that European lawyers had a positive contribution to make to American law. Through this organization a few exceptional European lawyers under the age of 35 were placed for retraining in American law schools so that they might be enabled to practice law in the United States. Stipends granted by the committee were matched by funds from the law schools to make this training possible.

Self-help groups, such as the American Association of Former European Jurists, set up as one of the professional services of the New World Club by the refugees themselves, also helped judges, lawyers, and clerks to retrain or to secure employment in allied fields (see chapter on refugee organizations).

4. *Social Workers.* As was true of many other professional groups, American social workers rallied to the aid of their European colleagues. Two principal agencies were set up through their efforts to help social workers from overseas become established in America. The first of these, Hospites, was established in 1933 through the initiative of a group of American social workers who had many international connections and felt a strong sense of responsibility for their colleagues in Europe. Through this organization money was sent to Europe to make small grants to social workers who were in distress. Social workers who came to this country also were given aid in various ways.

Another organization, the Committee on Displaced Social Workers, which had larger funds at its disposal, was formed during the years of 1937 and 1938 through the efforts of a group of individuals concerned with the problems of refugee social workers. This committee examined the credentials and qualifications of social workers, and sponsored the necessary re-education of 60 of the most promising applicants in American schools of social work. The New York School of Social Work, the School of Applied Social Sciences of Western Reserve University, the School of Social Administration of the University of Chicago, and other schools cooperated in the program, sometimes giving tuition scholarships to refugee applicants. This committee, independently organized, was recognized by the National Refugee Service as part of the over-all structure of services to refugees.

Through the National Federation of Settlements a small number of refugee social workers were placed in settlement houses throughout the United States.

5. *Other Occupational Groups.* Similar organizations helped many other occupational groups among the refugees. A special service for refugee librarians was established by the American Library Association to help them retrain and secure employment.

With the co-operation of the Jewish Agricultural Society, which had been functioning since 1900 to encourage farming among Jews in the United States, the National Refugee Service set up a special service for farmers. Refugees were trained and given loans through this service to help them purchase farms and start farming activities.

Also within the National Refugee Service structure special committees were set up for refugee musicians and rabbis. The service for musicians, called the National Committee for Refugee Musicians, was started in 1938 through the initiative of an American musician, Mark Brunswick, who served as chairman. Artists applying to the committee were auditioned and evaluated through the help of the Musicians Emergency Fund before placement was attempted.

The National Committee on Refugee Jewish Ministers was active in seeking openings for refugee rabbis with the co-operation of rabbinical groups and religious organizations throughout the country. Adjustment was assisted in other ways besides placement itself.

6. *Political Refugees.* Another important type of aid to special groups was that directed to the rescue of political refugees, anti-Fascists, labor leaders, and various intellectuals. A number of special committees were formed for this express purpose, and other committees set up special services to carry on this work.

The Jewish Labor Committee, established in 1933 by worker groups in this country for a variety of purposes, spent considerable funds and exerted much effort to help rescue intellectuals and labor leaders from Nazi concentration camps and firing squads. More than 800 such political refugees were rescued through the efforts of this organization alone.

The Joint Anti-Fascist Refugee Committee was active in giving aid to Spanish refugees, only a small number of whom were brought to the United States, most of them going to Mexico and other Latin-American countries. The Exiled Writers Committee, which rendered aid to Spanish refugees and refugees of other nationalities who had fought with the International Brigade in Spain, brought a dozen or so writers to this country before merging with the Joint Anti-Fascist Committee in 1942. The American Committee to Save Refugees, which aided refugees of various nationalities who had sought asylum in France to secure transportation to this hemisphere, likewise merged with the Joint Anti-Fascist Committee in 1942.

Another committee active in this field was the International Rescue and Relief Committee, and the two previously existing organizations of which it was formed. The International Relief Association had been giving aid since 1933 to individuals in Europe who had actively fought Fascism. The Emergency Rescue Committee had been set up in 1940 to help intellectuals, writers, artists, labor leaders, and musicians of proved democratic convictions to leave Europe. The work of these two committees was combined in 1942 into International Rescue and Relief Committee. Altogether through the work of these committees 2,000 anti-Fascists and intellectuals were brought to safety in the Western Hemisphere, less than 1,000 of whom came to the United States.

In 1941 the President's Advisory Committee on Political Refugees was appointed by the President for the specific and emergency purpose of aiding the emigration to the United States of political leaders, labor leaders, professionals, and liberals who were in immediate danger. Working from a list of 4,000 names, it carefully investigated the eligibility of individuals as opponents to Fascism, and a total of 2,000 such political refugees were brought to this country. The committee made special arrangements with the State Department and the Department of Justice to unblock the quotas and give preference to those in special danger who were also able to leave.

The work of rescue of anti-Fascists and other political refugees was also advanced through various committees of Christian church organizations. Prominent among these was the Unitarian Service Committee, which carried on a broad program of service to refugees in this country and abroad. Other denominations of the Protestant church established committees such as the Episcopal Committee for European Refugees and the Congregational Christian Committee for War Victims and Services, which, working through their various parishes, secured affidavits and funds for the rescue of a number of individuals.

7. *Students.* Refugee students also were given aid by several different agencies. Among the most active organizations aiding students was the International Student Service. This organization, with its chief office at Geneva, was founded in 1920 with the aim of providing a meeting ground where students from many nations could discuss their common problems. Since 1933 its energies have been devoted largely to helping student victims of Fascism to continue their education in other lands where they could study without interference. The United States Committee of the International Student Service during this period helped some 700 students. This committee was disbanded in July, 1943, due to disagreements about policy, and a new organization, the Student Service of America, took over its work with refugee students.

The Institute of International Education, which had been active for many years in arranging for exchange fellowships for students, likewise gave aid to refugee students. A total of more than 100 of them were granted scholarships and other services through its efforts.

Aid to refugee students was also an offspring of American student agitation. A student movement, starting in 1938 as a result of the Nazi pogroms, had its beginnings at Harvard University where the Harvard Committee to Aid Refugees was established. This movement stirred up support for aid to students in Nazi Europe and swept the colleges in various parts of the country and resulted in the establishment of the Intercollegiate Committee to Aid Student Refugees, which secured scholarships for them in 300 colleges. The Intercollegiate Committee was merged with International Student Service in 1939.

Assisting in the work with students were B'nai B'rith and the Hillel Foundation, which provided money grants and scholarships, and numerous fraternities and sororities, which gave room and board. The American Friends Service Committee, the Educational Alliance, the American Christian Committee for Refugees, and Vocational Service for Juniors were some of the other organizations which set up special services for refugee students.

The Refugee Scholar Fund, established and financed by the American Christian Committee for Refugees, has aided both young people and older students.

8. *Children.* The plight of refugee children aroused considerable concern in America and a number of organizations were devoted to their aid. In 1934 the German-Jewish Children's Aid (later called the European-Jewish Children's Aid) was formed to bring to this country small groups of refugee children from Nazi Europe. These children were placed in foster homes and supervised by approved child-caring agencies until they reached the age of 21. The United States Committee for the Care of European Children, formed in 1940, in addition to taking charge of British evacuees who came here for the duration only, helped bring over refugee children from continental Europe as regular immigrants. Through these two organizations a total of more than one thousand children were brought to this country under a corporate affidavit from continental Europe and placed in foster homes throughout the country. Another organization, the Non-Sectarian Committee, functioned briefly in 1939–1940 as sponsor for a plan by which a much larger scale migration of refugee children would be permitted. Congress, however, failed to pass the necessary legislation to permit such a migration, and the Committee disbanded (see chapter on Young Refugees).

Other projects gave aid of various sorts to refugee children who came here with their parents. A large number were sent to summer camps or to summer vacation homes through the actions of various committees. After-school play groups which took care of the children while their parents were at work helped solve some of the difficult problems of refugee family life.

OPINIONS OF REFUGEES AS TO HOW REFUGEE SERVICES COULD BE IMPROVED

In order to get further light on the adjustment problems of refugees as well as to learn their reaction to the refugee-service agencies and to get suggestions regarding the future role of these organizations, a question was included in the general questionnaire asking, "In what respects do you think the refugee service committees could help more toward the adjustment of recent immigrants to American life?" Around 3,800 replies to this question were received. Their frequency is indicated in the following table.

ANSWERS TO THE QUESTION: "IN WHAT RESPECTS DO YOU THINK THE REFUGEE SERVICE COMMITTEES COULD HELP MORE TOWARD THE ADJUSTMENT OF RECENT IMMIGRANTS TO AMERICAN LIFE?"

Suggestions	Total		Males		Females	
	Number	Per Cent	Number	Per Cent	Number	Per Cent
Total	3,817	100.0	2,246	100.0	1,571	100.0
Promote contacts with Americans	812	21.3	484	21.5	328	20.9
"Already doing a good job"	641	16.8	330	14.7	311	19.8
Teaching the English language and American ways	536	14.0	322	14.4	214	13.6
Helping more in finding jobs	360	9.4	219	9.8	141	9.0
No suggestions	369	9.7	189	8.4	180	11.5
Resettlement	262	6.9	182	8.1	80	5.1
More guidance in adjustment	190	5.0	116	5.2	74	4.7
More retraining	136	3.5	103	4.6	33	2.1
Promote understanding of immigrants	144	3.8	95	4.2	49	3.1
Treat immigrants as equals	137	3.6	75	3.3	62	3.9
Vocational guidance for intellectuals	95	2.5	54	2.4	41	2.6
Combat anti-Semitism	64	1.7	43	1.9	21	1.3
Other	71	1.8	34	1.5	37	2.4

One-fourth of the total replies indicated that the refugees believed the service committees were "doing their best" (16.8 per cent) or did not know how the services could be improved (9.7 per cent). Although an assessment of the work of service agencies was definitely not indicated by this question, which asked rather for suggestions for the extension of their services, the majority of the replies under these headings made favorable comments on the work they had done. Since many questionnaires were returned without suggestions as to how refugee services could be improved, it might be inferred that many of these individuals had also found the work of the service agencies satisfactory. Moreover, expressions of gratitude for the help given were of frequent occurrence both in life stories and in questionnaire replies.

Answers to this question make clear once again the high value placed by refugees on social and cultural adjustment. The suggestion most frequently made was that service agencies should devote more effort to promoting contacts between Americans and refugees. The refugees' emphasis on the need of help in this area, as shown by these answers, coincides with the high ranking they gave to the problem of making friends with Americans when listing their chief difficulties in this country (see preceding chapter).

Closely related to their stress of the need of help in achieving an adequate social adjustment is the emphasis the respondents placed on cultural adjustment. The answer given with the second greatest frequency was that service committees might have given more aid to refugees in learning the English language and American ways.

Although more help in social and cultural adjustment headed the list of suggested extensions of the work of refugee committees, many replies suggested that the committees should help more in finding jobs, especially in the cases of those with special problems. Criticism of the vocational guidance of intellectuals offered by general service agencies was often given. Many replies asserted that the placement divisions of some of these agencies had been staffed by individuals with inadequate understanding of opportunities for professionals and intellectuals, and of the way to deal with them. Several respondents declared that their adjustment had been considerably retarded by the attitude prevalent in certain of the refugee agencies that achievements in Europe were of little value here, and by the unwise advice that rooted in such attitudes.

Another group of answers suggested that some of the large organizations tended to handle refugees in a mechanical way and might well have given more care in guiding the refugees in their individual problems of adjustment. On the positive side a number of individuals said that they received just the kind of personal help and individual consideration they needed.

A substantial number of answers also suggested that the refugee committees extend their resettlement activities, and that they do more retraining. This would indicate that these programs have received the endorsement of a considerable number of refugees.

Another group of answers stressed the importance of educating the American public to the problems of the refugee through publications, lectures, and other means. Many others felt that more effort should be directed toward combating anti-Semitism in this country. All these answers indicated how important to the refugee was the attitudinal environment in which he lived.

Appraisal of the Total Program

The total program of refugee service served to promote an orderly absorption of the refugee group into the general population of this country. It did this on the whole effectively, especially in the sphere of providing for the material wants of the refugees. One indication of this is the fact that there is no case on record of a refugee having been deported as a public charge. Services in the field of relief, job placements, and occupational readjustment met a conspicuous need.

If any general criticism were to be made, it would be that the other aspects of the refugee's adjustment were somewhat less adequately handled by some of the major agencies. Owing in part, perhaps, to the pressure of time and the great number of applicants, some agencies tended to deal with refugees in a routine manner and did not show a deep understanding of their problems. The fact that refugees have resented this shows that the way in which help is given is often as important as the help extended. Refugees also feel that more help should have been extended in the fields of cultural and social adjustment, although it is easy to understand that more pressing problems would be given precedence by the organizations. A conspicuous exception to the inadequacies in this field is the work of the Quakers, although they never had to meet a problem of mass proportions.

The multiplicity of agencies at work in the field and the often inadequate co-ordination of their efforts has sometimes been criticized. The somewhat haphazard manner in which individual agencies were formed to meet particular needs of the refugees was the result of the emergency nature of the problem.

Unfortunately, refugee agencies sprang up in mushroom-like fashion to meet problems which were . . . emergent in character. We had to build shelters after the rains had started, and there was little time to plan whether they should be on this or that side of the street. The main thing was to get the people in out of the rain—and it was raining hard.[3]

All told, the service agencies were effective in cushioning the shock of refugee immigration, in preventing the refugees from becoming a public burden, and in promoting their adjustment. That the refugees, as subsequent chapters reveal, have adjusted themselves with remarkable rapidity, have placed little strain on American institutions, but on the contrary have been absorbed with relative ease, is due in no small measure to the work of the refugee-service agencies.

[3] Arthur Greenleigh, "The Work of Refugee Agencies in the United States," *Proceedings of the National Conference of Social Work*, 1941, p. 217.

CHAPTER VII

THE PROBLEM OF ECONOMIC ADJUSTMENT

The problem of getting a job and earning a living in a new country is difficult enough for the ordinary immigrant. It is far more serious for the refugee, for a number of reasons. His very occupational background is a handicap, at least in the initial stage of adjustment. The unskilled worker can move with relative ease from a manual job in his homeland to a similar position here. The requirements of knowledge of English and of American conditions are minor in his case. Far different is the situation facing a businessman, a teacher, a physician, or a writer. The language difficulty is almost prohibitive to immediate employment possibilities in their case. Moreover, the businessman must know American products and sales methods; the professional worker must learn the pattern of American professional life and practice; both need resources and connections such as come only in the course of time to established members of the community.

The intellectual type of immigrant has always had a more difficult problem. Unless he is a technician, he does not bring a commodity that America wants to buy, as does the laborer, and he must usually take whatever place he can among his fellow immigrants. No matter what his education and experience, he can often get work only as an unskilled laborer. Moreover, he frequently encounters more prejudice than does the unskilled laborer, which operates to prevent him from attaining a position to which his training would entitle him. This age-old problem has been more in evidence in the case of the refugees, for such an extraordinarily high proportion of them have been of the intellectual type.

The comparatively advanced age of the refugees, in contrast to the earlier immigrants, has presented a further handicap. Even the native American experiences difficulty in finding a new job in his own field after he has passed his fortieth birthday. How much more difficult it is for the immigrant without American experience and frequently forced to secure employment in an unfamiliar field! He might seek the alternative of establishing himself in business or in professional practice, but there he encounters obstacles of a financial nature.

With the exception of those who emigrated early in the Hitler regime, the refugees suffered confiscation of property and were allowed after 1937 to take out only 10 marks. The great majority of them thus arrived without funds. Often, as we shall see, they had to take menial jobs at first, and many have not yet found employment consonant with their former positions. Despite their necessity, owing to lack of resources, of taking any job that was offered, the refugees do not appear to have depressed wages for themselves or for Americans, probably because of their relatively small numbers. Nor, despite their ignorance of American working conditions and standards, do they appear to have been exploited to anything like the extent that earlier immigrants suffered. This is probably accounted for by the self-protection of their superior education and intelligence and by the assistance of friends, relatives, and social agencies.

Unless the newcomer happened to be an Einstein, a Fermi, a Maritain, or a Castiglioni, he lost through emigration all marks of his rank and had to regain them under completely changed circumstances. He had to learn all over again, to begin at the bottom, or to shift to a totally new field. Thus many an intellectual worker became a hand worker, an employer became an employee, a housewife became a wage earner, and a person of independent means became dependent on others. The need of doing hard physical labor, to which they were unaccustomed, was especially trying to the middle-aged and older people. The loss of status as well as the disruption of the former mode of life caused further distress.

In answer to the question "What has changed most in your way of life?" the refugees most frequently mentioned change of occupation (in the case of the women, becoming a wage earner) and other matters of an economic nature, as seen in the tabulation below. On the other hand, the replies were not all negative; some mentioned the positive gains of greater happiness, higher standard of living, more tolerant outlook, and greater independence.

The problem of change of occupation may be illustrated by the following statement by a German factory manager who arrived here at the age of 49 and is now a mechanic in Philadelphia.

"My wife got a housekeeping job and I got a job as an automobile mechanic. I had never done this work before and never had any experience, but I believe that if you try hard enough you can do almost anything you want to. I am not ashamed of the job or the work that I did there, but I am ashamed of the way the employer took advantage of me. He paid me $12.50 a week while all the other people working for him and doing the same work were getting $25 to $30 a week. I worked there for two and one-half years and he did increase the wages a little later, but very little. . . . When this country got into the war I wanted to work in a war plant. I thought I should be doing something to fight Hitler. I applied to different shipyards but they wouldn't employ me because I was an enemy alien. . . .

"I wrote to Washington to Paul McNutt of the War Manpower Commission. He

Replies to the Question: "What Has Changed Most in Your Way of Life?"

Reply	Males		Females	
	Number	Per Cent	Number	Per Cent
Total	2,251	100.0	1,865	100.0
Change of occupation	456	20.3	131	7.0
From employer to employee	209	9.3	19	1.0
Loss in social position	203	9.0	167	9.0
Less social life	175	7.8	161	8.6
Family separation	174	7.7	194	10.4
Work harder	129	5.7	140	7.5
Mode of living	114	5.1	108	5.8
Greater happiness	106	4.7	83	4.4
From mental to physical work	106	4.7	11	.6
Higher standard of living	74	3.3	44	2.4
More tolerant outlook	72	3.2	50	2.7
Less security	71	3.2	56	3.0
Greater hurry	64	2.8	54	2.9
Greater independence	58	2.6	91	4.9
Working conditions	58	2.6	17	.9
From civilian to army life	52	2.3	2	.1
Marriage here	50	2.2	40	2.1
Doing housework	30	1.3	156	8.4
Lack of servants	22	1.0	62	3.3
Dependence on children	18	.8	43	2.3
Becoming a wage earner	10	.4	236	12.7

answered my letter and sent me to the Manpower Commission here. They were all very nice to me but still I could get no job. I was still working as an automobile mechanic and went to Olney High School at night to learn sheet metal work. After I had been in school for three months my teacher told me that I was ready for a job and should try the shipyard again. I kept on trying and finally got a job at Cramp's Shipyard, where I am still working. I began to work there in June 1943. . . .

"I don't want to be a sheet metal worker all my life if I can help it. I know when the war is over I'll be laid off and I want to be ready for it. I have been taking a course at the International Correspondence School in business management, and I hope it will help me to get the right kind of job eventually."

Many of the professional and businessmen among the refugees had never before been faced with the necessity of applying for a job and had no idea how to go about job seeking. At times the refugee applicant heavily taxed the patience of the prospective employer by presenting a great number of testimonials and references and by furnishing much information that seemed irrelevant to a particular job application. Here he was merely following European custom. The refugee applicant was often in an awkward situation when applying for his first job, since his English was inadequate, his clothes and appearance foreign, and his feelings insecure. The various refugee-service committees made a special effort to help the refugees find jobs and the United States Employment Service also rendered considerable assistance and showed much good will. The refugees themselves frequently exhibited great ingenuity and resourcefulness. The following comment by an interviewer relates the efforts of an elderly German Jewish couple in Los Angeles to find some employment and become independent. The man, aged 70, was once a well-to-do manufacturer; his 68-year-old wife had never worked before.

The A's did not enjoy living with their children and being dependent on them. They chose to be on their own, rented an apartment, and set out to find work. Mr. A. had small green labels printed—"I do garden work of any kind. Call me by phone"— which he fastened on people's doors, and as a result he got many calls to tend lawns and gardens. At present they have about 20 steady customers, and are able to make a fair living. These two old people who had servants and gardeners on their own estate in Germany, now set out each morning and take care of gardens for other people. They are enjoying it and never complain of the hard work. Mr. A. tries to forget that he once was the owner of a factory which employed 500 people. He has so completely adjusted to his new life and occupation that he merits recognition. The A's show an excellent sense of humor and vigor.

Life in exile, even under the best conditions, is a hard lot. It was the refugee's added misfortune to be driven out during a time of economic depression when jobs everywhere were scarce or during a time of war when certain opportunities were closed to him because he had come from an enemy country. His status as an alien was an economic handicap in many ways. It restricted his chances of getting a job and it made him ineligible for work relief. The alien, under various state laws, is also ineligible to mothers' pensions, old-age assistance, and other forms of social security. More seriously, he is barred from numerous occupations. Every state in the Union has laws that withhold from the alien the right to engage in certain occupations. The most common form of prohibition lies in the field of the professions, especially medicine, dentistry, and the law.[1] Because of these legal barriers, the problem of retraining for other occupations assumes special importance in the case of refugees, a large proportion of whom were formerly in professional and mercantile positions. In some instances, trade-union rules have the same effect as these state laws. More commonly, however, the union requirement is one of first papers rather than full citizenship.

The entrance of America into the war both hindered and aided the refugees in their economic adjustment. A law passed by Congress in June, 1940, provided that all aliens desiring employment in war industries during wartime or during a state of emergency must first obtain consent of the War or Navy Department. When war was declared on Germany and Italy,

---

[1] Harold Fields, *The Refugee in the United States*, 1938, pp. 49–52, 71, 125–126; Harold Fields, "Where Shall the Alien Work?" *Social Forces*, Vol. XII, No. 2 (December, 1933), pp. 213–221.

many refugees found themselves falling within the technical classification of "enemy aliens," with restrictions on their employment and freedom of movement. This aggravated the suspicion of aliens held by many employers in peacetime and their employment became curtailed far beyond the legal restrictions. In 1942 the President and the Attorney General both issued statements against alien discrimination, pointing out that aliens might be freely employed in most war industries, and that they were excluded by law only from those phases of war production dealing with aircraft construction and specified secret processes. Toward the end of the year restrictions affecting the alien refugee group were eased, many barriers in the way of their employment, particularly in war industries, were removed, and discrimination was lessened through the action of the President's Committee on Fair Employment Practice (FEPC). The war demand for labor was so great that the year 1943 opened amid an upsurge of employment for the refugees, and in the course of the year practically every newcomer seeking work found employment, even though it was not necessarily in his former field or profession.

THE INITIAL STRUGGLE FOR A LIVELIHOOD

Except for those few who were fortunate enough to bring money or convertible goods or who were skilled in the technical professions or trades, the struggle for a bare living dominated the initial stages of the settlement of refugees in this country. The change these people had to undergo can hardly be overestimated. Here was the former factory owner who now peddled cakes and candy, or the manager of a department store who worked as a laborer in a cemetery. Others, as the following cases reveal, hired out as domestics, dishwashers, janitors, or took a variety of other menial jobs.

A former factory manager, who arrived in Philadelphia in 1940, states: "My wife and I went to Atlantic City where we got a job as a couple, she as cook and I as butler. We worked at this job for three months, or through the summer season, and it was really this job that gave us our start."

A graduate of an Austrian technical school writes: "I secured a position as maintenance man and my wife as chambermaid in an apartment hotel. I worked 70 hours a week and was paid $15, of which $5 was deducted for a basement apartment. My wife had to take care of 40 rooms a day and was paid $11 a week. There were no meals included." He is now an instructor in an engineering college in the Middle West.

The first job of a former textile businessman who settled in Detroit was as orderly in a hospital.

A classical scholar who arrived in 1938 got a job as dishwasher in a café in New York. He also handled garbage cans and ran freight elevators. He states that he met a variety of nationalities among his fellow workers—Greek, Italian, Puerto Rican, and French—but did not find them congenial nor an aid in his Americanization.

A former German judge worked for some time as dishwasher in the basement of a department store in San Francisco. "I have covered the whole range," he writes, "bus boy, kitchen helper, dishwasher, etc."

A former steel exporter from Germany states: "I began by peddling pencils and my wife was a waitress for a while. She made candy which I peddled, and I did a great many things. I did not earn any money, but I learned a great deal. I learned about American business and American people."

A former medical student writes: "When I arrived in this country I was penniless and had to make a living. During the first weeks I pasted little pieces of colored paper together to make Christmas angels, houses, trees, etc. Later I found a position as an accordion player in a Viennese restaurant during dinner hours. I worked an average of 16 to 18 hours daily and earned just enough to make my living and to support my mother."

More purposeful than usual were the menial jobs, such as sorting scrap metal or working furs, that many former merchants took in industries with which they were familiar, in order to gain knowledge of business practices in this country so that they could eventually resume their own businesses.

Many refugees had a variety of jobs at first. A former university professor writes:

"In all this time I spent in this country I never have been afraid to earn my daily bread in the really American way: I was a night watchman, a liquor salesman, twice I worked in junk yards, I was a clerk in a mattress factory, a packer in a grocery, a substitute in a senior high school (those were my lucky days), and even a male nurse. . . . I think I am more fit for an intellectual job."

A former judge, who arrived in 1939 and is now residing in Detroit, states: "Within the following years I had to change many times from one line to another. Among the jobs I mention the following: hotel clerk, horseback riding teacher in a summer camp, clothing salesman, furniture salesman, insurance agent, and lately I became a sales engineer in a packaging company for overseas shipping. This was possible only after having become an American citizen and after attending a special training course. In all jobs, whatever they were, I appreciated the democratic attitude between employer and employee, and also the immediate informality between colleagues."

A middle-aged former factory owner, arriving from Germany in 1940, and settling in Peoria, Illinois, worked variously as a porter and janitor in retail stores, delivery boy in an upholstering factory, cleaner of furs, and canvasser selling notions, before he secured a loan which enabled him to establish his present business of dry cleaning. He found no special difficulty in obtaining jobs, although his desires were primarily directed toward self-employment.

It would appear that refugee women experienced less difficulty than did the men in making the initial economic adjustment. The kind of work they did before emigrating was more transferable and they found it much easier to get a job than was true of the men. At least they could bake cakes and cookies which their husbands could sell. In the table cited above, it will be recalled that only 7 per cent of the women, in comparison with 20 per cent of the men, mentioned "change of occupation" as the greatest change in their experience, and that only 1 per cent of them as compared to 9 per cent of the men changed from employer to employee. Their main economic adjustment consisted in becoming wage earners for the first time (12.7 per cent). And here they took jobs chiefly in the household, or domestic, field with which they were already familiar. They met the change in status with more equanimity than the men, who experienced a greater sense of loss and of frustration. The role of husband and wife in the European household frequently became reversed, with the women becoming for a time the main support of the family, which increased the discomfiture of the men. Moreover, the women appear to have acquired English and American customs more readily and to have met with less prejudice at work, probably because they were regarded as only temporary competitors. Though their adjustment was less difficult, it does not follow that they had an easy time. Operating machines in factories, working in restaurants, and serving as domestics are hard tasks, especially to persons not accustomed to such employment.[2] The following excerpts from life stories and interviews illustrate the special situation of refugee women.

Mrs. S., from Czechoslovakia, whose husband had owned a factory worth $800,000, had had no work experience, but was employed upon her arrival here (in San Francisco) in a sewing room organized for emigres. From there she went out to get her own jobs sewing, and now explains that she is considered rather an expert seamstress and dressmaker and has a job which she enjoys.

A middle-aged Protestant woman from Germany, now working in a factory in Philadelphia, states: "I was not trained for anything, and the only thing I really could do was to cook in my own house. [After serving several years as a cook with a family] I started work in a factory making cases for bullets. The first two weeks they trained me. It was very simple, and very monotonous. At first I worked on a reamer machine, but now I'm on an assembly line."

A 49-year-old woman in San Francisco, widow of a German Jewish banker, states: "I came from a background of ease and luxury. I never had to do my own housework, but was surrounded by servants. It was not easy for me to adjust to being a servant myself, but I adjusted to it very quickly. I felt very happy in all my jobs and everybody has treated me in a respectful manner. All my employers have made an effort to make me feel at home and I never had the feeling of being a servant."

"I adjusted more easily than my husband," writes a Czech businesswoman, "as I spoke English quite well when I arrived. My husband had a difficult time learning the language. First he tried to get a job as a carpenter, but he didn't handle tools well enough to work like the American so he started selling brushes. I ran a home bakery business."

The necessity of taking such menial jobs as cited above and of adjusting to conditions far below their European skills, background, and income

[2] Cf. Freda Heilberg, "Experiences, Attitudes, and Problems of German Jewish Refugees," *Jewish Social Service Quarterly*, March, 1939, pp. 322–327; Vera Craener, "Frauen stellen sich um," *Aufbau*, December 12, 1945; "A Reporter at Large," *New Yorker*, June 3, 1939.

levels, was a distressing experience. The cultural background of the middle-class European made it hard for him to accept such a change of fortune. In contrast to America, a social stigma is attached to manual work. Whereas in America people are proud to have worked up from the bottom, in Europe one is proud of having spent one's whole life in one occupation, of having inherited wealth and economic position rather than of acquiring them.[3] The refugee therefore was not conditioned to accept easily the radical change in his economic and social status, and this fact caused much inner conflict and anxiety. The interviewers were frequently reassured that in Europe the refugee's social position and occupational status were much higher. Many refugees had done good work in their original fields and they felt that they could do good work again if only they were given a chance to utilize their training, experience, and talent. It seemed to them so much more difficult to make good even in the simplest job, in which they did not have any experience, than in the field where they had already proved that they could function efficiently. Many refugees became bitter, disgruntled, critical of their new environment, and sometimes arrogant. They forgot the dangers from which they had escaped and remembered only the life they had been leading at home before they had been threatened in their security. In most cases, however, the refugees accepted their changed fortunes with good grace, and displayed a courage and adjustability that are truly admirable. A case in point is that of a middle-aged Slovak businessman whose life history is given here.

From Businessman to Cook

It's New Year 1945. I look around in my living room where my wife, my children, Henry 11, Charlotte 7, and even my American-born Bobby, barely a week old, are having a good time, each after his own fashion, and I am happy again. . . . All of them are happy here in America—all feel the effect of America. The younger ones find it easier to be transplanted, but we parents also found it not too hard to become Americans, not only in name but in the full meaning of the term.

As I look around I can't help recalling the past. Born in a Slovakian hamlet, I attended the Slovakian public School (6 grades in one room), enrolling later in a Hungarian high school. (Slovakia at that time was a part of Hungary.) World War I found me in the middle of high school. A couple of months after graduation I was in the uniform of the Austrian Emperor's Army. I left the Army as a second lieutenant. Next year saw me in Vienna as a university student. There I majored in economics, studying also English, which, at that time, I didn't exactly know what it would be good for. I gained a fairly good knowledge of the language, and even had a chance to try it out in England as a student of a holiday course at the London University. Upon my return from London, I joined an English conversational club, which turned out to have been a wise thing.

Upon leaving school I joined a firm as a partner. The business proved to be successful, and began to flourish, when suddenly my partner died. This made me the sole owner of

---

[3] Gerhart Saenger, *Today's Refugees, Tomorrow's Citizens*, pp. 185–186.

the establishment with some debts to be paid to the widow. The next few years proved to be a succession of good years. I could therefore pay back everything and look upon the business with great pride as my very own. My married life, like my business, proved to be successful. I built a beautiful home where the happy laughter of Henry and Charlotte brought sunshine daily.

In 1935 everything suddenly changed. Hitler invaded Austria, and aroused the latent anti-Semitism. Everything was getting dark. Friends turned into enemies. Jews lost all rights of human beings. We had to wait nineteen months for our visa to America, and that year and a half was hell on earth. The most pathetic sight was my children. "Daddy, why aren't we allowed to sit down on this bench? Other people are sitting on benches. Daddy, isn't there any park that we could go to?" These were questions asked by my six-year-old son, but I could not answer them. . . .

Time passed slowly under the circumstances, very slowly. Our picture of America was gotten from books and movies about the country. One time America was the country where everybody was a millionaire; next time we saw in America nobody else but gangsters and racketeers; then, again, a country where people were sleeping in winter under the Brooklyn Bridge covered only with newspapers. One picture contradicted the other and no one therefore could be absolutely true.

Finally after 19 months of waiting we were notified we'll get our visas and before long we were on our way. . . . We arrived in New York on December 1, 1939. From there we were taken to our cousin in Atlantic City, where we spent about three weeks. I was soon made to understand that in America everybody has to work for a living. I found it to be a little rude at first, but when I got my first job as a dishwasher and earned my own dollars I realized that this rudeness really was a great help to me. I moved to a small apartment, managed to get along with very little, and soon all my experiences, Hitler, my own store, my friends, belonged to the past.

I washed dishes, scrubbed floors, but I "brought home the bacon" upon which my family thrived. The only thing that mattered was that I was told I did my job well. . . . I got a job in a hotel as a pantryman, made salads after a few weeks, and later was put in full charge of the kitchen. Atlantic City is a resort, however. Most of the jobs are seasonal. So I said to myself, "If you want to have a well-paid job all year around better move to a city where there are not two- but ten-month seasons." And so I moved to Philadelphia. Monday, when the papers carried the big headlines of the Pearl Harbor attack, I arrived here and Wednesday I was already working in a big chain restaurant as a salad-and-sandwich man. It was a wonderful job but the pay wasn't high enough. After working for ten months I left and was for a short time cook. Finally I landed in the delicatessen cafeteria line, where I am in charge of the kitchen. I have been on this job for about two years. It is a union job and pays well.

Well, this is another day. I am in the living room again. The children are preparing to go to school, the baby is being fed—all are satisfied. Settled, you would say. Yes, this country gave us shelter in the bitterest need. What can I, simple man, do to repay at least part of the debt I owe this country? Perhaps by becoming a good American citizen and bringing up my children to be good Americans. Our first papers are in our hands, and we are impatiently awaiting our final papers. When I compare my situation here with that in Europe, I come to the following conclusion: There I was a wealthy man, here I work for my daily bread. Nevertheless, I couldn't say that I was happier there than here.

CHAPTER VIII

OCCUPATIONAL ADJUSTMENT OF
THE REFUGEES

According to the Study Committee's questionnaire returns, 11,233 in number, 72.5 per cent of the refugees in the United States 16 years old and over are usually gainfully employed. This is true of 89 per cent of the males and 48 per cent of the females. These are higher percentages of employment, especially among the women, than is the case of the native American population. (In 1940, 79 per cent of all males and 25.4 per cent of all females in the United States 14 years old and over were reported by the Census Bureau as being in the labor force.) This reflects the generally lower income and greater need of employment on the part of refugees.

The occupational distribution of the refugees who are usually gainfully employed shows a high concentration in the white-collar fields, some two-thirds being engaged in professional, business management, or clerical occupations. In the case of the males, this is true of nearly three-fourths of the total. The women, however, are concentrated in order in semiskilled, clerical, and professional fields. In comparison with the occupational groups of the total body of employed workers in the United States, as seen in the following table, the refugees have a much higher percentage of professional and clerical workers, especially male; a higher percentage of female semiskilled workers; and a much lower percentage of unskilled and service workers of both sexes. If the farmers are eliminated from the proprietor and manager group, the refugees show a still higher proportion in business management than does the total body of American workers.

If the occupational distribution of the refugees in the United States is considered from the standpoint of religious affiliation, the Jewish groups show a relatively higher proportion of their number in business management, clerical, skilled and semiskilled occupations, and a lower proportion in the professions, while the Christians show the reverse. No outstanding difference in occupational structure appears when the data are further broken down by nationality or country of birth. Among Christian professional persons, teachers—mainly German and Austrian—comprise the largest number (36 per cent), followed by physicians and dentists (10 per

Per Cent Distribution of Refugees 1945 and of Total American Employed Workers 1940, by Major Occupation Group and Sex

Major occupation group	Total American workers*			Refugees		
	Total	Male	Female	Total	Male	Female
Total	100.0	100.0	100.0	100.0	100.0	100.0
Professional workers	7.4	5.5	13.2	21.3	22.6	18.5
Proprietors, managers and officials	19.7	24.5	5.2	21.1	26.5	9.3
Clerical and kindred workers	16.6	12.8	28.3	25.8	24.8	28.2
Skilled workers	11.2	14.5	1.0	8.8	10.4	5.3
Semiskilled workers	18.3	18.2	18.4	14.5	9.6	25.1
Unskilled and service workers	26.0	23.8	32.7	6.8	4.7	11.4
Occupation not reported	.8	.7	1.2	1.7	1.4	2.2

* *Sixteenth Census of the United States: 1940, Population*, Vol. II, pt. 1, p. 15.

cent), who are again mainly German and Austrian. Among Jewish professional persons, physicians and dentists rank first (23 per cent), followed by teachers (17 per cent), in both instances mainly German, Austrian, and Polish. The other professions, which are numerically less important, show a ranking, among the Christian refugees, of engineers, writers, artists, chemists, musicians, clergymen, and others, and among the Jewish refugees, of chemists, engineers, artists, writers, nurses, clergymen, musicians, and others. In the business management group, business owners rank first among both Christian and Jewish refugees, followed by managers and farmers. If all occupational groups are considered from the standpoint of their educational background, it appears that, although some university people are doing manual labor work, most are concentrated in professional and business management fields, while those of high school level or less constitute a majority of the workers in the other occupation groups.

Occupational Progression from First to Last or Present Job

The above data refer to the occupations of the refugees at the time they answered the questionnaire (extending from the fall of 1944 through the spring of 1945). Most of them, however, had been in the United States for a number of years, and we have seen in the preceding chapter how frequently their first job was menial or unskilled. The questionnaire provided some information on their work experience by asking for a report on the first job and the present or last one. It is thus possible to note the extent of their occupational adjustment by comparing the two. To ascertain whether there has been progression, retrogression, or no change in this respect, we may use as a standard the listing of major occupational groups given in the table above. This is considered by the U.S. Bureau of the Census as constituting a socio-economic ranking of occupations, ranging from professional pursuits at the top to unskilled labor at the bottom. Any movement of occupation upward on that scale may be considered as a progression, any movement downward as a retrogression, and remaining in the same category as no change. Some cases, such as persons entering gainful employment for the first time or those retiring from work, do not fit into the scheme and must be considered separately, as is done in the following table.

Occupational Change, from First to Last or Present Job in the United States, Among Refugees, by Sex

Occupational Change	Male		Female	
	Number	Per Cent	Number	Per Cent
Total	6,130	100.0	4,808	100.0
Never worked	341	5.6	1,648	34.3
Once worked, now housewife	——	——	449	9.3
Once worked, now student	16	.3	35	.7
Once worked, now retired	15	.2	——	——
Now working, formerly housewife	——	——	153	3.2
Now working, formerly student	77	1.2	117	2.4
Always worked, job progression	2,114	34.5	791	16.5
Always worked, no change	3,517	57.4	1,599	33.3
Always worked, job retrogression	50	.8	16	.3

The clear-cut cases of occupational change are the last three items in the table. Here it is definitely revealed that the great majority of the refugees, especially the men, either held on to their occupational status or improved it and that only a minute proportion lost ground. This becomes clearer if these cases are considered by themselves, as is done in the following table.

Change in Occupation Status among Refugees in the United States

Change	Total		Male		Female	
	Number	Per cent	Number	Per cent	Number	Per cent
Total	8,087	100.0	5,681	100.0	2,406	100.0
Upward	2,905	35.9	2,114	37.2	791	32.9
No change	5,116	63.3	3,517	61.9	1,599	66.5
Downward	66	0.8	50	0.9	16	0.6

It thus appears that fully a third of the refugees gainfully employed advanced in occupational status and that nearly two-thirds of them remained at the same level in which they had first found employment, while a negligible proportion retrograded. There was no appreciable difference in these respects between the various religious and nationality groups, except that the Jews, especially the Austrian, showed a somewhat higher percentage of occupational progression.

Occupation in Europe Compared to Occupation in the United States

How do the kinds of jobs refugees have in this country compare with the kinds of jobs they had in Europe before emigrating? To what extent have they been able to transfer their skills and continue in their former field of employment, and how has this differed among the various occupational categories? Failing to continue in their own field, into what other occupations have they gone? General answers to these questions may be gleaned from the following summary tables. More detailed information will be given later in the chapters on the businessmen and the various professional groups. Because of the different occupational situation of men and women, data will be given separately for each sex.

To consider first the male workers, the most striking revelation in the table is that in the case of each occupational group the largest single percentage of workers remained in the same category that they had been in abroad. It is also noteworthy that this tendency was most marked in the case of professional persons and skilled and semiskilled workers (the only instances of clear majority), which no doubt reflects the high degree of transferability of skills in these fields. There is much variation in this respect among professional persons, as is pointed out in detail in later chapters. The life stories and questionnaire comments reveal many instances where refugees with highly developed technical skills and professional knowledge readily found suitable employment and where skilled craftsmen like machinists, carpenters, painters, diamond cutters, jewelry makers, tailors, cooks, and butchers secured work almost immediately and at good wages, frequently better than they had abroad. Only a small amount of readjustment or re-education to fit into the American industrial scene was required. These workers also report that they encountered little or no discrimination in getting a job or while at work, since there was a demand for their type of services.

In the business field the most transferable skill appears to be the technique of selling. Nearly two-fifths of the refugees who had been business proprietors or managers in Europe continued as such in this country, while the next largest proportion of them, one fourth, obtained employment in allied fields as clerks, bookkeepers, agents, and salesmen. Nearly one-half of those who had been clerical and kindred workers in Europe found employment in that category here. A few advanced to business management or professional work, while nearly one-third became manual workers in industry.

Most skilled and semiskilled workers, as we have already seen, continued in the same occupational category. An appreciable percentage of both groups advanced to white-collar jobs; a very small proportion fell back to less

PER CENT DISTRIBUTION OF OCCUPATION IN EUROPE AND OCCUPATION IN THE UNITED STATES FOR MALE REFUGEES

Occupation in Europe	Total Known		Occupation in the United States							
	Number	Per Cent	Professional Workers	Prop. Mgrs. Off.	Clerks & Kindred Workers	Skilled Workers	Semi-skilled Workers	Un-skilled Workers	Students	Unemployed and Retired
Professional workers	1,436	100.0	66.9	8.9	12.4	3.8	2.7	1.9	.7	2.7
Proprietors, managers, officials	2,963	100.0	6.2	38.9	25.4	8.8	9.9	5.0	.1	5.7
Clerks & kindred workers	754	100.0	2.5	17.0	46.7	11.3	13.8	6.5	.1	2.1
Skilled workers	142	100.0	4.9	11.3	5.7	66.9	4.9	4.9	.7	.7
Semiskilled workers	78	100.0	1.3	12.8	7.7	7.7	62.8	7.7	—	—
Unskilled workers	31	100.0	3.2	12.9	6.5	9.7	29.0	38.7	—	—
Students	746	100.0	14.8	6.8	13.1	11.0	4.6	1.7	47.9	.1
Unemployed and retired	10	100.0	10.0	—	10.0	—	10.0	—	10.0	60.0

skilled occupations. Some three-fourths of the small group of unskilled workers, farm laborers, and servants continued in the same field, while the rest advanced chiefly to manual work requiring more skill. In this as in other fields, the refugees frequently took training courses to fit them for work in their former occupation or in a new one.

Still urgent is the problem of refugees who have not yet succeeded in getting into their former type of work in which they have had training and experience. In some instances, where there is little or no transferability of skill, such as the law, this is impossible. In other instances, the number of refugees in a highly specialized field, such as that of orchestra conductor, is greater than the possible demand for their services. But where it is feasible to resume their former occupations the refugees naturally desire to do so. It is a hardship and a blow to one's ego, after having owned or managed a large business, to become a minor employee, or after a university education to do simple clerical or manual work, or after having had a professional practice to become a technical assistant, and many refugees are unhappy in their present situations and dream of returning to their old places in Europe. On the other hand, this is an inevitable condition during a period of adjustment. The immigrant must first acquire an adequate knowledge of the language of the new country and of its mores and business methods before he can hope to assume a position comparable to that which he previously enjoyed in his homeland. As time goes on, the refugees have increasingly got back into their former occupational status, as the above tabulations of questionnaire returns reveal. There is still, however, a great deal of talent among them that is not fully utilized, to the detriment of both the refugees themselves and their adopted country.

The desire of the refugees to pull themselves out of poorly paid or menial jobs and to get into their former line of work has led in some instances to an insistent attitude which, in turn, has created an unfavorable reaction on the part of American employers. Some employers have complained that the new immigrants are too ambitious and overzealous. Others have objected to the emphasis some refugees place on European experience and methods, and charge that "they try to tell us how to run our business." On the other hand, there are plenty of instances where employers have taken the initiative and promoted refugee employees to higher positions and given them jobs more in line with their previous training and experience.

Turning now to the women refugees, we observe in the table below that, as in the case of the men, those who had been engaged in professional and in skilled or semiskilled work in Europe have been outstanding in their ability to follow the same type of occupation here. The business group of proprietors, managers, clerical and kindred workers have been least successful in this respect. The largest group of refugee women had been house-

wives abroad. While approximately three out of five of them are now
housewives here (frequently after having been gainfully employed during
the initial period of adjustment), the rest have been forced to take jobs
outside of the home, mainly as semiskilled factory operatives, dressmakers,
clerks, and salespeople. As in the case of the men, the career women among
the refugees who have not found positions in their own field of work are
anxious to do so. For example, women who were office workers in Europe
and who became domestics upon arrival here, and later took factory or
store jobs, are now seeking office work and are increasingly able to obtain
it. Meanwhile they have acquired a good knowledge of English and of
American business methods. This work history is an index of advancing adjustment.

Having discussed general categories of occupation, we may now go a
step further and investigate to what extent refugees, both men and women,
are following the same specific occupation here that they did in Europe.
This they would regard, by and large, as being "suitably employed." Involved in such employment is not only the question of transferability of
skill; there are also such factors as the demand for such services in this
country, legal restrictions, the attitude of employers and of fellow workers
or colleagues, the varying requirements as to adequacy of English and of
knowledge of American methods, all of which vary widely between specific
occupations.

To consider male refugees first, it is noteworthy that among the respondents to the questionnaire who were professional workers abroad,
chemists (76.7 per cent), physicians and dentists (76.7 per cent), and clergymen (71.7 per cent), followed closely by musicians (68.3 per cent), lead
in securing employment in the same occupation here. Then come professors
and teachers (60.5 per cent), engineers (55.0 per cent), artists (51.3 per
cent), and writers (36.4 per cent), with architects (10.0 per cent) and lawyers (5.8 per cent) bringing up the rear.

In the business management group, the record is less favorable, with the
following results: farm owners (46.5 per cent), business owners—numerically three-fourths of the total—(26.7 per cent), managers (19.7 per cent),
and bankers (7.4 per cent). Among the clerical and kindred workers, bookkeepers, etc. (42.0 per cent), salesmen (25.3 per cent), and the other clerical workers (32.3 per cent) are outstanding.

The skilled workers as a group, we have already seen, are noteworthy in
possessing a high degree of transferability of skill, 66.9 per cent of those
who were engaged in skilled work abroad being in the same occupational
category here. While the actual numbers are too small when the cases are
broken down into specific callings to give reliable percentages, it appears
that the skilled workers have found employment in their same craft in
roughly this order: tailors, painters, carpenters, machinists, furriers, tech-

PER CENT DISTRIBUTION OF OCCUPATION IN EUROPE AND OCCUPATION IN THE UNITED STATES FOR FEMALE REFUGEES

Occupation in Europe	Total Known		Occupation in the United States								
	Number	Per Cent	Professional Workers	Prop. Mgrs. Off.	Clerks & Kindred Workers	Skilled Workers	Semiskilled Workers	Unskilled Workers	House-Wives	Students	Unemployed and Retired
Professional workers	536	100.0	51.7	4.3	11.2	3.0	6.5	3.2	16.4	1.5	2.2
Proprietors, managers, officials	288	100.0	6.9	18.0	15.3	5.6	22.2	8.7	17.7	—	5.6
Clerks and kindred workers	431	100.0	2.3	4.4	36.7	2.1	15.5	8.8	29.0	.7	.5
Skilled workers	36	100.0	2.8	5.5	13.9	52.8	2.8	8.3	13.9	—	—
Semiskilled workers	101	100.0	2.0	2.0	6.9	2.0	58.4	3.9	23.8	—	1.0
Unskilled workers	49	100.0	2.0	8.2	4.1	—	12.2	38.8	28.6	2.0	4.1
Housewives	2,546	100.0	2.4	4.4	9.8	1.6	12.7	6.5	59.3	.1	3.2
Students	803	100.0	13.1	2.2	24.2	4.1	9.2	2.0	11.7	33.5	3.2
Unemployed and retired	46	100.0	4.3	4.3	13.1	4.3	21.8	6.5	28.3	4.3	13.1

nicians, printers, jewelers, and upholsterers, to mention just the leading examples. Among the semiskilled, the order is bakers, butchers (numerically most important), and machine operatives (the second largest group). Among the unskilled, 38.7 per cent are following the same occupation; the rest have improved their occupational status.

In the case of the women refugees, only 30 per cent of whom had a gainful occupation abroad, a generally lower proportion than is the situation with the men, are engaged in the same occupation here. Among professional women, physicians (56.9 per cent) and nurses (52.0 per cent) lead in this respect, and are followed by chemists (38.9 per cent), writers (37.9 per cent), professors and teachers (37.8 per cent), musicians (37.2 per cent), artists (32.4 per cent), and lawyers (13.3 per cent).

The proportion of women refugees engaged in the same occupation here as abroad is lowest in the business management field: business owners (15.4 per cent) and managers (12.3 per cent). A somewhat higher percentage of clerical and kindred workers follow the same occupation, namely, stenographers and typists (24.4 per cent), bookkeepers (23.3 per cent), saleswomen (21.1 per cent), other clerical workers (19.8 per cent).

The only important group of skilled workers among refugee women are the technicians, 57.1 per cent of whom are in the same type of work here. In the semiskilled category, the proportions following the same occupation in this country as abroad are: milliners (64.3 per cent), dressmakers (40.4 per cent), and practical nurses (35.3 per cent). The unskilled women workers are mainly domestic servants, 43.4 per cent of them remaining in this field over here.

Attention should also be drawn to the fact that, in addition to the above instances where refugees have found employment here in the same specific occupation which they followed abroad, some refugees have entered occupations in the same major grouping, so that they are on the same occupational level if not in the same special field. Both factors should be regarded as an index of occupational adjustment.

EMPLOYMENT STATUS

Of the 11,233 questionnaire returns, 8,360 were from persons who are usually gainfully employed, that is, in the labor force. Ninety per cent of these (7,530 in number) were employed at the time in some kind of work, whether or not it was in the occupation they had been trained in abroad, and 10 per cent, numbering 830, were unemployed and looking for work. In view of the special difficulties faced by the recent immigrants, this is a favorable employment situation. It is about the same degree of employment and unemployment that may be found, on an average, among all American workers. During the war years employment was at an unusually high level, probably over 90 per cent for native Americans. The refugees, too, gained by the wartime demand, though they still encountered restrictions due to alien status and other factors.

A smaller percentage of skilled workers (2.8 per cent) than of any other occupational group among the refugees were unemployed. The only un-employment reported by semiskilled workers was by dressmakers and nurses among the women. In the case of unskilled workers, 9 of the 11 respondents in this category who were unemployed were domestic servants. Among the numerically much larger white-collar groups, 5.9 per cent of the professional workers stated that they were unemployed, the proportion being highest among trained nurses, writers, and musicians and lowest among engineers and chemists. Of those refugees who had been proprie-tors, managers, or officials abroad, 5.3 per cent were unemployed, the rate of unemployment being noticeably less for those among them who had been sales representatives. In the category of clerical and kindred workers, 5.8 per cent were seeking work, this being especially the case with former in-surance agents and stenographers, and least with bookkeepers and account-ants and salespeople. The largest single group of respondents who said they were unemployed—280 or 10.9 per cent of their total number—were women whose occupation in Europe was that of housewife. Eight and nine-tenths per cent of those who were students in Europe were unemployed.

The reason for being unemployed was not stated by a third of the group. Approximately one-fifth—all women—gave as the reason "family responsi-bility," about 15 per cent ill-health, 11 per cent old age, and lesser propor-tions "in training," "between jobs," "no need to work," "can't find 'suitable' job," or other reasons.

INCOME AND FINANCIAL ASSISTANCE

Judging by the questionnaire returns, most of the refugees (75.3 per cent) are wholly dependent on their earnings, having no other source of income. The proportion declines steadily with advancing age groups, being 85.6 per cent of those 16 to 20 years old and 57.3 per cent of those over 60.

Replies were received from 4,775 men and 2,381 women regarding the amount of their average weekly earnings, which most commonly take the form of wages or salaries. The great majority of them were employed full time. The following table gives for each sex the distribution of earnings for full-time employment by main occupation groups in the United States.

This table clearly reveals the higher average earnings of men as com-pared with women, 64.4 per cent of the former earning over $50 per week and only 15.1 per cent of the latter. The most common weekly earnings of the women are between $20 and $40 a week; this is the case of three out of every five of them. On the other hand, three out of every five men earn between $50 and $75 a week. The same differential appears in each occupa-tional group, as is seen in a comparison of median weekly earnings. To give

Per Cent Distribution of Average Weekly Earnings for Full-Time Employment by Main Occupation in the United States and Sex

Main Occupation Group	Total Known		Average Weekly Earnings						
	Number	Per Cent	Under $20	$20–29	$30–39	$40–49	$50–74	$75–99	$100 and Over
I. Males									
Total known	4,649	100.0	1.2	5.3	11.2	17.9	31.0	14.4	19.0
Professional workers	1,117	100.0	.4	1.9	4.5	11.2	27.7	23.4	30.9
Proprietors and managers	1,149	100.0	1.1	2.6	4.3	9.7	27.7	17.4	37.2
Clerical and kindred workers	1,197	100.0	.8	7.8	18.9	25.1	31.4	9.1	6.9
Skilled workers	485	100.0	1.2	2.1	11.1	24.3	42.5	14.0	4.8
Semiskilled workers	475	100.0	.6	5.7	17.7	26.8	42.3	6.5	.4
Unskilled workers	226	100.0	8.4	27.5	25.7	23.0	12.8	1.3	1.3
II. Females									
Total known	1,912	100.0	6.2	31.2	29.2	18.3	9.9	2.4	2.8
Professional workers	348	100.0	2.9	15.2	25.9	27.0	17.8	5.7	5.5
Proprietors and managers	173	100.0	4.0	10.4	17.3	19.7	19.1	11.0	18.5
Clerical and kindred workers	573	100.0	3.1	35.3	37.9	17.6	5.6	.2	.3
Skilled workers	107	100.0	.9	21.5	25.3	23.4	24.3	3.7	.9
Semiskilled workers	503	100.0	4.8	39.2	32.2	16.7	6.7	.4	—
Unskilled workers	208	100.0	21.6	49.1	19.2	7.7	1.9	.5	—

a more complete picture, this may be compared with the range within which the majority of over three-fourths in each occupation fall.

Median and Most Frequent Range of Weekly Earnings for Each Major Occupation and Sex

Occupation group	Median		Range Including over 75% of all cases	
	Males	Females	Males	Females
Professional workers	$79.60	$42.30	Over $50	$20–74
Proprietors and managers	81.75	49.41	Over $50	Over $30
Clerical & kindred workers	49.00	33.09	$30–74	$20–49
Skilled workers	56.68	41.20	$40–99	$20–74
Semiskilled workers	49.76	31.91	$30–74	$20–49
Unskilled workers	35.60	25.83	$20–49	Under $20–39

The above table reveals the most typical weekly earnings of each major occupational group. As would be expected, professional workers and proprietors and managers have the largest average earnings. This is true of both sexes, though in the case of the women, professional workers average but little more than skilled workers. Earnings above $100 a week are noteworthy in the case of proprietors and managers of both sexes and of male professional workers. Both men and women skilled workers earn more than do clerical and kindred workers, whose earnings are on the same level as those of semiskilled workers. Although strictly comparable data are not available, the earnings of the refugees seem to be about the same as or slightly under those of the general working population at the time.[1]

Three-fourths of the refugees, as we have already seen, have no source of income other than their earnings. Of those with other sources, the largest single group, comprising 11.9 per cent of the total refugee population, have income derived from investments or savings. The questionnaire did not inquire into the amount of such income, but it appears in most cases to be of a supplementary nature rather than the sole source of income. In 3.5 per cent of the cases, friends or relatives are serving as a source of income; in not quite 1 per cent of the cases the source is an organization or committee. The balance of 8.6 per cent have a variety of other sources or failed to specify.

The above statement refers to the situation in 1945, or at the time of filling out the questionnaire. A different picture, so far as financial dependence on others is concerned, is presented if the whole period since arrival in this country is considered. Aside from the help obtained from members of the immediate family, which may be considered a normal and private matter, what proportion of the refugees have at one time or another since their arrival been financially assisted? To judge by the questionnaire returns,

[1] U.S. Department of Labor, Bureau of Labor Statistics, "City Family Expenditures and Savings in 1944," release Dec. 9, 1945.

73.7 per cent of the total group received no such assistance at all. Presumably they either soon found employment or had private funds or both. Seventeen and two-tenths per cent received financial assistance from a service organization or committee, the most important type of assistance received, 4 per cent from relatives other than members of the immediate family, and the remaining 5 per cent from friends or from a variety of sources.

An extremely small proportion of the refugees, as we have already seen, are now being financially assisted. Aside from the very recent arrivals, these are in the main more or less chronic cases of social maladjustment. The situation concerning this group and the factors underlying their failure to adjust are analyzed in Chapter IX.

SUCCESS IN ECONOMIC ADJUSTMENT

With the exception of a small minority who, because of extreme age, sickness, or family situation have been unable to work and become self-supporting, the refugees have become absorbed into the economic life of the country. Their occupational distribution corresponds to that of the general population except for an over-representation in the professional and clerical fields and an under-representation of unskilled laborers. Despite the over-representation, they have been relatively so few in numbers that they have not caused any serious competition or dislocation; in fact, in most communities they have not been conspicuous in any field. They have adapted themselves readily to American working conditions, bringing intelligence and a willingness to perform any task. What little complaint there has been has referred not to matters of efficiency but rather of attitude. Some of them have brought new skills or special knowledge which have contributed to the technical advance of our industry, as will be related in a later chapter. While the future outlook in regard to work opportunities for the older group, as they themselves realize, may not be as bright as under war conditions, since preference in obtaining peacetime jobs will be given to returning veterans, they will share with native Americans the opportunities that will be available. In the event of an economic depression in the near future, the refugees, being newcomers, may suffer unemployment to a greater extent than native Americans. On the other hand, such possible differential treatment may well be mitigated by the fact that the great majority of them will be citizens, acquainted with working conditions and personnel, and pretty well integrated into American industry.

Much material is available from individual case records regarding the successful economic adjustment of refugees. The following are typical instances. Similar evidence will be found in the life histories included in later chapters on businessmen, farmers, and professional workers.

Mr. S., a skilled worker, born in Russia, came here in 1939 from Germany. Since arrival the family has gone from almost complete pennilessness to comparative financial security, with Mr. S. earning an average of about $4,000 per year. For a year or so after arrival, he was unable to find satisfactory employment; this was his most serious obstacle to adjustment. He insisted on sticking to his trade, that of furrier, and was finally able to work out his situation by opening up a fur business himself. In this he was helped by the Jewish Welfare Society in the form of business loans, all of which have been repaid. He is well satisfied with economic conditions here, and explained several times during the interview that no matter what would have happened in Europe, he could never have become a businessman in his own right. He is anxious to show his appreciation of the good fortune he has found here, and has contributed substantially to the Community Fund and other organizations, purchased bonds, and donated blood. He recently became a citizen.

Mr. D., aged 60, was formerly a well-to-do businessman in Germany. Shortly after his arrival in Philadelphia he obtained a job as elevator operator and night watchman. In explanation he said that he did not care what the job was, that he was determined to take any job, so long as it was with an American firm, mingle with American people, learn to talk the language fluently, and work hard. He then took a job with a firm whose business was renting out evening clothes. He introduced ideas which led to a lowering of costs and an increase of business, and was soon making a very good salary. However, he did not feel that he should continue in this line after America's entry into the war and he sought a job in a defense industry, which he finally obtained despite his lack of citizenship. He had a minor position working at night. Observing an idle lathe, he asked if he couldn't learn to operate it. This he did and was soon making $60 a week as a lathe hand. Later, when his son left for military service, he was offered his position as salesman with a large firm. He has increased sales and is now making about $175 a week on what he describes as an easy job.

Mr. B., an engineer and statistician from Austria, who arrived in 1940 and settled in San Francisco, got his first position in the shipyards doing manual labor. Later he was given an opportunity to work in his specific field when the personnel department became aware of his college background and experience. He is able to accept the possibility that he may lose his job after the war if there should be mass unemployment.

Mr. R., aged 50, formerly a factory owner in Czechoslovakia, now a factory supervisor in San Francisco, first found employment as a houseman in hotels and resorts. He explained that he is extremely grateful for the fact that he has never had any difficulty finding a job and that he is earning at least a fair income. That he no longer has the security of his previous financial status does not worry him. He considers life in America much easier, and is glad not to have the responsibility of operating a large factory.

"At the end of six months," states a former Czech clothing manufacturer who arrived in 1942 and settled in Columbus, Ohio, "I took the job of a salesman selling Fuller brushes from house to house. I worked up a fairly good business and I now average $45 a week. I have the respect of my employer and the people with whom I come in contact and I enjoy the work. My hope is to establish myself in a business of my own. Naturally I do not have the sense of power that I had when I was running our large business in Europe. I am humble but content and ask for nothing more than to be permitted to live peacefully and earn my own way."

Within a short while after coming to Indianapolis Mr. C., formerly a store owner in Germany, secured a position as salesman with a national chain department store. During the past five years he has gradually elevated himself to the position of buyer in the men's furnishings department and is periodically called upon to travel to the headquarters of the organization to select merchandise for his department and also to attend staff meetings.

A middle-aged lawyer from Germany has adjusted himself by becoming a salesman in Los Angeles. He has been successful, being made a representative for the West Coast. He has a fine income and is well integrated on the job. States the interviewer: "One can hardly tell that he is an immigrant who has been only five years in this country. He has poise, ability, and to some degree the mannerisms of a typical American salesman."

A Dutch engineer, in his own line of work in Cincinnati, makes this general comment about the economic adjustment of refugees: "I feel that the success of the immigrant is dependent on the same things that make a person successful anywhere. Those who failed probably would have failed or have been no more than mediocre in their native country. The successful ones had the energy, ability, and adaptability required anywhere for survival in a highly competitive structure." There is much truth in this statement though it fails to allow for such important factors as chance or luck and a helping hand at the opportune moment.

CHAPTER IX

FACTORS IN THEIR SOCIAL ADJUSTMENT

The social adjustment of refugees, as of any group of immigrants, involves learning the language, customs, and ways of the new country, establishing social relationships, participating in organized activities, and otherwise becoming integrated into the life of the community. This process is both individual and social. The age and sex of the individual and his family relationship are factors which bear on the degree of success with which he becomes socially adjusted.

It might be stated as a rule that the adjustment of immigrants in their personal and social relations with Americans varies inversely with age. Children, because they are still in the formative stage, adjust most readily to life in a new environment and soon become practically indistinguishable from the native children. They learn English rapidly, associate freely with other children, and present no special problem. Having few or no ties to the European background, they do not know or long for any other life, as their parents may. They cannot therefore think of their future apart from America. This situation is treated in detail in a special chapter on the young refugee.

With older people the problem is different. As a middle-aged refugee from Rumania states: "Children need adjustment, older people need readjustment. Materially and psychologically adults are already shaped. They won't find much happiness in a new life where circumstances compel them to abandon all their background." Especially is this true of refugees of advanced years, who find it hard to make new friends, get used to new customs, and acquire a new language. Their social life beyond that of the family group must of necessity be found mainly among their *Landsleute*, or fellow countrymen.

Serious also, though to a much lesser degree, are the problems of middle-aged refugees, for the most part people who had established themselves in business or professions and in family and social relationships, and were substantial and respected members of the community and secure in their social status. The shock of emigration and transfer to a new setting where they had to begin all over again was more disturbing to them than to any other age group. This lessened their readiness to form new associations and establish intimate contacts with Americans of their age group. This situation has been rendered more difficult due to the fact that Americans of that age have generally crystallized their social relationships into social circles which are more or less fixed and are seldom penetrated.

It would appear that refugee women, on the whole, adjust themselves more readily to American life than do men. They are quicker in acquiring the language and in assimilating new customs. This situation differs from that found among earlier immigrants, where the women lagged behind the men in these respects. The explanation may be found in the difference in social class of the two types of immigrants. Refugee women, moreover, as we have already noted, have found it easier to get jobs, and they have accepted inferior types of work with more composure than the men. They have also attained numerous new privileges, while the men have had to surrender many of theirs.

"On the whole I adjusted much easier than my husband," states a German woman in her forties, a housewife here as abroad. "While I was very open-minded and ready to accept our new way of life, also had little language difficulty, my husband, on the contrary, found it much harder to adapt himself. He felt the responsibility for getting his family started again. Also, the fact that he who had always been an independent employer and found himself now looking for a job rested rather heavily upon him."

"For my wife," states a 29-year-old commercial artist, "this year was a much more real approach in respect to the finality of her life than my own. She was able, and I noticed this tendency more general with women refugees than with men, to approach the difficulties of every day and making a final decision for every day much more consciously than I."

A case worker reports the following contrasting situation of the adjustment of a former stage conductor in Europe, now 73 years old and unemployed here, and of his wife, aged 65, who taught theatrical art abroad and is a factory worker here. "Mrs. G. attends adult education classes for foreigners, and masters the language fairly well. Mr. G. has not made the least attempt to study the language, and talks German at all times. Mrs. G. mixes well with people. She joined a group of refugee women who meet monthly through a women's council. She is sociable and talks readily to Americans. She is also friendly and thinks well of American people. Mr. G. shuts himself out almost completely. He takes his daily walks, walks rapidly, not paying attention to other people, and is most unsociable. . . . He has given up writing and makes no attempt to do anything else. Occasionally he speaks of his wish to return to his home town, and he believes that he might regain his house and property."

In some instances the role of husband and wife in the European household became reversed, with the woman becoming the chief breadwinner of the family and also its mainstay.

It has sometimes happened that the failure of the man to adjust as satisfactorily as his wife and children has been a factor leading to his demoralization. An interviewer describes such a situation as follows:

While the children and the mother have adjusted fairly well, the father has fared poorly. His European position of dominance in the family has been destroyed. His past training as an attorney has been useless here. His entire physical condition has made it extremely difficult for him to develop new skills which would enable him to regain the social and financial prestige which he and the family enjoyed in the old country. He was for some time quite unable to support the family, and even at present his income is quite low. His wife was forced to seek employment to supplement the family's income. He himself after numerous unsuccessful efforts at self-employment and at wage labor was fortunate to find work on a semiskilled level in a local war plant. This economic inadequacy has caused a considerable weakening of his status in the family, despite the efforts of the other members to camouflage this before him. In a few short years he has become a physically and psychologically broken person.

The trauma of forced emigration and of readjustment has caused serious strains on the refugee family. The most extensive and serious example of this is the disruption and separation of families. Among refugees it is *usual* to be separated, husband from wife, children from parents; it is *unusual* for a whole family to be together. Never before in history have war and persecution led to family separation on so vast a scale. As a partial indication of the extent of the problem the International Red Cross in Geneva has received some 17,000,000 requests for information from dispersed families.[1] Bureaus to assist refugees to locate missing relatives have been set up in a number of countries, including the United States. Fully half (55.8 per cent) of all the refugees who answered the Study Committee's questionnaire stated that they had members of their immediate family abroad—by immediate family meaning husband and wife, parents and children, brothers and sisters. This situation was relatively less frequent among the Germans and Austrians than among other nationality groups, and was especially marked among the Netherlanders, Rumanians, Poles, and Hungarians, the varying circumstances surrounding the exodus from the various countries, as mentioned in Chapter I, probably accounting for the difference. A higher proportion of the Christian refugees, especially the Catholic, than of the Jewish have close relatives abroad. This no doubt reflects the fact that in the case of the Jews the persecution was directed at the whole "race" and the exodus assumed the form of a mass movement.

In about 5 per cent of the cases the refugee is separated from his or her spouse, including in some instances other close relatives as well. Similarly, about 13 per cent of the refugees here have children abroad, 44 per cent have parents, and 69 per cent brothers and sisters.

The following comments by refugees in the United States set forth various aspects of this problem of family separation. One of the most striking is the wide dispersal of family members as they fled for their lives to whatever countries throughout the world they could find admittance.

[1] *New York Times*, Aug. 17, 1944.

"Our whole family is scattered," states a Polish Jew who was deported from Germany. "My wife's mother when we last heard from her was in Shanghai, my father was killed in Belgium in 1941, my mother and one brother when we last heard were living in Belgium, two of my sisters were killed in Germany, and my only remaining sister is living here with me in Ohio."

The family of an Austrian chemist now living in San Francisco was separated as follows: His brother fled to Slovakia where he was murdered by the Gestapo; his sister with her husband escaped to Switzerland, their son to Palestine; another sister with her family eventually reached England, except for a daughter who could not escape in time and has disappeared; another brother and his wife fled to Paris, then to Switzerland.

"My mother died in Germany after my arrival in the United States," reports a 30-year-old teacher. "I have three sisters in Palestine and one in Holland, from whom I last heard two years ago through the Red Cross. I have one brother in England. My wife's parents, brother and sister are in Brazil."

States a German businessman who spent five weeks in a concentration camp in 1938: "I was compelled to separate my whole family to different countries: my son to England, my daughter to France [who later escaped to Switzerland], while my wife remained in Germany [later coming to the United States]."

The life of refugees is frequently dominated by their concern for relatives and friends left behind. This separation was listed as a prominent item in answer to the question "What has changed most in your way of life?" The refugee is more often than not filled with haunting fears for the fate of relatives who remained in Europe. In numerous instances the respondent to the questionnaire, when checking the box referring to members of his immediate family abroad, wrote in "if still alive," or placed a question mark after it, especially with reference to parents. Not only are they constantly worried about what has happened to their people, but many have a feeling of guilt that they escaped while some of their relatives did not.

"Sometimes," writes a former employee of the Austrian government, now a draftsman in Pittsburgh, "we feel guilty if we enjoy something and think of our family in Europe. These thoughts tie us more with the Old Country than anything else. German culture, science, and literature, which I enjoyed and loved, starts to pale out, but the bitterness about the sad fate of my brother, my sister-in-law with her little girl somewhere in Poland, my wife's father and two sisters, digs deeper and deeper into my being. Why should we be saved and not they? This question is one of the main reasons why I do not enjoy being here. It makes me critical of this country and the people, who take life much easier."

"Our only family problems," reports a German refugee in New Haven, "are our worries and sorrows about our nearest relatives whom we had to leave in Europe. We tried to bring my mother and my wife's parents over here, but the first was deported by the Nazis to Poland and died there and the two others were brought to the concentration camp in Theresienstadt where the father died. The sad news came to us only recently, years after it occurred, while we were still worrying and trying to bring them over."

"Now we are able to make a modest living," comments a former Austrian businessman now a draftsman in New York, "and to enjoy the freedom of this country. Can we indeed? We still have closest relatives in Austria, or in Germany, or in Poland—who knows? Are they still alive or not, and what was all their suffering? Will we ever get true information about their final fate?"

Mr. P., a Polish skilled worker in Philadelphia, had three sisters and three brothers in Vilna. About three months ago he heard that the whereabouts of the family were totally unknown. At this point in the interview he broke down completely and wept.

Because of the death or separation of the members of the family consequent to persecution and expulsion, the size of the refugee family in the United States is small. A special study made in Philadelphia of some 300 refugee families shows that in three out of five instances the group consists of two or three members only.

Among further effects of immigration on the refugee family may be mentioned the frequent financial dependence of parents on their grown children, changes in family life, and the appearance of cultural conflict between parents and children. In Europe the family as an institution appears to be more tightly organized and to have a stronger economic and emotional basis than is the situation in this country. Individual members of the family have less freedom and independence than in the typical American family. For the European the home appears to be more stable and to carry greater social significance than for the American, for he spends a great deal of his leisure time in it and builds his social life around it. Also more prestige accompanies home ownership. The European social system, based on class and authority, has had its reflection in family life. In Central Europe, particularly, is the family patriarchal. Men exercise a dominating role with respect to both their wives and their children. Where men brought up in military fashion were the masters, the children would naturally be expected to obey. They would not dare to contradict their parents openly.[2] Forms of deference toward parents are much more marked than in America. These aspects of refugee family relationships have undergone a change here. The male head of the family has tended to lose authority and status, and the women and children have experienced something approaching an emancipation.

A strained situation has developed especially in the relations between parents and children. Many refugee parents find it difficult to accept the idea that their children should have the freedom and independence enjoyed by American children. They complain that the children do not appreciate the European cultural values which mean so much to them. As one parent, a German businessman, states: "The greatest problem in adjusting to American life is due to the education of the children who feel that they know things much better than their parents and are much more Ameri-

[2] Cf. Ruth Z. Mann, "Refugee Adjustment," *Jewish Social Service Quarterly*, September, 1939; Martin Gumpert, *First Papers*, pp. 161–162.

canized. They look at them as old-fashioned, old-fogyish, European—and they are afraid a slip in the language or a slight accent of their parents may tell the story that the family is not what they call 100 per cent American." On the other hand, the children sometimes report that they feel handicapped by the attitudes of their parents and that their own problems often arise from the fact that their parents are not making as rapid an adjustment as they are. This is a familiar situation in all immigration movements and is not peculiar to the refugees.

Despite the stresses and strains, the family has been a pivotal point in the adjustment of the refugees, a secure mooring in a strange and difficult environment. In the great majority of cases it has weathered the terrible experience of persecution, expulsion, and transplanting to a new world, and emerged as a cohesive, harmonious, and well-integrated institution. In a small proportion of instances it has shown demoralization and failure to adjust.

Social Maladjustment

A special study of the failure to adjust, either financially or personally, was made by examining the case records of various social agencies serving refugees. These records show that only a small fraction of the total number of cases have required continued assistance, that the great majority have relatively soon been able to take care of themselves. Of the small residue still needing help, it appears that some of these will require assistance indefinitely, while others are marginal cases who may have periods of independence but will inevitably face maladjustment.

An analysis of dependency and maladjustment factors was made through the examination of 306 cases active with the National Refugee Service from June, 1944, to June, 1945, which may be considered as typical of the least well-adjusted group of refugees. Over 200 of these cases had been transferred, by agreement, to other New York City family agencies. Of the remainder, some had gone to institutions, such as hospitals and homes for the aged, and a few cases had been closed by the N.R.S. with problems left for the families themselves to cope with. The bulk of the "marginally" dependent come from this last group, while the so-called "chronic dependents" are found mainly in the transferred and institutionalized group.

As to their general background, the dependent group shows characteristics similar to those of the total body of refugees. They had enjoyed high economic and social status. The per cent of business and professional people (36.7 per cent and 21.7 per cent, respectively) among them was somewhat higher than in the general population. Only 1.3 per cent were manual laborers. A wide variety of nationality groups are represented. The Poles, however, particularly those who left Poland in the 1920's and established themselves in small businesses mainly in Austria, seem to be more heavily represented than in the refugee population as a whole, about 30 per cent being from this group. The greatest point of difference is in age, 161 of the family heads, or 52.6 per cent, being over 60 years old. Most of the dependent groups arrived here in 1939 and 1940 and hence had endured more terrifying experiences and had lost more of their resources than had the earlier arrivals.

To the social agency the refugee applicant represented a new type. Never before in its experience, not even during the depression, had such a group presented itself. The refugee's inexperience in taking help and the agency's early fumbling in meeting this new type of person further complicated the problem. The underlying factors, however, which made for maladjustment or marginal adjustment were not unique. The refugees in this respect showed no essential difference from other dependent persons. Generally it was a series of related events that resulted in failure for the family. Frequently the problems were not single but manifold and interdependent. They have been isolated here for convenience in treatment, with the most predominant problem taken to characterize the situation. In the majority of cases (52.6 per cent) the main factor was old age; in 27.5 per cent it was sickness; in 13.0 per cent it was a family situation involving women and children; and in the balance of the cases, 6.9 per cent, it was a variety of other conditions.

1. *Old Age*. In the old-age cases, the age range for family heads was from 60 to 85 years. The great majority were between 65 and 75 years of age. Having in the main come over in 1939–1940, these people were old on arrival. Moreover, nearly a third of them were here alone, and half were cases of childless old couples, in both instances lacking family members to care for them. In the few cases where there were children, they were either too young to work or, more commonly, earning too little to support the whole group.

Age alone was a factor for dependency in only 17 per cent of these cases. In the remaining, the head of the family was already affected by one or more of the debilitating diseases of age: the incidence of arteriosclerotic, cardiac, gall-bladder, diabetic, and hypertensive conditions being noticeably high. In 85 per cent of the cases of old couples, both members of the family were afflicted.

With severe handicaps of this sort it would obviously be impossible for these old people to attempt a new start toward economic independence, nor did they come with this expectation in mind. Migration to this country meant primarily safety and reunion with members of their family, with the normal hope that their younger relatives might provide for them. But the relatives, being mostly recent arrivals themselves, were having their own difficulties in getting started, and could ill assume the additional burden of supporting these old people. Frequently it was the inadequate earnings and excessive responsibilities of the younger relatives which led to social agency contact. Sometimes illness and other problems of the younger group led to dependency of the old.

Mr. S., aged 69, was a merchant in Vienna. He and Mrs. S., aged 62, came to the United States to join two sons, one who had been a lawyer abroad and the other a chemist. Mr. S. has diabetes and a cardiac condition, his wife has had a series of acute illnesses which has kept her bedridden. They came to the United States in 1939, and up to 1943 had made their home with the son who had been a lawyer. He was not working here in his profession, but nevertheless, out of his marginal salary he supported his parents. When he died suddenly of a heart attack in 1943, his wife did not keep up her relationship with her parents-in-law. The second son found only unskilled employment in the United States, and had his wife's people to support. Help from the social agency was needed after the first son's death in 1943.

The burden of caring for the old people inevitably produced strains and tensions. Relationships between younger and older members of the family, though formerly satisfactory, deteriorated. Hostilities and resentments previously controlled became more sharply expressed. In extreme cases this meant a final break between the two. Such was the case of the F's.

An old sick couple aged 75 and 73, the F's came to join a daughter and her husband, here in this country for ten years. The son-in-law, formerly well-to-do, had business reverses which led to a nervous breakdown. All his hostilities centered around the old people whose burden he strongly resented. To prevent a complete marital break-up of the young people, the F's left the home and severed relations with their daughter.

Dependency on a social agency was a new and unexpected situation to these old people. Their reactions to the experience were not unusual. Strong dependency patterns were revealed in a few instances. In one case a man "talked of having planned for agency help in Europe." In another, assistance was treated as an extension of a pension formerly enjoyed abroad. Some became depressed over taking relief, others reacted aggressively, were unable to accept any of the limitations set up, and strove to re-establish their former high status. A much larger number displayed a strong drive for independence and made attempts to find work. Jobs were not available at first, especially to old people. Moreover, these were mainly business and professional persons, for whose services there was little demand. As a result of the expansion of the war industries, however, many were able to find jobs, though these were mainly in a minor capacity, such as watchman, messenger, peddler, or delivery clerk, and the pay was too little for complete support.

It was not easy for these old people to forgo their independence, accept jobs on a lower level, and adjust to other drastic changes of fortune. For instance, it took Mr. K. a long time to become reconciled to his displacement in his profession.

Mr. K. is 70. He was a music teacher and orchestra conductor for 35 years in Vienna. His wife, aged 61, never worked. Mr. K. is a proud, aristocratic old man. It was hard for him to realize there was no place for him in the musical world. It was an added blow to think of his wife going to work. After four and a half years of taking help, Mrs. K. established a one-man business, stringing pearls, and Mr. K. got work in a factory about which he is now quite cheerful.

The greater number of the aged have little to look forward to. They are old and sick, and their children have low incomes. On the whole, they have accepted their new status philosophically. Financial dependency has not meant a complete withdrawal from living. All except a few have taken out their first citizenship papers. The overwhelming majority are preparing for final citizenship, studying English with considerable enthusiasm and competence. A number have shown interest in the history and culture of America, one 60-year-old woman having won a city-wide contest on this subject. Some, of course, have found it difficult to learn English, have ceased to struggle, and have aged rapidly. A few continue to live in the glorified past, when they were prosperous, had status, and were united with their family. Among the cases there was only one instance of senility, and another of complete disintegration of personality. On the whole, they present a picture of fortitude and capacity for change that is remarkable under the circumstances.

The findings of this sample study of the aged are corroborated by the experience of the Special Labor Aid Project of Refugee Relief Trustees, financed through the budget of the American Christian Committee for Refugees. This project was set up to help elderly refugee labor leaders, ranging in age from 55 to 85 years, some of them ill, and a large proportion unable psychologically to adjust themselves or to apply their abilities in a renumerative way to the American scene. Temporary or supplementary assistance is sufficient for many of them, while others continue to require substantial help.

2. *Illness.* In addition to the problem of sickness among the aged, illness resulted in dependency for the family in 27.5 per cent of the cases included in the sample study. Situations of physical illness were more common than those of mental illness or serious personality defects. In the great majority of cases it was the breadwinner who became ill. Most of them were between 45 and 60 years old. The illnesses were in the main those especially characteristic of middle age, such as cancer, cardiac conditions, and hemophilia. In addition, tuberculosis was of outstanding importance, affecting primarily family members under 45. Half the cases of dependency due to sickness developed within the first year after arrival in the United States, the other half by the end of the third year. In both instances it has been necessary to extend help for a long period of time. Frequently the illness was an aftermath of terrible experiences abroad.

Mr. A. was a barber in Vienna, where he made a comfortable living. He was beaten on the streets by storm troopers and crowds walked over his body. His home was taken away and he and his wife and child lived in cellars. Later when he was placed in a concentration camp he had to stand face to the wall with hands up in the air. After months in custody, he was asked to produce money for his release and when he did, he was told it was not enough, to get more. This went on several times. He was told, "You will never leave this place alive." He nearly went mad. Finally a Christian friend produced the cash. His health broken, he arrived in the United States in March, 1939, and by July he developed active tuberculosis.

As contrasted with the aged, this group came here with high hopes, and with full expectation of continuing their economic life in whatever sphere possible. Most of them did make a start and over half were well on the way toward good economic adjustment before ill-health interrupted their activity.

Mr. B., a small textile merchant in Vienna, came to this country in 1940 at the age of 40. He showed a good deal of initiative and independence, and found his own job. When taken ill with cancer of the intestines in 1943, he had a well established candy shop in Brooklyn, by which he had been supporting his wife and two children.

Mr. J., aged 57, fled from Hungary suddenly in 1939 after killing a Nazi who appropriated his restaurant. He was independent for three and a half years here as a porter in a hospital until organic seizures following a gastric ulcer condition left him very ill, with an unfavorable prognosis.

In this group, as in the aged, the interrelated problems of different members of the family proved to be complicating factors and retarded progress toward a return to independence. Moreover, about 40 per cent of this group were individuals here alone, which often meant expensive medical care and emotional components due to loneliness and isolation.

Families with children constituted about 40 per cent of the group. Here the family heads were in their forties. Most of the children were under 16. Naturally the illness of the breadwinner had its effect upon the rest of the family. Sometimes the breakdown of one member of the family was followed by the breakdown of a second member. Mr. A., whose concentration camp experience has already been mentioned and who developed tuberculosis shortly after his arrival, recovered sufficiently to be practically self-supporting, when immediately afterwards his wife developed cancer.

The percentage of recoveries and of return to work was high. The record of the tuberculous was particularly good. Sheltered employment, partial employment, retraining, all the available medical and social work tools were used effectively. Re-employment and independence within limitations of the handicap were often achieved.

Most of the physically ill cases might in a general way be classified as "marginal" dependents, with periods of ill-health followed by periods of recovery and work. The chances for complete independence depend in the final analysis on the degree to which responsibility can be shifted to the well members of the family, wherever there are such members.

The situation of the mentally ill and those with personality handicaps so severe as to interfere with employment and independence parallels to some extent that of the physically ill, though the outlook for the greater number may not be so hopeful. About 10 per cent of the 306 dependent cases analyzed were situations of people who were neurotic, unstable, or psychopathic in their behavior. The largest single group was composed of persons here without their families. Their problems were severe, and long periods of treatment, including institutional care, were needed in most cases. The successes are least numerous in this group, but are reassuring. An example is Mr. W.

Mr. W. came to the United States alone at the age of 20 and went to work on a farm. He had a mental breakdown in 1941 and needed a short period of institutional care. Upon his recovery he retrained and found work as a presser, and married an American girl. He has repaid his hospital bill.

In the family group of cases (about 25 per cent of the total), the breakdown of the breadwinner meant rearrangements and adjustments for the other members of the family. The effect on them was generally more serious than in the cases of physical illness, because of the nature of mental illness, the lack of understanding about it, and its distressing manifestations. What is most significant is that, considering their experiences, the cases of disintegration of personality were rare. This group is but a very small proportion of the total refugee population.

3. *Situations Involving Women and Children.* Grouped together in this category, constituting 13 per cent of the total, were mainly cases of women who were heads of households and responsible for support of their children, a few cases of children who came here without their parents, and of families where help was needed because of specific problems of the children. The great majority of the children, averaging two per family, were of school age.

This group thus had the very real problems of obtaining employment adequate enough to support a family and of proper care of the children while the mother was away at work. There were only one or two women with real skills from abroad which could be transferred to ready and effective work here. For the remainder it meant housework, unskilled factory labor, or simple retraining in preparation for jobs on lower wage levels, generally inadequate for full support of the family. The problems of housekeeping and of adequate supervision of the children at home while the mother was at work were not easy of solution, since such resources are generally inadequate.

The emotional experiences of these women ran the gamut from aggressive resourcefulness to complete capitulation. The general picture was one of unhappy, depressed people having difficulty in accepting separation from the husband and in taking over the role of the breadwinner. It displayed itself in neurotic, self-centered behavior, in various kinds of dependent attitudes, in retreat into illness to avoid work, in conflicts between staying home and working, and in rejection of the children.

Naturally the children were not unaware of the situation and consequently suffered. Some children had to shift for themselves. Some were shunted back and forth from their home to a foster home. Some had remained in foster homes and institutions for unduly long periods of time. While the majority of the children have been described as bright, making good school and social adjustments, there were several instances recorded of shyness, stammering, and other manifestations of insecurity, and also instances of behavior difficulty, some severe enough to necessitate assistance from a special agency dealing with such problems. Some of the older children also showed signs of strain. On the whole, however, they displayed evidence of stability and of promise of eventually taking over some of the responsibilities, even at the expense of curtailing their own educational plans. The following situations are typical.

Mrs. W., a very beautiful woman, was the favorite, pampered child of well-to-do parents. She was indulged in and protected by her husband. He died in a concentration camp and his ashes were sent to her. Coming here with two children, she retreated into illness to disguise her obvious dependency traits. The children are doing well—the boy studying to be a rabbi and the girl an excellent scholar.

Mrs. Z. came to the United States with three children. Her husband, who had a bakery business in Vienna, was last heard from in Buchenwald. She is a skilled underwear worker, but is frequently too depressed and unhappy to go to work, and indulges in many physical complaints which seem to have no basis. Of the children, the oldest girl has been retrained and is working. The second girl is a brilliant pupil and was awarded a scholarship to New York University. The boy, the youngest member of the family and described as intelligent and imaginative, has displayed predelinquency tendencies, staying out late and associating with bad companions.

These represent the residual cases of a much greater number with similar problems who seem to be able to function adequately. Women among the refugees have, by and large, had to play a greater role in contributing to the financial maintenance of the family than was the situation abroad. It has been easier for them to find work, they have adjusted more readily to a lower status and to jobs in the lower wage brackets.

The few cases of children here alone are representative of the situation where parents stayed behind and sent the children on to relatives. The relatives appeared unable or unwilling to carry the responsibility, the children seemed unattached and uprooted, and the basic problem was one of proper care and guidance.

In the remaining cases in this group, the problems of the family centered around that of the behavior problems of children. In most cases the neurotic unstable behavior of one or both parents, the rejection of the child, and the consequent insecurity contributed largely to the behavior difficulties. This group, too, is very small.

4. *Other Problems.* Except for two instances of marital conflict, the remaining cases represented people floundering around in their search for suitable employment. They were mainly professional persons who were obviously unable to continue in their former field and who had not yet accepted displacement to another type of work. Though most of the professional workers among the refugees have become adequately adjusted, there are a few still leaning upon the social agency, presenting difficult personality problems and requiring long periods of financial assistance.

In general, the total number of dependent refugees represent a small fraction of the total refugee population. They suffered abroad and have had disappointments here. On the whole, however, they have demonstrated a capacity for independence and for adjustment within their limitations. This plus the supportive role which agencies have played has helped many of them to effect at least partial adjustment.

CHAPTER X

THEIR SOCIAL AND CULTURAL ADJUSTMENT

The social and cultural adjustment of immigrants—their adoption of the language, manners, customs, and way of life of the native population and their incorporation into the native community—depends to a great extent upon the frequency and intimacy of contacts between the two groups. It is also dependent on such factors as the attitude of the newcomers toward assimilation, the attitude of the natives toward strangers in general or toward a particular nationality or race, the number of immigrants and the rate of entrance, the composition of the immigrant stream, and the manner of settlement. It is generally a slow process, involving generations; complete assimilation rarely occurs in the lifetime of the foreign-born individual. Progress in such adjustment is shown by admittance into competitive and personal relationships and by the acquisition of a common culture, as well as by the development of loyalty to the adopting group. Among the criteria of satisfactory adjustment may be noted, by way of illustration, a high degree of contact and communication, general acceptance, knowledge of the language and ways of life, participation in community affairs, intermarriage, and the acquisition of citizenship.

The situation of the refugees in this respect has been unusually favorable. They have become adjusted to a greater extent and in a shorter period of time than was the case with other immigrants of recent decades. This has been facilitated or promoted by their relatively small numbers, their wide distribution, their superior educational and cultural background, and their desire to become assimilated. Some account of the way they have fitted into American life has already been given. Further evidence is presented here and in the chapters immediately following.

Where Refugees Live

We have already seen, in Chapter IV, how the refugees are distributed in communities of varying sizes in practically every state in the Union. Within the communities in which they have settled, in what type of neighborhood do they live? Unlike other recent immigrants, they have not concentrated in special neighborhoods. Except in a few very large cities like New York and Chicago, they do not form colonies, but scatter throughout the city. They do, however, show a tendency to settle in parts of the city where others of their own nationality background live, following at the same time economic and social class lines. Frequently the refugees, especially those of the smaller nationality groups, have come to relatives already rooted in the community. Their pattern of distribution within the city is more like that of second- and third-generation Americans than of the foreign-born. This reflects their higher economic and social status, as well as their relatively small numbers. They are an urban people who were accustomed to live in the better sections of town, and they attempt to approximate their former standard of housing as closely as possible.

In the rare instances where the refugees have concentrated in immigrant-community fashion, they have settled in better neighborhoods than is usually the case. In Chicago, the largest refugee settlement is on the South Side (Kenwood, Hyde Park, and South Shore), in rental areas appreciably above the general city average. The second largest center is on the North Side (North Center, Lakeview, and Lincoln Park), in lower than average (except Lakeview) but not slum areas. The professional and business management classes are scattered in high-rent areas throughout the city. In New York, which is the one outstanding example of refugee residential concentration, the great majority of the refugees live in a few centers, notably Washington Heights and midtown Manhattan between Central Park and the Hudson River. Even here, they constitute only a small proportion of the population. Other and smaller centers may be found in the Bronx, the Lower East Side, where the poorest group lives, and in Queens, especially the Jackson Heights, Forest Hills, and Kew Gardens areas, where the younger and more assimilated group reside. With the exception of the Lower East Side, these centers of refugee settlement in New York are not slum or low-grade housing areas, but neighborhoods of comparatively modern homes. The wealthier refugees live in the good residential sections of Long Island or near Central Park and on Riverside Drive.

. The above statements concerning the settlement of refugees are based on the results of community surveys and of questionnaire returns. The questionnaire inquired into the type of neighborhood in which refugees were living and used as an index the proportion of recent immigrants in the neighborhood, whether there were none, few, or many. The results show that 34.1 per cent of the refugees throughout the United States were living in neighborhoods where there were no other recent immigrants. A larger proportion, 43.6 per cent, were residing in neighborhoods where a few recent immigrants lived. Only about a fifth of them (19.5 per cent) were in neighborhoods containing many recent immigrants. In this type of settlement the tendency would be to keep up old friendships at the expense of new ones and to perpetuate European culture at the expense of rapid acquisition of American. In 2.8 per cent of the replies, the proportion of foreigners in the neighborhood was not specified.

If the replies are broken down by religious groups and by nationality, it appears that the tendency to live in neighborhoods of no or few recent immigrants is more characteristic of the Christian than of the Jewish refugees, and of Italians, Hungarians, and Poles than of Germans, Austrians, Russians, and Czechs, to mention just the more important groups. Relative numbers are undoubtedly a factor, since the larger the immigrant group the greater the tendency to settle by themselves instead of scattering throughout the American community. We have already seen that the majority of the refugees are Jews and that the largest numbers have come from Germany, Austria, Poland, Czechoslovakia, and Russia.

Another factor in determining the type of neighborhood in which refugees settle is occupation. Professional persons show the greatest tendency to live in the more American neighborhoods, where there are few or no other recent immigrants, and they are followed by proprietors, managers, and officials. Semiskilled and clerical and kindred workers, more than any other occupational groups, tend to live in neighborhoods where recent immigrants are numerous. Length of time in the United States also is a factor. The figures do not form an unbroken progression, but the trend is sufficiently clear to warrant the generalization that the longer the immigrants live in this country the greater their tendency to live in more typically American neighborhoods. This is a mark of assimilation.

The proportion of immigrants living in a neighborhood also is a function of the size of the community. It is well known that immigrants have settled to a greater extent in our larger cities than in small towns and rural areas. The refugees are no exception. Hence the immigrant community is to be found primarily in large cities.

The refugees tend on the whole not only to live in more typically American neighborhoods but to settle permanently, as is indicated by their tendency to buy homes. Eighteen per cent of those who replied to the questionnaire owned their homes, which is a high proportion in view of both the short time they have been here and the large proportion living in big cities where tenancy rather than ownership is the general rule. The desire to own their homes is strong among the refugees and reflects their European background where great value was placed on home ownership and social prestige accompanied it. In some instances, however, refugees like native Americans have recently been buying homes, though they could ill afford it, because places to rent were not available. In the case of all immigrants, home ownership increases with length of time in the country. Among the refugees, the percentage owning their homes is above average for the group in the case of those who arrived before 1939, and below average for those who

Per cent Distribution of Types of Neighborhood in Which Refugees Live, by Size of Community

Type of neighborhood	Total	Size of Community							
		Under 2,500	2,500–9,999	10,000–24,999	25,000–99,999	100,000–499,999	500,000–999,999	1 million & over	New York
All cases	100.0	100.0	100.0	100.0	100.0	100.0	100.0	100.0	100.0
Not answered	4.7	2.4	3.5	4.0	3.7	4.3	4.2	5.5	6.0
No recent immigrants	32.5	46.9	36.7	50.6	42.9	37.5	34.2	29.7	16.3
Few recent immigrants	41.5	32.9	33.2	40.2	46.1	43.3	43.8	47.1	32.0
Numerous recent immigrants	18.6	14.8	24.7	2.4	5.3	12.2	15.4	14.7	42.5
Some, not specified	2.7	3.0	1.9	2.8	2.0	2.7	2.4	3.0	3.2

arrived subsequently. Home ownership varies also with size of community, in this case inversely.

WITH WHOM REFUGEES ASSOCIATE

Because of the type of neighborhood in which they live, among other factors, the refugees tend to associate more with native Americans than with their own group or other recent immigrants. Evidence on this point was obtained primarily from questionnaire returns. The general questionnaire of the Study Committee included a question regarding friends, which was answered by 97 per cent of the respondents. In 42.3 per cent of the cases the refugees reported their friends to be mainly native Americans, in 42.0 per cent to be mainly recent immigrants, and in 12.5 per cent to be about equally divided between the two. In an insignificant proportion of the cases, 0.2 per cent, the reply was that the person had no friends at all. The proportion having established friendships with native Americans is unusually high for an immigrant group, especially one that has been here so short a time.

The tendency to have American friends is most marked in the case of those refugees who live in neighborhoods where there are no other recent immigrants; it is least characteristic of those who live in neighborhoods where recent immigrants are numerous.

Forming friendships with native Americans is facilitated by residence in smaller communities. As the following table reveals, in communities of less than 100,000 population the friends of the refugees are in the majority of cases Americans. In cities of more than a million population, other recent immigrants outnumber Americans among the friends of the refugees. The conclusion is clear that intimate association with native Americans, and hence assimilation, is promoted by residence away from the largest centers of population as well as from neighborhoods where immigrants are numerous.

In general, the tendency to have friends among Americans rather than recent immigrants increases with length of residence in this country. It is nearly twice as marked in the case of refugees who have been here more than five years as compared to those who have been here a shorter period of time. A slightly larger proportion of male than of female refugees have their friends mainly among Americans. This is probably related to the higher rate of employment of men and their greater mobility. It is significant that housewives show the smallest percentage with American friends of any group. A much more striking difference appears when the cases are broken down by marital status. Some 68 per cent of single individuals state that their friends are mainly Americans in contrast to 39 per cent of the married, 29 per cent of the widowed, and 46 per cent of the divorced. Age is undoubtedly a factor accounting for this difference. The single are

PER CENT DISTRIBUTION OF TYPE OF FRIENDS BY SIZE OF COMMUNITY

Size of community	Total	Friends				
		Mainly Americans	Mainly recent immigrants	Half Americans, half recent immigrants	None	Not answered
Under 2,500	100.0	57.7	25.6	13.8	.5	2.4
2,500–9,999	100.0	61.2	27.6	8.0	.3	2.9
10,000–24,999	100.0	64.7	20.9	10.0	.4	4.0
25,000–99,999	100.0	57.5	29.5	11.2	.1	1.7
100,000–499,999	100.0	47.2	36.5	12.5	.2	3.6
500,000–999,999	100.0	43.4	41.8	12.4	.2	2.2
1,000,000 and over	100.0	39.4	44.7	12.9	.1	2.9
New York City	100.0	21.8	61.3	13.5	.1	3.3

younger, and hence more adaptable and active, participating more readily in community affairs. They also have greater need for social life than have the married. It is also because of their younger age, as well as their greater opportunity, that students lead all occupational groups in the proportion (77.3 per cent) associating mainly with native Americans. Of the gainfully employed, manual workers—unskilled (60.5 per cent), skilled (54.6 per cent), and semiskilled (48.6 per cent)—report their friends to be mainly Americans to a greater extent than do white-collar workers—professional persons (47.8 per cent), clerks and kindred workers (37.3 per cent), and proprietors and managers (34.6 per cent). This may reflect the readier acceptance of newcomers, the greater opportunity for meeting people, and the greater informality in some occupations as compared with others.

Among the Christian refugees, 62.7 per cent have mainly American friends, 23.9 per cent mainly recent immigrant friends, and 13.1 per cent friends divided about equally between the two; 0.3 per cent state they have no friends. Among the Jewish refugees, 40.3 per cent have mainly American friends, 46.8 per cent mainly recent immigrant friends, and 12.8 per cent friends equally divided between the two, with 0.1 per cent reporting no friends. In the case of the following nationality and religious groups more than half the respondents stated that their friends were mainly Americans: German, Austrian, Polish, Italian, Czech, Hungarian, and Netherlands Christians, and Italian, Hungarian, Polish and Russian Jews. Only one group, the Netherlands Jews, reported that in a majority of cases their friends were mainly recent immigrants. Groups reporting a percentage above average for friends mainly recent immigrants were German and Czech Jews and Russian and Austrian Christians.

There is no doubt about the desire on the part of refugees to know Americans and become their friends. Many have found it hard to accept the fact that the process of making friends is usually slow for the native American who is a newcomer in a community, let alone the immigrant. "If you cannot make friends, American friends," states an Austrian refugee, "the country remains strange." Some refugees have deliberately avoided limiting their associations to their own group and have sought opportunities to meet Americans, being prompted by the desire to become Americanized as soon as possible.

The respondents to the questionnaire listed "less social life" high in the ranking of changes in their way of life (see Chapter VII). It is significant that this was cited by a higher proportion of women than of men, as was also the case in citing "social isolation" and "making friends with Americans" as the greatest difficulty faced in adjusting to American life (see Chapter V).

Some of the refugees have commented that the refugee-service committees should do more to promote social contacts between them and native Americans, especially of the same social and educational class. A Polish businessman in New York thinks there is need for "a permanent and full-time USO for newcomers." The service committees have done much to enlarge and enrich the refugee's participation in American life, though frequently it has been on a group or organizational rather than an informal and personal basis.

Sometimes the refugees blame the attitude of native Americans for their difficulty in establishing friendly social contacts. It should be noted, however, that part of the difficulty lay in their erroneous assumption that the same pattern of informal social life, especially the family type, prevailed in this country as in Europe. From all sections of the country have come comments like the following:

"Americans do not bother to associate with us, to make us feel really at home; refugees are left to themselves." (Utah)

"Newcomers are not invited to the homes of Americans on a friendly basis." (Florida)

"It is awfully hard to get acquainted here in this country. American people don't seem to want to associate with us." (Pennsylvania)

"I was very anxious to meet Americans of my professional and cultural level, who could contribute toward my growth in the United States. Unfortunately I have had no opportunity to meet this kind of people." (California)

On the other hand, Mr. and Mrs. A., formerly of Frankfort and now residing in Kansas City, Missouri, state that although they have made very few American friends the American people are not to blame. "Our neighbors don't come together with Americans either. The fault lies mainly with ourselves and our timidity." An Austrian businessman in Philadelphia admonishes his fellow refugees: "Based upon my experience, the immigrant needs, above all, patience. It takes long, a few years probably, before you suddenly feel that you are already part of the community, that you mean something to some people, and that many mean something to you."

Difficulties in making social contacts that were much more frequently mentioned than the aloofness of Americans include such factors as advanced age, inadequate knowledge of English, low income, insecurity, and other conditions related to the refugee experience. The refugees' concern about relatives and friends left behind, which has overshadowed their lives with tragedy, has given them little stomach for the lighthearted interests of those about them. The fact that many came without means made them feel disadvantaged, and at times they felt they were being patronized. Frequently, even today, there is a great gap between their economic situation and their social standing. Many are so engrossed in the struggle for a livelihood that they have little time and energy for social activities.

The American acquaintances of Mr. F., an Austrian tailor, and his wife are pretty much limited to their business contacts. They feel that their opportunities for contact with Americans are limited because they do not have the money to join organizations nor the time to participate actively in community affairs. They feel a need for making friends but do not think they can take the initiative. They have occasionally been asked to join organizations which they felt they could not do, but they would have welcomed an invitation to an American's home, which they have not received.

States a middle-aged German woman employed as an office clerk in San Francisco: "Although I would have loved to make American friends I was more or less forced to seek the company of other immigrants with whom I could speak the same language, if I wanted any social contacts. I know that many immigrants have gone through the same experience. We are all anxious to make American friends or to meet Americans, but do not seem to succeed in doing so."

"One of the reasons for the difficulties of our adjustment," states a scholar," is doubtless the fact that our economic situation is entirely incongruent with our social standing. That means that we do not have the money to lead the same social life as we were used to on the other side and as those Americans do who would meet with this standing."

Some refugees, especially those who have been here longer, report that they now have as many friends as they had in their homelands and are leading as rich a cultural life. Refugees who have traveled extensively in the United States have experienced an advantage in becoming acquainted and in learning American ways.

Mr. P., a German residing in Los Angeles, travels a great deal because of his job as a salesman, and consequently meets many people and many different situations. This has made him a well-rounded person. He has mastered the English language and converses easily. He has also developed a fine sense of humor.

Other factors—some personal, some situational—have facilitated social contacts and assimilation. For example, an Austrian in Youngstown, Ohio, states: "It was easy for me to get acquainted since I taught bridge, and knew how to play cards, which was one reason why people invited me to their homes." Intermarriage is an outstandingly effective means. A Polish refugee from Germany relates:

"My wife, an American-born girl to whom I owe everything I am now, introduced me gradually to the American way of life. Her American environment became mine. She was my best English teacher. It was not easy. One had to overlook pride, give up a good deal of intellectual musing, one had to adopt a different sense of value, particularly in the evaluation of individuals with whom one deals. But I made the grade. Last, but not least, through our marriage I was regarded from the very outset as one of the gang, a newcomer, yes, but not a refugee with the usual connotation of pity and distrust."

WHOM REFUGEES MARRY

Twenty per cent of both the men and the women who replied to the questionnaire had married since their arrival in the United States. The most typical marriage was with other refugees, this being the case of 62.4 per cent of the males and 71.4 per cent of the females. A small proportion (5.9 per cent of the males, 10.5 per cent of the females) married immigrants who had arrived here before 1933. In 30.2 per cent of the cases of male refugees marrying and 17.0 per cent of female refugees the marriage was with a native American. These are unusually high percentages of intermarriage for a foreign-born group, and they indicate a rapid rate of assimilation.

This evidence of assimilability is further borne out by examination of the nationality background of the native Americans whom the refugees married. The general rule in intermarriage between foreign-born and native Americans, as has been revealed in special studies,[1] is that most persons choose mates of their own nationality or ethnic background, as, for example, an Italian immigrant marrying a person born in the United States of Italian extraction. It is usually only in the second or third generation that internationality marriages become common. In the case of the refugees, however, as the following table indicates, the native Americans they married were in the majority of instances (77.5 per cent of the persons refugee men married, and 64.8 per cent of those whom refugee women married) of different nationality background. Internationality marriages were also common, especially in the case of male refugees (50 per cent), in matings between refugees and earlier immigrants. Whereas nationality lines are rather readily crossed, marriage tends strongly to be kept within the same religious faith. This is the general rule, characteristic of all immigrant groups, and native Americans as well. The refugees are no excep-

[1] Julius Drachsler, *Democracy and Assimilation*, 1920, part II; Bessie B. Wessel, *An Ethnic Survey of Woonsocket, Rhode Island*, 1931; Niles Carpenter, *Immigrants and Their Children*, 1927; New York State Department of Health, *Marriage Statistics, New York State, 1921–1924*, 1928.

Per Cent Distribution by Nationality Background and Religion of Persons Whom Refugees Have Married in the United States

Married Since Arrival	Males				Females			
	Total	Married "Recent" Immigrant	Married "Immigrant before 1933"	Married Native American	Total	Married "Recent" Immigrant	Married "Immigrant before 1933"	Married Native American
All Cases	100.0	100.0	100.0	100.0	100.0	100.0	100.0	100.0
Same Nationality	61.4	85.4	44.6	15.1	72.2	84.5	73.9	20.0
Same religious faith	55.2	76.7	37.5	14.0	66.5	77.5	69.3	19.0
Different religious faith	5.7	8.0	7.1	.7	5.4	6.6	4.6	1.0
Religious faith unknown	.5	.7	—	.4	.3	.4	—	—
Different Nationality	35.6	13.9	50.0	77.5	23.2	13.3	23.1	64.8
Same religious faith	27.1	11.5	42.9	56.1	19.0	11.3	18.5	51.4
Different religious faith	8.2	2.4	7.1	20.4	4.2	2.0	4.6	13.4
Religious faith unknown	.3	—	—	1.0	—	—	—	—
Nationality Unknown	3.0	.7	5.4	7.4	4.6	2.2	3.0	15.2
Same religious faith	2.1	.2	1.8	6.3	2.8	1.1	1.5	10.5
Different religious faith	.1	—	—	.4	.3	—	—	1.9
Religious faith unknown	.8	.5	3.6	.7	1.5	1.1	1.5	2.8

tion, although the percentages of those marrying native Americans of different religious faith appear unusually high.

Knowledge of English

Nothing is more basic in the adjustment of the immigrant than knowledge of the language of the new country. Without this means of communication, the immigrant is tremendously handicapped in securing employment, associating with the natives, and learning the customs of the country.

The refugees have made an extraordinary record in acquiring a knowledge of English.[2] It is safe to say that no other non-English-speaking immigrant group has learned English so rapidly and so well in a comparable period of time. Many reasons account for this, including the superior educational background of the refugees, their cosmopolitan outlook, their feeling for language and the high value they place upon it, and their desire to become assimilated. A considerable proportion of them knew languages other than their own, including English. The study of English was part of the regular education of the intellectual group, and many refugees had had business connections or moved in cosmopolitan circles where a knowledge of English was required.

Attending school in this country has naturally been effective in acquiring a knowledge of the language. The children have learned English in a remarkably short period of time; language has been, at most, only a temporary handicap, and instances are numerous where refugee children have won essay contests and prizes in English composition. Three-fourths of the adults answering the questionnaire had attended school in the United States, a proportion high above the average for a recent immigrant group. Also unusual is the large proportion (approximately 40 per cent) attending secondary or trade schools, colleges, and professional schools. The most common type of institution attended in the United States was the English and citizenship class. Over a third of the respondents had been to such classes, including persons over 70 years old. The great majority were between 40 and 60 years of age. Also exceptional is the age distribution of refugees attending college or professional school, most of them being between 30 and 50. The need of retraining in their profession or in another field is the main reason for persons of that age attending institutions of higher learning, and it is evidence of both the educational background of these immigrants and their desire to resume their former occupational status.

The unusual progress made by refugees in learning English is borne out

---

[2] One refugee, after graduate study here, has become an expert in how to write simple and readable English. Rudolf Flesch, *Marks of Readable Style*, Teachers College, Columbia University, Contributions to Education, No. 897, New York, 1943; *The Art of Plain Talk*, New York, Harper & Brothers, 1946.

in several ways by the findings of the Study. Although some of the questionnaires sent out by the Study Committee were printed in German, with refugees of advanced age in mind, it was found that there was little need for them. What few German questionnaires were distributed, moreover, were returned in many cases with the answers in English. The life-story material likewise showed a surprisingly good mastery of English, and in many cases of American slang, as the reader may have already observed from the excerpts quoted. Another indication that English was widely known among the group is the fact that it was commonly used in the home. Information on this point was collected through a special study of refugee families in Philadelphia which was made as part of the general investigation. According to that study, English was the only language commonly spoken in the home in 41.5 per cent of the families, and it was a subsidiary language in an additional 26 per cent of them.

Language Commonly Spoken in the Home of Refugees in Philadelphia

Total families	335
Not answered	20
Total answered	315
English	131
German	78
English and German	51
German and English	26
Yiddish	17
English and Yiddish	5
Hungarian	2
Russian	2
French	2
Polish, Yiddish, and German	1

Naturally refugees speak English with varying degrees of skill. In this variation, age is probably the most important factor. The children, with the characteristic adaptability of the young, have learned the language with greatest ease and rapidity. Refugee children in this country have had, in addition, the added advantage of intensive training in American schools and constant contact with American children. At the other end of the age scale, the old people have experienced the greatest difficulty in mastering a new language. They have had, moreover, restricted contacts outside of their own group, have found it hard to identify themselves with the new country, and as a result have seldom attained any considerable knowledge of English. A 54-year-old housewife living in San Francisco declares:

"My mother is too old to adapt and does not speak the language. She has a few old German friends whom she sees often but otherwise has few contacts except the immediate family. My husband will never feel 100 per cent American. This is probably due to the language difficulties. I have not found things so hard because I speak the language fluently. I had an English governess as a child and was always gifted in languages."

Further evidence of the progress refugees have made in acquiring a knowledge of English is seen in the answer to the item in the Study questionnaire regarding the type of newspaper read. The overwhelming majority—94.6 per cent of the men and 92.5 per cent of the women—stated that they read mainly English-language newspapers. The small proportion reading in the main non-English-language papers was composed in three out of four cases of persons over 50 years old, in half of the cases of persons over 60.

EVALUATION BY REFUGEES OF THEIR LIVING CONDITIONS AND SOCIAL STATUS HERE AS COMPARED TO EUROPE

As an indication of the degree of adjustment of the refugees and their integration into the community, the respondents to the questionnaire were asked to compare their present economic and social status with their situation in pre-Hitler Europe. The question was in two parts, the first referring to their living conditions—housing, food, clothing, and other material aspects of the standard of living. Most of the refugees now feel that their living conditions are the same as (47.6 per cent) or better than (26.6 per cent) those they enjoyed in Europe. This is particularly true of clerical and kindred workers (86.1 per cent) and still more so of the skilled (96.6 per cent), semiskilled (93.6 per cent), and unskilled workers (96.2 per cent). It is also characteristic of persons under 40 years of age. On the other hand, among the professional and business people, the majority report their living conditions as being the same or worse (78.6 and 77.9 per cent, respectively). A proportion below average of these groups (21.4 and 22.1 per cent, respectively, as compared with 26.6 per cent of the total) regard their living conditions as better than they were in Europe. The age groups above 40, in over 75 per cent of the cases, report their present living conditions as the same or poorer. There is little difference between the sexes except for a slight tendency on the part of the men to give a more favorable evaluation. There are no marked differences between the various nationality and religious groups, except that a little larger proportion of the Christians said their living conditions were poorer; and a corresponding lower proportion said they were the same.

Length of residence in this country and type of community and neighborhood where they live also are factors associated with the evaluation of living conditions. Those refugees who arrived before July, 1939, are above the average in estimating their present living conditions as the same as or better than they were in Europe and markedly below average in estimating them as poorer. The reverse is generally true of those who arrived subsequently and have had less time in which to become adjusted. The percentage of respondents reporting their living conditions as "better" was above average in the case of those living in cities of 100,000 to 1,000,000 population, the percentage reporting "poorer" was marked in the case of those residing in New York City and, at the other extreme, in communities of 2,500 to 10,000 population. In regard to type of neighborhood in which the respondents lived, the closer it approached the American type (with few or no other recent immigrants) the higher the percentage reporting their living conditions as better, and the closer it approached the immigrant-community type (from few to many recent immigrants) the higher the percentage reporting their living conditions as poorer.

The above findings indicate in general that the refugees have emerged or are emerging from the initial struggle to earn a living and that the majority of them have improved their economic status to the point where they live as well as or better than they did in Europe. This has quickened their integration since it has made them feel more secure and contented. The younger refugees and those less well established and less favorably situated in Europe present a more favorable evaluation since they had more to gain or less to lose in migration to this country. They have profited by the higher material standard of living here, as is illustrated, for example, by the wage earner who commented, "In Europe only the very wealthy had autos. Here, we have one." On the other hand, a comment typical of the formerly well-to-do business or professional person is the following: "The adjustment from living in something like a 20-room house to living in a 3-room apartment is difficult. Our economic condition is below our European standard, but we prefer having less in a free country."

A different picture is presented when the replies to the question regarding social status—place in the community, social life, etc.—are considered, even though there is a high correlation between social status and living conditions. For example, 83.1 per cent of those who reported their social status as being higher here than in Europe also reported their living conditions as being better, and 50.9 per cent of those who regarded their social status as lower also regarded their living conditions as poorer. The difference in the response to the two questions lies in the fact that most of the refugees feel that they have lost more in social than in economic standing. The great majority of the refugees replied that their present social status is the same (49.2 per cent) or lower (38.9 per cent) than it was in Europe. Only 11.9 per cent felt that their social status was higher here.

The tendency to view their present social status as the same as it was in Europe or lower was marked among professional persons (94.1 per cent), proprietors and managers (90.8 per cent), clerks and kindred workers (88.0 per cent), and housewives (90.4 per cent). On the other hand, more than three-fourths of the students (77.7 per cent), skilled (84.4 per cent), semiskilled (84.0 per cent), and unskilled (95.9 per cent) workers regard their social status here as being the same as or higher than it was in Europe. There are no differences between the evaluations made by Christians and Jews. Length of time in this country, however, is an important factor, since with one minor exception the shorter the period of time refugees have been in the United States the higher the proportion who feel that their social status is lower. In other words, it takes time to regain a former social status or to improve it just as it takes time to regain or improve one's standard of living conditions. From the refugee's viewpoint, it is easier to accomplish the latter than the former.

All the evidence seems to indicate that economic adjustment proceeds more easily and rapidly than social adjustment. This derives in part from the fact that, although there is an interrelation between the two, the latter is somewhat conditional upon the former. It requires an income above what is needed for the necessities of life in order to participate in social and cultural activities, and when the immigrant is engrossed in the struggle for a livelihood he has little time or energy left for such pursuits.

Much more so than other immigrants, the refugees are concerned about their social status. This is not only because of their superior economic, educational, and cultural background. It is due also to the fact that in Europe, especially in Germany, social station and titles were highly prized, inordinately so from the American standpoint. Even though the refugee is now living in this country where the social distance between various occupations is less felt than in Europe and where a man is judged more by what he is than what he does, he is conditioned to think in terms of the old country rather than the new, and to him occupational readjustment means not only an economic setback but a social degradation as well. His bitter and painful feeling of loss in social status has at times led, as was noted in earlier chapters, to compensatory reactions that many Americans find unattractive. No human being could endure the experience that has been the refugee's fate—to be driven out of one's homeland, separated from family and friends, deprived of property and position, if not actually physically abused, and forced to start life anew in a strange country—no one could endure this experience without a wrench and without impairment of his spiritual life. The psychological problems of the refugee will be solved long after his economic and social problems, if indeed, except for the young children, they can be solved at all. In many cases the tragedy of the refugee's experience will be stamped upon his soul to the end.

CHAPTER XI

ORGANIZED LIFE OF THE REFUGEES

REFUGEE ORGANIZATIONS

The refugee of today, like the immigrant of earlier periods, has set up his own organizations, for the purpose both of aiding him in his social, cultural, and economic adjustment in this country and of furnishing him with a medium through which he could participate in the kind of social and cultural life to which he was accustomed abroad. In the urban, sophisticated society from which he came there existed most of the different types of organizations found here. If he was of the Jewish faith, he belonged to the *Kulturgemeinde* or Jewish community, which was a state-recognized institution and to which practically all Jews automatically belonged. Being a member of this community meant participating in a great variety of organizations and activities sponsored by it. These were the *Vereine* (associations), organized for social and cultural purposes, the *Bruederschaften* (brotherhoods), and other types organized for economic, social, and cultural purposes. Aside from these, there were general, nonsectarian organizations, societies, and clubs to which he might and often did belong. The refugee in his homeland also was familiar with a number of international organizations, such as the Masonic Order and B'nai B'rith, branches of which existed in almost every country.

The refugees, upon arriving here, were thus far from lacking a familiarity with organizational life and its techniques. They were therefore ready and willing to join organizations. This is especially true of the Jewish refugee. While many joined American organizations, many others formed their own.

In setting up their organizations, the refugees often made use of the techniques that were familiar to them in the old country, borrowing, of course, freely from the organizational methods current in this country. In some instances, they took over and adapted to their new needs organizations already in existence. An outstanding example of this is the New World Club, which was, under a different name, established by earlier German immigrants in this country. In other cases, the organizations were transplanted from the Old World. In most cases, they were more or less new creations called forth by circumstances.

There are, at the present time, some 150 organizations, including congregations, formed by refugees, two-thirds of them being located in New York City. In the main, they are Jewish organizations. This is to be explained, of course, by the larger number of Jewish refugees as well as by the traditionally greater tendency among Jews to organize.

The refugee organizations are of different types. They can be divided into the following major classes: mutual aid; trade and professional; social, cultural, and recreational. Extensive diversification by type, however, has been possible only in New York, where refugee concentration is heavy. The German refugees, being the largest single group and having wide organizational experience, lead in the number of organizations established. Their largest organization is the New World Club.

The Austrians for a long time were merged with the Germans, and their first attempts at separate organization came late in 1938, when the bulk of the Austrians began coming here. Their numbers were quite sizable after that, but they showed nowhere near the same degree of interest in organization as the Germans. Most likely this is because the Austrians are not so homogeneous a group as the Germans. Upon arriving in this country, many joined established local groups of Galicians, Czechs, Hungarians, etc., depending upon the territory of the former Austro-Hungarian Empire from which they came. Up to 1944, there were few separate Austrian groups, but in that year and the year following a number of organizations of Austrians suddenly sprang up, one in Boston, one in Chicago, another in Los Angeles, and several new ones in New York.

The Polish refugees, although fewer in number, also formed several well-functioning organizations. In addition to the National Organization of Polish Jews, their largest and most active association, they maintain a number of others. The professional people among them; namely, scholars, lawyers, physicians, musicians, and engineers, are especially well organized.

Similarly the Russians, despite the smallness of the group, have a large number of societies. Some of these represent adaptations of organizations they had maintained in their places of former refuge—for the Russians, America was often a second or even a third haven of refuge—while others are more or less new creations. Perhaps the experience the Russians have had as refugees, as well as their homogeneity, has made it possible for them to form and re-form themselves into little groups with considerable ease.

The remaining nationality groups have shown less skill as well as less need to develop societies of their own. Although each has made an attempt to organize in one way or another, few such attempts have been successful. Their small numbers often made it impractical or even impossible for them to organize effectively. The Italians afford an example. In the case of other groups, the lack of organizations has been due primarily to the temporary nature of their stay in the United States.

Refugee organizations, on the whole, as we have seen, belong to one of the three major classes: the social and cultural associations; mutual aid and fraternal societies; trade and professional groups. This classification does not imply that any one of them is exclusively of one type or another, as there is considerable overlapping. In a sense each combines, to a greater or lesser extent, the features of all three. Within each of these three classes there is considerable diversification, of course, depending upon the type of membership.

Within the first class are to be found such organizations as the above-mentioned New World Club, as well as smaller, purely local, societies. These societies, organized primarily along nationality lines, admit all refugees coming from the same country. Another type included in this class are the so-called *Landsmannschaften,* or societies of persons coming from the same town or region abroad. In this class of societies may also be found the few youth groups, organized primarily for sport and recreation. Within the second class are included the so-called self-help societies, transplanted fraternal orders and college fraternities, and special branches of American fraternal orders. In the third class are to be found societies of doctors, lawyers, musicians, and other professional groups, as well as trade organizations. Some of these societies are bound together by "roof organizations," or federations. In addition, there are among the Jewish refugees a number of congregations similar in pattern to other Jewish congregations in this country. The majority of these are located in New York City.

In general, the refugee societies follow the well-known American organizational pattern. They have the usual officers, a president, one or more vice-presidents, a secretary, a treasurer, and an executive board, all elected on a democratic basis. A committee made up of officers or members of the executive board is responsible for handling the business of the group. The membership is kept in touch with the activities of the organization through bulletins and similar means.

The membership of these societies is drawn mainly from the middle-aged and elderly groups who comprise the majority of the refugees. As far as the youth is concerned, most adolescents and young people tend to merge with general youth groups, in so far as they become members of organizations at all. Moreover, all these organizations consist mainly of men, which is in line with the European pattern. Women, however, have come to participate more and more in their activities—undoubtedly an American influence. Some organizations also maintain women's auxiliaries, with functions similar to those of their American counterparts.

The refugee organizations show, nevertheless, some distinctive features.

The natural gaiety and sociability of the European finds considerable expression in these societies. Every meeting, every get-together, is generally the occasion for a social evening, a meeting of old friends, a reminiscing over the past, and an exchange of present experiences. Hardly a meeting is complete without its "Kaffee und Kuchen," often delicious home-baked pastries prepared by the ladies. Holidays, both secular and religious, provide the opportunity for more elaborate entertainment. The "Sylvester-Feier," or New Year's celebration, is one of the gayest occasions. The use of large halls for elaborate dances, with big-name bands and special entertainment by the best of refugee talent, is quite usual in cities with large refugee organizations. Other religious festivals among the Jewish refugees, such as Hanukkah, Purim, and Succoth, are equally observed by celebrations.

The love of outdoors is exemplified in the frequent hikes arranged by various organizations. Instead of going out for automobile rides, many of the refugees seem to enjoy roaming in the countryside around the city. Young, middle-aged, and even older people all like to participate in organized walks. While mainly social in character, these hikes are valuable in helping the refugees to get better acquainted with the surrounding territory. The hikes are usually three or more hours in length, the starting point being the end of a subway run.

The cultural phase receives great emphasis in the activities of refugee organizations, which may be explained primarily by the intellectual sophistication of many of the members. In the large organizations, it is not uncommon for a distinguished refugee, literary man, scholar, or artist, to read a paper on a serious subject. Programs devoted to an analysis of the "Flemish Masters at the Metropolitan Museum," "Scenes from Goethe's Faust," "Readings from Heine" reveal the high caliber of such gatherings. Musical evenings devoted to the "Songs of Schubert and Strauss," "Chopin Waltzes," or "Italian Street Songs" are typical. In arranging for these evenings, the refugees have, of course, the advantage of being able to draw upon the best of their talented countrymen, thus lending to the programs an unusually high quality.

Most of the refugee organizations display a great interest in promoting the Americanization of their members. Discussions on American history, the differences between their own and American customs, American ways of living, American politics, American economic life, and differences in the training and practices of the various professional groups occur frequently on their programs. "What is the difference between the American and the German way of life?" "A Bavarian studies America," "Living Democracy," "American Unions and their Rights," "Women in Immigration," "The Contribution of the Immigrant to the American Way of life"—are typical of the topics brought up for discussion and analysis.

All the larger and some of the smaller organizations maintain English and citizenship classes. The drive for language perfection which the refugees manifest is indeed extraordinary. Many of these classes are primarily concerned with removing the foreign accent or perfecting the grammar of their "students" rather than teaching elementary English.

Most of the meetings of the refugee organizations are conducted in the native tongue of their members, this being, of course, one of the basic reasons why they have their own organization. English, however, is more and more resorted to. Gradually announcements of programs, bulletins, etc., are being printed in English and some meetings are conducted in that language.

The vast majority of refugee societies engaged in various activities in behalf of the war effort. Red Cross activities, bond drives, group blood donations, parcels to soldiers, civilian defense, all were carried on with a great deal of enthusiasm and actively participated in by a large proportion of the membership. So important an activity did the refugees consider this to be that to co-ordinate their efforts, they established an Immigrants' Victory Council, which included most refugee organizations. The council championed the right of immigrants to participate in all aspects of the civilian defense program, and was effective in having discriminatory rules changed.

Another type of activity common to all these organizations is that concerned with social welfare. Mutual aid of some kind is a feature of practically every group. Some organizations, like Selfhelp, Inc., have this as their main objective. It is, of course, financially impossible for these recent immigrant organizations to carry the main burden of assisting their fellow countrymen. The help of the various American service agencies, described in a previous chapter, is therefore indispensable. The welfare programs of the refugee societies do, however, render extremely important services to their members. Small amounts of aid are given in emergencies, and extra budgetary needs are frequently taken care of. Other services also are rendered. Thus one group in New York is responsible for setting up two nursery schools for children and another, in co-operation with an American organization, for establishing a boarding home for aged persons. On the other hand, while these organizations have been useful in helping to care for their own, they have also aided in the general welfare program of the communities in which they live. This is evidenced by the extent to which these organizations share in various fund drives and join the community councils of social agencies.

The organizations of recent immigrants have, of course, all along shown great concern for relatives and friends left behind. The bitterness the refugees feel toward their native lands which persecuted them and their desire for integration into the American scene have by no means resulted in a forgetfulness of their fellow countrymen not so fortunate as they are, or a complete indifference to the destiny of their former homeland. The "rehabilitation sections" of their societies are concerned not merely with the sending of packages and money abroad, with the locating and reuniting of families, but are also working closely with American and international societies in formulating plans for reconstruction and rehabilitation. The extent of their concern with regard to these problems is evidenced not merely in rehabilitative activities, but also in the amount of time and effort devoted to them at their meetings.

The activities of the larger refugee organizations are extensive. The New World Club sponsors all types of social, educational, and cultural activities, including the publication of a newspaper, the *Aufbau*. It includes many subdivisions and affiliated groups, two kindergartens, home-nursing and nutrition groups, three youth groups, a boys' club, a physicians' group, an employment office, a sport group, a philatelic group, and a cemetery association. The Blue Card, a self-help organization, is another of its affiliates.

A similar organization, but much less extensive in its activities, is the National Organization of Polish Jews, with a membership of 1,000, mainly middle-aged professional and business people. Like the New World Club, it has a large network of activities, cultural, social, educational, and welfare. Other nationality organizations—the Netherlands Jewish Society, the Italian Jewish Club, the T. G. Masaryk Society, the Luxembourg Jewish Information Office—all carry on similar activities, though on a much smaller scale.

Most of the organizations, as mentioned above, are to be found in New York City. Outside of New York, refugee organizations exist only in the larger centers of refugee population and are mainly of the social cultural type. They are mainly German-Austrian in membership. The refugee organizations range in number of members from about a score to 2,000. Both the New World Club in New York City and the Jewish Club of 1933 in Los Angeles have 2,000 members each.

Noteworthy among refugee organizations are the *Landsmannschaften*. There are a number of these functioning, particularly in New York City. Their aims and objectives are the same as those of similar societies earlier established in this country—to afford an opportunity for people coming from the same town or region in the old country to get together and help one another.

There are two refugee veterans' organizations, both Jewish, which have been transplanted here from Germany and from Austria. In both of these countries the Jewish veterans of World War I had effective organizations, the one in Austria having had a membership, in 1938, of over 20,000 and the one in Germany having been even larger. Their purpose here, in addition to protecting their rights as veterans and of aiding each other, is to fight Nazism and anti-Semitism in general. "Good citizenship" is still a major part of their program, but instead of emphasizing good citizenship in their native land it is now American citizenship to which they are directing their energies. Aside from these major objectives, the veterans' organizations are also carrying on various social and cultural activities.

Out of a dozen or more independent youth societies formerly existing there remains now only one. This is the Austro-American Youth Council. A number of the large societies and congregations, however, maintain youth sections. The decline of the youth groups is due primarily to the rapidity with which the young refugee desires to become part of American life. "Our members have lost interest and have joined American groups" is the usual reply of former leaders to the question as to why their organizations have declined or disappeared. Another factor in this decline is the large-scale drafting of the youth into the Army. The survival of the Austro-American Youth group as a strong independent organization with well-attended weekly meetings is largely due to the efforts of the considerable female membership. Of the 200 members in this group 90 were drafted into the armed forces. The hope of refugee leadership for a revival in youth groups seems to be indicated by statements that describe their status as "temporarily dissolved" or "temporarily suspended."

Separate religious organizations or congregations have been developed almost exclusively by the Jewish refugees. There are 22 such congregations in New York and 9 in various other large cities of the country. The refugee congregations follow closely the pattern of American congregations. While most of them have been established by the Germans and are predominantly German in membership, in New York City the Austrians, French, Belgians, and Luxembourgeois each have a congregation of their own. The Italians, Yugoslavs, and some of the Southeastern European Jews, on the other hand, have joined the existing Sephardic congregations, while the Hungarians, Poles, and Russians have joined existing congregations of their particular nationality groups.

The refugee congregations not only provide for the spiritual needs of the newcomers but also make it possible for them to retain some continuity with their life in the past. This is achieved through services conducted in the European manner, prayers in the mother tongue, and the use of old familiar melodies. In addition, most of the congregations conduct their own cultural and social programs designed to keep alive the cohesiveness of the group as well as to help in the adjustment of the members to American life. Some congregations have educational activities as well, maintaining Sunday schools and different kinds of courses for adults. Burial societies are generally an integral part of the congregational activities. In a few instances, however, such societies are separately organized. A number of congregations have bulletins, issued monthly or at regular intervals.

On the whole, the refugee congregations have adapted themselves to the situation in their new homeland. Abroad the congregation was the center of Jewish community life; in fact it was the Jewish community. This is not the case here. "In the United States the immigrant finds a strict separation of 'Church and State,' powerful Jewish organizations of charitable, social, and cultural nature, big and little 'congregations,' all types of religious groupings with luxurious synagogues and community centers, but no Jewish Community."[1] The synagogue therefore has had to adjust itself to this new situation, which it has done by engaging in activities similar to those found in American congregations.

There are a number of professional organizations among the refugees. While the majority have been created by the newcomers, there are a few of older immigrant origin now largely dominated by refugees. These societies are, on the whole, nonsectarian and nation-wide in membership. In the case of some groups, principally the Poles, Austrians, and Russians, however, the members are almost all of the same nationality.

Our records show five active societies of lawyers, three of physicians, two of economists, two of writers, two of journalists, and one each of dentists, chemists, engineers, musicians, former bank employees, and one of diamond merchants, although the last-mentioned organization is more in the nature of a guild than a professional society. In size of membership these societies range from a tiny group of six Jewish journalists to a lawyers' organization of close to 800 members.

The main purpose of these societies is to help the professional person prepare for employment in his field in America through group lectures, discussions, demonstrations, as well as courses of instruction in special subjects. They also aid individual members to establish and maintain contacts with American institutions within their particular fields. Another important function is to provide some place where the individual's social and professional status can, despite the loss of former prestige, still have some meaning.

Both the number and size of the lawyers' groups are indicative of the very serious problems these professionals have had in their vocational adjustment and their need for mutual aid. Because of this, the lawyers' societies are among the largest and most active of the professional groups. A feature characterizing practically all these societies during wartime was the offer of technical assistance to the United States government, thus contributing freely of their knowledge and experience. In the postwar period these organizations continue to render valuable service along similar lines. Most of them, in addition to serving their group professionally, have a variety of social and cultural programs.

[1] Adolf Kober, "Immigration and Congregational Life," *Aufbau*, Dec. 22, 1944.

An interesting type of organization is the college fraternity, which is a transplanted society of former college students. There are ten such fraternities among the refugees. Three are "roof organizations," or federations, the others are individual fraternity clubs. All are reconstituted organizations from abroad, and their main purpose is to continue to "maintain friendships and brotherly relationships." Some are German and some Austrian in origin. All are Jewish, two being Zionist in orientation. These organizations are small in size since only a fraction of the total membership was able to come here. These former university people of professional and business status find that gathering together with their fraternity brothers helps them bolster up their former prestige which is constantly being threatened by their changed situation.

The sport organizations, like the fraternities, are revivals of former organizations abroad. There are four in New York City and six more elsewhere in the country. Most of the sport organizations are small in size. Their main interests are such sports as soccer, tennis, table tennis, ping-pong, swimming, wrestling, track, field skiing, and the like. The two best known sport groups among the refugees are the Hakoah and the Maccabees, both Zionist organizations, the one Austrian in origin and the other German. The development of sport organizations, like other youth organizations, was retarded by the entrance of young men into the Army, and by the desire and ability of youths to break away from strictly refugee activities and to become part of American groups.

Practically every shade of European political opinion can be found represented in the refugee political societies. The Social Democrats of Germany and Austria, the de Gaullists of France, the followers of Count Karolyi in Hungary, and a number of other political parties are each constituted in some kind of organization. These organizations are usually nation-wide and nonsectarian in membership. They are generally headed by a committee which governs the activities of the organization and which reaches the membership through publications rather than through meetings, general membership meetings being infrequent. Most of the organizations have their own publications.

The interest of refugees in these political groups in no sense is an indication of disloyalty to their adopted country. It is only natural for many to be interested in the lot of their former homelands. Their understanding of the situation abroad, their sympathy for the plight of their friends and relatives, the need for helping them have led many to participate in these societies.

The so-called self-help organizations, already referred to, perform a most important function among the refugees. There are three such major organizations in existence. These are Selfhelp of Emigres from Central Europe, Inc., and its four branches in other parts of the country, Help and

Reconstruction, and the Blue Card, a New World Club group. All these organizations are nonsectarian. The chief aims of these organizations are "to give interim help for immigrants, advice, and material assistance," "to interpret the immigrant to the American and American ways to the newcomer," as well as "to co-operate with other organizations and co-ordinate activities with such other organizations to avoid needless duplication of effort."

In promoting this kind of program these societies can point to some very considerable achievements. Selfhelp, for instance, maintains an active employment service, primarily for household jobs, and in 1942 placed 1,275 persons. It has collected, reconditioned, and distributed clothing to refugees receiving assistance from the Council of Jewish Women and the National Refugee Service. It maintains a visiting nurse and housekeeping service available in cases of sickness or other emergencies. It also maintains a furnished-room directory and a legal-aid service. In co-operation with the National Refugee Service and other agencies it has assisted in the placement of children in camps and private homes throughout the country. With the American Friends Service Committee it helped establish the Co-operative Residence Club, a home for elderly refugees. Similarly, the Blue Card has contributed to the establishment of nursing schools, summer camps, and nursing homes for elderly, sick refugees. Help and Reconstruction has engaged in similar activities.

The activities of these mutual-aid societies are international in scope. Selfhelp of Emigres has maintained offices in England, Shanghai, and Switzerland. It has set up special groups to deal with problems of refugees in different camps in France and Spain. It has also co-operated with the Red Cross and other national and international welfare agencies in some of their activities.

Several organizations have been developed to co-ordinate the activities of the individual societies. They are the so-called "roof organizations." Their main purpose is to hold the groups together, to centralize and unify their activities, to guide and advise them on special problems, and to stimulate new activities. They have helped to interpret to the aliens their legal rights. They have particularly sought to clarify the rights of "enemy aliens." They have served as the voice of the refugees and have assisted in interpreting to the public and to American authorities the needs and abilities of the newcomers. There are three such roof organizations: the American Federation of Jews from Central Europe, Inc., the Conference of Jewish Immigrant Congregations, and the Immigrants' Victory Council.

It is difficult at this time to predict the future of all these refugee organizations. They are all comparatively new. They all arose to meet some general or specific need within the immigrant group. Most of them have managed to maintain not only their membership, but also the active interest of their members. Only one type of society speaks pessimistically of its future, namely, the transplanted fraternities, one of whose leaders writes: "As no new members are accepted, our organization is only a friendship club as long as present members are alive," adding that "our organization will cease to exist upon the passing away of our present members." Some of the professional societies describe their outlook as "fair" or "only fair," one group indicating that its members are too busy at the moment to come to meetings. The indications seem to be that as the problems of the refugees approach solution, the individual's interest wanes and he seeks to identify himself as completely as possible with the American community. Some of the smaller *Landsmannschaften*, particularly those outside of New York, see their future as "doubtful," statements like the following being typical: "Since integration of our members has progressed well, the club is losing members."

The larger and stronger groups, particularly the congregations, seem to feel that they are fulfilling needs that will continue indefinitely. Their optimism is evident from such statements as "prosperous," "good," "very good," in response to a question regarding their outlook. The congregations' hope for the future is built largely upon the possibility of attracting native-born members. "Our congregation wishes to Americanize itself more and more and build itself into an establishment of which the Jewry of our town will be proud," writes the secretary of a Cleveland congregation. Similarly, a rabbi of a successful organization in New York writes: "It is hoped that our congregation will outgrow its purpose and become a full-fledged American Jewish Congregation. That process will be hastened by returning veterans."

This process of adaptation is noted also in many other well-functioning societies. The first problems and needs of the immigrants have already been met. New postwar problems seem to be emerging and these societies are making an effort to meet them. The main problems, as a leader of the refugee community of Los Angeles sees them, are the reuniting of separated families, problems of postwar employment, and the fight against discrimination.

THE REFUGEE PRESS

Like earlier immigrants, the refugees are maintaining a press of their own. Although, as brought out elsewhere in this book, the vast majority of the refugees read the general American newspapers and periodicals and few depend exclusively upon newspapers in their own language, the refugee publications seem to fill a definite need. This need is not so much for a paper printed in their native language—this can be met by existing foreign-language papers which are, of course, read by the refugees—as for a paper that represents their special interests—social, economic, and political—which for a considerable period of time after their arrival remain their very own. The foreign-language papers which are published here by their respective nationality groups have in the course of time become Americanized; they are largely American papers published in a foreign tongue; even the very language has been Anglicized and is somewhat strange-sounding to the newcomers. The refugee, therefore, has need of an organ that speaks to him intimately, that understands and is concerned with his problems, and this he finds in his own publications.

The refugees publish about a dozen papers with a national or international circulation. The languages in which they are printed include German, French, Polish, Italian, Spanish, and Greek. These publications are monthlies, biweeklies, or weeklies, none being published daily. Undoubtedly the most outstanding among the weeklies is the German-language *Aufbau* (Reconstruction), published in New York by German Jewish refugees. This publication, which grew from a mere bulletin, established in 1934, is a 28-page weekly paper of regular newspaper format with a national and international circulation, in 1944, of about 35,000 copies. Next in importance, from the point of view of size of circulation, are the New York-published French weeklies *Pour la Victoire* (For Victory) and *France-Amérique* (France-America) with national and foreign circulations, in 1945, of 29,000 and 20,000, respectively. In addition, the French also publish a monthly, *République Française*, a luxury publication with a more limited appeal. The Austrian refugees are represented by four monthlies, namely, the *Austro-American Tribune, Austrian Labor Information, Austrian Labor News,* and *Austria,* and the Polish by one weekly, *Tygodnik Polski* (Polish Weekly), one semimonthly, *Nasza Trybuna* (Our Tribune), and one English-language monthly, *Poland Fights.* All these, too, are published in New York. In addition to the *Aufbau,* the Jewish refugees from Germany maintain a German-English biweekly, the *Jewish Way.* The Italian, Spanish, Greek, and Hungarian refugees have each a publication of their own, which are respectively *L'Italia Libera* (Free Italy), *España Libre* (Free Spain), the *Free Press,* and *Harc* (Fight).

What is common to all these publications is their anti-Fascist sentiment. Beyond that, they differ to a greater or lesser extent in their political orientation and interest. Politically they vary from the radical-socialist, Soviet-friendly orientation of the *Austrian Labor News* to the conservative-monarchist *Austria.* In between are publications representing all shades of liberalism and conservatism. Practically all are non-Communist, some, particularly *Pour la Victoire* and *Tygodnik Polski,* being strongly anti-Soviet.

It is only natural that the refugee papers take a vital interest in European events, especially those occurring in countries close to them. All, therefore, feature articles, dispatches, "letters," etc., that deal with one or another aspect of life there. Some maintain special correspondents here and abroad, while others rely primarily upon reprinting news items and articles from American newspapers. A large part of the space is, therefore, given over to European news. Often items seemingly unimportant to the general American press are prominently featured and commented upon at length in the refugee press, because of this special interest.

Most refugee papers contain some English-language items, ranging from part of a column to a whole section. In some cases this serves the purpose of acquainting the general public with something the paper wants to convey to it, while in others the objective is to arouse the interest of the Americanized youth.

Each of these publications tends, of course, to promote its special views and interests. Many of the papers have been carrying on among their readers propaganda for one or another political cause, with the hope also of influencing American public opinion in general.

As is to be expected, all refugee papers carry items, articles, stories, accounts, and pictures about the homelands which the refugees have left behind. Nostalgic stories about towns and their landmarks are often included. Many of the papers also maintain a so-called search service for the purpose of locating missing persons or for reuniting separated members of families. Other features common to most are correspondents' letters from various localities in the United States and abroad harboring important refugee colonies, reviews and criticisms of works of literature, music, art, and the theatre, stressing particularly those involving refugees in one way or another. Some carry literary essays, short stories, poems, and even scholarly treatises. The *Aufbau* has a special Hollywood correspondent with a column "Hollywood Calling," patterned after similar columns in some of the general American newspapers. The refugee press in general displays a strong literary and esthetic bent.

The interests and needs of the readers of these papers, the refugees, may also be gauged from the type of local news items, announcements, and advertisements found in them. Many carry items regarding activities of refugee organizations and groups in New York and other cities. The following two items, taken from *Aufbau*, illustrate this.

SEE NEW YORK FIRST

Tours and trips to introduce immigrants to Americans and the American way of life. No reservations required; for information apply at 67 West 44th Street, NYC. (VA 6–3168). Not responsible for any accidents. For members (who produce fully paid membership cards) free: for guests 15 cents; Saturdays. Sundays and holidays: members free; guests 25 cents. Additional expenses (such as carfares, etc.) will be announced separately.

WELCOME HOME PARTY

ALL OUR BOYS (and girls) are cordially invited to our next party which will be held on Wednesday, January 9, at the home of the Uptown Youth Group, 164th St. This will be a friendly get-together whereby boys meet girls and where we'll have an opportunity to talk things over and make plans for the further development of OUR BOYS' CLUB.

The *Aufbau* and the *Jewish Way*, adhering to the custom of some Jewish papers in Europe, contain a brief commentary by an outstanding rabbi on the weekly portion of the Pentateuch read in the synagogue. Announcements of births, engagements, weddings, deaths, and greetings on various occasions occupy considerable space in some papers. Advertisements for mates, which is also a European practice, is another frequent feature. The following advertisements, taken from the *Aufbau*, are typical.

I cannot offer you more than I am, I cannot promise you more than I have. But what I am and have is yours, should we come to the understanding, which is essential between mature humans, who consider joining in matrimony.

I am in my early forties, independent, in good professional standing, a veteran of this war in perfect health, a naturalized citizen of German-Jewish extraction.

I like to get in contact with lady, who thinks realistically about every day's life, but appreciates also "the better things." Your answer should contain your latest photograph, which will be returned without delay. Box N.I. 152-M

YOUNG SCIENTIST

Doctor, in excellent position, with good appearance and live sense of humor, desires the acquaintance of a very pretty and intelligent girl (18–23). Object: Matrimony. Please enclose photograph with first letter in English or German. Box G.M. 349-M

CHARMING LADY

40 years old, very good looking, intelligent, seeks acquaintance with fine refined gentlemen, willing to help in business. Object matrimony. G.I. 4625-M

Although the bulk of the commercial advertisers are refugee business establishments and professionals, not a few are American. Frequently the owner of an establishment or a professional worker will insert in parentheses under his name the city from which he has come and his connections abroad. Advertisements of preparations for exterminating mice and especially bedbugs are very frequent and occupy considerable space. Advertisements of toilet articles feature preparations of European origin and taste. One also frequently encounters advertisements of patent medicines claiming to be exactly like the ones readers used in Vienna, Berlin, Mannheim, or some other city.

Some of the refugee papers were established primarily for political propaganda purposes. These will undoubtedly disappear with the change in conditions and circumstances responsible for their appearance. Some, on the other hand, seem to cater to the needs of a considerable number of the new Americans. They help them in their adjustment to the American scene, interpreting American life to them, and, hence, will undoubtedly continue to exist for some time to come.

Participation of the Refugees in Organizational and Community Life

The refugees tend to join American organizations to a much greater extent than former immigrants. This is undoubtedly to be explained by their greater desire as well as readiness to become part of American life. Although, as seen above, the refugees have created and are maintaining a variety of organizations of their own, the majority have joined American organizations. These are usually, but not always, organizations maintained

Per Cent Distribution of Participation in American and Recent Immigrant Organizations, by Date of Arrival

Date of Arrival by Fiscal Years	Total Known		Type of Organization			
	Number	Per Cent	Only American	Only Recent Immigrant	American and Recent Immigrant	No Participation
All Cases	8,296	100.0	59.8	15.5	17.6	7.1
1933	9	100.0	55.5	33.3	11.1	—
1934	141	100.0	71.6	9.2	14.2	5.0
1935	138	100.0	68.9	4.3	22.5	4.3
1936	231	100.0	70.1	10.0	14.3	5.6
1937	561	100.0	69.7	7.8	18.4	4.1
1938	967	100.0	60.3	13.4	20.0	6.3
1939	2,458	100.0	61.8	14.6	17.9	5.7
1940	2,246	100.0	56.3	18.5	17.7	7.5
1941	1,063	100.0	55.9	19.4	16.6	8.1
1942	308	100.0	48.4	21.1	14.6	15.9
1943	90	100.0	57.8	14.4	11.1	16.7
1944	58	100.0	51.7	19.0	10.3	19.0
1945	26	100.0	50.0	15.4	—	34.6

by nationality or religious groups to which they belong. Moreover, many of those joining refugee societies also belong at the same time to American organizations. Only a small minority, particularly of those who have been here a considerable period of time, belong exclusively to organizations established by the refugees themselves.

As shown in the above table about 60 per cent of all those belonging to organizations are members of organizations with a predominantly American membership. It is interesting to note that only a comparatively small percentage do not participate in any organized life. From the same table it is also evident that those who have been here longer tend to join American organizations to a greater extent than those who have been here a briefer period. The latter show a greater tendency to belong to exclusively refugee organizations, and they also show the largest percentages of non-participation. All this may, of course, be explained in terms of the greater degree of acculturation of those who have been here a longer period.

There is also a high correlation between the size of community and the degree of participation of refugees in predominantly American organizations. As a glance at the following table shows, the largest percentage

Per Cent Distribution of Participation in American and Recent Immigrant Organizations, by Size of Community

	Total Known		Type of Organization			
					American	
				Only	and	No
			Only	Recent	Recent	Partici-
Size of Community	Number	Per Cent	American	Immigrant	Immigrant	pation
All Cases	8,296	100.0	59.8	15.5	17.6	7.1
Under 2,500	284	100.0	82.1	3.9	5.9	8.1
2,500–9,999	302	100.0	73.5	6.6	12.3	7.6
10,000–24,999	207	100.0	78.3	3.8	11.6	6.3
25,000–99,999	667	100.0	71.8	7.0	13.1	8.1
100,000–499,999	2,212	100.0	76.8	7.4	10.2	5.6
500,000–999,999	1,474	100.0	48.8	20.7	23.2	7.3
1,000,000 and over	1,628	100.0	47.0	24.0	21.6	7.4
New York City	1,522	100.0	44.7	22.9	24.4	8.0

belonging to American organizations is to be found among refugees living in the smallest communities, namely, those under 2,500 population. Participation in American organizations is in general much greater in communities with less than 500,000 population than in larger ones. Since it is in the largest cities that the greatest concentration of refugees has occurred it is natural that there should be greater organizational activity on the part of refugees there and hence that more of them should belong to their own organizations.

As far as religious groupings are concerned, analysis shows that the Protestants among the refugees have the highest percentage belonging to American organizations only, while the Jews have the largest proportion among those joining refugee organizations. The Catholics occupy a middle position, having at the same time the largest percentage of nonparticipants. As regards the Greek Catholics, they constitute too small a number to make it possible to arrive at any definite conclusion.

The refugees, on the whole, as is borne out by reports on communities throughout the country, are becoming integrated into general community life at a comparatively rapid pace. This is especially true of the children and young adults. "We consider," states a report from St. Louis, "that there has been an exceedingly high rate of integration of most of the group. . . . There has been a good deal of intermarriage." A report from Detroit states: "They [the refugees] have joined established organizations. . . . Considering the brief time [less than five years for most], the integration has been remarkably well." From Chattanooga, to cite another illustration, the report includes the following statement: "Most of the refugees had achieved citizenship and there was practically no program left which, in the opinion of the Refugee Committee, warranted their maintaining a separate committee."

The desire on the part of the refugees to adjust themselves to and become part of American life is noticed everywhere. The following two excerpts from autobiographical sketches, one from a young housewife in Decatur, Michigan, and the other from a young chemist in Dayton, Ohio, are typical of many.

"I have made friends both among the Americans and Europeans. We find just as many cultural opportunities here as in Europe. . . . Our recreation now consists of music, reading, horseback riding, visiting with friends. We definitely want to stay in the United States. I can't think of any other country where I'd rather bring up children. My husband is satisfied. He is working in his special field, progressing both professionally and financially, and is happy. My daughter has started school—and because she had not quite reached the public school age (she lacked about two weeks), we have enrolled her in a Catholic school for the first grade."

"We try to be active in many organizations in order to get better acquainted with the people with whom we live, to learn their ways of likes and dislikes, and, too, to master our English better and better. We hardly ever speak German except when writing to our both parents. . . ."

Nevertheless, some refugees, because of their background and experiences abroad and here are either forced or prefer to seek their associates from among their own group, thus remaining aloof from the American community. Some individuals with a superior educational and social background find that only by mixing with their former townsmen can they continue to enjoy their former respect and social status. They are bitterly disappointed in the way people in this country tend to judge a person by his financial status rather than his education or social background.

Such individuals usually seek the company of their countrymen and tend to join organizations and groups established by the refugees, particularly the *Landsmannschaft* type of organization, where their former status is recognized and appreciated, and where they feel at home. Again, there are those who tend to associate with members of their own refugee or general nationality group because of their unfortunate experiences in Germany.

They feel drawn toward their group as a reaction to the untold cruelties suffered at the hands of Nazis in Germany. On the other hand, there are those who are forced to associate primarily with their countrymen because of the discrimination they have experienced here. A Jewish refugee businessman living in Philadelphia writes that he "was surprised by the anti-Semitism in this country and the degree of segregation of Jewish people." And an electrical engineer from Bavaria stated in an interview:

> In his native town where there were 800 Jews there were relatively few completely Jewish organizations, it being the custom of Jewish people to mingle more generally among non-Jewish people than is true here. It was his opinion that if anti-Semitism were propagated by the government here as it was in Germany that the man in the street would be much more ready to accept it than were the people of his own community in Bavaria.

Complaints of Jewish refugees that they are being discriminated against by their American co-religionists are also met with. This is expressed in the following statement taken from an interview with a German Jewish refugee in a New England city:

> Mr. G. senses a feeling of antagonism toward them on the part of the Jewish community. . . . Mr. G. ascribes this to the general carry-over of Old-World antagonisms, Eastern-European vs. German Jews, a lack of knowledge of each other and small incidents.

The majority of refugees, however, as stated above, do not encounter much difficulty in being accepted by the communities in which they live and are successful in making the proper adjustment to American life.

CHAPTER XII

THE REFUGEES AS CITIZENS

We have already noted that the vast majority of the refugees admitted on permanent visas to this country intend to remain. In the replies to the Study Committee's questionnaire, 96.5 per cent stated that they had no intention of returning to their former homeland or of settling in other countries. They seek to identify themselves completely with America. We have also noted the high proportion of refugees who have attended English and citizenship classes and other institutions of adult education to learn the language and ways of their adopted land and prepare for naturalization. They have not only eagerly enrolled in the public school classes but have also utilized the facilities offered by private organizations such as churches, settlements, and youth associations. The outstanding private organization in this field has been the Committee for Refugee Education, in New York, which has given instruction to thousands of refugees and pioneered in the development of special teaching materials. Further evidence of the refugees' desire to become Americans and their progress in this respect is seen in their acquisition of citizenship, their military service, aid in the war effort, and other manifestations of their loyalty and attachment to the United States.

THE ATTAINMENT OF CITIZENSHIP

The refugees exhibit an unusual desire to become naturalized. Many of them take out their first papers almost immediately after their arrival. Only an insignificant number of them have failed to apply. They are tremendously impressed with the privileges of citizenship. They feel intense allegiance to this country and do not want to be known as refugees but as new Americans. The following comments are typical of their attitude.

"I wish to remain in the U.S.A. and become an American citizen. After almost 12 years of enforced wandering, one has the desire to have a home and a base to stand on; also, my children have already become completely American in mind and behavior and I wish to give them the legal rights an American citizen enjoys. For myself I desire the feeling of security—to be at home some place in the world." (German Protestant actor, an active anti-Nazi who arrived in 1941; New York)

"Both my wife and I took out our first papers the first day we got here." (German Jewish factory manager; Philadelphia)

"My wife and I are now ready to apply for citizenship. My daughter is a little worried because I can't speak English well, and she thinks I will not get my citizenship. But I'll say to the judge. 'I love America.' " (Austrian, aged 81; San Francisco)

Similar material has appeared in newspaper stories, especially on the emotional reaction to the attainment of citizenship. The following are typical examples.

Ellen Schwanneke, 28-year-old native of Berlin, who was starred in the German motion picture, "Maedchen in Uniform" in 1932, wept hysterically as she took the oath of allegiance in New York. "This means so much to me," she explained later, adding, "I hate Hitler and all he represents." (*New York Times*, Dec. 19, 1944)

German-born Mrs. Anna Kost Oehlke, 57 years old, residing in Miami, Florida, had but one regret, that she would die before she could take the oath as an American citizen. Federal Judge John W. Holland learned of her dying wish, and found that she had met all naturalization requirements except for the oath of allegiance. By ambulance Mrs. Oehlke was taken to the Federal Court where she lifted her frail hand and smiled as Judge Holland administered the oath. (*New York Times*, Aug. 1, 1945)

To the refugees, most of whom had been deprived of their full rights as citizens in their homelands and many of whom had been rendered stateless, the attainment of American citizenship is a matter of great moment. The event is often marked by celebrations, the exchange of gifts, and notices in the foreign-language press. The refugees become enthusiastic citizens, showing great appreciation of the democratic principles underlying our government, because they are in an excellent position to contrast the freedom of democracy with the tyranny of Fascism.

How many refugees have attained American citizenship? This question cannot be answered officially, since no statistics are available for refugees as distinct from immigrants generally. The official data of the Immigration and Naturalization Service are not kept by country of birth or by race or people, but by country of former allegiance. The latter, however, would be a satisfactory index if data were also available by date of arrival, so that the refugees could be distinguished from other and earlier arrivals. On the other hand, the material gathered by the Study Committee, which is presented below, provides an accurate indication of the citizenship status of refugees. Before considering it, however, the general situation regarding naturalization in recent years may well be examined.

Naturalization statistics on a nation-wide scale have been collected since 1907. As the accompanying graph indicates, a sharp drop in the number of naturalizations began in 1929 and continued until about 1935. This was owing in part to the increased cost of naturalization and in part to the financial depression. Since 1935 the demand for American citizenship has steadily increased, reaching the unprecedented peak of 441,979 certificates granted in 1944. The threatening situation in Europe, the outbreak of war, and the nation-wide registration of all aliens in the United States in 1940 are important causes for this increased demand. The coming of the refugees also is a factor, since it coincides with this upward trend in naturali-

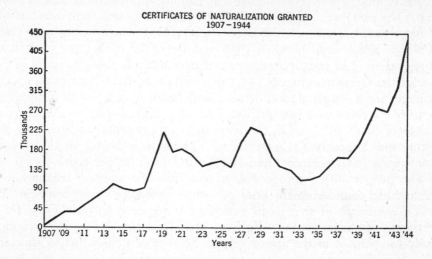

zation. This most active period of naturalization has occurred during a time of drastic reduction in immigration, with the result that the number of aliens naturalized has greatly exceeded the number of aliens admitted, and the alien population of the country has shown a substantial net decrease.

Noteworthy among the cases of naturalization during the war years were those of noncitizens in our armed forces. For many reasons, psychological as well as practical, it was important that members of our armed forces be citizens. Especially was it so in the case of "enemy aliens" and aliens who were natives of enemy-occupied or enemy-dominated countries—a classification including many refugees—whose lack of American citizenship might mean death if they were captured. Congress acknowledged this in the Second War Powers Act in 1942 by simplifying the naturalization requirements for members of the armed forces, permitting them to secure citizenship after three months' honorable service. This act also authorized naturalization through administrative processes and outside of the United States. By the end of 1944, 101,653 noncitizens in our armed forces had been naturalized, 10,997 of them overseas, even in the actual combat areas. This is the first time in American history that citizenship was granted outside the boundaries of the United States.

Specific information on the naturalization of refugees is provided by the investigation conducted by the Study Committee. Of the total number of respondents to the questionnaire who were eligible to apply for citizenship, that is, were at least 18 years old—11,074 in number—exactly 50 per cent had already attained citizenship and the rest were in various stages of attaining it. Of the latter, 2.7 per cent had applied for first papers, 29.3 per cent had received their first papers, and 17.1 per cent had applied for their second or final papers. The number who had not applied for first papers (99, or 0.9 per cent) was negligible. This atypical group was composed mainly of older people (half of them over 50, one-third over 60 years old) most of whom had arrived between 1939 and 1941, the peak years of refugee immigration. The rate of attainment of citizenship is above average in the case of the German refugees (53.7 per cent) who have been here, on the average, for a longer period of time and hence have a larger proportion of their numbers who can qualify. The next highest rate is the Austrian (48.6 per cent), followed by the Russian (43.9 per cent), Italian (42.2 per cent), and Yugoslav (41.9 per cent). The rate is lowest in the case of Rumanians (23.5 per cent) and Netherlanders (15.2 per cent).

The proportion of refugees who have already attained citizenship is remarkable, considering the brief period of time they have been here. By law, a minimum of five years' residence is required to be eligible for a certificate of naturalization. We have already noted the special exception made for persons in the armed forces. Because of delays due to shortage of naturalization examiners and various administrative reasons, which was a serious problem until 1943, the actual time required was commonly six to seven years, especially in the more congested districts of New York, Boston, Detroit, Buffalo, Chicago, Los Angeles, and San Francisco, where a very large proportion of the refugees resided.

A refinement of the questionnaire returns, which limits the cases to those refugees who are over 21 years of age and who have resided here five years or more, gives a more accurate and revealing picture of the attainment of citizenship, for these are the only persons, with the exception of those in the armed services, who are eligible for full citizenship. On this basis, 82.7 per cent of the refugees have already attained citizenship, 11.1 per cent have applied for their second papers, 5.5 per cent have applied for or received their first papers, and less than 1 per cent have failed to take any step toward the attainment of American citizenship. A higher percentage of men than of women refugees and of Jews than of Christians have attained citizenship.

THE REFUGEES AS "ENEMY ALIENS"

When America entered the war, many refugees who had not been here long enough to become citizens found themselves, along with other aliens born in countries with which the United States was at war, technically "enemy aliens," with limitations on their personal freedom. Though the

PER CENT DISTRIBUTION OF CITIZENSHIP STATUS OF REFUGEES, 1945, BY RELIGION AND SEX, FOR THOSE AGE 21 AND OVER WHO HAVE RESIDED IN THE UNITED STATES FIVE YEARS OR LONGER

	Total			Religion					
Citizenship Status	Total	Male	Fe-male	Jew-ish	Prot-es-tant	Ro-man Cath-olic	Greek Ortho-dox	No Reli-gious Affili-ation	Un-known
Total Known	100.0	100.0	100.0	100.0	100.0	100.0	100.0	100.0	100.0
Nondeclarant alien	.7	.4	1.0	.5	1.0	3.9	5.7	—	—
First papers applied for	.8	.7	1.0	.7	1.0	3.4	2.9	1.3	—
First papers received	4.7	4.0	5.6	4.0	6.8	10.7	17.1	5.3	—
Second papers applied for	11.1	9.8	12.8	10.8	13.0	15.0	8.6	4.0	16.2
Citizenship attained	82.7	85.1	79.6	84.0	78.2	67.0	65.7	89.4	83.8

refugees and other loyal aliens in this category suffered some limitations, frustrations, and discrimination and were hampered in securing employment in war industries and participating in the military and civilian defense of the nation, the government handled the problem justly and efficiently. The United States was better prepared to handle the alien problem in this world war than in the last one. The Immigration and Naturalization Service had obtained information about all aliens through the Alien Registration Act of 1940. The Federal Bureau of Investigation (FBI) had collected a great amount of information concerning possible subversive elements and had compiled a list of aliens from Axis countries who might prove dangerous to the national security. On the night of December 7, 1941, the most dangerous persons in this group were taken into custody; in the following weeks a number of others were apprehended. Each arrest was made on the basis of information concerning the specific alien taken into custody. No dragnet techniques or indiscriminate large-scale raids were used. Thus, we fortunately avoided repetition of the hysteria of 1917 and 1918, which culminated in the "deportation delirium of 1920."

Of the five million aliens registered in 1940, approximately 1,100,000 were, by the fact of war, immediately classified as "enemy aliens," and restrictions were imposed on their freedom of movement, their right to live in areas designated as necessary to defense, their possession of certain articles, including cameras, short-wave radios, and firearms. But it was soon discovered that the great majority of them were more properly designated friendly "aliens of enemy nationality." Included among them were the Italians, numbering over 600,000, who were, late in 1942, exempted as a group. A new division called the Alien Enemy Control Unit was created in the Department of Justice to supervise the alien enemies and to hear and review the cases of those apprehended by the FBI.[1] Only a small proportion of these aliens proved to be hostile or disloyal to this country. These were interned. Only 23,000 enemy aliens had to be taken into custody for questioning, and the number interned never exceeded 10,000.[2]

It was feared at one time that enemy agents might enter the United States under the guise of refugees. So carefully was immigration controlled that practically none entered this way. In fact, it would have been impossible for anyone continuously and successfully to pretend to be an anti-Nazi refugee, because there were so many genuine anti-Nazi refugees here who could expose such a fake.[3] Indeed, no case has been announced of spies and subversive elements who could claim to be refugees. Though it is difficult to make an accurate statement on this matter, since the Alien Enemy Control Unit, like the Immigration Service, has never included the classification of refugee in its filing system, this much can be safely stated: "the incidence of refugees in the Alien Enemy Program was negligible." This is an official statement by the Department of Justice. Thomas M. Cooley, II, Assistant to the Director of the Alien Enemy Control Unit, has stated further, in a letter to the Study Committee dated December 12, 1945:

> I might add unofficially that I was the Head of the Review Section which reviewed all Alien Enemy cases up to approximately the beginning of 1944, and I do not recall a single case in which a person I would consider properly classified as a refugee was found to be engaging in subversive or other harmful activities. It is true that occasionally persons appearing before our Hearing Boards attempted to pass themselves off as refugees in order to confuse the issue or disprove the charges against them. But it is my opinion that in none of these cases was refugee status actually involved.

The overwhelming demonstration of the loyalty of the "enemy aliens" led to a provision for exempting from this classification all persons certified, after investigation, as loyal to the United States, and thus permitting them to apply for naturalization. This was provided by executive order on March 20, 1942 and extended by executive order on August 27, 1943. Only a minimum investigation was required in the case of aliens with children serving in the armed forces of the United States, housewives whose husbands were citizens, aliens over 65 years of age, and aliens who came here to escape persecution in the countries of their origin. Some 200,000 of those technically classed as "enemy aliens," including numerous refugees, thus found it possible to conclude their naturalization.

---

[1] John Edgar Hoover, "Alien Enemy Control," *Iowa Law Review*, Vol. 29, No. 3 (March, 1944).

[2] Ugo Carusi, "Our Post-War Immigration Policy," Common Council for American Unity, *Interpreter Releases*, Aug. 27, 1945, p. 230; Eugene M. Culp, "Alien Enemy Paroles," *Monthly Review*, Immigration and Naturalization Service, October, 1945, pp. 204–208.

[3] Hans Lamm, "I Am an 'Enemy Alien,'" *Common Ground*, Summer, 1942, p. 16.

The refugee community proved itself to be overwhelmingly on the side of democracy, and aided in the war effort in every way. Perhaps no segment of our national population has been more wholehearted in its condemnation of Fascism and Nazism than the refugees who had been victims of such oppression.

The great majority of the refugees desire nothing more than to be absorbed permanently as United States citizens; hence they are not politically organized and they show little active concern about future political developments in their former homelands. This seems to be especially true of the German Jewish refugees. Only a small proportion of the recent immigrants were political refugees who had been active in European political movements opposed by the Axis. Included among the political refugees are government officials, royal families, writers, and scholars—officially or unofficially recognized leaders—who have endeavored to spread their political views and in some instances have established refugee societies with political purposes looking toward postwar conditions in their homelands and trying to affect American opinion on foreign policy. There is no unity among them, even within a given nationality group. Frictions and differences that existed in the old country are continued here. This situation prevails particularly among the Poles, Yugoslavs, Lithuanians and other Baltic peoples, Ukrainian nationalists, Austrians, and the French. This is the traditional picture of the political activities of foreign-born groups in the United States. The governments-in-exile have been no more successful than European governments in the past in their endeavor to induce their American compatriots to come under their leadership. The great majority of all immigrants, and particularly of refugees, lose active interest in political affairs in their former homelands as time goes on and assimilation proceeds, and they develop attachment and loyalty to the United States.

REFUGEES IN THE ARMED FORCES

Like other immigrants and children of immigrants, the refugees have demonstrated not only their undivided loyalty to the United States, but their readiness to defend it with their lives. Our enemies expected that a nation made up of people of many nationalities would be disunited. Instead of becoming divided, however, we grew more unified. They attempted to incite racial dissension, but failed. The GIs in particular have learned that loyalty, courage, and sacrifice have nothing to do with race, nationality, or creed.

To cite just one instance of the part that the foreign-born and their children have played in our armed forces in the war, it is noteworthy that of the six servicemen who participated in the historic flag raising at Iwo Jima three were unquestionably of foreign origin: Sergeant Henry C.

Hansen, from Somerville, Massachusetts, of Scandinavian origin; Pfc. René A. Gagnon (marine) from Manchester, New Hampshire, of French-Canadian origin; and Sergeant Michael Strank from Johnstown, Pennsylvania, of Carpatho-Russian origin, coming from Czechoslovakia. A fourth member of the group, Pfc. Ira H. Hayes, is a full-blooded Pima Indian from Arizona. Hansen and Strank were later killed in action.

Rumors, Nazi-inspired, have been current to the effect that American Jews did not play their full part in the military effort, yet in World War II, as in every other war in our history, they carried their full share and played a great and commendable part in the defense of Americanism.[4] Some 500,000 Jews were in the nation's armed services in the war just concluded, and studies made by the Bureau of War Records of the Jewish Welfare Board indicate that the rate of enlistment or induction was at least as high for Jews as for the general population.[5]

Rumors have also been spread that refugees did not serve in the armed forces proportionately to the rest of the population, that they attempted to dodge the draft or that they were not accepted for military service as being enemy aliens. As an example of the extreme type of allegation, we may note that an anti-Semitic sheet called *Bible News Flashes*, April, 1945 issue, defined a refugee as "a man who comes boo-hooing to the U. S. because he's too cowardly to fight like real men do in Europe." As a matter of fact, the Selective Training and Service Act made aliens as fully liable to service as citizens. All resident male aliens within the designated age groups had to register, whether they were of enemy or of neutral nationality. Neutral aliens might claim exemption from military service, but doing so barred them forever from American citizenship. Aliens of enemy nationality were accepted for military service after the armed forces or the Director of the Selective Service System made an investigation and determined their acceptability. The great majority of the refugees who were still aliens were of enemy nationality, but as anti-Nazis were generally acceptable. Refugees who had already become citizens were of course in the same category as native-born citizens. Aliens were not eligible to enlist, and in certain special services citizenship of a number of years' standing was required. Within these limitations imposed by American law and regulation, refugees—aliens and citizens alike—entered the armed forces to the same extent as native Americans.

The report for 1943–1944 of the Director of Selective Service states:[6]

The number of aliens inducted into the United States armed forces has not been large in proportion to the total number of inductees. The number is slightly over 1 per

[4] J. George Fredman and Louis A. Falk, *Jews in American Wars*, 1942.

[5] Samuel C. Kohs, *Jews in the United States Armed Forces*, Yiddish Scientific Institute (YIVO), 1945.

[6] *Selective Service as the Tide of War Turns, the 3rd Report of the Director of Selective Service, 1943–1944*, Washington, 1945, pp. 235, 240.

cent of the total registrants in the age group. . . . Nevertheless, the percentage is almost identical with the alien population as it relates to the citizen population of the United States, the proportion of which is about 1.02. In other words, the aliens residing in the United States have contributed their share to the armed forces. . . . Most aliens have entered the armed service willingly and, according to reports furnished to us, have served faithfully.

In a study conducted by the Bureau of War Records of the National Jewish Welfare Board in 27 widely scattered cities it was reported as of December 23, 1943, that "of the male refugees, 18 to 44 years of age inclusive, 34 per cent were in the armed forces of this country. It is interesting to note that this percentage is almost exactly the same as that for the total number of men in the armed forces from the entire United States."[7] The Study Committee received questionnaire returns from 602 refugees in the armed services. They constitute 33 per cent of the male respondents of military age. It is also noteworthy that 32 per cent of all respondents to the questionnaire mentioned military service by family members in answer to the question on contributions or service to the war effort.

The refugees were already geared to the necessity of fighting for a democratic way of life and, as some of the cases cited below reveal, had a special reason for fighting Nazism. No systematic effort was made by the Study Committee to gather information about the activities, awards, or special services of refugees in the armed forces. The following instances were culled incidentally from newspapers and from casual comments on questionnaires and in life stories.

When Ernest Stock was inducted in the Army on May 3, 1943, he hoped he would be sent to Europe, which might give him an opportunity to locate his father who had been confined to the Buchenwald concentration camp and unable to flee to the United States with the rest of the family. Because he spoke French, German, Spanish, Flemish, and English fluently, Ernest was assigned to the Army's Criminal Investigation Division. He is now a technical sergeant. In May 1945 he located his father who had managed to escape to Utrecht, Netherlands. (New York Times, June 3, 1945)

M/Sgt. Bernard Bernkof who had arrived in this country in 1937, had enlisted in the Army a month after Pearl Harbor, and had been in the European campaign since D-plus-4, winning the Bronze Star for "an argument I had with some Krauts crossing the Seine," found his father and mother alive in the ruins of Cologne. (New York Times, March 9, 1945)

States an AP dispatch, datelined April 27, 1945, at the Southern Okinawa Front: "A slim, wiry Jewish boy who fled Nazi intolerance is rapidly becoming a legend in the fighting for Okinawa. He feels that because he found sanctuary in the United States he has a debt to pay, but his mates in the 106th Infantry, 27th Division, say it's all paid and anything else—if he lives—will be pure interest. His name is Leo Rosskam, 27, a former

[7] Samuel C. Kohs, op. cit., p. 12.

sandwich maker in a Bronx delicatessen. Before that he had spent six months in Germany's Buchenwald concentration camp, where he felt the pain of Nazi torture. He escaped and fled to the United States in July, 1939. Two years later he enlisted in the Army." He has been awarded the Distinguished Service Cross.

Helmuth Ameicah, 20, whose family fled from Nazi persecution in Germany in 1936 to Shanghai to Manila to Samal Island, got a measure of revenge nine years later when he led American troops to skilfully hidden Japanese naval guns on Samal Island which were firing on 24th Division infantrymen around Davao. (*New Haven Evening Register*, May 25, 1945)

Frequently refugees in the armed services were given special assignments where knowledge of the language and terrain of the enemy-occupied countries was required. Many are the refugees who have been decorated for special acts of bravery. The following instances are but a few out of literally hundreds.

Lt. Richard Stern, who fled from Germany to New York in 1937, has the Bronze Star. Comments his sister, "We like it much better than the Iron Cross that father got as a German mess sergeant in the other war." (*New York Post*, Feb. 2, 1945)

M/Sgt. Walter Mitener, a sculptor in civilian life, who learned after his arrival here that his parents had committed suicide to avoid deportation to Poland, said that he knew what he was fighting for. He received the Silver Star and a commission as lieutenant for capturing 400 Germans. "I just talked them into surrender." (Excerpt from letter)

A German-born American soldier, Klaus Mann, son of Thomas Mann, famed Nobel Prize-winning novelist, captured in Prague a notorious American traitor, Edward Leo Delaney, who broadcast propaganda throughout the war over the Nazi radio. (*New York Times*, June 30, 1945)

A huge collection of priceless Jewish manuscripts, paintings, and other cultural objects stolen by the Nazis all over Europe was recovered at Hungen, Germany, by a unit of the Third Army led by an Austrian refugee, Lieut. Robert Schoenfeld of Brooklyn. (*New York World-Telegram*, April 11, 1945)

Although he has accumulated 97 points toward discharge, S/Sgt. Eric W. Lange feels that he may be classified as essential, now that he has been made mayor of a small town in Bavaria by the Allied Military Government. His knowledge of the German language and countryside brought about his metamorphosis from infantry squad leader. Lange, who came to New York in 1941, participated in the Normandy invasion on D-day, received the Bronze Star for heroism, and fought in the Aachen, Ardennes, and Munich campaigns. He has been decorated five times. (*New York Times*, June 5, 1945)

A great many refugees have been used as interpreters and for cross-examining German prisoners of war. One of them, Capt. Herbert Cohn of Cedarhurst, New York, was the chief interpreter when the last Nazi government was dissolved by the Allies on May 23, 1945, and Grand Admiral Karl Doenitz, General Gustav Jodl, and other members of Germany's "Government," High Command and General Staff were arrested. (*New York Times*, May 24, 1945)

Many refugees also served in our counter-intelligence corps. Concerning the work of this nature against the Nazis in Austria, it is stated: "Our side of the hide-and-seek game was from the start made easier here by the presence of a fabulous young OSS officer named Rudolf von Ripper, himself a native of Austria. Anti-Nazi at the time of the *Anschluss*, von Ripper sent his regards to Hitler and Co. in the form of bleak caricatures and drawings. In 1938 he spent nine months in a concentration camp, then escaped to the United States. In due course he became a cloak-and-dagger man and returned to Europe. On a daring assignment he penetrated the Nazi lines in Austria and preceded our troops to Salzburg by some ten days. Hidden by relatives and friends, he collected valuable intelligence on fleeing officials and their rendezvous in the mountains." (Edgar Snow, "They're Getting Their Alibis Ready," *Saturday Evening Post*, July 28, 1945, p. 12)

Many refugees made the supreme sacrifice for their new homeland and for liberty. The total number who were killed in the war is not known, but that it was relatively large is indicated by the fact that by the end of 1944 at least 78 readers of one refugee newspaper, *Aufbau*, had died for their country.

AID IN THE WAR EFFORT

On the home front, the refugees contributed generously to the various war activities. Only 27 of the 11,233 who replied to the questionnaire stated specifically that they had not contributed to the war effort, and only 376 left the question blank. Even if all of these cases are interpreted negatively, it remains that 96.5 per cent of the total group made some contribution, an extraordinary record. The most common type of contribution was the purchase of war bonds. Ninety-one and three-tenths per cent of the total group purchased war bonds. If we eliminate those who did not answer this question, the percentage rises to 94.9 per cent. The refugees in this respect stand second to none. Also remarkable is their record regarding blood donations, one-third of the respondents having given to the blood bank, many of them several times. No comparable figures are available, since the American Red Cross does not keep a record of the number of individuals who have given blood. It does, however, have a record of those who have given blood three times or more, though no national compilation has yet been made. From the evidence at hand, it would appear that few, if any, groups in the population have a record superior to that of the refugees. Among them it became a common practice, emotionally reinforced, to make blood donations. The refugee journal *Aufbau* has regularly included a list of those who have contributed eight or more times. Refugees strove to make this honor roll. Among the respondents to the questionnaire were many who had given blood repeatedly. In the life stories, comments like the following were very frequent:

"As our contribution to the war effort I can say that we buy war bonds regularly, not only at the time of drives. I am a regular blood donor at the Red Cross. I have given a pint of blood twelve times and intend to continue as long as possible." (German upholsterer, 44; Cincinnati)

"My husband hopes to get a better job when he will be an American citizen next year. He gave his blood to the Blood Bank ten times." (Wife of German lawyer in Columbus, Ohio)

Mr. S. organized and was made chairman of the Blood Donor League in his place of employment. He himself contributed blood on fourteen different occasions. Mrs. S. knitted continuously for the Red Cross. In addition, the couple have been buying war bonds through the payroll plan and extra ones wherever possible. (Interviewer's report on German middle-aged couple in Indianapolis)

"We are contributing to the Community and War Fund. We are buying bonds. My wife and I gave, together, 25 pints of blood to the Red Cross." (Stage director; Chicago)

The variety of services or contributions by either individuals or family units is noteworthy.

Mr. P.'s son entered the Army before the war started and his daughter became an Army nurse soon after she completed her training here in Philadelphia. At the beginning of the war, Mr. P. tried to give up his business and go into a defense plant where he offered to do special work in glider construction, which he had studied at some length in Germany. His offer to do this was rejected because of his age. He has been a consistent blood donor and purchaser of war bonds. (Interviewer's account)

Like many other refugees who furnished maps, pictures, city plans, street guides and other material and data for the use of the Allied Armies, an Austrian draftsman in New York states: "I sent a collection of maps and guide books from the European theater of war to Washington and I got a letter from the War Department thanking me for important information concerning the mountain warfare in the Alps."

The G's and their firm have been on the honor roll for oversubscribing their quota of war bonds. They contribute as generously as they can to war relief. Mr. G. and his daughter have both been blood donors. (Interview with Czechoslovak factory owner in Milwaukee)

Thirty-two per cent of the respondents to the questionnaire reported military service by family members, which was the next most frequent contribution to the war effort after purchase of war bonds and blood donations. Only a small proportion of the refugees engaged in civilian defense activities since aliens were not permitted to become air-raid wardens, auxiliary firemen, or to participate in other protective services. They did, however, make the most of opportunities open to them in such activities as sale of war stamps and bonds, salvage, knitting for the Red Cross, first-aid assistance in child care centers, service as nurses' aides, etc., since these activities lacked the barriers, both actual and psychological, that existed toward newcomers in the case of the protective services.

Striking also is the number of different contributions or services to the war effort. Of the great mass of the respondents to the questionnaire answering this question, only 0.2 per cent had made no contribution, while 13.2 per cent had made one type of contribution, 33.0 per cent two types, 34.6 per cent three types, 15.2 per cent four types, 3.6 per cent five types, and 0.2 per cent six types. The very high incidence of three and four contributions is noteworthy. It is especially characteristic of the younger age group, from 16 to 40 years of age.

A special type of war service was rendered by the refugee scientists, scholars, industrialists, technicians, and other experts, either directly in government service or through the universities and private industries. Because of their intimate knowledge of the languages, industries, public utilities, and governments of enemy countries—a knowledge not matched by that of native Americans—there was a great demand for their services. To facilitate their employment, several files or rosters of foreign experts were compiled and made available to government agencies. A refugee, Dr. Fausto R. Pitigliani, established a Roster of Alien Specialized Personnel, listing 2,250 individuals in the natural sciences, technologies, social sciences, medicine, and business, who not only had valuable specialties to offer but also a particular knowledge of the industries, plants, commercial and social conditions of enemy countries. Under the auspices of Professor C. J. Friedrich's Seminar on Administrative Science at the Graduate School of Public Administration, Harvard University, a Survey of Foreign Experts was carried on during 1942–1943. The actual administrative detail was undertaken by Mr. F. P. Hellin, a refugee businessman from Austria. It covered about 300 businessmen and industrialists who had recently come to this country, mainly from Germany and Austria. The results of the survey proved so useful to the United States government that in the summer of 1943 it was taken over by the Board of Economic Warfare and continued as the United States Government Survey of Foreign Experts. The detailed knowledge possessed by these experts was effectively utilized in both military and economic warfare, as for example in bombing operations by revealing the location of hidden munitions plants and by advising with regard to the timing of bombing operations so that they would be most effective. It was a refugee, for instance, who described the heavy-water plant in German-held Norway, used in connection with atomic bomb research, which was subsequently demolished by Allied bombers.

The Army availed itself of the services of several thousand German citizens now here who had expert technical knowledge of the water plants, telephone systems, etc., in German cities. The Office of Strategic Services, the central intelligence agency which assembled strategic information needed by the joint chiefs of staff at Washington and strategic and tactical information needed by the commanders of the various theaters of war, used a number of refugees for specialized services. Refugees assisted also in psychological warfare. An article by a refugee psychiatrist, Dr. W. Eliasberg, on German philosophy and German psychological warfare, which appeared in the *Journal of Social Psychology* in 1943, was of value in our effort to direct such warfare against Germany. During the war the Foreign Broadcast Intelligence Service employed eight refugees, four of whom were European-language monitors, three were foreign broadcast analysts, and one was a wire editor. In a letter to the Study Committee, dated November 16, 1945, Russell M. Shepherd, Director of Foreign Broadcast Intelligence Service, stated:

The quality of performance of these refugees varied with the individual to a certain extent, but was generally on a high level. . . . Almost everyone in this group was of German extraction and his special contribution was his knowledge of German geography, politics, social structure, and personalities. . . . The outstanding refugee on our staff was Hans Speier, who was chief of the German Analysis Section from the summer of 1942 to May of 1944. He was in charge of the preparation of regular and special reports dealing with the characteristics and content of German broadcasts. In addition, he testified on those subjects in legal action against alleged Axis sympathizers in this country. Speier's particular capabilities for the job were the result not only of his academic work in Germany but of the research work he did on German propaganda after coming to the United States. He is without question one of the leading experts in the world on propaganda techniques.

Prominent among the government agencies employing refugees was the Office of War Information, in part because it was one of the few not having citizenship requirement. Its need for writers, editors, and speakers who could answer German propaganda in the German language was met by refugees, among others.

In World War II science and technology played a role unsurpassed in the history of warfare. To a certain extent the war became a struggle between opposing scientists. It became an operation of great military significance, for example, to capture Dr. Otto Hahn, German atom scientist, and remove him from Germany. Similarly it weakened the enemy and strengthened the Allies to assist in the migration from enemy territory of anti-Nazi and anti-Fascist leaders in the natural sciences and technologies. The enemy through its racialist doctrines helped in handicapping itself by expelling scientists who were "non-Aryans." Literally hundreds of refugee scientists, especially in the United States, made substantial contributions to the success of Allied arms.

Some of these scientists worked on the government's research program either directly or indirectly through universities and private industries. Others made contributions out of their independent research activities. For example, Professor Karl Sollner, a refugee scientist at the University of Minnesota, was a co-inventor of a portable device to enable shipwrecked sailors and airmen to convert sea water into drinking water. A Polish engineer, T. Janiszewski, invented a new type of portable demountable

V-type deck bridge which became standard U.S. Army equipment. An Austrian, Alfred Schwarz, research director for an optical company, designed a synchronized shutter used by Air Force and Signal Corps photographers. Czech specialists in the glass industry brought in a number of secret processes that were utilized in plane manufacture and in plastics. Iron and steel men from the Skoda Works contributed special knowledge and skill to the manufacture of munitions. These are just typical examples of the extensive contribution made by refugees to the war effort.

Most dramatic of the new discoveries was the development of the atomic bomb, which turned into a race between German and Allied scientists. Ironically enough, Germany started the experiments, but we finished them. In this we were aided by refugee scientists, a number of whom had been expelled by the Nazis because they were Jews. Among them were Albert Einstein, who provided the mathematical equation which showed just what the relation of matter to energy is and how one can be converted into the other, and whose letter to President Roosevelt resulted in the appointment of the Advisory Committee on Uranium; Dr. Lise Meitner, who discovered with Professor Otto Hahn the important clue to the release of atom energy, fled to Denmark where she communicated her results to Dr. O. Frisch, a physicist likewise driven from Germany, and worked with Dr. Neils Bohr, a Nobel Prize winner, until the German occupation in April, 1940, when she escaped to Sweden and continued her research work, the results of which were sent to the United States; Dr. Bohr, formulator of the theory on which the atomic bomb is based, who was whisked from the grasp of the Nazis in his occupied homeland, went to England and also came to the United States where he assisted in developing the atomic bomb; Professor Rudulf Peierls and Dr. Franz Eugen Simon, two German physicists who fled to England where they participated in the British part of the program; Dr. Enrico Fermi, Italy's foremost physicist and a Nobel Prize winner, a refugee to the United States, who discovered how easily a slow neutron can slip into an atom to burst its nucleus and release terrific energy and who also did much to show how the chain reaction could be controlled; and numerous refugees of other nationalities who assisted in bringing the bomb to perfection. As the *New York Times* of August 8, 1945, remarked editorially: "Though the credit for having forestalled Germany must go to the air forces that bombed German research laboratories where secret weapons were developed, we have some reason to thank Hitler and Mussolini for handicapping themselves. The Fuehrer's irrational glorification of Nordics and Il Duce's acceptance of the Nuremberg policy had the result of presenting us with some of the best physicists of Germany and Italy and of occupied countries. . . . There must be scores of others who were not mentioned in the official announcements—engineers, technicians, chemists, physicists of distinction, all gifts of Hitler and Mussolini."

CHAPTER XIII

YOUNG REFUGEES

A special role in the history of refugees coming to the United States since Hitler's rise to power has been played by the young refugees who came here as children and who are growing up to be the American citizens of today and tomorrow. It is of great interest to learn how well these young people, whose early years were marked by persecution, flight and transplantation to a new environment, have been able to adjust themselves.

Of the estimated total of some 250,000 refugees who came to the United States between 1933 and 1944, about 37,000, or nearly 15 per cent, arrived here under the age of 16. This total of refugee children includes all children born in Germany who came here since 1933, those born in Spain arriving since 1937, and those born in Austria, Poland, Italy, Czechoslovakia, and other countries of Europe affected by Nazi persecution and aggression arriving since 1938. It includes only children who were admitted to the United States as regular quota immigrants, and does not include the British children, numbering between four and five thousand, who came here as visitors for the duration only and are termed "evacuees" rather than "refugees."

The proportion of children in the total refugee immigration since 1933 is similar to the proportion of children among immigrants in general during that period and also during the earlier period from 1925 to 1933. The number of boys in the total group of refugee children was somewhat higher (19,041) than the number of girls (18,206).

The majority of these refugee children came to this country with one or both of their parents as part of a family group. Although many families migrated intact or were able to reassemble in this country, many others were not so fortunate. Frequently one of the parents, usually the father, had been imprisoned in a concentration camp or killed before the emigration of the rest of the family. In other cases the family had succeeded in fleeing as far as the frontier before one of the parents was arrested and sent back while the rest of the family continued their journey. Sometimes in the process of flight the family became separated, and individual members spent years in one country after another trying unsuccessfully to arrange for immigration into the United States.

Another group of refugee children were sent by their parents directly to relatives in this country in order to avoid the perils and hardships of persecution and war. These children were admitted as quota immigrants on the personal affidavits of their relatives and have continued under the care of these relatives until they have become old enough to be self-supporting. Most of these children will doubtless remain residents of the United States, since in many cases their parents have been killed by the Nazis. Where one or both parents have survived they will probably plan to immigrate to this country to join their children when conditions permit.

In addition to the children who came to the United States with one or both parents or who came directly to relatives here, more than one thousand children arrived from continental Europe unaccompanied by their parents as the charges of child-caring organizations established for the express purpose of caring for them. The admission of these children was made possible by an agreement with the immigration authorities which permitted the use of the corporate affidavit of an organization in place of the usual personal affidavit. These unaccompanied European children came here as quota immigrants, in contrast to the British children evacuees who were admitted as visitors for the duration only and most of whom had returned to their homes by the fall of 1945. The refugee children were placed in foster homes in communities throughout the country, as were the British children, and supervised by child-caring agencies until they should reach the age of 21.

For our special study of refugee children, the case records of these unaccompanied children have been especially valuable. No comparable source of data regarding other refugee children in this country was available. But, although the situation of these children differed in some respects from that of the larger group, notably in the fact that most of them were living with foster parents rather than with their own parents and were receiving the assistance of case-work supervision, all refugee children had much in common. The process of their general social and cultural adjustment, in school and at work, was basically similar. Moreover, 218 of the children who arrived here unaccompanied were later joined by their parents, and others of them were placed with relatives by the organization in charge. A careful study was made of the individual case records of the children on file in the national offices of the organizations sponsoring them. On the basis of these records, plus special reports sent in by case workers in charge of children still under care, the degree of success of their adjustment was estimated, and the various factors and processes underlying it were analyzed.

In addition to these data on the unaccompanied children, various other sources were utilized. A special report on the adjustment of refugee children was included in the community reports from towns and cities throughout the country. Information concerning the children of individual families was excerpted from the life stories written by adult refugees and a number of life stories were written by refugees who arrived here as children. The answers of young people to the general questionnaire also were examined. A special study was made of refugee children in New York City schools where large numbers of refugee children had been or were still enrolled. Interviews were likewise held with workers in agencies handling problem children regarding the refugee children referred to them. From all these data a fairly comprehensive picture of refugee children in the United States was obtained.

EXPERIENCES OF REFUGEE CHILDREN IN EUROPE

Some knowledge of the life of these children in Nazi Europe is necessary to an understanding of the problems involved in their adjustment here. The experiences of individual children before coming here, and the extent to which they have been affected by these experiences, are not always easy to determine. Many children seem to have forgotten much of their past experience or to be reluctant to talk about it. It is clear, however, that the group as a whole had undergone hardships and anxieties, the pain of separation from home and friends, persecution and danger, not usually the lot of childhood. In general those arriving in the later years had undergone more disturbing experiences than those who came over during the earlier years of the movement. They had seen Nazism developed to its extreme of ruthlessness and terror; they had often faced years of disrupted family life, of internment in refugee camps, of flight from one country to another, and had been subject to the hazards and deprivations of war.

Many children arriving even in the earlier years of the Nazi regime had undergone disturbing experiences. The Jewish children who had lived under Hitler for even a few years had seen the development of Nazi anti-Semitism in their home communities. They had found their life circumscribed by restrictions as to where they might go and what they might do. They had seen their families become depressed and fearful, their sources of income cut off or threatened, and their people subjected to humiliations. Many had suffered from hunger and deprivation. It was probably in school that the children felt most directly the pressures of the new regime, although the destruction of their happy, secure home life left an indelible impression upon them.

Essays written by refugee children in American schools reveal that even the children who came here at an early age have a vivid remembrance of the humiliations they suffered before leaving Europe. Their strongly patriotic note was not included for effect, according to the teachers, but sprang from a genuine admiration of their adopted land. Through hearing such recitals of life under Fascist dictatorship, American school children have often been taught a deeper appreciation of the meaning of democracy.

Myself as a Refugee
(written by a pupil in the seventh grade)

With experiences of the German persecution of the Jews, I am writing this.

About two years ago when I was still in Germany in school one morning our teacher came into the room and said, "Do you want the Jews in our class?" "No," said the children, "we don't want them." Then we had to go to another room and the teacher asked his class the same question and they said, "No." So we went from one teacher to another. At last we went to our official teacher and he gave us a beating and told us to sit down.

This is only a little theme about my private life, but it will give you an idea how the Jews in Germany have suffered.

Now you can understand why I like and appreciate the American people and schools so much and I say to myself, "Be a good American!"

The pogroms of November, 1938, violent assaults on the persons and property of the Jewish people, were witnessed by many of the children. Some had seen their fathers sent away to concentration camp and had lived through months of suspense as to their fate. Forcibly impressed on many young minds was the horrible significance of these camps and other practices of the Nazis.

After the pogroms of November, 1938, the Nazis embarked upon a ruthless policy of expulsion of the Jews. From some sections of Germany Jews were deported wholesale and dumped into France. Also many families fled to France to escape internment. Frequently the children were the first members of the family to leave. Not only Jewish children, but children whose parents had opposed the Nazis in any way were among those fleeing to safety.

The hospitality of France to these children and to the refugee families who fled there was markedly generous in the period previous to the invasion. But with the establishment of the Vichy government France's policy became much less humanitarian. The tremendous flow of refugees into France had created a hopeless problem, and they were, under the new government, interned by the thousands in refugee camps where conditions were almost as bad as in the concentration camps of Germany.

The situation of Jewish children left in Germany, Austria, and other countries under Nazi control grew increasingly desperate, and flight became for them, as for the adults, a race with death. For Nazi ruthlessness in its later stages of development made no exception of the children and the threat to their lives became increasingly ominous. Children were often placed in concentration camps with their parents, deported with other children of the same age or with their parents, and finally, as the revelations of the crematoria of Lublin and Belsen have proved, slaughtered along with the adults.

THE PROGRAM FOR UNACCOMPANIED REFUGEE CHILDREN

Recognition of the dangers and horrors faced by children in Europe led to the organization of a special program to admit unaccompanied children to this country. This program, in spite of efforts to make it more extensive, never developed into a large-scale plan of rescue of European refugee children. It did, however, bring to a safe haven more than one thousand children from continental Europe through a carefully conceived plan which safeguarded them and helped them to make an adjustment in their new homeland.

The plan for the admission of unaccompanied refugee children was instituted in 1934, or shortly after Hitler's accession to power. In that year the European-Jewish Children's Aid (at first called the German-Jewish Children's Aid) was founded through the activity of several groups, prominent among which were the Joint Consultative Council and the National Conference of Jewish Social Welfare. The groups responsible for the establishment of this organization had reached an agreement with the immigration authorities as to how refugee children, unaccompanied by their parents, might be admitted to the United States. The plan agreed upon permitted the admission of refugee children under the age of 16 on a corporate affidavit by which the European-Jewish Children's Aid guaranteed that the children would not become public charges, that they would attend school regularly until the age of 16, and that they would not be gainfully employed until then. The children were to be placed in suitable foster homes carefully investigated by child-caring agencies throughout the country that had been approved by state departments of public welfare, and were to be supervised by these agencies until they reached the age of 21. The success of the whole program was due in large part to this careful planning.

Up to 1940 the European-Jewish Children's Aid was the only organization sponsoring the admission of refugee children from Europe. Funds for its support were raised in the early years by contributions from various foundations and private individuals. From 1938 to 1941 the National Council of Jewish Women, which had previously made substantial contributions, assumed complete financial responsibility. Since 1941 the National Refugee Service has taken financial responsibility for this agency and has integrated it into its general structure of refugee services, although the European-Jewish Children's Aid maintains its corporate identity.

Before the year 1938 the policy of admitting small groups of children within the quota restrictions was accepted as a satisfactory agreement. Since the quota from Germany was not filled before July, 1938, it was a relatively simple matter to bring over children whose parents desired their emigration and who met the immigration requirements. In that year, however, the situation in Central Europe became so acute, and the pressure upon Jews in Germany so insistent, that the applications for quota visas far exceeded the number allowed. Because of the large number of adults applying for visas, only a small proportion of the children's applications could be given favorable consideration, and they began to pile up by the thousands in European consular offices.

At this time, in view of the desperate plight of the Jews in Germany and Austria, other countries began to make liberal concessions to allow refugee children admission. France sheltered thousands of both children and adults in a spontaneous movement shared in by organizations, philanthropists, and civilian population. England through the efforts of the British Inter-Aid Committee for the Care of Children Coming from Germany, had before the outbreak of war admitted nearly 10,000 refugee children, more than 6,000 of whom were Jewish. A legal loophole was found for the admission of an additional 10,000 children on the condition that they leave England after reaching their majority.

The comparatively small part being played by the United States in the rescue of refugee children at this time led to many expressions of dissatisfaction that we, as a democratic nation, were not more vigorously sharing in the work of relieving the victims of persecution. This type of sentiment led to a movement for relaxation of immigration restrictions to permit the entry of larger numbers of refugee children, which culminated in the introduction of several bills, most conspicuous of which was the Wagner-Rogers bill introduced in 1939. This bill provided for the admission to the United States within a two-year period of a maximum of 20,000 refugee children of all faiths under the age of 14, outside the quota restrictions. It was supported by the newly formed National Non-Sectarian Committee, which proposed to assume responsibility for the placement of the children in foster homes of their own faith. The bill was discussed extensively in the immigration committees, but never came to a vote in either house of Congress. Considerable opposition to it had been expressed on the grounds that such legislation might be an opening wedge to loosen present immigration restrictions, that the United States should first take care of its own neglected boys and girls, and that "America should be kept for the Americans."[1] With the failure of the Wagner-Rogers bill and other efforts to allow a large-scale immigration of unaccompanied refugee children, their immigration continued, as it had begun, as a small-scale and closely controlled program.

As a result, the Non-Sectarian Committee, which had purposed to function in the case of a large-scale immigration of refugee children, disbanded in favor of the United States Committee for the Care of European Chil-

[1] Y.W.C.A. National Board, *Public Affairs News Service*, Series No. 3, Bulletin No. VII, March 23, 1939.

dren, a committee backed by many of the same people as the Non-Sectarian
Committee, which proposed to sponsor the quota admission of all refugee
children. The United States Committee was organized in June, 1940, under the sponsorship of Mrs. Franklin D. Roosevelt. A large share of its
work was devoted to bringing 840 British child evacuees to this country for
the duration and supervising their adjustment while here. In the period
1940–1944 the committee brought over independently, in addition to the
British children, a total of 86 children from the continent of Europe, including 40 Spanish Loyalists, and co-operated with the European-Jewish
Children's Aid in bringing over 350 Continental Jewish children. These
children were brought over on the affidavit of the United States Committee, but their adjustment has been supervised by the European-Jewish Children's Aid. Costs for this joint program have been shared by both agencies.

NUMBER OF UNACCOMPANIED CHILDREN ADMITTED AND COMPOSITION OF THE GROUP

The details of the program for unaccompanied children admitted as
quota immigrants are of special interest because such a migration of children
to new homes in the United States is unique in our history, and because the
plan by which they were settled here has provided a valuable experiment
in the transplantation of children. The statement made by President Truman on December 22, 1945, that he hopes large numbers of orphaned children from Europe will be admitted to this country in the future, gives it
added significance.

Altogether a total of 1,035 children came to this country on the program
during the years 1934–1944, or an average of about 100 a year. The largest
number of children coming in any one year arrived in 1941 when the joint
program with the United States Committee had begun to function to aid
children in new areas, and before the entry of the United States into the
war had closed American consular offices in Germany and Austria. The
rescue of children then became increasingly difficult. From 1942 on, only
children who had already found refuge outside the war zone could be
brought to this country. During 1944 only 9 unaccompanied children arrived here; during the first half of 1945, only 6. (In the spring of 1946 the
immigration of such children from conquered and liberated areas was resumed under the same program.)

Although the majority of the children brought over on the program were
German, the group included children of many other nationalities. The program was originally set up to aid Jewish children residing in Germany, and
nearly all of the 433 children coming over between 1934 and 1940 were
German by birth, although 41 were of Polish parentage. With the spread of
Nazi control to Austria, Poland, France, and Belgium, the program began
to include children from these countries.

ADMISSIONS OF UNACCOMPANIED CHILDREN, BY YEAR OF ARRIVAL

1934	53
1935	106
1936	76
1937	92
1938	74
1939	32
1940	118
1941	260
1942	88
1943	127
1944	9
Total	1,035

As to the parental stock of the total group, 621 were of German parentage, 249 of Polish, 57 of Austrian, 40 of Spanish, 12 of Czech, 12 of Russian, and the remaining 44 children were of Hungarian, Rumanian, Syrian, or Portuguese parentage.

The number of boys (627) sent over on the program exceeded the number of girls (408). The tendency to send boys rather than girls was much more marked in the early years of the migration. The children ranged in age from 2 to 16. Three-fourths of them were 12 years old or over. Since some of the children arrived here as much as ten years ago, a sizable number of the group have now attained adult status. These children came from middle-class and lower middle-class families. In most cases the fathers had earned their living through business or commercial pursuits.

SELECTION OF CHILDREN

As larger and larger numbers of Jewish families were affected by forced impoverishment and other forms of persecution, it became clear that the program for unaccompanied children could never hope to bring to this country all the children needing adequate care. The Jewish organizations aiding in the selection in Europe favored those children in direst need. Later, when the lives of all Jewish children were menaced, the agencies concentrated on the rescue of any children for whom a chance to escape remained open.

Children selected for immigration to the United States under this program had to meet definite qualifications. They must be under 16 years of age, physically and mentally healthy, and to come from normal homes. They must be children whose parents were willing to have them leave home and who had no relatives or friends in the United States financially able to provide acceptable individual affidavits of support. The agency did not propose to bring children here for adoption, but rather to leave the way open for eventual reunion with the parents if that proved possible. Children were not to be included on the program if their parents had been able to secure affidavits on a family basis. However, in the rush to rescue as many individuals as possible in the period following the pogroms of 1938 this ruling was somewhat relaxed, and some children were brought over whose parents had been able to obtain affidavits; a number of these parents later succeeded in coming to this country.

SPECIAL EXPERIENCES OF UNACCOMPANIED CHILDREN BEFORE ARRIVAL

The children arriving on this program had for the most part faced particularly disturbing experiences before coming here, for in the main they represented the children on whom persecution and war had borne with unusual hardship.

Leaving their parents was inevitably one of the most painful of their experiences, in part because of the ominous outlook for the parents' future. A few children have written accounts of their leavetaking. Some of them, such as the following, written by a boy who left Germany in 1936, reconstruct the atmosphere of the home they were forced to leave:

This was the morning of my departure. . . . At 5 o'clock my father called me. I dressed in my best clothes and went downstairs to eat breakfast. The table was laden with all kinds of cakes. I sat down without saying a word, for I could not find anything to say, although usually I am scarcely bothered with having to hunt words. I had always been fond of cake, especially the ones my mother had baked for me that day, but somehow I was unable to eat them, and the chocolate milk did not at all suit my taste. I finally dropped my attempts to eat, when I saw that the appetite of the others was not exactly good either.

Then came the saddest moment of all, the moment I dreaded more than all the troubles in life. I had to bid farewell to my parents and sister. . . . The time flew by, minutes seemed seconds, and at every tick of the clock my heart beat faster. Only 15 minutes yet. My hand was resting in my grandfather's. I dared not look up, dared not look at his face, that cheerful always smiling face, that was now wet with tears. Then he kissed me with fervor and murmured an indistinct goodbye and good-luck. Then I rested on my mother's breast. No longer could I hold back my own tears. She said nothing, she only held me, pressed me against her body and wept. . . .

States a boy who left Germany in 1938, and after spending two years in children's homes in France came to the United States:

"Our parents' sacrifice in sending us away was great, but greater was their love for us to see us happy, free and joyful. . . . One part of my heart was full of joy because of having escaped from a land of slavery, but the other part of my heart was dark, full of grief for my parents and all my folks who were left behind."

Most of the children brought to the United States after 1941 came here after years of wandering, hardship, and uncertainty. Many of the children had been forced to say farewell to their parents under particularly painful circumstances. The terse summaries in their case records often tell a tragic story:

> Her father was sent to Dachau in 1938. In 1939 she went with a transport to a children's home in France. She lived in three different colonies there. Her father was released from Dachau, but her parents were expelled from Germany to the Camp de Gurs in 1940. She saw her father for an evening, her mother for six minutes before she left France.

In June of 1941 a group of 111 children, assembled from children's homes and refugee camps throughout unoccupied France, arrived in the United States in one shipload. An account of these children has been written by the doctor who with his wife had served as their escort on the train from Marseilles to Lisbon. When he collected them at the Marseilles Quaker office, he found that "on their thin, tired faces was written a heartrending tale of suffering and privation." His description of the beginning of his train trip with them follows:

> As the train begins to get under way, I consult my list of names and begin to acquaint myself with the boys and girls. On each child's white identification card are several descriptive phrases which tell a pitiful story. On one card I read: "Father died in concentration camp at Buchenwald." Another declares: "Mother died in French internment camp at Gurs." A third adds, "Parents sent to Lublin." Only two words appear on a fourth: "Parents unknown." I suddenly find myself choking and gasping for air. Ashamed to let the children see my tears, I hurry out of the car.[2]

This trainload of children passed through Oloran, the nearest station to the Camp de Gurs, where some of the children had previously been interned and where many of them still had parents and relatives. Through the intercession of the Organization for Protection of the Health of the Jews it had been arranged that the train make a stop there so that the children might bid their parents farewell. The doctor describes the scene of the reunion:

> The train is approaching the station at Oloran. All the children rush to the window in anticipation. "They are here!" they shout as they bend forward. With a screeching of brakes, the train comes to an abrupt halt. A loud cry, more piercing than any mechanical noise, suddenly rends the air. From the train comes the answering call of over a hundred shrill voices. Mothers, fathers, and kin, with the last ounces of strength in their frail bodies, suddenly tear through the cordon of gendarmes and dash to the doors of the train. Their scrawny hands, quivering with excitement, are raised to quiet the young ones. As the children pour out of the train, their parents and relatives hug them tightly, forgetting for this moment that their own clothes are indescribably dirty

[2] I. Chomski, "Children in Exile," *Contemporary Jewish Record*, October, 1941, p. 522.

and shabby. They haven't the time to take such matters into consideration. The train leaves in three minutes. These moments never will return.

He goes on to say that, before the children left, they tried to cram into their parents' hands and into their mouths bread which they had saved, unbeknown to their escorts, from their day's rations.

As to the fate of the parents of most of these children, it is easy to hazard a guess that few survived. Some concrete information is already available through agency records. After the end of hostilities further information concerning the fate of the parents began to be sent to the agencies from Europe. A large proportion of those about whom information has been received have been ascertained to be dead. In no case so far have both parents left in Germany been found to have survived.

Besides the Jewish children, there were many others whose lives had been gravely disturbed prior to their entry into this country. The forty Spanish children who arrived in the United States in 1942 had faced a particularly long period of migration and life in refugee camps. Belonging to families who had served the Loyalist cause during the Spanish Civil War, most of them had been evacuated from their original villages as early as 1936, had been forced back in a series of evacuations, as the front receded, until with the collapse of the Loyalist forces they had fled to France for refuge. Many of them had lived through bombings and had lost one or both parents or brothers and sisters during the war. At the time they were invited to come to the United States, some of them had been reunited with the surviving members of their families and were living under conditions of privation in Marseilles and near-by communities, but the majority were being cared for in Quaker refugee camps.

Among the children arriving in this country in 1943 and 1944 were several who had had particularly perilous adventures. Some of these children had learned at an early age to live by their wits, and had done much of the planning for their own escape. Confronted by constant danger, having to depend on begging and thieving much of the time for a livelihood, a number of these "lost children of Europe" had of necessity drifted away from the moral code of their families in their struggle to survive. More basic, however, than the habits they had acquired during their years of wandering was the effect of this experience upon their emotional development. Some had spent so much of their lives away from their families that they had never known close relationships with other human beings and had little capacity for affection.

ARRIVAL IN THE UNITED STATES

In spite of the upsetting experiences they had faced, the refugee children who arrived in the United States before 1941 were surprisingly normal in appearance and behavior, although a number of them were undersized and showed other effects of undernourishment. It was only those who arrived in the later years, after a long period of wandering and life in refugee camps, that lived up to the picture of pathetic waifs that the term "refugee children" is apt to bring to mind.

The children who came during the earlier years tended to accept their life in the new country with a healthy optimism. They enjoyed the adventure of the trip across the ocean. To many of them the arrival in America was the realization of a long dream, a release from the hardships and humiliations of life in Europe. As one boy describes the entrance of his ship into New York harbor:

"Every one of us felt overjoyed and our eyes were wet with tears, thrilled at the sight of this land of liberty and justice for all. My dreams were finally realized—being in America."

As soon as they arrived in New York these children began to enjoy the sights and thrills of the big city. People who expected to feel sorry for the refugee children were sometimes surprised (almost disappointed) to see them shouting and waving from the windows of trains and buses, and to realize that, in spite of all the suffering they had witnessed, they were "just kids."

These children rapidly identified themselves with their new country. Reports made by individuals in charge of their reception agree that they were in the main surprisingly normal in behavior. However, some of the children, especially those who had recently been separated from their parents, showed symptoms of extreme homesickness upon arrival, cried themselves to sleep at night, and did not join into the activities of the group. But the distress of many children at the separation from their parents was eased by the conviction that by coming to America they could help rescue their parents. They set out without delay and with extreme determination to try to obtain affidavits for them. This raised a real problem for the agencies sponsoring their entry, because from the viewpoint of the immigration authorities the admission of these refugee children was to be undertaken in such a way that it not be used to augment adult immigration. It was hard to explain this to the children, however.

Naturally there was great variation in the reactions of the children to arrival here, depending upon their recent experiences and upon their general personality make-up. Younger children were nearly always bemused and bewildered for a time. The children who came during 1939 and 1940 were found to be much more obviously upset and shaken by their experiences than those who came earlier. Anxiety about their parents and concern over their own placement were, moreover, shown in various ways, such as by hyperactivity, aggressiveness, voracious eating, bed-wetting, suspiciousness, and fearfulness, symptoms which are commonly observed among children separated from their parents. Yet on the whole the behavior of even the arrivals during this late period was amazingly normal.

The children arriving here after 1941, who had spent years in refugee camps or in children's homes or in wandering, were generally too far below par physically and too confused emotionally to enter immediately and enthusiastically into the life of their new country. These children had to be retained in reception homes or institutions for a considerable time until they were ready for foster home placement. It was found to be impossible to escort them around New York to see the sights, as had been done for the earlier arrivals. They had neither the energy nor the interest. It was a sufficiently new experience for them to get used to having enough food to eat and to be able to play a few simple games in the yard of their reception home. Sad-eyed and serious, having struggled for long to maintain life itself, they had to learn how to play and be children again. But the recuperative power of children is extraordinary. Most of them started to gain weight immediately, some as much as 10 to 20 pounds within a few weeks. Only a negligible number failed to show rapid physical progress.

The attitudes of the new arrivals toward America were interesting and varied. Many had heard so long of America as a land of fulfillment that they expected everything about the country to be wonderful and perfect. This was especially true of the younger children and those from less sophisticated environments. A number of these children had the attitude of little urchins entering into fairyland. Common was the notion of America as a land of plenty, to be enjoyed to the fullest. As one small girl shouted to her previous companion in parting at the station: "I wish you loads of fun, lots of ice cream, and lots of money!" ("*Viel Spass, viel ice cream, und viel Geld!*")

Other children who were older and came from a more sophisticated environment showed a more intelligent curiosity regarding America. They were full of questions about the new communities to which they were to be sent, and sometimes surprised the social workers with the fund of accurate information they managed to acquire before they started on their new journey. Other children were especially interested in such questions as the treatment of the Negro in the United States, and the role of anti-Semitism. Some of these children insisted on being taken for a tour of Harlem shortly after their arrival. They asked many questions regarding democracy and American institutions.

It was clear that, although many children were still suffering from their experiences in Europe and were preoccupied by concern for their families, most of them were eager and ready to embark upon their new life in this country.

SEPARATION FROM PARENTS

The children who came to this country without their parents, either on the program for unaccompanied children or directly to relatives, faced an especially difficult problem: they had to become adjusted to separation from their own parents and to living in a foster home as well as to life in a new and strange country. In general, this, like other phases of their adjustment, was rapid and successful, although some of the children were upset for a long time by the loss of their parents. The younger children were usually most upset and bewildered by the separation during their early days here. Although they felt the loss of their parents most acutely at first, like most young children they were usually better able to accept substitute parents and in the end to make a more complete adjustment than the children coming at a later age.

The emotional reactions of the children to being sent away from their parents depended in part on the situation in Europe at the time they left. The children who left home in the early years of the Hitler regime could see less plainly the necessity for being sent away, and this affected their emotional adjustment. Children who came in the later years were usually well aware of the reasons why their parents had sent them to America. Their chief source of anxiety was concern over their parents' fate. Those who arrived while emigration from Central Europe was still possible were in many cases preoccupied with efforts to secure affidavits and sponsors for their parents' immigration to this country. In the great majority of cases, however, the immigration of the parents was prevented by deportation or the outbreak of war, and the great hopes of the children were shattered. Those children who arrived in the later years when rescue was impossible were often gravely disturbed by anxiety over their parents but had to face the fact that there was no possibility of bringing them aid. Case records describe the reaction of some of these children. For example:

When the social workers at the reception home visited R. B., a boy of sixteen who had left Europe shortly after his parents' deportation to Poland, he was found to be very tense and depressed. He said he could not run around like the other children. His heart was too full. He could not forget his thoughts about his parents. . . . He had been reading the *Aufbau* and had learned of the mass slaughtering that was still going on in Polish towns among the Jews. . . . Later R. agreed that there was nothing for him to do to help his family. As sad as it was, he had to face this. . . . R. was stammering badly that day, another symptom of his inner strain.

Although the anxiety of some of the children regarding their parents was very obvious, in other cases it was expressed only indirectly and many children had apparently begun to adjust to the separation by the time they reached this country. This was particularly true of the children who had already been separated from their parents for some months or years before their arrival in the United States.

The contrast between their own living conditions and the privation being experienced by their parents often aroused strong emotional reactions. Plentifulness of food sometimes seemed to have such an effect. To quote from two case records:

> I believe that part of Luis' attack of homesickness was produced by the three large platefuls of eggs which appeared at the breakfast table following the cereal and toast. We found with several of the refugee children a very deep sensitiveness to "plenty" of any kind, which reminds them of the lack of these things which their parents are experiencing.

> G. appears to have a compulsive desire to consume a great deal of food very quickly at every meal and appears to "shovel" the food into his mouth, as if afraid that he will not be able to get any more. For a long time he would cry about his mother at every meal, saying that here he was being able to have something to eat and he did not know what his mother would be eating.

It is hard to tell what proportion of the children continued for years to feel deeply their separation from their parents or to know just how much they suffered from it. Many children tended to cover up their real feelings and to speak little of their parents. Yet it is clear that for a large number the separation was far from easy. While escape for the parents was still possible, many children bent every effort to help them come to this country, spent nearly all of their free time at work, saved every cent, and tried frantically to secure affidavits for them. Some of the children showed an amazing adaptability in accepting the tragic fate of their parents, even after years of hope and effort in their behalf. The following case history is typical of a number of children who showed themselves to be able to carry on and to identify themselves with their new life and country, even after tremendous emotional frustration.

> Kurt, like many other refugee children, was brought to this country through the efforts of a social agency and placed in a foster home. When he arrived here his chief aim in life was to help rescue his father and mother. He wanted to go right to work to save money for this purpose, and only gradually became reconciled to the fact that he had to go to school and could work only after school hours.

> Although helping his family appeared to be his sole concern, he did his school work well and willingly and made a number of friends. He continued to plan and work for the rescue of his parents. In February, 1939, however, came the news that his father had died in a concentration camp. This was a heavy blow to him, but he bore it stoically. He then redoubled his efforts to help rescue his mother.

> In spite of all his anxieties and his full work schedule, Kurt adjusted himself surprisingly well. He did excellently in his school work, was interested in school activities, and

wrote for the school paper. He did much Red Cross and other war work, and was especially honored by being sent to Washington as a delegate to a Red Cross convention. In addition, he played basketball and was a member of several young people's clubs.

In January, 1940, Kurt received the shocking news that his mother, too, had died in a concentration camp. In spite of this tragic experience and the utter failure of all his plans he continued his normal life with courage and purpose. He was graduated from high school with honors. He was very eager to enter the army, but was rejected because he was an "enemy alien." He appealed his case successfully and was finally inducted. Upon being made a citizen while in training, he wrote to his foster parents as well as to the agency that helped to bring him here that this was the greatest day in his life and that he was "mighty proud" of what he believed to be his greatest achievement. He was sent overseas for combat service. His foster mother is anxiously awaiting the return of her "hero son."

The concern of children over their parents and their grief at separation were not always so obvious. Sometimes children seemed to wish to draw a veil over the early part of their lives, and seldom mentioned their parents, yet nonetheless missed them. The subject was almost too painful for them to wish to discuss it. Occasionally some child who for years had given the appearance of having become happily reconciled to the parting would break down and blurt out a story of loneliness and heartache which he had long tried to mask.

Although there is ample evidence that many refugee children found it difficult to accept separation from their parents, the large majority appear to have finally become adjusted to it. Most of them have been able to fit into their foster homes and build up warm relations with their foster parents, to enter happily into their work and play, and to accept the responsibilities of approaching adulthood. They seem to have pushed back from their consciousness the memories of sadness and pain in order to make the most of what life in their new home has to offer.

Adjustment in the Foster Home

The placement of these children in foster homes in communities throughout the country was pivotal to the generally good adjustment they have made. Their integration into normal American home life facilitated their cultural assimilation and gave them an entree into the social life of the community.

In all cases homes were selected with great care to accord with the religious background of the children and their special needs. Both free homes, in which the foster parents accepted financial responsibility for the child, and boarding homes, subsidized by child-caring agencies, were used.

After placement in foster homes, the children were continually supervised by local child-caring agencies under the guidance of the national organizations sponsoring their admission to this country. The children were told that if they were not happy in their foster home they could try another. Transfers or new placements were made whenever it seemed to be to the best interest of the child. Sometimes the adjustment in the foster home was smooth and rapid, and a warm emotional relationship between foster parents and child soon developed. In other cases adjustment was slow and was preceded by a period of difficulties in finding the right home for the child and in settling misunderstandings with foster parents. Whereas with the younger children a close emotional relationship was often rapidly established, with the older children this usually developed only gradually from more impersonal relationships.

An analysis was made of the degree of success in foster-home adjustment of those children who were not later rejoined by their parents. Of these children, 71.4 per cent eventually succeeded in making a good adjustment to their foster homes. Most of them were declared to have been accepted as family members and to have established close relationships with their foster parents. The extent to which these children considered their new homes real homes is shown by the large number of the boys in the Army who have returned to them when on furlough and by the active correspondence they have carried on with their foster parents.

On the other hand, there were some children whose adjustment was in general satisfactory but lacked the positive elements described above. These children adjusted to their new homes on a "boarding home" basis. That is, they faced no real problems in the home but failed to accept their foster parents in any sense as real parents. Some of these children still felt close ties to their own parents and did not wish to build up close relationships with other adults. For instance, certain children when asked why they did not call their foster parents "mother" and "dad" would explain that they had "parents in Europe." The majority of the children who thus remained emotionally aloof from their new homes were those who arrived here after the age of 11. By and large, most of the children, even the older ones, found a satisfactory life in the foster home.

In some instances adjustment in the foster home, while not a failure, was nevertheless not clearly satisfactory. These were rated as only "fair" adjustments. They represented 19.6 per cent of the total. Included among these cases were older children who did not have a long enough time under foster-home care before they became self-supporting and moved away. Other placements though of longer duration, were never really successful but represented a sort of *modus vivendi* relationship. In these instances, personality traits of the children often made adjustment difficult. On the other hand, difficulties were presented by lack of understanding and warmth on the part of the foster parents, by their setting too high standards and thus creating tension for the children, by overemphasis on discipline and conformity, and by other shortcomings.

The foster-home adjustment of some of the children was completely unsuccessful. Such cases, rated "poor," represented 9.0 per cent of the total. Some of these children had to be removed from foster homes and placed in institutions because they seemed to be completely unable to adapt themselves. Others remained in the home but were thoroughly difficult and unhappy children. In some instances the difficulties were caused by inherent personality traits of the children, in others by the traumatic parting with their parents which resulted in hostile, suspicious attitudes toward adults, in negativism and defiance, or in complete lack of emotional responsiveness. Even the most understanding foster parents sometimes found it impossible to establish a satisfactory relationship with such children.

About one-fifth of the children who came over on the unaccompanied program were placed at least for a time with relatives, most of whom were subsidized by the agency for the care of the children and all of whom were supervised. Placements with relatives were not always successful, however, and nearly 20 per cent of these children were later transferred to other homes. The analysis revealed that the number of good adjustments with relatives was slightly lower than with other placements. In general, the records of this group indicate that children sent to the homes of relatives needed supervision by children's agencies as much as those placed in foster homes.

We have already noted that of the 1,035 children coming over on the program, 218 were later joined by one or both parents who succeeded in immigrating into the United States. In some cases children were very happy to be reunited with their parents, and their adjustment was considerably improved in consequence. In other cases problems were presented by the reunion, because the children had already accepted their foster parents as parents, were well Americanized, and somewhat resented having to share their parents' tribulations in adjustment. But most of the children seemed proud and happy to welcome their parents and help them become established in the new homeland.

PERSONALITY PROBLEMS IN ADJUSTMENT

It was in the sphere of emotional development that the impact of refugee experience struck with greatest force on the children. Whereas the adult refugee faced many problems of adjustment as an immigrant, in learning to adapt himself to a new country and its culture, this phase of adjustment took place automatically for the young refugee. His chief difficulties resulted rather from the emotional upset consequent to his uprooting and other painful experiences during the formative years of his personality development.

The majority of refugee children are now described as "normal, happy children," and many made an easy, smooth adjustment to life in this country, but it is clear nevertheless that a sizable proportion gave evidence of being emotionally disturbed for a period of time after their arrival here. Some of the children who in the end made a successful adjustment passed through a difficult period before their fears and feelings of insecurity were overcome.

A good many of the children appeared to be nervous and restless for a time after their arrival. Some of them stuttered or showed other symptoms of nervous tension. Others displayed their insecurity through aggressive behavior, or were shy and withdrawn for a time.

According to evidence from the schools, a small number of refugee children presented rather serious problems for a time. In all these cases the maladjustment could be explained either by the experiences of the children before leaving Europe or by the attitudes of their parents. One little boy, who was "all jerks" and whom the school found impossible to teach, had, it was discovered, seen his grandfather tortured and killed before his very eyes. One little girl, who was nervous and run down, could not sleep, lied, and was difficult in the group, had been bombed and evacuated from her home before being brought here by her parents. Another little girl who had been in a bombing and conflagration was subject to "mob hysteria." Although her behavior was normal at other times, whenever a large group assembled she would begin to scream and become hysterical. She was a problem for a year or so, but after that her symptoms disappeared and she made a satisfactory adjustment. Some children who had experienced Nazi persecution seemed for a time to imitate their Nazi oppressors, laughed and jeered at other children and bullied them unmercifully. Of several children exhibiting such abnormal behavior, independently reported by different schools, most were declared to have overcome these tendencies in a few years. Sometimes when the source of the child's anxiety was removed the behavior improved rapidly. For example, one boy who was deceitful and a troublemaker in school had parents in a concentration camp in France. As soon as word came of the liberation of France his social attitudes began to change and he rapidly achieved a normal adjustment.

Many times the maladjustment of the children was clearly traced to the parents. Usually a nervous child was found to have parents who were even more nervous, and an arrogant child a very arrogant parent. Many of the parents were having difficulty in becoming adjusted to this country and their poor adjustment was reflected in the children. As the parents gained security the children's symptoms of maladjustment began to diminish. Sometimes the attitudes of the parents created problems for the children. Some parents were overambitious for their children (or "extra-energetic," as one principal expressed it) and pushed them too hard toward academic achievement. Occasionally parents seemed overeager to reassert their rights in this land of liberty, and at times encouraged their children to indulge in antisocial behavior on the theory that they were in a land where they could do as they pleased. In one or two instances reported by schools such attitudes were marked enough to constitute severe maladjustment of both parents and children.

Whereas adjustment problems of children coming here with their parents were often related to those of their parents, children coming here unaccompanied, as we have already seen, faced emotional problems resulting from the traumatic separation from their parents or from the emotional isolation in which as wanderers or refugee camp inmates they had lived. Some children among the later arrivals presented problems, less because of emotional maladjustment than because of the peculiar habits they had acquired or their lack of understanding of accepted values. Some children had lived by their wits for a long time in Europe, begging and stealing in order to sustain life. Some had been accustomed to searching for their food in garbage cans and continued to do this even after reaching this country where it was no longer necessary. Naturally these children took a while to learn normal social standards as well as to make other adjustments.

The role of the social case worker in aiding the adjustment of the group of unaccompanied children was most important. These children were constantly supervised by a social agency until they reached the age of 21 and those with special problems were given intensive case-work treatment. The response to such treatment was in general excellent. Analysis of the case records of the unaccompanied children reveals that in 67.6 per cent of the cases the personality adjustment was good, in 27.8 per cent fair, and in only 4.6 per cent poor.

SOCIAL ADJUSTMENT

A predominant motif in all material regarding refugee children is the theme of their rapid cultural and social adjustment. To quote from some community background reports:

The children have moved more rapidly and further [than the adults] in the direction of community participation. They have found American friends, participate in American interests and activities, and in culture, speech and other areas have become quite American. (Peoria, Ill.)

The children have shown the greatest progress. . . . They are participating in community life to the fullest. Their friends and contacts are non-sectarian as well as Jewish. They have quickly absorbed the American way of life. (Rochester, N.Y.)

Schools likewise report that the refugee children have within a short time been accepted by the other children, have often been elected to school offices, and have been granted their due place in all extracurricular activities. Some teachers believe that refugee children have even been exalted by their schoolmates because of their distinctive backgrounds. Failure to adjust has been solely an individual rather than a group problem, according to nearly all reports.

Many of the life stories include glowing accounts of the successful cultural and social adaptation of the younger members of the family. The following is typical:

"My children entered school immediately we arrived in San Francisco. They overcame the language difficulties very rapidly and especially my son was promoted very quickly. They made friends with American boys and girls and felt from the beginning that they were fully accepted. While my children at the time of our arrival in New York did not speak any English, they spoke it quite fluently by the time we arrived in San Francisco [a few months later]. They lost their foreign accent very quickly and my daughter has brought home quite a few trophies from oratory contests. My son went through high school with straight A's and graduated as a life member of the California Scholarship Federation. He started college with a scholarship and has taken great interest in the associated student's organization. He was president of the honor student society and is the president of the Student YMCA in B———. He is acting president of the Race Relations Committee and of the Fair Employment Practices Committee at the university. He enjoys social life too and believes that outside activities are just as important as his studies."

The ease and rapidity of social adjustment appear in general to vary inversely with age. The older children, who remembered more of the European background, found it relatively difficult to make new friends and accept a new cultural pattern. Many of the young refugees responding to the general questionnaire, who arrived in this country at the age of 15 or older, mention the fact that they had some trouble in finding friends, especially among native Americans. They also mention the fact that problems were created by their different cultural background. Similar evidence appears in the records of the unaccompanied children. The proportion of children achieving a good social adjustment was higher among those children who arrived here at an early age than among those who were older. This proportion varies from about 80 per cent in the case of children coming under the age of 8 to about 40 per cent of those coming between the ages of 13 and 16.

For the unaccompanied group, as for the other children, the major instruments of social integration into the life of the young people of their community were the schools, the Scouts, the Y's, and various neighborhood groups. On the other hand, the social adjustment of numerous refugee children was handicapped by out-of-school employment which their straitened circumstances made necessary. Many of these children did part-time work after school and on Saturdays in order to earn their own spending money or in order to save money for the purpose of eventually helping their parents to immigrate to the United States. Some of the children, however, carried an amazing schedule of work and study and yet found time to hold important school offices and to take part in other school and community affairs. Another factor which retarded the social adjustment of some of the refugee children, as revealed by the records of unaccompanied children and the reports of schoolteachers, was the serious religious attitude of many orthodox Jewish boys. Some of these boys devoted so much of their time to religious studies during their first years here that they found little time for play and friendships. Most of these children, however, tended to become more relaxed in their religious attitudes after a few years in this country and to fit into the less orthodox pattern of the American Jewish community.

THE REFUGEE STUDENT

Young refugees as a group have made a fine showing in the schools and colleges they have attended in this country. All schools participating in the study declared that refugee children had shown remarkable adaptability to their new environment. Although some children had shown the effects of their unfortunate experiences during the first weeks or months in school, most of these had made rapid strides in overcoming their anxieties and gaining a sense of security. Most schools declared that the refugee children had been well accepted by their schoolmates, had received their share of elective offices, had mixed easily with the other children and entered into extracurricular activities. A number had won outstanding popularity in their school group and attained positions of leadership. Records of refugee students in colleges also show that those who had been in any sense a problem were an exception to the rule.

All schools emphasized how rapidly the children had learned English and become Americanized. At the time the survey was conducted, in 1945, four or five years after the peak of refugee immigration to the United States, most of the children, especially those in the elementary schools, were indistinguishable from the other children. Only through consultation with school records was it possible to locate the refugee children and thus to provide specific information about them.

It is clear that language presented only a temporary handicap for the children coming here before the age of 16. In some schools special classes in English were set up during the years when the largest number of refugee children were enrolled. In general, however, the schools did not find it necessary to set up special English classes, but adopted instead the plan of placing the children for a time in classes below their proper level, where they could learn the language without special aid, and then promoted them rapidly. The refugee children, moreover, learned a great deal of English just by associating with other children. In general, the younger they were the faster they learned. Only those above elementary school age on arrival had difficulty in losing their accent.

A number of the refugee children knew some English before they entered the schools. Some had studied it before leaving their homes in Europe; others had spent some time in England en route to this country and arrived here with an "Oxford accent."

In spite of language handicaps the academic work of the young refugees has not only been up to standard, but by many educators is considered to have been above the average of American students. There is no doubt, moreover, that in proportion to the size of the total group there has been an unusual number of outstanding students at all levels of education.

The marked proficiency of young refugees in their school work has been conspicuous in communities throughout the United States according to the reports received. In New York City, where a special study was conducted of refugee children in the schools, the general opinion was held that the group as a whole had made a superior record, or at the least that it had contained an unusually high proportion of outstanding students. Even at the elementary level many schools commented on the good work done by refugee children, and their general interest in their studies. At the high school level there was greater evidence of superior work. All high schools commented on the large number of refugee children who had made the honor societies of the school.

Further light is thrown on the caliber of the school work of refugee children by the case records of the thousand unaccompanied children. Information on this point was available for about two-thirds of them. Of the total known group, 33.7 per cent had done very good or outstanding work in school, many of whom had been awarded special honors, prizes, and scholarships; 31.9 per cent had done good work, 26.9 per cent fair work, and 7.5 per cent poor work. There were more boys than girls with an outstanding academic record.

Various explanations are given by different educators for the unusual showing of young refugees in the field of scholarship. A number of them believe the explanation to lie in the selective quality of refugee immigration, that in the main only the more intelligent families were able to plan and effect an escape from Nazi Europe. Others stress not the native intelligence of the group, but the great emphasis placed by refugee families as a whole on scholarly achievements. They feel that the intellectual environment of refugee families provides a stimulus to studious endeavor and gives refugee children an advantage over young Americans. Some educators do not believe that as a whole the young refugees are a superior group so far as native intelligence goes, but that the good work habits, thoroughness, and precision learned in European schools, combined with greater striving in the educational field, have produced a superior record. Also it appears that, especially among the older children, young refugees who have had difficulties in social adjustment tend to concentrate all efforts for recognition in the field of scholarship.

Schools often commented that rather than constituting a problem the presence of young refugees had contributed much to the life of the schools. They had stimulated interest in world affairs, in languages, in literary and artistic pursuits, as well as awakening new interest in scholarship itself. Most of the colleges which gave scholarships to refugee students also commented on the real contributions these students had made to campus life through their breadth of outlook on international affairs and their wide cultural interests.

OUTSTANDING YOUNG REFUGEES

An incontrovertible fact in the story of young refugees in this country is the large number of outstanding and talented individuals among them. From all sides accounts were sent in of young people whose achievements had been truly amazing—children here only a few years who made distinguished academic records, were accorded places of prominence in school life, and were already launched upon promising careers. Nearly all schools could cite numerous instances of young refugees who had been valedictorians of their class, won contests, been awarded prizes and scholarships, or distinguished themselves in musical, literary, or artistic lines.

One refugee boy from Vienna who was graduated from George Washington High School in New York City in 1945—a high school with an average enrollment of 4,000 students—made the highest record of any student attending the school in the last twenty-five years. Graduated at the age of 16, after five years in this country, he won the Hearst National American History Prize of $1,000 and several other important prizes and medals. At this same school, another refugee boy, from Hungary, who was graduated a year or two before, had made the second highest record in a quarter century. He had been valedictorian of his class, president of the honor society, president of the mathematics club, president of the chess club, and in general taken a prominent role in school life. Examples of young refugees of similar achievements in various communities throughout the country are too numerous to cite. A number of them have obtained scholarships and fellowships for graduate study in some of the nation's leading institutions. Some have already made notable scientific contributions through their own researches (one young scientist was present at the atomic bomb test off Bikini Atoll in the Pacific). Several are teaching at well-known colleges and universities.

It is possible to quote only one or two examples of the many accounts received that reveal the high caliber of some of these refugee children. Here is a statement written early in 1945 at the request of a local co-operating committee by a refugee boy in New Jersey who arrived in this country at the age of 12 and is now 18:

I started at the age of twelve in the regular Public Grammar School, in the first grade. Within less than two years I graduated from this grammar school with Honor Roll grades. In high school, from which I shall graduate this month, I have done well; I am the valedictorian of my class, and have been voted "the one most likely to succeed." In school I have had many activities. I have served on the Student Council for many terms, at times being member and chairman of different committees. I have been elected to membership by the faculty of the school to the National Honor Society. I served as president of the Mathematics Club, as acting president of the Public Speaking Club, later as chairman of the Program Committee. I am a member of the Advisory Council to the Student Council, and have been chosen by the principal to serve on the two-man Assembly Planning Committee. Because of the shortage of teachers, I have often substituted. . . .

I have also done my share in the war effort. I am serving as a captain of a group of fire-watchers under the Civilian Defense setup. My greatest contribution, however, is in the field of bond selling. I originated the idea, which by now has spread all over the country, of Youth Bond Drives. The High School Club Council of the local Y.M.-Y.W.H.A., at my insistence and under my leadership sponsored two such Youth Bond Drives. . . . During the Youth Bond Drive, we were on WPAT daily for five minutes for two months; I wrote all the scripts. December 7th, I conducted a whole hour and a half program on WPAT. During Youth Week, I was program director of station WPAT.

This paper almost sounds like bragging, but it was not intended for that purpose. I have purposely omitted my name. Besides the things I have mentioned I have done many other communal tasks some of which I do not want to mention. . . . I hope this paper will show that all immigrants do not merely take from America, but also contribute. This matter of immigration is a "give-and-take."

The following is an account of a Polish youth who came to this country in 1941, with his parents and a younger brother:

Having had only one year of high school in Poland, he had difficulties with his admission to the University of California in Berkeley. After much endeavor he was admitted on the condition that if his average record for the Inter-session and Summer session were B, he would get a chance to take the admission test. He got A's in all subjects and was admitted as a regular student to the department of chemistry without examinations. In two years and three months he finished the four year course and got his B.S. degree with honors. He earned the sympathy and respect of his professors and classmates both on the campus and in the International House where he lived more than a year, and was elected vice-president of the board in charge of the men's department.

During his studies he did research on war chemistry problems, and was elected to Sigma Xi, the honorary scientific society. The professors with whom he did research on war chemicals proposed after his graduation permanent collaboration, which would have meant deferment from military service. He declined the offer, however, to enlist as a paratrooper. In 1944 he was killed in action in Germany.

YOUNG REFUGEES IN THE ARMED FORCES

The marked patriotism of young refugees from the elementary grades up is the source of constant comment. Having learned at an early age the meaning of tyranny and oppression, liberty and democracy have great significance for them, and with the idealism of youth they are less critical than their elders of the shortcomings of their new homeland. "Why I Love America," "What America Means to Me," "Old Glory," are subjects frequently chosen by young refugees for essays and poems. Through them, many schools report, a new appreciation of the blessings of America is given the other pupils.

It is not surprising, therefore, that young refugees entered into the fighting forces of our country with unusual enthusiasm in the recent war. The case records of the boys coming over on the unaccompanied program tell a striking tale of patriotism. Many of the boys tried to enlist, but were prevented by their "enemy alien" status. One boy went so far as to enlist with the Canadian Air Force and was later killed in action.

In the end, of the 352 boys on the unaccompanied program who had become 18 before 1944, 259 are known to have served in the armed forces. Others undoubtedly also served, but record is lacking because they had passed from agency care. At least twelve are known to have been killed in action.

GENERAL ADJUSTMENT—CONCLUSION

Refugee children have adjusted themselves to life in this country with relative ease and speed as compared to the older generation. This might be expected, for the young are in general much more adaptable than their elders, and acquire a new language, new attitudes, and new customs with greater facility. Moreover, refugees who came here at an early age were spared the profound cultural and psychological conflicts springing from strong attachments to the old country and a former way of life, which complicated the adjustment of many adults. Whereas the older refugees were subjected to the strain of disrupting well-established careers and lifelong associations and starting anew, young people have been able to plan their life and work in terms of the adopted country.

Refugees, in their life stories, often recount the details of the rapid progress of their children in school, their swift assimilation, and their favorable reception by other children. Although some refugee parents complain that their children have become so completely Americanized that they reject their cultural background and show no interest in the old-country language, customs, and values which still have meaning for the adults, the majority of these parents are proud of their children's success in becoming adapted to America. Many adults who have experienced difficulty in becoming adjusted to life in this country derive their greatest satisfaction from the successes of their children and from plans for their future.

Community reports, which are concerned with the broad outlines of the adjustment of the total group of children, rather than with individual variations, present a uniformly bright picture of their successful adjustment.

There has, of course, been much variation in the type of success achieved by individual members of the group. There have been failures, and other cases where adjustment has been dubious. In general all evidence indicates, however, that such cases constitute a small proportion of the total.

Special data regarding the proportion of children attaining a generally good over-all adjustment is presented by the Study Committee's analysis of the case records of the more than one thousand refugee children who came to this country unaccompanied by their parents as the charges of child-caring agencies. These records were studied with the object of evaluating not only the adjustment of each individual child in the home, the school, and the community, but of estimating how adequate the over-all adjustment had been. Special reports from case workers aided in the appraisal. The study rated individual children in the group according to the degree of their success in adjustment from "very good" to "poor," with the following results:

12.8 per cent of the children, rated as "very good," have made a conspicuously good adjustment in all areas of life and are in general outstanding because of their well-rounded personalities and unusual potentialities.

45.0 per cent of the children, rated as "good," have likewise made a successful over-all adjustment, are emotionally well balanced, are leading a normally active social life, and have very good chances of becoming happy, responsible adults.

20.8 per cent of the children, rated as "fairly good," have also made a satisfactory adjustment in the home, the school, and the community, but one which contains less positive elements than those in the first two groups.

16.4 per cent of the total group were rated as having made only a "fair" adjustment. This rating indicated that the children continued to face problems which made their future somewhat uncertain. Some of the children rated "fair," however, may still be in the initial process of adjustment, requiring a longer time than most children to make the transition.

3.2 per cent only of the total group were rated as having made a "poor" adjustment. This rating indicated that the children were thoroughly maladjusted people. They had failed to adjust in nearly every area of life and continued to present problems of behavior and emotional instability.

In 1.8 per cent of the cases sufficient data for evaluating adjustment were not available.

Factors of sex and nationality background seem to have played only a minor role in the adjustment of these refugee children. Girls and boys adjusted themselves with almost exactly the same degree of success. Nationality background likewise was found to have no important bearing on the type of adjustment achieved, although children of Polish and German background had somewhat higher ratings than those of other national stocks, even when the year of arrival, as indicating different circumstances of emigration, was taken into consideration. Only the unaccompanied Austrian children had made a conspicuously poor record. This was probably the result of the rapidity with which the Nazi regime had overtaken Austria, and the poor preparation the children had received for leaving home.

The type of adjustment made by the children varied to some extent with the year of their arrival in this country. Although the children arriving in 1934, the first year of the program, made a high percentage of successful adjustments, those coming in 1935 received a lower rating. This large group of children had perhaps been selected less carefully than the smaller group coming the first year and had placed a heavy strain on the newly organized program. Children coming in these earliest years, moreover, were less able to see the necessity for being sent away from home, and this affected their adjustment. Children coming during the years 1936 through 1939 made a better showing in general than those arriving later. This was doubtless in part the result of the less extended periods of hardship and persecution they had suffered before reaching this country. The fact that those who have been here only two or three years may still be in the process of adjustment must also be taken into consideration. On the whole, even the children who had spent years in wandering or in children's homes or refugee camps responded remarkably well to the conditions of their new life and many have made a good general adjustment.

The degree of success in adjustment is related in some measure to the age at which the children reached this country. In general those who arrived here at an earlier age have made a more successful adjustment. This is easy to explain because younger children are in the main more adaptable, find it less difficult to accept substitute parents, and are more apt to forget their past life. On the other hand, although those reaching here at 16 have failed to make as large a proportion of thoroughly successful adjustments, none coming at this age has definitely failed (rated "poor"). This suggests a high degree of stability in the more mature group.

Persecution, flight, and in many cases separation from parents were experienced by refugee children at a critical time in their emotional development. It might be feared that such experiences would have proved so profoundly disturbing that an adequate adjustment in this country would have been gravely impaired. It seems clear, however, that in most cases no severe and enduring emotional injury was sustained and that the majority of the children were able to adjust themselves to life here with striking success.

Young refugees, on the whole, have proved a stable and responsible segment of American youth. They have made an excellent adjustment in the

GENERAL ADJUSTMENT OF UNACCOMPANIED CHILDREN BY AGE ON ARRIVAL

Age on Arrival	Total		Good		Fairly Good		Fair		Poor		Unknown	
	No.	%	No.	%	No.	%	No.	%	No.	%	No.	%
All Cases	1035	100.0	598	57.8	215	20.8	170	16.4	33	3.2	19	1.8
Under 5 yrs.	7	100.0	5	71.4	0	—	1	14.3	0	—	1	14.3
5 "	3	100.0	3	100.0	0	—	0	—	0	—	0	—
6 "	14	100.0	5	35.7	4	28.6	3	21.4	0	—	2	14.3
7 "	15	100.0	11	73.3	1	6.7	1	6.7	2	13.3	0	—
8 "	23	100.0	13	56.5	6	26.1	3	13.0	0	—	1	4.3
9 "	41	100.0	26	63.4	8	19.5	4	9.8	1	2.4	2	4.9
10 "	57	100.0	33	57.9	11	19.3	10	17.5	3	5.3	0	—
11 "	93	100.0	59	63.5	17	18.3	13	14.0	2	2.1	2	2.1
12 "	126	100.0	70	55.6	30	23.8	21	16.7	3	2.3	2	1.6
13 "	170	100.0	97	57.1	32	18.8	30	17.6	8	4.7	3	1.8
14 "	187	100.0	110	58.8	40	21.4	26	13.9	9	4.8	2	1.1
15 "	176	100.0	102	58.0	35	19.9	32	18.2	5	2.8	2	1.1
16 and over	123	100.0	64	52.1	31	25.2	26	21.1	0	—	2	1.6

home, the school, and the community. They fought bravely in the recent war. They appear in general to be a superior group who are making the most of their opportunities and who promise to contribute much to the enrichment of American society.

Scores of millions of Europeans were driven from their homes and millions from their native countries from 1933 to the end of World War II.

Over 1,000,000 were still homeless and uprooted in Central and Western Europe nearly two years after the fighting ended. Hundreds of thousands were in "DP" centers and refugee camps.

270,000 had found haven in the United States

Remnant of a refugee family (Photo from the Newspaper PM)

Tattooed death-camp numbers (New York Daily News Photo)

Concentration camp survivors reach New York

Immigrant refugee family (Photo from the Newspaper PM)

Many were welcomed by relatives after long separation. Voluntary welfare agencies aided their resettlement and Americanization.

Brother and sister reunited on a New York Pier (Photo from the Newspaper PM)

Father and Son

Man and family

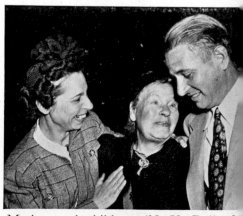

Mother and children (N. Y. Daily News Photo)

Many refugees were outstanding in the arts, science, and industry —"Hitler's gift to America."

arc Chagall, France, leading painter of the modern school

Jacques Lipchitz, France, noted sculptor

Konrad Heiden, Germany, author of

Otto Zoff, Czechoslovakian, author of

This country acquired twelve refugee Nobel Prize winners and hundreds of other men and women of almost equal distinction.

Hans Habe, Hungary, author of
"A Thousand Shall Fall"

Franz Werfel, Czechoslovakia, author of
"The Song of Bernadette"

Wanda Landowska, Poland, harpsichordist

Heinrich Mann, Germany, author of
"Henry, King of France"

same proportion as all Americans.

Sgt. Frederick Mayer of the OSS, decorated for exploits behind German lines

Sgt. Werner Katz of Merrill's Marauders, Burma campaign

Bernard Stern—(Left) German soldier in France, 1917—and the same Bernard Stern—(Right) American GI in Italy, 1944

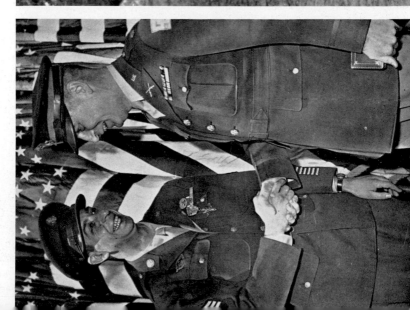

T/4 Leo Rosskamm, survivor of Buchenwald, receiving D.S.C. for heroism on Okinawa

Refugees introduced new industries employing many Americans.
Practically all soon were useful members of their communities.
Over 99 per cent planned to become United States citizens.

Refugee war worker

Former refugee now an American farm

Small plant making a new confection, started by refugees

CHAPTER XIV

BUSINESSMEN AND MANUFACTURERS

Business and professional people constitute the most important elements among the refugees who came to the United States. Hence, their adjustment and activities as well as their problems should be considered in some detail. Special chapters on these groups follow, with material based not only on the general questionnaire returns but also on the findings of special questionnaire studies, the analysis of the records of various special committees dealing with these classes, extensive interviewing, and other types of investigation.

The largest of these classes as to occupational background—indeed, the largest single occupational group among the refugees—is that of owners, proprietors, and managers of business and industrial establishments. Questions concerning them to which answers were sought include the following: In what types of business or industry were they engaged abroad, and in what types are they engaged here? To what extent have they continued in the same field? What special difficulties or advantages have they experienced in transferring their activities from Europe to America? How well have they fared? Have they created employment opportunities for American workers? Are they competing unduly with American businessmen? Are they producing any goods not previously manufactured here but imported? Have they introduced any new products, new processes, or new skills? Have they developed our foreign trade? Have they produced materials for use in the war effort? What in general have been the economic effects of their immigration? To have attempted to make a census of refugee business enterprises and to follow out all the complicated ramifications of their activities and the economic effects upon the country would have been beyond the scope of the Study. It is possible, however, from the results of various sample studies and other data to arrive at a pretty clear indication of the role of the refugee in this field of economic endeavor. These sources and the main findings are cited below. The case of refugee farming enterprises is treated separately.

Our general questionnaire returns included replies from 2,604 individuals who had been in business for themselves in Europe before being forced to emigrate. Of this group 31.2 per cent (slightly higher among the Christian than the Jewish refugees) had been engaged in manufacturing, 56.2 per cent in wholesale or retail trade (appreciably higher among the Jews than the Christians), 2.2 per cent in export-import, 1.9 per cent in finance, 6.6 per cent in services, and the balance of 1.9 per cent in other fields. These enterprises ranged from small individual or family undertakings with no outside employees (3.4 per cent) to large firms with over 100 employees (14.6 per cent), sometimes with several thousand. Half of them had more than 10 employees. The general picture is that of a fairly substantial business group.

The number of respondents to the general questionnaire who were in business for themselves in the United States was appreciably less, namely 1,006. About two-thirds of them were the same individuals who had been in business in Europe; the rest entered business for the first time in the United States. Immigration has therefore involved a considerable loss to the business group. Most of them had suffered confiscation or destruction of their business in Nazi Europe and most of them have been unable as yet to establish themselves in business here. Of the various types of businesses, wholesale and especially retail trade appears to be the most readily transferable, as measured by the percentage of those who were in the field abroad and have continued in it here; finance ranks second in this respect, closely followed by manufacturing, while export-import and service businesses rank fourth and fifth.

Some of the refugee businessmen and industrialists experienced no difficulty in establishing themselves here. These were mainly persons who had been in America before and knew the country and language, who had connections here which they had established when in business abroad, who managed to bring over considerable capital, or who possessed special skills and patented processes. In numerous instances the refugee merchant or manufacturer had been conducting a business that had been in his family for generations and which he had begun to learn at an early age. Among Europeans—especially, it would seem, among Jews—it has long been the custom for the son or sons to enter the father's business, beginning as a sort of apprentice, learning all aspects thoroughly, and eventually taking over. This accumulated skill plus knowledge in some instances of special processes and trade secrets proved to be an asset not only in Europe but in setting up in business here. Some of the refugee manufacturers even brought special machinery with them from Europe. In a special study made of 271 refugee business enterprises (questionnaire form is included in Appendix B), it was found that 60 per cent of them were the same as had been conducted in Europe. Similar findings were reported in an investigation made of refugee entrepreneurs in 1941.[1] This high degree of transferability was marked in

[1] Sophia M. Robison, *Refugees at Work*, 1942, pp. 41–45.

the clothing, leather, and diamond industries and in the field of general merchandise.

Much more commonly the refugee businessmen have experienced great difficulties in occupational adjustment in this country. The majority of them have thus far been unable to go into business for themselves and have taken clerical, skilled labor, and other jobs. Many were not prepared to go into business because of their insufficient knowledge of English, of conditions in this country, and of American business methods. When they attempted it under those circumstances their business ventures not infrequently failed. It was also not easy to start a business during the depression or later during the wartime scarcity of materials. Moreover, many of them lacked adequate capital. A few, including some large capitalists, managed to get out of Europe most of their wealth, amounting in all probably to several hundred million dollars, but the majority, especially those coming after 1938, had suffered confiscation of their property, forced sales, or other losses. Some of these started in business here on a shoestring, some were aided in establishing business enterprises by loans from refugee-service agencies—especially men over 40 for whom the opportunity for employment was limited and self-employment appeared to be the answer—while others took selling or similar jobs while they acquired sufficient experience and capital to venture on their own. As examples of the assistance given by refugee service agencies, the following cases are typical:

Mr. R. and his wife had manufactured fine quality handbags in Paris before they were forced to emigrate. Escaping with only enough money for their passage, they arrived in the United States in 1942. Mr. R. found a job but had to give it up because of ill-health. The Central Loan Trust, affiliate of the National Refugee Service, decided that the R.'s could become self-supporting if they were financed in setting up their former business, and accordingly granted them a loan of $850. With this as a springboard they were able to obtain additional financing and re-establish their enterprise. They now employ 10 workers in their plant and are expanding their business. They have repaid the money advanced to them.

The local refugee committee in Indianapolis secured a loan of $500 for Mr. H., which with his savings enabled him to buy a grocery store. By arranging monthly payments to the former owner, he paid off the entire debt within eighteen months. The interviewer, watching Mr. H. wait on his customers, was impressed by the courtesy and friendliness existing between them. Mr. H. belongs to the Retail Grocers Association of Indianapolis and is most cooperative in abiding by their rules and regulations.

The following illustrations of how they got started are taken from the case histories of refugee business enterprises which were obtained by the Study Committee in co-operation with the American Federation of Jews from Central Europe.

"About one year I was employed in a department store," states the owner of a food products concern in Indianapolis. "During this time I was eagerly learning the American language and American business ways. Then I started with a small capital as wholesale wagon jobber in distributing food. Today I employ four people and my customers are glad to deal with us."

"I started business in 1939 with an investment of approximately $10,000 which I managed to bring with me to this country. At first, only my brother, also a refugee, helped me, and we had no other employees. Today we are a partnership and employ an average of over 30 people, and are doing quite well." (Manufacturers of decorative linens in New York)

"When I came to this country in 1939 I had exactly $4.60 in my pocket. I worked for the Fuller Brush Co. for about four months, left New York City, and settled in New England. At first I traveled for a small concern for about 16 months and after that I started my own business with all the savings I was able to make, $90." (Wholesale confectioner in Boston, with a present capital investment of $5,000, and employing 7 workers, 3 of whom are native Americans)

A German shoe manufacturer who had employed about 2,000 people came to New York in 1939 where he opened a factory, starting with very few employees. He now employs 250, all but 25 of whom are Americans.

"I started in 1941 with no employees and with no experience," says a manufacturer of shoulder pads who in Germany had run a printing plant. "After one year of struggling along and acquiring experience, I expanded gradually. We now have an established enterprise with a name for quality pads for which there is a bigger demand than the existing firms can handle." (Employs 35 workers, most of whom are refugees)

Frequent are the stories of great struggle at first, of lack of knowledge and experience, of inadequate capital, and of beginning in a small way with no employees. Not uncommonly the business was started in the home with the assistance of the refugee's wife and children, and later moved to a factory loft where employees were hired. Thus, a food specialty company in Brookline, Massachusetts, with a nation-wide distribution was founded in 1939 in a home kitchen, a leading firm in the manufacture of plastic jewelry in New York City was started by a refugee couple in 1940, an infants' shoe factory in Philadelphia now employing 15 workers was started by a refugee and his wife in their two-room apartment, a leather goods concern in Boston which occupies 10,000 square feet and employs 40 workers was begun by a refugee who styled a sample line in his home with the help of his wife who stitched the items, and a ladies' apparel manufacturer in Albuquerque whose "garments are styled so differently that there is no competition to speak of" and who cannot now "fill even a small portion of our orders" started in business in his home with the assistance of his wife. Similar instances of the establishment of successful businesses, large and small, from such meager beginnings by dint of hard work are numerous; they include a great variety of products or goods and come from communities throughout the country, including such widely separated cities as Boston, New York, Trenton, Philadelphia, Pittsburgh, Buffalo, Chicago, Peoria, Indianapolis, Milwaukee, St. Louis, and Austin.

The following life story, written by a refugee who had been an executive of a large knitting mill in Vienna and who eventually established a similar business in Cleveland, is an eloquent testimony of the resourcefulness, capability, and high standards characteristic of many refugee businessmen:

"The first few days in New York were a big disappointment. I was forlorn in strange surroundings; the fright of persecution and deportation were still in my bones. I would have been very glad to get some real advice as to how I, with my previous experience, could best fit into a new life in a new country which I wanted to make my home forever, and which I desired to serve by every possible means.

"As I had a cousin in Cleveland, I left for Cleveland on April 10 by bus. Arriving at Euclid Avenue on a dark rainy day, the outlook was drab, dismal, and depressing. So this was to be my home! I waited at the bus terminal an hour for my cousin to pick me up, because I had informed him the time of arrival, but did not know of the difference between Eastern time and Cleveland time.

"As my small supply of money had dwindled I started out immediately to look for a job. The biggest handicap was the lack of language, of which I had some knowledge, but in which I could not express myself fluently. I was looking around for days, calling on strange people, sometimes getting a warm welcome, sometimes refused admittance, sometimes offered some money, which I refused because I did not want charity. I wanted work, but couldn't get it. At one time I didn't eat lunch for two days, to save a few cents for carfare.

"I finally got some work in a mattress factory. After talking to the owner for an hour, he told me he was very sorry that he had no work which would be suitable for me. I saw the dirty windows in his factory and offered to clean them for him. He seemed surprised, and, glancing at my good quality expensive-looking European suit, he asked me if I was really serious. My answer was, of course, that I was ready to start right away. He said my clothes were too good for such work, to come back and start the next morning.

"I rushed to tell my cousin the good news and right away to buy some work clothes. I could not wash the windows after all, because I was not a member of the Window Cleaners Union, and so started to wash the walls in the showroom and then did general porter's work for 25 cents an hour. This work seemed heaven to me in spite of the fact that I wasn't used to it and that my hands became infected by the chemicals used in the cleaning preparation. But I had a chance to talk with some of the workers in the factory, improve my English, and learn about unions, wages, hour and labor laws, etc.

"I still tried to get into the trade which I knew best in Europe. I was employed for almost 15 years as an executive in one of the biggest knitting mills in Vienna, which had 3,600 employees and branches all over Europe, and had gone through all departments.

"After six weeks, through some recommendations, I finally secured a job in the designing department of one of the Cleveland knit-goods manufacturers, but my knowledge of designing was of no value to them because my tastes called for too expensive merchandise, too expensive for the low-priced mass production articles of this concern. After a slack season I was laid off and tried to go into the knit-goods business from another angle.

"I started in the packing room of another firm, giving out home work, but left this job for the reason that the working hours were too irregular. Two days a week I was taking a course in English and History and had to leave at five o'clock, which wasn't always possible. The woman who ran the factory told me she couldn't see why I wanted to go to school. She said when she came to this country she worked 7 days a week for $5 and did not go to school and 'look where I am now!'

"After searching again for three or four weeks somebody advised me to go to New York because there was more opportunity there for a designer. I borrowed some money from a relative, went to New York in July, without knowing a soul, and walked the hot pavements for weeks trying to get a job as a designer. . . . In New York I could not obtain a job because there was a strong union, and I did not have the money to pay the initiation fee.

"So, back to Cleveland, where I finally found a job as a machine operator. With my small knowledge I would have been considered just a beginning apprentice in Europe, but here I found I was actually considered a knitter! . . .

"In the back of my mind there was always the thought of starting my own business. In a year and a half, after gaining more knowledge about American working conditions, combined with knowledge I brought from Europe, I thought I was ready for that big enterprise of my own.

"Accordingly, I went to New York, bought one machine, rented a small room for $20 a month, light, heat, and cleaning included. I kept on working at my job, working nights, Saturdays and Sundays in my own place. . . . Finally I obtained enough business to permit me to quit my job. I bought another machine, hired another man and three more girls.

"I had to devote more time to outside contact work, running around for supplies, trying to sell, etc., so in order not to leave my machine idle I hired a second man. Business started to grow. I came in contact with a sales organization which secured more business for me, so I decided upon expanding. I bought eight more machines, rented a bigger space, and after I had convinced myself that the business would be a success I felt no hesitation in borrowing some capital to finance the expansion. I started to manufacture on a real scale. My payrolls kept on growing. I soon employed 40 people. The bank readily loaned me money on Accounts Receivable, because they were all highly rated in Dun and Bradstreet. . . . Although I did not relax my quality standards I was able to price them on a mass production basis, which is possible only in the United States. . . .

"I tried to keep my factory going for 12 months a year, and can proudly say that since 1940 we never laid off our workers for lack of orders. We sold our products the first three months of the year for delivery from April to October, and we always had enough re-orders to keep production going without interruption. Through the arrangement with the bank I was able to finance my production for advance deliveries at a low rate of interest. Interest payments naturally gave me a lower net profit, but kept the place going the whole year, and assured my employees steady work. This was at a time when other knitting mills were working seasonally and laying off workers for periods of a few weeks to a few months at a time.

"My first 7 employees were all experienced native Americans. Later on, however, I started to train male refugees, mostly in the older age group, because I knew from my own experience how hard it was for a man of 40 or over to find any kind of a job in this country. This later proved to be a lucky stroke for me, because having older men, I was not so hard hit by the draft regulations and the flow of labor to war plants, and as the men increased in skill, their wages, on a piece-work basis, increased accordingly. At the present time we have 15 men and about 40 women working.

"From the start I was shocked at conditions in factories here. I wanted to improve the working conditions in my own place, figuring out that working people, including myself, spend at least one-third of their lives at work, and that they should have surroundings as comfortable and as pleasant as possible. I started with improving the lighting, installing a fluorescent light for almost every man and one or two such lights over each work table.

"Lack of money prevented me from doing more then, but I tried to do my best. I was always a firm believer in sharing profits. From the first year in business I started to give a small bonus to all my workers at the end of the fiscal year, which I have continued to do within the limitations of present Wage Stabilization Laws.

"In the summer of 1943 the government took over the building where we were located and we had to move. At the time it seemed like a disaster. It entailed heavy expenses and a lot of other things. It turned out to be fortunate, however, because I secured space in a downtown building occupying one and one-half floors. Now part of my dreams were realized as I could improve the working conditions considerably, by providing for the workers a larger, lighter and airier space, attractively painted in soft colors, and by adding some more and better equipment and lunch rooms for men and women.

"It was not an easy task to pull through the critical time of the war, when I was sometimes faced with the possibility of a complete shutdown for lack of materials because of our equipment not being adaptable for government work. But somehow we struggled through and I managed to keep our organization together. . . . As soon as conditions permit I am ready to put my plans for further improvements and expansion into effect. I may be able then to provide work for about 50 more people.

"At the present time we have six men serving in the armed forces, whom we promised jobs when they return. But one, who was a refugee from Italy, will never return. He was killed in action, back on his native soil, on the beachhead of Anzio.

"On the whole, America, my adopted country, has treated me far better than I expected. My own experience has taught me that anyone having resourcefulness and determination can achieve as much of a success as any native American.

"America is the country of opportunity if you don't lose courage in the beginning stages. Actually, one's former experience and abilities are never really lost, but it may take some time until one really finds himself and creates a satisfying, constructive life."

As is evident in the cases cited above, refugee businessmen have opened up employment opportunities for both Americans and refugees. Hence this type of immigration has not been competitive with American labor but just the opposite. Also, by providing employment opportunities for refugee workers, refugee businessmen and industrialists have not only kept them from competing with American workers but have aided materially in their adjustment. As was indicated in the life story just cited, they have given jobs to older refugees, among others, who would have found it otherwise difficult or impossible to secure employment. Moreover, in a number of instances they have retrained refugees who were unable to pursue their former calling, such as lawyers, teachers, other professional and business people, and given them a means to self-support.

Exactly how many Americans have been given jobs because of the establishment of refugee enterprises is unknown, but several sample studies indicate that the number is considerable. To be sure, most of the new enterprises are small; the majority of the thousand businessmen who replied to the general questionnaire had fewer than five employees each. Some 27 per cent of them employed between 5 and 100, and 2 per cent more than 100. There were several instances of machine tool manufacturers with over 200 employees, of textile concerns with over 300, and of shoe manufacturers with over 500. The largest refugee business enterprise known to the Study Committee was a munitions plant in the New York area employing 1,700 people. One thing is clear: the proportion of Americans among the employees of refugee business enterprises is very high. A study made in 1939 of 64 refugee firms revealed that 734 or 78 per cent of the workers were Americans, while 206 were refugees.[2] In a survey made in 1941 of 715 such enterprises, employing approximately 9,000 workers, two-thirds of the employees were Americans.[3] The special study of 271 refugee enterprises conducted by the American Federation of Jews from Central Europe in co-operation with the Study Committee disclosed that 80 per cent of the 8,620 employees were Americans.

It is also significant that in not a few instances refugee businessmen have opened up factories that had been idle and given employment to Americans who had long been out of work. For example, a former German industrialist has restored prosperity to the small city of Waverly, Iowa, by reopening a sugar refinery which had been shut down for two decades. A refugee textile manufacturer in 1941 rented a mill that had been closed for two years to produce the same merchandise he had manufactured in Europe; he expanded his business to include a second mill, and exported his product to Sweden and South American countries. The plant operated by another refugee concern manufacturing sole leather had been idle for some years and the townspeople who had been wholly dependent on it were unemployed and on relief. Under refugee management the capacity of the plant has been expanded, its product improved, and the level of wages raised. An American machine and tool works that was failing was acquired by two refugees who had been in that industry abroad. They revived and expanded the business and recently moved into larger quarters. Two refugee diamond cutters, six weeks after their arrival here in 1939, set up in

[2] National Coordinating Committee, *Survey of Refugee Business Enterprises*, 1939, manuscript.
[3] Sophia M. Robison, *Refugees at Work*, 1942, p. 52.

business and hired 15 cutters who had been unemployed for years. These are but a few illustrations of the economic advantage to this country, especially in the period before wartime prosperity, resulting from the introduction of refugee capital and business enterprise.

The capital investment of 158 refugee business and industrial enterprises which replied to this question in the Study Committee's special questionnaire ranged from less than $1,000 (9 cases) to over $1,000,000 (1 case) and totaled between $10 and $12 million. The value of the average annual production, as reported by 191 firms, was under $50,000 in the case of 30 enterprises, between $50,000 and $100,000 in the case of 24, between $100,-000 and $1,000,000 in the case of 111, and over $1 million in the case of 26. These figures are not presented as typical or representative of all refugee business enterprises, since the total situation is not known, but merely as indicative of the contribution to the economic life of the nation which they have made.

The gain to the United States from the immigration of refugee businessmen is further evidenced in the new types of products, new processes and skills which they have introduced. Some indication of the fields of business which they have entered and where they have made these contributions is given in the following table covering 880 such enterprises. These data were obtained from the replies to the special business questionnaire the Study Committee utilized and from a classified list of refugee business firms compiled by a philanthropic fund-raising organization in the New York area. A breakdown by nationality also is given.

Since small retail merchants were excluded from both lists, these 880 firms may be taken as typical of the more substantial refugee business enterprises. They also represent types of enterprise that are characteristically European innovations here. Certain of them call for special comment because of their relative importance or of special interest.

Outstanding in many respects among the refugee business enterprises in this country is the diamond industry. Until Hitler overran Europe, Antwerp and Amsterdam were the diamond centers of the world. Thanks to his action, that position is now occupied by New York City. When the Germans invaded the Low Countries one of their first moves was to loot the diamond industry,[4] not only for the wealth in jewels but because the diamond industry is a powerful war industry. Before and during the invasion many of the diamond dealers, cutters, and polishers fled, carrying with them what stocks they could. About 4,000 polishers fled to Palestine, about 1,000 merchants and polishers went to Cuba, a few to England and other countries, but the largest single group came to the United States, estimated at about 1,000 Belgian-Dutch diamond merchants and 4,000 to 5,000 workers. It has been estimated that from 1936 to 1941 cut diamonds in the value

[4] Meyer Levin, "The World's Greatest Diamond Robbery," *Liberty*, March 17, 1945, pp. 28, 73.

TYPES OF REFUGEE BUSINESS AND INDUSTRIAL ENTERPRISES IN THE NEW YORK AREA, BY NATIONALITY BACKGROUND OF OWNER

Type of Enterprise or of Product	Total	Nationality Background of Owner											
		Austrian	Belgian	Czech.	Dutch	French	German	Hungarian	Italian	Polish	Russian	Swiss	All Others
Total	880	51	19	78	130	77	236	29	19	37	131	63	10
Banking, brokerage	76	3	1	6	14	12	25	3	1	—	3	8	—
Chemicals, synthetics, etc.	32	—	—	2	2	1	14	1	—	9	1	2	—
Clothing	40	4	—	6	3	2	10	1	1	—	9	4	—
Clothing accessories	30	3	—	3	—	4	8	—	—	1	5	6	—
Cosmetics	16	1	—	1	4	6	3	—	1	—	—	—	—
Decorative arts	21	—	—	1	—	6	11	1	—	—	—	—	2
Export-import	58	4	2	4	6	6	20	—	5	—	6	5	—
Food products	32	4	—	4	6	1	13	1	1	—	2	—	—
Furs	52	3	1	1	2	13	—	1	2	1	28	—	—
General merchandise	25	4	—	5	2	1	4	1	1	1	4	2	—
Gloves	18	1	—	1	1	1	9	1	—	1	2	1	—
Hides and skins	32	3	—	2	—	—	18	—	1	1	7	—	—
Housefurnishings	17	3	—	1	1	—	4	1	1	—	2	4	—
Jewelry and diamonds	143	3	14	7	47	20	8	6	—	6	14	18	—
Leather goods	17	3	—	—	—	—	10	1	—	1	2	—	—
Machinery and machine tools	29	1	—	8	4	—	6	—	—	1	7	—	2
Metal and mineral products	30	—	—	1	2	1	19	1	—	—	4	2	—
Novelties and toys	26	2	—	3	—	2	18	—	—	1	—	—	1
Publishing and printing	19	1	—	1	6	—	5	1	1	1	3	—	—
Real estate and construction	29	—	—	—	4	2	5	7	1	3	6	1	—
Shoes	15	—	—	3	1	—	6	—	1	1	1	2	—
Textiles	32	1	1	3	5	—	3	2	1	4	4	6	3
Tobacco	14	1	—	—	5	2	3	—	1	—	2	—	2
Miscellaneous	77	7	—	16	14	2	14	4	1	3	14	2	—

of $132 million were shipped to the United States;[5] in addition a large quantity of rough or unprocessed diamonds were brought in.

Prior to this immigration there had been a small number of diamond merchants and producers, organized in a Diamond Dealers' Club, with about 500 employees throughout the country. There are now two other clubs: the Diamond Center, Inc., with a membership of 580, at least 90 per cent of whom are refugees, and the United Diamond Manufacturers Association, with a membership that overlaps with those of the other two groups. As was the case in Europe, these organizations are essentially merchant guilds and exchanges. The Study Committee compiled a list of 424 diamond firms operated by refugees. They were not included in the above table since information on the nationality of the owners was not obtained. With the growth of the diamond industry here, the diamond workers have become highly organized. A long period of apprenticeship or training, ranging up to three or more years, is required to become a highly skilled worker. In Europe it was the custom to charge for apprenticeship. Here the practice became modified and the apprentices are paid, but at a low rate. They are induced to undertake this long period of training for minimum wages because of the high earnings of experienced workers, which average $100 a week and reach as high as $400 a week for the more skilled artisans. Many Americans have entered this trade, being taught by the skilled refugee workers.

The Netherlands and particularly the Belgian government are anxious to have the diamond merchants and producers return. During World War I, when the Belgian diamond people had to flee, they found refuge in the Netherlands, but after the end of the war they returned to Belgium when the government offered many inducements. This time, however, many will not return. Not only is the economic situation abroad uncertain, but there is fear that anti-Semitism in years of German occupation has left its impression. Some of the larger merchants, especially the Dutch, will likely return, but the chances are that many, if not most, will remain here and that New York will continue to be a world center of the diamond industry.[6]

Along with the diamond workers, recent immigration has included an appreciable number of jewelry manufacturers and of highly trained jewelers—especially French and Austrian—experienced in original artistic as well as skilled work. Some were international leaders as stylists and fashion designers, and many of their products have been original enough to receive American patents. These high-grade jewelers have readily found positions at high salaries with either American or refugee jewelry concerns. During

[5] Sylvia F. Porter, "Refugee Gold Rush," *American Magazine*, October, 1942.

[6] Data on the diamond industry obtained through interviews with the president of the Diamond Center, Inc., the secretary of the Diamond Workers Union, the president of the International Jewelry Workers' Union, officials of the Belgian Embassy and Information Center, from articles in *Aufbau*, Oct. 27 and Dec. 20, 1944, and from questionnaire returns.

the war, some of the jewelry firms were converted to make medical instruments for the Army and Navy.

Numerically prominent in the list of refugee businesses given above are the bankers, brokers, and other financiers. Actually, many of them have found it difficult to adjust themselves since their knowledge of finance was limited to conditions in Germany and other European countries. A few individuals, such as the former executive of the Berlin Chamber of Commerce, succeeded in obtaining leading positions in large American banks, and a few financial houses of international reputation were able to establish firms which have achieved recognition, but many of those who salvaged considerable capital from their former homelands have not been able to put it to productive use. Some have maintained themselves by clever manipulation of their capital and have established themselves as brokers or obtained positions in American financial houses. Some have engaged in speculation in the stock market or in real estate; this is discussed in another chapter where certain complaints against refugees are considered. If international banking and finance, which is highly developed in London but of little significance in New York, should be further developed here in the postwar period, these people, by virtue of their knowledge of European conditions and languages, would be able to play a prominent role. At some future time it might come about that the German and other refugee financiers will have promoted the development of commerce in the United States in a way similar to what the Spanish refugees of an earlier century did in Amsterdam, Salonika, and London.[7] As is mentioned in detail below, refugee businessmen have already exerted considerable influence in the development of American export-import business.

Outstanding among other fields of business which refugees have entered are furs, clothing, textiles, leather goods, food products, chemicals, and machine and precision tools. Certain nationality differences appear, as revealed in the preceding table. For example, the French are concentrated in the luxury trades, the Russians are outstanding in the fur industry, the Belgians, Dutch, Russians, and Swiss in the jewelry and diamond industries, the Germans in chemicals, metals and mineral products, hides and skins, and novelties and toys, the Czechs in machinery and machine tools, and so forth. In these various fields the refugees have frequently introduced types of business which they or their families had been carrying on for years abroad, producing articles not previously manufactured here. The following case histories, selected from among many, may serve as illustrations.

The ancestors of Mr. R., who came to the United States from Czechoslovakia in 1937, had been glaziers in Lieben, the Jewish suburb of Prague, for about 250 years. In 1830

[7] Walter Floersheimer, "Finanzmaenner im Neuen Feld," *Aufbau*, Dec. 22, 1944, p. 44.

his paternal forebears established a factory for glass products in northern Bohemia. One hundred years later the family employed 2,500 workers in their firm which exported Bohemian glass to the United States, East Asia, South America, and South Africa. When Mr. R. fled to the United States he brought along the well-established export relations of his firm and became export agent for a number of American glass factories. Besides that he developed a new photochemical process of glass printing and is now producing radio dials, advertising signs, and advertising mirrors.

The well-known Goldscheider ceramics works of Vienna, established in the eighteenth century, was taken over by the Nazis in 1938. The family came to the United States in 1939 and established the Goldscheider-Everlast Ceramics Works in Trenton, New Jersey. They employ 75 workers, some of them refugees who had been in their employ in Vienna, others American craftsmen including artists to create designs in line with American tastes.

The former manager of the Berlin metal industrialists association, forced out after the Nazis came to power, emigrated to France and then to Czechoslovakia where he studied the production of flints for cigar and cigarette lighters, gas lamps, welders' and miners' lamps, sparkling toys, etc. He established a plant in Prague in which the complete process of producing such flints was carried on. Previously the chemical and technical parts of the process had been done by different factories. The Nazi attack on Czechoslovakia forced him to emigrate to the United States. In 1939 he formed a partnership with another refugee, formerly a member of one of Berlin's leading metal industrialist families, for the production of flints here, in a factory in New Jersey. They invested $40,000 in their plant, and employ American as well as refugee workers whom they had to train for the special work to be done. The factory is almost unique in the world.

A German and two Viennese specialists in manufacturing art leather goods established a plant soon after their arrival here in 1939 for the production of pipe and tobacco pouches, pocketbooks and other leather goods of the famous Viennese kind. They design their goods themselves, which are sold in leading American stores and also exported to South America, Canada, and until the beginning of the war, to England and other countries. They use American sewing machines, leather, talon zippers, linings, etc. for their goods, which were formerly imported from Vienna. They employ American workers, whom they have trained, as well as refugees who were skilled in this work abroad.

Shortly before the attack on Pearl Harbor, a precision tool and die company was started here by some Austrian manufacturers to produce high-class precision instruments for civilian use, the same industry they had conducted abroad. With the outbreak of war, the company switched to war production, and has been awarded the Army and Navy E for excellence three times in succession. Based on the European system of highly developed individual skill, the company has developed a specialty and has introduced new methods and procedures. It has trained many refugees who were lawyers, clerks, or other white-collar workers abroad to be highly paid mechanics. The company employs "Americans, old immigrants and new immigrants from all over the world, whites, blacks, and yellows, males and females, of all nationalities and creeds."

Some refugee business enterprises are directly competitive with American. Others, although producing goods already manufactured here, are nevertheless noncompetitive since they represent export concerns which have been transplanted from Europe and which are continuing here their old export trade to South America, Africa, and elsewhere. Still others are noncompetitive inasmuch as they are producing goods not previously manufactured here but imported from Europe. Moreover, many refugee concerns have introduced new products, new processes, or new skills. Some inkling as to how extensive such contributions to American economy have been is given by the results of the special study combining questionnaire and interview methods which the Study Committee made in co-operation with the American Federation of Jews from Central Europe. Of the 158 refugee concerns in this group that were engaged in manufacturing, 69 were producing goods not previously manufactured in the United States. Of the total group, 50 had introduced new products, 22 new processes, 16 patents, 7 secret formulas, and 13 new skills. If the same proportion should hold true for the total number of refugee industries in this country, the result would be a considerable addition to the economic life of the nation and a source of increased employment opportunities.

The following are examples of refugee enterprises which have been a net gain to American industry:

Mr. T., a 51-year-old Dutch Jew, invented a portable hydraulic tool for bending pipes, which he has patented and is producing in Milwaukee. He found a ready market for his product because there was no such machine available here before. He is also exporting it to twenty countries.

Mr. W., who had been the owner of a factory making rubber shoes in southern Germany, employing 1,500 workers, created a sandal combined of a rubber sole and leather ribbons. He adapted this sandal to the American taste and had it patented in 1939. He is now manufacturing it "with American employees, using American machines, American leather, American rubber soles, and American accessories" for his product.

A former Austrian shoe manufacturer is manufacturing a new type of sponge rubber sole, for which he has a U.S. patent, in Waynesville, North Carolina, where he employs 320 workers. In near-by Asheville, a former German leather manufacturer is also helping to build up a new industry based on the same new manufacturing process utilizing sponge rubber. He employs 300 workers. Both have produced goods for the Army and Navy.

In 1941, Dr. Robert Freund came to this country with his secret formula for color printing and started an enterprise, called the Twin Editions, making color reproductions of art masterpieces. From art schools, art galleries, universities, and other sources have come appraisals such as these: "the finest and most accurate reproductions from oil paintings which have been made in this country," "a service which has long been needed in this country," "Americans can thank Hitler for one thing: they need no longer import the world's finest color reproductions of art masterpieces," "while the Nazis have senselessly stripped Germany and Austria of their finest talents, this country has gained immeasurably."

Space limitations prohibit further case illustrations. The following listing is therefore given of some of the new products being manufactured here in enterprises established by refugees. They are based on inventions and new processes and skills that were either introduced into this country from Europe or developed here. Many of them have been patented in the United States.

NEW PRODUCTS AND NEW PROCESSES INTRODUCED BY REFUGEE BUSINESS AND INDUSTRIAL ENTERPRISES

Chemicals, synthetics, etc.—Water plastic paint in powder form; emulsified casein paint; paint or enamel remover; "Mellolite," a new material for lamp shading; a chemically treated shoe polishing cloth; oxygen shaving preparation; the use of waste material for the manufacture of caffeine alkaloid, an essential ingredient for medicinal products; medicated bandages; an instant-dry ink.

Clothing and clothing accessories—New fur-lined coat; ladies' leather jackets; English-style woolen socks; hand-crocheted and -knitted sweaters, mittens, and slippers; high-grade knitted goods Viennese style; new clothing styles; shopping bags; knitting bags.

Decorative arts—A versatile bust form for window displays; new display materials; composition figurines; new designs.

Foods—A new kind of wafers; cookies; cakes; "Lebkuchen" (a kind of spice cake); a domestic cheese to replace an imported one; new types of candy; European chocolates; fruit preserves and syrup; a soluble coffee extract; process of dehydrating food; coatings for nuts; special packaging of extracts of citrus fruit.

Furs—Mouton, a new process fur, invented and patented by a Hungarian refugee.

Gloves—New types and patented processes of glove manufacture; rayon gloves; hand sewn leather gloves; knitted gloves and mittens.

Animal hair and hides—New qualities of hair as substitute for goods rendered unavailable by the war; special processing of raw wool.

Leather and leather goods—New upper leather splits; new lining splits; waterproofed sole splits; leather arch supports; various patented leather goods; hand-made small leather goods; fine leather billfolds and pocketbooks; leather compacts and cigarette cases; photo cases; wardrobe luggage.

Machines and tools—Portable engraving machine; slotting machine; milling machine; rubber mold for metal casting; new machine designs; special machinery for the nonferrous metal industry; new designs of tools and dies; drawing instruments; surgical instruments.

Novelties and toys—Miniature auto license plates for key rings; cataline match holders; sculptured dolls; figurines; new style of artificial flowers; new types of lamps; new toys and gift articles; toy animals; wooden toys, ladies belts, and other wood novelties; novelties for window displays; goods in "Florentine technique"; three-dimensional pin-up figures; novelties combining artificial leather and glass.

Publishing, printing, photography—Patented process of microfilm reproduction; color photography; quick photography; special kind of photo finishing; picture making in third dimension; a special photoelectric light meter; an electronic timer; new type of exposure meter; reproductive work from microfilm for public and commercial purposes; texted photo series for magazines; photographic archive; true color printing; quality prints; bookbindings; scientific publications.

Shoes—French boudoir slippers; infants' wear; sandals; new manufacturing processes; new styles.

Textiles—A new-process wool; tie fabrics; new kind of fabric called Timmie Tuft; hand-blocked linen fabrics; laces and embroideries.

Miscellaneous—Ski equipment; patented electric sign; package carrier; celluloid specialties; special kind of writing desk; lapel watch; new production in woodware; harmonicas and accordions; pitch pipes; various glass products; wax-treated spot carbon; a synthetic wax; fuel oil emulsifier and sludge remover; filtermass for breweries; Italian vermouth; "magic writing pad"; horsehair brushes; carved moldings; fine boxes for perfumes and cosmetics; new furniture designs; fluorescent fixtures; military laces.

In addition to the instances cited above, culled from the returns to the special questionnaire on business enterprises, there were a number of replies to the general questionnaire that mentioned the attainment of U.S. patents for such miscellaneous items as a new geographic globe, a coffee-brewing device, new gauges for open presser, self-setting table, a toy set, new type of agricultural tractor, a right and left turn signal device, a new diabetic food sweetener, a method of purifying drinking water, an automatic machine for the printing industry, an office folder, a new type of incinerator, and a score of other devices. We do not know how many of these items are actually being manufactured.

Many refugee businessmen and manufacturers have also reported to the Study Committee on new processes and secret formulas they have introduced in the manufacture of lotions and pharmaceutical products, including digitalis glucosides formerly manufactured only in France; in the production of synthetic rubber; in making wood alcohol from waste timber; in the manufacture of plastics, synthetic resins, and building materials, and numerous other chemical processes; in the manufacture of flavorings and drinks, the treatment of wood used in smoking meat products, the processing of meat, and the dehydration of food; in glass manufacture, the decorating of glassware, and electric sealing methods; in dyeing shoes; in textile printing; in manufacturing large decalcomania posters for advertising purposes; in weaving and knitting mills; in the manufacture of tools, dies, and precision instruments; in jewelry manufacture; in the production of airplane parts and munitions; and in scores of other ways.

Seventy-five of the 271 concerns answering our special questionnaire on business and industrial enterprises established by refugees produced goods for the war effort. In some of the instances they manufactured general merchandise items for the use of the armed forces such as gloves and mittens (one concern alone produced over 200,000 pairs for the armed forces), clothing, military lace, shoes, sleeping bags, leather bags for Wacs and nurses, dehydrated foods, soluble coffee, and countless other items. In other instances they manufactured directly materials used in warfare, sometimes doing highly confidential work and obtaining the highest priorities. The latter situation was especially true in the case of firms in the fields of chemicals and synthetics and precision instruments, and those engaged in research. A number of refugee concerns had munitions contracts and were awarded Army and Navy E's for excellence of product and for surpassing production schedule. One refugee set up a factory for manufacturing war materials out of powdered metal, a revolutionary process. The diamond and jewelry industries supplied essential material for making precision instruments and for equipping planes, tanks, warships, and submarines. A Polish engineer established a factory which manufactured rayon for parachutes. A German businessman produced safety devices for workers on aircraft machines. Other industrialists, technicians, and experts in many fields contributed greatly to the war effort, the full story of which has not yet been revealed.

Another distinctive contribution of refugee businessmen and industrialists to American economy, and one which will become of increasing importance in the postwar period, is the development of our foreign trade. Of the 271 refugee enterprises answering our special questionnaire, 72 were exporting or importing goods. Half of them were carrying on an export or import trade which they had developed before emigrating to this country. Prominent among the products they were exporting from the United States to countries all over the world (over 30 separate countries and every continent were specifically mentioned) were machine and precision tools, metal products, textiles, food products, novelties and toys, paper products, books, photo supplies, leather goods, animal hides and hair, clothing, shoes, and tobacco products. Goods in similar fields also were imported and in addition diamonds and other precious stones, jewelry, synthetics and chemicals, and wood products. In some instances the imported goods were of a type urgently needed for military purposes.

Many of the refugee businessmen engaged in export-import trade here are making use of their long-established business connections throughout the world. They brought with them their former customer lists, experience in foreign trade, and knowledge of the market. In some instances they are carrying on here an export trade they formerly had conducted from Europe. For example, a number of export businesses in animal hides and hair were transferred from European countries to New York; a Dutch concern with agents in the principal cities of the world transferred here its export business in construction materials, paper, and chemicals; some French shippers of wines and liquors now operate from the United States; and an 80-year-old German firm dealing in hops and tapioca flour is now carrying on its former business here. Some of these concerns are manufacturing for export products not previously manufactured here; others are exporting goods that formerly were exported solely or mainly from Europe. Many are now selling American merchandise to their former customers, utilizing their business connections and their special knowledge of the tastes and needs of the foreign countries. For example, a German concern exporting hardware was re-established in the United States and before the war started exporting American goods to the Scandinavian countries, the Netherlands, and elsewhere. It expects to open up extensive new markets for American products in various European countries, South Africa, and Asia where it formerly had business connections. A former Austrian dress manufacturer who sold almost his entire production to foreign countries states: "After having established my business here I contacted my old business friends and as a result of the confidence they had in me after our business dealings of several decades they have entrusted me with their orders for American merchandise." A German metal goods company with world-wide distribution, which has been transferred to New York, expects to expand its activities greatly when world trade is resumed; "we are only interested," the company states, "in furthering the sale of American products and are creating new markets for American manufacturers."

Especially noteworthy is the influence of refugee export enterprises in the South American field. Before the war most of the business with South America was in the hands of Europeans. An important reason for this was the intimate knowledge European exporters had of the requirements of these countries and their willingness to cater to their demands. Few American firms would bother to deliver to South American customers exactly what they needed. A number of European concerns that had specialized in this field are now, because of refugee immigration, continuing it from this country. Typical is the case of the German shirt manufacturer who transferred his factory here and is now employing American labor to supply his Latin-American customers as before, or the Polish exporter of pharmaceuticals who is carrying on his same business with Latin America but from San Francisco. Some of these refugee exporters have made suggestions to American companies regarding the making and packaging of goods in accordance with the specifications of South American customers, and some have developed an export business for American firms which had never exported before.

In thus furthering American trade with her southern neighbors the refugee businessmen have not only utilized their old connections but have established new ones among their relatives and acquaintances who fled to these countries. Besides the refugees who came to the United States, at least 125,000 went to Latin America and many thousands to other countries. Many of them have kept in touch with one another and established business connections. Thus the world-wide dispersal of refugees has laid a basis for the development of international trade. For example, a former dealer in complicated types of German and Swiss timepieces, who came to the United States where he represented two Swiss watch factories, has developed an export business with Central and South America through agents, old friends of his, who emigrated there. Or, to illustrate the reverse action, two German refugees in the United States have established a partnership for importing mahogany wood carvings from Haiti, a new industry that has been developed there by refugees of their acquaintance. It is not exaggerating to say that the refugee businessman and manufacturer have made the United States much more export-conscious than it was before and that the future will see an expansion of American foreign trade for which they can claim much credit. In this and other ways refugee immigration has demonstrably enriched American economy.

THE REFUGEE FARMER

The story of the refugees who have taken up farming provides an interesting chapter in the history of the occupational adjustment of the newcomers. Along with the 1,006 refugees replying to the Study Committee's questionnaire who became business owners here there were 194 who became farm owners. Of these, 180 were Jewish. Despite the popular belief that the Jew has neither desire nor aptitude for farming, there is much evidence in Russia, Palestine, the United States, and elsewhere that under favorable conditions this originally rural people, forbidden for centuries by the laws of European countries from owning land and engaging in agriculture, is eager to till the soil and can do so successfully. Some of the refugee farmers in the United States had been farmers or cattle dealers abroad. The great majority, however, had been business and professional people, who entered farming for the first time here, frequently after retraining.

The most important agency assisting refugees to settle on farms has been the Jewish Agricultural Society, which was founded in 1900 by the Baron de Hirsch Fund and the Jewish Colonization Association to encourage agriculture among Jews in the United States. It advises prospective farm buyers, helps in the selection of suitable farms, makes loans, maintains an agricultural extension department and a farm employment bureau, advises on all phases of farming, and renders other services. Beginning in 1935 it developed a special program to establish refugees on farms, and it opened a training farm for them at Bound Brook, New Jersey. By the end of 1944 it had settled 456 refugee families on farms in Connecticut, Florida, Illinois, Indiana, Michigan, Missouri, Massachusetts, New Hampshire, New Jersey, New York, North Carolina, Pennsylvania, and Virginia. Many refugees have also settled on farms independently. The society estimates that all told more than 3,000 of those who fled the Nazi terror are now securely anchored on American farms, and that the ratio of refugee farmers to the total body of refugees is already about the same as that of the old-line Jewish farm group (approximately 100,000) to the total Jewish population of the United States. Of the 456 refugee families settled through the efforts of the J.A.S., 412, or 90 per cent, are still on their farms. More than half the loans aggregating over $500,000 advanced to them have already been repaid and nearly the same proportion of the farm loans (some $63,000) administered by the society for other agencies, mainly the National Refugee Service. This excellent record is partly the result of favorable farming conditions; it also reflects the intelligence and enterprise of the refugee farmers.[8]

With the co-operation of the Jewish Agricultural Society, the Study Committee made a survey of refugees in agriculture, using for this purpose a special questionnaire regarding farm activities, to be filled out by the head of the farm family. This was to accompany the general questionnaire. One hundred and thirty-two replies were received. While twelve states, ranging from Massachusetts to California and from New York to Florida, were represented, nearly three-fourths of the replies came from New Jersey. Eighty per cent of the respondents were producing poultry and eggs. This concentration in area and in type of farming is a true picture as tested by the records of the Jewish Agricultural Society. The largest refugee farm settlements are in and around Vineland, Farmingdale, and Toms River, New Jersey; Binghamton and Middletown, New York; and Lebanon and Brooklyn, Connecticut. Next to raising poultry and eggs, dairy farming is the favored branch, accounting for 13.6 per cent of the cases. The remaining 6 per cent of the respondents were producing vegetables, livestock, field crops, forest products, and fruits and nuts.

Only about 10 per cent of these refugee farmers had been farm owners abroad. Some 60 per cent had been business owners, the rest professional workers, clerks, and salespeople. The various nationalities were represented in about the same proportion as in the total refugee group. Practically all the respondents were married, and the family members, most commonly two in number though ranging up to five, worked regularly on the farm. Most of the farmsteads were of the "family type," that is, farms that can be operated by the farmer and his family with a minimum of hired help, and where products are raised both for home consumption and for the market. About one-third of the farmers employed outside help, most frequently one or two workers and mainly native Americans.

These refugee farmers were not only self-supporting but the great majority of them had no source of income other than the farm. All but 7 of

[8] Jewish Agricultural Society, *Annual Report of the Managing Director*, 1944, pp. 22–23; cf. Gabriel Davidson, "His Ancestral Calling," *Commonweal*, Nov. 17, 1944.

the 132 cases plan to continue in farming. Three intend to leave because unable to get help, two for reasons of health and old age, one because of family complications, and one to return to Europe. Forty-five per cent of them have already attained citizenship; only one individual has failed to apply.

From the life stories of a number of these refugee farmers it appears that they have made a good economic adjustment and have established friendly community relations:

Mr. E., aged 37, had been a small farmer and cattle dealer in Germany before his property was destroyed by the Nazis and he was forced to emigrate. Arriving here in 1939 he went to Iowa where he rented a small farm but could not make a living on it, and he did not have sufficient money to buy or rent a larger one. He moved then to Pennsylvania where he rented pastures and started raising cattle, buying them when small and selling them in the fall. He succeeded to the extent that in 1943 he was able to buy a farm of 72 acres. Besides buying and selling cattle he keeps a herd of cows and sells milk. He has a tenant on the farm who helps him. He is following the same occupation as in Germany and making a success of it. He is very well satisfied with life in America and intends to remain here permanently.

A German lawyer and his wife, who arrived in the fall of 1938, trained to be farmers and in 1941 undertook to manage a farm of their own in Michigan. The wife writes as follows: "We love our farm, we love the people, and we love the whole nation. We do our utmost to produce as much food as we possibly can and so help our country. Our baby was born here. We have our citizenship papers and it was one of our greatest days. We were home again! In winter we are both active. I am the secretary-treasurer of the Farm Bureau and Home Extension Club. I am a member of the Eastern Star and Mothers Club. My husband is a Mason and we both take active part in our local discussion Forum. My husband now holds a small job with the AAA and is active in other fields of agriculture. We have only Gentile friends and yet they respect wholly our way of life. We appreciate the way they meet us and for their respect which we in return give them the same. This is the way of being one people and one nation. I wish more people would remember that you can't only take but must give in return, and giving in return is getting happiness for yourself. It is a great nation we are privileged to live in."

The following life story is that of a wealthy German industrialist who became a farmer by the mere chance that some property in California which he bought in Germany from the heirs of the former owner turned out to be a fruit farm. With the aid of his family and the neighbors and by much perseverance he has become a successful farmer. The family has also made an admirable social adjustment, and each of the five members has been outstanding as a good citizen. The story is also a tribute to the friendliness and helpfulness of the native American community. Above average in intelligence and in willingness to work, this family is a distinct asset to the nation.

From Industrialist to Farmer

"I was junior partner of the firm of F. & W. which manufactured heavy cotton textiles, such as tents and hammocks. I had never done any farming, although I liked to cultivate the roses in my garden. We lived in Kassel, which is a big city. . . .

"The first thought that it really would be necessary for us to leave Germany came to us in 1935. At that time the senior member of my firm died. In his will he stated specifically that I was to become senior partner after his death and was to have the leading voice in the management of the firm. When this became known, I was taken to court. The Judge locked me in a room with certain papers which relinquished all claim to control of the firm and told me I would never leave the room until I had signed. I knew that this meant we could not remain in Germany but it was hard to decide to leave and the family were divided as to where we should go. My wife and Paul were anxious to go to Palestine. They felt a great interest in the work being carried on there and thought they would like to become a part of it. Carl and I wanted to go to some English-speaking country but did not care whether it was the United States, Australia, or New Zealand. We came to the United States entirely by chance.

"In 1936 we saw an advertisement in a newspaper of property for sale in California. The property was to be sold for cash only, to be paid in German marks. The former owner had passed away in California in 1934 and the heirs were Aryan German citizens. We decided to try to buy the property and were successful. . . . Although the purchase was made in 1936, we did not actually immigrate until 1937. We left Germany with 10 marks each in our pockets.

"We landed in San Francisco in May, 1937. We were able to prepay the entire trip in German marks and the whole family made the trip together. We realize that we were extremely fortunate. We were allowed to transfer certain funds to both the American and British ships on which we travelled. This gave us a few dollars for our necessary expenses when we landed.

"I knew a good deal about the United States commercially as our firm bought its cotton in this country and we had a good many customers here. My wife and I had both studied English in school but had not used it for over 30 years. We had no idea that we would like this country so much. We love it, and if we could return to our former life with all our former possessions, we would not want to do it. We have never had nor dreamed of such wonderful experiences as the friendship and help that our neighbors here have given us. We did not like New York but we like everything about California.

"When we arrived in San Francisco, we found that we owned two houses and five lots in San Francisco, an acre in Mountain View and 20 acres in Los Altos, the latter all in apricot orchard and including a house. On May 4, the day after our arrival, we went to Los Altos to see the property. It was in terrible condition. The place was full of rats and mice, and the upstairs room, where the last owner had died, had not been cleaned since. Even the bedding was still on the bed. We had to stay in San Francisco for a week and during that time went down to Los Altos every day to clean the house. That was when we met the first of our wonderful neighbors. Dr. H., who lived next door, came every day and helped us clean. On May 10 we moved into the house. We had no furniture, as our furniture was still on the way. We slept on straw on the floor.

"Then began our work here on the farm. We found a tractor which did not run. My two sons repaired it and got it working and a neighbor came over and did the first cultivating for us. This is the most wonderful place in the world. All the neighbors have been helpful. We were never allowed to pay our neighbors for anything they did for us except the little favors we have been able to do for them. We came in May, and in July we had a light apricot crop of 11 tons, as nothing had been done for the trees. The neighbors came over and taught us how to pick and how to dry the crop. Late in 1937 we decided to buy a cow. One of the neighbors came over every day, morning and night, for six weeks until my wife learned to milk the cow. After we had the cow we sold milk and butter and in that way got a little cash.

"At about the same time our two big lift vans arrived with the furniture. One of our new friends gave us a little extra lumber which he had in his yard, and suggested that we use our lift vans and this lumber to build a chicken house. We got pamphlets from the University of California and found them extremely easy to follow. The boys and I built the chicken house. We started with 24 chickens. Now we have 1,000 laying hens and 400 baby chicks. We produce only eggs, and last year we totaled between 14,000 and 15,000 dozen. We have built additional chicken houses as we needed them, doing all the work ourselves. We learned mostly out of pamphlets from the University of California, but one of the neighbors whom we met here helped to teach us to take care of the chickens. My daughter is now engaged to marry his son. The only bad luck we had with the place was that 100 pear trees had the blight. I had to take them out. I felt terrible to do it but the neighbors told me I would just have to.

"One thing that made us decide to go into farming was that we wanted to be on our own after our experiences in Germany. We did not want to be dependent on other people or to be in contact with them. But the way the neighbors treated us here and the wonderful things they have done for us have made us feel that we are really part of this community.

"For years we did all the orchard work ourselves, except the spraying, in addition to taking care of the chickens and the building of the chicken houses. For the last couple of years we have rented out the orchard. We are not young enough any more to do so much work, and the chickens are more important and more profitable. We keep an eye on our tenant and see that he takes proper care of the orchard. This year our crop amounted to 53 tons, in contrast to 11 tons in the year we arrived.

"Our main object has always been a good education for the children. Carl was graduated in Germany as a radio engineer. We were able to send him to the University of California and he got his degree of Master of Science there. He has been steadily employed as a radio engineer. When drafted, he was given an exemption at the request of his firm. As soon as he became a citizen he tried to volunteer in the army, but the firm for which he was working stated that he was necessary to them and refused to give him up; he was, therefore, not accepted by the army. He is now going to do research for Westinghouse. He had had offers from them before but did not want to leave. Now the work offered him is too important to refuse. Paul studied chemistry at the University here and was graduated. He now works at the California School of Technology on secret war work and is also able to study for his Ph.D. Ruth had only 4 years of school in Germany. She had to go to a Jewish school there. These schools were good but were terribly crowded. Ruth started to go to grammar school as soon as she arrived in Los Altos. She used to come home in tears every day as she did not know a word of English. One of the neighbors who had been a school teacher before her marriage offered to give Ruth private lessons in English every day. This helped her greatly. In addition, she found the teachers very kind and helpful. She was graduated from Palo Alto High School, and is now studying at San Jose State College to become a nurse.

"Our only regret is that my wife and I have not had a chance to learn good English. Due to our work, we can never leave the place. We work even at night, candling the eggs. We also regret very much the lack of time to read. The children, of course, have had opportunity for study. As soon as Carl goes East, he plans to take lessons in pronunciation so as to lose his German accent. The only thing that we dislike are the American newspapers. We find the papers hard to understand, particularly the headlines, and we do not like the way they publish scandals. We think it is terrible that they give so much space to stories like that of Charlie Chaplin and Joan Barry when there is so much of interest and importance.

"We belong to a Jewish Congregation in Menlo Park and to two cooperative farmers' organizations. Our sons belong to professional radio and engineering societies, and Ruth belongs to a pre-nursing sorority. We have a delightful social life with our good neighbors. They always come to our home, as we are unable to leave very often, and we are able to enjoy good music and interesting talks together. Excepting Ruth, who was too young, we all voted at the last election.

"We feel that our whole way of life is helpful to the war effort. Farming is essential, and we are building up our farm so that it can produce far more food than ever before. Both our sons are in essential war work, and our daughter is studying nursing. Naturally we all buy bonds. In addition, I was able to give information and maps to the Board of Economic Warfare. The man that came to interview me for this had another appointment and telephoned from here that the information I was able to give him was so important that he would not leave. He stayed until 6 o'clock that evening. . . ."

CHAPTER XV

PHYSICIANS

The skill of the physician is readily transferable. Yet refugee physicians have experienced great difficulty in adjustment and have aroused more opposition than any other professional group. In part this has been due to fear of their competition and in part to the control exercised by American medicine, the most highly organized of all the professions. This situation is not peculiar to the United States. As a result of the economic depression of the 1930's and the growing unemployment, most Western countries became more and more protectionist against competition by foreign professionals, especially doctors and lawyers. At the instigation of professional organizations, quotas for foreign workers were introduced in many European countries and laws were passed, setting up citizenship and other requirements, which virtually excluded them from professional practice. Generally it has been the medical profession that has been most intransigent and also most successful in preventing foreign competition.[1] It was during this antiforeign trend that the forced migration of refugee professionals occurred.

Although the physicians comprise the largest single group of professional people among the refugees coming to the United States, they are not numerous. According to official immigration statistics, the total number of physicians and dentists, including medical students and nonpractitioners, admitted to the United States from all countries in the period from July 1, 1932, to June 30, 1944, was 6,426 or an average of 535 a year. Not all of these were by any means refugees. The latter would number 4,657 on the basis of immigrants whose last country of permanent residence was in Europe, and 5,480 on the basis of selected "races and peoples." On the generous assumption that all physicians and dentists admitted from these sources during the entire period 1933–1944 were refugees, the number would be not far from 5,000. They amount to about 3 per cent of the total number of physicians and surgeons (165,629) enumerated by the 1940 census. There is thus no support for the assertion made by *Medical Economics* in February, 1939, that foreign doctors were "coming in droves" nor, as we shall see, for the picture it painted of unrestricted immigration,

[1] Walter M. Kotschnig, *Unemployment in the Learned Professions*, London, 1937.

unfair competition of emigres with American doctors, and low standards of medical treatment. Also exaggerated and misleading are the figures on "refugee physicians" released by some state medical boards, which are based, not on the foreign-born but on those graduated from foreign medical schools, a category which includes many native Americans. To gain some balance and perspective on the situation, it is well to note that the total number of immigrant physicians over the entire period is about equal to the number of graduates in a single year from American medical schools.

In the case of the refugee physicians our information is based largely on the returns of a special questionnaire that was mailed to 4,774 physicians and dentists throughout the country. This master list was built up by utilizing the files of the National Committee for Resettlement of Foreign Physicians and adding to them the names and addresses of refugee physicians obtained in a nation-wide survey conducted by local committees cooperating with the Study Committee. Some 709 questionnaires were returned unclaimed because the address was incorrect or the person was in the Army. Of the questionnaires presumably reaching their destination, 4,065 in number, 1,676 were returned. This is a rate of 40 per cent, which is unusually high for a survey using the method of a mailed questionnaire and extraordinary in view of the fact that the questionnaire was not anonymous but called for name and address. Only 23 had to be discarded because of insufficient information. Fifty-three were received too late to be included. The net number used in the Study was 1,600, which covers approximately one-third of all the refugee physicians and dentists in the United States.

That this sample is not only adequate in size but also representative according to known characteristics of the group is borne out by a comparison of the findings with the tabulations as of July, 1944, of the Central Index of Refugee Physicians, Dentists, and Medical Scientists. This index was based on the records of the National Committee for Resettlement of Foreign Physicians, supplemented by data from the American Medical Directory, the Office of Procurement and Assignment Service of the War Manpower Commission, and other sources. The findings of the Study Committee tally closely with those based on the Central Index with reference to age, sex, marital status, country of birth, and former specialty. The Study cases show a somewhat lower proportion of Jews, a wider geographic distribution, and a higher percentage naturalized and licensed.[2] The time difference of a year between the two studies explains some of the differences in the findings. The inclusion in the questionnaire study of persons not known to service agencies as well as agency cases also is a factor.

[2] National Refugee Service, Division of Statistics, *Central Index of Refugee Physicians, Dentists, and Medical Scientists and Tabulations as of July, 1944*, mimeographed, Aug. 31, 1944.

CHARACTERISTICS

The questionnaire returns utilized in the analysis that follows came from 455 different communities in 41 states, the District of Columbia, and the Virgin Islands. The largest group, constituting about 55 per cent of the total, is located in New York State, including nearly 40 per cent in New York City. This concentration is undoubtedly due to the fact that New York City, aside from being the port of entry of nine-tenths of the total group, is located in one of the few states with a comparatively liberal licensing policy. About 25 per cent of the refugee physicians are located in Illinois, Ohio, California, and Massachusetts, and the remaining 20 per cent in other states or areas. The tendency to remain in New York is more characteristic of the Jewish, especially French, Russian, and Polish, than of the Christian physicians, and of specialists than of general practitioners, medical scientists, and public health workers. Refugee physicians reside in communities of all size groups, as the accompanying table discloses. Except for the greater concentration of Jews in New York City and of Christians in other cities of a million or more population, there is no appreciable religious difference in the distribution of refugee physicians by size of community.

PER CENT DISTRIBUTION OF REFUGEE PHYSICIANS BY SIZE OF COMMUNITY

	Total		Jewish		Non-Jewish	
Size of community	Number	Per cent	Number	Per cent	Number	Per cent
Total	1,600	100.0	1,318	100.0	282	100.0
Under 2,500	151	9.5	123	9.3	28	9.9
2,500–9,999	116	7.3	92	7.0	24	8.5
10,000–24,999	110	6.9	85	6.4	25	8.9
25,000–99,999	143	8.9	113	8.6	30	10.6
100,000–499,999	183	11.4	154	11.7	29	10.3
500,000–999,999	115	7.2	95	7.2	20	7.1
1,000,000 and over	143	8.9	101	7.7	42	14.9
New York City	639	39.9	555	42.1	84	29.8

The background and characteristics of refugee physicians, as revealed by the sample study, are as follows. Over one-half were born in Germany, and about one-fifth in Austria. The remaining quarter were born in other European countries. The country of birth was also the country of last citizenship in the case of practically all the Germans and Austrians and three-fourths of the Hungarians and Italians. In the case, however, of those born in Poland, Czechoslovakia, France, and particularly Russia, the majority had a different country of citizenship. A similar picture is presented when the country where medical training was obtained is compared to the country of birth.

PER CENT DISTRIBUTION OF REFUGEE PHYSICIANS BY COUNTRY OF BIRTH AND COUNTRY OF
GRADUATION FROM MEDICAL SCHOOL

	Country of Birth	Country of Graduation
Germany	57.6	58.2
Austria	19.0	24.7
Poland	6.9	0.9
Hungary	4.6	2.4
Czechoslovakia	4.2	3.5
U.S.S.R.	2.3	0.1
Italy	1.3	3.6
France	.7	1.5
Switzerland	.4	4.1
All others	3.0	1.0
	100.0	100.0

Most of the refugee physicians who were born in Germany or Austria graduated from medical schools located in those countries. Graduation from medical schools in countries other than their country of birth was especially marked in the case of the Russian and French, who showed a preference for German schools, and the Poles and Czechoslovaks, who attended chiefly Austrian schools. By and large, Austrian medical schools attracted a greater proportion and variety of nationalities than did any others.

Approximately 83 per cent of the respondents to the questionnaire were Jewish, 10 per cent Protestant, 5 per cent Roman Catholics, and 2 per cent other faiths or having no religious affiliation. Males comprised 87 per cent and females 13 per cent of the group. Considered by age on arrival, the refugee physicians were primarily a middle-aged group, in the most active years of productive work.

AGE DISTRIBUTION

	Percentages			
	Age on arrival		Present age (1945)	
Age groups	Male	Female	Male	Female
Total	100.0	100.0	100.0	100.0
21–30 years	19.2	35.0	.8	4.9
31–40 "	29.1	30.0	24.5	39.4
41–50 "	34.5	28.1	37.1	34.0
51–60 "	13.7	5.9	27.4	18.7
61–70 "	3.4	1.0	8.8	2.5
71 and over	.1	—	1.4	.5

As shown by the accompanying graph, the peak year of arrival was 1939, and the curve of arrivals of physicians answering the questionnaire follows closely that of all physicians from Europe, a further indication of the representativeness of our sample.

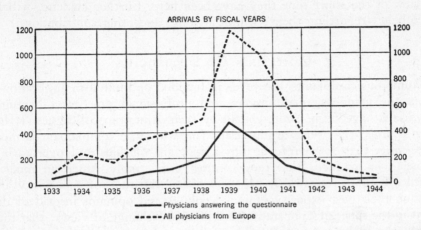

ARRIVALS BY FISCAL YEARS

——— Physicians answering the questionnaire
▪▪▪▪▪ All physicians from Europe

Ninety-five per cent of the Jewish physicians and 93 per cent of the Christian came on permanent visas, and practically all who arrived on temporary visas later changed their status to permit permanent residence. Most of the physicians, like other refugees, came to escape persecution. This was true of 97.1 per cent of the Jews and 73.5 per cent of the Christians. An additional 20.3 per cent of the Christians emigrated because of political reasons. A minor percentage of both came to join members of the family, to improve their economic condition, or to visit.

As to their professional activity abroad, nearly 90 per cent were licensed physicians. Those not licensed to practice included medical students (8.4 per cent of the total group) and some of those in institutional, research, or other positions where a license was not required. The majority of the men physicians had been engaged in private practice. The next largest number held institutional positions, and were followed by those in research and teaching. Minor proportions had been engaged in public health work or held government positions. A smaller proportion of the women had been engaged in private practice and in research and teaching, and a larger proportion had held institutional positions. Nearly three-fourths of the physicians were specialists in one branch of medicine or another. About 6 per cent of the men and 9 per cent of the women were dentists.

Some of these physicians were young and inexperienced, some had had inadequate training, some were of mediocre ability, but the great majority were highly qualified and some were outstanding men of international reputation. The countries of refugee emigration suffered a serious loss in the flight of this group, especially of the medical scientists. As an objective evaluation of their quality it may be stated that at least 67 of them are listed in *American Men of Science* (1944 edition), a remarkable record in view of the short time they have been here. Further evidence will be cited below regarding their scientific writings and other contributions.

COMPLAINTS AND DIFFICULTIES

Numerous complaints—however ill-founded or limited in application—about the manners, qualifications, and professional practices of refugee physicians have been made, chiefly by their American colleagues. It has been charged that refugee physicians (or, when the complainant is more discerning, that *some* refugee physicians) are officious and overbearing, Prussian in manner; that they contrast unfavorably American medical practice with European; that they exhibit an attitude of superiority and rely on their past experiences and deeply rooted opinions instead of displaying the spirit of co-operation and mutual exchange of views; that they follow the European custom of carrying on controversies in public regarding claims for priority in scientific discoveries; that their training is inferior to American, especially with regard to clinical experience; that they offer serious competition, especially in New York and other large cities where they have concentrated; that they charge lower fees, advertise for patients, and engage in other unprofessional practices; and that they have replaced American doctors who left for military service.

As applied to some individuals the complaints are justified, but as is usually the case in intergroup relations characteristics observable in the few come to be attributed indiscriminately to the entire group and specific incidents become inflated into generalities. Some refugee physicians do have manners and attitudes that Americans find irritating; there is an inevitable clash between European and American ways which persists until the immigrant becomes Americanized. European, especially German, medical schools emphasize research and specialization rather than broad clinical experience, which becomes a handicap when the refugee physician is forced to take up general practice. A number of refugee physicians have reduced fees and advertised—a practice not peculiar to them. It is significant that specific charges of unethical practice or malpractice have been infrequent and that proved cases have been exceedingly rare. Although the competition of refugee physicians has undoubtedly been felt occasionally, especially in some of the larger cities, it has been greatly exaggerated. Many refugee physicians have settled in rural areas and small towns where American doctors have been reluctant to take up practice. Moreover, the nation has been experiencing a dearth rather than a surplus of doctors. Many eligible refugee physicians joined the armed forces, while others took over the practices of Americans with the understanding that they would relinquish them upon the latter's return. All told, the extent of the competition could not have been great because the total number of refugee physicians, not all of whom were practitioners, is, as we have seen, only 3 per cent of the number of physicians in America.

One fact appears perfectly clear, as judged by community surveys and other evidence: American physicians, more than any other professional group, have feared possible refugee competition and have taken measures to protect themselves against it. With notable exceptions, the attitude of American physicians has been one of resentment and hostility, which in some instances has taken the form of deliberate propaganda and the spreading of rumors. From the community relations standpoint, the physicians more than any other occupational group among the refugees have met with an unfavorable reaction, not so much among the people in general as among other doctors. They are practically the only group that has encountered any sustained anti-refugee sentiment. While anti-Semitism plays a part, the opposition is more broadly gauged. It appears to stem primarily from economic motivations.

The reaction of refugee physicians to their reception and experience in this country varies from disillusionment and resentment to gratitude and admiration.

States a young Austrian physician, now an instructor in bacteriology: "When I landed here [in 1939] the immigration officer, after finding out that I was a physician, took my hand, shook it, and said, 'I am glad you came here, doc. Maybe you will help to make those doctor's fees cheaper.' Somehow this formulates all my experiences: not the slightest antagonism by the people in general, on the contrary almost enthusiastic welcome, but some antagonism within the profession, although, I admit, less than one could expect and less than one might encounter in Europe."

A German physician comments on his questionnaire: "In the field of science the victims of Hitler's persecution expected a more helpful attitude [on the part] of the American scientists. We thought that especially in the United States science has been regarded as universal and independent from race prejudices. Instead, we found in many instances discrimination. In most states of the United States even experienced and internationally recognized medical scientists were regarded as undesirable by their colleagues. It was a bitter disappointment for the best of those who in the pre-Hitler days were honored by American scientific institutions."

"Among my friends," writes a German-Jewish doctor in New York City, "I find a good mixture of Jews and Gentiles, men and women from all walks of life. There is only one exception, and this may be of some significance. I met a considerable number of American doctors and have worked for them and with them. Never did I achieve any social contact with any of these men, no matter how friendly and pleasant our professional relations might have been. I am rather sure that most of my fellow-refugee physicians have had a similar experience."

"After all is said and done," writes a refugee physician in the Medical Corps, "you cannot help feeling cheated of your rights as a professional man and as a citizen. I might be quite happy to become a general practitioner in Maryland, but I will always resent, yes, I hope I will always resent, that the secretary of the Minnesota Medical Board can keep me from becoming a G.P. in Minnesota. . . . I wish I could believe that concern for the public welfare was the moving idea of all this legislation restricting foreign-trained physicians."

"The only real difficulty I encountered in this country," states a German Protestant who was a medical student abroad, "was to find admission at a medical school. I found everything I had hoped to have left behind me forever in Europe: prejudice, narrow-mindedness, arrogance, suspicion, selfishness, and a huge superiority complex. I wrote to all medical schools in the country. There are 64 . . . I kept on writing and applying to all 64 medical schools for three whole years. Eastern schools would not accept a refugee student, western schools would not accept a student from the East, southern schools would not consider someone from New York. The reasons were all different ones but the result was always that I would not be admitted. . . . Then I learned that there was an unofficial but very definite agreement among all medical schools not to admit any European student unless he went through a complete American education, with college, pre-med schooling, etc. This was of course quite impossible for me since I could never hope to obtain sufficient funds for such a protracted enterprise. Therefore I chose the only remaining way out: I went to Middlesex University, a medical school which was not approved by the American Medical Association." (This person is now an intern in New York)

Prevented by the Nazis from enrolling for the last semester and obtaining his degree in the Medical School of the University of Vienna, and rejected by American medical schools, J. S. joined the U.S. Army and is now a laboratory technician in an Army general hospital in the Pacific.

On the other hand, favorable comments are not lacking.

"I was very well received by almost all of my American colleagues," states a German Jewish doctor, "especially those of the older age groups."

"I wish to express my profoundest gratitude towards this country and particularly its medical profession. They have given us European physicians the possibility to resettle and to practice. No other country in the world displayed such unusual fairness and hospitality. Due to this generous attitude the large majority of immigrant physicians are now in a position to make a decent living, and so am I. But as far as my scientific endeavors in research, clinical work and teaching are concerned, I am sorry to say that I did not get any assistance whatsoever."

A captain in the Medical Corps writes: "I only wish to say that the chance my wife and I were given to start life afresh after it had seemed near its end is something that cannot be forgotten. I shall also never forget that this country has given me the chance to raise my head again as man among men, as equal among equals."

Writes a lieutenant in the Medical Corps from a camp in Texas: "I suppose every one of us who has a little more ambition both as a physician and a citizen than merely to eke

out a livelihood has reasons for despair at times when it looks as if the only class of people in whose eyes he could not live down a foreign degree are his own professional brothers. The mere fact that a committee of American doctors, as outstanding for their names
and fame as for their humanity, continues to work to improve the professional situation
of a mixed bunch of immigrants—this is one of those things that makes you feel sure
that this is the most wonderful country in the world, worth working for no matter what
gripes you."

Half the physicians who replied to the questionnaire, 52.4 per cent to
be exact, stated that they had encountered special difficulties in carrying
on their professional activity in the United States. The frequency with
which special difficulties were experienced is indicated in the following
table.

Per Cent Distribution of Special Difficulties Encountered

Difficulty	Per cent
Restrictions imposed by local medical organizations	30.0
Legal restrictions	23.7
Lack of working capital	14.7
Differences in professional practices in Europe and the United States	8.0
Insufficient knowledge of English	5.5
Own physical condition	3.9
Other or not specified	14.2
Total	100.0

In a small proportion of cases, refugee physicians experienced difficulty
in establishing themselves in this country because of their own physical
condition. This was a problem of advanced age, ordinary sickness, or disability due to persecution abroad. Language was mentioned as a special
difficulty in only 5.5 per cent of the replies, a much smaller percentage
than in the case of other refugees and especially of those, like writers,
teachers, and actors, whose profession is tied to language. The language
difficulty was more severe among the Hungarian and Slavic groups. It was
felt especially in taking examinations for licensure. Wherever it existed it
tended to force the physicians to remain in cities where there was a large
population of their own nationality.

Approximately four out of every five respondents to the questionnaire
had received some education in the United States. About 27 per cent of
them had attended English and citizenship classes, 41 per cent had tutored
for the state medical board examination, and 9 per cent had attended medical or dental school.

The refugee physician faced special difficulties unknown to the graduates of approved American medical schools in taking state medical board examinations. The examination is given in English, which is a foreign language to him. He frequently had to take it without an adequate period of preparation, and had to prepare for it while working to support himself and family. Many of them had completed their training ten or more years ago and thus were not recently associated with academic life. These difficulties largely account for the fact that refugees have failed more frequently than American applicants, who in the majority of cases had just been graduated from medical school. Nevertheless, the state board examinations have not proved an insuperable barrier to graduates of foreign medical schools permitted to take them. Of the respondents to the questionnaire, 88 per cent had succeeded in obtaining a license. Those unlicensed include mainly students, persons studying for licensing examinations, and persons who had left the field of medicine.

The following statement is taken from the life story of a German physician born in 1893, who arrived here in 1939.

"I shall never forget how much I was struck by the sight of the assemblies of hundreds of candidates for the Medical State Board Examination in New York City. In Europe we did not have written tests in the field of medicine, and the silent question sheet had a horrifying effect. . . . The mixture of noisy and unworried American youngsters and quiet, pale, and tense-looking, gray-haired or bald-headed candidates from Old Europe was certainly the main feature of these gatherings. Two generations and two continents were striving toward the same objective. This thought meant some comfort to me, even if I had to admit that I belonged to the party with the gray hair. Watching one or another of my young American-born colleagues, I realized how easily words and phrases came to them, while I had to spend precious time in an effort to find the proper terms and to formulate my statements in a way that I thought adequate for a professional examination of such high standard. I believe that almost every refugee physician had similar experiences, shortcomings, and inhibitions, and I am certain that I do not exaggerate when I say that many of them deserve great credit and high praise for their will power, diligence, and perseverance, which enabled them, despite their age, despite their difficult economic situation, and last but not least, despite the tribulations most of them had undergone, to obtain their licenses to practice medicine and again to become active members of their old professional group, physicians."

Differences in professional practices here as compared to Europe naturally led to problems of adjustment, but it is significant that this was mentioned in only 8 per cent of the instances as a special difficulty, thus probably indicating the high degree of transferability of knowledge and skill in the medical field. This seems to be a reasonable interpretation in view of the fact that disease, as well as the means to combat it, is not confined to national frontiers. More important as a handicap was the lack of working capital. Most of the refugee physicians arrived without means or with insufficient means to set up adequately in practice. The expense of securing new equipment and suitable office space was considerable. Many, at least at the start, had to put up with inadequate equipment and combine office with residence, often in quarters lacking conveniences and located in poor neighborhoods. On the other hand, some fortunate physicians who immigrated early and were able to salvage much or most of their wealth have up-to-date offices in the best districts. But more important than all these difficulties together have been the restrictions imposed by medical organizations and state laws.

Restrictive Measures

The professions differ from most occupations in that many of them require licenses. This is especially true of medicine, where the requirements are particularly rigid with respect to both state laws and the regulations of the state medical examining boards. In the case of foreign physicians there are special and additional requirements to be met for licensure, which can only be interpreted as discrimination against them. As the number of refugee physicians increased, new legislation and new rulings, sponsored by medical societies, were adopted for the primary purpose of protecting native physicians from the new competition. As a consequence, by 1943 licensing examinations were, in effect, closed to aliens in all states except New York and Massachusetts. In a few other states selected candidates might be admitted. This discrimination contributed directly to the congregation of refugee physicians in certain communities. The increasing tendency of licensing boards to withdraw reciprocity from those states in which emigres have been admitted to licensure has presented a further barrier to the equitable distribution of qualified refugees. Moreover, the National Board of Medical Examiners, which issues licenses after examinations that are valid in most states after endorsement, refused to accept, beginning February 15, 1942, applications from graduates of any medical schools in Continental Europe, though it might make an exception in the case of persons who had acquired full citizenship and who presented certain special credentials and endorsements.

Among the various restrictions that serve to bar emigre physicians from pursuing their professional careers, the most serious is the requirement of full citizenship before admission to a licensing examination. This is required by law or by regulations of state licensing boards in twenty-eight states, and it is frequently accompanied by other restrictions. In 1938 it was recommended by the House of Delegates of the American Medical Association as a prerequisite to medical licensure. On the other hand, a number of leading American physicians and legal authorities have raised the question whether this requirement has any bearing on medical standards.[3] It appears to have been prompted by considerations of competition rather than of competence, to have been inspired by a desire to protect the "rights" of American physicians. The connection between skill in medicine and citizenship is not obvious. After all, the human body and its ailments are pretty much the same the world over. Not only is this requirement in direct violation of our best traditions, but its constitutionality is distinctly questionable.

In support of alien exclusion it has been urged that doctors have many public and official duties and that a physician who is a citizen will be better able to co-operate with the state in carrying out its policies than one who is foreign-trained and an alien. Good medical practice, however, is taught in Europe as well as America, and the alien physician can soon learn the provisions of our health laws. Moreover, if an alien physician is in the process of becoming a citizen there can be no doubt of his personal or civic responsibility. The citizenship requirement is not only unfair but it is also futile, for it is not a permanent barrier to licensure. It simply bars an otherwise qualified person from the pursuit of his professional career for at least five years. The result is liable to be deterioration of professional skill and acumen and loss of morale. The New York State law, which requires only first papers before licensure, and revocation of the license if full citizenship is not obtained within ten years of its issuance, is a model which all other states might well follow.

In addition to the citizenship requirement there are other recent laws and state board rulings that deliberately impose prerequisites to licensure which are difficult or impossible for the refugee applicant to meet. It is evident from the kinds of bars that have been erected in many states that while they have served in some instances to protect the American public against a lowering of standards they have served primarily to safeguard the interests of American physicians. These restrictions include refusal to admit to a licensing examination graduates of European medical schools unless the application was signed by the dean of the school (this in the case of persons who were driven out of countries of refugee emigration, with which we later were at war!), requiring certification of medical diplomas by a United States consul (though no consular offices were open in these countries during the war), requiring that the country of the applicant must grant reciprocity to American licentiates (California law), restricting licenses to graduates of approved American or Canadian schools (some 27

[3] "Refugees and the Professions," *Harvard Law Review*, 1939, Vol. LIII, No. 1; David L. Edsall, "The Emigré Physician in American Medicine," *Journal of the American Medical Association*, Vol. 114 (March 23, 1940), pp. 1068–1073; David L. Edsall and Tracy J. Putnam, "The Emigré Physician in America, 1941," *Journal of the American Medical Association*, Vol. 117 (Nov. 29, 1941), pp. 1881–1888; Alfred E. Cohn, "Exiled Physicians in the United States," *American Scholar*, Summer, 1943; Ernest W. Puttkammer, *Alien Enemies and Alien Friends in the United States*, 1943, pp. 6–8.

states including the District of Columbia), excluding graduates of foreign schools on the grounds of insufficient information concerning their standards (a medical board ruling in at least 12 states), and requiring internship in an American hospital, even though the individual may have practiced for years and won distinction in his field (15 states including the District of Columbia).

In regard to the last-mentioned requirement, there is no doubt that one or two years of internship in an American hospital is desirable before licensure, especially in the case of the younger men. Refugee physicians agree with this, even regarding it as essential to real adjustment in this country for men up to early middle age. But no distinction is made in the ruling between recent graduates and those of long standing. Justice and wisdom dictate that, in the case of men of middle age and over who have had abundant clinical experience, such a requirement is not necessary. As a general rule, the more highly trained a man is the less desirable does retraining become. It may be a boon to students and young graduates, it becomes a catastrophe for the fully trained physician.

Most stringent and protectionist are the restrictions requiring graduation from an approved American school before admission to the state licensing examination and those excluding graduates of foreign schools not rated by the American Medical Association. These restrictions bar native Americans who take their training abroad because of the limited enrollment of American medical schools, as well as Europeans, and graduates of British and other leading universities as well as of less reputable ones. It is quite true that Continental schools that came under the Nazi regime deteriorated and that it has been difficult to evaluate them since 1934. It is sensible and just to bar graduates from such schools *after* the change, but no one can justify a retroactive ruling which bars graduates of the leading European schools of earlier years. The majority of the refugee physicians were graduated before Hitler came to power. That these schools were of high standard is indicated by the statement of the Council on Medical Education and Hospitals of the American Medical Association as recently as 1929:

With the requirements of two or more years of premedical study, medical education in the United States is now on a par with the requirements of other countries.

While there has been no opportunity for visiting and inspecting such schools, nor have official reports been received from them, nevertheless a list of foreign medical schools is available and is used by our National Board of Medical Examiners; this list is virtually the same as that issued by the Royal College of Physicians in the British Empire. Blanket exclusion of Continental schools cannot logically be supported by any group which has accepted the National Board certificate. The fair thing to do would be to evaluate foreign physicians on their own merits and by examination rather than reject them by ukase.

To illustrate some of the legal obstacles and technicalities encountered by the refugee physician, we may cite a few cases involving the regulations of Ohio, which is by no means the most illiberal state.

A woman physician writes: "My husband, who was professor of internal medicine at the University of Jena, took the State Board in November, 1941 in Columbus, and passed in full immediately. The following month he was appointed full-time pathologist at the City Hospital." [Shortly thereafter he died and Mrs. S., on whom fell the support of the children, decided to work again as a physician.] "In Ohio, meanwhile, non-citizens were not any more accepted for the State Board. I have worked for nine months in T.B. work and left my position to prepare for the Medical State Board. I had hoped to find some part-time work as a physician during this time, which was not possible. I will try to find work as a camp physician in summer time and afterwards to take again a residency."

Dr. F., a tuberculosis specialist, not here long enough to become a citizen, was licensed in New York and then moved to Ohio. He writes: "The State of Ohio had abolished the reciprocity existing between it and New York just when I went there, and also asked for final citizenship papers as requirement for admission to the State Board. By that, it was made impossible for me to stay there, so I returned to New York."

Dr. G., a pathologist, licensed in Illinois, moved to Ohio to take a hospital position. He wished to become an American specialty board diplomate but encountered these legal and other difficulties: "Although I had fulfilled the educational requirements to take the examination of the American Board of Pathology, I was not admitted to the examination because I was unable to become a member of any national medical society such as the American Medical Association. Reasons: residing in Chicago and having an Illinois license, I would have been admitted had I been a citizen at that time, which I was not. Residing in Toledo and being a citizen, I could not be admitted because I have no Ohio license. A license in Ohio is necessary to become a member of the A.M.A. To obtain a license in the State of Ohio, I would have to submit a license to practice medicine from the country where I graduated as Doctor of Medicine. I submitted a document to the State Medical Board of Ohio, which was given to all German Jewish physicians until 1937 on request in case they fulfilled the necessary requirements to practice medicine, though they actually were prohibited to do so and did not receive a license (*Approbationsurkunde*). The originality of this document was not questioned. However, my application was turned down because the signature was not that of the *Preussische Minister des Inneren* but only by his direction and signed by one of the undersecretaries. I was told that in case I should bring this document with the signature of this official I would be licensed in Ohio by reciprocity with Illinois. I was also requested to bring a certificate of the Dean of the Medical Faculty of the University of Bonn of recent date on one of the application blanks of the State Medical Board of Ohio, though we were at war with Germany."

An Austrian woman doctor, noncitizen, residing in Cleveland, states bitterly: "I have no hopes whatsoever. Medicine is considered in this country as a business and he who takes it as a profession cannot compete. This business spirit of the American physicians

has provided the State of Ohio with regulations to keep out newcomers from any practice. All medical and daily papers are full of despair about the insufficient number of
trained psychiatrists, but my 20 years of psychiatric experience and my credentials are
not sufficient for an admission to the State Board Examination, although sufficient to
work for the fellow who cashes the check."

In a class with restrictive rulings toward applicants for licenses is the
action of some county and state medical societies denying membership
to foreign physicians who are licensed. Some require citizenship, others
have ruled that applicants must be graduates of approved American schools.
According to a bylaw adopted in 1942, the Massachusetts Medical Society
forbids membership to doctors until they have been licensed five years.
These provisions not only withhold membership in a professional society,
which is considered the natural prerequisite to good standing in the medical
fraternity, but also deny them hospital privileges, which are often conditional on medical society membership and essential to adequate medical
practice. Such action has been protested by a number of leading physicians
in Massachusetts who state that no proof has been offered that it protects
medical standards or that the training of refugee doctors is inadequate.
These requirements are degrading to the licensed emigre with first papers
who is doing his best to become a reputable member of the community.
The reason behind such rulings must be fear of competition or prejudice.

The general effect of these provisions is to delay medical society membership or hospital affiliation until the requirements can be met. Of the
respondents to the questionnaire, 68 per cent had by 1945 attained membership in a county medical or dental society and 57 per cent had hospital
affiliation. In regard to the latter, however, it should be noted that only
two-thirds of the refugee physicians were engaged in private practice and
hence had a need for hospital privileges.

The dentists have had a tougher row to hoe than the physicians, though
with some justification, since European dentistry, which is simply one of
the medical specialties, is technically inferior to American dentistry. Consequently, the refugee dentists have had to take training in American dental
schools. Indeed, in practically every state dental licensure is restricted to
graduates of approved American or Canadian schools. A minimum of one
or two years' (in three states four years') retraining has generally been
required. Even after graduation, the refugee dentist is not allowed to practice in at least thirty-two states of the Union (no information on this point
could be secured from four states) until he has attained full citizenship.
Those who have qualified have never been considered by the profession
as outsiders or competitors, and they have generally been successful. On
the other hand, it has been hard for the older practitioners and those with
little money to get the needed retraining. Of the dentists who answered

the Study Committee questionnaire, 30 per cent had left their specialty, half of whom had also left the field of medicine.

The state laws on medical licensure were passed and the licensing boards were created to protect the community from undesirable or unqualified physicians. Nowhere has the power been given to regulate the number of physicians permitted to practice in any state. Nevertheless, the economic self-interest of American physicians has been an important factor in formulating requirements and interpreting them, with the object of preventing competition. This situation is not peculiar to America. Sir Norman Angell[4] writes regarding the situation in England:

To find a so-called "Trade Union" type of outlook in its extremest and narrowest form one must turn, not to the Trade Unions, but to the organised professions. Permission for an alien professional man to practise in our country has to be obtained first from the Home Office, and secondly from the official organisations which control registration for their respective professions. Thus there are two major handicaps in the obstacle race. In the case of the British Medical Association, zeal to protect themselves from competition has reached so high a pitch, that, in comparison with their attitude, that of the Home Office seems to shine by its liberality and high-mindedness. In 1938 the Home Office was ready to allow admission to 500 Austrian Jewish doctors. Under the energetic pressure of the B.M.A., the number was reduced to 50, and it was stipulated that even doctors of the highest attainments must first submit to a two years "retraining" before being allowed to practise.

The new regulations to keep foreign physicians out of practice were passed at a time when, because of the national emergency, the nation was experiencing an acute need for physicians. About 55,000 of the nation's 165,000 physicians practicing before the war went into the armed services, leaving a skeleton staff to care for ordinary civilian needs and the special requirements of defense production centers. This shortage of physicians promises to continue in the future, because of the failure to defer premedical students, the desire of young Army doctors who went through the speeded-up wartime training program to return to school, and the new postwar demands. The American Council on Education and the National Research Council describe the outlook in the medical field as extremely serious, and estimate that there will be 19,000 fewer doctors available for civilians, compared with the prewar period.[5] In August, 1945, the government announced a program to enroll 12,000 war veterans in medical and dental schools in a drive to meet the postwar need for physicians and dentists. Paul V. McNutt, manpower chief, said the nation urgently needed 35,000 more doctors. Many more physicians would be needed than were available before the war, it was stated, since the postwar needs of the armed

[4] *We and the Refugee*, London, 1939, p. 240.
[5] *New York Times*, June 13, 1945.

forces alone would be 15,000 doctors, the veterans' administration will need another 15,000, and an undetermined number will be required in liberated areas.[6] It will be a problem to provide these extra physicians in the near future without lowering the standards of medical education.

During the entire period of the emergency little was done to utilize the services of the several thousand refugee physicians, despite their desire to continue in their profession and to aid in the war effort. Little use was also made, except partially in three or four states, of the device of temporary or war-duration license, a procedure adopted in England where over a thousand emigre doctors were drawn into the wartime medical structure. Our Immigration and Naturalization Service did what it could by speeding up the naturalization process for alien physicians so that they might qualify for examination in states where citizenship is required. The Army illogically declined to give the foreign physician a commission in the Medical Corps if he was not a citizen, but drafted him as a private if he was of the right age and physically sound and not in a medically "essential" post. For the Navy Medical Corps citizenship plus 12 years residence in the United States was required. After V-E day, the postcitizenship residence requirement was reduced to one year, but though many applied, to date none has been accepted. Even alien physicians inducted or enlisted as privates, who became eligible for citizenship after three months' service according to special wartime ruling, were denied after 1942 the privilege of applying for a commission in the Medical Corps, if they were of "enemy alien" origin. Other requirements besides citizenship stood in the way.

The result of this policy was to reject most of the refugee physicians who offered their services and to dislocate a disproportionate number of native American physicians for war duty. The Procurement and Assignment Service, which was responsible for military recruitment of medical personnel and for assigning physicians to critical shortage areas in this country, did, however, co-operate in a plan to utilize the services of refugee physicians in civilian life, such as temporary positions in hospitals, special positions in medical schools, and service in war-shortage areas and in rural communities, where they were rated as essential and thus deferred. Much valuable service was rendered in this way, though state laws and regulations were a limiting factor. A number of refugee doctors were placed on a *locum tenens* basis, an arrangement whereby they carried on the practices of American medical men serving in the armed forces, paying them a percentage of the income from the practice, and agreeing to leave after the war. Under this policy, the refugee physician, far from displacing the American doctor called to military service, actually protected his practice, holding it intact until he returned.

Also in co-operation with the Procurement and Assignment Service a

[6] *New York Times*, Aug. 21, 1945.

number of refugee physicians were placed in small towns and rural districts hitherto lacking in medical care. Many more would have been so placed had it not been for the numerous licensure restrictions. Small communities that had never had a doctor or where the doctor had left for the war were anxious to avail themselves of the services of refugee physicians, but were frequently estopped by legal and semilegal obstacles. In New York State, by way of contrast, where only first papers are required for admission to a licensing examination, such communities have received medical care more frequently than elsewhere. The following case is typical of the wartime emergency service that refugee physicians rendered. There would have been more instances of this sort if regulations of medical practice had permitted.

In October, 1944, the assistance of the National Committee for Resettlement of Foreign Physicians was sought by the citizens of Vinalhaven, a small island 15 miles off the coast of Maine, with a population of 1,500. The inhabitants, consisting chiefly of fishermen and workers in granite quarries, were desperately in need of medical services since their former physician had gone to war. An appeal throughout the state had failed to secure a new physician. There was considerable illness and several deaths had occurred. A local committee was organized to search for a doctor, and the chairman came to New York for this purpose.

The National Committee was able to secure for them the services of a refugee physician, Dr. Schymen Nussbaum, aged 32, who had come to the United States in 1940. Polish by birth, he had received his medical education in Italy. Dr. Nussbaum had applied for a commission in the Army, but was rejected for physical reasons. His brother, also a refugee physician, obtained a captaincy in the Medical Corps and served for a long time overseas. Dr. Nussbaum, who was anxious to serve on the home front, had a medical license in New York State, but was not eligible for one in Maine where full citizenship is required. He nevertheless went to Vinalhaven in November, 1944, on the chance that he might be granted a temporary license there. Meanwhile he performed first-aid work without fees. In response to popular demand, the State of Maine granted him a temporary license for the duration of the war and he began to practice officially in December. The natives of the island were extremely grateful for his services and he became a respected member of the community. He practiced there until December, 1945, when the former physician returned from military service, grateful that his practice had been maintained and that the health of the community was at a high level as a result of Dr. Nussbaum's skilled and faithful work. Dr. Nussbaum then returned to New York, where he plans to train for specialty work in psychiatry. Being an emigre physician, however, and one who does not have veteran status, he is handicapped in obtaining a suitable position in his chosen field.

Many such communities where refugee physicians have located are enjoying better medical service than they ever had before.

The following account of practice in a mountain community—Konnarock, Virginia—was written by Dr. Heinz C. Meyer, born in Germany in 1899, graduated from Goettingen in 1923, engaged in private practice until

1938, when he came to the United States as a political refugee. He is now, quite literally, a medical missionary. When asked to compare his professional activity in the United States with his normal situation in Europe, he replied, "No comparison possible." He has described his work as follows:

"What struck me most at the start of my medical work at Konnarock was the unproportionately high occurrence of increased blood pressure in relatively young people, especially young women who had had several children within a few years. Another impressive feature was the high incidence of infected tonsils, decayed teeth, and what was called 'rheumatism.' In the beginning, there appeared to be no possibility, however, of co-ordinating all those findings of physical and mental peculiarities until, at the end of February, 1940, about six weeks after I had opened my office, a man came to me who had been paralyzed in his right foot due to neuritis of the sciatic nerve since 1936. He complained that he was now losing strength in the other leg and that he was afraid of becoming totally disabled.

"About six years before that time, in 1934, I had started to treat neuritis with injections of vitamin B, and had seen marvelous results. This treatment was based on a comparison with a disease rather prevalent in the Far East. It was known at that time that the dry form of beriberi, which presents itself in severe neuritis ending in paralysis, was caused by malnutrition where polished rice furnished the main food, and that it could be cured by addition of extracts of rice polishings to the diet or by injecting them.

"After a few injections, this man, whom I mentioned before, had improved and could do his farming again. This was the point at which the veil of secrecy began to disappear. When, consequently, we started to study the nutritional standards of our patients, we found a totally insufficient nutrition as far as variation or balance was concerned. The direction was now given, and so we started our campaign on improving the condition.

"What was to be done was chiefly this: to convince the people that the greatest part of their trouble was caused by the fact that their food was insufficient and that they had to change their eating habits at the very start of their attempt to better their health. Better health would enable them to work better and thereby earn more money. And this, in turn, would improve their whole situation. . . . Then began the slow, tedious process of educating the people to change their eating habits, to think of their health in terms of food, and to improve their farming methods. . . .

"It did not deter me when children called me names while I was driving through the community or the adults made jokes about my talking about food. . . . Nutritional education, however, is only part of our work. Emphasis on calisthenics, exercises for beginning deformities at trunk or feet, building up of general resistance by promoting sun bathing for children and regular cleanliness and cool showers for everyone are another; but it would lead too far to go into details about all that.

"Are there results? Definitely yes! The improvement of the physical health condition is qualitatively similar to that observed by Dr. Spies of the Hillman Nutrition Clinic at Birmingham, Alabama, who reported on one hundred war workers who were restored to health within a few weeks of nutritional treatment after having been disabled for a long time. Our figures, of course, are much smaller. However, I do not believe that I exaggerate when I say that I had several dozens of patients whose disability was solely due to malnutrition and whose treatment consisted only in dieting and vitamins. . . .

"The work which we are doing at Konnarock is our answer to this country and its people who did everything for us without asking, who gave us home and work and peace and freedom without requiring any guarantee except loyalty. It should be visualized as our means of paying down a debt, which is so great as to make us work at it as long as we may be given to live; as our expression of gratefulness to this nation and its government for permitting us to enter this great haven of rescue for the persecuted all over the world, and to the United Lutheran Church in America and its welfare organizations who located us in the mountains of Virginia and helped us materially and spiritually to overcome the difficulties of the beginnings of our readjustment. And lastly, it is our way of returning to the people of this specific part of the state for the friendliness and helpfulness which we were offered by a great many of them. If our efforts should be allowed to bear the fruit, which I wish they would, I should like to call their results a *Hymn of Thanks.*"

COMMITTEES ASSISTING REFUGEE PHYSICIANS

Besides the assistance rendered them by the general refugee-service organizations, refugee physicians have been aided by two important committees set up by American physicians who were keenly aware of the problems of the immigrants and anxious to extend a helping hand to their foreign colleagues. The financial support in both instances has come mainly from the National Refugee Service. The first of these, the Emergency Committee in Aid of Displaced Foreign Physicians, was established in the fall of 1933. In 1939 it changed its name to the Emergency Committee in Aid of Displaced Foreign Medical Scientists. Its main objectives have been to supply information and advice regarding opportunities for medical research and teaching in the United States and to place in full-time research positions a limited number of specially qualified foreign physicians by furnishing stipends for their maintenance. The committee has been careful to avoid assignments that might result in injury to American physicians or create professional competition with them. The grants were made only at the request of universities or hospitals and the funds were derived from sources which would not otherwise have been available to those institutions. The grants were usually for a period of one year. During the period of its greatest activity, the academic years from 1934–1935 to 1941–1942, the committee made 215 grants to 125 different medical scientists. The grants averaged $1,351. The total amount awarded was $294,075, about one-third of which came from supplementary sources. Many of the grantees have since made notable places for themselves in American science.

In 1940 this committee merged offices and secretaryships with the National Committee for Resettlement of Foreign Physicians, which had been formed in 1939 by a group of farseeing and patriotic American doctors. This organization, with a number of co-operating committees in cities throughout the country, has been sensitive to the need of protecting American physicians from unfair competition by emigres, and has striven to place refugee doctors in sections of the United States where medical care is inadequate or completely lacking. It has been the policy of the committee to require that before refugee candidates take the licensing examination they complete a year of internship in an American hospital, take out their first citizenship papers, pass an English examination, and receive a favorable professional evaluation by an advisory board of American physicians. The committee has made a special effort to resettle refugee physicians away from large cities where competition is keenest and into rural areas where physicians are urgently needed, and also to effect a more equitable distribution between states. This process has become increasingly difficult due to new laws and regulations barring the practice of foreign-trained physicians. Since its inception the committee has placed over 1,700 of these physicians in laboratories, in hospitals as interns or residents, in private practice, or in research and teaching. If necessary, loans have been extended for purposes of study or other preparation for practice, to supplement income, or to set physicians up in practice. Much care has been taken to place the proper physician in the proper position and to prepare the community for his reception. No serious complaints or maladjustments have occurred in the vast majority of such placements.

Professional and Social Adjustment

Through the questionnaire returns the Study Committee gathered considerable evidence regarding the professional and social adjustment of refugee physicians. Like other refugees, the physicians frequently had to accept at first menial jobs; like other professionals, many had to take non-professional positions. Nearly a fifth of them are still in other types of work, such as business or industry, or are unemployed. The great majority, however, have remained in the professional field, though often in lesser roles than they had enjoyed abroad. Women physicians especially found it difficult to resume medical practice.

In comparing major professional activity abroad with that here, it is noteworthy, in the case of the men physicians, that 82.5 per cent of those who had been in private medical practice abroad were in the same activity here. In the comparable situation among the dentists, the percentage was 58.5 per cent. On the other hand, only 38.3 per cent of those engaged in research or teaching abroad, 28.1 per cent of those in hospital positions, and none of those in governmental or public health positions were engaged in the same activity here. Among the women physicians the percentages of those engaged in the same professional activity abroad and here were: private medical practice, 59.3 per cent; private dental practice, 54.5 per cent; research or teaching, 25 per cent; hospital positions, 28.9 per cent; and governmental or public health positions, zero per cent. It may be concluded that either there is greater transferability of skill in private practice as compared with other medical activities or that the social and cultural adjustment is easier in that field, or both.

At the time of the Study, the overwhelming majority of the respondents, 1,569 out of 1,600, were still in the field of medicine or dentistry, although in many cases in minor and nonpractitioner positions. Many of those who had left the field intended to return; among them the proportion of dentists was unusually high. Legal restrictions were the main reason why these people had left the field.

Eighty-eight per cent of those who replied to the questionnaire had obtained a medical or dental license to practice. In 7.3 per cent of the cases the license was obtained by endorsement of foreign credentials, the rest by examination. On the general matter of licensing by endorsement, it may be stated here, on the authority of the head of the New York State Board of Medical Examiners, that from 1932 to September, 1936, when this general procedure ceased, a total of only 632 foreign-trained physicians received licenses here by endorsement. Since 1936 there have been only four instances, each by virtue of an international reputation in medical science.

Fifty-six respondents were diplomates of the National Board of Medical Examiners, having passed this highest type of examination, and were thus eligible to practice in most of the states. One hundred and eighteen were diplomates of an American specialty board, a great distinction for the specialist. Psychiatrists and neurologists were outstanding in this respect. Because of the common citizenship requirement for licensure, citizenship status and, as a concomitant, length of residence in the United States are important factors. Seventy per cent of those licensed were citizens, the rest had all taken steps toward the attainment of citizenship. From 90 to 100 per cent of those who had been here for six years or longer were licensed. Because it requires only first citizenship papers for admission to the licensing examination, New York leads all states where refugee physicians have been licensed, accounting for 59.6 per cent of the cases. The order of the more important other states where refugee physicians have been licensed is Illinois (9.6 per cent), California (5.1 per cent), Ohio (4.9 per cent), Massachusetts (4.8 per cent), Connecticut (2.1 per cent), and New Jersey (2.1 per cent).

The present professional activity of refugee physicians, as indicated by the questionnaire returns, is summarized, by sex, in the following table. The tendency to enter private practice or take hospital positions is a little more marked among the Jewish than the Christian physicians, while a higher proportion of the Christian than Jewish have obtained governmental or public health and especially research or teaching positions. In general, the longer the refugee physicians have been in the United States the higher the proportion engaged in private practice and the lower the proportion in hospital positions. This reflects the fact that time is required for citizenship and hence licensure to practice, and meanwhile the physician takes an institutional position where a license is not required. The tendency to engage in private medical practice is marked in the case of New York City and in communities of under 25,000 population, while the proportion employed in hospital positions is above average in communities of all size groups below 500,000. Research and teaching positions are largely located

PER CENT DISTRIBUTION BY PRESENT PROFESSIONAL ACTIVITY

Activity	Males	Females
Private medical practice	72.9	54.4
Private dental practice	3.5	5.5
Hospital positions	14.8	27.5
Research or teaching	6.5	3.8
Governmental or public health positions	2.3	8.8
Total	100.0	100.0

in New York, Massachusetts, Illinois, Ohio, Pennsylvania, Connecticut, and California, and in the larger cities of those states.

It may be recalled that nearly three-fourths of the refugee physicians had been specialists in Europe, with the tendency to specialize being more characteristic of women (76.4 per cent) than of men (72.5 per cent) physicians. Here the proportion specializing is less—52 per cent of the men and 64 per cent of the women. Internal medicine and psychiatry are the leading specialties among the men, with dermatology, dentistry, obstetrics, and ear, nose, and throat taking second place in a long list of specialties. Among the women physicians, psychiatry and pediatrics rank first, with lesser numbers in dentistry, tuberculosis, pathology, internal medicine, and all others. The tendency to follow the same specialty here as abroad is most marked in the case of psychiatry, ear, nose, and throat, and dentistry.

In 77.5 per cent of the cases, the present professional position of the refugee physician was obtained through his own efforts. This was especially true of those in private practice. Ten per cent obtained their present position through the National Committee for Resettlement of Foreign Physicians, 7.7 per cent through friends and relatives, 2.6 per cent through commercial agencies, 1.0 per cent through the Procurement and Assignment Service, and 1.3 per cent through other organizations.

Eighty per cent of the refugee physicians professionally engaged regard their present position as permanent. This is most true of those in private medical or dental practice and in research or teaching and least true of those in hospital and governmental or public health positions. Eighty-five per cent of the group did not expect that their position or affiliation would cease after the war. The exceptions were mainly those in private practice on a *locum tenens* or assistantship basis and those in hospital positions, especially the residents and pathologists.

The occupational adjustment of refugee physicians is further measured by their earnings and the extent of their economic independence. Covering the entire period since their arrival in this country, 43.6 per cent of the physicians had at one time or another received financial assistance, mainly from an organization or committee, to a much lesser extent from friends and relatives. At the time of replying to the questionnaire (the first half of 1945), 79.6 per cent of the physicians were deriving their entire income from their earnings, 11.5 per cent had in addition income from investments and savings, only 2.6 per cent had financial assistance from an organization or committee or from friends and relatives, and the remaining 6.3 per cent had income from other courses or failed to answer the question.

Ninety-five per cent of the respondents to the questionnaire who were engaged in professional activity reported on the amount of their earnings. The results are given in the accompanying table, where it is also indicated whether or not maintenance was provided in addition. The provision of maintenance applied to only one case out of every eight, and was mainly a feature of hospital employment. The earnings in these instances were appreciably less than in the noninstitutional positions, being most typically between $100 and $250 a month.

From the table it will be seen that over half of the refugee physicians who are engaged in professional activity in positions where they do not live in, that is, where maintenance is not provided, have gross earnings that average over $500 a month. Nearly one-third average between $250 and $500 per month. The earnings of the men physicians are appreciably higher than those of the women. Private practice is clearly the most financially rewarding, being the only type of activity in which more than half of the physicians and dentists take in $500 or more per month. All told, the picture is one of good economic adjustment where the refugee physician has been given an opportunity to engage in professional activity.

The respondents to the questionnaire were also asked if they had experienced any advantages in their professional activity here as compared to their normal situation in Europe, and if so, to specify. Only 387 of the 1,600 respondents commented on this matter.

The largest single group of respondents thought there were no superior advantages in professional practice here as compared with Europe. This attitude was more characteristic of the women physicians, who have experienced greater difficulty in adjustment than have the men. The restrictions affecting licensing, hospital affiliation, and medical society membership loom large in the minds of those refugee physicians who have experienced no advantage here as compared to Europe. The large proportion not replying at all to this question further implies a negative attitude.

PER CENT DISTRIBUTION OF AVERAGE GROSS MONTHLY EARNINGS, BY SEX, FOR REFUGEE PHYSICIANS EMPLOYED IN THEIR PROFESSION

	Without Maintenance						With Maintenance					
	Number	Per Cent	Under $100	$100 249	$250 499	$500 and Over	Number	Per Cent	Under $100	$100 249	$250 499	$500 and Over
Males	1,069	100.0	1.0	10.4	31.3	57.3	137	100.0	16.8	56.9	24.8	1.5
Females	139	100.0	7.9	28.8	38.1	25.2	35	100.0	22.9	65.7	11.4	—
All Cases	1,208	100.0	1.8	12.5	32.0	53.7	172	100.0	18.0	58.7	22.1	1.2
Private medical practice	948	100.0	1.5	8.7	29.4	60.4	17	—	23.5	64.7	11.8	—
Private dental practice	53	100.0	5.7	15.1	26.4	52.8	—					
Hospital positions	96	100.0	3.1	38.5	27.1	31.3	137	100.0	17.5	61.3	20.5	.7
Research or teaching	75	100.0	—	22.7	62.6	14.7	12	100.0	25.0	16.6	50.0	8.4
Governmental or public health positions	36	100.0	5.6	19.4	58.3	16.7	6	100.0	—	66.7	33.3	—

About 10 per cent of the men and 5 per cent of the women physicians replying thought our hospital affiliations were better and our internship more practical than in Europe. As one doctor commented: "Hospitals are more accessible for the general practitioner than in Germany, where the large hospitals have a completely closed staff." Eliciting a larger proportion of favorable comments were matters relating to scientific standards and opportunities, such as better research facilities, better graduate courses, more opportunities for keeping abreast of scientific accomplishment, and a more congenial academic atmosphere. The role of the hospital with regular clinical-pathological conferences, an institution unknown in continental Europe, as a stimulant for keeping scientific knowledge up to date is given special mention. On the other hand, some refugee physicians believe there are more facilities for research in Europe—more assistants available, more support of research that does not promise immediate practical application, more appreciation of extreme accuracy, and more opportunities for publication, especially of long papers. According to them, the medical journals of Germany are more specialized, extensive, and indispensable to pure research than ours.

About the same proportion of respondents find more advantages in the practice of medicine here than in Europe. These cover a variety of items such as greater remuneration, a "wider field," more opportunity for specialization and for professional progress, better professional relations with other physicians, the absence here of state sickness insurance (no *Kranken-kassen* or sick funds), and better relations with patients. Whereas many of the nonmedical refugees regard the absence of compulsory sickness insurance here as a handicap and a factor of insecurity, the refugee physicians tend to regard it as an asset. Typical comments are these:

"I enjoy not having socialized medicine which is factory work, not scientific medical work."

"I think the private practice of medicine far superior to the sociological plan in Germany."

With regard to the physician-patient relationship, some respondents state that American patients place more confidence in the physician and are less inclined to question his work. One states: "After you explain something to a patient, the frequent answer is, 'Well, you're the doctor.'" Another comments:

"In Europe the ties between doctor and patient are much more emotional. The doctor by his well-versed social attitude somehow has to impress the patient by his superior social position (which he usually truly has). As soon as the patient 'looks up to him' he will be obedient and undergo all required procedures, will be a 'good' patient, a very thankful patient (much more so than here), and a completely trusting patient.

"Here the opposite is true. The patient . . . will from the beginning do everything to co-operate because he is hopeful, he believes in 'science' and even if the doctor is bad, something good will result from all these procedures. For the average American there is 'something good,' 'something hopeful' around every corner."

Finally, a small percentage of physicians who commented on this item in the questionnaire stated they found less discrimination in medical practice here, more fairness, and a greater tendency for professional development to depend on ability, in a keenly competitive field, than on name, family, race, or religion.

With regard to the social adjustment of the refugee physicians and their integration into community life, we may note first their tendency to reside in neighborhoods where native Americans predominate. Only about one-fifth of the physicians are living in neighborhoods of the immigrant-community type. In New York City, however, where there is a notable concentration of refugee physicians, one-third of them live in such neighborhoods. The great majority, especially outside of New York City, reside in neighborhoods where other refugees are relatively few in number or absent, and thus are favorably situated so far as opportunity for association with native Americans is concerned.

As a result of this situation and other factors, it is not surprising that 51.2 per cent of the physicians report that their friends are mainly Americans. The percentage of cases where the friends are mainly Americans varies inversely, almost in perfect progression, by size of community, ranging from 70 to 80 per cent in the very small communities to under 50 per cent in cities of over 500,000 population to 33 per cent in New York City. The tendency to have mainly American friends is more marked among the men than the women physicians and among those under 50 years of age, especially those under 40, than those who are older. It is also more characteristic of those who have been a longer time in this country, being the rule only in the case of those who have been here six years or longer and amounting to 70 per cent of the cases with residence of nine years or more.

Home ownership also varies directly with length of residence. The overall percentage of home ownership is 20.5 per cent, a high proportion for a recent immigrant group and indicative of both economic and social adjustment and of intention to remain here permanently. The percentage of home ownership is somewhat higher in smaller than in larger sized communities and among Christians than among Jews.

Twenty-two per cent of the refugee physicians had married since their arrival in this country. That nearly two out of every five marriages of these recent arrivals were with native Americans is indicative of ready social acceptance and assimilability.

Integration into community life, as measured by membership in American organizations, also has proceeded apace. Only 7 per cent of the physicians replying do not belong to any organizations, whether fraternal, professional, civic, social, or other kinds. The most common type of organization in which they participate actively is that with mainly American membership; this was true of 68.4 per cent of the respondents. Only 4.6 per cent participated in refugee organizations only, while 20.0 per cent belonged to organizations of the greatly mixed, refugee and American, type. The tendency to participate in the American type of organization is more characteristic of those residing in communities of less than 500,000 population than in the larger cities, though it is the rule everywhere. It is also slightly more characteristic of men than of women and especially marked among those under 40 years of age.

The citizenship record of the refugee physicians is remarkable. Aside from four respondents who were citizens on arrival, that is, repatriates, and three who were on temporary visas and hence not eligible, the questionnaire returns reveal that no refugee physician has failed to apply for his first citizenship papers and that two-thirds of them (66.4 per cent), as compared with one-half of the general refugee group, have already become citizens. Among the factors accounting for this are the longer average period of residence of the physicians and their special incentive to attain citizenship so as to become eligible to take licensing examinations. The percentage who have attained citizenship is highest among the German physicians, most likely explainable by the fact that they have been here a longer time and hence more able to meet the minimum residence requirement of five years.

Whether aliens or citizens, the physicians, like other refugees, contributed to the war effort through military service, purchase of war bonds, blood donations, and other ways. Only 4 out of the 1,600 respondents specifically stated that they had made no contribution, whether able to or not, while 26 left the question unanswered. The great majority of the respondents had made from two to four types of contributions. A frequent complaint by the men was that because of citizenship and other requirements they were not accepted for service in the Army Medical Corps, though, as we have seen, some did attain this objective. A number of them had assisted in medical examinations for the Selective Service System for which they held certificates of appreciation for uncompensated services.

Ninety-seven per cent of the respondents to the physicians' questionnaire stated that they intend to remain permanently in the United States. The few who intend to return to Europe or are undecided about their postwar residence plans are mainly Austrians, Hungarians, Poles, and Czechoslovaks. They are largely an older group, those unlicensed, and those anxious to aid in the reconstruction of their former homelands. Prominent among the latter are the Slavic groups, especially the Poles. From the medical as well as other standpoints, Poland probably suffered more than other countries, most of her physicians being killed and her medical institutions destroyed. Many of the refugee physicians would like to help in postwar reconstruction in Europe if they could do so without losing their American citizenship. According to our laws, if any naturalized citizen should reside for two years in the foreign state from which he came, or for five years in any other foreign state, it shall be presumed that he has ceased to be an American citizen. This presumption may, however, be overcome on the presentation of satisfactory evidence to a diplomatic or consular official of the United States under regulations prescribed by the State Department.

The future plans and hopes of the refugee physicians in the United States consist largely in continuing in their present professional activity or finding employment in the type of activity they had been engaged in abroad, improving their scientific training, and gaining more professional status.

The largest single group of those answering this question hope to continue in their present activity, which they find satisfactory. Others would like to specialize, do research, teach, or get into the type of professional work they were trained for. Many of these are in hospital or other positions which are temporary or intermediate to the assumption of private practice. Frequently they are holding these positions pending the attainment of a license. Some expect to lose their present positions when the Army doctors return to civilian life. Competition, they think, will be keen, and if the returning veterans should encounter difficulties the refugee physicians will be the scapegoat. Already they have been blamed for the serious shortage of office space, though the number of refugees in private practice is less than 3 per cent of the total body of American physicians. More commonly, however, the refugee physicians feel that after being here five or more years they are pretty well adjusted and assimilated and that the years to come will be less difficult than those which have passed.

Despite the difficulties of readjustment in a new country, refugee physicians have contributed to the advancement of medical science and practice. American medicine has benefited by the achievements of many of those refugees who were given a chance to resume their work in medical research, clinical work, and teaching. One of the respondents to the questionnaire received the annual prize of the American Association of Obstetricians, Gynecologists and Abdominal Surgeons for the discovery of the theoa cone in human and mammalian ovaries. Another was co-founder and officer of the Association for Advancement of Psychotherapy. Some have been appointed to the editorial boards of professional journals, such as the *Journal of Immunology*, the *Journal of Investigative Dermatology*, and the *An-*

nals of Allergy. Twelve reported on the discovery of new principles and the invention of new techniques, some of which have been patented. One hundred and nine had published books or scientific papers since their arrival in the United States, reporting on their research in a great variety of fields. The total number of such publications runs into the hundreds. These contributions of the respondents to the questionnaire, along with their practical medical service, are indicative of the benefits that have already accrued from the immigration of refugee physicians.

CHAPTER XVI

LAWYERS

‖‖

According to official immigration figures, between 1,800 and 2,000 immigrant lawyers came to the United States from Europe during the period 1933–1944. Many of these were refugees. A former barrister, who has been active in building up a card file of former European jurists in exile, had been able to account for 755 such in the United States as of January, 1945. He stated that, in time, this list might include as many as 1,000 from Germany alone. Compared to the total number of 180,483 lawyers in the United States as reported in the 1940 census, however, immigrant lawyers constitute at most but a very small proportion.

What happened to these lawyers when they reached the United States? How many succeeded in retraining so that they could continue to practice their former profession? How many were obliged to go into less congenial fields?

Before attempting to answer these questions, let us consider the law as a profession. The law is not like music or mathematics; it is not a profession with an international vocabulary. As a specialty it is narrow. Of all fields it is one of the most difficult in which to make a contribution in a strange country. As a refugee lawyer expressed it: "The law is a dogmatic science. To pick up a European jurist and set him down in the American legal atmosphere is like taking up a theologian who has been trained in Rome and putting him down in a lamasery in Tibet. In each setting the same God is worshipped, but the manner and philosophy are very, very different."

Much more is involved, however, than certain obvious hazards experienced by any foreigner who would acquire a working knowledge of Anglo-Saxon law and establish the connections necessary to build up his practice here. One of these is pointed out by Marie Ginsberg in her article, "Adjustment of the Professional Refugee":[1]

As to the lawyers, the possibility of their continuing as jurists in foreign countries is practically excluded. Except for a small proportion who specialize in comparative and international law, the lawyers are for the most part very limited even in their practice of

[1] *Annals of the American Academy of Political and Social Science*, Vol. 203, May, 1939, pp. 157–158.

German law. The custom has been to practice a high degree of specialization; thus, one will confine himself to matters of taxation, another to problems of tenancy, another to insurance, and so forth. If they have been doing this for a great number of years, they are obviously unfitted for an entire reorganization of their knowledge in a foreign law system. So, on the whole, only a very few, and those among the younger men, are able to qualify for legal practice in a new country. Of course, commerce and industry can absorb a certain number of these former lawyers.

From the standpoint of employment possibilities, the legal profession is one which has come close to overcrowding, at least in the large cities, however great may be the need for more and better lawyers in "under-lawyered" areas. This situation was intensified during the depression.[2] Actually, the number of lawyers in the United States in proportion to the population had dropped from 140 for every 100,000 inhabitants in 1930 to 137 per 100,000 inhabitants in 1940. Yet the fact remains that professional opportunities in large cities are inadequate as measured by the number of lawyers available. Thus the distribution of lawyers is a factor to consider as well as their total number.

In terms of the refugee lawyer, the difficulties of converting his knowledge to fit a new legal system, and the alleged overcrowding in the profession, added up to an almost insurmountable obstacle in the way of continuing his professional career. In order to persevere, he must inevitably retrain—a costly process taking at least two years of intensive study during which he could not hope to be self-supporting or contribute to the support of his family. At the end of this period he could not be sure of gainful employment.

Nor could the European lawyer or professor of law hope for much in the way of a teaching position on an American law faculty (although there were a handful who succeeded in finding such appointments). In 1939, the secretary of the American Committee for the Guidance of Professional Personnel stated categorically: "The very basis of my committee's work has been the assumption that European professors could not secure teaching positions and therefore required retraining."

Yet to the former lawyer whose heart was bound up in his profession, no other occupation seemed so desirable as the law. In spite of this strong predilection, once in the United States, the lawyers turned their hands to many kinds of work. They were not lazy, and did not disdain manual labor while waiting for a chance to get back into the law. One found a job as bottle washer in a factory; another worked successively as a fireman, a mechanic, and an unskilled workman. A third became in turn fireman, night watchman, and shipfitter. A fortunate few found white-collar jobs—selling insurance, translating documents, handling real estate, teaching school.

[2] Cf. Walter M. Kotsching, *Unemployment in the Learned Professions*, 1937, p. 152.

But whatever their temporary occupation might be, one and all yearned after the law. To some, dropping out of the legal profession meant unbearable loss of professional status and self-respect:

"In spite of my conscious struggle to keep myself in touch with people of my professional interest," wrote a refugee lawyer, 44 years of age, who arrived in San Francisco in 1939, "in spite of my conscious struggle to maintain myself on a level of professional standard—I began to realize that I was sliding down. I felt that the life I led, the difficulties and disappointments, was showing its effects on me. I began to catch myself losing confidence, self-assurance, freedom, which I had always experienced before, of meeting people of my own level. I also noticed a change not only in my exterior looks—my clothing, etc.,—but also in my manners, thinking and my inner self. I became self-conscious and that gave me the feeling that I maybe was 'a failure' after all."

While refugee lawyers freely declared that they had suffered a greater loss in professional status than any other refugee group, Americans frequently retorted that refugee lawyers gave themselves unwarranted airs—considered their European education superior to that of Americans and felt that they were entitled to preferential treatment. Occasionally American colleagues alleged that when refugees sought subsidies to enable them to study American law for a two- or three-year period they were in effect begging to be translated to the ivory tower of academic life where they would not have to do manual work.

It was impossible, however, to overlook the wistfulness of the appeals of the refugee lawyers themselves, with their unmistakable air of earnestness:

"I think, it is impossible for me to become again lawyer," wrote one. "I like to tell you, that my transportation-business is growing nicely, so that I make a good living. Beside this I try to do my duty; I became Auxiliary Fireman and help in refugee-organizations. I am still very interested in law; if you should see any possibility, please let me know it."

"I had put it in my blockhead to stick to my line," declared another more eloquently than elegantly, "not to desert the Law to whom I have served for almost twenty-five years with the fervor of a lover, but there were 'collateral' obstacles which I could not surmount or avoid."

"I am working as a night nurse with 84 hours of duty and therefore have nearly no private contact with American people," wrote another. "But I have one call and hope and wish to come back to my former faculty. I was a lawyer with all my heart, and I strive to resume my former calling."

It was the steadfastness of such men as these that was finally rewarded by the establishment of a special organization—the American Committee for the Guidance of Professional Personnel—which was instrumental in retraining a selected group of refugee lawyers. This committee (later to

develop into the Committee for the Re-education of Refugee Lawyers)
came into existence in 1938 because a group of outstanding and public-
spirited men including John W. Davis, C. J. Friedrich of Harvard University, and David Riesman, Jr., then professor at the University of Buffalo
Law School, believed that refugee scholars had a positive contribution to
make to American law. Professor Riesman as secretary vigorously expressed his committee's viewpoint when he declared:

"I believed, and I have not been disabused of this belief, that we would find five or
ten refugees of exceptional ability and personal adaptability who would be equipped to
do some real cross-fertilization, not so much of comparative law or European legal methodology as of the social sciences in which, much more than the average American lawyers, they had been steeped by training and inclination. On the basis of intrinsic capacity, men such as these, if there is a chance of placing them in law schools, or in research
jobs, would seem to have as much to contribute as American law school professors already
placed, and perhaps a little bit more because of their ability to combine in one person
the multiple skills that law teaching now seeks. Many of our men have done exception-
ally well academically in the law schools where they have gone."

It was the committee's plan to place a few exceptional European lawyers
in American law schools for retraining on the basis of a special two-year
course which would enable them to practice in the United States. The applicant had first to be accepted by the selection committee, and then by a
law school. Following this, the law school was expected to raise enough
money to satisfy the conditions imposed by the committee, and then, with
the law school and the committee both co-operating, a modest stipend sufficient to take care of living expenses and tuition would be granted the applicant. The committee found it desirable that those persons retrained
should follow the regular law course required of American undergraduate
legal students. In the words of a consultant dean: "From the point of view
of placement also, I am persuaded it is of the first importance that these
men be stamped as regular graduates of the Law Schools, not men who
have taken some marked special course."

What the committee sought "both in application forms and interviews,"
explained Professor Riesman, "was to discover men of youthful vigor and
energy, of ready adaptability, who had something special to contribute to
the practice of law in the United States."

The committee limited its assistance to men and women 35 years old or
less, believing that after that age a person's chances after retraining were
slight. In spite of this restriction, jurists of all ages turned to the committee
for guidance with the result that its files are a rich source of information
about the refugee lawyer population. Refugees of every European nationality were considered, and during its first year the committee received some
135 applications.

The committee undertook to raise money to cover a limited number of stipends by turning to the legal profession itself:

"The retraining of refugee lawyers is too small and unexciting a venture to appeal to the usual charitable donors," explained the committee's secretary. "We have felt all along that the appeals should be made to the bar not so much because lawyers offer the best market for securing funds, but because part of the point of the program was to secure their sympathetic understanding of the plight of their brethren of the bar who had come here from other lands."

With the funds secured, the committee was able to assist nine scholars during the academic year 1939–1940 while some nineteen others studied with the Committee's help during 1940–1941. In all, the committee's final report states, "a total of twenty-eight men were enabled to undergo retraining courses at twenty-one different colleges and universities, scattered over a sufficiently wide area to be fairly representative of the whole United States."

There was not much ready money available, however, to help the would-be student, for as someone ruefully remarked, "nobody is particularly interested in helping lawyers along." A fairly typical response, too, was that expressed by an eastern university whose spokesman said: "We have felt here that we could not use our so-called research funds for purely relief purposes, though there have been several cases in which our hearts have influenced our heads."

Meanwhile law schools all over the country were receiving direct applications for fellowships, in many cases from refugees who had been in the United States for some years and who had already had the benefit of several years of professional law training. In these instances schools tended to encourage the applicant to go into practice rather than to continue advanced work. Subsidies when given were usually reserved for the benefit of men who had not as yet had the benefit of any American legal training.

The Riesman Committee with its extremely limited number of fellowships, and the law schools themselves, were generally speaking the only agencies which offered direct financial help in retraining refugee jurists. Among the immigrant lawyers and judges themselves, particularly among the older ones, there was a good deal of bitterness because the large refugee-service organizations had given subsidies to medical men enabling them to retrain in their profession but had in the main withheld financial assistance from lawyers.

Among American organizations, however, the point of view was widely held that, taking into account the attitude of local student groups in the law schools, it was doubtful whether any service agency could have enlisted good will in the universities for a substantial number of refugee lawyers. The arrival in the law schools of these displaced people en masse would almost certainly have aroused antagonism to a degree prejudicial to the entire refugee movement. The agencies furthermore believed that in order to succeed as a lawyer one needed many contacts among businessmen so as to secure employment from or through them. This took time. Without such contacts one must have capital with which to open one's own office. Few refugee lawyers could command either contacts or capital, and refugee organizations, judging lawyers to be a less good risk than doctors whose skill was much more transferable, were unwilling to appropriate the funds necessary to support individuals for the three to five years that might elapse before they could begin to be self-supporting in the law. It was this line of reasoning that led to the establishment of programs to retrain lawyers in other fields or to facilitate their immediate employment in business enterprises, factories, or such occupations as might offer.

In spite of the formidable obstacles standing in their way, it is known that at least some 175 former lawyers succeeded in retraining in their field in the United States. This figure, which is at best a partial one, was secured by writing to deans of law schools and consulting the records of a number of service agencies.

Once the refugee was slated for formal retraining, either with the help of the Committee for the Re-education of Refugee Lawyers or a university or both, or through the use of such personal funds as he might have at his disposal, there were still other factors than those already discussed which confronted him. One of these was prejudice on the part of the American community. One refugee lawyer wrote in discouragement as his studies drew to a close:

"I do not believe that I could find a position anywhere in the United States. I do not know whether this is due to Anti-Semitism or Xenophobia or personal shortcomings, but after these two years I have to say, that I do not think that former lawyers should study law once more in the United States."

Another had to say:

"I am most anxious to join a reputable law firm either in New York or in the South or West, but repeated efforts in New York have taught me that my Jewish descent or my German birthplace are, in the alternate, or cumulatively, almost insuperable handicaps."

But far and away the most basic difficulty confronting the foreign student was the difference in conception between American and European law and methods of legal study here and abroad. A representative of a great eastern law school remarked of refugee lawyers, "the foreign background in many cases seems to me to hinder them in acquiring common-law ways. So many of them seem to think that the baggage they carry is sufficient justification for carrying it no matter where they are going." The dean of a northern university analyzed the difficulties of foreign students exposed to the case method of study:

"It is simple enough for a well-trained German lawyer to digest quickly our statutory materials or to learn legal principles from texts or such a thing as the Restatement, but it is difficult for them to get the feel of our use of cases. Much of their own training has to be rooted out. Deeply rooted habits of thought which have become very nearly instinctive and which are conditioned reflexes to the very problems which arouse in us quite a different reflex have to be replaced. Unfortunately, it does not matter how good or bad their thinking may be on these problems relative to the thinking of American lawyers. If they are going to compete in the kind of game we play, they will have to think in the way we do."

It must not be forgotten that the process of retraining was frequently undertaken when the newcomer was still suffering from mental, physical, and emotional strains. Frequently the lawyer approached the scholarship committee after having undergone trying experiences, as this typical case reveals:

"I practised as independent lawyer for about two years and was forbidden to practise law on 23rd day of June, 1938, because I was a Jew. I was sent to a concentration camp without any reason and trial and was released after six months and twenty days. . . ."

There was a former German lawyer who had become a victim of his sense of duty as a member of the legal profession. "This man, who is neither a Jew nor an open enemy of the National Socialist regime, has been persecuted and driven out of Germany for the mere reason of having dared to defend prisoners in political cases. The man seems to have not only courage but also other high personal qualities." Such instances could be multiplied indefinitely.

There was ever-present worry about absent relatives, and the destruction of a way of life. Occasionally these emotional stresses carried over into student life, as the following instance chosen from a great number indicates:

He is a nervous taut personality still unadjusted to the shock of having been torn from a secure life in Munich with an affluent family and excellent opportunities for the future. His mother is a Jewess, which prevented him from completing his doctorate in law at Munich. . . . He becomes nervous in exams and finds the classroom discussion difficult to follow due to the Americanisms tossed about.

Perusal of letters written by refugees in training indicates that they were frequently recipients of harrowing news from abroad. This was true of all refugees, but the younger group more frequently had parents and grandparents still living in Europe than did their older colleagues.

It was under these conditions that many of the lawyers retrained. Moreover, the student usually worked to earn part of his expenses, which, combined with his heavy hours of classroom and study assignments, was taxing:

> Forced to leave Germany, he now does clerical work in the office of a paper mill, at the same time studying law at New York University night school.

> He is working for his board washing dishes at the University Hospital. This will keep the expense down so that I think the effort is worthwhile.

A student's own description of his work and study at a law school is illuminating:

> "I might say that I have become completely Americanized during this period. I live in one of the dormitories, and steady, friendly intercourse with the students helped me a lot in taking on American habits and customs. . . . I have acquired a very wide knowledge of American law. This semester I am taking again twenty-one hours in the following courses. . . . The work is rather heavy, but I can manage it, and I hope to hold the same academic standing and average as last year. Besides my studies, I work about twenty hours for the college, but this part is rather nominal, as it seems to be well understood that, with a heavy load like I take, there is not much time left. In addition, I participate in various college activities. I sponsor a quiz program like 'Information, Please.' I write a column for the weekly college paper. I take part in various sport activities, and I won last year's championship in table tennis, and I went into the finals of the state championship matches."

When the refugee lawyer had finished his training, he must take bar examinations if he would practice. There are no figures available as to the number of European jurists who took and passed such examinations. A former Austrian lawyer estimated the number to be "some 70-odd" as of the end of 1944; a German refugee lawyer declared early in 1945 that this was "much too high a figure."

Following the arduous years of retraining and the taking of bar examinations, the lawyer must try to launch himself in professional life. Some Americans feared lest the struggle prove so great that the refugee would give up the battle and try to make for himself a life of research in the universities. The first obstacle he encountered was the citizenship requirement before he could be admitted to practice. According to the article on "Refugees and the Professions" which appeared in the *Harvard Law Review* in 1939 (Vol. LIII, No. 1):

> In thirty-nine jurisdictions full citizenship is a prerequisite to admission to the bar. A variety of apologia have been adduced in answer to the contention that such a requirement denies to aliens the equal protection of the laws. Thus it has been said that the profession requires an appreciation of the spirit of American political institutions; that attorneys as officers of the court should be citizens; that an alien cannot take an oath to support the Constitution; and that a war between the United States and the alien's country might result in seizure of the alien, with resultant injury to his clients. It has also

been suggested that diversity of citizenship might serve to remove the lawyer from the traditional control of the state over its bar.

In seven jurisdictions whose legislatures have imposed no citizenship requirement, the omission has been nullified by regulations of the state supreme court or board of bar examiners. While the possibility of successful attack upon these regulations may be doubtful, the advisability of requiring citizenship seems rather a question for legislative determination than an aspect of the power of court or bar to establish criteria of training and character. And an attack on the validity of such an action of the court or bar might well succeed where the legislature has specified a lesser requirement.

Citizenship papers during war years were slow in coming through.

The war increased employment opportunities, but prejudice against refugees sometimes presented an obstacle, as a letter written in February, 1942, by a Boston attorney pointed out:

"Since the war there has been a greater need for lawyers and I have had some hopes that the situation would ease. At the same time, some of the firms have been made more —and unduly—suspicious by the war itself and one man, who I had hoped to place with a downtown firm which is in desperate need of personnel, recently informed me that they could not take a refugee."

By June of 1942, and thereafter up through the end of 1944, when the Riesman Committee became inactive, hopeful reports were filtering in:

"One of our two graduating refugee lawyers has gotten a job with a very good law firm in Manitowoc, Wisconsin, and starts in today," a dean wrote. "They will pay him enough to live on and he and I are both very happy about the outcome."

"As you might know," a refugee jurist wrote, "I have graduated from Harvard Law School and obtained a position with ———— [a prominent law firm]. I hope you have received the last issue of the Louisiana Law Review in which one of my articles has been published. Another article dealing with corporation law has been accepted for publication by the Iowa Law Review."

"I found a position with the law firm of ————," wrote another, "and feel myself nicely settled again."

In studying so minutely this group which sought or succeeded in securing retraining—a group interesting because it revealed so intimately the interplay of American and European legal concepts and the interrelations of American and European jurists—we have been dealing for the most part with a younger group of men and women. In the words of an American attorney who had been a refugee himself: "The refugee lawyers who succeeded 'just in earning a living' in the legal profession are probably all less than 40 now. They came into the United States when they were between 25 and 35."

And yet a number of older men retrained, heroically enduring the same difficulties which nearly engulfed their younger colleagues. It would be pleasant to report that many of them are now engaged in successful practice. Where they are in the law, however, it is usually with firms where they advise on questions of foreign law or draw up legal documents. Usually they do not draw up briefs or appear in court. Younger men sometimes ask of this senior group why they were willing to make the terrific sacrifices of time and health when they must have known how meager would be the rewards.

Now and then a refugee lawyer made the transition from menial work to academic life:

"In my particular case," wrote one, "it meant the change from a floorwalker in an all-night hash house on 42nd Street and 7th Ave., in New York City to a member of the ———— University faculty within less than 5 years."

There was a certain amount of formal retraining of refugee lawyers to enable them to enter other professions and occupations, although no over-all figures are available. A student at the New York School of Social Work[3] reported as of August, 1940, that of 114 individuals known to have studied or practiced law abroad in Germany whose records she studied in the relief, service and resettlement division of the National Refugee Service, 26 had "retrained" to fit them for the following employment:

As Certified Public Accountants	6
As lawyer	1
As sales persons	6
As craftsmen or skilled workers	4
For service jobs	8
For manual labor	1
	26

Accountancy offered one of the most congenial fields for many refugee lawyers, although it required arduous training or close independent study.

A number of lawyers came to the schools of social work to retrain as case workers. Others, who were interested in children's courts, juvenile delinquency, and crime prevention, regretted their inability to enter the social-work field in the United States without formal training.

There was recognition of the needs of foreign lawyers who could not pursue the study of American law here to familiarize themselves with American legal phraseology. Such a need was met by the formation of special classes like those described below:

As an illustration of language education in a special field, we should like to refer to the classes in American terminology of law as they are conducted at the Free French University. Dr. Ernst Fraenkel was in charge of such a class for almost a year. It was attended by an average of 30 refugee lawyers. The purpose of these classes is to familiarize

[3] Marjorie S. Dammann, *The Employment Problems of the Refugee Lawyer*, unpublished.

former European jurists with the principal concepts of American law. These students do not intend to practice law in this country. But they hope that their total adjustment may become easier by being able to understand problems which are particularly close to their interest. Moreover, the knowledge of the American legal terminology may help people with a legal background to get jobs in which the understanding of legal questions is essential. Former lawyers are trained in this class to read decisions of American courts, Federal and State statutes and typical American contracts.[4]

It is noteworthy that these courses for refugees were not given by American lawyers. Occasionally in the records one finds quite outspoken criticism of Americans. One refugee lawyer reported that he had sought work opportunities from American lawyers of his own nationality background. They had been unresponsive. "This disappointed me very much," the lawyer stated in an interview, "because I had thought that clerical posts in law firms would afford excellent opportunities for refugee lawyers—opportunities which would be infinitely better for them than having to work in factories . . . I tried to interest American lawyers in the personal affairs of the refugees, asking, where there seemed to be no employment opportunities, whether they would not supply scholarships for studies in international law. There just wasn't any response. Perhaps they were afraid of competition from the newcomers." Sometimes the refugee came to regard American jurists with scorn. "I wouldn't want to go back to law again, even if I could," asserted a former factory manager and lawyer from Europe who was working as a mechanic here. "In this country law hasn't the same standing as it had in Germany. There it was regarded as even a higher profession than medicine." Another refugee jurist was reported as saying that "the moral level here among American lawyers was very low. She did not wish to compete with them, neither did her friends."

With or without retraining, lawyers spread out into other fields. An Austrian attorney stated that the bulk of the lawyers he knew had become accountants. Some few went into the factories, some became diamond polishers and leather-goods workers, some founded independent businesses (such as printing establishments) which gave work to other Americans as well as refugees, while others became umbrella makers, and so forth. He personally knew of two who had been admitted to the bar. Other refugee jurists were doing as he himself was doing—that is, giving opinions to American lawyers and sometimes to clients. Another Austrian attorney remarked in an interview that a few of the older men he knew had retired and, without definite occupation to keep their minds active, had died. Many younger people were in business—exporting, importing, real estate, and insurance brokerage.

[4] *Selver-Fraenkel Report on Social Adjustment of Refugees*, National Refugee Service, 1943, unpublished.

A Polish jurist said that his co-nationals were for the most part in real estate or other white-collar occupations.

A German reported that a number of his group were now insurance, real estate or stock brokers, or had gone into commerce and industry, or into the service of the government.

A Russian lawyer, who stated that very few members of his group had retrained as lawyers and taken their bar examinations, described his own business activities as confined largely to consulting with his compatriots on matters pertaining to visas and foreign funds control, giving opinions on questions of foreign law, and serving as interpreter in American courts. He has clients who are still in Europe whose business affairs he handles. He also works on Treasury Department reports.

Opportunities during the war years for obtaining jobs were brilliant compared to what they had been in the preceding period, the Russian lawyer went on to say. Compatriots of his had secured jobs in the Office of War Information, or were teaching Russian, or had been engaged by the Office of Strategic Services, Foreign Economic Administration, and the like.

From every side came stories of refugee lawyers in government bureaus —Office of Censorship, Treasury Department, Office of Price Administration, military occupation services, and others. An American commented cynically that for many of these refugees military government and the allied fields into which they went had simply been a "racket" which they exploited. Actually, this charge emanated from a few officers of medium rank in the occupation forces and had little or no justification in fact. The experience of the United Nations Relief and Rehabilitation Administration with refugees to America whom it has employed has been very satisfactory, according to a special report it prepared for the Study Committee in February, 1946. Nearly half of the 87 refugees employed through the headquarters office in Washington were professional people, including lawyers, doctors, teachers, and social workers. Many were given important assignments in their respective fields, in capacities "where their European experience has been very helpful to the Administration." About half of the group were sent on overseas assignments.

One of the most striking examples of contributions made by former European jurists to the American prosecution of the war and the administration of problems growing out of the conflict, was that of Dr. Robert M. W. Kempner, a former German lawyer and judge. "This former concentration camp inmate who came to the United States as a refugee on the very day when the war broke out," as Raymond Daniell described him in a signed news story in the *New York Times* of January 17, 1946, became a member of Justice Robert H. Jackson's prosecution staff at the Nuremberg trial of German war criminals.

A sample group of 311 lawyers reached by the Study Committee's questionnaire reported their present occupations as follows:

A total of 78 remained in professional life, of whom, however, only 19 were lawyers in the United States. It is interesting that an equal number became professors or teachers—almost certainly not of legal subjects.

In the nonprofessional fields, where the great majority were forced to seek employment, it is worthy of note that 27 became owners of businesses and 33 managers or officials. The largest single group, 122, or about 40 per cent of the total, took jobs as bookkeepers, salespeople, or other white-collar workers. Twenty-nine were employed as skilled, semiskilled, or unskilled laborers. Of the total, 13, or 4.2 per cent, were unemployed, not counting 2 students and 4 housewives.

Of the 311 lawyers responding to the Study Committee's questionnaire, 49.2 per cent had already become citizens, while 32.4 per cent had received their first papers and an additional 15.4 per cent had applied for their second papers. Of this segment of the refugee lawyer population, none expressed any desire to return to Europe. Twenty-nine of the respondents declared that they felt they had made special contributions to American life ranging from publications by 24 of this number to patents on inventions by 2.

Before closing this section, mention must be made of the strong organizational life among refugee lawyers in this country (see Chapter XI). Almost every language group developed its special association to promote occupational opportunities for its members and to provide a meeting place where questions interesting to the legal profession could be debated. In some instances, special publications and even periodicals were sponsored. A number of these groups concerned themselves also with the complicated problems of the restoration of civil and property rights to victims of Nazi oppression on the theory that the people who could present the best documented claims and the most tightly drawn schemes for restitution would fare best at the peace table.

CHAPTER XVII

PROFESSORS AND SCIENTISTS

||||||||||||||||||||||||||||||||||||||||||||||||||||||||||||||||||||||||||||||||||||||||||||||||||||||||||||||||||||||||||||||||||||||||||||||||||||||||||||||||

UNIVERSITY PROFESSORS

Hitler became Chancellor of Germany on January 30, 1933. Little more than two months later, the law "to reconstruct the Civil Service" initiated a series of cataclysmic measures "calculated to ensure the loyalty of civil servants, under which the university faculties were to lose from 15 to 20 per cent of their personnel."[1] As of 1937, dismissals of German university teachers had reached the following proportions:[2]

CLASSIFICATION OF DISMISSED SCHOLARS BY ACADEMIC STATUS

"University Teachers"[1]		
Ordentliche Professoren	313	
Ausserordentliche Professoren	109	
Nichtbeamtete Ausserordentliche Professoren	284	
Professoren *in honoris causa*	75	
Privatdozenten	322	
Lektoren	11	
Beauftragte Dozenten	13	
Teachers of unknown rank	18	
Total	1,145	1,145
Assistants		232
Employees of Non-University Scientific Institutes[2]		133
Recent Graduates		105
Intellectuals[3]		69
Grand Total[4]		1,684

[1] *Universitäten* (including *Medizinische Akademie Düsseldorf* and *Staatliche Akademie Braunsberg*), 953; *Technische Hochschulen*, 158; *Handelshochschulen*, 28; others, 6.
[2] Branch Institutes of the *Kaiser Wilhelm-Gesellschaft*, 33; hospitals, 27; *Robert Koch Institut für Infektionskrankheiten*, 6; industrial research, 3; other scientific institutions, State foundations, etc., 65.
[3] Libraries, 15 (7 from the *Preussische Staatsbibliothek*); teachers, 24 (music 12, art 2, normal schools 2, vocational school 1, adult schools (*Volkshochschulen*), 5); government officials, 6; museum officials, 11; editors, 5; free-lance writers, 3; musicians and conductors, 4; one banker.
[4] 1,615 men, 64 women, and 5 cases of "no information."

But the expulsion of scholars did not stop with Germany. As Nazi domination swept beyond the borders of the Reich, university professors of Jewish "race" or of unacceptable political views throughout continental Europe

[1] Edward Yarnall Hartshorne, Jr., *The German Universities and National Socialism*, 1937, p. 16.
[2] *Ibid.*, p. 93.

were uprooted. At first, many scholars bided their time, believing, in happy ignorance of what lay in store for them, that the Hitler regime would pass and that the old order would soon be restored. Some picked themselves up with promptitude and went to neighboring countries which, like Great Britain, France, Italy, Switzerland, and the Low Countries, extended hospitality. Some, like Fritz Haber of synthetic nitrogen fame, made the ultimate protest against Nazi doctrine and committed suicide. Some accepted calls which overseas universities spontaneously accorded them. Others sought desperately to go abroad, but did not find the means immediately to emigrate. For some, deliverance from the Nazi yoke did not come for many years. For a number, a long and dreadful odyssey led eventually to the New World.

To judge from the replies of 425 refugee professors and teachers to the Study Committee's questionnaire, one-half of them found similar positions here and an additional 17 per cent secured other professional jobs. Of those who obtained positions as professors or teachers, 57 per cent were Christians, 36 per cent Jews, and 7 per cent of no indicated religion. Slightly more than half of them were Germans, nearly one-fourth were Austrians, and the rest came from various nationality backgrounds.

The displaced professor coming to the United States entered in the main into an environment that was well prepared for his coming. Keen awareness of his plight existed on the part of American educators. As early as May, 1933, the American Association of University Professors adopted a resolution expressing concern that freedom of teaching and learning in Germany had been subordinated to political and other considerations irrelevant to scientific research and scholarship, and recording its sympathy for members of the teaching profession who had been subjected to intolerant treatment. Solidarity among intellectuals transcended national barriers and responsible American teachers voiced their sense of moral obligation to help colleagues who were victims of Nazi oppression in Europe.

There was strong appreciation among college administrators and many faculty members of the contribution which world-renowned scientists and scholars could make to the academic life of the country. A number of invitations to outstanding displaced professors in Europe went out in the first months following the Hitler decrees. Some of these invitations were extended on the basis of funds already in university budgets. With the aid of funds from foundations and refugee organizations, however, it was possible even for small colleges impoverished by the depression to secure for one or two years the services of distinguished foreign scholars. In practice, many institutions all over the country, ranging from the smaller colleges to the large universities, proved eager to take advantage of special funds available for the assistance of refugee professors and the enrichment of American education.

Yet thoughtful administrators saw that the picture had its dark as well as its light side. Although they might accept no formal obligation in the name of their institution to keep on the refugee scholar at the close of his contract, they did not see how they could altogether escape an implied moral commitment to retain him, which would be difficult if not impossible in the face of reduced budgets. Professors from Europe who were already approaching retirement age presented an especially grave problem since, in entering a university faculty, they could take advantage only in the most limited way of existing pension plans, and would shortly find themselves without any means of livelihood.

Colleges and universities throughout the country were struggling in the trough of the depression. Many had had to cut the salaries of their faculty members, while the American Association of University Professors stated in October, 1933, that 246 publicly or privately controlled colleges and universities with a total faculty of over 27,000 reported slightly more than 2,000 persons dropped since June, 1930, over half of whom were instructors or assistants.

Faced with the threat of unemployment and enforced change of occupation, young instructors as well as their older colleagues who had suffered as the depression deepened could not invariably be counted on to welcome newcomers who might in time take the places they regarded as rightfully theirs and block the ladder of academic advancement. This point of view met with sympathy on the part of administrators, alumni, and friends of the colleges. Side by side with the desire to enrich the college curriculum and uphold *Lehrfreiheit* and *Lernfreiheit* was the feeling that "our own come first." The situation was fraught with dangerous implications. Sentiment early took the form that only outstanding scholars among the refugees should be taken on, and that in every case where there were Americans of sufficient stature to fill openings they should be given preference over refugees. Public-spirited Americans eager to assist victims of Fascist oppression in the German universities thus had to search for a formula by means of which they could place foreign scholars to the greatest advantage of American higher education without creating uneasiness and antagonism among American academicians and particularly without working a hardship upon the younger members of the American teaching profession who still had their way to make. Philanthropic agencies and institutions working to assist refugee scholars also had to take this problem into account in their planning.

As already indicated, the more fortunate among the refugees came on calls from universities and colleges which wanted their services, their salaries occasionally being provided by foundations and organizations interested in upholding academic freedom and in contributing to the enrichment of

American educational life. In some instances the institutions themselves met the entire cost of the scholars' salaries. Often the expense would be shared between the institutions and the various funding bodies.

One of the most important centers to provide a locus at which refugee scholars could gather to carry on their academic careers was the New School for Social Research in New York City, an institution of higher adult education. By October of 1933, the New School, under its director, Dr. Alvin Johnson, had established a graduate faculty to which were called some fourteen distinguished scholars in the social and political sciences who had been displaced from German universities because of race, religion, or political views. As the European situation grew progressively more disturbed, the New School expanded its activities until its original faculty was joined by many professors and scholars from Axis-dominated countries. From the beginning it was the aim of the New School to create an atmosphere in which the displaced scholars would be able to keep alive the traditions and methods that had been the glory of their universities.

This purpose differed somewhat from that which guided the activities of the Emergency Committee in Aid of Displaced Foreign Scholars, an organization established in the early summer of 1933 under the leadership of Dr. Stephen Duggan, Director of the Institute of International Education, New York City, who became its first secretary. The committee's program of grants-in-aid and fellowships assisted refugee professors by enabling them, through stipends paid directly to American institutions, to teach or carry on research work in universities and colleges throughout the country where they as foreigners would form but a minute proportion of any given faculty. Although the Emergency Committee did not for many years develop an active placement program, it stood ready to furnish information about distinguished foreign scholars to college deans and presidents upon request. The committee had expended over a million dollars in grants-in-aid and fellowships before closing its work in June, 1945, and had assisted 335 individuals for periods ranging from one year to seven.

In 1936, the Oberlaender Trust of the Carl Schurz Memorial Foundation of Philadelphia under the leadership of Dr. Wilbur K. Thomas voted to use part of its funds to assist scholars from Germany and Austria who wanted to establish themselves permanently in this country. The Trust, like the so-called Scholars Committee, did not function as a relief organization but undertook to help refugees in finding positions and by supplementing their salaries if the amount offered by the institution was insufficient to cover living expenses. The Oberlaender Trust asked that the institution be prepared to keep the grantee if he made good, and required it to make some contribution to the scholar's salary from its own budget as an evidence of good faith. Approximately 330 individuals benefited either by direct grants or by grants made to institutions toward their salaries through the Oberlaender Trust Program, in the course of which a sum of $310,000 was expended.

During the period 1934 through 1940, the Carnegie Corporation granted to universities the sum of $110,155 which enabled them to secure the services of displaced German scholars. About one-fifth of this money was spent in the United States and the rest in the British dominions.

The Rockefeller Foundation, in line with its interest in supporting scholarship and scientific inquiry, assisted foreign scholars who had been driven out of their universities and research institutions by means of three interrelated programs, in the course of which 303 individual scholars were aided and $1,410,778 expended. The first of these programs, in effect from 1933 to 1939, operated both in America and in Europe. In the United States it came to the assistance of a number of scholars in whom the Emergency Committee in Aid of Displaced Foreign Scholars also was interested. A second program, operating from 1940 to 1945, continued the work of the earlier plan, but with grants made from the Foundation's regular grant-in-aid appropriations rather than out of special funds. With the invasion of Norway, Denmark, the Low Countries, and France, and the intensification of the war on England, the Foundation faced a situation in which time was of the essence. In order to cope with the urgent necessity of extricating scholars and scientists as rapidly as possible from overrun countries, it turned to the New School for Social Research as an institution of university standing which could issue without undue delay bona fide teaching invitations to distinguished refugee scholars. Under the aegis of the Foundation and the New School, and with the help of certain other institutions, a number of celebrated French, Belgian, Italian, and other teachers and scientists were brought together in New York at the Ecole Libre des Hautes Etudes and sister faculties, and at several American institutions of higher learning.

A special project for refugee scholars and professionals was instituted by the American Christian Committee for Refugees in 1943. During the course of its subcommittee's work, a total of 42 scholars were assisted through direct subventions.

Toward the end of 1940, the Catholic Committee for Refugees developed its own program to aid Catholic refugee scholars, through the agency of which these scholars might be subsidized for a brief period in order to enable them to qualify for professorships, fellowships, and other opportunities in which they could exercise their vocation or (in the cases of some) devote themselves to writing until permanent integration into American life could be effected.

The American Friends Service Committee attempted to place refugee teachers and professors in secondary schools and colleges. Seminars and cooperative workshops were held by the Friends at which scholars and teachers were given opportunities to mingle with American teachers and students, observe methods of classroom instruction, participate in actual teaching programs, and acquire practical knowledge of the American language and folkways.

In addition to the various organizations and groups with programs to assist refugee scholars initiated by American good will, several associations were established among the refugees themselves to give advice and, through various forms of self-taxation, financial assistance to the most needy. Of such sort was the Notgemeinschaft Deutscher Wissenschaftler im Ausland, active through its New York office in behalf of deposed scholars domiciled in the United States. As the Americanization process made itself felt, the local Notgemeinschaft changed its name to the Association of Immigrant Scholars. Selfhelp of Emigres from Central Europe, Inc., an organization which numbered on its board a good many displaced intellectuals, carried on a similar program.

The foregoing paragraphs have indicated that there were scholars who came into the United States on invitation from institutions of higher learning, and that there were others, entering on quota or as visitors, who desired to find their way into academic life. It is a commonplace to suggest that the latter group needed all the assistance it could obtain. College jobs were scarce, and foreigners were not always welcome. The foreign scholar was advised first of all to use his letters of introduction, look up scientific colleagues with whom he had exchanged opinions on scholarly topics in correspondence, attend meetings and congresses of scholarly societies where he could let himself be seen and make known his availability for university appointment ("But I'm not accustomed to advertising myself," the professor would usually say. "It wasn't good taste to do that where I came from— and anyway, where would I get the money to go out to Cleveland to attend the annual meeting of the ——— Society?"), and perhaps to apply to fee-charging teacher-placement agencies.

The wife of a refugee scientist has described her husband's experiences:

"My husband is a zoologist. As a scientist he was known in many lands, and everywhere he was received as a distinguished and honored guest. When the storm clouds of Nazism broke over Europe, we felt confident that somewhere among the many scientific institutions which so often had solicited his cooperation or which, even, had elected him their honorary member, there would be surely a place for him to continue his work in his chosen field. His years of experience, his standing as a scientist, would undoubtedly be of value in trying to obtain employment in the United States. And so he came to America.

"But how different was it now. He who had been an esteemed collaborator, whose advice in special questions had always been appreciated, he was, now, only an immigrant —one among the thousands of immigrants coming to America as a haven of refuge, seeking employment and a chance to begin life anew in a strange land. Not yet did he realize all this. Not until he had traveled throughout the country seeking out every scientific institution which might have need of his services and his abilities. Bewildering and disheartening were the answers he received. Everyone was cordial but regretful. They would like to have him as a member of their staff, but their staff was complete, and unfortunately there were not sufficient funds to employ an additional member."

In spite of the manifold difficulties attending the process, however, we know that many refugee scholars, thanks to their great abilities and the good will and generosity of American friends and colleagues, did succeed in securing teaching posts in American colleges and universities.

Once introduced into American academic life, the so-called "adjustment" of refugee scholars was partly a question of individual temperament, partly a matter of circumstances over which they had little or no control. Not only were they strangers in a strange land, seeking entrance into a profession in which job opportunities were limited; not only was their general ability to get along well with people severely taxed in the strain and stress of new surroundings; but immigrant professors were subject to sharp scrutiny on three rather specialized counts: their relations with the student body, their relations with colleagues on the faculty, and their contributions to the intellectual life of the college.

Let us admit at the outset that language difficulties heavily burdened the new professor. Certainly language was a barrier which frequently came between the refugee professor and his American students. It is unhappily true that the latter, more often than not, are allergic to foreign accents and have little patience with lecturers struggling with an alien idiom. Although many educated foreigners while still in Europe acquired a book knowledge of English as part of their cultural equipment and, once in the United States, were not long in achieving a close enough acquaintance with the spoken language to suffice for simple conversational exchanges, they were apt nevertheless to find it an exasperating and emotionally frustrating experience to have to lecture clearly and precisely before a classroom of undergraduates. When the lecture must be followed by a period of open discussion and debate, the situation became a severe test of linguistic ability and nervous equilibrium.

Another bar between the foreign professor and his students was the difference in attitude which characterized the European as distinguished from the American professor. The former had developed to a fine art the technique of social distance from his students. Whether this provided him with an armament against the importunities of daily life or whether it served solely to make him seem more important in the eyes of those whom he would instruct, the fact is that he held himself quite aloof from the student body. His American counterpart, on the other hand, is accustomed to encourage the members of his class to approach him freely and talk with him about their problems. Whereas the European student's contact with his professor usually ends with the close of the lecture hour, the American student sees his professor frequently for conferences and at discussion groups, meets him again at faculty teas, and may occasionally be invited to his home.

The testimony of a foreign scholar on this point is interesting inasmuch as it is concrete:

The American student expects not only guidance but also personal interest from his instructor. I had to learn this very soon. The European professor keeps office hours, but he is not supposed to have more than two or three hours per week available to the students. Even if he is in his office he keeps his door closed and does not expect to be approached about matters other than problems closely related to his field. . . .

American professors practice the open-door policy. I have learned to do the same. My office door is always open when I am in, and quite frequently a head looks in and a friendly girl's or boy's voice asks: "Are you very busy or may I come in a minute?" There are various reasons why students want to talk to their instructors: there are quizzes and grades, there may be prospective jobs to be discussed with the instructor, there are term papers and reports, experiments and books to be talked over. But some come in "just to talk to you" and some "have problems."[3]

Not only did foreign scholars have to accommodate themselves to a more personalized manner of teaching than they had previously known, they had also to study the subtle differences in educational outlook here and abroad. Whereas in Europe education for scholarship is the primary aim, in America the emphasis is on education for citizenship. Not all European professors entered this country with a clear idea of what our system of higher education stood for. Textbooks on education gave a clue, but as one of the emigre professors put it:

It takes a long time for anyone not born or brought up in this country to realize . . . that . . . the primary aim of a college, at least potentially, is to educate members of a democratic society, that it includes among its functions the training of mind and character, of social attitude and political behavior.[4]

Thus it will be seen that the foreign professor had to learn to see his relationship to his students as something more than a framework within which to transmit information and knowledge and provide professional training. This concept was the more difficult to grasp in that, to the observer of European background, the American liberal arts college inevitably resembled a European secondary school. Dr. Walter M. Kotschnig[5] reminds us:

Compulsory attendance, a rigid system of credits, which in spite of notable exceptions is still very general, study under close supervision and control are all elements which indicate the secondary-school character of a large section of American college life.

[3] Erna Barschak, *My American Adventure*, New York, 1945, pp., 118, 119.
[4] Richard Krautheimer, "On Liberal Education," *Bulletin, Vassar College*, Vol. 35, No. 2, April, 1945.
[5] *Unemployment in the Learned Professions*, London, 1937, p. 19.

It was found that many professors who had taught at large European universities feared to lose prestige by accepting a position at a small American college, or once in such an institution struggled to extricate themselves. There was little initial acceptance of the point of view so current in American educational circles, that the best introduction to a teaching career in institutions of higher learning is the small but good American college—much as it is said that the journalist secures his best experience and training on the newspaper of some small town.

When it came to his relations with his colleagues and the college community, there were many pitfalls for the unwary refugee professor. It was hard for the newcomer who had been a person of eminence abroad to realize that younger, less illustrious colleagues on the university faculty might have seniority rights. He had to learn not to be "snooty" or to antagonize his fellow professors by an appearance of superiority. He must not continually speak of his own past importance, even though by so doing he could bolster his own morale. He must not be outspokenly critical of American ways. Above all, he must not act "as if he were conferring a boon upon American education by descending upon it," as one American educator put it.

The list of prohibitions was endless. He must, for example, guard against too much forthrightness in publications. As Professor Whyte points out in comparing German and American ways:

The tone of scientific or intellectual controversy in writing is also different. Though German scholars have long since outgrown the bitter, war-like tone that characterized a major "wissenschaftlicher Streit" a generation ago, they still frequently attack contrary opinions with an unsparing and devastating directness. Americans who feel inwardly called upon to register their dissent in writing usually do so much more amiably. They will often take the sting from their criticisms by first pointing out the virtues of the article they intend to attack, and then they will proceed to a calm analysis of its defects— an analysis which again is characterized by the posing of questions, expressions of doubt, or other indirections rather than by direct, head-on collisions.[6]

It was unwise for the refugee teacher constantly to press his claim for renewal of appointment or for tenure or to hold a college president who had given him a job to the strict letter of the contract, written, implied, or imagined. Yet many refugee scholars did just that, partly from their natural fear as foreigners of being cheated in a strange country and partly because literalness and exactitude were an integral part of their make-up. This led to the charge sometimes heard that the refugee scholars tended to regard as rights what were in effect privileges, were "litigious," or insisted "on their pound of flesh." Individual college presidents also expressed resentment over what they termed "pressure" from refugee faculty members

[6] John Whyte, *American Words and Ways*, New York, 1943, pp. 147–148.

who introduced a succession of friends and relatives seeking for jobs in the same institutions.

Differences in social customs and manners presented special problems. The professor was usually accompanied by wife and children, who must find acceptance among faculty wives and children, many of whom were not well acquainted with foreigners. The European housewife, less accustomed than her American counterpart to doing her own work, was surprised and sometimes vocal about the scarcity and high cost of domestic help. European husbands, after the first shock of seeing American professors help their wives wash the dishes, mind the baby, sweep the rugs, and put up the screens, soon found they had to learn to fit into the routine themselves, since in America college professors' salaries are far from munificent. Displaced scholars, like other refugees, were struck by the fact that, although the general standard of living in the United States is quite high, middle-class professional incomes are not such as to make possible much more than a relatively simple style of existence. Faced with the necessity of setting up housekeeping again in a new country—purchasing furniture, dishes, cooking utensils, linens, or arranging for transportation of former possessions; of laying aside travel money in order occasionally to attend conferences of learned societies where one might read a paper and hear job opportunities discussed; of putting children through school and college or preparing them for a vocation—faced with all these charges upon his salary, the displaced scholar had difficulty in making ends meet.

In a number of college and university faculties, American teachers out of the kindness of their hearts assessed themselves to provide a fund from which refugee professors might be assisted. With a personal stake in the matter, it was human and natural that these same American teachers and even some of their friends and colleagues should take a certain interest in the manner in which foreign scholars and their families adjusted themselves to the economic factors in their new environment. Unfortunately minor points of friction arose, of which one is perhaps a typical example: the almost universal desire of European parents to provide piano lessons for their youngsters. Campus wives and mothers, struggling to make their own budgets stretch to meet necessities and honor their commitments, were a little inclined to regard piano lessons as out of line. Not all refugee scholars, however, could budget for such items. Many had to try to scrape together money to send back to relatives overseas.

However straitened might be their circumstances and however depleted emotionally they might be as a result of demands made upon their sympathies by family members still abroad, the refugee professors must meet certain social obligations. In daily contacts the personality of the refugee and his family made the greatest difference, particularly in the small college community. A tactless wife, or one who imposed on faculty members' hospitality, or who nagged members of the faculty to "do something" for her husband, could ruin her husband's American career. Equally resented was the strong-minded wife who took the president's wife aside to tell her how the college should be run or who lectured her neighbors on how to keep house. Children, on the other hand, were readily accepted and found a short cut to Americanization through the public school system.

The professor must show himself to be outward-going and a "good mixer," but must not indicate that he took his position as a member of the faculty too much for granted. If the refugee scholar did not attempt to establish friendly relations with his colleagues and their families he was criticized for being "high hat." If he entertained them too lavishly he was suspected of being a show-off or possessing an exalted sense of his own importance. In all things he must walk the tightrope between obsequiousness and real humility of spirit, between generosity and ostentation. It was incumbent upon him to adapt himself to American ways, if he could discover what they were; so small a thing as continued insistence upon the Continental custom of dining at eight, if it caused difficulty with domestics, could antagonize a small community.

It would be idle to suggest that the adjustment process was an easy one. There can have been few refugee scholars who did not meet with problems on that score. The inflexible, the very old, and the deeply troubled suffered most. "My father died a year ago," the son of a celebrated scientist said; then added quietly, "It was best for him. He was so unhappy, he never could have adjusted." "Dr. Y. took his own life when he was suffering a period of depression that was unbearable to him," a college administrator wrote.

Stories of maladjustment arouse more interest than those of happy accommodation to new environments and situations, and the case-work agencies are not called in to assist people happily and productively disposed in their new surroundings. For every record of infelicity there were at least five telling of a cheerful acceptance of living and working conditions and a readiness to like and be liked by new associates.

Unsung for the most part was the refugee wife who labored humbly and quietly to make the exile's home happy, who did *not* antagonize faculty wives, and who struggled to understand her new circumstances and to learn to do without beloved objects once taken for granted.

As has already been indicated, some jealousy of the refugee professor on the part of American colleagues was inevitable. Charges were made that foreign scholars, particularly in the language field, were competing unfairly by accepting lower salaries than American university graduates, thus aggravating the employment problem faced by the latter group. It was alleged that in certain eastern universities Americans who had been awarded the rank of instructor faced a diminished chance of professional advancement because of the eminent and well-qualified foreign professors who were being introduced at the top. An institution on the West Coast, which prided itself on its liberality in the matter of refugee appointments, stated that its faculty had grown jealous of its prerogatives and had reached the point of watching each new appointment. There were enough instances of American faculty members who publicly declared that they had been displaced by refugee professors whose salary was supplied by outside sources to give color to the general charge that refugee scholars were displacing American professors. As the president of a midwestern college said in 1938: "Much as I sympathize with our friends across the sea, and much as I would like to help them, I cannot see how I am justified in the present situation when there are so many splendid teachers in America still looking for jobs, in doing too much to encourage these friends of ours from abroad to look for actual employment."

Refugee professors were least popular with their colleagues when they were numerous enough to form a foreign bloc on the campus. It was usually the policy of administrators to watch closely for signs that the saturation point had been reached. This was done primarily out of consideration for the rights of American faculty members, but also in order to avoid arousing anti-refugee sentiment by flooding the colleges with refugee teachers. It was generally held that one or two foreign scholars were all the small college could take care of. In the large universities the presence of European professors was more apt to be accepted as a matter of course or to pass unnoticed, but in these institutions no less than in the small colleges it was believed that the rights and privileges of American personnel had to be protected.

The foreign scholar who was too "radical" politically for the community in which he found himself had a difficult time, while the refugee whose talents were too creative for a narrow environment suffered even as an American in the same situation would have done. It was a real question as to how much anti-Jewish feeling existed on college campuses throughout the country, for there were few overt expressions of such a sentiment. Some observers remarked that, while there was little expressed antagonism and prejudice against Jews, there was present in all faculties a fear of numbers.

When it came to the contribution that refugee scholars had made to the intellectual life of the college, most qualified observers believed that the sum total of such contributions was impressive indeed. Their numerous publications and research achievements were cited, as were their insistence upon high standards of scholarship, the breadth and richness of their experience, and the combination of social, intellectual, and political background which they brought with them to the college campus. "The stir of discussion and traffic of ideas which they stimulated and promoted" was spoken of with appreciation, as was the "ferment" they introduced into scholarly life.

It was felt that European scholars could contribute more fruitfully in certain fields than in others. Foreigners were reputed to fit best into the teaching of "universal" subjects such as mathematics, philosophy, physics, and biology. In the social sciences, where American material was required, the refugee scholar was not sought after. It was commonly said in the early days of the scholarly migration that musicology and art history were fields in which refugees could make the most welcome contribution. Some fear existed at the outset lest the introduction of too many European physicists and mathematicians might endanger the future of young Americans starting out on their scientific careers. By the time the war was under way, however, every refugee physicist and mathematician was certain that his talents would be used to the utmost and that he would in fact come to be regarded as a public servant.

The refugee scholar was considered better as a teacher of graduate students than of undergraduates (but one university president remarked that "the experiment was most successful with those who came for special research projects and who thus worked individually and not as members of established departments of instruction"). A field representative of the Emergency Committee in Aid of Displaced Foreign Scholars reported in 1940 that, where opportunities for the placement of refugee scholars existed, men who could undertake classroom teaching were greatly preferred to researchers, for whom there was little demand. "Scholarship, pleasing personality, command of English, assimilability in the community were qualities sought in filling any vacancy." The same observer added that there was a feeling that "the foreign degree requirements emphasizing minutiae do not equip a man for the American classroom, and in some cases, the very length of the list of publications which a man submits militates against him as he may make too much of too little."

Not only could and did the refugee scholars contribute to the intellectual enrichment of the college and university, they were also uniquely placed to render a service to American life. Many of the professors came to earn the love and esteem not only of their associates but of members of the wider community outside the campus as well. They were frequently musical or artistic, and added to the amenities by forming or joining string quartets and choral societies, giving lectures on aesthetics and art history before adult education groups, and directing plays and operettas. The wives of many were talented in arts and crafts, and among them were sculptresses, painters, pianists, and weavers who brought their own special gifts to the cultural and avocational life of the community.

One of the strongest and most tangible of all contributions which the refugee scholar made to his new country was in connection with the war effort. Here the scientific gifts of the refugees were used to the fullest possible extent in the development and testing of implements of war, while the art historians mapped monuments and historic sites in areas to be bombed and economists and technicians indicated strategic points for aircraft penetration. Many philologists, political scientists, and historians were called upon to serve in Language and Area instruction for the Army Specialized Training Program and for the Navy V–12 projects.

In summing up the "adjustment" of refugee scholars—if indeed such a summing up is possible—it should be said that in spite of the greatest difficulties of a personal and emotional nature, foreign professors tended gradually to be so absorbed into American academic life that as the years went by many people came literally to forget that they had been refugees. The focus shifted slowly but surely in the course of time until at last the stereotype of "German-Jew" no longer jumped to the minds of university people when the word "refugee" was uttered. In January, 1945, the vice-chancellor of a large American university was asked in conversation whether he had any refugee scholars on his campus. His reply was somewhat unexpected. "Oh, yes," he said, "we have several Chinese refugees, and are expecting several Hindus." Intrigued, the interviewer put the same question to a number of administrators, only to receive similar replies.

Particularly during the war years, a dramatic and accelerated process of adjustment was evident. During this period of teacher shortage, the colleges needed people badly and were glad if never before to employ refugees. Except where security regulations interfered, refugee professors were accepted on the same basis as native Americans. To the demands which were made upon them they responded with loyalty, promptitude, and intelligence.[7]

It may have been that, at the beginning, a mistake was made in expecting too much of the foreign scholar. That he should bring with him to the college campus a wealth of scholarship, charm of manner, and an impeccable command of English plus a delightful wife and family and no personal problems of any kind with which to plague administrators and colleagues was to ask a great deal. It should have been obvious from the outset that refugee professors were human beings, with human virtues and frailties, and that among human beings a certain law of averages obtains. The great scientist is not invariably a magnetic public speaker, and the successful classroom teacher may meet defeat at home (about which all the neighborhood may ultimately hear) from an unloving and unadjusted family. So it is with American teachers, and so it was bound to be with refugees. Not all could claim a perfect score on all counts, but many contributed gifts of great

[7] See forthcoming book, *The Rescue of Science and Learning,* by Stephen Duggan and Betty Drury, for collection of letters from college and university presidents on the subject of refugee scholars.

price. It must by now, however, be abundantly clear that only an archangel could have measured up to all the specifications commonly drawn up for "guest professors."

Foreign scholars had difficulty in adjusting to heavy teaching loads and committee assignments which interfered with research activities. "As a whole, the schedule of a teacher does not allow much outside work," a refugee teaching on the faculty of an American university wrote, "but I do not stand alone when it comes to a 17-hour schedule being in conflict with scholarly work."

Foreign professors were enthusiastic about the eagerness to learn and the mental capacity of American students in the municipal universities, but frequently deplored the lack of intellectual curiosity of the well-to-do student found in the expensive "upper-class" colleges.

In many communities the refugee scholars are now American citizens, sharing the concerns and problems which face their native-born colleagues. If in a number of instances they still feel themselves to be "foreigners," they realize that this is the inevitable fate of men and women transplanted in mature life. A feeling of foreignness is seldom thrown off in the first generation. A few—a very few—have become 100 per cent Americans, but natural good taste prevented most refugee scholars from the ultimate absurdity of one of their number who, after encountering personal difficulty in finding a permanent place for himself, complained bitterly after he became a citizen about "the way refugee scholars are taking jobs away from Americans."

The sober words of the president of an eastern college throw as much light as any other single source upon the whole subject of the refugee scholar:

"What has impressed me most," he wrote to the office of the Emergency Committee in Aid of Displaced Foreign Scholars, "is not the difficulty which the Germans in particular have in adapting their Teutonic background and experience to the American undergraduate scene—and it should be borne in mind that these men have been teaching in an undergraduate institution—as their success in making the adjustment. There is no question that the presence of these foreign scholars has enriched American education. It has provided a great diversity of points of view, and it has brought to us many men of distinction."

From the files of the Emergency Committee in Aid of Displaced Foreign Scholars, from the American Friends Service Committee, from bulletins and publications of learned societies, from interviews and from the study of press clippings, the Study Committee was enabled to build up a list of 1,457 professors, teachers, intellectuals, and other scientific and scholarly personnel who had sought refuge in the United States.

Of these the largest number (707) was found in the so-called professorial group—that is, the group composed of men and women who were formerly attached to European universities, Hochschulen, or the equivalent, as professors, Privatdozenten or Dozenten (or their equivalent, in non-German-speaking countries), assistants, researchers, lecturers or the like.

It was a matter of the greatest interest to learn that of these 707 refugees who had formerly been on university faculties, no less than 523 succeeded in entering American college or university life in a teaching or research capacity at some time following their arrival in this country. This is not to say that all of these 523 men and women were occupying an academic post when last heard from, but rather that the entire group had had some opportunity to secure experience of and initiation into American university life—experience which in some instances led to permanent appointment. This introduction might have taken the form of a temporary instructorship, a visiting professorship, a teaching appointment under the Army Specialized Training Program, or a faculty appointment carrying with it all rights and privileges accorded faculty members. From information available it is known that at least 6 of the 523 who broke into American academic circles remained to become heads of college or university departments.

The broad fields of study represented by the 707 "professors" are indicated below. These have been taken as far as possible from the designation used in connection with the scholar on or before his arrival in the United States. It is known, however, that a number of men and women have had to change their disciplines in order to meet American market requirements. It will be understood, of course, that a certain amount of leeway in interpretation has been inevitable where the "professor" had one or more fields of interest in Europe, or where American usage did not follow the European classification strictly.

Of special interest is the large number of teachers of law. On the basis of admittedly incomplete information, it is estimated that not many more than 15 or 20 of the total of 74 found college or university posts where they were able to teach in their own field. Government, economics, political science, criminology, ancient history, and language and literature were disciplines to which a number of legal scholars turned. The field of physics was almost as well represented as the law, with a total of 71 scholars. In view of the heavy demand for physicists in connection with programs centering around nuclear fission, the presence of these scientists in the United States was of positive value. As least 8 men in the group, plus one scholar usually listed among chemists, were known to have been directly engaged in atomic energy research.

On the whole, however, this list of disciplines cannot be taken as a measure of the demand in the United States for teachers or scientists in various fields. Scholars entered the country prepared to teach a given subject, as, for example, language and literature. Often, however, circumstances obliged

Fields of Study of 707 Refugee Professors now in the United States

Law	74
Physics	71
Medical Science	71
Language and Literature	65
Chemistry	63
Economics	60
Mathematics	53
History	45
Philosophy	44
Art and Archaeology	33
Psychology	25
Sociology	19
Unclear or Miscellaneous	17
Biology	15
Music and Musicology	10
Political Science	9
Engineering	7
Theology	7
Astronomy	6
Zoology	5
Anthropology	4
Education	3
Geology and Geography	1
Total	707

them to seek a new orientation and develop specialties which were not so adequately covered in the American curriculum.

Because of the initial difficulty of securing a foothold in the colleges and universities, it was thought that a number of men and women from the professorial field in Europe might have accepted secondary school posts as stopgaps, and then found themselves blocked at this level. An attempt was therefore made to examine the employment records of the 707 "professors" where this material was available in any detail, and determine whether an appreciable number of the group appeared to have been sidetracked in secondary school teaching. On the basis of such information as the Study Committee had at its disposal, it was not evident that sidetracking of this sort had taken place in more than a handful of instances, although there were cases where foreign scholars had had their introduction to the American teaching field through secondary schools, not remaining long in them, however, before going on to college or university posts.

An interesting note, quite outside the calculations pertaining to the 707 professorial refugees, but important to take into consideration at this point, concerns 36 other refugees who had not belonged to the professorial group in Europe in so far as biographical material revealed, but who, in spite of this limitation, occupationally speaking, became professors or assistant professors in this country.

No section on refugee scholarship would be complete without mention of the teaching and research centers at which the refugees congregated in great strength.

There is, for example, the Institute of Social Research which, in December of 1944 celebrated ten years on Morningside Heights in New York City.[8] The institute, established in 1923 on the campus of the University of Frankfurt am Main, after being forced out of Germany by Hitlerism was obliged to seek temporary asylum in Switzerland, France, and England. It settled down at last in New York City under the auspices of Columbia University. With a staff of collaborators drawn largely from refugee social scientists, some of whom were to enter the service of the United States government during the war years, and an advisory committee of American scientists, the institute "endeavors—under different skies—to carry on the mission originally assigned to it more than twenty years ago: to inquire into the character of modern society; to investigate the problems of changes in social structure; and to develop new conceptual and methodological tools appropriate for this task." The institute's European periodical, *Zeitschrift für Sozialforschung,* was transformed in the summer of 1940 into *Studies in Philosophy and Social Science,* written entirely in English and published by the institute.

The Yiddish Scientific Institute, YIVO, which came to New York from Vilno, Poland, at the outbreak of the war, developed in this country its own establishment and research staff of refugee scholars. Its research director, Dr. Max Weinreich, stated that since 1940 over 7,000 pages of research material had been published by the institute covering work in the fields of sociology, linguistics, history, and the like. The institute also publishes three periodicals, the *Yivo Bleter,* Journal of the Yiddish Scientific Institute; the *Yidishe Shprakh,* which appears every two months; and *News of the Yivo,* a bimonthly in Yiddish and English; and maintains a Yiddish library and reading room. Before the advent of the YIVO, Dr. Weinreich declared, the field of Jewish social studies in this country had been largely neglected.

Reference has been made elsewhere to the New School for Social Research and its faculty of displaced foreign scholars. The number of celebrated intellectuals who were welcomed to the New School by Dr. Alvin Johnson, its director, is considerable, and they, together with their celebrated American colleagues, have made the New School an outstanding institution of adult higher education in the United States.

In the New York area and environs, several other institutions were markedly hospitable to exiled scholars and, in turn, derived substantial scholarly benefits from their presence.

[8] *Institute of Social Research: Ten Years on Morningside Heights, A Report on the Institute's History, 1934 to 1944,* December, 1944.

The Institute of Fine Arts of New York University under the direction of its chairman, Professor Walter W. S. Cook, was quick to see the advantage of adding to its already fine faculty a number of distinguished refugee art historians and archaeologists, who have attracted students from far and wide.

The Iranian Institute and School of Asiatic Studies enriched its already full curriculum with many offerings made possible by the talents of refugee scholars, particularly, although not exclusively, in the field of linguistics.

The Institute for Advanced Study in Princeton, New Jersey, under the direction successively of Dr. Abraham Flexner and Dr. Frank Aydelotte, welcomed to its staff a number of important scholars from overseas, of whom the most celebrated was Albert Einstein.

SECONDARY SCHOOL TEACHERS

So far we have been considering the scholars who found their way into American university careers. A number of refugee intellectuals, however, were enabled to enter American education through secondary school teaching, generally through the private schools but once in a great while through the public school system where substitute teaching gave them an entering wedge. Teaching posts in general were eagerly sought after, and refugees who could not get into the colleges found that the preparatory schools served as an outlet for their eagerness to impart knowledge and satisfied to a considerable extent their desire for status. Inevitably there were difficulties, however. Professors and teachers who had been accustomed to dealing with students on the adult level now had to simplify their teaching to meet the needs of immature minds.

Another hazard came from the fact that many of the positions available were institutional posts where living in, with a certain amount of responsibility for dormitory supervision, was a requirement. Disciplinary problems encountered in the preparatory schools are of a special sort, and one is best equipped to cope with them if one has a fluent command of English and a working knowledge of the folkways of American youth. The headmaster of one school in which a refugee had given a very creditable account of himself as a teacher made this comment:

"I feel that his discipline was weak not because he lacked the force but because he was an alien. This alone is a great handicap in an American boys' private school. I believe that he is better qualified to teach older boys than younger boys. I feel that he would be successful with older boys."

Aside from the ability to impose discipline, to teach well, and to overcome the students' feeling of strangeness with a foreigner, were certain intangibles of personality, address, "good breeding," and background that profoundly affected the refugees' chances of finding a teaching post in the private school world. Not all refugees any more than all Americans were possessed of the combination of attributes considered desirable. Where personal qualifications, scholarly background, and teaching ability were favorable, mutually rewarding placements occasionally resulted.

The College Work Shop, operated by the American Friends Service Committee at Haverford, Pennsylvania, offered an excellent orientation experience to foreigners who needed to acquire flexibility in the use of language and a working acquaintance with American ways. Many scholars found their stay at Haverford rich in human values.

Some secondary school teachers, a number of curators, several museum directors, and teachers of adult education in Europe also succeeded in getting into higher education in the United States. A few young scholars—"entry applicants," as it were—were fortunate enough to secure college posts as well.

Most secondary school teachers in the refugee group were delighted to find opportunities to enter the secondary school field here. Few were so fortunate, however, as the one who wrote:

"It was relatively easy for me to get a start in my profession as a teacher and since I have been teaching for more than twenty-five years and was always very fond of teaching I am grateful for the opportunity to continue this work. I arrived with my family in November, 1937, in ———. After half a year already I was teaching in a private school and substituting in the public schools. Due to my previous study in Germany and my experience the [State] Department of Education granted me a certificate for the following majors: mathematics, French, German, and psychology. . . . Now I am teaching in the same public school system. . . ."

A young woman who had been a student in Germany found her way into the school system through substitute teaching:

"Since I have been in ——— I have been very fortunate. I managed right away to secure a position teaching civics in summer school. For this year, and maybe longer, I have a long-term substituting job teaching Spanish, German and English at another ——— high school. I love my work, enjoy my students and like the people with whom I work. All my colleagues have been extremely kind and helpful."

More often the way to a teaching post was strewn with difficulties:

The difficulties in continuing her profession as a kindergarten teacher proved insurmountable, especially the accent [a social worker wrote of a recent immigrant]. Therefore she decided to take up tailoring which she had learned before embarking on her career as a kindergarten teacher. After working as a power machine operator she was able to combine her knowledge of tailoring by conducting a vocational class in women's tailoring at one of the city's evening high schools. She now works during the day as sewing supervisor for a War Relief Organization.

Statistically the picture presented by the 277 teachers in the special group studied is the following. One hundred eighty-one were men and 96 women. Of the entire number, 76 went into some form of nonuniversity teaching here. Seventy-two other former teachers obtained faculty appointments in American colleges, universities, normal schools or junior colleges, in spite of the fact that they had not belonged to the so-called professorial group in Europe. One of these men even became head of his department. In all, therefore, 148 of the total number of 277 found some sort of teaching job in this country.

The European professional experience of the group was of this sort:

Secondary School	130
Miscellaneous; bridging several fields; undetermined	77
Adult Education	41
Teacher-training	11
Kindergarten or Nursery School, etc.	7
Elementary School	6
Physical Education	5
Total	277

The group was predominantly German. In addition to the refugees who were teachers in Europe, the Study Committee found 17 others not clearly deriving from the teaching field who became teachers here.

Nonuniversity Scientists and Other Scholars

For practical purposes, scientists and intellectuals whose records did not show former affiliation with a European institution of university standing were considered separately. Actually the borderline between these scientists and the men and women known as "professors" is a shadowy one and the distinction between the groups somewhat artificial, since many of the professors will go down in the annals as eminent scientists of their day, while it is by no means certain, on the basis of incomplete information, that a number of the so-called "scientists and other scholars" had not at some time or other enjoyed a university connection.

They exhibited disappointingly few characteristics of a homogeneous group, for their number included scientifically inclined men and women of all kinds, from independent researchers in archaeology, ancient languages, and the fine arts to dye chemists employed in the woolen industry. Their distribution by fields of study is given in the following table.

That their fields do not follow the same frequency pattern as did those of the "professors" is not without interest. Whereas there is a high proportion of chemists in both groups, there are more proportionately among the nonuniversity scholars than among the academicians, indicating perhaps a slight preference for industry among the chemists. Although the law led as

Fields of Study of 424 Non-University Scientists and Other Scholars

Chemistry	81
Economics	66
Music and Musicology	40
Art and Archaeology	35
Physics	29
History	21
Undetermined or Miscellaneous	19
Philosophy	18
Sociology	16
Mathematics	14
Language and Literature	14
Political Science	14
Psychology	10
Biology	10
Medicine	6
Anthropology	6
Astronomy	5
Engineering	5
Law	4
Bacteriology	3
Theology and Religion	3
Architecture	2
Education	2
Zoology	1
Total	424

a field of specialization in the professorial group, it occurs low on the list of the nonuniversity scholars. The high incidence of language and literature specialists among the professors as against its rather minimal occurrence among the nonuniversity scholars points perhaps to the fact that philologists and other students of language found the most congenial surroundings for their studies within rather than outside of university halls.

One hundred and thirty of the so-called "nonuniversity scientists and other scholars" had established a connection with an American college or university after their arrival in this country. Four had found museum posts, and 66 were affiliated with scholarly or scientific institutes of one sort or another. Industry claimed 31, and American business absorbed 3. Two went into government jobs, 7 had engaged in defense work or war jobs, 7 were private researchers, and 5 found teaching jobs on a noncollegiate level.

In a world inflamed by war, scientific and technological activity tends to receive more notice than research carried on in the humanities. Meticulous and inspired work on an Etruscan dictionary, on Secret Chromatic Art and the Netherlands Motet, on the philosophy of Kierkegaard, on the precursors of Le Corbusier, on Poussin, on the history of the theater or of the dance—projects among hundreds of others to which refugee scholars have devoted their talents and understanding with almost sacrificial zeal—re-

ceive less than their just share of attention. Knowledge of languages—
Annamese, Iranian, Ethiopian—of Chinese sociology, of European cultural
monuments, can be diverted in one form or another to practical wartime
uses. But it is the refugee scientists who worked on nuclear fission, on aero-
dynamics, on meteorology, on ballistics and on engineering devices, whose
researches were immediately and eagerly demanded because of their practical and terrible applicability.

The astonishing factor in the whole situation is that, with the sky dark
with war clouds, Nazi Germany permitted so many of its leading scholars
and scientists to leave its camp to go into exile. Scientific personnel fled to
Great Britain and the United States by the hundreds. In a report on science
and its social relations[9] it is stated that "more than half of the leading 300
American mathematicians are engaged full time in the mathematics underlying the mechanical engineering of war weapons. There are today more of
the leading German mathematicians in the United States than there are in
Germany." The article goes on to state that the staff of the *Zentralblatt für
Mathematik und ihre Grenzgebiete* was disrupted by the Germans in 1938,
but that Otto Neugebauer, formerly of the *Zentralblatt* in Europe, who
had been called to the United States, edited the newly started American
abstracting journal, *Mathematical Reviews*.

The quality of the refugee scientists coming to the United States is indicated by the fact that at least 300 of them are listed in the current editions
of *American Men of Science* and *Who's Who in America*, 23 being listed
in both directories. Among the group are 38 physicists, 6 of them Nobel
Prize winners; 38 chemists, including 2 Nobel Prize winners; 42 mathematicians; 58 in medical and 15 in biological sciences, one of whom won the
Nobel Prize; 9 astronomers; 8 psychologists; 7 meteorologists; 12 in the
social sciences; and 4 in engineering.

Not only was the scientific and technological achievement of Axis countries reduced by refugee emigration, but that of the United Nations, especially America, increased. This had an important bearing on the outcome
of the war. The full story of the role of scientists in the successful prosecution of the war has not yet revealed, but there is no doubt that refugee
scientists played a distinguished role. For example, Dr. Ernst Berl, who had
been chief chemist for Austria-Hungary in World War I, came as a refugee
to the United States in 1933 and turned his world-renowned skill in chemistry and explosives against the Axis nations. He was a member of the
United States Explosives Advisory Committee and co-operated with the
United States Chemical Warfare Service and the Navy Ordnance Department. In regard to his peacetime contributions, it may be noted that he
discovered a method of artificially producing coal and oil.

[9] Walter B. Cannon and Richard M. Field, "International Relations in Science," *Chronica
Botanica*, Vol. 9, No. 4 (Autumn, 1945).

A number of refugee scientists had worked in the field of atomic energy. Hans Bethe, who in the 1930's had advanced a theory which is now generally accepted, explaining the heat of the sun by a cycle of nuclear changes involving carbon, hydrogen, nitrogen, and oxygen, and leading eventually to the formation of helium, came to the United States from Nazi Germany. Enrico Fermi, who with his colleagues first studied the results of the bombardment of uranium by neutrons in 1934, left Europe for the United States during the Hitler years. So did Albert Einstein, James Franck, and many other celebrated men of science. *Atomic Energy for Military Purposes: The Official Report on the Development of the Atomic Bomb under the Auspices of the United States Government, 1940–1945,* by Henry De-Wolf Smyth, contains this interesting statement (p. 45):

The announcement of the hypothesis of fission and its experimental confirmation took place in January 1939. . . . There was immediate interest in the possible military use of the large amounts of energy released in fission. At that time American-born nuclear physicists were so unaccustomed to the idea of using their science for military purposes that they hardly realized what needed to be done. Consequently the early efforts both at restricting publication and at getting government support were stimulated largely by a small group of foreign-born physicists centering on L. Szilard and including E. Wigner, E. Teller, V. F. Weisskopf, and E. Fermi.

The names of at least nine refugee scientists have appeared in connection with the development in this country of the atomic bomb, and others may become public as more of the details of the project become common property.

The tremendously practical contributions made by the refugee scientists to their new homeland during time of war will certainly have their counterpart in the peacetime world. They have proved themselves beyond any doubt loyal and patriotic members of American society, ready to share with their new compatriots their intellectual gifts and achievements.

CHAPTER XVIII

ARTISTS AND WRITERS

|||||||||||||||||||||||||||||||||||||||||||||||||||||||||||||||||||||||||||||||||||||||||||||||||||||||||||||||||||||||||||||||||||||||||||||||||||||||||

REFUGEE ARTISTS

Any discussion of refugee artists is liable to be overshadowed by the great names among them—Lipchitz, Zadkine, Masson, Mondrian, Kisling, Breton, Duchamp, Tanguy, Chagall, Léger, and many others—who gave to the migration its distinctive quality. Even before Hitler swept over Europe, such artists as these were already celebrated in this country, thanks to the efforts of institutions like the Museum of Modern Art in New York and the enterprise of art dealers. When they came to the United States their canvases and sculpture were fashionable and commanded high prices, while the artists themselves were lionized and enjoyed a veritable *succès fou*.

The impact of this group was enormous, and should not be minimized, but it would be less than accurate to overlook the many earnest, devoted artists, for our purposes often nameless and unnumbered, who came in on the quota from 1933 on, intent on practicing their art and earning a living. Immigration figures show that some 717 sculptors and artists migrated from Europe to the United States during the period 1933–1944. Just what proportion of these were refugees we cannot say, since government statistics furnish no clue. It is evident, however, that there were in effect two groups of artists who arrived during the years of Nazi domination, one of which might be characterized as the "immigrant artists" and the other as the "guest artists." Their problems and reactions were not necessarily the same.

By the same token that the general public is likely to think of the artistic immigration as consisting mainly of a few top names, so the layman is apt to identify the refugee group chiefly with the School of Paris. There is some reason for this misconception. Just as the musical center of the world had passed to the United States as the war advanced, and in the same measure that the fashion center shifted from Paris to New York and California, so was the art capital lifted bodily out of Paris as the tides of Nazism swept over Europe, and set down in the New World. Although a few celebrated artists remained behind—Matisse, who "saw no reason why, as a Frenchman, he should have to think of going,"[1] Picasso, Brancusi, Maillol, who

[1] Varian Fry, *Surrender on Demand*, New York, 1945, p. 157.

died in Paris during the war years, and Derain, whom Kisling is reported to have accused of being Fascist[2]—the fall of France was announced and attended by a wholesale exodus of artists both gifted and famous, the extent of which, qualitatively speaking, has probably never been seen before in the history of Western civilization. These artists inevitably set their stamp on the group.

To speak of the "adjustment" of the French artists in the United States is perhaps an inept choice of terms. A shrewd guess is permissible that the degree of their adjustment to American life was in direct proportion to their willingness to become adjusted. The special problems of the group as they appeared to American observers were presented in capsule form by Robert Coates in the *New Yorker* of May 5, 1945:

> On the whole, the position of the refugee artists in this country has been a tough one, and the complaints that have occasionally been levelled at them by American painters and others should be considered with that fact in mind. If they've been cliquey—and it's true that a good many of them have—it should be remembered that the pulls of old friendships and associations are strong, particularly in a foreign country. If they've shown a certain condescension at times toward American art, it should be acknowledged that, in a historical sense at least, that attitude was justified; the French tradition may quite possibly be dying, but it isn't dead yet, and every Frenchman, big or little, carries with him the prestige of Renoir and Cézanne and all the others who have made the wheels of the world go round, artistically, for the past seventy-five years. Add the fact that these men did not really want to come here in the precise way they came, hurriedly and in flight, and with all the regrets and uncertainties that such a way of coming entails, and you have a fair explanation of any recalcitrance in their attitudes.

There have been Americans who complained that relatively few of the members of the group had any desire to learn fluent English. It was alleged that in certain instances there was a marked rejection of the language on the part of this or that artist, "accompanied by a deliberate exaggeration of Gallic mannerisms and habits of dress imported from Europe." (On examination this might prove in some cases to be nothing more deadly than retaining a foreign beard or haircut or refusing to give up an old beret.) One artist, a refugee of non-French background, exclaimed, "They have an inferiority complex occasioned in part by the fall of France, and this makes them violently assertive of their own personality and of their own nationalism." He went on to say that this was true not only of native French artists but of the Poles and Russians who had adopted France as their spiritual home. As a group they tended to blame the United States for their own feeling of frustration and strangeness. "They do not like America, and they resent the fact that they have had to accept 'American charity.'" (Parenthetically it should be said that "charity" usually took the form of cash

[2] Harry Henderson and Sam Shaw, "Art for Profit's Sake," *Collier's*, Nov. 25, 1945, p. 22.

payments for the artist's salable commodity—his canvases or his sculpture.)

Artists long established in the United States deplored the tendency of French artists to keep to themselves and concentrate on returning to Europe. Many of the artists, it is true, were frank to say that they regarded their residence here as a temporary exile, and that when travel became possible after the war they would return to their homeland. The relative merits of the New and Old World atmospheres were discussed and some difference of opinion was evident.

"I am too much of a Parisian to want to stay in New York indefinitely," one refugee artist said. "In Paris the very air was full of competition. Here I can go for days without painting anything."

"In Paris," earnestly declared a refugee painter in an interview, "if you did not like painting, did not like to read but preferred to play cards, you simply said you didn't want to go look at paintings or read, but went and played cards instead. In the United States, everyone must go by the exhibition and by the concert—but he doesn't know what it's all about."

Said André Masson, "Years ago Henri Matisse told me the light here was wonderful. It is true . . . magnificent!"

"In Europe," a member of the French School explained, "it was 'l'art pour l'art,' and not just whether you could sell what you painted."

Contrary to general expectations, many of the French artists will not return to France to live when postwar travel becomes possible, asserts Mr. Monroe Wheeler, Director of Exhibitions and Publications at the Museum of Modern Art. They find life in the United States extremely stimulating and sympathetic. Some of these artists would find the atmosphere of disaster and destruction in Europe unpropitious to their work and constrictive of their style if they should return. Many of those who do go back will almost certainly want to have a re-entry permit so that they can return to the United States from time to time. From other sources has come information about refugee artists who have made plans to become naturalized Americans, with the intention of spending part of each year in Europe and part in the United States.

On some of these artists the influence of American life has been greater than on others. Competent critics declare that the canvases of Tanguy and Tchelitchew are better than those they produced abroad. Where the refugee artist has failed, declared Robert Coates in the New Yorker article previously mentioned, "is in not taking full advantage pictorially of the physical facts of the country itself. I would cite André Masson . . . as one of the few exceptions."

From the foregoing pages, with their differing points of view and conflicting testimony, it will be seen that it is difficult to be categorical about the French artists in exile; their final story has yet to be written, and for the moment it can only be said that they are typical of no group but their own.

In addition to the French artists, there were the men and women who came directly from Germany and Austria in the early and middle thirties —many of whom owed their inspiration to Germany rather than to France. There were Yugoslavs, Rumanians, and Netherlanders. There were the famous and influential men from the Bauhaus, that art center established in Germany in 1919 in an attempt to integrate arts and crafts and train the artist to take his place in the machine age. There were artists of great potentialities whose talents had not been recognized in Europe but whose artistic development in this country often won critical acclaim and in some cases resulted in successful sales. There were distinguished painters like Eugen Spiro who had played a leading part in the artistic life of Germany as president of the Berliner Secession (1916 to 1933); there was Arthur Szyk, the Polish cartoonist upon whose head Hitler had put a price, and Antonín Pelč, satirist and caricaturist from Czechoslovakia.

For all the artists of prominence who had "arrived," and who could go back to Europe almost at will when postwar conditions should permit, there were many others, primarily from Central Europe, who had no place to which to return and no strong desire to go back to anything. Their number included not only the strong and talented professionals but also the pedestrian, workaday artists who had their way to make. For most of them the vocation of artist meant not only fulfillment of artistic aspirations but also a means of livelihood. In this country, perhaps even more so than in Europe, the artist has always had to struggle to live. With very few exceptions, artists cannot make a living wholly from their art but have to supplement their slender earnings by activity in other occupations. As one refugee artist who had been here for some years expressed it: "The degree of economic security of the artist differs here and in Europe. In the United States the artist is not so integrated a part of society as he is abroad. It is a matter of pure good luck here if he manages to support himself in his profession."

Teaching has been one of the few related sources of income for American artists, and the refugee, like the American, has had to try to augment earnings by securing private pupils or by affiliating himself with an art school. Even so celebrated a sculptor as Ossip Zadkine turned to this field.

Some refugee artists declared that art training abroad was more thorough than it is here. In the United States, stated one, there are "too many teachers and too many classes." Large American art classes of twenty-five or thirty pupils were derided as "sheer nonsense." "Americans do not stick to things as much as Europeans," asserted a refugee painter. "A Spanish sculptor I know told me that in Europe he had four pupils who stayed with him five years; in this country he has had some two or three hundred pupils, none of whom stayed more than two months."

In general, refugee artists were welcomed by their American colleagues.

"There isn't much resentment against us on the part of American artists," a painter from Germany said. "It seems to me Americans have proved ready to co-operate and meet us on equal terms."

"It is an unquestioned fact that we welcome these refugee artists," an American painter said in reply to direct questioning. "This is a tendency not only among their fellow artists, but on the part of the general public as well. The Whitney Museum is going to give an exhibit shortly of the works of refugee artists. Up to now the Whitney Museum has been limited to Americans. That is certainly an excellent example of the way the community in general has received them."

Although refugee artists were usually accepted by fellow craftsmen in the field of applied art, resentment occasionally flared up against them in the schools and universities, where it was alleged that they were taking positions which rightly belonged to Americans. One of the most pointed criticisms was leveled at the appointment of a newcomer as chairman of the art department of a New York City college and of several other newcomers as art instructors. The *Art Digest* of April 15, 1944, cited a resolution and protest made by the American Artists Professional League to the Board of Higher Education of the City of New Work which contained these words:

"The League knows there are plenty of American instructors who are peers or superior to any of those who have been employed on the faculty, and it would be remiss in its duty to American artists if it did not protest vigorously, both against this notable discrimination and against this infiltration and teaching of their alien ideologies in an American college which is supported by American tax-payers.

"Especially is this discrimination hard to understand when our American artists are now experiencing the most difficult times in their history. The League insists they should have first call."

A number of refugee artists deplored the absence of government subsidies which might have permitted a greater number of talented people to study in the art schools for longer periods of time than was habitual under the American system. The foreigner believed that American artists were for the most part unable to spend sufficient time at their art studies to bring their talents to fruition. Not only was this deemed unfortunate for art in general, but the European artist regretted that he had to compete commercially against a great many American artists, of whom only a small number might be his peers in training, skill, and artistic development. He contended, therefore, that success in the American art world depended more upon the artist's personality and general attractiveness than upon his craftsmanship.

Some bitterness was expressed by refugees about the practice of buying one's way.

"In Europe once you had a good exhibition which was well and favorably received, you had a fair chance of making your mark," stated an artist. "Here it is different. Everything depends on money. Exhibitions are bought by money, publicity is bought by money. It is not only the quality of your work, but the stir you can make in the press that determines your success."

Refugees were at a special disadvantage in the art market inasmuch as many of them had been obliged to leave their artistic productions as well as the tools of their trade behind them in Europe. This often meant that new equipment must be purchased. Translated into dollars and cents the artists' needs become quite worrisome. A refugee painter estimated his weekly living and working expenses as of January, 1943, as follows:

The approximate cost of my living expenses amount to	$ 8.00
Rent and light for studio and living accommodation	9.00
Material, brushes, paint, pastel and canvases—this figure can only be calculated on an average based on work accomplished over some longer period	6.00
Model	6.00
	$29.00

This was independent of "initial expenses to purchase necessary equipment such as an easel and the most essential furniture—bed, chair, table, etc., $100.00."

Sculptors even more than painters had difficulty in getting along. "Sculpture in general is not much appreciated in the United States," sadly commented a leading American artist. Not only is the demand for the sculptor's work limited; materials are costly, and it takes a long time to produce the number of pieces required for an exhibition. A case record reads:

X wants to complete 14–16 pieces of sculpture to exhibit by winter of next year. Estimates that four small blocks [of stone] would cost $100; a block of 64 cubic feet would cost $360, while one of 56 cubic feet would cost $180.

No special committees existed to help the artists from Europe. The Emergency Committee in Aid of Displaced Foreign Scholars, and the Refugee Scholar Fund connected with the American Christian Committee for Refugees and the Institute of International Education, undertook projects which assisted temporarily some half dozen refugee painters and sculptors, and the Oberlaender Trust assisted others, but for the most part immigrant artists turned to the service agencies as such for help in meeting their needs. With the limited funds available, few could hope for aid to enable them to continue in their poorly paid profession. Distracted, more than one refugee artist turned to private sources of assistance, sometimes with attendant misfortunes:

"Mr. A. offered me some money to cast some bronze and buy some pieces of marble if I would give him 40 per cent of the selling price of the statues. This would not have been so terrible if every gallery would not ask me another 30 per cent when I would do an exhibition which brings about to nothing my earnings."

Refugee artists prevented from working because of lack of materials or of money for living expenses, with the resultant uneasiness of mind that accompanied these handicaps, resisted retraining for other forms of employment as long as they could. Without the means of practicing their vocation they found themselves floundering in a strange element and showed signs of strain and anxiety. Even to be kept away from the exercise of their profession long enough to undergo an "orientation experience" provided by well-meaning friends proved a painful ordeal. The poignant account taken from the record of an impassioned woman painter, plunged into a job as summer camp counselor to help her get the "feel" of her new country, does not describe an isolated case:

She is extremely nervous and discouraged. Needs rest and quiet, and a chance to sit down quietly and *paint*. They've all done too good a job on readjusting this woman. They should leave her alone and stop trying to teach her English. Then she could get some work done, and it would make her feel better.

As in the other professions, in order to assist the man of the family to forge ahead with his art, the wife frequently labored to contribute to the family income:

"My wife works in the department of an aviation concern. Her salary is 40 dollars a week, and we are living on her salary only. No one in our family can be of any help. We live in a studio for which rent is 70 dollars a month, and you will realize that with a family of two small children not the slightest sum can be taken for my work."

Some artists went into commercial art work and allied fields. Others had to give up their art altogether.

Yet in spite of numerous difficulties which beset him, the refugee artist's lot had its compensations. He was better off by far than the writer, whose skills were not readily transferable, and not much less well off than the musician, who could command an international audience. Once they had acquired a working knowledge of the folkways of their new country, had lost to some extent their feeling of strangeness, and had acquired the materials and tools of their trade, artists from overseas were not essentially more disadvantaged than their American colleagues. Art exhibitions commonly include works by members of the new group, and in New York the Museum of Modern Art and the Whitney Museum are among the galleries which have put on shows devoted exclusively to the productions of the immigrant artists.

When the Study Committee came to consider statistically the cases of artists, it wanted to obtain a sample which would include refugee artists from varying ethnic and religious groups domiciled all over the United States. This sample it obtained through its questionnaire, which brought in responses from 126 artists, not all of whom, however, answered every question fully enough to furnish adequate information on each point.

From a study of these questionnaire replies, certain facts emerge which give character to the group. It might have been thought, for example, that refugee artists would have tended to cluster in the New York area. Actually the answers of 95 who replied to the question concerning dispersal from port of entry disprove this belief. Of 65 male artists who entered the United States through the port of New York, 66.2 per cent left the metropolitan area, while 33.8 per cent remained. Comparable figures for females show that, out of a total of 30, 80 per cent left and 20 per cent remained.

A reassuringly large number continued to be active in their own field. Of 73 male and female artists replying to this section of the questionnaire, 31 stated that their main occupation in the United States was art. It is interesting to note that 10 of the group became professors or teachers. Only one was unemployed.

Information about the religion and country of origin of our sample group of artists shows that 88 were Jewish, 33 non-Jewish, and 5 of no or unspecified religious affiliation. Fifty-eight came from Germany, 38 from Austria, 3 from Poland, 10 from Czechoslovakia, 2 from the U.S.S.R., 5 from Hungary, 2 from Italy, 3 from the Netherlands, 1 from France, and 4 from other countries.

With regard to citizenship, they made a fairly good showing in view of the short time they have been here. Of a total of 74 artists who replied to the question concerning naturalization 29, or 39.2 per cent, had attained citizenship. Thirteen others had applied for their second papers, 30 more had received their first papers, and 2 others had made application for first papers. Not one of these artists had failed to take steps toward naturalization.

By accumulating material about artists known to the American Friends Service Committee and the Emergency Committee in Aid of Displaced Foreign Scholars, and by following notices in newspapers and journals, a second list of some 166 refugee artists was built up. This list differed from that obtained from the questionnaire in several important respects. It was not anonymous, and hence permitted of assembling material on each case from numerous sources; and it contained probably more names of famous artists than did the questionnaire returns. On the debit side there was some danger lest it contain a few artists who were not authentic refugees. It was, furthermore, probably not a true sample of the entire refugee artist population inasmuch as it was heavily weighted on the side of the well-known people whose activities were chronicled in art publications and newspapers.

In this group of 166, there were 130 men and 36 women. Ninety were painters, 18 sculptors, 8 cartoonists, 7 designers, 8 art teachers, 31 miscellaneous or unclassified artists, and 4 were in graphic arts. Astonishing as it may seem, 141 of these refugee artists were active in the field of art—that is to say, although they may have had to turn their hands to other occupations in order to help support themselves, they were still able to produce art works.

A strikingly large proportion—108 out of the total of 166 artists—reported exhibitions. A number of these were one-man shows. Almost all exhibitions were in substantial galleries, well regarded in the art world, and some were in institutions of the caliber of the Metropolitan Museum, Brooklyn Museum, Pennsylvania Academy of Fine Arts, and the Chicago Art Institute. Three of these artists were listed in *Who's Who in America*.

Twenty-four known members of the group of 166 men and women had taught in the United States—18 in colleges or universities and 6 in noncollegiate institutions.

Finally, how may we assess the contributions which refugee artists have made to the life and art of this country? Judged by any standards, these have been important. There have been critics who have seen refugee artists as a corrective influence, as did R. H. Turnbull of the *San Francisco Argonaut,* as quoted in the *Art Digest* of January 1, 1942:

It is to be hoped . . . that artists and public alike will recognize that in the long run American art will probably profit greatly by the presence of stimulating and challenging personalities in our midst. For the blunt fact is that American artists have always tended to be timid and backward in theorizing about their work, and there are even "Regional Schools," self-styled, which pride themselves on assuming an ostrich-like attitude towards any intellectual development or activity. Roughly speaking, one might say that the spirit of isolationism is more strongly entrenched in American art than in any other side of our cultural life, and at this time in our history it is hard to find any kind words to say about the spirit of Isolationism.

There are those who feel that European art is some twenty-five years ahead of American art and that refugee artists have formed a vanguard exerting a strong influence in the direction of modernism. Particularly in the field of advertising and commercial art has the presence of refugee artists loosened up the traditional style, it is claimed.

In some circles it is believed that the "pull" of the foreign artist is past; "that students in general still get excited about European artists, but as for the long-established artists, in this country, their style has probably already been formed." In such cases, the contribution made by the refugee artists has been "perhaps an indirect one." It has been pointed out that the surrealists and abstract artists have been helped and stimulated by the presence in this country of outstanding exponents of their department of art who had come from Europe. The entrance of sound sculptors among the refugees was welcomed "because we had very few good sculptors here."

In the last analysis, the question seems to resolve itself not into a discussion as to whether European art has been better than American art and could thus by its introduction effect an improvement in the existing order, but rather to a realization and acceptance of the fact that any art form can profit by cross-fertilization. Creative talents like those of Masson, Breton, Ernst, Kisling, and Lipchitz—to name only a handful from among the large number of distinguished refugee artists—were bound to have an energizing influence in their field. Thus it would make little difference whether or not these same artists should elect to return to Europe; their vitalizing and stimulating effect would have been felt.

Refugee Writers

During the years from 1933 to 1945, many writers left continental Europe as refugees. Poets, playwrights, editors, journalists, and novelists —they formed a highly articulate group prone to express their opinions freely on subjects near to their heart. Their political views were usually a matter of record, and when these ran counter to Nazi ideology, as was not infrequently the case, continued residence in overrun countries was uncomfortable or impossible. "Aryanism" or "non-Aryanism" made little difference: Jews and Christians alike held strong views about what we have come to call the Four Freedoms.

There were men of heroic stature who spoke their minds without counting the cost, like the poet Fritz von Unruh, member of an aristocratic German family who had been converted to democracy during World War I and publicly denounced Nazism at the Sportpalast in 1932 before 25,000 people at the foundation of the "Iron Front" directed against Hitler. There was Siegfried Kracauer, whose account of the Reichstag fire published after Hitler came to power was regarded by many as the boldest piece of oppositional writing in Germany at that time. There were writers who were active as interpreters of the democratic spirit in the Underground. Many paid a steep price for their outspokenness.

As the Germans threatened to engulf Europe, some refugee writers saw nothing but chaos ahead and chose self-destruction.

We learned, for instance [writes Varian Fry], that Ernst Weiss, the Czech novelist, had taken poison in his room in Paris when the Germans entered the city; that Irmgard Keun, a German novelist, author of a best-seller in the days of the Republic, *Das Kunstseidene Maedchen—The Artsilk Girl*—had also committed suicide when the Germans took Paris; that Walter Hasenclever, the German playwright, had killed himself with an overdose of veronal in the concentration camp at Les Milles, not far from Marseille;

that Karl Einstein, the art critic and specialist on Negro sculpture, had hanged himself at the Spanish frontier when he found he couldn't get across . . ."[3]

Some, like Heinrich Mann and the Feuchtwangers, chose flight. Fry[4] tells us of the Franz Werfels:

> They had fled from Paris to Lourdes, where they had sought the protection of the Church, they said. While waiting there, Werfel had begun a new novel, *The Song of Bernadette*. When they realized that they would never be able to leave France from Lourdes, they came to Marseille to get the American visas which were ready for them at the Consulate. . . . Werfel, despairing of ever getting an exit visa, had decided to have himself demobilized in Casablanca. But . . . there was real danger that he would be detected and arrested if he tried. When I persuaded him to drop that plan, he began to think of going through Spain. He got a letter from the Czech Consul saying that Cordell Hull had invited him to go to the United States to lecture, and letters from French Catholic dignitaries to Spanish Church and lay officials asking them to give all help and protection to one of the leading Catholic writers of our times. . . . (Actually Werfel is a Jew.)

Then there were the scores of writers who met with persecution because of their religion. Finally, there were a number of writers who migrated simply because they felt embarrassment and honest shame over political events within their own countries.

Precisely how many refugee writers came into the United States during the period of Nazi domination of Europe we do not know. Immigration figures show that during the years from 1933 to 1944 a total of 1,907 "literary and scientific persons" entered the country from Europe. Not all were what we understand as writers, journalists, editors; certainly not all were refugees. The figure is therefore high for our purposes. Compared with the total of 77,619 authors, editors and reporters in the United States as recorded in the 1940 census, even a maximum of 1,907 authors would seem at most like a drop in the bucket. Of only one thing can we be fairly certain—that the refugee writers included more famous names in proportion to the size of the group than did any other professional class.

To few of the writers, well known or obscure, politically minded or aesthetically inclined, did economic adjustment come easily. The exception might be found in the small group of celebrated authors whose works had for years been known in this country through the medium of translation. Present in small numbers, too, were the well-to-do writers visiting the country as tourists rather than as exiles. For the great majority the matter of making their way in this country was fraught with difficulties. Of all

[3] Varian Fry, *Surrender on Demand*, 1945, p. 31.
[4] *Ibid.*, pp. 6, 57.

professions, that of writers—next to that of artists—is the one at which
one is least likely to make a living. Even the American writer who owns
English as his native tongue and handles it with fluency and grace faces
a life of hardship in a highly competitive occupation if he would support
himself from his craft. The foreign writer who must learn to acquire
proficiency in a new language, or submit to having his work translated by
a strange hand and mind, is in a doubly trying situation. It was early evident that there would be little opportunity for the European writer to continue publishing in his own language once he had come to this country. As
Marie Ginsberg pointed out in May of 1939 in writing of German authors:

> The outlook is not very promising, as the market for German books which cannot be
> sold in the great German-speaking areas—Germany, Austria, and Czechoslovakia—is
> necessarily very restricted. However, several new publishing houses have been created
> outside Germany, notably in Switzerland and the Netherlands, which print the works
> of emigrant writers.[5]

The essence of the literary artist's work is stylistic precision. A feeling
for style in a strange language may be acquired rather quickly, but a command of style in the new idiom takes years to acquire. Before being able
to express oneself with subtlety and distinction, many hazards have to be
overcome. For the refugee writers, therefore, there was little help but to
turn to professional translators. Thomas Mann comments in correspondence that "there are writers of great talent who, in their own country and
in Europe were highly estimated . . . and who have hardly become visible or audible in this country, apparently because an adequate reproduction of their style in another language offers too many difficulties." Few
refugee poets have been able to find adequate translators to render their
verse into English.

Novelists might or might not retain something of the essence of their
novels after the translators were through with them. Many an author
whose entire success had depended upon the color and spirit of words found
that the intrinsic charm of his novels was lost in translation. Probably the
playwrights had as difficult a time as any writers, since no art form is more
deeply embedded in the poetry of language than is the drama. Best off
of all, perhaps, were the writers on historical subjects whose work, largely
factual or interpretative, suffered least in translation, and those stubborn
and industrious compilers to whom the act of translation is actually beneficial inasmuch as it sometimes improves upon the original.

Occasionally a refugee writer has broken away from the pattern. One
novelist who now writes all his books in the language of his new country says:

[5] Marie Ginsberg, "Adjustment of the Professional Refugee," *Annals of the American Academy
of Political and Social Science*, Vol. 203 (May, 1939), p. 158.

"Convinced that to rely on translations—as most emigre writers do—will in the long run hardly do for an author who wants to make his permanent home in this country, I have spent whatever spare time was left to me on improving my English."

In spite of the great difficulties inherent in the task, we have it on good authority that there is a small group of foreign authors who are turning out books in English rather than their native language, among them Hans Natonek, Robert Pick, Annette Kolb, Hertha Pauli, and Maria Gleit. The last two mentioned are writing juvenile fiction.[6] Varian Fry[7] suggests that the reason certain refugee writers of adult books have taken to juveniles now that they are writing in English is because it is easier to write for children in a new language than it would be to write for their elders.

Once in a great while a foreigner's prose will be so happily rendered that the translation will not be an obstacle to understanding, but rather a bridge. So it is in a recent novel of Erich Maria Remarque, *Arch of Triumph*, about which a reviewer[8] has said, "The translation by Walter Sorrell and Denver Lindsay is so fine it is never noticeable as a translation at all."

Refugee writers were of all kinds, sizes and shapes, but if there was one common trait which seemed to characterize them all it was their determination to continue as creative writers. In vain did case workers and vocational counselors in the social agencies urge upon the writers the necessity of embracing other occupations in order to become self-supporting. Writers reported with more surprise than pleasure conversations with social workers anxious to direct their clients to more profitable fields. "You were an author in Europe? Well, you know you don't have to write *here;* we can get you a good job with lots of money." Authors fitted into agency patterns about as imperfectly as did the artists, and were apt to be considerably more critical than their professional colleagues in evaluating the services offered by the refugee organizations.

The refugee writer was often prepared to accept monastic privation and sue for "only the bare necessities of living" if he could get on with his work. "Freedom from financial anxiety" in many cases meant only a small stipend sufficient to provide a few groceries and a roof over one's head. Determination to engage in creative writing thus often worked severe hardship on the author and his family. Rather than retrain—learn a trade, accept a factory post, look for a clerical job, run errands—the author was frequently content to subsist on a small allowance granted by a relief agency.

[6] An informant tells us, on this point: "Hertha Pauli has just finished a book for adults, *I Lift My Lamp,* and also wrote a biography of Nobel. Maria Gleit is now at work on a novel for adults."

[7] Varian Fry, "What Has Happened to Them Since," *Publishers' Weekly,* Vol. 147 (June 23, 1945), No. 25.

[8] Orville Prescott, "Review of *Arch of Triumph* by Erich Maria Remarque," *New York Times,* Jan. 21, 1946.

Within the married group, the nonliterary spouse frequently became the breadwinner, "suffering privation for a spiritual cause," as one worker put it. A middle-aged woman, suffering from cancer, supported her family as long as she could while her husband struggled to re-establish himself as a writer. Often the earnings of a single member of the family were not enough to maintain the writer and his brood. An authoress writing in 1942 said:

"A refugee from Germany, I have been in this country for two years. My husband, a writer and editor by profession, has been working as a packer and a porter for about a year in order to support us. However, the job pays only $20 a week and he may lose it any day. . . . Since we have to support my mother and our six-year-old child, I too was compelled to take any odd job I could find. That is why I was not able to stick to my literary work. . . ."

The writer who tried to live from the income of his writings alone, without accepting the help of agencies or of other members of his family, had especially difficult problems:

"I have been able to support myself on a very modest basis since I came to this country, a penniless immigrant, more than three years ago," wrote a refugee. "I worked on many an odd job, and practically never in my line. . . . At present, my only income is derived from occasional honorariums for book reviews and equally occasional fees reading manuscripts. On the average, this income amounts to $25.00 a month."

Unquestionably one of the major difficulties faced by refugee men of letters in securing employment outside their own field was that once they obtained a full-time job sufficiently remunerative to support them they had little leisure in which to carry on their writing.

"I need not point out to you," explained one of them, "that the writing of a book of about 500 pages in an adopted language cannot be done as a side line. There also is an amount of time pressure involved. . . . You will understand my anxiety to devote the bulk of my time to its completion."

For such a group, therefore, part-time jobs became of major importance. Translating jobs when available were useful because they could be done in spare time. Occasionally, but not very profitably, lecture engagements could be obtained. In the case of lesser known writers, these might be opportunities to speak before church groups, clubs, or educational gatherings. Frequently there was no honorarium, since such gatherings served primarily to extend hospitality to the newcomer rather than as profit-making activities. In all platform appearances, however, the question of proficiency in the English language was of great importance. Lectures in foreign languages were sometimes arranged, but outside of such institutions as the University in Exile, or modern language groups, they reached a limited audience. The war introduced still another element of discomfort, much as it had done twenty-five years earlier:

Since the United States entered the war [reads the record of a refugee author] he has not done extensive lecturing, since he does not feel that addresses in the German language are appropriate at this time. His spoken English is not quite up to lecture-platform standards.

Refugee writers perhaps more than any other group except the physicians needed the counsel of people who could help them understand the American scene, vocationally and culturally. Too often their own plans for their professional future were made without any knowledge of economic conditions in the new country or of the literary taste of the American public, or of ways of shaping their articles and books to satisfy that taste. They knew nothing of channels for marketing literary productions, of ways and means of establishing contact with people and groups who could bring them in touch with publishers. It was frequently demonstrated that they needed help with regard to contracts for their manuscripts. The following letter reports a rather commonly encountered problem:

I wonder if you are actually sure [wrote an American to a refugee] that the ————— Press will publish your book once the translation is completed. The reason I ask is this. I have now seen a number of refugees misled by the American brand of courtesy which is a very different thing from the German forthrightness. This courtesy often leads a rejection of a manuscript to look like an acceptance, and only a lawyer could tell you that it is not. For example, recently a refugee sent a manuscript to [the name of a nationally known and reputable magazine has been deleted here] and received a beautifully written rejection slip following the usual American formula, "We are very much interested in your work. We hope at some time to be able to publish it," etc. After waiting several months he angrily asked them for a check and was amazed to learn that they never had any idea of publishing it. Hence before you lay out the money for translation, I would suggest that you be absolutely sure that the ————— Press is contractually bound.

An American editor remarked that many refugees wanted to write magazine articles because that was reported to be a fairly easy way to make lots of money, but had little idea of what editors here required. Refugees either produced highly popularized papers which wrote down to their readers or else turned out heavy articles which, like chapters from scientific or philosophical treatises, had little appeal for the general reading public. Their literary employment in Europe had not prepared them well for the highly competitive branch of writing that supplies the slick American magazines. In spite of the manifold difficulties, it is a matter of record that many scenario writers from Europe were successful in Hollywood, while a number worked on radio scripts.

Recognizing the special needs of the refugee writers, and realizing that as a group they did not accept or work too happily with the professional case worker, the agencies set up special projects designed to help a limited number of gifted writers, artists, and professionals. One of the first of these was the Rosenwald Fellowships, made available under the auspices of the Emergency Committee in Aid of Displaced Foreign Scholars during 1942 and 1943. Under this plan, eight writers secured fellowships enabling them to concentrate on their writing for a period of time that was usually of a year's duration. With this subsidy, several authors succeeded in bringing to completion books which were subsequently published on regular publishing terms. The experience of the Refugee Scholar Fund, established in the spring of 1943 by the American Christian Committee for Refugees in co-operation with the Institute of International Education, was similar. Stipends were granted for six writers. We are told that they hewed very close to their original occupation, deviating no further than to editorial work, publicity, research, library service, or teaching. At least one of them has published. The American Committee for Scholars, Writers and Artists, which came into existence in the summer of 1945 following the termination of work by the Emergency Committee in Aid of Displaced Foreign Scholars, has attempted to carry on a program similar to that which earlier assisted professional and intellectual groups.

It is a characteristic of the literary temperament to require recognition and encouragement from fellow craftsmen. To the everlasting credit of American writers it should be noted that they extended to their distressed colleagues from Europe a welcome that was warm, spontaneous, and generous. Individuals in the profession opened their homes and their pocketbooks to the newcomers and helped a number of them to secure a breathing space during which they could recuperate mentally and physically after their shattering experiences in Nazi Europe. Writers' groups subscribed funds for the relief and rescue of refugee authors. The activities of the American Center of the P.E.N. were described by Mrs. Jane Hudson, Executive Secretary, in a letter of December 6, 1945, as follows:

We did not have what could be called a formal program for refugee writers, but we did try to help in all the ways at our disposal. We raised money, both by projects such as a tea in conjunction with Lord and Taylor at which Jules Romains, Maeterlinck, and other prominent refugees spoke, and by an appeal to our membership. . . . We also entertained them in P.E.N. homes, arranged for them to meet American writers and publishers, helped arrange a symposium at New York University at which several of them spoke, etc. Our Foreign Writers Committee catalogued over 75 of them, and did its best to meet their individual needs. . . .

The P.E.N. did try to facilitate the entry into this country of quite a few writers. We wrote countless letters and sent cables to American authorities abroad, and found people here to sign affidavits. We also worked with the Emergency Rescue Committee in specific cases, sometimes contributing money.

Individuals like the Henry Seidel Canbys and Dorothy Canfield Fisher were indefatigable in their efforts in behalf of the group, and many European authors owed their start in this country to the advice and help of such interested colleagues. No less important than monetary assistance were the friendly services which built morale. The annals abound in anecdotes both touching and comical which attest to the awareness and intelligent sympathy of the American hosts. One true story tells of a refugee author who became lonely and despondent to a degree where he could no longer work. As his brooding settled into melancholia, an American writer of his acquaintance came to the rescue and adopted a dog for him at the Bide-A-Wee Shelter. The story ends on a pleasant note: encouraged by the companionship of his new-found friend, the refugee writer found heart to face the vicissitudes of daily life.

It is sometimes said, exaggeratedly to be sure, that every refugee author had a chance to get one book published here. Unfortunately this book would often prove unacceptable to American tastes or would suffer so badly in translation as to lose all quality of distinction. After this initial failure, the refugee author was seldom called upon to publish again. A number of excellent novels are probably interred in bureau drawers of refugee boardinghouses as a result.

A great deal of theorizing has gone on about the type of subject matter which the refugee writer should utilize. Writers themselves have said that in order to be successful the refugee must either learn to know and understand the American scene and draw his subjects from it—that is to say, put his roots down in American soil—or else confine himself to international topics of universal appeal.

As was to be expected, the subjects of the first crop of books actually published by refugees grew out of their own recent experiences and concerns: refugees in flight, life in a French concentration camp, experiences of a newly arrived immigrant, social consequences of Fascism, effect of war conditions upon children, the life of Hitler, persecution, and the Underground.

Subjects proposed by refugees who sought stipends to enable them to follow their professional bent for a year were chosen in a manner that suggested a willingness to adapt themselves to the American market as well as a desire to please their sponsors. Refugees offered to write about American music, about Lincoln, about American generals. They tried their hand at plays about official Washington and sketches for the radio on American themes. Many writers were preoccupied with the collapse of European civilization in the perennial conflict between Germany and France, with the displacement of populations with all that that implied in the way of adjustments, with the reconstruction of Central Europe, with the re-education of Europe, with German youth; some were concerned with allegories and fantasies which would depict obliquely the spirit of the times; some, as is the case in any group of writers, dealt with great figures of the past; one wished to write about Death.

Refugee writers who continue production in foreign languages have found small audiences. Whereas in Europe there was at one time a Yiddish reading public of several million people, such readers in the United States are numbered only in the thousands. Yiddish journalists from abroad have not succeeded for the most part in obtaining jobs on Yiddish newspapers here since the supply so far exceeds the demand. A number of Yiddish writers are working in factories, some were taken into the armed forces, and others have found posts in institutions of science and learning. Some make a precarious living from writing occasional articles or publishing an infrequent book.

Austrians have contended that they had a harder time establishing themselves in the writing craft than did their German colleagues "who came on an earlier boat." Poles complained about the small number of their compatriots interested in Polish-language literature in exile. They pointed out that compared to the Polish reading public in the United States, the Italo-American group of readers interested in Italian literature and art was considerably larger and more sympathetic. If Poles were to be heard in this country, they must learn to write in English. Several distinguished Spanish writers have found places in American colleges, where they continue to make their influence felt through the medium of self-expression.

French writers, however, have found outlets for publications in French. A number of books have been published by French-speaking authors in exile by houses in the United States specializing in French offerings. Several French newspapers, to which writers in exile contributed, are published weekly. A periodical, *République Française*, founded by a group of scholars, scientists, and other persons interested in democratic thought, appears monthly.

The war years brought new employment opportunities for the writers' skills. A number of well-known refugees, including Leo Lania, the novelist, Walter Mehring, poet, and André Breton, writer and leader of the surrealist movement in art, were able to contribute to the war effort through their work for OWI. For several years during this period a European author was production manager for Alfred A. Knopf, publisher. A number have written successfully for the movies. At least one, Emilio Lussu, has returned to Europe where he is active politically as are, according to Varian Fry, several others of the Italian writers who passed through the doors of the Emergency Rescue Committee. Hermann Kesser and his wife have returned to Switzerland, where he is busy with play productions and publications. Some of the best known and most highly appreciated of the writers in exile have died, among them Stefan Zweig, Franz Werfel, Bruno Frank, Valeriu Marcu, the Rumanian historian, and Antoine de St. Exupéry. Among the group whose work has not yet been widely presented to an American public are Heinrich Mann who since his arrival in the United States has published a novel, *Lidice*, in Mexico under the auspices of El Libro Libre, the Free German publishing house, and another of whose novels is expected to appear in 1946 in a translation by Ludwig Lewisohn. Barthold Fles, who supplies this information about Mann, goes on to speak about two other writers whose names have appeared but little here:

Leonhard Frank and Alfred Doeblin, both in Hollywood, have continued to turn out novels in their native tongue in full confidence that after the war they would find publishers in their native country. Doeblin, whose "Berlin Alexanderplatz" was brought out by Viking years ago, has been at work on a tetralogy set in Berlin between the two world wars. It would seem their confidence was justified.

From other sources comes word of refugee writers currently approached by foreign publishers for German-language books to be published in Switzerland. Contact with European publishers is also developing in Holland, France, and Sweden. Restrictions imposed by wartime conditions upon the international transfer of currency continue, however, to hamper completion of such arrangements. But with the revival of publishing abroad, the exiled writers in this country should find their lot greatly improved.

To assist it in its consideration of recent immigrants in the field of letters, the Study Committee obtained from the files of several organizations which had worked closely with writers, as well as from newspaper and magazine clippings, material about 326 refugee writers known to have entered the United States. While these data had a limited usefulness from a statistical standpoint, they furnished a great deal of helpful and detailed information about individuals in the group, some of which has been incorporated in this section. A few additional facts drawn from the 326 cases may be of interest.

Of the group of 326, it was found that 295 were men and only 31 were women. A total of 138 writers out of the entire group were reported to have worked in their own field since arrival in the United States.

Their distribution as to specialty was as follows: biographers, 7; dramatists, 11; scenarists, 47; journalists, 112; novelists, 18; poets, 14; and writers in more than one branch of literature or writers on miscellaneous subjects, 117. In the light of what was discovered from other sources, it was not surprising to find that only 40 of the 112 journalists continued to write after coming to this country.

In the records of the 326 writers there were notes of the publication of numerous articles. Special honors included literary awards granted by the American Academy of Arts and Letters to Hermann Broch, Josef Wittlin, Hugo Ignotus, and Richard Beer-Hoffmann, and a citation from the National Conference of Christians and Jews to Franz Werfel for the "promotion of amity, understanding and co-operation among the varied cultural groups" that compose the population of the United States.

As gleaned from material obtained about these 326 refugee writers (no one of whom was directly solicited for information bearing on any point here discussed), contributions made by them to the war effort included the following activities: teaching in the Army Specialized Training Program by three writers; employment in the OWI of seven refugee writers, and the translation into German by one of them of *The Raft* by Trumbull and the *U.S. Pocket History* by Nevins and Commager for the use of OWI overseas; work by two of them with the OSS. One had written broadcasts for Station WRUL and published a book on Axis Military Tactics; one "broadcast during the fighting in Europe literally from trench to trench." Two were contributors to a German Reader to be published for use in postwar German schools. These cases are merely indicative of the activities of refugee writers in the war effort. Perhaps their outstanding contribution was in translating into German the American books sent to Europe by the Council on Books under OWI.

As for the Study Committee's own questionnaire, there were 129 writers who responded. The present age of the group shows the greatest concentration between 41 and 50, although there are now 6 who are 71 years old or older.

Of 86 writers responding to a question dealing with country of birth and religion, 41 were Jewish, 38 non-Jewish, and 7 of no or unknown religion. Thirty-six were German, 22 Austrian, 3 Polish, 3 Czech, 9 Russian, 6 Hungarian, 1 Italian, 3 Dutch, 2 French, and one Yugoslav. The questionnaire does not show that writers inevitably clustered about New York City. Out of 107 who stated that they had entered the United States through the Port of New York, nearly as many chose to leave the port area as decided to remain in it. (The division was 50 who left as against 57 who remained.)

Of the total group of writers answering the questionnaire, 38 per cent had become citizens. Most the remainder had taken steps toward the attainment of citizenship. Only five, all of whom entered during 1940, had failed to apply for naturalization.

Counting the 71 writers who remained in their profession, and taking special note of 16 others who became professors or teachers, it is interesting to observe that 87 of the 129 former writers replying to the questionnaire remained in some form of professional life.

In spite of the manifold difficulties facing refugee writers, there is perhaps no other department save applied art in which newcomers have scored so many outstanding successes as they have in the field of letters. Some of these successes have been material, while some have been of the spirit. Eighteen of these writers are listed in *Who's Who in America*. The three Nobel Prize winners in the group—Maurice Maeterlinck, Sigrid Undset, and Thomas Mann—and celebrated figures like André Maurois (who in 1945 joined the faculty of the University of Kansas City) and Henry Bernstein, playwright of a score of *pièces bien faites*, have been an inspiration to young American writers. The presence in this country of such men as Emil Ludwig, Franz Werfel, Stefan Zweig, Ferenc Molnar, Richard Beer-Hoffmann, Walter Mehring, Josef Wittlin, Berthold Viertel, Egon Hostovsky, Lion Feuchtwanger, Erich Maria Remarque, Jules Romains, Alfred Polgar, Erich Kahler, Hermann Broch, Paul Schrecker, Fritz von Unruh, and Konrad Heiden, has added luster to the American literary scene.

The words of Varian Fry,[9] who, as representative in Europe of the Emergency Rescue Committee, personally assisted many of the celebrated writers and professional people to escape to the United States and who has followed their careers here with an informed and lively concern, hold a special interest for everyone who is interested in refugee writers. In summing up "what has happened to them since," he states:

Most of them are very active indeed, and most of them are writing. Once a writer, always a writer, I guess. Many of them have greatly enriched our leisure hours, and some of them have greatly enriched our publishers, our printers and binders, our booksellers and our motion picture producers.

Not that there would have been any dearth of books to publish and make into movies if they hadn't come. But it is not only good to know that they were able to come, and to go on working. It is also good to know that so many of them have had considerable success. It shows not only how much opportunity America still has to offer the newcomer to its shores; it shows also how much the newcomer to its shores has to offer to America. It was no purely humanitarian gesture of ours to let these people in. We profited enormously from it. We got some of the best minds Europe has produced in a generation.

And yet there are some people who still want to cut off all immigration!

[9] Varian Fry, "What Has Happened to Them Since," *Publishers' Weekly*, Vol. 147 (June 23, 1945), No. 25.

CHAPTER XIX

OTHER PROFESSIONS

It is often said that the degree to which skills can be transferred from one country to another determines the extent of the refugee professional's success in the New World. The corollary to this, of course, is that language is one of the prime factors affecting the transferability of skills. Where language is not the only medium of expression with which the refugee professional deals (as, for example, in the field of music), the newcomer has had a better than average chance to make his way. In the next breath it must be admitted that even in those fields where language would be thought to be of prime importance, as in stage and screen art, tremendous individual successes have been scored by refugees. Clergymen, given time, have made a successful adaptation in measure not only as they mastered the new language but, even more vital than that, acquired a sound working knowledge of American folkways. Social workers and librarians had special problems not rooted in language. Their difficulties came rather from the fact that they sought admission to professions which had rigid entrance requirements, methods highly developed for use in the American scene, and a body of knowledge best interpreted to either the foreigner or the native through the medium of instruction in professional schools. The occupational initiation of both the social worker and the librarian has had usually to be deferred until a somewhat lengthy period of formal instruction had been successfully completed. Social work and library service appear to have represented fields for which refugees who came from other professions in Europe might retrain rather than occupations with a large membership drawn from European social workers and librarians respectively. Architects and engineers also have entered occupations with high professional standards and formalized codes of practice, but as the generous attitude of their American colleagues imposed fewer restrictions at the outset than did certain of the more jealously guarded professions (as, for example, medicine), they were able in due course to find their place and perform a useful service in community life.

A rapid glance at the experiences of refugees in these professions will serve to make the above points more clear.

Musicians

With regard to musicians, it must be realized that there are few plainly labeled "refugee musicians" in the sense that there are refugee painters or refugee lawyers. Musicians are migratory artists. America has a tradition of receiving guest artists which goes back at least to the eighteenth century. Certainly long before Hitler came to power, European musicians came frequently to the United States on concert tours, at the conclusion of which they might return to the Continent or go on to South America to fill additional engagements. Their return to the United States within a year or two of a successful season was confidently awaited, and in the perpetual going and coming of foreign musicians they have never been a novelty among us.

With the establishment of the Nazi regime, however, a greatly increased number of musicians came to this country from Europe, while many who were already in the United States remained here. In the group of the emigres and the self-exiled there were many world-famous figures: Arturo Toscanini, Bruno Walter, Wanda Landowska, Lotte Lehmann, Ernst Krenek, Jaromil Weinberger, and Darius Milhaud are only a few of the names that come immediately to mind. In addition to the world-renowned, there were many others of international reputation for sound musicianship. In the group, also, were the young musicians, the struggling musicians, and the lesser talents who laid claim to no great distinction in the world of music.

_ Many of those who were already famous continued to concertize, to find their way into the established organizations—philharmonic societies, opera associations, choral groups—and in certain instances into the field of light opera. Others had to have patience. As Mark Brunswick, Chairman of the National Committee for Refugee Musicians and President of the American Section of the International Society for Contemporary Music, stated in an article entitled "Refugee Musicians in America" in the January 26, 1946, issue of _The Saturday Review of Literature,_

> The refugee musician from Europe was bewildered when he found that apart from orchestras and the very limited field of music and private teaching, there were few normal careers available for him. He was expected to hit the jack-pot by giving a Town Hall concert and become famous overnight, or to vanish into obscurity.

The relative absence of opera houses in this country, which had flourished in Europe by the hundreds, was a source of hardship to the refugee. Mr. Brunswick reminds us that the European opera houses gave employment to "large numbers of solo singers, choral singers, orchestral musicians, coaches, conductors, producers, composers—all possible kinds of musicians" in a way which had no counterpart in this country.

Yet good vocalists in general were in demand, for "good vocalists do not come along in every generation," as one Polish musician put it. Some sang in synagogues and churches; others, like Jarmila Novotna and John Garris, sang in grand opera. Even distinguished exponents of the art of singing had their problems, however, as one less immediately successful than his fellows admitted when discussing his expenses:

"Since I am in this country, I have tried to get an engagement in one of the theatres, but due to the small number of first tenors needed and especially for the French reper-toire and the competition, I have not succeeded as yet. To make a living I started to give lessons, but it takes time to build up a sufficiently important group to meet my expenses [for which] I would need a sum of $150 a month. I am compelled to keep a decent apartment, the type of which I am occupying now and for which I have to pay $75 a month, because I have to teach in my apartment."

Instrumentalists found themselves in an especially favorable position with the coming of the war years. Many replacements were necessary as the manpower shortage made itself felt. By the winter of 1942, the chairman of the National Committee for Refugee Musicians was able to say in cor-respondence: "In general . . . the position of a good orchestra player is decidedly better now than it ever was. All our orchestra players have found jobs if they were willing to leave New York." Pianists for the most part— unless they were Schnabels or Serkins—found their main source of revenue in teaching. Least fortunate of all were the conductors, for, although there were many European conductors of the first rank in the refugee group, the number of American orchestras which could support a first-class leader was extremely limited. Furthermore, as a prominent educator remarked, "More than one hundred years ago, Berlioz said that the hardest thing about conducting was to get the opportunity."

Although there was the inevitable jealousy that exists in the musical world as surely as it does in any of the professions, musicians in general believe in open competition. Doors were not inexorably shut to refugees in the field simply because they were outsiders. Mr. Brunswick's comment in the article previously cited is illuminating:

The newly arrived refugee found people and organizations ready to give help and guidance to him. Often made-work programs were adopted to tide the refugees over the bad initial period, enabling them to keep up the practice of their art. In New York, for instance, privately financed concerts were given in the public schools in which many refugee musicians participated. This gave them a feeling of renewed functioning and yet was in no way unfair to our indigenous musicians. Some foundations made grants for outstanding refugee musicians and musicologists, enabling educational institutions whose financial resources were limited to have them on their staffs. Sectarian and non-sectarian organizations administered financial relief in cases of extreme need until a self-supporting job could be found.

The National Committee for Refugee Musicians, which operated in close association with the National Refugee Service, was able during a peak immigration year, 1940, to make 607 placements in the field of music and arrange for single engagements in 1,937 instances. Over 1,000 cases were active on the committee's list during that year.

A smooth relationship was early developed between the National Refugee Service and the Musicians Emergency Fund, Inc., an organization which, according to Erika Mann and Eric Estorick, "while formed primarily to aid American musicians, has co-operated by giving advice, by evaluating the proficiency of musicians coming from Germany and Austria, and by advising about possible positions." Both of these organizations auditioned and rated applicants for employment.

Refugee musicians were accepted in unions and protective organizations. A refugee musician might freely join Local 802 of the American Federation of Musicians, for example, provided only that he had his $50 initiation fee. In some cases, this sum was advanced to the client as a loan by the National Refugee Service. The union made no downward adjustment in the amount of the fee, however, in consideration of the refugee's financial circumstances.

Music publishers responded to the need of foreign musicians rather generously, extending their facilities so that compositions might be evaluated and in some instances accepted for publication. Moreover, they gave refugees employment as proofreaders, arrangers, and editors, although some individuals complained bitterly that these assignments did not give them a living wage.

Refugee musicians had frequent opportunities to appear as performers or to hear their pieces played over local radio stations. Both WNYC and WQXR in the New York area featured such occasions. While such "appearances" provided an excellent source of publicity for the refugee musician, they were not immediately remunerative.

Many artists continued to rely for their main source of livelihood, in the United States as they had done in Europe, upon teaching. This might consist in teaching individual pupils or in securing small paid posts at the conservatories, settlement houses, and music schools. In New York City it was sometimes said that there was at least one refugee on the staff of each of these institutions.

The war hit many music schools badly, however, and took away most of their male students. Wrote one musician in 1943, a composer by choice who had been teaching general music classes:

"I am not able to rely any more on the salary of my teaching position in [name of Eastern city deleted] which I held for 4 years, as classes are emptied through leave of pupils for the army and the director still has not decided whether he can renew my contract or not. But even in the best case, assuming my return in spite of those facts, it would be limited to a teaching period of approximately 4 months as it has happened last year. My income would be increased only by about $200 for the whole year. In regard to the question of other means of support: my wife, who is an appointed piano teacher at the same school, is earning $1,800 a year which are reduced by taxes and train fare to not quite $1,200 a year, which by the high cost of living and the necessity to maintain a certain minimum standard is hardly enough for the needs of one person."

Composers, vocalists, instrumentalists and—with the greatest frequency of all—musicologists, turned to the colleges and universities as preferred places in which to teach.

Once in institutions of higher learning, refugee musicians led a full life. A pianist-musicologist wrote happily from a small college in 1942:

"I am very fond of my work. It is many-sided and stimulating. I have six piano students, give a course on 'Reading of Music,' another one on 'Survey of the History of Music' and lead the a cappella choir, in which we perform the music treated in the history course. Our rector asked me to give an additional course on 'The Culture of the Renaissance' in the next term. This will be a fine opportunity to give an integrated picture of the period, which is nearest to my heart. . . . My wife participates in the ensemble as a violinist and violist. She has also been appointed a member of the State Symphony Orchestra as a violist. In early November she was away for four days on her first tour with the Orchestra. She likes the work and is, of course, quite glad to see something of the country on these occasions."

Community services were frequently expected of the refugee teacher:

"I have been invited to be the guest conductor of a band clinic which will take place in a near-by city next week. I shall work with, and give instruction to, eleven different bands and a girls' glee club of 150 voices during two days, and then conduct the entire group of around 300 on Friday evening in a concert."

The reaction of college presidents to the presence of refugee musicians ran the entire gamut. "He's a marvelous addition to our college," one administrator declared enthusiastically. "He has built up the music department and brought us a lot of new students. In addition, the people in the town like him." Another said glumly, "He's as good as, but no better than, the American teachers. If I had to choose between letting him go and letting one of the Americans go, I'd let him go." Another comment frequently heard was: "He's too good for the college. He has more music in his little finger than all the rest of the faculty put together."

General comments made by refugee musicians during 1945 were revealing.

"My experiences, one-sidedly made in the musical and college fields, may not be of general value," observed an Austrian Protestant who was living in California. "However, I found that in those two fields the main obstacles will arise from a certain *fear* of the native-born musicians and teachers that the immigrants are better or at least considered better [on account of European training] by students and the public."

A former concert pianist, a German Jew, stated of a city in northwestern United States that "it is not really music-minded." He also found that the other music teachers in the community made things "a little difficult" rather than trying to work things out together as they might have done.

In general, the agencies felt that it took at least two years' financing on the average before an individual refugee musician could get on his feet. This was even with the best introductions and contacts, and the benefit of a European reputation. It seemed to be the consensus that men among the refugee musicians were able to cleave to their profession in the United States, while women had not been so fortunate, having been obliged frequently to go into other lines of work and practice music only as a side line or avocation. The group as a whole had been quite successful, however, or as one person close to the musical practitioners remarked, "Refugee musicians have got jobs, all right—in fact, some of them have done pretty well for themselves. Everybody seems to be busy, and there is plenty of activity which will probably mean jobs for everybody for a long time to come."

From the Musicians Committee of the National Refugee Service and from other sources, including newspaper clippings, records of the Emergency Committee in Aid of Displaced Foreign Scholars and the American Friends Committee, and from interviews, the Study Committee obtained the names of some 1,015 musicians, of whom it could be said that at least 150 were working once more in their own field. (Actually, many more than this number were probably employed in one form or another of musical occupation.) Within the broad field of music, the occupations of these refugees might be broken down as follows:

Conductors		107
Composers		69
Vocalists		215
Instrumentalists		330
String	140	
Wind	53	
Piano and Other Percussion	137	
Teachers		275
Miscellaneous		19
Total		1,015

To this number might have been added the cantors listed through the committee on religious functionaries of the National Refugee Service. This was not done, however, except in a few cases where the cantor was primarily a secular musician who sang only infrequently at religious services.

Twenty-six of these refugee musicians were listed in *Who's Who in America*. They included 8 conductors, 7 composers, 4 singers, 3 pianists, 3 violinists, and 1 musicologist.

The group has contributed much to the cultural life of the nation. They have published musical compositions, furthered the study of musical history, concertized, directed philharmonic orchestras, founded orchestras and choral groups, and put on opera productions.

STAGE AND SCREEN ARTISTS

One of the professions with the broadest social outlook, most marked cosmopolitanism, and most tolerant and hospitable attitude toward the newcomers is the stage. In spite of the traditional open-mindedness of the dramatic profession, however, actors have found it exceedingly hard to re-establish themselves in this country. The reasons are not difficult to find.

First and most important is the language barrier. As Erwin Piscator says, "No element is so strongly bound up in nationalism as is the drama of a country. . . . The poetry of language is the centre of every theatre even in the naturalistic school." Although an Oscar Karlweiss may declare, "Language is no difficulty. When I first came I acted a role like a parrot, without understanding a word, and I got wonderful notices!"[1] the fact remains that there were few foreign actors who found a *Jacobowsky and the Colonel* in which to play a title role. Mady Christians and Oskar Homolka scored over and over again in plays which attracted good audiences, while Verich and Voskovec, erstwhile comedy team from Prague, delighted their public in Shakespeare, but these foreign actors, all of whom acquired a greater or lesser degree of promise, were exceptions which proved the rule.

Language, however, was not the only drawback. As a prominent American producer expressed it: "Many refugee actors had very important positions on the European stage, and it was with the utmost psychological difficulty that they accepted minor roles here. To be relegated to a subordinate place had a devastating effect upon the actor's ego—that quality which is so basic a part of the actor's make-up."

Some Americans maintain that European actors, as well as European directors and producers, hold firmly to the belief that everything in Europe was better than it is here. It is alleged that foreigners did not realize that the American theater was the way it was because it was a genuinely American product. Acting techniques used here differed from those in Europe, with the result that foreign actors had a great deal to learn in adjusting themselves to American methods and staging.

[1] *New York Times*, Nov. 18, 1945.

Contrary theories on the staging and presenting of plays made for an area of confusion between representatives of the two continents:

"The European concept of the theatre is totally different from that held in the United States," a refugee explained. "Here a play is little more than a dramatized reading of a script. Abroad, on the other hand, a play is a vehicle or nucleus around which a rich structure embodying details of acting, presentation, production, costuming, and so forth, may be built up. The play itself may be a very simple thing provided it is treated as a vehicle for expansion and development at the hands of its director. In the United States a play is cast as much for its actors as anything else; in Europe the actor was merged as part of the group.

"Abroad," he went on to say, "the director was a *creator* and not just an interpreter. It was the director who made a physical production out of a play, giving it dimensions and the breath of life. The director in Europe had absolute *carte blanche*. No one would think of telling a director what to do with his play. It was his property, his own creation. Here in this country the director can write his own ticket only after he has made a big success, and then only so long as he continues to be successful. . . ."

The Study Committee built up a list of 273 refugees connected with the stage and screen by using the files of the Emergency Committee in Aid of Displaced Foreign Scholars and of the American Friends Service Committee, and utilizing also clippings from theater programs and from the drama pages of the English and foreign-language press. We have no way of testing the representativeness of this sample. The number, 273, is roughly a third of the total number of actors reported by immigration authorities as entering the United States from Europe between 1933 and 1944. (The immigration figure is 767 if based on selected "races or peoples," or 836 according to Europe as the place of last residence.) It is not known, however, just what proportion of the immigrant European actors were refugees, although undoubtedly they constituted a majority.

Two actors, two dancers, two stage directors, and a movie art director were listed in *Who's Who in America*, whose coverage of this field, as well as of art, has been admittedly inadequate.

Kurt Hellmer, in an article entitled "Berlin und Wien am Broadway," which appeared in the *Aufbau* of December 22, 1944, listed nearly 80 refugee actors and actresses who had appeared on the American stage. His list included such well-known names as those of Albert and Else Bassermann (*Embezzled Heaven*), Sig Arno (*Song of Norway*), Edith Angold (*Professor Mamlock, Knickerbocker Holiday, The Barber Had Two Sons,* and *Tomorrow the World*), Adrienne Gessner (*Another Sun, Claudia, Thank you, Svoboda,* and *I Remember Mama*), and Marianne Stewart, née Schuenzel (*Jacobowsky and the Colonel*). Long, too, was his list of stage managers and producers, among them Paul Czinner, Otto Preminger, Erwin Piscator, Herbert Graf, Berthold Viertel, and Max Reinhardt.

DRAMATIC ARTISTS KNOWN TO THE STUDY COMMITTEE

	Number	Those Still in Same Field
Actors		
Stage	65	29
Screen	85	17
Producers		
Stage	5	2
Screen	15	5
Directors		
Stage	15	6
Screen	30	9
Managers		
Stage	6	2
Screen	—	—
Teachers		
Stage	7	7
Screen	1	1
Miscellaneous or Unclassified		
Stage	3	—
Screen	—	—
Artists in the Field of the Dance		
Teachers	22	5
Performers	19	2
Total	273	85

The Study Committee did not succeed in making much contact with representatives of the motion-picture industry and cannot, therefore, report any original research on refugees in this field. It is widely known, however, that of the Frenchmen now prominent in film circles in this country many had already had Hollywood contracts before leaving Europe. Such directors as René Clair, Julien Duvivier, and Jean Renoir, for example, came into an industry that was waiting to welcome them. Whether or not many of the refugee group would return to Europe after conditions there had settled down was uncertain; those who might choose to return would maintain the contacts they had in the United States. It was felt that the cross-fertilization of ideas resulting from the sojourn in this country of the many talented artists driven out by Hitler would almost certainly redound to the benefit of the native industry while at the same time it could not fail to have a stimulating effect upon emigre art itself.

Hans Kafka's article, "What Our Immigration Did for Hollywood—and Vice Versa," which also appeared in the anniversary number of *Aufbau* of December 22, 1944, listed some 90 refugee screen actors in the United States, some 33 directors, 23 producers, 59 screen writers, and 19 composers for the films. Some of these names reappear in several classifications, as is quite natural from an occupational standpoint, so that there is a certain amount of duplication. For comparative purposes, it should be noted that a number of names are included which relate to persons who entered the United States prior to the period covered by the present Study.

Before closing this section on dramatic artists, a word should be said about refugee dancers. Just how many came to the United States is not certain. It has been said that comparatively few German dancers, with the exception of the younger and more adventurous ones, came to this country during the Hitler years. Some who left Germany went to Paris, others settled in London, while a number of the top people in the profession were thought to be "hibernating" in country retreats in rural Germany where they were not molested. "For the most part," a well-known dancer stated, "there is a tendency always to go where the group goes, and groups of dancers did not come to the United States."

Thanks to organizations like the Friends, refugees who had not been able to continue as teachers of the dance were given contacts which enabled them to enter other fields, as, for example, body building, posture, and other forms of physical education.

RELIGIOUS FUNCTIONARIES

There is probably no more interesting or varied group in the whole company of refugees from Nazism than the religious functionaries. The Study Committee recorded data about some 491 of their number who had come to the United States, of whom all but a few were rabbis, cantors, religious teachers, schochtim, mohelim, and others of the Jewish faith. The Study Committee has no reason to believe that the group about which it was able to obtain material represents a true cross section of the nearly 2,500 clergymen who were known to come into the United States from Europe during the period 1933–1944. It prefers to suggest rather that the group is one which will offer to future students a rich source of information about the attitudes and characteristics of Jewish immigrant clergymen during the fateful years of Hitler domination.

It must be pointed out that the problems represented by this group strike so deeply into the roots of Jewish religious and community life that they merit a separate study. A brief summary such as the present one can do no more than hint at the nature of these problems, illustrate certain facets of them, cite several examples of adjustments made by individuals within the group, and tentatively offer such figures as suggest possible conclusions.

On December 1, 1938, the National Refugee Service set up a committee to serve refugee rabbis. This committee had a threefold function. First of all, it worked closely with the Migration Department of the National Refugee Service in an attempt to help foreign rabbis and religious functionaries migrate to the United States. (It must be remembered that in order to enable a foreign minister to enter the United States as a nonquota immigrant there must be secured for him a bona fide "call" from a duly organized congregation together with a promise of at least a minimum salary of $1,500 per annum.) In the second place, it strove to find placement opportunities for refugee religious functionaries in this country. Third, in co-operation with the Jewish Theological Seminary of America, to which the National Refugee Service was to appropriate funds for this service in 1939, it retrained a number of religious functionaries so that they might adapt themselves to American community and congregational needs.

Rabbi Alexander J. Burnstein, Secretary of the Committee on Refugee Jewish Ministers of the National Refugee Service, early recognized the need for financial help to supplement the inadequate salaries of rabbinical contracts which he and other religious leaders had been able to secure for the group, as well as the need for providing financial assistance for the elderly unemployable refugee rabbis and scholars ineligible for the National Refugee Service's help. An agreement was accordingly reached whereby the Central Conference of American Rabbis, the Union of Orthodox Rabbis, and the Rabbinical Assembly of America undertook to try to engage capable rabbis still abroad as assistants or co-workers in refugee work in the larger cities where there were great numbers of refugees. Plans were laid to canvass certain small towns with a view to finding posts for a number of displaced synagogue functionaries. A series of subventions were provided by the Central Conference of American Rabbis to make possible the engagement at certain Jewish institutions of higher learning of elderly, scholarly rabbis who would find difficulty in American placements. Subsidies were also made available to small congregations unable immediately to pay the salaries of refugee clergymen. It was hoped in such instances that the local community or congregations would eventually take over full financial responsibility. The retraining of a number of younger liberal rabbis also was envisaged as a possibility.

At the initiative of the National Refugee Service, and with the active support and co-operation of outside interested groups, this program went forward for some four and a half years. On May 27, 1943, following discontinuance of financial assistance in behalf of certain clients by outside co-operating agencies, the National Refugee Service took stock anew of the situation and outlined what it considered the problem of religious functionaries.[2] This was mainly a problem of resettlement and placement arising out of the fact that the refugee religious functionaries—especially the Polish and Russian—were generally much more orthodox than American Jewish congregations desired and were insistent on adhering to their traditional pattern of religious education and practice, dating back to the

[2] Report entitled *Problem of Religious Functionaires*, submitted as an interoffice memorandum at the National Refugee Service on May 27, 1943, by Laura G. Rubin and Morris Salganik.

Middle Ages, which was not acceptable even to American orthodox groups.

At the time the above memorandum was formulated, the agency had a total case load of 75 religious functionaries, of whom 46 were orthodox, 18 conservative, and 11 reformed. Occupationally they were distributed as follows: rabbis, 34; cantors, 22; schochtim (ritual slaughterers of fowl and cattle), 5; teachers, 6; shamus (a sexton), 1; Talmudist (scholar), 1; scribe (a strictly orthodox person versed in Hebraic law who copies the Torah and other religious writings on parchment), 1; mashgihim (inspectors and supervisors of the preparation of kosher food), 2; rabbinical students, 3.

The European rabbi came from a culture in which Jewish life was a community institution to one in which it was a congregational function. In the words of a former German rabbi:

"Jewish life in Germany was different from Jewish life here in that in Germany the Jewish community was a legal part of the population. Jewish babies were born into it and unless Jewish people indicated their desire to leave the community officially they were always regarded as a part of it and were assessed taxes for the maintenance of Jewish institutions. In this country, there is no corporate body of Jewry, but an aggregation of small congregations all over the country."

The rabbi in Europe did not follow any one set pattern. He may have been a clergyman who looked after neighborhood functions of a limited sort; gave advice; studied the Talmud; perhaps engaged in a small business in association with his wife. One orthodox clergyman had been, for example, not only rabbi, but mohel (circumcizer), baal kore (reader of the scrolls in the synagogue), and schochet as well. The rabbi may have been a great scholar and sage, leading a life of intense study and contemplation. Or he may have been a man of action, playing a highly important role in the city-wide community.

It could not have been easy to find a suitable post for each of these rabbis in the new country. Reformed rabbis appear to have been more easily placed than their conservative or orthodox colleagues. The supply of European rabbis was considerably in excess of the demand for their services. Congregations were loath to consider men over 40 or at the most 45, believing that younger men had more energy, ambition, and flexibility than the older clergymen. Congregations tended to look ahead with concern to the moment when retirement and pensions would become immediately pressing considerations.

Inevitably, language was a stumbling block, whether for orthodox or non-orthodox groups.

Since your knowledge of Yiddish is meager [an American rabbi wrote a refugee in 1942], your chances of locating a position in any orthodox congregation are none too promising.

Our committee will be disinclined to consider Dr. J. because of his German background [a midwestern community leader stated in 1941]. His Hebrew pronunciation would be unintelligible to our group since they all have Russian-Polish backgrounds and their sons have been trained along the same lines. I had in the past invited refugee rabbis to our congregation, fine men, largely cultured men, but whose Hebrew expressions were decidedly against them.

Most important of all, however, were those subtle differences "in mentality and background between the native-born Jew and the rabbi who came here recently, which cannot be easily ignored, and which frequently undermine the prestige and influence of the rabbi among the young in his congregation."

Although the placement situation was at no time especially bright, and many synagogue officials were finding their way into other fields of activity, the National Refugee Service was able to announce as early as 1940 that 119 rabbis and other functionaries had been placed during that year in cities and towns throughout the country.

Salaries were not large and, as previously indicated, supplementation was frequently necessary. Certain of the orthodox rabbis opened little synagogues of their own, refugee or otherwise, but because of the smallness of their congregations were able to earn at most only a few dollars a week. The records are full of engrossing accounts of refugees who found American congregations. It can truly be said that the correspondence on this subject is a study in itself.

Some foreign rabbis, as already noted, had refugee congregations. Others had "adjusted" so completely to American institutions as to be completely out of touch with the refugees right in their own communities. Synagogues and temples ranged in size from single rooms and simple stucco buildings to large church-communityhouse structures complete with gymnasium, swimming pool, and meeting rooms.

Refugee rabbis co-operated in community activities and contributed to the war effort.

"I conduct Jewish services in several neighboring army camps," wrote one minister. "For Rosh Hashonah and Yom Kippur we expect more than 400 soldiers at our services. We succeeded in giving home hospitality to 421 soldiers. That is something, if you consider that the congregation has only 52 members, and that only 61 Jewish families live in this community."

Here and there in the records are striking instances of interfaith co-operation. The rabbi of a small community allowed the use of his synagogue to an Episcopalian congregation temporarily without a home. Reported a refugee rabbi from the South:

"There is hardly a week in which I have not to lecture in or to address Christian clubs one to four times. I think that this strengthened my position within the community most. I spoke in almost all civic clubs in town and the neighboring places. I was the main speaker at a convention of social workers that was held here, spoke to the students of the ———— Teachers College, to the several hundred civil servants that were employed here at the office of Soil Conservation Service, to the women of the Central Presbyterian Church on brotherhood day, four times to different groups of the First Methodist Church, being attended by 25 to 150 persons, to different schools and high schools, to the Red Cross and many others."

Rabbis themselves and Hebrew scholars from Europe, interviewed in 1945, agreed that most refugee rabbis had fared well rather than ill in the United States.

With very few exceptions, almost all of the refugee rabbis are placed [a European professor of Jewish Studies reported]. This is partly, however, because there is such a demand at the present time for clergymen in the Armed Forces.

In general I think rabbis adjusted themselves very well [the spiritual leader of an important congregation declared]. One thing which counted for a good deal in their favor was the fact that their rabbinical ordination was internationally valid. It was necessary for European rabbis to obtain a "secular" doctor's degree in a university, such as the Ph.D. or Dr. Juris. This had insured the possession of a broad liberal education, a fact which is much appreciated here.

The majority of Jews in this country came from Poland and Russia up to a few years ago and Polish-speaking rabbis accordingly had little difficulty in finding groups here with which they could communicate. Positions for German-speaking rabbis had to be established artificially [a refugee rabbi stated].

The majority of European rabbis who came here now have pulpits [another refugee said]. Few have had to change from their own field, although I know of three who could not continue their work. Of these, two are now working in factories, and one is a superintendent in a building. For the most part, refugee rabbis found small congregations, which were of course scattered all over the country and not localized in New York City. Some established their own congregations.

One great source of difficulty in the placement of cantors was the fact that few of them were prepared to use the East European modes of chanting such as are employed in American synagogues. As an American rabbi explained the situation:

The German type of Chasanuth [method of chanting] is not needed or desired in this country. We have had the same problem with all the German cantors, even the best ones. Their Nusach [order of service] is sufficiently different from the one that is in vogue in this country to make congregations feel ill at ease during their davening [praying]. Even the most gifted and outstanding German cantors had to undergo many ordeals and painstaking training before they could adjust themselves to American congregations. For the difficulty relates not only to the Nusach but also to the manner of their pronunciation of the Hebrew words and general pulpit manner.

Cantors as well as other religious functionaries were continually urged to go outside their own profession. "After all," one rabbi said, "the great Spinoza was a lens grinder by profession." Some worked in factories. One was assistant manager of a motion-picture theater seven nights a week. Another did "bitter strong work—sweeping floors."

The National Refugee Service stated in its "Report on the Unit for Refugee Religious Functionaires" of November 11, 1943, that

> The majority of [the cantors] are employed in other types of employment . . . A number have full year jobs as cantors, but the pay is about $1,200 annually. All of these cantors are asking either for full time positions as cantors with salary sufficient to maintain themselves; others who are content with their present employment are requesting us to locate cantorial openings for weekends and holidays to supplement their incomes. . . . Some of the cantors have other skills. They may be Hebrew teachers, and occasionally schochtim or mohelim. They are also baal koreas and baal tfilas.

Yet here and there in the records appear statements like the one which follows:

> Cantor A.'s contract was recently renewed and a raise was granted to him again by the congregation. He receives now a regular salary of $40 per week, and side-money for concerts, weddings, etc., brings it up to about $200 per month. Mr. A. stressed repeatedly how happy he is in the congregation and in his work.

Another cantor, who was established in New England, had been mentioned as winner in a nation-wide contest in synagogue music.

Pleased comments came from congregations here and there:

> His singing of the Rosh Hashonah, Shabbas Shuva and Yom Kippur music was more than satisfactory; it was uplifting and inspirational. It is clear that his many years of experience in Germany has made the singing of Synagogue music second nature to him. He willingly and easily made whatever adjustments were necessary to make the service as he sang it in Germany suit the needs of an American Jewish congregation.

Consideration of these two main groups, the rabbis and the cantors, will give some idea of the setting into which the refugee religious functionaries came, and of the special problems which they, in a sense, brought with them. As for the secondary groups, the National Refugee Service made certain generalizations concerning its own case load on November 11, 1943:

> Although we have several people who are listed as being schochtim, we are unable to fill the occasional requests for a schochet in some of the smaller communities because as mentioned previously the salary is frequently insufficient to maintain a family. . . .
> The few mashgihim who are on our rolls are elderly people who at one time have

been considered unemployable, but who might now be available for the employment market. Some are amenable to this plan, and we have referred them for such employment.

In the case of the Hebrew teachers, we run up against the difficulty that frequently they are unable to speak sufficient English to satisfy the local organizations. Many of the latter also insist on local training. . . . Most of the teachers have been willing to accept other types of employment.

SOCIAL WORKERS

In the welfare field the market for social workers has changed greatly since the early days of refugee migration, when there was little demand for the services of case workers from overseas, to the present time when all social workers are at a premium, and even refugees in the over-age group are now employed.

Retraining of refugee social workers has been considered necessary and desirable in order to enable them to enter the profession at a level of preparation and competence equal to that of Americans entering the field. In contrast to the American emphasis on intensive professional training in schools of social work, supplemented of course by units of field work which are integrated into the schools' own program, European practice has laid far greater stress on what may be broadly called vocational or in-service training. Although schools of social work formed part of the educational structure of European countries, a great number of men and women in the field were there by virtue of administrative and legal training rather than formal training in what we know as case work. So true is this that it is a matter of the utmost difficulty to determine, out of a group of refugees employed in the administration of social services in Europe, which ones were "social workers," which were legal advisers, and which were experts in the field of public administration. In the period that followed the close of World War I, practically all private social agencies in Germany, for example, were crushed. Social welfare became government controlled, and under government auspices it was natural that the legal and fiscal aspects of the program should predominate.

Experts in the field state that during the early years of the Hitler regime the majority of the social workers were asked to remain in Germany to administer the government program of social services. Those workers who left the country were for the most part socialists, pacifists, and men and women with relatives or other connections in the United States. They arrived in fairly small numbers, however, until about 1937 when a sharp increase in their number made evident the need for a special committee which would accept responsibility for the group, examine their credentials, evaluate their qualifications and experience, advise them about retraining possibilities, and steer them toward work opportunities in this country. Holding that it would be unwise and impractical to attempt to care for refugee social workers as clients of case work agencies, representatives of various agencies concerned with the problems of refugees met and established the Committee on Displaced Foreign Social Workers.

As the work of this group developed, and as its interpretation of the refugee social worker to American colleagues met with an increasingly interested and sympathetic response, official recognition of the committee was sought from the National Refugee Service. Along with recognition, which was accorded, came financial support, so that in addition to counseling services the committee was able to extend a number of loans to refugee social workers in need of retraining. A number of schools of social work generously granted fellowships or supplementary assistance in certain cases.

After training had been completed, however, the refugee still had to start at the bottom of the scale and work up. Older people with long years of experience in social administration found this particularly distasteful, as they did the necessity of accepting a low beginning wage. One of the great difficulties immediately facing the refugee worker was the need of adjusting to the framework of the American social agency, and accepting supervision with its formal system of periodic work-and-personality evaluation. The experienced European worker had known relatively greater freedom abroad and had enjoyed greater latitude in working out his own solutions to problems on the job than the average American who was accustomed to his earned position in the hierarchy of case worker, case work supervisor, department head, and organizational director, and who had learned to accept "supervision."

Both refugees who had retrained and those who could not or would not undergo such preparation for American social work, tended to resent the attitude which they sensed and occasionally heard voiced to the effect that all their ideas of welfare work were wrong, *qua* European. One individual exclaimed bitterly, "Surely there must be a carry-over from one country to another of professional experience." Another refugee declared that American agencies were doing now "what we did in Europe fifty years ago."

Europeans who had had close contact with social work abroad, although not themselves actively engaged in the field, regretted that the profession in this country was closed to them without special training.

A number of men and women who had worked in other fields in Europe —such as, for example, the law—were drawn to welfare work in this country and joined the ranks of former social workers who were training in the field. That they became skilled practitioners has been abundantly proved. According to one of their colleagues in the United States, those

who had been psychoanalyzed in Europe became the best case workers
here—not because they had been psychoanalyzed so much as because the
process taught them what case work could mean.

Throughout the years of the migration, settlement houses proved particularly hospitable toward refugee social workers, and many a foreign
worker spent his first weeks in this country in a room set aside for him at
one of the settlement houses. Henry Street Settlement in New York, for
instance, played frequent host to many members of the profession. Neighborhood houses had pressed for the admission of refugee social workers,
not alone for humanitarian reasons, although these admittedly loomed
large, but also because it was in the tradition of the settlement house to be
vitally interested in current happenings. Refugees brought the outside
world very close to the settlement house, and helped neighborhood people
understand what was going on in Europe.

Today many refugee social workers are in positions of considerable responsibility. A number are in supervisory positions, and at least three are
head workers in settlement houses. One refugee has "done a splendid job
counseling other refugees and veterans." Another is in the leadership
training department of the Girl Scouts. Some four or five have become
professors of social work or sociology in universities and colleges. A number are working directly with the churches in carrying on social programs.
In the New York area, almost every private agency has one or more
refugee workers on its staff.

LIBRARIANS

The material which the Study Committee collected did not indicate that
many refugees who had been librarians in Europe retrained for that profession in the United States. The field was one, however, which had a very
real appeal for men and women in general who cared for scholarly pursuits, and a number of refugees who were interested in entering library
work found help and advice through the American Library Association
Committee on Refugee Librarians created in June, 1940, "to aid, in co-
operation with other committees of the American Library Association and
other agencies, refugee librarians seeking occupation and contacts in the
country; to give advice to those foreigners trained in other related professions, considering retraining for librarianship; to accumulate information
on uncommon language and other resources of foreign librarians for the
use of librarians considering the employment of additional staff members."

Refugees were counseled about opportunities in the field of library
service and more particularly about their own suitability for entrance into
that field. In certain cases refugees were explicitly advised against training
for librarianship because of over-age, absence of sufficient evidence of adjustability, and personality handicaps, as well as because, after thorough

discussion of the field with them, it was determined that they had not been sufficiently informed of the duties and activities they would be expected to perform, the chances for advancement, the wage scale and working hours.

To an American librarian, library work in this country and abroad suggested two very different careers. The European librarian is more apt to be a bibliographer than a librarian working with people, as he would be in the United States where the emphasis is placed on the human and socialized side of library work. Here the profession is considered primarily a service occupation, like social work. The librarian works with the public, striving to make available to everyone who needs his help the riches of literature and art, as well as the precise information on the sciences and near sciences that is to be found between the covers of books, periodicals, pamphlets, and other publications.

In the opinion of at least one American with wide contacts the field was not an easy one for refugees to enter. The dean of an important library school stated that placement problems for such a group as had studied at his institution were considerable. While refugee scholars who were specialists in certain disciplines, once trained in library science, might find an opportunity to work within their field of specialization, it was a very real question whether it was not better for the counselor to advise the refugee who did not have a field of specialization to enter another occupation than library work. Then, too, the matter of advancement presents difficulties. At best it takes a librarian a long time to work up through the ranks. Salaries are low in comparison with those found in comparable occupations.

European students themselves analyzed job chances in this way, pointing out, however, that it had proved impossible to generalize since each case has been different.

Inasmuch as library service is a field in which special schooling is a prerequisite to employment at the professional level, refugees who were determined to enter the field sought to secure training at one of the accredited professional schools or at a school of library science connected with a university.

Some 98 refugee librarians were known to the Study Committee through lists supplied by the School of Library Service of Columbia University, the Graduate Library School of the University of Chicago, Pratt Institute, and from other sources. Most of them are known to have taken some form of library training in this country and to be engaged in library work. Overall reports indicate that the typical European library student was a mature person who has made a good adjustment to professional life. Some of the group are obviously headed for distinguished appointments or positions of leadership but it is to be expected that they will advance up through the ranks as native Americans themselves must do. Many refugees who trained as librarians, however, have gone into other fields of work, such as teaching and government service. In this connection the following comment on refugee librarians from a placement officer of an eastern university is of interest:

. . . notwithstanding the group of men who are in the armed forces, a much higher percentage of women have remained in the professional field following graduation. At least two factors are of importance here: one, the financial returns have not been sufficient to hold the men in the profession, and two, we have the feeling that the women have made the adjustment from European to American points of view more easily and quickly, and as a result have become more efficient librarians.

ENGINEERS

Refugee engineers have proved to be an energetic and enterprising group, of marked adaptability and initiative, for whom the war emergency created many employment opportunities. They have had to struggle against relatively few of those prohibitions which hindered the free entrance of most refugees into the professional life of this country. According to the *Harvard Law Review*,[3] their situation even before the United States entered the war was distinctly favorable:

Of those states that have a registration system for engineers [all except five and Washington, D.C.], only two require citizenship; seven others require first papers. In many states graduation from an approved college or a number of years of experience is necessary in order to be eligible for an examination; in a few states, once the minimum qualifications are met, an examination is discretionary with the board. In other states, experience of a specific character, graduation from an approved school plus experience, or membership in the National Council of State Boards of Engineering Examiners or in the National Bureau of Engineering Registration may be accepted by the board, as a substitute for the examination. In some states the board may likewise waive the examination where the applicant has a license as an engineer in a foreign country or in a foreign country which reciprocates.

In spite of the fact that few discriminatory measures existed, it would be somewhat far from the truth to suggest that these foreign engineers were invariably welcomed by their American colleagues. Severe criticism of their training was occasionally heard. When asked about postwar opportunities for refugee engineers, an American representative of the profession replied sharply:

"There will be a personnel shortage after the war, all right, but the need will be for well-trained American engineers and physicists and not for foreign engineers. European-trained engineers are simply not good enough; our industry will not have them. I don't know just what it is about the man with foreign training—he is usually a hound for detail and carries every calculation out to fourteen places. American boys like accuracy, too, but they know how to get it with the help of machines."

[3] "Refugees and the Professions," Vol. LIII, No. 1 (1939), pp. 117–118.

A German Protestant engineer from the metropolitan area pointed mildly to a certain fear of competition on the part of Americans:

"The main change is the surrounding and that I have not the many professional friends as I had in all countries of Europe. This is not the country's fault, of course. But it can be said that the same [now] colleagues who were so friendly to visitors from foreign countries are icicles when the famous competitor from Europe settles in their midst."

There was more than a touch of "America for the Americans" in the comment of a native engineer:

"There will be a great deal of rebuilding to be done in Europe. It would be a good thing if refugees would go back and undertake this task. In so doing, they would leave the field here open for our young American engineers."

None of the attitudes or opinions indicated above appears to have prevented the effective employment of refugee engineers in their own or cognate fields.

"I was hired as a draftsman in one of the then Defense Plants and I have held this same position for more than five years," wrote in 1945 an Austrian Protestant, who had been a designer and mechanical engineer abroad. "In addition to this I suggested and worked out several courses in mathematics and mechanical subjects for the war-training program of the local university."

Mr. M. specializes in cutting machines for textiles of various kinds including synthetic rubber [an interviewer reports of a German Jewish electrical engineer]. He takes great pride in the fact that he designed the machine used in the last step in the process of making synthetic rubber used by the Standard Oil Company. He has also designed machines which were used in cutting material employed in the manufacture of boats for the Navy.

His work has been largely research [the description of another electrical engineer from Germany reads] and he was able to help develop a vacuum-sealed rectifier power tube. He remained in this department until June, 1944, when he was transferred to his present work which is a secret project for the United States Army. His experiences at work have been very satisfying professionally and in his relations with his fellow employees. He has always felt welcome there, experiencing no discrimination. He was admitted to membership into the American Institute of Electrical Engineers.

The general situation of refugee engineers is mirrored by the experience of one of the nationality groups. Although his organization had been brought into existence in order to take care of the group of Polish technologists, Mr. Henryk Kozmian, Chairman of Polonia Technica, stated that in actual practice there had been little need of assistance. In his three years as head, no one had come to ask him for a grant or a loan. It was true, he said, that some of the older men among the engineers had had a hard time of it. The younger engineers, however, were employed—some at very good salaries, a number in quite important posts. He was constantly amazed at the tremendous adaptibility of the Polish engineers, he declared. Scarcely any of the refugees, even those who were most successful, were working in their own specialty. A chemical engineer with a fine reputation abroad, whom he knew, had worked himself into an excellent position as mechanical engineer for one of the large concerns. A good architect from Warsaw was now engaged in electrical engineering.

A number of refugee engineers entered universities and schools of technology, where there appears to have been no feeling against them but rather an appreciation of what they could bring.

As the war continued, opportunities at the level of higher education became more numerous. In general, however, teachers and instructors called to American institutions had come out of the university and Hochschule system in Europe, and as such they were considered in this Study under the blanket heading of "professors and other scientists."

At least four refugee engineers are listed in *American Men of Science*. A number of those replying to the Study Committee questionnaire reported inventions, some of which were patented, publications, and technical contributions to production for the war effort.

ARCHITECTS

The refugee architect found himself in a situation which was roughly comparable to that of the engineer. Although the personal welcome extended to him varied according to local conditions and individual viewpoints, prejudices, or predilections of American colleagues, he did not meet with active discrimination. The regulations covering the practice of architecture, as outlined in the *Harvard Law Review*[4] during 1939, are significant in the light of their broad tolerance of foreign training and experience. In those states which have a registration system, stated experience or study is usually necessary. Where examinations are required, frequent exceptions are permitted in the discretion of the state board, such as where the applicant has had ten years' experience as an architect or three years' experience plus a diploma from an approved architectural school, or where he has been registered as an architect in a foreign country, although in addition the foreign country must sometimes reciprocate. Not more than six states require citizenship; twelve require first papers.

As of October, 1945, refugee architects not yet citizens of the United States were not barred from membership in their professional association, the American Institute of Architects, although the New York Chapter was considering a proposal that none but citizens be admitted to full membership.

From the foregoing it may be inferred that there was little of the or-

[4] "Refugees and the Professions," Vol. LIII, No. 1 (1939), pp. 121–122.

ganized blocking of refugee practitioners in the field of architecture such as existed, for instance, in the field of medicine. Yet individual American architects have resented their European colleagues, or stated grudgingly that there were both good and bad ones in the group. "Some want to become good citizens and contribute to the life of this country," a New York architect averred; adding, "others want to get as much money as they can and then go back where they came from." American architects do not resent competition as such, it was said, but they do resent the ease with which refugees who have practiced architecture abroad can get their licenses (by endorsement) compared to the great difficulty experienced by American students who must pass a severe licensing examination. There was a tendency to praise the work of architects and industrial designers from the Northern European countries but to disparage the work of their colleagues from the south.

Americans readily admitted that there were noted names among the newcomers—Eric Mendelsohn, Serge Chermayeff, Martin Wagner, Siegfried Giedion, Ludwig Mies van der Rohe, and such representatives of the Bauhaus as Walter Gropius and Marcel Breuer. There could not fail to be great interest when former associates of that famous school became exponents in this country of the aims and ideals of one of the leading aesthetic movements of our time.

Strictly, the Bauhaus [Ger.: *to build house*] was an art center established 1919 in Weimar, Germany, by Walter Gropius, a modern German architect who is now chairman of the department of architecture at Harvard University [the *Art Digest* of Dec. 15, 1938, stated].

The Bauhaus idea is a concept, as old as ancient Egypt, that artist and craftsman are one, that any division between the two is false and "arrogant"; that only through the conscious co-operative effort of all craftsmen can a really great work of art result. It aimed to bring a fundamental unity to modern life, and its ultimate, distant goal was "the collective building" which (like the Temple of Karnak, the Parthenon, and Chartres) would be the work of many craftsmen—painters, carpenters, architects, sculptors, designers, etc.—all working harmoniously with the materials and tools at hand. . . .

Most of the former masters of the Bauhaus are now here: Gropius and Marcel Breuer are at Harvard, Moholy-Nagy at Chicago (former director of the erstwhile "New Bauhaus"), Feininger and Alexander Schawinsky are in New York, Josef Albers at Black Mountain College, North Carolina.

Men like Werner Hegemann have exerted their influence on American planning, and the publications of such leaders as Walter Curt Behrendt and Paul Zucker have added greatly to our understanding of architectural problems and city planning. At least five refugee architects have received the recognition of being listed in *Who's Who in America*.

As expressed by a European architect, the great contribution that refugee architects were able to make in the United States was their introduction of the social concept of architecture. As a result of the immigration of refugee architects there is much more happening now in the realm of social thinking, he declared, adding, "This more or less dates back to the coming of Gropius. . . . Every little school of architecture has had at least to take into account the new teachings. As a result of the new concepts introduced into architectural education within the last ten years, the younger generation is now approaching the problem of building for modern life with an entirely changed outlook. And in the schools," he concluded, "we are not so much interested in the formal results they achieve as we are in the way they approach the problem."

CHAPTER XX

WHAT AMERICANS THINK OF THE REFUGEES

The general reaction of Americans toward the refugees may be summed up as one of compassion for the victims of persecution seeking a haven here, and of appreciation of the contribution this superior group of immigrants is making to American life. The refugees report that, on the whole, Americans have shown an attitude of friendliness and helpfulness. As the number of refugees increased, however, a certain amount of antagonism developed. Refugees began to be looked upon as serious competitors, especially by certain professional and wage-earning groups and in certain communities. These fears were allayed with the increased demand for manpower brought about by war conditions.

Nevertheless, a certain degree of resentment has persisted in certain quarters and against certain groups of refugees. This is not an uncommon occurrence in American history, since newcomers frequently have been regarded with enmity and accused of possessing undesirable traits and of offering serious competition.

From colonial days on, there has been opposition to immigrants because of their foreign ways, foreign language, different religion, economic competition, poverty, and crime. In general, prejudice toward foreign nationalities has been directed chiefly against groups which have recently arrived in large numbers. It has shifted from Germans to Irish to Scandinavians to South Europeans. The despised alien of yesterday becomes the 100 per cent American of today and joins the native-born in scorn of freshly arrived nationals. People already settled here do not as a rule welcome newcomers. The Indians resented the coming of the first white men who tried to settle on this continent, and succeeding generations of white men have resented the coming of others after they themselves had become comfortably settled. Native-born Americans opposed to recent immigration often fail to realize that similar complaints were made against their parents and grandparents who came hopefully to these shores. The following quotations are examples of expressions of prejudice against immigrants during the nineteenth century.

1819: The tide of emigration still sets to the United States. Never before perhaps, except in the last year, did so many persons from Europe reach our shores. . . . We regret that it is so. . . . We have always until just now greeted the stranger on his arrival here with pleasure. There was room enough for all that would come. . . . Now, however, our population in most of the maritime districts and in some parts of the interior also, seems too thick . . . and that hitherto sure refuge of the industrious, foreign emigrant, the western country, is overstocked by domestic emigration. [*Niles' Weekly Register*, Sept. 18, 1819, p. 36]

1835: *Then*, we were few, feeble, and scattered. *Now*, we are numerous, strong, and concentrated. *Then*, our accessions of immigration were real accessions of strength from the ranks of the learned and the good, from the enlightened mechanic and artisan and intelligent husbandman. *Now*, immigration is the accession of weakness, from the ignorant and the vicious, or the priest-ridden slaves of Ireland and Germany, or the outcast tenants of the poorhouses and prisons of Europe. ["Imminent Dangers to the Free Institutions of the United States through Foreign Immigration," by "An American" (S. F. B. Morse), 1835]

1859: The prodigious influx of Irish during the past twenty years has created a large Irish class apart from the rest of the people, poor, ignorant, helpless, and degraded, contemned by Americans, used as tools by politicians of all parties, doing all the hard work and menial duties of the country, and filling the jails and almshouses, almost to the exclusion of everybody else. [Journalist's letter, March 16, 1859, in *Life and Letters of Edwin Lawrence Godkin*, edited by Rollo Ogden, 1907, Vol. 1, p. 181]

1873: A very large percentage of vice and crime in the United States, especially in the great cities, is chargeable to European immigration. The police statistics of New York show that the vast majority of prisoners arrested for criminal offences are of European birth; and of these, again, the great majority are natives of Ireland. [Joseph P. Thompson, *Church and State in the United States*, 1873, p. 128]

1898: An inquiry addressed by the New York Bureau of Labor to officers of labor organizations elicited the following reply from the Brotherhood of Carpenters and Joiners No. 382, of New York: "Immigrants from Northern Europe—Danes and Swedes—interfere very much with the keeping up of the wages in the trade. That is the principal thing we find fault with." [*Annual Report of the New York Bureau of Labor Statistics*, 1898, p. 1047]

American politics has never been free from what historians term "native Americanism"—the antagonism between native Americans and the foreign-born. From time to time, intensified by propaganda and organization, it has assumed the form of an organized movement. Examples are the Native American movement which began about 1835, the Know-Nothing movement of the 1850's, the American Protective Association movement of the late 1880's and early 1890's, and the Ku-Klux Klan movement of the 1920's. While the various movements were concerned with the issues of the day, they had this in common: an opposition to aliens and foreign-born citizens and prejudice toward racial and religious groups, notably Negroes, Jews, and Catholics.

At the present time, a similar movement is under way, represented by such organizations as the American Nationalist party, the America First party, and the resurgent Ku-Klux Klan. There are various segments of the current nationalist movement, such as the Fundamentalist group, the Christian Front group, and the Pan-German group, but in general the views held in common are: anti-alienism, racial and religious hate, opposition to the underlying philosophy of the New Deal, isolationism, dislike of labor unions, and distrust of democracy.[1]

The present movement differs from earlier movements in that it has imported from Europe, especially from Germany, its pattern of prejudice, particularly anti-Semitism. This world-wide propaganda was part of the Nazi plan to arouse ethnic hatred and create disunion. Anti-alien feeling, which is a basic plank in the platform of every American Fascist group, is directed against the refugees, among others, partly because the majority of them are Jews and partly because the refugees form a solid focus of anti-Fascist opinion. Under our present laws there is little protection against the vicious propaganda and deliberate falsehoods circulated by such hate groups, for they concern classes and races, not individuals. The Fascists strike at "Reds," "democrats," "Jews," "liberals," "Negroes," Catholics," and run little risk of prosecution for libel. A group is too vague, the courts hold, too large to be defamed. However, it may be possible to curb hate-mongers through other means, such as sedition statutes and the Federal Foreign Agents Registration Act.[2] The history of earlier movements reveals that such organizations tend shortly to disappear through internal dissension, their own excesses, ridicule, and public enlightenment.

How widespread such nationalist prejudices are it is impossible to say. Many Americans have recognized the threat that this movement presents to the unity and welfare of the nation. Attempts have been made to counteract the movement by such organizations as the National Conference of Christians and Jews, numerous church bodies, and the C.I.O. National Committee to Abolish Racial Discrimination. Various programs of inter-cultural education have been initiated by these and other organizations. The federal government and a few state legislatures have either considered or passed fair employment practice laws designed to eliminate discrimination in employment on account of race, nationality, or creed.

COMPLAINTS AND ALLEGATIONS AGAINST REFUGEES

It is an old American custom, as we have seen, to depict the latest arrivals on our shores as strange creatures, whose presence threatens to undermine

[1] Tom O'Connor, " 'Nationalists' Take over U.S. Fascist Drive," *PM*, May 27, 1945; "Hate Groups Differ on How to Run U.S.A.," *PM*, May 28, 1945; Freda Kirchwey, "In Defense of Refugees," *Nation*, Aug. 31, 1940, pp. 163–164.

[2] Charles Olson, "People v. the Fascist, U.S. (1944)," *Survey Graphic*, August, 1944, pp. 356–357; U.S. Department of Justice, *The Foreign Agents Registration Act of 1938, as Amended, 1942.*

the American way of life. This is not to say that immigrants have not created problems. Nor is it to deny that an inevitable culture conflict exists between different customs, manners, and values, which can be lessened only through assimilation. It is to say, however, that the attitude toward newcomers is often alarmist and grossly exaggerated and that in some instances it represents a deliberate attempt to foster enmity.

Such criticism of immigrants is a Hydra-headed monster. As soon as one rumor is spiked several more spring up to take its place. It is also impossible to answer such broad generalizations as "refugees have bad manners" except to note that in any group there are bound to be some people with undesirable traits. It is a common practice, characteristic of stereotyped thinking, to ascribe to a whole group traits observable in a few individuals. For example, refugees as a whole are often judged by the few and casual contacts individual Americans may have with a small and selected number of them. This tendency has been fostered by the appearance of articles critical of certain refugees that have appeared in magazines of national circulation such as *Life* and *Look*. It does little good for the article to carry the editorial comment that it applies to only a few individuals. The unusual attention and spread given the subject create the impression that it is of general application and of considerable moment. As an aid to discriminating thinking, one can, however, point out the proportion of the group of which the complaint may legitimately be made.

Another common psychological trait, evident in intergroup relations, is to regard as vices of the outsider what are deemed virtues of the in-group member, such as self-assurance and financial success; or to deplore in the case of the native but to consider as unpardonable in the case of the immigrant unacceptable behavior, such as sharp dealing and objectionable manners.

Anti-refugee sentiments, like anti-immigrant or anti-ethnic feelings in general, are characteristically distorted and exaggerated. We have already seen how inaccurate is the notion that "the country is being flooded with refugees." Let us now examine some of the more common complaints and charges and rumors concerning the refugees themselves.

An allegation frequently made during the depression was to the effect that refugees were usurping the jobs of Americans and prolonging the depression. Stated the American Immigration Conference Board in a pamphlet published in 1939:

We cannot give away our jobs to foreigners and, at the same time, provide jobs for our unemployed. We haven't jobs enough for both. . . . The United States will never get out of the depression, nor provide work for the jobless, neither will we ever take the millions off relief rolls until drastic legislative steps are taken to safeguard American jobs for Americans.

This statement was designed to create the impression that the country was being flooded with immigrants who were throwing Americans out of work. The total number of immigrants admitted during the depression, however, was so small that it could have had but the slightest effect on unemployment. The excess of arrivals over departures, 1931–1940, was only 68,693. Moreover, a majority of the recent immigrants were not wage earners but housewives, young children, and people too old to work. Finally, to obtain a visa the prospective immigrant had to show that he or his sponsors had sufficient means for his maintenance so that he would not become a public charge. Some of the immigrants, instead of taking jobs away from Americans, brought in capital and started new enterprises which gave employment to Americans.

No one can say categorically that no recent immigrant or refugee has taken a job from an American. But neither is there any ground for assertions that thousands of Americans have been displaced by refugee workmen. Such allegations, when run to earth, generally prove to be fantastic exaggerations. Consider, for example, the rumor that Americans were being displaced from factory jobs in Shelton, Connecticut. The Connecticut Department of Labor made an investigation in six or more plants in the city, and Deputy Commissioner John C. Ready reported: "Investigation disclosed that one refugee has been employed in one of the plants as an elevator operator. This job was created for him and no one was displaced."[3]

Examine also the story that New York department stores were hiring refugees and firing Americans. An embellishment of this story was to the effect that customers had to carry German dictionaries along when shopping. This rumor, spread by a whispering campaign, became so prevalent in November, 1938, that a group of large stores issued a forthright denial. Among those issuing statements printed in the New York press were executives of R. H. Macy and Company, Lord and Taylor, the Associated Dry Goods Corporation, Hearn's, Gimbel's, Stern Brothers, and Bloomingdale's. The statement by Delos Walker, vice-president of Macy's, was as follows:

For some months past we have heard from time to time an utterly false and malicious rumor to the effect that store people in New York have been let go to hire refugees from Europe. Now the papers have heard the rumor, and have asked us what we know about it.

So far as this store is concerned not one word of truth supports such a statement.

The plain fact is that none of our employees has been displaced by a refugee. The further and self-evident fact is that we share the deep and natural public sympathy for the plight of any refugee from any form of oppression or persecution. We ignored the rumor, believing it to be so preposterous that it would die of its own absurdity. We did not choose to dignify it by comment.

But the rumor has persisted. We are forced to the conclusion that the only thing

[3] National Board, Y.W.C.A., *Meet the Refugees*, 1940, p. 17.

that could plant it in the minds of innocent and well-meaning people is organized and systematic propaganda, using the innocent as carriers in a whispering campaign.

So, perhaps, the best thing for all concerned now is just to speak right out in public and say that the rumor is a plain falsehood, and to say it with all the emphasis that can be placed on it.

Since then, some of the stores have issued sworn affidavits as to the number of refugees employed. Richard H. Brown, vice-president of Abraham and Strauss, Inc., Brooklyn, a store with 2,719 employees, on March 28, 1939, said, "To my knowledge, no employee has been discharged and replaced by a refugee from any foreign country." Miss Elizabeth Westgate, director of personnel for Bloomingdale Brothers, Inc., a store employing 2,563 people, declared:

"The total number of people in our employ who might be classified as refugees is eleven. Of these, two were employed in 1936, seven in 1937, one in 1938, and one in 1939. Of the eleven, only one is employed in selling. Of the others, one was employed as an executive in our Berlin office, one was employed in our Vienna office. Not a single person has at any time been discharged from our employ in order to make room for a refugee."[4]

In Pittsburgh, where similar rumors became current, the Better Business Bureau appointed a committee of leading citizens to check the employment records of five large department stores which had been named in the rumors. The committee found that out of approximately 8,000 full-time employees of these stores none was a refugee and that out of approximately 3,600 part-time employees no refugees were employed at the time of the investigation, but seven had been employed in the past, none for longer than a two months' period.[5] Similar rumors regarding department stores in Milwaukee were found to have no basis in fact.[6] In all these instances the rumors were part of an anti-Semitic campaign, for the stores maligned were Jewish owned or managed.

Similar rumors have been current about refugees in Hollywood replacing American movie workers who entered military service, and so forth, which are either baseless or exaggerated out of all resemblance to the facts, but the above illustrations should suffice.

Attention, however, should be given to the complaints against refugee physicians, the largest single group of professional people among the refugees. American physicians have complained about the competition of refugee physicians, especially where the latter have replaced Americans who left for military service. Although the competition of refugee physicians has un-

[4] Henry Smith Leiper, "Those German Refugees," *Current History*, May, 1939.
[5] National Board, Y.W.C.A., *op. cit.*, pp. 16–17.
[6] Report on Community Backgrounds and Attitudes, Milwaukee, ms. p. 13.

doubtedly been felt occasionally, especially in some of the larger cities, it has been greatly exaggerated. The total number of refugee physicians, not all of whom were practitioners, was only 3 per cent of the number of physicians in America. Not all of them by any means, as we have seen in the chapter on the refugee physician, succeeded in entering private practice. Moreover, the nation has been experiencing a dearth rather than a surplus of doctors. It should be noted that many of the eligible refugee physicians joined the armed forces, while others took over the practices of Americans with the understanding that they would relinquish them upon the latter's return. Still others settled in small communities previously lacking the services of a physician. Despite these facts, or in ignorance of them, Senator Nye has referred to "astounding tales . . . of the extent to which refugee doctors are taking over practice in some of our larger cities, in some communities in such numbers as to enable them to dominate," and he has read into the *Congressional Record* (May 19, 1944, pp. 4781–4782) a scurrilous column, "Cuckoos in the Nest," by columnist Frank C. Waldrop, which appeared in the *Washington Times-Herald,* referring to refugee doctors as "second-raters," "unscrupulous," "inexperienced," "quacks and rascals," "small-fry bunglers," and "invaders."

Another group of refugees who have been singled out for adverse comment are the rich emigres, particularly the "café-society" set among them. Although numerically a very small group, they have been highly conspicuous and have attracted attention out of proportion to their numbers and significance. The average American is familiar with the Ellis Island immigrant draped in a shawl or wearing a sealskin hat. But the immigrant arriving by clipper or luxury liner, preceded by a bank deposit or carrying a million dollars' worth of jewels or bringing a fortune in art, is a novelty to him, an item of "news."

According to the excellent study by the editors of *Fortune* magazine,[7] the rich refugees may be grouped under three headings: society, royalty, and businessmen and their families. The first group came here mainly for safety, sometimes for greater comfort; the second, chiefly for political reasons; the third, to make a living or to live upon a previously deposited fortune. The third category is the most important group, and the one likely to remain here permanently. But the other two groups are the ones who have attracted attention, being the natural prey of gossip writers and society columnists. Especially has the spotlight of publicity been turned on that minority among them who constitute the flighty, conspicuous-spending International Set, or what is called here the Café-Society Group. In Europe, they differed sharply from real "society," which was a stable group to which certain people belonged by right of birth or were admitted on account of

[7] "Rich Refugees," *Fortune,* Vol. XXIII, No. 2 (February, 1941), pp. 81, 145–146, 148–150, 153–154.

unusual accomplishment, a group whose behavior was inconspicuous and who constituted the ruling classes.

While the International Set among the refugees, like any other group of people, is made up of the good, the bad, and the indifferent, its behavior on the whole, as related by society columnists like Cholly Knickerbocker, Walter Winchell, and Patricia Coffin, has shocked many Americans and brought discredit on the refugee group. Conspicuous consumption, which is deplored by many people in normal times, appears especially reprehensible during depression or war, on the part of either natives or foreigners, and quite incongruous in the case of people who have fled to another country for safety. This group, it has been charged (with characteristic exaggeration), has not only "taken over" exclusive hotels, "overrun" fashionable resorts, and "paraded" in expensive restaurants and night clubs, but has often behaved in a self-assertive, ostentatious, and rude manner.[8] These criticisms have usually emanated from Americans who themselves frequent such places. But as is so often the case, characteristics of the few have been attributed to members of the entire group, and Americans observing the refugee café-society group or reading of their antics have frequently erroneously assumed that all or most refugees are of that type, whereas they constitute but a small percentage even of the wealthy, who in turn are a small minority of the total group. The same may be said of America's own "idle rich."

The careless spending of this International Set, however, has contributed much to the prosperity of the entertainment establishments and luxury stores. Rich refugees have sponsored the development of many a ski and sports center and supported many an art gallery through perilous times.[9]

Among the businessmen contingent of the rich refugee group, according to the *Fortune* article, the little entrepreneur has shown more initiative and more rugged individualism than his big brother. The smaller refugee businessmen have sought hitherto unexplored markets in which to develop business, have founded enterprises for noncompetitive novelties hitherto obtainable only in Europe, or have expanded long-established American branches of European firms that have lost most of their other business. At the same time, there are a number of wealthy industrialists and financiers who have transferred their fortunes here, or what remained of them, and engaged in business activity. Examples are Jan Bat'a (shoes) and Hans Petschek (metals) from Czechoslovakia, Fritz von Opel (oil) and Jacob Goldschmidt (broker) from Germany, D. N. Heineman (electric utilities) and Dr. Anton Philips (radio) and numerous diamond dealers from the Low Countries, Captains Constantin Rethymnis and Nikolas Kulukundis

---

[8] Emily Post, "The Refugees," *New York Herald Tribune*, May 28, 1944; S. F. Porter, "Refugee Gold Rush," *American Magazine*, October, 1942; "Rules for Refugeees, Royal or Otherwise, While in America," *Life*, Dec. 16, 1940; "May We Offer Apologies for 'Life's' Boorishness?" *PM*, Dec. 24, 1940.

[9] S. F. Porter, "Refugee Gold Rush," *American Magazine*, October, 1942, p. 88.

(shipping) from Greece, Baron Edouard de Rothschild and André Meyer (banking), Emile Mathis (automobiles), and Pierre Wertheimer (perfume) from France. In an earlier chapter the activities and contributions of refugee businessmen have been considered in some detail.

Complaints have continued to be heard about the alleged amassing of wealth by refugees dealing in the stock market and real estate and engaging in other large financial operations. More specifically it has been claimed that they have avoided paying taxes through loopholes in the law, have engaged in sharp practices, been interested in speculation rather than investment, and have promoted inflation. There is some truth behind these assertions. The number of refugees, however, engaged in large-scale business transactions is small, and their effect has been greatly exaggerated. The actions objected to are not illegal, nor are they characteristic of the group. While some individuals have been sharp in their dealings and have taken advantage of looseness of the laws, the evidence indicates that the practices of the great majority of them have been ethical according to American business standards.

How much capital the refugees brought to this country is unknown, but S. F. Porter, financial writer for the *New York Post*, estimates that from 1935 to 1942 wealth in gold, jewels, art, etc., amounting to $5,230,700,000 was brought in.[10] The editors of *Fortune* estimate that from 1934 to 1941 private transfers of gold amounted to five billion dollars and that an appreciable part of this, perhaps several hundred million dollars, represents refugee capital.

When the collapse of the European countries began, the U.S. Treasury was faced with the problem of the control of these foreign holdings, governmental and private. In order to prevent money belonging to nationals of conquered countries falling into German hands, the United States government ordered that all foreign assets should be frozen. This idea was first applied in 1940 to Norway and Denmark and extended the following year to Germany, Italy, and the rest of the invaded or occupied countries. Thus many foreigners arriving here with the comfortable assurance of wealth in American banks were unable to lay hands on it easily. Supervision of alien cash and securities, friendly as well as enemy alien, was left with the Foreign Funds Control of the Treasury Department. Its value exceeds eight billion dollars.[11] What fraction of it belongs to the refugee is unknown, but it must be exceedingly small.

In 1941 the government ordered a census of all foreign-owned property in the United States, and placed it in charge of the Alien Property Custodian. Any person using funds originating in enemy or occupied countries

---

[10] *Ibid.*

[11] Henry F. Pringle, "The Alien-Property Riddle," *Saturday Evening Post*, June 30, 1945, pp. 19, 81–82.

had first to obtain a license from the Federal Reserve Bank for every expenditure. A general license was granted for living, traveling, and similar personal expenses not exceeding $500 per month. This restriction was liberalized in 1941 and 1942 with respect to bona fide immigrants and refugees. A special license was required for withdrawals for any other purpose, such as starting a business, buying real estate, or making any other purchase, the nature, purpose, and amount of the transaction being stated in detail in the application.[12] The withdrawals were frequently in cash, which sometimes had the unfortunate effect of leading to rumors of "hidden money." This regulation has been inconvenient, but, as the editors of *Fortune* remarked, thanks to such paternalism the refugees at least had the assurance that their money was still safe in the banks and not commandeered by the invaders of their homelands.

Most of their funds available to them the refugees have used to establish manufacturing or other business enterprises, to buy into well-established American firms, or to invest. A favorite field of investment has been American railroad securities, for the following reasons. Before World War I the United States looked to Europe for much of its financing. Especially was this true of the railroads, whose securities were widely sold in Europe, particularly in Great Britain, Germany, and the Netherlands. In Germany the financing was handled by international bankers often connected through family relationship with American investment banking houses. These were located mainly in Frankfort, Munich, Hannover, Hamburg, Cologne, and later, Berlin. Knowledge of American railroads was very common among financial people in Germany, though they knew very little about the American political setup and the role of the government in this field. When the refugees came here, in the middle 1930's, they frequently invested in railroad securities because they knew this field better than any other. Prices were at rock bottom, which was a further inducement. Conditions in this field were such that they might have lost, but they were saved by the improved situation brought about by the war.[13]

A certain amount of the capital of the refugees, however, has been mobile, seeking short-time employment. This it has found chiefly in stock market transactions and real estate deals. For certain refugees with means the stock market has offered a special attraction. These are the "nonresident aliens," here on temporary visas, who are exempted from taxation on profits from transactions on securities or commodities exchanges. Under Section 211 (B) of the Internal Revenue Code Act of 1936, nonresident aliens "not engaged in trade or business in the United States and not having a place of business therein" need not make a tax return on any capital gains, whether on a

---

[12] U.S. Treasury Department, *Documents Pertaining to Foreign Funds Control*, March 30, 1944; "The Control of Foreign Funds," *Banking*, August, 1941, pp. 24–25.

[13] Interview with a former German international banker.

turnover within six months or longer. A nonresident alien cannot ordinarily claim the exemption if he has, while in the United States, earned compensation for personal services, participated in commercial or industrial activities, or bought and sold property.

Some financial columnists in newspapers have written that 250,000 non-resident aliens,[14] mostly rich refugees,[15] have taken $800,000,000 in tax-free profits out of stock market transactions. It is highly questionable whether there are that many non-resident aliens in the United States, and certainly they are not all engaged in Wall Street operations. The number of refugees here on temporary visas is only about 15,000, and there is no evidence that they are characteristically stock market speculators. Columnist Leslie Gould censures the aliens for what can only be regarded as a shortcoming in our law, calling them "speculators who have lived out the war in the safety and comfort of the U.S.A.," and making such further critical comments as: "the contribution to the war of these refugees has been about nil," "they duck military service when they can," and "they escape paying taxes needed to finance the war." So far as any official and public record is concerned, the Study Committee is aware of only one case, that of an international financier, who has been indicted for draft evasion.

An editorial in the *New Work World-Telegram* on July 19, 1945, takes a sound and balanced view:

> We have no reason to be angry with our alien visitors. They don't write our tax laws. Congress does that. They don't interpret and apply our tax laws. The Bureau of Internal Revenue does that. The present law, with the loophole through which aliens have operated, was enacted in the piping peacetime of 1936. Aliens here on temporary visas were presumed to be taxed by their own governments, and Congress gave them relief from double taxation, partly because that was the fair thing to do and partly to encourage other governments to stop the double-taxation of Americans temporarily residing in their lands.
>
> It was a good enough law for peacetime. But with the war in Europe, many of our alien visitors couldn't go home, and thousands more came over here and stayed. Their governments were overthrown and couldn't tax their incomes here. And our Congress was too busy with the war, or too unconcerned, to change the law to fit changed conditions. Meanwhile, thousands of aliens, while not technically engaged in making profits, are free of taxation by our government or any other.
>
> Congress should change the law to recapture a fair share of those profits. . . .

A bill to eliminate this exemption was introduced in Congress in May, 1945, but at present writing no action has been taken on it. Meanwhile the Internal Revenue Bureau has instructed its field officers to scrutinize care-

[14] Henry J. Taylor, "Move to Collect 200 Million Tax on Alien Profits," *New York World-Telegram*, July 18, 1945; "Tax Bureau in Drive on Alien Profits," *ibid.*, July 23, 1945.

[15] Leslie Gould, "How to End Aliens' Tax Racket and Make 'Em Pay," *New York Journal-American*, July 18, 1945; "The Aliens' Tax Racket—Others Are Waking Up," *ibid.*, July 19, 1945.

fully all claims for exemption from the capital gains tax so as to make sure that those who claim to be nonresident aliens are not in fact residents of the United States.[16] If any aliens have been improperly claiming this exemption, they will be discovered and the full tax levy imposed. It should further be noted that before any alien may depart from this country he must have a tax clearance certificate, indicating that he has satisfied all the tax claims against him.

Refugees with funds to invest have also been interested in real estate. Several reasons account for this interest, one of which derives from their European background. In Europe, prestige goes with ownership—of one's home, place of business, or factory. Real estate is regarded as an investment, is kept in the family for generations and constantly improved. Refugees think that Americans, especially in the large cities, have little pride in ownership. Speculation in real estate, such as is common in New York and other large cities, was a new idea to them, which some have adopted as they have picked up other practices here. Real estate has been a favorite field for investment for the further reason that the refugees, whose funds were limited to what they had been able to salvage from their possessions in Europe, felt the need of being careful, and real property appeared to be a sound and secure investment. Moreover, many of them, especially the Germans, had suffered from the ruinous inflation after World War I, and believed that real estate was more stable than liquid investments.

When the refugees first arrived here, real estate prices were at rock bottom, and provided a tempting offer to persons with ready funds. Such persons could not immediately enter business, because they did not know American business methods nor have sufficient knowledge of English, but they could buy real estate. This they did individually or through American firms. Only later did a few refugees set up as real estate dealers and operators. The real estate activities of refugees have consisted in buying their homes, buying other property as a long-term investment, and engaging in short-term operations of a speculative character. It is the last-mentioned type that has given rise to certain complaints and rumors.

It has been alleged that refugees have bought a great deal of real estate, that they have sometimes used sharp practices and taken advantage of the looseness of the laws, that they have "milked" the property and caused inflated values. In an effort to find out how widespread such allegations are and how valid, the Study Committee, with the aid of its local co-operating committees, made inquiry in many of the large centers of population throughout the country. In the following cities investigation revealed that there were no refugees in the real estate business, nor instances of real estate speculation by refugees, that refugee property purchases were of the long-term investment type, mainly their own homes, and that there was no evi-

[16] *New York Times*, June 29, 1945.

dence or complaint of practices contrary to the accepted standards in the field: Baltimore, Buffalo, Cincinnati, Cleveland, Hartford, Indianapolis, Milwaukee, New Haven, Newark, Pittsburgh, Portland (Oregon), Providence, Seattle, St. Louis, and Washington, D.C. The same applies also to Westchester County, New York. In the case of New Haven it was pointed out that there had been some large absentee purchases of business property by refugees in New York, presumably for investment purposes. In four cities—Chicago, Detroit, Rochester, and San Francisco—there has been some real estate activity by refugees, generally of the character of long-term investment and in accordance with recognized business practice, and giving rise to no complaints nor even rumors. Only in Los Angeles, Philadelphia, and New York did the Study Committee discover any complaints and grounds for criticism.

In fast-growing Los Angeles there have long been extensive real estate operations of both a speculative and an investment character. Some refugees have entered the field. In a few instances their deals have occasioned some criticism but not sufficient to be a ground for complaint against refugee operators as such. In Philadelphia, refugees have not engaged heavily in real estate but their operations have been largely of a short-term nature and speculative—a question of buying and selling at a profit. There has been considerable talk among American real estate operators about unethical practice on the part of some of the refugee group. It appears that there has doubtless been some sharp dealing, but that it has been minor and, as usual, subject to considerable exaggeration.

New York City is the real center of real estate activity by refugees and of complaints against them. To understand the situation there, one must first have a background of the real estate business in that city. This may be stated briefly as follows, being based on interviews with leading real estate men. New York real estate operations are largely speculative; they are normally more for speculation than for investment; property is commonly purchased for a term and then resold. The key person is the operator, who stimulates the market by his deals, as owner or agent, and the activity spreads to individuals, banks, mortgage companies, and other holders of real estate. If held in check, and if conducted with long-range view as to the real value of property, the activities of operators are regarded as beneficial. The practices of some operators, both Jewish and Gentile but more commonly the former than the latter, however, are viewed as questionable. These consist in buying on terms rather than price, paying more than the present appraisal and taking a lower rate of return, thus creating a fictitious market. Such operators buy for cash or ninety days, refinance, get a higher appraisal, and sell for an advance. Sometimes the cash is suspected of being "hidden money," kept in safe-deposit boxes or elsewhere and not declared for income tax purposes. Such operators, it is further complained, do not keep up the property or improve it, but bleed or "milk" it, expecting soon to dispose of it. Their interest is in financing rather than in real estate. Their actions are not illegal, but in some instances, with the aid of lawyers, they negotiate sharp and shrewd deals and create complicated systems of ownership, such as cause concern to conservative real estate interests. It should be noted that, while Jews are more often criticized than Gentiles in this respect, the reliable Jewish operators have a reputation second to none for honesty, community interest, and integrity.

Only a few refugees have entered real estate business in New York. They are not as successful as Americans when they undertake to manage property, since they are not conversant with American conditions. Many more refugees concerned with real estate buy through operators, commonly of their own nationality background, either for investment or speculation. Since their assets are liquid, frequently being funds impounded by the U.S. Treasury and released for specific purposes such as buying real estate, the refugees have increased the number of cash operations, thus unwittingly giving rise to rumors of "hidden money." Some refugees brought over their possessions in jewelry and diamonds which they have used to barter for real estate or other property. Incidentally, barter appears to be a fairly common practice in Europe. In one instance a refugee astounded the officers of a savings bank by offering to exchange $3 million worth of diamonds for a hotel which the bank owned. The bank declined the deal. This was not a naïve proposal on the part of the refugee but a shrewd proposition. By thus trading equity for equity, he would avoid taxation. The bank would not suffer, since it does not have to pay an income tax. If the refugee had sold the diamonds and paid cash for the hotel, he would have been obliged to pay a tax on the transaction and include it in his income tax return. His diamonds were worth three million dollars if bartered. If sold, their value would have been appreciably less.

Despite the complaints of sharp dealing and unacceptable business practices of some refugees, it is generally agreed by New York real estate interests that the effect of refugee enterprise in this field has been beneficial. The refugees put new life into the realty market. They came during the depression when real estate was in a slump and banks and other interests were reluctant to put money into it. They supplied much "risk capital" in this and other fields at a time when boldness was needed. Favorably conditioned toward real estate by their European background, and finding prices extremely low and money tight, they took over many properties for cash, trusting on an upturn in the market. They guessed correctly, and the coming of the war brought a demand for real estate such as New York has seldom seen, and a great increase in values. The actual holdings by refugees in New York are insignificant in relation to the total amount of real estate, but they have had a stimulating effect out of proportion to their size, and

American real estate operators as well as refugees have benefited thereby.

In sharp contrast to the complaints about the rich refugees are those about the alleged radicals and communists among the refugee group. Here the allegations are not merely exaggerations but appear to be deliberate misrepresentations. Many refugees are depicted as being "dangerous radicals," "political and social agitators," and "Marxists"; they are said to be indoctrinating our country with un-American ideas, and inserting themselves into our Government to control its thinking. It is even claimed that "the air waves are controlled by paid refugees, some of whom can hardly speak English." Such allegations have come primarily from the reactionary press and from representatives of the current nationalist movement in the United States, who tend to label all their opponents as "communists." There are some socialists among the refugee group, and many liberals, but the great majority are business and professional people, exponents of the capitalistic system and conservatively inclined. They unite, however, in their opposition to Fascism in any form, for they have all been victims of its tyranny and oppression. As we have already seen in a preceding chapter, there are no grounds for questioning the attachment and loyalty of the refugees to the principles of our democratic form of government.

A much more common complaint concerning refugees, and one which has some justification, is that which relates to certain of their personality traits or attitudes. It has frequently been complained, for example, that many of the refugees, especially the German, have been arrogant, demanding, overbearing, and contentious. Their air of superiority and high degree of self-assurance have irritated many Americans, including their well-wishers. There is no doubt that these traits characterize some individuals, as is true of any other group. There is also no doubt that some refugees have bad manners.

In some instances, however, what is interpreted as arrogance may be due to compensation for the loss of status and indignities that many refugees have suffered or merely to the difference between European and American behavior patterns. Many refugees feel that they must find some way to tell us that they were respected and successful in their former life. Sensitiveness and a feeling of insecurity have led others to adopt a superior attitude. Furthermore, some of the traits objected to are characteristic of the social habits of the middle- and upper-classes of continental Europe, for instance, their manner toward servants. It is considered correct in Europe to berate any servant or employee who makes a mistake. Criticisms are made more directly than here, where class lines are not fixed or rigid, and with a sort of punitive intention. It also appears to be a European custom to handle goods in a store, examine them critically before making a purchase, carefully check the bill in a restaurant, and in other ways behave in a manner that while acceptable in Europe is irritating to Americans. These are just some of the numerous ways in which conflict of culture traits occurs when peoples of different backgrounds are brought together. It tends to disappear as the immigrants learn and adopt American practices.

Objection has also been made to the habit of certain refugees of constantly contrasting unfavorably their condition here with their former social and economic status in Europe. Many Americans have been irritated at the frequent reference to the excellent living conditions, numerous servants, high social status, and superior cultural advantages these refugees say they had abroad, and retort that if their lot was so much better there, why don't they return. This type of refugee is known as the "bei-uns," meaning that "with us" or "as was the situation with us" such-and-such was the case. Some listeners think that there is a good deal of exaggeration about the former status, that "apparently all refugees must have been millionaires and university graduates." Certain jokes have become current, frequently told by refugees themselves concerning the "bei-uns" type of individual, jokes to the effect that this exaggeration has spread even to the animal kingdom. For example, two German dachshunds met in America and one of them told the other about his beautiful basket at home in Germany. The other replied, "That's nothing. In Europe I was a St. Bernard." Or another version: a little Pekingese dog from Vienna was being pushed around by a Boston terrier. "You wouldn't dare do that in Vienna," said the Pekingese. "There I was a St. Bernard."

Again, this reaction on the part of certain refugees may be explained as an attempt to compensate for their loss of status, which is a real and distressing experience. A large proportion of the refugees did have a status above average, socially, economically, and educationally. Moreover, it was possible to live in comfortable circumstances and have servants on a much smaller income in Europe than is possible in the United States. To point to the past with pride and to visualize it in the brightest colors reflects a desire to regain a prestige that has suddenly been wrested away. It is a form of self-protection against a feeling of inferiority which may easily arise when the refugee, in comparison with his former social and economic status, finds himself on a much lower level and living in a country which often considers immigrants as socially inferior. This tendency to boast of the past, like the other reactions mentioned above, is a passing phase, disappearing as soon as the refugee feels at home in America.

One further charge against refugees may be considered: their alleged ungratefulness. If this is so, it is definitely the exception rather than the rule. The Study indicates that most refugees feel a profound gratitude to America. What has been interpreted in some instances as ingratitude may be, rather, the failure of the refugee to marvel at our technical progress and level of cultural development and to reject all his attachments to his former life and appear as though reborn. Moreover, there are some Americans who expect the refugees to show continuing humility, gratefulness, and a willingness to accept a low standard of living. Their attitude dates back to dealings with immigrants of earlier periods, who were quite unlike the present-day refugees in educational and cultural background.

The reaction of the refugee to the trying experience of having his world upturned, his life shattered, and of being driven from his native land, varies, of course, with the individual. While some were never able to get over the shock and committed suicide after arrival here or succumbed to emotional disturbances, and while others developed inferiority feelings and various unpleasing reactions, the great majority have shown extraordinary adaptability, have not let the change of fortune affect their outlook on life, but have set out courageously to rebuild their shattered lives. In the life stories and questionnaires appear many comments like the following:

"I resolved not to let the past hinder my adjustment to this country, and therefore speak no German and have accepted the American standard of equality in place of the European scale of values which emphasizes education, manners and class distinction." (Former medical student in Austria, now shipping clerk in Philadelphia)

"Immigrants should be taught to forget the past in every respect; it is immaterial what someone used to be and used to possess." (Middle-aged German businessman, now salesmanager in New York)

"Forget the past, master the present, prepare for the future." (German businessman in Los Angeles)

"Those people who are always talking about their old country and how wonderful it was, forget the inconveniences they had to put up with there." (Spanish woman, teacher in Philadelphia)

"I try to do everything in the American way. . . . But we wish and pray not to be 'the refugee,' the 'newcomer' any more, but to be fully accepted." (Czechoslovak housewife, Cleveland)

"Very often we could prevent misunderstandings and difficulties if we would think more and say less. We have had other family education, other traditions, customs and points of view than the American has, and therefore, we should keep silent, and learn." (Factory executive in Germany, factory worker in Dayton)

"We have been very careful not to be conspicuous or do anything that would antagonize people. Newcomers should be a good example to others." (Czech exporter, now housewife in San Francisco)

As is evident in some of these quotations, the refugees are aware that some of their attitudes or the attitudes of some of their fellows have been a cause of complaint. A former rabbi in Germany, now a social work executive in Paterson, New Jersey, has set forth some rules for refugees. He writes:

One has to embrace the following precepts: (1) But for the grace of God you would be in an extermination camp. Never forget that and be grateful for your existence. (2) It is primarily up to you to transform your existence into a worthwhile life according to your ability. (3) Don't indulge in idle reminiscences of your past achievements on the other side of the ocean. It will only retard your progress and your finding your proper place. (4) Work hard and remember that those who came before you at the end of the 19th and the beginning of the 20th century worked harder and were less prepared in terms of education. (5) Try to overcome your superiority complex of European culture in your daily contacts. Americans are proud of their achievements and will not accept belittling them in any way.

And a German physician, who is also a successful author, writes:[17]

We, the emigres, have arrived here in the hour of decision. We have our own urgent, wretched problems. We must earn our bread, learn the language, understand our environment. True, the longing and sadness in our breast are understandable. Our arrogance is not. We are, after all, rescued fugitives. We stand in an awakening world that heretofore was strange and closed to us. We have the good fortune to stand by the side of our friends instead of bearing the yoke of our enemies. Our place is here. We must today begin to build the roof that shall be our indestructible shield for the future. We must make greater sacrifices, must be bolder and more steadfast than our new neighbors. Only then can we salvage our past as Europeans.

REACTION OF THE AMERICAN COMMUNITY

To gain some perspective of the effect of the coming of the refugees on the attitude of Americans toward them, the Study Committee, with the assistance of its local co-operating committees, made a survey of community backgrounds and attitudes in some fifty towns and cities throughout the United States. The communities, ranging in size of population from Winona, Minnesota, with 22,490 people, to New York City with its 7,454,995, are listed below.

CALIFORNIA: Los Angeles, Oakland, Santa Barbara, Stockton
CONNECTICUT: Bridgeport, Hartford
DISTRICT OF COLUMBIA: Washington
FLORIDA: St. Petersburg
GEORGIA: Atlanta
ILLINOIS: Chicago, Peoria, Springfield
INDIANA: Bloomington, Indianapolis, Marion
KANSAS: Kansas City
MARYLAND: Baltimore
MASSACHUSETTS: Lawrence
MICHIGAN: Detroit, Kalamazoo
MINNESOTA: Duluth, St. Paul, Winona
MISSISSIPPI: Vicksburg
MISSOURI: Kansas City, St. Louis
NEW JERSEY: Elizabeth, Paterson
NEW YORK: Buffalo, Elmira, New York City, Rochester, Utica, Westchester County

[17] Martin Gumpert, *First Papers*, 1941, p. 197.

NORTH CAROLINA: Asheville
OHIO: Akron, Canton, Cincinnati, Cleveland, Columbus, Dayton, Youngstown
OKLAHOMA: Oklahoma City, Tulsa
PENNSYLVANIA: Harrisburg, Philadelphia, Pittsburgh, Scranton
TEXAS: Austin, Dallas, Houston, San Antonio
WASHINGTON: Seattle, Tacoma
WISCONSIN: Madison, Milwaukee

It will be observed that all sections of the country were included except the Mountain Division, where immigrants, including refugees, are insignificant in number. Through the assistance of the field representatives of one of the Committee's sponsoring agencies, the National Refugee Service, this section was represented by reports concerning Great Falls, Montana; and Colorado Springs, Colorado, where refugees had been resettled. Such field reports were used also in the case of Austin and Mankato, Minnesota.

The general results show clearly that, except in a few large centers, the number of refugees is so small that unless attention is drawn to them the community as a whole is hardly aware of their presence. Most communities have no firsthand knowledge and hence no valid opinion about the refugees in their midst. This is not surprising since the refugees constitute less than 3 per cent of the foreign-born white population (enumerated as 11,419,138 in 1940) and a minute percentage, scarcely $\frac{2}{10}$ of 1 per cent, of the total population (131,669,275) of the country. Moreover, they are widely distributed despite a concentration in New York.

In most communities the only contact with refugees is on an individual basis, with the personal reactions depending on the type of people involved. This appears to be particularly the case in the very small communities, where the refugees, often numbering only one family or at most a few, must of necessity be known as individuals, not groups. Here the reactions vary from "well liked," "well adjusted," "fit into all community activities," with their counterparts of the refugees referring to the friendliness and helpfulness of their American neighbors, to complaints about refugees "wanting too much," "not being appreciative," "remaining aloof," and "being arrogant." In general, where the number of refugees is small, their integration into local community life is facilitated. Further evidence on this point is presented in earlier chapters, on adjustment. This is true regardless of the size of the community, though it is more frequently associated with the smaller ones. On the other hand, some very small communities are provincial in outlook, suspicious of newcomers, especially if foreign-born, and less tolerant than some large cosmopolitan cities.

Another impression borne out by the community surveys is that, whereas the attitude toward the individual refugee is generally friendly and helpful, there is a hesitant feeling about refugees or other immigrants in the plural sense. Thinking about the individual is favorable, about the group is fearful. Individuals are accepted, but the idea of an immigration movement meets with apprehension. The nation appears to be convinced of the desirability of the present policy of restriction of immigration. The statements that recent immigration has been unusually small in amount and that only a sixth of the quota has been used since 1931 are received with gratified surprise. Remembrance of mass unemployment during the depression is still vivid and opinion is strong against unrestricted immigration for fear of competition for jobs. The fear has also been expressed by both Jews and Christians that if there should be large-scale immigration of refugees, the majority of them Jews, it would increase anti-Semitism in this country. Even with the small number of Jewish refugees already admitted there has been an increase of anti-Semitic feelings in some communities, especially where, like Milwaukee and New York, there is a large German population receptive to Nazi propaganda, and where, like these cities plus Detroit and Chicago, there is a large Polish element still influenced by Old World attitudes.

The arrival of refugees during the depression years gave rise to some resentment, since it was feared that they would displace native workmen. Employers were reluctant to hire them. Rumors, greatly exaggerated, became current that refugees were being hired in place of native Americans. Actually the refugees had a more difficult time in securing employment and many failed to do so except in menial and more or less noncompetitive jobs. Even later under the wartime demand, refugees experienced difficulty in getting war-factory jobs, being denied them by law in some instances as being aliens and in other instances by the preference of employers for citizens. The community attitude, where the labor market was tight, was negative and cold. These criticisms diminished as the resettlement program of the refugee-service agencies got under way and as employment conditions improved. Fortunately, the peak of the refugee immigration occurred when war conditions were bringing about a demand for labor, and soon the country was calling for every available hand.

It was largely because of the fear of their competition that certain classes of refugees got a more unfavorable reception than others. This was true to some extent, and in some communities, of laborers and merchants, but it was particularly the case with professional groups, especially the physicians. In fact, it is safe to say that no occupational group among the refugees has had a worse reception than the physicians. Various obstacles were put in their way to prevent them from obtaining a license or from carrying on a satisfactory practice. The main effect, as was seen in the chapter on the refugee physicians, has been to delay rather than prevent them from resuming their professional activity. The extent of the competition, as we have already noted, has been greatly exaggerated.

The reception which the refugees have received at the hands of their own nationality groups already resident here has been ambivalent. In general the nationality groups have welcomed the refugees, protected, helped, and taught them; their generosity, both individually and organizationally, has been outstanding. On the other hand, there has been some lack of sympathy and conflict and, as has always been the case in immigration, representatives of their own nationality groups have taken the lead in exploiting the new arrivals. In some instances the absence of congeniality between the refugees and their fellow nationals here has been due to a difference in class background. Most of the Polish-Americans and Italian-Americans, for example, are simple people from the lower-income and less-educated groups in their homelands, while the refugees belong in general to the more privileged classes. They are often inclined to be cool and suspicious toward the newcomers and to take the attitude that "we did hard manual labor to get where we are; you do the way we did."

American Jews have not always welcomed their co-religionists among the refugees. In some instances they have feared their competition, in others that they might increase anti-Semitism. Many of the Jewish refugees, on the other hand, resent the role and status that the average American Jew assumes. Some, like the Belgians, dislike the organization of Jewish life here, regarding even the social services and communal organizations as commercialized, reduced to a business. In numerous instances there is conflict of culture, the refugees, although Jews, being at the same time Germans, Poles, Czechs, etc., while the American group, though deriving from similar backgrounds, being essentially Americans. The age old division between German and Eastern European Jews prevails to some extent in an intensified degree, the former regarding themselves as a superior group and representing Western rather than Eastern culture. The majority of the Jewish refugees are German, who have little in common with the majority of America's foreign-born Jews, who are Eastern European, mainly Russian and Polish. They have little affinity with German-American Jews, since these are mainly second, third, or earlier generation and Americans, not Germans. On the other hand, some Polish and Russian Jews feel prejudice toward the German Jews because of their alleged mistreatment of Eastern Jews in the past and their unsympathetic attitude toward Palestine.

The Jewish group is by no means united and of one accord, and varying attitudes toward the refugees may be found in different Jewish communities. But on the whole, American Jews, like Jews throughout the world, are deeply disturbed at the tragic fate of their co-religionists at the hands of the Nazis and determined to do all they can to aid the survivors. Immigration to the United States is just one of many proposals to solve the problem of those who are unable or unwilling to return to their former homelands. Many American Jews would like to bring here their relatives among such nonrepatriables but they express no sentiment for letting the bars of immigration down. Their attitude, like that of most Americans, is in favor of retaining the present policy of restriction, neither opening the gates wide nor making the laws more strict.

In general, the attitude of the American community toward the refugees has been preponderantly sympathetic and helpful. This has been demonstrated individually and through refugee-service committees and other social agencies. The behavior and reactions of the newcomers themselves have been a factor in creating a favorable impression. They have not become public charges or public nuisances, nor are they regarded in any way as a burden on the community. Their special skills have been recognized as an asset and their contributions in many spheres appreciated.

CHAPTER XXI

SOLUTION OF THE REFUGEE PROBLEM
AND ITS INTERNATIONAL ASPECTS

"The fact that a person is a refugee from tyranny does not make him a hero or a saint," commented the *New York Times* editorially on January 27, 1945. "It does prove that he does not like tyranny or cannot get on with it, points which are in his favor. In this country since the rise of Nazism and kindred tyrannies we have had refugees of various kinds, some living pretty comfortably on property they were able to take out, some in poverty, some just average human beings, some far above the average. On the whole, this immigration, tiny in numbers, has been extraordinarily high in quality. We are the richer because of it. In knowledge and wisdom, even in dollars and cents, we have gained by providing sanctuary." In its Report to the President, November 9, 1942, the Board of Appeals on Visa Cases stated: "The United States is admitting many people who will be of distinct value in our national life. Often these can contribute directly and immediately toward the well being of the nation. Illustrations are found in the cases of physicians, now greatly needed, physicists and chemists of proven ability, mechanics, artisans and others. Some persons admitted have demonstrated artistic ability of a high order, others are scholars of international reputation. A group particularly worthy of mention is that comprising former democratic leaders in territory now Axis controlled. Many courageous men who vigorously opposed the rise of the dictators have escaped the anger of the Nazis and have safely reached the United States." Similar testimony is abundant. It all points to the conclusion that, while refugees have received the great boon of a sanctuary, the adopting country has benefited as much, if not more, from their coming.

EFFECTS ON AMERICAN LIFE

The weight of the evidence pro and con cited in the chapters above demonstrates that by and large the refugees have shown unusual adaptability, that in a short period of time they have gone a long way toward becoming a part of the nation, that they have presented little or no problem to the American community, and that they have had a beneficial effect upon this country out of proportion to their numbers. This evidence is nation-wide in scope and based on firsthand and verifiable information. The experience of other countries that have received refugees may be cited for comparative purposes.

In his classic treatise, *The Refugee Problem* (London, 1939), Sir John Hope Simpson has stated that the conditions in which final absorption of the refugees can occur are of a legal, political, economic, and cultural character, and that these conditions must be fulfilled in any country before its refugee problem is finally solved. It may be stated quite literally that these conditions have been met to an extraordinary degree in America owing to the relatively small size of the problem, the selective quality of the immigrants, the remarkable absorptive power of the country, and the favorable traditions, institutions, and other characteristics of this greatest of all immigrant-receiving countries.

Legal Absorption. Legal absorption of refugees, as of other immigrants, is symbolized by naturalization. Until naturalized, the refugee, however generously treated, is legally an alien, has no enforceable rights, may be subject to expulsion, and may be legally restricted in place of residence and in opportunities of employment. The United States has long been outstanding among nations in its generous and comprehensive provision of the right of naturalization. This was provided for in the Constitution, and the United States has taken the lead in formulating the principle and in insisting upon its recognition. As an immigrant-receiving country it could take no other position: it was impossible for the millions of immigrants to retain their old allegiance and it was undesirable that they should have any less rights, whether at home or abroad, than the native-born citizens. Naturalization in this country thus became a regular procedure open to all (except later denied to Asiatics), and not a rare or special privilege. We thus avoided the creation of alien minorities so common in Europe.

While evidence regarding the naturalization of refugees in various countries is incomplete, it nevertheless appears that the proportion naturalized is less in other countries, with the exception of Palestine, than in the United States and that in some instances domestic laws operate to perpetuate statelessness or alien status. It also appears that in some countries the political and patriotic loyalties of certain nationalities among the refugees have deterred them from applying for citizenship. In the United States, the immigration of refugees has been marked by a great upsurge in the number of naturalizations, and the overwhelming majority of the refugees have either already become citizens or are in the process of attaining citizenship.

Political. The refugee, even though naturalized, states Sir John Hope Simpson in his world survey, is not in a condition favorable to final absorption if he has not minimum political security or if he retains actively political external loyalties or the refugee mentality. The majority of the refugees

throughout the world have a minimum political security; the great exception is provided by the unrepatriables—those who do not want to be repatriated or who for various reasons cannot return to their former homeland.
In some countries, especially in those adjoining their country of origin, refugees have at times contributed to their insecurity and that of their fellow
refugees by their political activity designed to influence developments in
their former homeland. Others have retained the "refugee mentality,"
that is, have preferred to remain unassimilated and have exploited their
position as refugees for political purposes. This political difficulty, marked
among Russian, Polish, and Balkan refugees in Europe, rarely occurs in
English-speaking countries.

In the United States, as was brought out in Chapters XI and XII above,
there has been only a minor amount of political activity on the part of
refugees concerned with developments in their countries of origin and attempting to influence American opinion on this score. The great majority of
the refugees have broken definitely and finally with the past and have no
intention of returning to Europe. Especially is this the situation with the
Jews, who make up the largest segment of the group. The characteristic
reaction of our refugees has been the desire to identify themselves completely with America. They have shown great appreciation of the democratic principles underlying our government and have demonstrated their
loyalty to the United States by their services in the war effort and in other
ways.

Economic. Economically the refugee cannot achieve absorption without
employment and security of livelihood. The country expelling the refugees
seldom permits them to take out their property and rarely gives adequate
compensation. This general tendency was carried to an extreme by the
Nazis, with the result that most of the refugees reached a haven, here as
elsewhere, with little or no means. Almost the whole burden of relief and
humanitarian work for all groups of refugees has fallen on private organizations and a few interested governments. The refugees arriving in the
United States were fortunate for the additional reason that they had so
many relatives and friends here to assist them. The work of the private
organizations is beyond praise. It is one of the extraordinary features of the
history of refugee movements that voluntary philanthropic effort has repeatedly and successfully met the initial relief burden until the process of
employment has restored the refugees to minimum economic independence.
At no time has this been demonstrated to greater effect than during the
present refugee movement.

The dictum that the right to work cannot be separated from the right of
asylum has suffered in fulfillment even in countries with a liberal tradition,
owing mainly to the economic depression prevailing in most countries dur-

ing the early period of the refugee movement. Some governments restricted or forbade their employment, and trade unions and professional organizations adopted obstructionist and exclusive policies.

Compared to the action of other countries offering a haven, the situation in the United States was favorable in this respect. There was no federal legislation restricting employment opportunities except that forbidding employment to "enemy aliens" in certain war industries. The various state and federal laws requiring citizenship as a condition of employment in certain occupations and of admission to the benefits of certain government services were of long standing and no new measures were enacted to obstruct the refugees with the exception of the professions, notably medicine and dentistry.

Some fear was expressed during the depression that the refugees would take jobs away from Americans, but actually little or no such competition occurred. A large proportion of the newcomers were old people, housewives, and children, who did not compete in the labor market; an appreciable number of others were in noncompetitive occupations or in fields, like skilled labor, where a demand existed. The number of refugees was so small in comparison both to the total American labor force and to those in specific occupations that the amount of competition could not have been appreciable. Besides, many refugees unable to transfer their skills or to secure employment in their former field were retrained for vocations where labor was scarce. It should also be noted that their immigration not merely increased the supply of labor but increased the demand for labor as well, for the refugees were also consumers and thus helped to give employment to others.

Instead of taking jobs away from Americans, the refugees have increased job opportunities and been an economic asset to the country. Immigration in general has often had that effect, as the history of the United States amply demonstrates. Refugee immigration is striking in this respect, since refugees more than ordinary immigrants are likely to bring with them capital and to possess professional and technical skills which cannot help but be of value to the country. While the amount of capital brought by refugees to the United States is unknown, we have already noted that it has been estimated at many million dollars. Much of it was brought in at a time when "risk capital" was scarce, and it had a beneficial and stimulating effect on the market. Much of it was invested in new enterprises which gave employment to many thousand American workers.

The refugees also brought their special skills and experience as free gifts to their country of refuge. Europe had borne the costly investment of rearing, educating, and training them and made us a present in the shape of ready-made workers. This has always been one of the economic gains of an immigrant-receiving country, in that it profits by the skill and experience of the immigrants, who usually come as mature individuals and full-fledged workers, without having had to bear the cost of this capital investment. This has been especially marked in the case of the refugees, who are more educated, more skilled, and more experienced in business and the professions than the ordinary run of immigrants. Their ability and special knowledge have been contributed to the economic advantage of the country, as seen in the introduction of new products and new processes, and in the development of our foreign trade.

Social and Cultural. The final absorption of the refugee group involves the acquisition of the culture of the country of refuge and integration into its social life. Indispensable in this process is knowledge of the language of the country. Except for some of the older generation, the refugees in the United States have displayed phenomenal adaptability in this respect. It is not exaggerating to say that no non-English-speaking group of immigrants has learned English so rapidly and so well in a comparable period of time.

Education of the children in the schools of the country, rather than in special schools established by immigrants for the purpose of retaining the language and culture of the parents, also is basic. This has been especially characteristic of the United States where attendance at school is compulsory and where the younger generation of refugees is growing up in the American school system with a real acquaintance with the language and culture of the country and with increasingly intimate social contacts with American-born children. No group among the refugees has had a more brilliant record of adjustment or has become more completely absorbed than the children.

The high educational and cultural level of the refugees has been both an asset and a handicap in their Americanization and general adjustment. On the one hand, their assimilation has been fostered by their educational proficiency, their cosmopolitan outlook, their knowledge of other countries and languages than their own, their wide travel, and their associations with people of different cultural backgrounds. On the other hand, as the history of immigration reveals, the absorption of working-class people and peasants has been easier than that of intellectuals. Not only is there more demand for the services of the former, but their economic adjustment is much simpler. Americanization for them means an adjustment to a higher standard of living than that they previously knew; for the intellectuals it involves an adjustment to a lower standard of living than what they were accustomed to before immigrating. The loss in social and economic status which most of the refugees suffered was a most trying experience for them, all the more so since they came from a cultural background that placed an unusually high value on status. Moreover, it appears to require more effort on the part of the intellectual, in contrast to the untutored, to change his habits of thinking, acting, and feeling. This probably derives from the fact that the intellectual is more aware of cultural values, more inclined to weigh the differences between the culture of the adopted land and that of his country of origin, and more insistent on acquiring a thorough understanding even of the refinements of the new culture. In other words, his cultural adjustment is on a higher level, and hence more difficult and intricate.

There is no question that the attitude of the refugees is favorable to assimilation. No group of immigrants has been more keenly convinced of the necessity and desirability of identifying themselves mentally, economically, and spiritually with this country. This is a characteristic of the refugee type of immigration.

There are, of course, individual differences in attitude toward cultural absorption as there are in the degree of success in becoming assimilated. While most want to forget the old country as quickly as possible, a few, especially of the older generation and of the upper class, cannot forget their cultural background and they contrast it favorably with their situation here. The very fact that it is impossible to return to the old country, that they must stay here whether they like it or not, tends to make some refugees dissatisfied. In contrast to those who think that practically everything was better in the old country are those at the other extreme, who would discard their cultural background as one would a shirt, ignore the German language and pre-Hitler culture, and even banish their memories. The great middle group appreciate deeply what America has done by opening her gates to them, try hard to master English, fit into the American way of life, and become loyal citizens.

It takes time to acquire a new culture; complete absorption is a matter of a generation rather than a lifetime. The great body of evidence presented in preceding chapters clearly indicates that the refugees have made extraordinary progress toward attaining that goal. This has been promoted, in addition to the factors mentioned above, by their relatively small numbers, their wide distribution, and their general acceptance.

From all over the country comes evidence of the contribution by refugees to the cultural life of the community, especially in the fields of music, science, art, and education. America has been enriched incalculably by the thousands of artists, scientists, scholars, engineers, and craftsmen who found refuge here. There have always been notable individuals among the immigrants to this country—men who have created new industries, made important inventions and discoveries, and made outstanding contributions to the welfare of the nation in every branch of activity—but the number and proportion of such renowned people have been unusually high among the present-day refugees. Some indication of their achievements has already been given. Their contributions in the future will be even greater. The countries that came under Axis domination have been impoverished and their reconstruction will be slow and incomplete because they either killed off or drove out their best scientific and technical brains. In more ways than one Nazism and Fascism were attacks on civilization. The countries upholding these doctrines have brought about their own ruin, while the democratic countries offering sanctuary have gained immeasurably.

The four general conditions for final absorption of refugees, mentioned above, exist in the highest degree in the United States. In many European countries, by way of contrast, the governments have largely failed to create those factors necessary to ensure conditions of complete absorption, while in their turn the refugees, particularly the older generation and certain irredentist nationalities, as a general rule have failed to adopt that attitude toward the country of refuge which would facilitate the emergence of those conditions. Many refugees in Europe have retained hopes of repatriation, and in some instances neither they nor the countries of refuge have regarded absorption as the desirable solution.

In the United States, on the other hand, with its long-established traditions as an immigrant-receiving country, the attitude toward refugees as toward other immigrants has been strongly in favor of absorption. The United States makes no legal differentiation between refugees and immigrants. The refugees have entered, as the country expected them to, with the intention of becoming Americans, and they have taken out their first citizenship papers at the earliest possible moment. There is no thought of return to the former homeland. The very geographic location of the country, involving a land and sea voyage of several thousand miles, creates in the refugee embarking for America a feeling of divorce from the past. This attitude is strengthened by his being admitted for permanent residence. Wherever he settles he finds incentives, even pressures, on all sides to become assimilated. No region has been settled by any one nationality, there are no permanent minority groups with special legislation defining their rights, immigrants are treated as individuals rather than members of a nationality group, and the way is open to all to become full-fledged American citizens. Under these circumstances, no specifically refugee problem exists in the United States; there is simply the immigrant problem, a problem which has existed throughout our entire history and which has been solved in each generation with good judgment and justice, to the development and enrichment of American society.

THE EXPERIENCE OF OTHER COUNTRIES

Although extensive scientific inquiries similar to this one have not, to our knowledge, been carried on in other countries in which refugees have found a home, there is nevertheless a certain amount of information about the experience of some of these countries that might well be considered.

In Great Britain the sympathy evoked by the calamity that created so many exiles was tempered by the fear that they might become a source of economic competition, and a very restrictive policy of immigration was pursued. Emphasis was placed on the admission only of aliens with economic resources adequate for their re-establishment. The one possible exception to this generalization—the admission of Jewish refugees from Germany—was the result of the extraordinary effort and generosity of the Jewish community in Great Britain in undertaking unconditional responsibility for their support. The British government made it a condition of the admission of refugees that they should not enter employment without express permission, although those with capital were encouraged to establish their own businesses. Before an alien could work he had to secure from the Home Office a permit which was granted only if his employer was able to prove that the work could not be done by a Briton.

As it actually turned out, the number of British workers given employment by refugees was far greater than the number of refugees admitted. By 1945, some 450 factories had been established by refugees which were giving employment to some 30,000 Britons. About one-third of these factories were set up on the government's Trading Estates, first established in 1934, within easy reach of the then economically depressed areas. The Trading Estates were intended to serve a twofold purpose: to revive industry locally, and to establish and develop industries and crafts that had been carried on for years by experts in Germany, Austria, and Czechoslovakia, who sought a new home in Great Britain. The refugee industries produce a great variety of products, prominent among them being furs (the whole valuable fur trade of Leipzig was transferred to England), leather bags, leather gloves and other leather goods, furnishing materials, food products, silk printing, ladies' clothing, novelty woolens, and electrical equipment. The Home Secretary has stated that the contribution which refugees had made to the economic and industrial life of the country was considerable.

It is difficult to measure the contributions made by refugee scholars and scientists, but it may be noted that one of the three residents of Great Britain winning the 1945 Nobel Prize for physiology and medicine was a German refugee, Dr. Ernst B. Chain, now professor at Oxford University. The refugees participated wholeheartedly in the war effort. Several refugee scientists shared in the atomic bomb investigations carried on in England, about 6,000 refugees fought with His Majesty's forces, many of them having been killed in action, and many thousands did essential war work. There was not a single case of espionage in which a refugee was involved. In short, the evidence available indicates that when the full story is known the refugees will prove to have made a valuable contribution to the economic and cultural development of Great Britain.[1]

It is estimated that about 6,000 refugees from Nazi persecution entered Canada. According to figures provided by the Department of Trade and Commerce in Ottawa, from 1939 to 1942 refugees established 130 industries with a capital investment of $39,218,332, employed 9,530 workers, and produced goods valued at $42,555,008. The industries included textiles, wood and paper products, iron and iron products, chemicals, animal products, nonmetallic mineral products, and others. The Wartime Information Board made a survey in 1943 of 45 "refugee industries" with reference to Canada's wartime production. These industries turned out that year $31,556,500 worth of goods, of which more than two-thirds was direct war material. They gave employment to more than 5,000 people, of whom 87 per cent were Canadians. Twenty-three of these industries claimed to have introduced new skills, new techniques, or new products to Canada.[2]

Mexico was the first of the Latin-American countries to receive any significant number of refugees, estimated at some 25,000. Most of the newcomers were Spaniards who fled Franco's reprisals, but Frenchmen, Greeks, Poles, some 2,000 Jews, and other nationalities of formerly Axis-occupied Europe were represented. Few of the refugees brought capital, but they brought the more valuable assets of experience, ambition, technical and professional skills, and new ideas, which they contributed to Mexican life. Nearly 4,000 farmers, mostly Spanish, were among the arrivals; they have helped increase the production of agricultural staples. Refugees have established a number of factories in textiles, leather goods, furniture, cutlery, machine tools (the first one in the country), brushes, glue, wine, and citrus products. These refugee ventures have not only provided employment for many thousand Mexicans but have raised living standards by producing cheaply at home goods which formerly were imported, hence beyond the reach of most buyers.

In the cultural field, the immigration has resulted in educational and scientific progress. In 1938 the first Spanish intellectuals to arrive were helped to establish the Casa de España, an informal institute offering advanced studies to young Mexicans. By 1940, the Spanish House became the College of Mexico, with 15 Mexicans, 17 Spaniards, 2 Frenchmen, and 1 Czech on its faculty. Aided by the government and by American founda-

[1] Sir John Hope Simpson, The Refugee Problem, 1939, pp. 342–344, 605; London Spectator, Jan. 20, 1939; Israel Cohen, "Refugees Have Substantially Enriched Many Countries in which They Have Found a Home," Rescue Information Bulletin of HIAS, Sept. 15, 1945, pp. 7–8; Sir Norman Angell, We and the Refugee, 1939; New York Times, May 3, June 13, and Oct. 26, 1945.
[2] Wartime Information Board, "Refugee Industries Contribute to Canada's Wartime Production," 1943; Vancouver (B.C.) Sun, "The 'Liabilities' Turn Out to be Substantial Assets," reprinted in Rescue Information Bulletin of HIAS, September, 1945, p. 8; Canadian National Committee on Refugees, "Beginning Anew," Bulletin No. 1, January, 1945.

tions, it has developed a program to fill the gaps in Mexican cultural life wherever they exist. Its medical men have set up a laboratory of physical and pathological studies at the National University and revitalized other courses there. Doctors were scattered over the country instead of flocking into Mexico City. A publishing house founded by refugee writers, dramatists, and poets has already established a market for its publications throughout Latin America and now has branches in Argentina, Chile, and Uruguay. Refugees have met with a certain amount of rivalry and envy on the part of Mexicans, which is natural and to be expected, but it appears that Mexico regards the influx of these refugees in the light of a genuine contribution to the national life of the republic.[3]

At the Evian Conference called by President Roosevelt in 1938 to discuss the urgent refugee problem, only one country came forward with an outright offer to take in the uprooted and homeless people for large-scale colonization. That was the little Dominican Republic. The government backed up the invitation by contributing a 26,000-acre estate at Sosua. Out of the offer grew the first planned refugee colony in the Western Hemisphere. According to information provided in February, 1946, by the Dominican Republic Settlement Association, Inc., only a few hundred Europeans had settled in Santo Domingo under this colonization scheme. They were farming on a co-operative basis and planning to establish new industries. The project is still considered to be on an experimental basis to determine whether European settlers can work under subtropical conditions and maintain without outside aid a standard of living considerably above the very low standard of the native laboring population. A serious obstacle to the development of a resettlement project of this type is the cost, estimated at $1,600 per settler.[4]

In the Dominican Republic there are also about 1,200 Spanish refugees, who arrived shortly after the end of the Spanish Civil War, worn out from the ravages of war, the rigors of the concentration camp, and the effects of disease and malnutrition. Without means, equipment, and the backing of any group that could extend help over a long period of time, they were quickly plunged into abject misery, and for years they have lived at the level of the poorest natives. Most of the group had been professional people, intellectuals, tradesmen, and businessmen; they show little or no aptitude for agriculture or for group action in meeting their problems. The country is undeveloped from a business and industrial standpoint. The per-

[3] Michael Sully, "New Blood in Old Mexico," *Current History*, Vol. 5 (1943), pp. 40–44; Ray Josephs, "Light and Shadow in Mexico," *National Jewish Monthly*, Vol. 59, No. 6 (February, 1945) pp. 178–179, 193; interview with Professor Alfredo Mendizabal, March, 1945.

[4] Earl P. Hanson, "The Americas and the Refugees," *American Mercury*, Vol. LII, No. 205 (January, 1941), pp. 45, 51–52; Joseph A. Rosen, "New Neighbors in Sosua," *Survey Graphic*, September, 1941; Brookings Institution, *Refugee Settlement in the Dominican Republic*, 1942, pp. 34–35; National Planning Association, *Europe's Uprooted People*, September, 1944, pp. 42–43.

manent colonization of this group in the Dominican Republic seems inadvisable, and plans are being worked out for their emigration to other Latin-American countries.[5]

Some estimates are available regarding the number of Jewish refugees in Latin America, said to number at the end of 1943 some 114,000. Among the countries with appreciable numbers are: Argentina with 50,000; Brazil, 25,000; Chile, 12,000; Uruguay, 7,000; and Bolivia, 5,000. A contrasting situation is presented in reports on Bolivia and Chile.

Before 1938 when the first fugitives from Hitler arrived in Bolivia, there were between 200 and 250 Jews in the country. The refugee immigration brought in about 5,000, though deliberately exaggerated estimates up to 40,000 have been circulated. The newcomers were soon under fire directed by old-line Germans, whose influence in Bolivia is said to be tremendous. Adjusting themselves to the new life in Bolivia, without money and position, was not easy. Nevertheless, some starting from scratch have established sizable businesses in textiles, furniture, hotels and restaurants. The Polish Jews seem to have adapted themselves more easily and to be more successful. Most of the refugees, it is said, would be happy to leave for almost any other country that would admit them. Some 1,500 have already gone to other South American countries.

Few Latin-American republics have increased their Jewish population as quickly as has Chile, and in few are Jews treated as well. It is estimated that 25,000 Jews now live in Chile, about half of whom arrived between 1933, when the Nazi anti-Semitic drive began, and 1939, when immigration to South America was halted. The sudden influx of German-speaking Jews created new problems and strains for the long-settled, Spanish-speaking Jewish community and the older European immigrants of Russian and Polish descent. Co-operation between the groups, however, has been successfully worked out, and the Chilean Jewish community has prevented any refugee from becoming a public charge, has helped via loans and other aid to establish many small businesses and other enterprises, and has begun to plan for further postwar immigration. Like Brazil and Argentina, Chile wants industrialists and technicians as well as agriculturalists.[6]

The Refugee a World Problem

The end of the war has not meant the end of the refugee problem. Left in the wake of the war's devastation throughout the world were some sixty million men, women, and children who upon liberation from Axis hands were stranded far from their homes. On V-E day an estimated twenty million of them were homeless in various European countries and by the

[5] Janet Siebold, "Spanish Refugees in Dominican Republic," American Christian Committee for Refugees, *Newscast*, September-October, 1944, p. 1.

[6] Ray Josephs, "Chile's Jews Have Unity," *National Jewish Monthly*, October, 1944, pp. 40–41; "Bolivia Seethes with Hatred," *ibid.*, September, 1944, pp. 10–11.

end of 1945 there were still in Europe some twelve million displaced persons. It will take years before these uprooted millions are restored, and for some it will never happen. The displaced persons include, besides the refugees from Nazi tryanny, five other categories: war fugitives or evacuees, prisoners of war, forced laborers, political and racial prisoners freed from concentration camps, and Axis soldiers and civilians remaining in United Nations countries when the war ended.[7]

Many of them (nearly 6,000,000 by the end of 1945) have been and most of them will eventually be returned home. Some may be absorbed in the place of actual residence. Many others, however, cannot or do not want to return to their country of origin because of changes in state boundaries, in type of government, in political allegiance, or because of fear of political, racial, or religious persecution. Many have been rendered stateless, and others would be unable to enjoy the protection of the government. While some of the persons affected by this situation are Jews who survived the Nazi attempt at extermination, the majority are Russians, Poles, Germans, Yugoslavs, Latvians, Lithuanians, Estonians, Spaniards, Ruthenians, and Ukrainians. Such persons will either have to remain where they are or find a new home.

This group of so-called "unrepatriables" is estimated to number at least a million in Europe. In addition to those unable or unwilling to be repatriated it includes persons of undiscoverable nationality—adults and young people who because of Axis brutality, long starvation and privation have become mentally unbalanced and do not know where they came from; and orphans and other children who have lost track of their parents.

The problem of displaced people is so vast and complex and involves so many countries throughout the world that it can be solved only by international co-operation. The special problem of the unrepatriables is peculiarly an international question. Obviously, these "people without a country" cannot be deserted, to wander about the world, driven from country to country by immigration restrictions or national decrees. The existence of large groups outcast from normal national, civic, and social ties, unable to earn a livelihood or have normal family lives, and largely deprived of everyday responsibilities as well as rights, would constitute a danger to society and to world peace.

Steps have been taken to establish international authorities to deal with postwar migration problems. The United Nations Relief and Rehabilitation Administration (UNRRA) was created in 1943 to provide emergency relief in supplies and special services. Among these services is caring for

[7] Fred K. Hoehler, *Europe's Homeless Millions*, Foreign Policy Association Headlines Series No. 54, November-December, 1945; National Planning Association, *Europe's Uprooted People, the Relocation of Displaced Population*, Planning Pamphlet No. 36, September, 1944; Eugene M. Kulischer, *Displacement of Population in Europe*, 1943.

displaced persons. With the assistance of voluntary relief agencies, the military authorities, and the governments of the territories in which the displaced people are found, UNRRA had by the end of 1945 repatriated several million persons and was giving relief to additional millions and helping in the problem of reconstruction.

To care for those displaced persons who cannot be repatriated is the responsibility of the Intergovernmental Committee on Refugees. This committee was formed as a result of the conference called on the initiative of the United States at Evian, France, in 1938 to aid the victims of Nazi persecution. In 1943 it was reorganized and its scope widened to include "all persons, wherever they may be, who, as a result of events in Europe, have had to leave, or may have to leave, their countries of residence because of the danger to their lives or liberties on account of their race, religion or political beliefs."[8] Its functions are to preserve, maintain, and transport such persons, so far as this may be necessary and practicable. Thirty-six governments are members of the committee, including thirty-four United Nations governments and two neutrals, Sweden and Switzerland.

The legal protection of stateless persons and the task of finding places of permanent resettlement for unrepatriables will have to be undertaken by the IGC or by the assumption of such responsibility by the United Nations organization. At a meeting of the United Nations in London on February 13, 1946, the General Assembly adopted a resolution that recognized the problem as an international one, specified that there should be no enforced repatriation, and recommended that a special committee be established to examine the problem. On February 16, the Special Committee on Refugees and Displaced Persons was appointed, with a membership representing some twenty countries, to study the problem and to recommend to the United Nations plans and means for dealing with it. Upon recommendation of this committee, the Economic and Social Council voted to establish a specialized agency, to be known as the International Refugee Organization, which would repatriate those refugees and displaced persons who desire to return to their countries of origin and would care for, and eventually resettle and re-establish, those who present valid objections to being repatriated. On October 3, 1946, it approved the proposed constitution of the IRO and transmitted it to the General Assembly. In December the approval of the General Assembly was voted. UNRRA and the IGC were to continue their refugee activities pending the ratification of the International Refugee Organization constitution, including budgetary provisions, by the requisite minimum of fifteen countries.

In the formulation of a program for migration and resettlement, a decision will have to be reached on questions such as these: Where shall the

[8] Intergovernmental Committee on Refugees, *Report of the Fourth Plenary Session, August 15–17, 1944,* London, 1944, p. 4.

unrepatriables or refugees be settled? Shall the resettlement be a mass movement to relatively uninhabited areas selected for colonization or by immigration of individuals and family units to developed countries? What is to be the role of Palestine both as a country of immigration and as a national home for the Jewish people? What is the outlook for immigration into Western countries? What are the opportunities in underpopulated countries like Canada and Australia and those of Central and South America, and what will their attitude be?

After World War I the general trend in immigration countries was in the direction of increasingly restrictive immigration policies. Especially was this the case in the United States, which was the first country to adopt a quota system and is still one of the few in the Western Hemisphere to have a quota law. Will there be a similar trend now that World War II is over? Can the United States justly urge other nations of the world to accept refugees unless it accepts a share of the burden itself? It would be strange indeed, especially at this time when the lives and liberties of millions throughout the world are endangered, if we, with our proud tradition as a refuge for the oppressed, should refuse to bear our share of a great human problem by closing our gates.

That the United States will remain true to its traditions despite the sentiment in some quarters to prohibit or reduce further immigration is promised by the action taken by President Truman on December 22, 1945, in ordering that displaced persons and refugees in Europe be admitted to this country up to the limit permitted by our immigration laws. The directive urged that priority be given to orphaned children, who will be cared for by child-welfare agencies. Said the President: "I consider that common decency and the fundamental comradeship of all human beings require us to do what lies within our power to see that our established immigration quotas are used in order to reduce human suffering. I am taking the necessary steps to see that this is done as quickly as possible." He added: "I feel that it is essential that we do this ourselves to show our good faith in requesting other nations to open their doors for this purpose."

NATIONAL AND LOCAL AGENCIES PARTICI-
PATING IN THE STUDY

Community	*Co-operating Agency*	*Representative*
ALABAMA		
Birmingham	Birmingham Co-ordinating Committee	Mrs. Benjamin A. Roth
Montgomery	Jewish Federation of Montgomery	Mrs. Lucien Loeb
ARIZONA		
Tucson	Tucson Jewish Community Council	Mrs. Lee Berner
ARKANSAS		
Little Rock	Federation of Jewish Charities	Mrs. Elsa K. Rosenthal
CALIFORNIA		
Bakersfield	Bakersfield Refugee Committee	Dr. H. Lionel Klakoff
Fresno	Jewish Co-ordinating Committee	Rabbi David L. Greenberg
Los Angeles	International Institute	Miss Sue Wagner
	Jewish Social Service Bureau	Miss Freda Mohr
	Los Angeles Committee for Christian Refugees	Rev. W. Bertrand Stevens
Oakland	International Institute of Alameda County	Mrs. Wilhelmine W. Yoakum
	Oakland Jewish Federation	Harry J. Sapper
Pasadena	American Friends Service Committee	David Henly
Sacramento	Sacramento Committee for Service to Emigres	Oscar A. Mathews
San Diego	United Jewish Fund of San Diego	Sol Stone
San Francisco	American Friends Service Committee	Mrs. Josephine Duvenack
	International Institute	Miss Grace Love
	San Francisco Committee for Service to Emigres	Hyman Kaplan
San Jose	Refugee Committee of San Jose Jewish Federation	Philip Hammer
Santa Barbara	Santa Barbara Refugee Committee	Miss Mary Halliday
Santa Cruz	B'nai B'rith Center	Sam Magidson
Santa Monica	Santa Monica Refugee Committee	Miss Irmgard Level
Stockton	Jewish Welfare Association	Mrs. Sam Frankenheimer
Vallejo	Jewish Welfare Board	Isidore Meyers

Community	Co-operating Agency	Representative
COLORADO		
Denver	Denver Co-ordinating Committee for Immigrants	Isidore Hilb
CONNECTI-CUT		
Bridgeport	International Institute	Miss Lena Kelly
	Jewish Welfare Bureau	Fred J. Stern
Danbury	Danbury Refugee Committee	Rabbi Jerome Malino
Hartford	Refugee Service of Hartford	Jacob Little
	Hartford Theological Seminary	Dr. E. Jerome Johanson
New Haven	Jewish Family Service of New Haven	Isidor E. Offenbach
	New Haven Committee for Christian Refugees	Mrs. George H. Gray
	New Haven Council of Social Agencies	Miss Adah Attwood
Stamford	Stamford Jewish Community Center	Paul Kulick
Waterbury	Waterbury Refugee Committee	Mrs. Harry Klampkin
DELAWARE		
Wilmington	Jewish Federation of Delaware	Ben V. Codor
DISTRICT OF COLUMBIA	Jewish Social Service Agency, Committee for Refugee Services	Mrs. Marguerite N. Mayer
FLORIDA		
Miami	Jewish Social Service Bureau	Mrs. Sadye Rose
St. Petersburg	United Jewish Appeal	Edward Goldman
GEORGIA		
Atlanta	Atlanta Federation for Jewish Social Service	Edward M. Kahn
Columbus	Columbus Refugee Committee	Mrs. Simon Schwob
Savannah	Jewish Educational Alliance	Rabbi Jerome Lebovitz
ILLINOIS		
Aurora	Aurora Resettlement Committee	Mrs. J. E. Alschuler
Chicago	American Friends Service Committee	Edwin Morgenroth
	Jewish Social Service Bureau	Miss Virginia Frank
	United Charities of Chicago	Mrs. Elsa Englander
East St. Louis	Jewish Federation of Southern Illinois	Morris Appelman
Peoria	Jewish Community Council & Welfare Fund	Oscar A. Mintzer
Rockford	Jewish Community Council	Paul Windmueller
Springfield	Springfield Jewish Federation	Ralph Segalman
INDIANA		
Bloomington	B'nai B'rith Hillel Foundation at Indiana University	Dr. Alfred Jospe
Fort Wayne	Fort Wayne Jewish Federation	Mrs. Abe Beck
Gary	Gary Refugee Committee	Milton Dreyfus
	International Institute	Miss Esther Tappan

Community	Co-operating Agency	Representative
Indianapolis	Jewish Federation of Indianapolis	H. Joseph Hyman
Marion	Marion Jewish Federation	Sam Fleck
South Bend	Young Women's Christian Association	Miss Dorothy Johnson
IOWA		
Des Moines	Jewish Welfare Fund	Sidney Spiegelman
KENTUCKY		
Louisville	Kentucky Refugee Committee	Charles Strull
LOUISIANA		
Alexandria	Jewish Welfare Federation of Central Louisiana	Morris J. Weiss
New Orleans	New Orleans Committee for Refugee Service	David Fichman
MAINE		
Bangor	Bangor Hebrew Community Center	Joseph Perlberg
Lewiston	International Institute	Miss Mary Dailydaite
		Dr. Henry I. Hershall
	Lewiston-Auburn Jewish Federation	Oscar Goldman
MARYLAND		
Baltimore	International Center, Y.W.C.A.	Miss Helen Garvin
	Refugee Adjustment Committee	Miss Edith L. Lauer
MASSACHU-SETTS		
Boston	Boston Committee for Refugees	Miss Dora Margolis
	International Institute of Boston	Mrs. Louisa S. Neumann
Brockton	Brockton Refugee Committee	Dewey D. Stone
Cambridge	New England Division, The American Christian Committee for Refugees, Inc.	Mrs. Oliver Cope
		Mrs. George Selleck
Fall River	Fall River Refugee Committee	Myer N. Sobiloff
Holyoke	Jewish Community Center	Isidore Ziff
Lawrence	International Institute, Y.W.C.A.	Miss Anna B. MacIntosh
Springfield	Family Welfare Association	Miss Sara M. Dill
	Jewish Social Service Bureau acting for Springfield Co-ordinating Committee for Refugees	Miss Jessie Josolowitz
Worcester	Worcester Refugee Committee	Jacob Gross
MICHIGAN		
Detroit	Council of Social Agencies	Miss Florence G. Cassidy
	Resettlement Service	Harold Silver
Flint	B'nai B'rith	B. M. Pelauin
	International Institute	Miss Anna Ratzesberger
Kalamazoo	Kalamazoo Resettlement Committee	Mrs. Eric Snyder
Saginaw	Saginaw Christian Refugee Committee	Rev. Garfield Hafermehl

Community	*Co-operating Agency*	*Representative*
MINNESOTA		
Duluth	Jewish Social Service Agency	Miss Frieda Fostoff
Minneapolis	Minneapolis Committee for Refugee Service	Mrs. Arthur Brin
St. Paul	International Institute	Miss Eleanor D. Deringer
		Miss Evelyn Apitz
	St. Paul Refugee Service Division	Miss Clara M. Diamond
Winona	Winona Refugee Committee	Mrs. M. A. Goldberg
MISSISSIPPI		
Vicksburg	Jewish Welfare Federation	Rabbi Stanley R. Brav
MISSOURI		
Kansas City	United Jewish Social Services	Miss Emelie Levin
St. Louis	International Institute	Miss Harriett F. Ryan
	Jewish Social Service Bureau	Miss Frieda Romalis
NEBRASKA		
Omaha	Omaha Co-ordinating Committee	Mrs. Grace D. Saferstein
NEW JERSEY		
Atlantic City	Federation of Jewish Charities	Miss Kate Rosenberg
Bayonne	Jewish Community Center	Ben A. Siegel
Belleville	Belleville Refugee Committee	Rabbi Herman Schwartz
Camden	Federation of Jewish Charities	Dan S. Rosenberg
Elizabeth	Elizabeth Refugee Service	Miss Sophia Gordon
Newark	Jewish Community Council of Essex County	Herman Pekarsky
	Jewish Social Service	Mrs. Frances Berson
Passaic	Passaic Section, National Council of Jewish Women	Mrs. Abraham Mandel
Paterson	Jewish Community Council	Dr. Solomon Geld
	Y.W.C.A.	Miss Charlotte O. Colin
Perth Amboy	Council of Jewish Organizations	Henry Schoss
Trenton	Jewish Family Welfare Bureau	Miss Edith Abraams
Vineland	Beth Israel Congregation	Leon M. Bardfeld
NEW YORK		
Albany	Albany Jewish Social Service	Mrs. Rose B. Freund
Buffalo	Buffalo Refugee Service	Miss Celia Weinberg
	International Institute	Mrs. Elizabeth G. Ponafidine
Elmira	Elmira Refugee Committee	Mrs. Werner Bloch
Kingston	Kingston Refugee Committee	Artnur B. Ewig
Newburgh	United Jewish Charities	Meyer J. Rider
New York	American Christian Committee for Refugees	Miss Aroos Benneyan
	American Federation of International Institutes	Mrs. Edith T. Bremer
	American Federation of Jews from Central Europe, Inc.	Rudolf Callmann
		Sol Levy

Community	Co-operating Agency	Representative
New York	American Friends of Czechoslovakia	Dr. Ruga Stuerm
	American Friends Service Committee	Miss Olive Whitson
	Austrian Action	Count Ferdinand Czernin
	Austro-American Association	Dr. Lili Spitzer
	Austro-American Youth Council	Mrs. Maria Jensen
	Brooklyn Bureau of Charities	Miss Elizabeth Dexter
	Catholic Committee for Refugees	Rev. Emil N. Komora
		A. Dietsche
	Committee for Refugee Education	Miss Hannah Moriarta
	Community Service Society	Miss Anna Kempshall
	Congregation Adath Jeshurun of West Bronx, Inc.	Morris Wolf
	Congregation Ahawath Torah of Washington Heights, Inc.	Max Oppenheimer
	Congregation Beth Hillel, Inc.	Dr. Leo Baerwald
	Congregation Chevra Gemiluth Chesed	Fred Marks
	Congregation Emes Wozedek	Rabbi Max Koppel
	Congregation Gates of Hope	Bernhard Seelig
	Congregation Machane Chodos, Inc.	Eugene Rothenberger
	Congregation Ramath Orah	Dr. Robert Serebrenik
	Diamond Center, Inc.	Moses Torczyner
	European-Jewish Children's Aid, Inc.	Miss Lotte Marcuse
	French Press and Information Service	Miss Blanche Finley
	Gesellschaft der Breslauer Freunde	Alfred Kalischer
	Hebrew Sheltering and Immigrant Aid Society	Isaac Asofsky
	Immigrant Jewish War Veterans	Leopold Landenberger
	International Rescue and Relief Committee, Inc.	Miss Sheba Strunsky
	Italia Libera	G. Tagliocozzo
	Jewish Agricultural Society	Gabriel Davidson
	Jewish Labor Committee	Jacob Pat
	Jews from Hesse	Albert Mayer
	Kartell Konvent	Dr. Frederick S. Aron
	Maennerbund 1911	Alfred Kalischer
	Mazzini Society	Umberto Gualtieri
	National Committee for Resettlement of Foreign Physicians	Miss Lucille Segal
		Mrs. Laura G. Rubin
	National Council of Jewish Women, New York Section	Miss Sonia Shaffer
	National Organization of Polish Jews	Joseph Ghon
	National Refugee Service, Inc.	Ralph Astrofsky
	Netherlands Jewish Society, Inc.	Alex Boekman
	New School for Social Research	Prof. Hans Staudinger
		Dr. Else Staudinger

Community	*Co-operating Agency*	*Representative*
New York	New World Club	Fred H. Bielefeld
	Organization of Jews from Wuerttemberg	Dr. Walter Strauss
	Polish General Workers' Bund	Sasha Erlich
	Polish Social Service Bureau	Miss Maria Ostrowska
	Polish War Refugees Association	Mrs. Marie Gurtler
	Prospect Unity Club	Albert Mayer
	Selfhelp of Emigres from Central Europe, Inc.	Dr. Fred S. Weissman
	T. G. Masaryk Club	Joseph Stein
	Union of Jews from France	Mrs. Sophie Klatchkine
	Union of Russian Jews	Julius Bruskus
	Union of Yugoslav Jews	Roman Smucer
	United American-Jewish Organizations of Austrian Origin	Ernest Stiasny
	United Rumanian Jews of America	Sol Rosman
	United States Committee for the Care of European Children	Miss M. Ingeborg Olsen
	Young Women's Christian Association, National Board	Miss Grace H. Stuff
		Miss Margaret Gerard
	Young Women's Christian Association, International Center	Miss Kyra Malkowsky
	Young Women's Christian Association, Central Branch, Brooklyn	Mrs. Gladys S. Fraser
Niagara Falls	Jewish Federation	Mrs. Joseph H. Chinkers
Poughkeepsie	Jewish Community Center	Mrs. Martin Leiser
Rochester	Jewish Social Service Bureau	Miss Eva Ravnitzky
Schenectady	Schenectady Refugee Committee of the Jewish Community Council	Samuel Weingarten
Syracuse	Jewish Social Service Bureau	Max Stern
	Syracuse Refugee Committee	Mrs. Malcolm E. Peabody
Troy	United Jewish Charities	Fred. A. Glass
Utica	The Citizens Bureau	Frederick W. Kincaid, Jr.
White Plains	Westchester Committee for Refugees, Inc.	William Frank
NORTH CAROLINA		
Asheville	Asheville Refugee Committee	Mrs. Gustav Lichtenfels
Winston-Salem	Jewish Community Council	Rabbi Frank Rosenthal
OHIO		
Akron	Jewish Social Service Federation	Miss Malvyn Wachner
Canton	Canton Jewish Community Center	Mrs. Ruth A. Wilkof
Cincinnati	Cincinnati Committee for Refugees	Maurice J. Sievers
	Cincinnati Committee for Christian Refugees	Mrs. Robert Coady

Community	Co-operating Agency	Representative
Cincinnati	Citizenship Council	John G. Olmstead
Cleveland	Cleveland Committee for Christian Refugees	Harry O. Way
	Jewish Family Service Association, Refugee Service Committee	Miss Rae Carp
	Y.W.C.A.	Miss Margaret Fergusson
Columbus	American Friends Service Committee	John Cavanaugh
	Jewish Welfare Federation	Miss Rose C. Javis
Dayton	Jewish Community Council	Benjamin R. Rosenberg
	Y.W.C.A.	Miss Evelyn C. Bassett
Mansfield	B'nai B'rith	A. J. Goldsmith
Portsmouth	Jewish Welfare Association	William Atlas
Springfield	Springfield United Jewish Welfare Fund	Mrs. Anne G. Buckfirer
Steubenville	Jewish Community Council	Sam Fisher
Toledo	Council of Social Agencies	Eugene Shenefield
Youngstown	Jewish Federation of Youngstown	Morris A. Ross
OKLAHOMA		
Oklahoma City	Oklahoma City Jewish Community Council	Ben Stark
Tulsa	Tulsa Jewish Community Council	Emil Salomon
OREGON		
Portland	Oregon Emigre Committee of Federated Jewish Societies	Max Hirsch
PENNSYL-VANIA		
Easton	Jewish Community Council	Jack Sher
Erie	Jewish Community Council	Mrs. Milton Schaffner
Harrisburg	United Jewish Community	Cecil Toback
Lancaster	Refugee Resettlement Committee	Mrs. Sydney Breuer
Philadelphia	American Friends Service Committee	Mrs. Kathleen Hambly Hanstein
	International Institute	Miss Marion Lantz
	Jewish Welfare Society	Ben Sprafkin
Pittsburgh	Alleghany County Committee for Christian Refugees	H. Boyd Edwards
	American Service Institute of Alleghany County	Miss Mary E. Blake
	Jewish Social Service Bureau	Miss Zena Saul
	Tri-State Co-ordinating Council	Stanley Engel
Scranton	Scranton Immigration Committee	Miss Helen Rubel
Wilkes-Barre	Jewish Welfare Agency	Mrs. Cosmar P. Long
RHODE ISLAND		
Providence	International Institute	Miss Katherine L. Lawless
	Rhode Island Refugee Service, Inc.	Miss Florence H. Parker

Community	*Co-operative Agency*	*Representative*
SOUTH CAROLINA		
Charleston	National Resettlement Committee	Maier N. Triest
TENNESSEE		
Chattanooga	Chattanooga Refugee Committee	George Berke
Memphis	Federation of Jewish Welfare Agencies	Mrs. Ruth Marks
Nashville	Jewish Community Council	Mrs. A. S. Weinbaum, Jr.
TEXAS		
Austin	Austin Refugee Committee	Alfred Schweizer
Dallas	Jewish Welfare Federation	Miss Bertha Goslin
Fort Worth	Jewish Federation (Refugee Committee)	I. H. Ginsburg
Houston	Refugee Service Committee	Mrs. Howard Heyman
San Antonio	International Institute	Miss Marguerite M. Manzer
	Jewish Social Service Federation	Miss Hannah Hirshberg
UTAH		
Salt Lake City	Salt Lake City Refugee Committee	Rabbi Alvin S. Luchs
VIRGINIA		
Norfolk	Jewish Family Welfare Bureau	Miss Sadie Routenberg
Roanoke	Community Relations Committee	Julius Fisher
WASHINGTON		
Seattle	American Friends Service Committee	Floyd Schmoe
	Washington Emigre Bureau	Mrs. Marianne K. Weingarten
Tacoma	Tacoma Refugee Committe	Fred D. Lippman
WEST VIRGINIA		
Huntington	Huntington Refugee Committee	Roger H. Liepmann
Wheeling	War Service Committee	Mrs. Kermit A. Rosenberg
WISCONSIN		
Madison	Madison Refugee Committee (Jewish)	Rabbi Manfred Swarsensky
	Madison Refugee Committee	Rev. Francis J. Bloodgood
Milwaukee	International Institute of Milwaukee County	Miss Elizabeth A. Campbell
	Jewish Social Service Association	Miss Rebecca Tenenbaum
	Milwaukee Committee for Refugees	Miss Elizabeth A. Campbell
	Milwaukee Public Schools, Department of Education	Miss Dorothy E. Enderis
Oshkosh	Oshkosh Jewish Welfare Fund	Simon Horwitz
Racine	Racine Co-ordinating Committee	Ben Schwartz

Questionnaire Returns by States and Number of Communities

States	Total Number of Communities (unduplicated)	Total Number of returns	General Questionnaires Number of Communities	General Questionnaires Number of returns	Physicians Questionnaires Number of Communities	Physicians Questionnaires Number of returns
Total	873	12,833	638	11,233	459	1,600
Alabama	4	16	4	14	2	2
Arizona	2	4	2	4	—	—
Arkansas	3	14	3	13	1	1
California	54	1,232	46	1,149	28	83
Colorado	8	106	6	97	5	9
Connecticut	38	300	29	262	20	38
Delaware	4	61	4	59	2	2
District of Columbia	1	186	1	182	1	4
Florida	6	25	6	25	—	—
Georgia	4	41	3	38	2	3
Idaho	—	—	—	—	—	—
Illinois	52	778	31	632	35	146
Indiana	7	155	7	147	4	8
Iowa	11	27	6	17	8	10
Kansas	5	5	3	3	2	2
Kentucky	8	69	5	63	4	6
Louisiana	3	5	3	4	1	1
Maine	11	16	4	4	11	12
Maryland	19	242	12	219	10	23
Massachusetts	63	774	46	701	35	73
Michigan	14	353	12	335	7	18
Minnesota	5	103	5	101	2	2
Mississippi	2	7	1	6	1	1
Missouri	8	274	6	258	4	16
Montana	—	—	—	—	—	—
Nebraska	3	20	2	18	2	2
Nevada	—	—	—	—	—	—
New Hampshire	8	19	7	16	3	3
New Jersey	79	615	70	567	28	48
New Mexico	1	1	—	—	1	1
New York	203	3,600	110	2,724	148	876
North Carolina	11	48	10	45	3	3
North Dakota	4	5	4	4	1	1
Ohio	46	1,117	32	1,033	26	84
Oklahoma	3	42	3	40	2	2
Oregon	6	204	6	199	1	5
Pennsylvania	76	1,221	73	1,188	10	33
Rhode Island	6	220	6	218	1	2
South Carolina	3	6	3	5	1	1
South Dakota	2	2	1	1	1	1
Tennessee	7	44	6	40	3	4
Texas	16	241	10	220	11	21
Utah	6	39	5	38	1	1
Vermont	4	10	4	10	—	—
Virginia	21	76	13	51	14	25
Washington	12	169	11	160	5	9
West Virginia	10	20	7	9	7	11
Wisconsin	13	320	10	314	4	6
Wyoming	—	—	—	—	—	—
Virgin Islands	1	1	—	—	1	1

STUDY FORMS

IIIIIIIIIIIIIIIIIIIIIIIIIIIIIIIIIIIIIIIIIIIIIIIIIIIIIIIIIIIIIIIIIIIIIIIIIIIIIIIIIIIIIIIIIIIIIIIIIIIIIIIIIIIIIIIIIIIIIIIIIIIIIIIIIII

COMMITTEE FOR THE STUDY OF RECENT IMMIGRATION FROM EUROPE
139 CENTRE STREET, NEW YORK 13, N.Y.

Sponsored by the American Christian Committee for Refugees, the American Friends
Service Committee, the Catholic Committee for Refugees, the National Refugee
Service, and the United States Committee for the Care of European Children

QUESTIONNAIRE FOR IMMIGRANTS FROM EUROPE ARRIVING SINCE JANUARY 1, 1933

To Newcomers to the United States:

This questionnaire is being distributed among immigrants of all nationalities and religious groups who have come to the United States since Hitler's rise to power. It will
provide basic data for a nation-wide study of the adjustment of recent immigrants to
conditions here, and their effect on American life. Little reliable information is available on this subject, while rumors and misconceptions are widespread. Our aim is to
get at the facts and present an impartial and accurate picture which, we hope, will result
in a better understanding of the newcomers and their place in America.

Since these facts can best be obtained from the recent immigrants themselves, we are
appealing directly to you. Only with your assistance can the study be completed and
its aims realized. Will you please co-operate by answering all questions frankly and
accurately? *You need not sign your name.*

Committee for the Study of
Recent Immigration from Europe

NOTE: *The term "recent immigrant," as used in this questionnaire, applies to all persons of European origin who have arrived in the United States since January 1, 1933, whether they have come
on a permanent or a temporary visa. The questionnaire is to be answered only by those who are at
present 16 years old and over. It is an individual, not a family questionnaire, and therefore all members of the family over 16 should fill one out individually. If any family member is temporarily
absent because of service in the American armed forces or other reasons, a questionnaire should be
filled out for him or her.*

This questionnaire is intended for all occupational groups among the recent immigrants except physicians and dentists. This group is being covered in a special study.

CHECK PROPER BOX ☒ OR WRITE OUT ANSWER WHERE LINE IS GIVEN.

Date...Town and State...................................

1. Sex: Male ☐   Female ☐   2. Year of birth................   3. County of birth.................
4. Mother tongue.....................   5. Country of last citizenship (European)....................

6. Religion:
{ Protestant ☐
Jewish ☐
Roman Catholic ☐
Greek Orthodox ☐
Other (specify)................... }

7. Marital Status:
{ Single ☐
Married ☐
Widowed ☐
Divorced ☐ }

8. Principal or usual occupation in Europe...
(Example: carpenter, music teacher, dentist, shipping clerk, bookkeeper, university professor, housewife, student.)
If in business for yourself, state: Line of business.........................Number of employees.........
Was your enterprise: { Manufacturing ☐
Selling: wholesale ☐   retail ☐ }

9. Education in Europe: Give highest type of school attended.........................
and number of years completed.............................. If degree or certificate was received, specify kind......................and institution by which granted...................

10. Date of arrival in the U.S. (month and year)...............   11. Port of entry in the U.S...........

12. Immigration status on arrival: permanent visa ☐   temporary visa ☐
If admitted on temporary visa: { has attempt been made to change status? Yes ☐   No ☐
has status been changed? Yes ☐   No ☐ }

13. MAIN reason for emigrating:
to improve economic or social condition ☐   to avoid anticipated religious or racial persecution ☐

to join other members of your family ☐   to escape actual religious or racial persecution ☐

to visit (business, pleasure, study, etc.) ☐   opposition to political regime ☐

14. What members of your immediate family are: In the U.S.   Abroad
(Do not include those who have gone abroad for military service)

husband or wife ☐ ☐
parent or parents ☐ ☐
child or children ☐ ☐
brothers or sisters ☐ ☐
none ☐ ☐

15. Present citizenship status: first papers not applied for ☐   first papers applied for ☐
first papers received ☐ second papers applied for ☐ citizenship attained ☐

16. Principal or usual occupation in the U.S....................................
(If student, state type of school and class)
If in business for yourself, state: Line of business.................. Number of employees...........
Is your enterprise: { Manufacturing ☐
Selling: wholesale ☐   retail ☐ }

17. List MAIN occupations since arrival in the U.S. ....
(If in the Armed Forces, indicate branch of service and rank)   (first job)

(present or last job)

Do Not Write in Squares Below.

		1	2		3		4		5		6	7	8		ac		b	9
c	10		11	12	13	14		15	16	a		b	17	18	19	20	21	22
b	c	23	c	24	25	26	27	28		29		30		31	32	33		

18. If usually gainfully employed (work for pay or in business for self) are you employed at present? Yes ☐   No ☐   If No, state reason................

19. Present WEEKLY average earnings (before deductions): Under $10 ☐ $10–19 ☐ $20–29 ☐ $30–39 ☐ $40–49 ☐ $50–74 ☐ $75–99 ☐ $100 or more ☐   Do you work: full time ☐   part time ☐

20. Have you other sources of income at present? Yes ☐   No ☐   If Yes, check source: investments or savings ☐   friends or relatives ☐   organization or committee ☐   other ☐

21. Since your arrival, have you been assisted financially by anyone outside of your immediate family?
Yes ☐   No ☐   If Yes, by: other relatives ☐   friends ☐   organization or committee ☐

22. Have you married since your arrival in the U.S.? Yes ☐   No ☐

If Yes, check a, b, and c {
a. Did you marry: another recent immigrant ☐   an immigrant who arrived before 1933 ☐   a native American ☐
b. Was he or she a member of your nationality group? Yes ☐   No ☐
c. Was he or she of the same religious faith? Yes ☐   No ☐

23. Education in the U.S.: Check type of school or class attended: none ☐   citizenship class ☐   elementary school ☐   high school ☐   trade school ☐   business school ☐   college ☐   professional school ☐   other (specify)...................Degree or certificate received...........

24. Do you read: mainly English-language newspapers ☐   mainly non-English newspapers ☐

25. In the neighborhood in which you live, are there other recent immigrant families? Yes ☐   No ☐   If Yes, are they: relatively numerous ☐   relatively few ☐

26. Home or living quarters: owned ☐   rented ☐

27. Are your friends: mainly Americans ☐   mainly other recent immigrants ☐

28. What types of organizations do you participate in actively? Indicate whether the membership is mainly:

	American	Recent Immigrant
fraternal or mutual aid	☐	☐
trade or professional	☐	☐
religious	☐	☐
civic or community	☐	☐
cultural	☐	☐
social or recreational	☐	☐
other (specify type)		

29. Contributions or service to the war effort:
purchase of war bonds ☐   civilian defense work ☐
blood donations ☐   military service by family members ☐
contributions to war relief ☐   other (specify) ....

30. Have you experienced discrimination or prejudice here? Yes ☐   No ☐
If Yes, was it: in obtaining a place to live ☐   while at work ☐
in trying to aid the war effort ☐   in social relations ☐
in getting a job ☐   in school ☐
in other ways (specify) ....

31. As compared to your normal situation in Europe, do you consider your present living conditions (such as housing, food, clothing, etc.): better ☐   poorer ☐   about the same ☐

32. As compared to your normal situation in Europe, do you consider your present social status (such as place in the community, social life, etc.): higher ☐   lower ☐   about the same ☐

33. After the war, CONDITIONS PERMITTING, do you intend to: return to live in Europe ☐ remain permanently in the U.S. ☐   settle elsewhere ☐   If undecided, why? ....

34. What do you regard as the greatest difficulties or problems which you personally have faced in adjusting to American life?

35. In what respects do you think the refugee service committees could help more toward the adjustment of recent immigrants to American life?

36. What aspects of American life do you regard as most satisfying?

37. What has changed most in your way of life?

38. List special achievements and contributions since your arrival in the United States, such as publications, musical compositions, artistic productions, new manufacturing processes, inventions. (Specify)

The Committee will be very glad to receive essays on personal experiences of recent immigrants in the United States. Such life stories may be submitted by children as well as by adults. They should be sent to—

Committee for the Study of Recent Immigration from Europe
139 Centre Street, New York 13, N. Y.

COMMITTEE FOR THE STUDY OF RECENT IMMIGRATION FROM EUROPE
139 Centre Street, New York 13, N.Y.

To Local Committees or Agencies Co-operating in the Study of Recent Immigration from Europe:

INSTRUCTIONS REGARDING THE QUESTIONNAIRE

Persons to Whom the Questionnaire Applies: The questionnaire is intended for immigrants of European origin who arrived in the United States after January 1, 1933. It applies to those on temporary visa as well as those admitted for permanent residence. It includes all such recent immigrants of European origin whether or not they are "refugees." Since the questionnaire is an individual, not a family questionnaire, care should be taken that not merely the family head but as many as possible of the members of the family over sixteen fill out a form.

Groups Not to Be Included: (a) Recent immigrants who are or were members of the medical profession—practicing physicians, medical scientists, medical students—are not to be included, since they will be covered in a special questionnaire. Specifically, this means those who hold a medical degree obtained either in Europe or the United States. (b) Children now under the care of the European-Jewish Children's Aid, Inc., or the U.S. Committee for the Care of European Children are not to be included, since they are being covered in a special study. (c) The questionnaire is not to be filled out by anyone under sixteen years of age.

Coverage: Where there is only a small number of recent immigrants in a community, practically all of them should fill out a questionnaire. In communities with hundreds or thousands of recent immigrants an adequate sample will suffice. Since the aim is to obtain a nation-wide total of thousands of replies, the local sample should be as large as possible. It certainly should be 5 to 10 per cent and we hope it will be much larger.

Representativeness of Sample: Though a wide distribution is important it is equally essential that the returns be representative of the total number of recent immigrants, especially with regard to such major categories as age groups, sex, religion, nationality, education, and occupation. Those not served by social agencies as well as agency clients, should be included.

Methods of Reaching Individuals Not Known to Local Committees: The chief difficulty will be experienced in reaching recent immigrants not already known to service agencies. They may be reached through various methods, depending on the size of the community, including the following: (a) *Through organizations*, such as recent immigrant societies or clubs, congregations, English and citizenship classes, fraternal organizations, social settlements, community centers, international institutes, youth organizations, colleges, and other institutions. (b) *Through individuals*, such as refugee acquaintances among board members and social workers. A recent immigrant thus reached may serve to bring in other recent immigrants among his own circle of friends. (c) *Through publicity* in agency bulletins, newspapers, and other publications.

Method of Distribution: Any method or combination of methods of distribution best suited to the local situation may be employed. The questionnaires may be mailed where a list of names and addresses is available. In this case, a covering letter should accompany the questionnaire and an envelope addressed to the local committee should be enclosed. They may be distributed through recent immigrant clubs or other organizations, following a talk to the groups or to their officers. Such an occasion may be used to have questionnaires filled out then and there. Social workers may distribute them personally to their appropriate clients as well as other recent immigrants known to them. It would be very helpful if the local committee or agency would call in a few recent immigrant leaders, take them into its confidence, and get their advice and co-operation as to ways of procedure. The services of lay people or volunteers may well be utilized in distributing, interpreting, and collecting the questionnaires.

The questionnaires are designed to be filled out by recent immigrants individually and at their leisure. Since the questionnaire is self-explanatory and the questions simple to answer, an interview should not be necessary, though some individuals may need assistance in filling out the questionnaire.

Collection and Forwarding of Questionnaires: The completed questionnaires should be returned to the local committee or agency, so that it will be able to check on the coverage. The agency should not wait until all forms are in before forwarding them, but as soon as a fair number have been received it should send them on to the *Committee for the Study of Recent Immigration from Europe, 139 Centre Street, New York 13, N.Y.* Forms received subsequently by the agency should be forwarded later but within the time limit mentioned below. If the quantity is large, the forms should be sent by express collect to avoid excessive mailing cost.

Time Limit: A maximum of six weeks after receipt of the questionnaires has been set as the time limit for this part of the general study. Communities with a small number of recent immigrants should be able to complete the task in about two weeks. The time limit is necessitated by the requirement that the report of the Committee be published by next Fall.

Anonymity: Since the questionnaire does not call for a signature, there will be complete anonymity as far as the Study Committee is concerned. The question of preserving anonymity may arise, however, on the local level. In such case, it may be handled by having the recent immigrants return their questionnaires to the local committee in sealed envelopes. In general, however, it is not expected that any such problem will occur, since the majority of recent immigrants will know the local committee or agency and have confidence in it. In fact, many recent immigrants may feel more inclined to participate in the study if it is not too impersonal and "secret."

Local Community Organization: Main reliance for the local studies will rest on the local refugee committees affiliated with the national organizations sponsoring the study and on social agencies, especially those with a program for the foreign born. In communities where two or more such committees or agencies are participating, each will be advised of the other's cooperation and of the persons representing them in the study. In communities where there exists but one such committee, it will have to assume responsibility for covering all recent immigrants of whatever nationality or religion. If it so desires, it may, of course, ask for the collaboration of other agencies or individuals in the community. Each community is to follow its own plan of organizing the task before it. Some may want to proceed informally and not set up a co-ordinating committee. Others may prefer to establish a special community-wide committee or to seek the sponsorship of a general community agency. In the larger communities there may be need to clear for duplications. This should not, however, be a serious problem, since no person is likely to fill out more than one questionnaire; and he can readily be advised not to.

Assistance Available from National Committees: Some of the national agencies participating in the Study have field representatives whose services may be made available in the case of special problems arising in connection with the Study. The local committees should feel free to call upon the national agencies with which they co-operate, or upon the Study Committee directly, for such assistance as may be necessary.

Special Requests to the Local Committees or Agencies

(a) *Names and Addresses of Physicians and Dentists.* If you have not already been asked to send to the National Committee for the Resettlement of Foreign Physicians, 139 Centre Street, New York 13, N.Y., the names of physicians and dentists, will you kindly do so. The Physicians Committee is trying to complete its registry of all foreign physicians and dentists who arrived in the United States after 1933. This master list will be used for mailing a special questionnaire to this group as part of a study which the Physicians Committee and the Committee for the Study of Recent Immigration from Europe are making jointly. We are interested in receiving names and present addresses, but feel that it is important as well to list those individuals who have previously lived in your community, but are now elsewhere, and whose present addresses may or may not be known. Identifying information such as name of wife, country of origin, and previous cities of residence in the United States would be helpful, if you can provide it.

(b) *Names and Addresses of Organizations of Recent Immigrants.* As part of the source material for the Study, we are interested in data concerning the types, functions, and activities of organizations established by and for recent immigrants. A schedule has been prepared for this purpose, which will be mailed directly by the Study Committee to the officers of such organizations. To help complete our list, will you please send to us the names and addresses of such organizations in your community, and include, if possible, the names of the officers to whom the form should be sent. If you should prefer to distribute these schedules yourselves and mail them to us, please advise us, and we shall be pleased to arrange it.

(c) *Special Local Studies*. We shall be glad to receive copies of any special studies or surveys of recent immigrants, whether published or not, that may have been made in your community.

Committee for the Study of
Recent Immigration from Europe

COMMITTEE FOR THE STUDY OF RECENT IMMIGRATION FROM EUROPE
139 Centre Street, New York 13, N.Y.

LIFE STORIES OF RECENT IMMIGRANTS
Guide for Interviewers

Purpose: These life stories will form part of the source material for a nation-wide study of immigrants from Europe who have come to the United States since January 1, 1933. Through them it is hoped to secure a more detailed and intimate picture of the processes of adjustment and to gain greater insight into the problems and attitudes of the recent immigrant than could be obtained by the questionnaire method alone. Moreover, it is expected that much more of the family situation will be brought out in these life stories than is possible in the questionnaire, which is designed for the individual.

Method: In contrast to the questionnaires, which are to be distributed widely, the life stories should be obtained from a comparatively few recent immigrants in each community. Roughly, the ratio should be one life story to every ten questionnaires in communities with a small number of recent immigrants and one in twenty to thirty in communities with a large number. The aim is to secure, not numerous, but *typical* cases. They should be representative, as nearly as possible, of the total recent immigrant group in the community with regard to age, sex, religion, nationality, occupation, and education. It is especially important to include representatives of business, professional, and wage-earning groups. Physicians and dentists, however, should not be included, since they are being covered in a special study. While various age groups and both sexes should be represented in the total of life stories obtained, it is not necessary to include them in each category, such as occupation or nationality.

A special effort should be made to get life stories from recent immigrants not served by social agencies as well as from agency clients. Care should be taken that the cases are not all success stories. The general run of immigrants and the less successful should be included as well as those whose achievements are outstanding.

The stress in the interview should be upon the experience of the individual immigrant, though the family situation is to be included both in the specific data and in the narrative. Although some information concerning his life in Europe should be included, the major emphasis should be on his life since his arrival in the United States. In the main this should be the story of the person interviewed, and he should be allowed to follow his own sequence in his account. Some direction will, however, doubtless be needed to cover the pertinent points, particularly the specific data. The story should be recorded as nearly as possible in the words of the person interviewed. The interviewer should not include his own interpretations in the body of the narrative, but may add on separate sheets his interpretation of the story, and his appraisal of the degree of adjustment and the chief problems of the recent immigrant.

In sending the material to the Study Committee the true name of the interviewee need not be used. In the published study the name of neither the individual nor the community will be mentioned. Except in the case of prominent persons, and then only with their expressed consent, these life stories will be used anonymously.

Suggested Topics for the Interview

Except for the Specific Data, these topics are suggested merely as a guide. They are not intended to limit the narrator's account of his experiences and reactions. The life stories should be typewritten double-spaced, and may be as long as necessary to give a well-rounded picture of the individual and his experiences. The heading of each life story should include the date and the name of the town and state.

Specific Data: Sex. Age. Marital status. Present occupation. Country of birth. Nationality. Religion. Year of arrival. Immigration status on arrival. Naturalization status. Size of family living together as a unit. Other members of the family and relationship; their age, sex, and occupation.

Background in Europe: Education and occupation of adult members of family in Europe; their place in the community, and their social and cultural life. Reasons for emigrating. Experiences in getting out of Europe and assistance received. Other countries of refuge and reasons for coming to the United States. Notions about the United States prior to arrival.

Arrival in the United States and First Impressions: Financial resources and physical condition upon arrival. Aid from agencies, friends, or relatives. First living accommodations. First impressions: aspects of American life found interesting, those found difficult to comprehend, and those regarded unfavorably. Chief difficulties in getting oriented. Port of entry, and other communities lived in since arrival; reasons for moving or staying.

Family Situation: General living conditions. Changes in family life since arrival. Family problems. Differences in degree of adjustment of various members. Family dislocation: members in the United States and abroad; plans for reuniting.

Economic Adjustment: Employment history. Difficulties in getting a job. Transferability of skill. Present occupation and earnings. Difficulties experienced at work. Prospects for the future. Attitude of employer and fellow-workers. Labor union experience. Degree of satisfaction with economic conditions here, as compared with Europe.

Social and Cultural Adjustment: Acquaintances among Americans and degree of intimacy. Membership in organizations. Recreational life. Facility with English. Education here. Participation in political activities. Aid in the war effort. Degree of satisfaction with social and cultural life here. Obstacles to adjustment. Prejudice or discrimination experienced. Favorable or unfavorable attitude toward Americans and American life. Assimilation thought desirable or undesirable. Desire to return or remain. Future plans and hopes for self and children.

Note: Interviewer's Comments should be written on separate sheets and attached to the life story. It will be helpful if the comments are signed by the interviewer.

Please send completed stories promptly to:

Committee for the Study of Recent Immigration from Europe
139 Centre Street, New York 13, N.Y.

COMMITTEE FOR THE STUDY OF RECENT IMMIGRATION FROM EUROPE
139 Centre Street, New York 13, N.Y.

REPORT ON COMMUNITY BACKGROUNDS AND ATTITUDES

Purpose: In order to round out the study of immigration from Europe since January 1, 1933, information is needed regarding the communities in which recent immigrants have settled and the reactions of these communities toward them. This information, by providing the community setting, will supplement the data regarding the adjustment of the individual obtained through the questionnaire and the life story.

Method: The following report on the local community does not call for a special survey or any extensive research, but may be based on information already available. It should be made by an individual who possesses an understanding of the community and the problems of the recent immigrant. In addition to drawing upon his own knowledge of the situation he may find it helpful to confer with other persons having an insight into local conditions. Wherever possible, concrete instances should be cited in support of the generalizations made. If the space provided below is not sufficient, comments may be written on separate sheets and attached to this report.

I. GENERAL CHARACTERISTICS OF THE COMMUNITY

Town and State ....

Type of community (such as manufacturing, commercial, residential, agricultural, resort, etc.)
....

Chief industries ....
....

Main occupational pursuits ....
....

General employment opportunities ....
....

Climate of opinion: conservative or liberal ....
....
....

Size of the population ....
Chief racial and nationality groups ....
....

Major religious groupings and their approximate sizes ....
....

Nature and extent of divisions and conflicts between groups in the community ....
....
....
....
....

Attitudes toward racial and national minorities ....
....
....
....
....

II. Characteristics of the Recent Immigrant Group

Estimated size of the recent immigrant group ....

Composition by nationality and religion ....

Manner and circumstances of settlement in the community ....

....

....

Degree of residential concentration ....

General occupational distribution ....

....

Extent of separate organizational life ....

....

Extent to which the recent immigrants have become integrated into the general community......

....

....

....

....

The adjustment of the children of recent immigrants in the home, the school, and the community

....

....

....

....

....

III. Attitude of the Community Toward Recent Immigrants

General community reactions ....

....

....

The reactions of particular groups in the community, favorable and unfavorable ....

....

....

....

Complaints against special groups of recent immigrants ....

....

....

Opinion as to the effects of recent immigrants on the economic, political, social and cultural life of
the community ....

....

....

....

Filled out by ....

Address ....

COMMITTEE FOR THE STUDY OF RECENT IMMIGRATION FROM EUROPE
139 Centre Street, New York 13, N.Y.

Sponsored by the American Christian Committee for Refugees, the American
Friends Service Committee, the Catholic Committee for Refugees,
the National Refugee Service, and the United States
Committee for the Care of European Children.

INFORMATION REGARDING ORGANIZATIONS OF RECENT IMMIGRANTS

1. Name of organization ....
2. Address of meeting place .... Tel. ....
3. Date organized .... 4. Incorporated? Yes .... No ....
5. Is your organization a revival of a former organization in Old Country? Yes .... No ....
6. Purpose:
   a. Main reasons for organizing ....

   b. Changes in purpose since first organized. Explain: ....

   c. Does organization have Constitution and By-laws? Yes .... No ....
      (If yes, please enclose copy.)
   d. In the case of religious organizations, indicate, if Jewish, whether Orthodox ....
      Conservative .... Reformed ....; if Christian, give denomination ....
      How often are services held? .... Average attendance .... Language used ....
7. Membership:
   a. Number of members: Total .... Men .... Women .... Children ....
   b. Size of membership: Increased? .... Decreased? .... Reasons: ....

   c. Age groups (Give approximate percents): Young .... Middle Aged .... Elderly ....
   d. European nationality background of majority of members ....
      Other nationalities represented: ....
   e. Religion of majority of members ....
   f. Approximate percent of members: Recent immigrants (since 1933) .... Older
      immigrants (before 1933) .... Native Americans ....
   g. Who is eligible for membership? ....
      How are members secured? ....
      Has there been any change in either respect? Explain: ....
8. Officers:

a.	Names of present officers	Positions	Date of induction
	(1)	....	....
	(2)	....	....
	(3)	....	....
	(4)	....	....

   b. Officers: Elected? .... How often? .... By whom? ....
            Appointed? .... How often? .... By whom? ....
9. Activities:
   a. Business meetings: How often held? .... Open to non-members? Yes .... No ....
      Average attendance .... Language used .... Minutes kept? Yes .... No ....
   b. Social functions: Types ....
      How often held? .... Average attendance ....
      Open to non-members? Yes .... No .... Language used ....
   c. Cultural activities: Types ....
      How often held? .... Average attendance ....
      Open to non-members? Yes .... No .... Language used ....

d. Religious activities: Types ....
   How often held? .... Average attendance ....
   Language used ....
e. Other activities: Describe ....

f. Publications (Newspapers, bulletins, newsletters, annual reports, etc.) Yes .... No ....

Type	How often issued	Date of 1st issue
....	....	....
....	....	....
....	....	....

(Please enclose sample copies)

g. Who is responsible for planning activities? Chairman .... Board ....
   Committee .... General membership ....
10. Finances:
   a. Sources of income (check): Membership dues .... Contributions ....
      Income from entertainments .... Other sources (specify) ....

   b. Types of expenditures (check): Running expenses .... Benefit payments to members
      .... Contributions to causes (specify): ....

   Other types of expenditures: ....
11. Affiliation with other organizations: Give names of organizations and type of relationship
   ....
   ....
   ....

12. What is the outlook for the future of the organization? ....
   ....
   ....
   ....

Filled out by ....
Office held ....
Address ....
Date ....

COMMITTEE FOR THE STUDY OF RECENT IMMIGRATION FROM EUROPE
139 Centre Street, New York 13, N.Y.

Sponsored by the American Christian Committee for Refugees, the American
Friends Service Committee, the Catholic Committee for Refugees,
the National Refugee Service, and the United States
Committee for the Care of European Children.

QUESTIONNAIRE FOR PHYSICIANS AND DENTISTS FROM EUROPE
ARRIVING SINCE JANUARY 1, 1933

To Physicians and Dentists:

This questionnaire is designed for European physicians and dentists who have arrived
in the United States since Hitler's rise to power. It will help provide basic data for a
nation-wide study which is being conducted among recent immigrants of all nationalities
and religious groups to determine the adjustment of these newcomers to conditions here,
and their effect on American life. Little reliable information is available in this area,
although rumors and misconceptions are widespread. Our aim is to get at the facts and

present an impartial and accurate picture which, we hope, will result in a better understanding of the newcomers and their place in America.

Since these facts can best be obtained from the recent immigrants themselves, we are appealing directly to you. Only with your assistance can the study be completed and its aims realized. Will you please co-operate with us?

If your husband or wife is also a physician or dentist, please be sure that each of you fills out a questionnaire. The two questionnaires should then be returned together.

If you know any other physicians or dentists who have arrived since January 1, 1933 and who have not received a copy of this questionnaire, please send us their names and addresses and we will be glad to see that they obtain copies.

Information given by you will be held in the strictest confidence. Names or other identifying information will not be used in any published report. The data will be treated only statistically. If there is any question you prefer not to answer, leave it blank, but please fill out the rest of the questionnaire.

Committee for the Study of
Recent Immigration from Europe

CHECK PROPER BOX ☒ OR WRITE OUT ANSWER WHERE LINE IS GIVEN

Name...Date..............................
Address...
Street   Town   State

1. Sex: Male ☐ Female ☐   2. Year of birth ....   3. Country of birth ....
4. Mother tongue ....   5. Country of last citizenship (European) ....

6. Religion:
- Protestant ☐
- Jewish ☐
- Roman Catholic ☐
- Greek Orthodox ☐
- Other (specify) ....

7. Marital Status:
- Single ☐
- Married ☐
- Widowed ☐
- Divorced ☐

8. Professional activity in Europe: In what branch of medicine did you specialize? ....
Was your MAJOR activity: private practice ☐ public health ☐ research ☐ teaching ☐ other full-time institutional employment ☐ government employment ☐ other (specify)

State honorary or other positions and institution ....
----

9. Medical education in Europe: State medical schools attended, and place and date of graduation ....

Specify degree, diploma, or certificate obtained .... Were you licensed to practice? Yes ☐ No ☐ If Yes, in what countries? ....

10. Date of arrival in the U.S. (month and year) ....   11. Port of entry in the U.S. ....

12. Immigration status on arrival: permanent visa ☐ temporary visa ☐
If admitted on temporary visa: { has attempt been made to change status? Yes ☐ No ☐ / has status been changed? Yes ☐ No ☐

13. MAIN reason for emigrating:
- to improve economic or social condition ☐   to avoid anticipated religious or racial persecution ☐
- to join other members of your family ☐   to escape actual religious or racial persecution ☐
- to visit (business, pleasure, study, etc.) ☐   opposition to political regime ☐

14. What members of your immediate family are: Living with you   Living elsewhere in the U.S.   Abroad (Do not include those who have gone abroad for military service)

     husband or wife ☐ ☐ ☐
     parent or parents ☐ ☐ ☐
     child or children ☐ ☐ ☐
     brothers or sisters ☐ ☐ ☐
     none ☐ ☐ ☐

15. Present citizenship status: first papers not applied for ☐   first papers applied for ☐   first papers received ☐   second papers applied for ☐   citizenship attained ☐   U.S. citizen on entry ☐

Do Not Write in Squares Below.

1	2	3	4	5	6	7	8	9	10	11	12	13	14	15	16	17	18	19	20
21	22	23	24	25	26	27	28	29	30	31	32	33	34	35	36	37	38	39	40
41	42	43	44	45	46	47	48	49	50	51	52	53	54	55	56	57	58	59	60
61	62	63	64	65	66	67	68	69	70	71	72	73	74	75	76	77	78	79	80

16. Education in the U.S.: Check type of school or class attended: none ☐   English class ☐   citizenship class ☐   tutoring or coaching class for State Board Examinations ☐   medical school ☐   other (specify) ....   Degree or certificate received ....

17. Present licensure status in the U.S.: Do you hold a license to practice? Yes ☐   No ☐
If Yes, medical ☐   dental ☐   By examination ☐   by endorsement of foreign credentials ☐
Specify state or states in which you are licensed and date of license ....

If NOT licensed in the U.S., have you applied for State Board Examinations? Yes ☐   No ☐
If Yes, in which states? ....
     Have you been accepted for State Board Examinations? Yes ☐   No ☐   If Yes, in which states? .... If No, in which states, and why?

     Have you taken State Board Examinations? Yes ☐   No ☐   If Yes, in which states?

     Results: passed in full ☐   passed in part ☐   failed ☐   If examinations were taken in more than one state, give results in each ....
Are you a diplomate of the National Board of Medical Examiners? Yes ☐   No ☐   If Yes, give date ....
Are you a diplomate of an American Specialty Board? Yes ☐   No ☐   If Yes, give date ....

18. List MAIN occupations, non-professional as well as professional, since your arrival in the U.S. Please be specific. If in the Armed Forces, indicate branch of service and rank. If in school full time, state institution and year when course will be completed.

     ....
     (First job)
     ....
     ....
     ....
     ....
     (Present or last job)

19. Are you gainfully employed (work for a salary, in private practice, or both) at present? Yes ☐ No ☐   If you have left the field of medicine or dentistry, do you intend to return to it? Yes ☐ No ☐

20. Present average gross MONTHLY earnings: Under $100 ☐ $100–249 ☐ $250–499 ☐ $500 or more ☐   Is maintenance provided in addition to salary? Yes ☐   No ☐

21. Have you other sources of income at present? Yes ☐   No ☐   If Yes, check source: investments or savings ☐   friends or relatives ☐   organization or committee ☐   other ☐

22. Since your arrival, have you been assisted financially by anyone outside of your immediate family? Yes ☐   No ☐   If Yes, by: other relatives ☐   friends ☐   organization or committee ☐

23. Present professional activity: medical or dental student ☐   studying for licensing examinations ☐   private practice ☐   locum tenens ☐   assistant to private practitioner ☐   teaching ☐   research ☐   public health ☐   industrial medicine ☐   internship ☐   residency ☐ other hospital or institutional appointment (specify) .... other activity (specify) ....
Are you specializing at the present time? Yes ☐   No ☐   If Yes, state in which branch of medicine ....

24. Nature of present position or activity: permanent ☐   temporary ☐
Do you think your present position or affiliation will cease when the war is over? Yes ☐ No ☐ How was your present professional position obtained? independently ☐   commercial agency ☐   National Committee for Resettlement of Foreign Physicians ☐   local committee ☐   friends ☐   other (specify) ....

25. If in private practice, do you have hospital affiliation? Yes ☐   No ☐   If No, state why ....
....
Are you a member of the county medical society? Yes ☐   No ☐   If No, have you applied? Yes ☐   No ☐   If you have applied, what action has been taken? ....
....

26. Have you married since your arrival in the U.S.? Yes ☐   No ☐
If Yes, check a, b, and c:
  a. Did you marry: another recent immigrant ☐   an immigrant who arrived before 1933 ☐   a native American ☐
  b. Was he or she a member of your nationality group? Yes ☐ No ☐
  c. Was he or she of the same religious faith? Yes ☐   No ☐

27. In the neighborhood in which you live, are there other recent immigrant families? Yes ☐ No ☐   If Yes, are they: relatively numerous ☐   relatively few ☐

28. Home or living quarters: owned ☐   rented ☐

29. Are your friends: mainly Americans ☐   mainly other recent immigrants ☐

30. What types of organizations do you participate in actively? Indicate whether the membership is mainly:

	American	Recent Immigrant
fraternal or mutual aid	☐	☐
professional	☐	☐
religious	☐	☐
civic or community	☐	☐
cultural	☐	☐
social or recreational	☐	☐
other (specify type)		

31. Contributions or service to the war effort:
purchase of war bonds ☐   civilian defense work ☐
blood donations ☐   military service by family members ☐
contributions to war relief ☐   other (specify) ....

32. Have you encountered any special difficulties in carrying on your professional activity in the U.S.? Yes ☐   No ☐   If Yes, were they because of:
legal restrictions ☐   restrictions imposed by local medical organizations ☐
lack of working capital ☐   differences in professional practices in Europe and the U.S. ☐
insufficient knowledge of English ☐   your own physical condition ☐
other factors (specify) ....

33. Have you experienced any advantages in your professional activity in the U.S. as compared to your normal situation in Europe? Specify ....

34. After the war, CONDITIONS PERMITTING, do you intend to: return to live in Europe ☐ remain permanently in the U.S. ☐ move to a country other than European ☐ If undecided, why? ....

35. What are your future plans and hopes with respect to your professional activities in the U.S.?
....
....
....
....

36. List special achievements and contributions (professional, scientific, scholarly, and so forth) since your arrival in the U.S. ....
....
....
....
....
....

The Committee will be very glad to receive essays on personal experiences of recent immigrants in the United States. Such life stories should be sent to—

Committee for the Study of Recent Immigration from Europe
139 Centre Street, New York 13, N.Y.

COMMITTEE FOR THE STUDY OF RECENT IMMIGRATION FROM EUROPE
139 Centre Street, New York 13, N.Y.

Sponsored by the American Christian Committee for Refugees, the American Friends Service Committee, the Catholic Committee for Refugees, the National Refugee Service, and the United States Committee for the Care of European Children.

QUESTIONNAIRE ON BUSINESS AND INDUSTRIAL ENTERPRISES ESTABLISHED BY RECENT* EUROPEAN IMMIGRANTS

* By "recent immigrants" is meant those who arrived in the United States after January 1, 1933.

1. Type of ownership: corporation ☐ partnership ☐ single ownership ☐ Did you establish ☐ or acquire ☐ the enterprise? Year established or acquired ....
2. Year of your arrival in the U.S. .... Religious affiliation ....
Country of last (European) citizenship ....
If a partnership, is your partner also a recent* immigrant? Yes ☐ No ☐
If a corporation, are the chief stockholders also recent* immigrants? Yes ☐ No ☐
3. Type of enterprise (i.e., manufacturing, wholesale or retail trade, export-import, etc.) ....
....
Type of product or goods ....
4. (Reply to this question is very important, as it indicates the size and significance of the enterprise, but may be omitted if preferred).
Capital investment: $..
Average value of production or amount of business done annually: $..
Average value of goods exported annually: $..
Average amount of wages paid annually: $..
5. Number of employees: .... How many are recent immigrants? ....

6. Goods sold: in domestic market ☐ in foreign market ☐ If in foreign market, in what countries? ....
Goods imported: Yes ☐ No ☐ If Yes, from what countries? ....
....
Was your import or export trade developed by you before you immigrated? Yes ☐ No ☐
7. Is your business or industry the same as you conducted in Europe? Yes ☐ No ☐ If No, what was your occupation or business in Europe? ....
8. If in manufacturing, are you producing goods not previously manufactured here? Yes ☐ No ☐ Explain ....
9. Have you introduced: a new product ☐ a new process ☐ a patent ☐ a secret formula ☐ a new skill ☐ Describe briefly ....
....
....
....
10. Are you producing materials for use in the war effort? Yes ☐ No ☐
11. Give here a brief account of the history of your enterprise:
....
....
....
....
....
....
....
....
Name of enterprise: ....
Address: ....

Note:

(1) If you have any material describing or illustrating your product or business, the Committee will appreciate receiving copies of it.

(2) If you know of any other recent immigrants who have established new enterprises, will you please send us their names and addresses.

* * * * * * * * * *

Please return this questionnaire to:

Committee for the Study of Recent Immigration from Europe
139 Centre Street, New York 13, N.Y.

SCHEDULE FOR STUDY OF UNACCOMPANIED CHILDREN

Name .... Location of foster homes ....
EJCA affidavit ....
Sponsoring agency: U.S. Committee alone .... Still under care ....
Joint program .... Discharged ....
Religion .... Nationality and country emigrated from ....
Sex: M .... Date of birth .... Present age ....
F .... Date of arrival .... Age at arrival ....
Location of real parents ....
Location of siblings ....
Foster Home adjustment: Good .... Fair .... Poor ....
Problems in Foster-home ....
....

Personality adjustment: Good .... Fair .... Poor ....
Personality problems or distinctive traits ....
....

Social adjustment: Good .... Fair .... Poor ....
  Problems: ....
....
  Activities: ....
Health: Good .... Fair .... Poor ....
  Health problems ....
Educational adjustment: Advanced .... Normal .... Retarded ....
  Level of education achieved ....
  Quality of work or special distinctions ....
  Special aptitudes ....
Plans or ambitions for vocational life ....
Paid jobs held ....
Service in Armed Forces, Yes............ No .... Comments: ....
Married, Yes............ No .... To member of what group .... No. of children ....
Summary of adjustment ....
....
....
....

DISTINGUISHED REFUGEES

═══

NOBEL PRIZE WINNERS WHO CAME TO THE
UNITED STATES SINCE 1933

Name	*Field*
Peter J. W. Debye	Chemistry
Albert Einstein	Physics
Enrico Fermi	Physics
James Franck	Physics
Victor Francis Hess	Physics
Otto Loewi	Pharmacology
Maurice Maeterlinck	Literature
Thomas Mann	Literature
Otto Meyerhof	Biochemistry
Wolfgang Pauli	Physics
Otto Stern	Physics
Sigrid Undset	Literature

REFUGEES LISTED IN *WHO'S WHO IN AMERICA* (1944–45)

Name	*Field or Occupation*	*Country of Birth or last residence*
Maurice Abravanel	Music—Conductor	Greece
George Balanchine	Dancer	Russia
**Walter Curt Behrendt	Architect	Germany
*Ernst Berl	Chemistry	Austria
*Hans Albrecht Bethe	Physics	Germany
Charles Boyer	Actor	France
Karl Brandt	Agricultural Economist	Germany
Paul Breisach	Music—Conductor	Austria
Marcel Lajos Breuer	Architect	Hungary
Goetz A. Briefs	Economist	Germany
Adolf Busch	Music—Violin	Germany
Salvador Dali	Art	Spain

* Listed also in *American Men of Science*
** Deceased

REFWGEES LISTED IN *WHO'S WHO IN AMERICA* (1944–45) (*Cont.*)

Name	Field or Occupation	Country of Birth or last residence
*Peter J. W. Debye	Chemistry	Netherlands
Fernando de los Rios	Diplomat—Political Science	Spain
**Antoine de Saint Exupéry	Aviator—Author	France
*Albert Einstein	Physics	Germany
*Kasimir Fajans	Physical Chemistry	Poland
Nina Fedorova	Writer	Russia
*Enrico Fermi	Physics	Italy
Lion Feuchtwanger	Writer	Germany
*James Franck	Physical Chemistry	Germany
Philipp Frank	Physics	Austria
Rene Fülop-Miller	Writer	Roumania
Jean Gabin	Actor—Movies	France
*Richard Benedikt Gold- schmidt	Zoology	Germany
Oskar Maria Graf	Writer	Germany
Walter Gropius	Architecture	Germany
*Jacques Hadamard	Theoretical Mathematics	France
Laszlo Halasz	Music—Conductor	Hungary
Oscar Halecki	History	Poland
*Victor Francis Hess	Physics	Austria
Hans Heymann	Economist	Germany
Paul Hindemith	Music—Composer	Germany
Hajo Holborn	History	Germany
Harry Horner	Art Director—Movies	Austria
Vladimir Horowitz	Music—Pianist	Russia
Werner W. Jaeger	Classical Philology	Germany
Herbert Janssen	Singer	Germany
Otto Klemperer	Music—Conductor	Germany
*Wolfgang Köhler	Psychology	Esthonia
Hans Kohn	History	Czechoslovakia
Erich Wolfgang Korngold	Composer—Conductor	Austria
**Karl Landsteiner	Medical Research	Austria
Lotte Lehmann	Singer	Germany
Erich Leinsdorf	Music—Conductor	Austria
*Kurt Lewin	Psychology	Germany
Prince Hubertus zu Loewen- stein	Political Science	Austria
*Otto Loewi	Pharmacology	Germany
Emil Ludwig	Author	Germany
Maurice Maeterlinck	Poet-Dramatist	Belgium

* Listed also in *American Men of Science*
** Deceased

REFUGEES LISTED IN *WHO'S WHO IN AMERICA* (1944–45) *(Cont.)*

Name	*Field or Occupation*	*Country of Birth or last residence*
**Bronislaw Malinowski	Anthropology	Poland
Alfred Manes	Economics—Insurance	Germany
Erika Mann	Author—Actress	Germany
Heinrich Mann	Writer	Germany
Thomas Mann	Author	Germany
*Otto Marburg	Neurology	Austria
Jacques Maritain	Philosophy	France
André Maurois	Writer	France
*Leonor Michaelis	Medical Research	Germany
Ludwig Mies van der Rohe	Architect	Netherlands
Darius Milhaud	Music—Composer	France
Nathan Milstein	Music—Violinist	Russia
David Mitrany	Political Science—Author	Rumania
Ferenc Molnar	Author	Hungary
Frank Munk	Economics	Czechoslovakia
*Carl Alexander Neuberg	Biochemistry	Germany
*Otto Neugebauer	Mathematics	Austria
Jarmila Novotna	Opera Singer	Czechoslovakia
Erwin Piscator	Theater Director	Germany
Luis Quintanilla	Artist—Painter	Spain
*Wilhelm Raab	Medicine	Austria
Louis Raemaekers	Art—Cartoonist	Netherlands
**Max Reinhardt	Theater—Director	Austria
Erich Maria Remarque	Author	Germany
Jules Romains	Author	France
**Arthur Rosenberg	History—Government Service	Germany
Eugen Rosenstock-Huessy	Law—Social Philosophy	Germany
*Bruno Rossi	Physics	Italy
*Reinhold Rüdenberg	Electrical Engineering	Germany
Curt Sachs	Musicologist—Critic	Germany
Artur Schnabel	Pianist	Austria
Arnold Schoenberg	Composer—Teacher	Austria
Rudolf Serkin	Pianist	Czechoslovakia
Igor Stravinsky	Music—Composer	Russia
Alexander Sved	Singer	Hungary
*Harald Ulrik Sverdrup	Meteorologist—Oceanographer	Norway
*Gabor Szegö	Mathematics	Hungary
George Szell	Conductor—Pianist	Czechoslovakia
Joseph Szigeti	Violinist	Hungary
Paul Johannes Tillich	Theology—Philosophy	Germany

* Listed also in *American Men of Science*
** Deceased

REFUGEES LISTED IN *WHO'S WHO IN AMERICA* (1944–45) (*Cont.*)

Name	Field or Occupation	Country of Birth or last residence
Ernst Toch	Composer	Austria
Arturo Toscanini	Conductor	Italy
Robert Ulich	Education	Germany
Sigrid Undset	Author	Norway
Herbert von Beckerath	Economics	Germany
Martin Wagner	Architect	Germany
Bruno Walter	Conductor	Germany
Kurt Weill	Composer	Germany
**Franz Werfel	Author	Czechoslovakia
*Herman Weyl	Mathematics	Germany
Vera Zorina	Dancer	Norway
Carl Zuckmayer	Author-Playwright	Germany
**Stefan Zweig	Author	Austria

* Listed also in *American Men of Science*
** Deceased

REFUGEES LISTED IN *AMERICAN MEN OF SCIENCE* (1944)

Name	Field or Occupation	Country of Birth or last residence
Felix T. Adler	Physics	Switzerland
Leo Alexander	Neurology, Psychiatry	Austria
András Angyal	Psychiatry	Hungary
Ludwik Anigstein	Medical Microbiology	Poland
Camillo Artom	Biochemistry	Italy
Pierre V. Auger	Physics	France
Reinhold Baer	Mathematics	Germany
Georg Barkan	Biochemistry, Pharmacology	Russia
Clemens Ernst Benda	Neuropsychiatry	Germany
Tibor Benedek	Dermatology	Hungary
Oscar Benesi	Anatomy	Hungary
Max Bergmann	Chemistry, Biochemistry	Germany
Peter Gabriel Bergmann	Physics	Germany
*Ernst Berl	Chemistry	Czechoslovakia
Felix Bernstein	Biometry	Germany
Eric W. Beth	Physics	Austria
*Hans Albrecht Bethe	Theoretical Physics	France
Erwin R. Biel	Climatology, Meteorology	Austria
Z. William Birnbaum	Mathematics, Statistics	Poland
Jacob A. B. Bjerknes	Meteorology	Sweden
Felix Bloch	Physics	Switzerland

* Listed also in *Who's Who in America*

REFUGEES LISTED IN *AMERICAN MEN OF SCIENCE* (1944) *(Cont.)*

Name	Field or Occupation	Country of Birth or last residence
Konrad E. Bloch	Biological Chemistry	Germany
Robert Bloch	Botany	Germany
Salomon Bochner	Mathematics	Poland
Richard Brauer	Mathematics	Germany
Leon Brillouin	Physics	France
Jan O. M. Broek	Economic Geography	Netherlands
Walter V. Burg	Analytical Chemistry	Germany
Ernst Caspari	Genetics	Germany
Hans M. Cassel	Physical Chemistry	Germany
Arturo Castiglioni	History of Medicine	Italy
Erwin Chargaff	Chemistry	Austria
Claude Chevalley	Mathematics	S. Africa
Victor Conrad	Climatology, Geophysics	Austria
Richard Courant	Mathematics	Germany
Sergio De Benedetti	Experimental Physics	Italy
Peter P. H. De Bruyn	Histology	Netherlands
*Peter J. W. Debye	Chemistry, Electrical Engineering	Netherlands
Paul F. de Gara	Bacteriology, Immunology	Austria
Max Dehn	Mathematics	Germany
Max Delbrück	Biology	Germany
Alexis B. Dember	Physics	Germany
Tamara Dembo	Psychology	Russia
Konrad Dobriner	Medicine, Biochemistry	Germany
Jean Dufrenoy	Plant Pathology	France
Tilly Edinger	Vertebrate Paleontology	Germany
Maximilian R. Ehrenstein	Chemistry	Germany
William E. Ehrich	Pathology	Germany
*Albert Einstein	Theoretical Physics	Germany
Hans Michael Elias	Embryology	Germany
Boris Ephrussi	Zoology	Russia
Paul Erdös	Mathematics	Hungary
Immanuel Estermann	Physics	Germany
*Kasimir Fajans	Physical Chemistry	Poland
Ugo Fano	Theoretical Physics, Biology	Italy
*Enrico Fermi	Physics	Italy
Ernst Fischer	Physiology	Germany
Piero P. Foà	Experimental Medicine	Italy
Heins L. Fraenkel-Conrat	Biochemistry	Germany
*James Franck	Physics	Germany
Fritz W. Fromm	Chemistry	Germany
Frieda W. Fuchs	Microbiology	Germany

* Listed also in *Who's Who in America*

REFUGEES LISTED IN *AMERICAN MEN OF SCIENCE* (1944) *(Cont.)*

Name	Field or Occupation	Country of Birth or last residence
Walter M. Fuchs	Chemistry	Austria
Sergei I. Gaposchkin	Astronomy	Russia
Hilda Geiringer	Mathematics	Austria
Kurt Gödel	Mathematics	Czechoslovakia
*Richard B. Goldschmidt	Zoology	Germany
Ernest F. Goldsmith	Internal Medicine	Germany
Kurt Goldstein	Psychiatry, Neurology	Germany
Michael Golomb	Mathematics	Germany
Bernhard Gottlieb	Dental Pathology	Poland
Emil J. Gumbel	Mathematical Statistics	Germany
Paul György	Pediatrics	Hungary
Fritz Haas	Zoology	Germany
*Jacques Hadamard	Theoretical Mathematics	France
Viktor Hamburger	Zoology	Germany
Poul Arne Hansen	Bacteriology	Denmark
Zaboj Vincent Harvalik	Physical Chemistry	Yugoslavia
Bernhard Haurwitz	Meteorology	Germany
Thorleif G. Hegge	Psychology, Education	Norway
Ernst D. Hellinger	Mathematics	Germany
Edward Helly	Mathematics	Austria
Olaf Helmer	Mathematics	Germany
Max Herzberger	Optics	Germany
Leo Hess	Internal Medicine	Austria
*Victor Francis Hess	Physics	Austria
Paul F. A. Hoefer	Clinical Neurology, Neurophysiology	Germany
Jörgen Holmboe	Meteorology	Norway
Imre Horner	Physiological Chemistry, Immunology	Hungary
Hugo Iltis	Botany, Genetics	Czechoslovakia
George Jaffé	Theoretical Physics	Russia
Fritz John	Mathematics	Germany
Henri A. Jordan	Mathematics	Belgium
Franz J. Kallmann	Psychiatry	Germany
Boris G. Karpov	Astronomy	Russia
Gerhard Katz	Pharmacology	Germany
Walter Kempner	Medicine, Physiology	Germany
Paul Kimmelstiel	Pathology	Germany
Heinrich G. Kobrak	Medicine, Physiology	Germany
Ervand Kogbetliantz	Mathematics	Russia
*Wolfgang Köhler	Psychology	Esthonia

* Listed also in *Who's Who in America*

REFUGEES LISTED IN *AMERICAN MEN OF SCIENCE* (1944) *(Cont.)*

Name	Field or Occupation	Country of Birth or last residence
Zdeněk Kopal	Astronomy	Czechoslovakia
Arthur Korn	Mathematics, Physics, Electrical Engineering	Germany
Maurice Kraitchik	Mathematics	Russia
Hartwig Kuhlenbeck	Anatomy, Neurology	Germany
Ernst Lachman	Anatomy	Germany
Rudolf Ladenburg	Physics	Germany
Gustav Land	Astronomy	Germany
Helmut Landsberg	Geophysics	Germany
Rolf Landshoff	Theoretical Physics	Germany
Karl O. Lange	Aeronautical Meteorology	Germany
Willy Lange	Chemistry	Germany
Alois Langer	Chemistry	Czechoslovakia
Charles P. Leblond	Endocrinology	France
Philippe Le Corbeille	Engineering	France
Irene Levis	Chemistry	Germany
Fritz Levy	Clinical Pathology	Germany
Frederick H. Lewey	Neurophysiology, Neuropathology	Germany
*Kurt Lewin	Child Psychology	Germany
Hans Lewy	Mathematics	Germany
Leopold Lichtwitz	Medicine	Germany
Julius E. Lips	Anthropology	Germany
W. Siegfried Loewe	Pharmacology	Germany
*Otto Loewi	Pharmacology, Physiology	Germany
Charles Loewner	Mathematics	Czechoslovakia
Julian P. Maes	Physiology	Belgium
Adolf Magnus-Levy	Internal Medicine	Germany
Szolem Mandelbrojt	Mathematics	Poland
*Otto Marburg	Neurology	Germany
Erich A. Marx	Physics	Germany
Lore Marx	Obstetrics, Gynecology	Germany
Walter Marx	Biochemistry	Germany
Walther Mayer	Mathematics	Austria
Otto Meyerhof	Biochemistry	Germany
*Leonor Michaelis	Physical Chemistry	Germany
Rudolph L. B. Minkowski	Astronomy, Physics	France
Richard von Mises	Mathematics	Austria
Stanislaw Mrozowski	Physics	Poland
Ernst Mylon	Experimental Medicine	Germany
Erwin Neter	Bacteriology, Immunology	Germany
*Carl A. Neuberg	Biochemistry	Germany

* Listed also in *Who's Who in America*

REFUGEES LISTED IN *AMERICAN MEN OF SCIENCE* (1944) (*Cont.*)

Name	Field or Occupation	Country of Birth or last residence
*Otto Neugebauer	Mathematics, History of Science	Austria
Hans Neurath	Biochemistry, Physical Chemistry	Austria
Lothar Wolfgang Nordheim	Theoretical Physics	Germany
Josef Novak	Gynecology, Obstetrics	Czechoslovakia
Severo Ochoa	Medicine	Spain
Isaac Opatowski	Mathematical Physics, Applied Mechanics, Mathematical Biology	Poland
Balint Orban	Oral Histology	Hungary
Wolfgang Pauli	Physics	Austria
Francis Henri Perrin	Physical Chemistry	France
George Placzek	Physics	Czechoslovakia
George Polya	Mathematics	Hungary
Richard Prager	Astronomy	Germany
Peter Pringsheim	Physical Chemistry	Germany
*Wilhelm Raab	Internal Medicine, Pathological Physiology	Austria
Eugene I. Rabinowitch	Physical Chemistry	Russia
Hans Rademacher	Mathematics	Germany
Otto Redlich	Physical Chemistry	Austria
Wilhelm Reich	Sexeconomy	Austria
Fritz Reiche	Theoretical Physics	Germany
Richard Kohn Richards	Pharmacology, Therapeutics	Poland
Maria A. Rickers-Ovsiankina	Psychology	Russia
Meinhard Robinow	Pediatrics	Germany
Hans R. Rosenberg	Organic Chemistry	Germany
Arthur Rosenthal	Mathematics	Germany
Otto Rosenthal	Biochemistry	Germany
*Bruno Rossi	Physics	Italy
*Reinhold Rüdenberg	Electrical Engineering	Germany
Henri S. Sack	Applied Physics	Switzerland
Michael A. Sadowsky	Applied Mathematics	Russia
Mario Giorgio Salvadori	Civil Engineering	Italy
William George Sawitz	Parasitology	Germany
Otto Schales	Chemistry	Germany
Marcel Schein	Physics	Czechoslovakia
Rudolf Schindler	Gastroenterology	Germany
Joseph Z. Schneider	Chemistry, Economics	Czechoslovakia
Klaus Schocken	Physics	Germany
Guenter Schwarz	Physics	Germany
Martin Schwarzschild	Astronomy, Astrophysics	Germany

* Listed also in *Who's Who in America*

REFUGEES LISTED IN *AMERICAN MEN OF SCIENCE* (1944) (*Cont.*)

Name	Field or Occupation	Country of Birth or last residence
Carl L. Siegel	Mathematics	Germany
Robert Simha	Physical Chemistry	Austria
Rolf Singer	Mycology	Germany
Roman Smoluchowski	Physics	Poland
Karl Sollner	Chemistry	Austria
Hertha D. E. Sponer	Physics	Germany
Joseph Stasney	Pathology, Hematology	Hungary
Gabriel Steiner	Neuropathology	Germany
Curt Stern	Zoology	Germany
Otto Stern	Physics	Germany
*Harald Ulrik Sverdrup	Oceanography, Meteorology	Norway
Wojciech Swietoslawski	Physical Chemistry	Poland
Pol Swings	Astronomy, Astrophysics	Belgium
Otto Szász	Mathematics	Hungary
*Gabor Szegö	Mathematics	Hungary
Alfred Tarski	Mathematics, Logic	Poland
Edward Teller	Physics	Hungary
Siegfried J. Thannhauser	Medicine	Germany
Carl H. W. Tiedcke	Chemistry	Germany
Gerhard Tintner	Mathematical Economics	Germany
Franz Urbach	Physics	Austria
Theodor von Brand	Physiology, Parasitology	Germany
Fritz J. von Gutfeld	Bacteriology	Germany
Arthur von Hippel	Electrical Engineering	Germany
Heinrich B. Waelsch	Biochemistry	Czechoslovakia
Wolfgang Wasow	Mathematics	Switzerland
André Weil	Mathematics	France
Herman Weil	Chemistry, Metallurgy, Physics	France
Alexander Weinstein	Mathematics	Russia
Arnold Weissberger	Organic Chemistry	Germany
J. Richard Weissenberg	Histology, Embryology, Zoology	Germany
Heinz Werner	Psychology	Austria
*Herman Weyl	Mathematics	Germany
Maria Wiener	Bacteriology	Czechoslovakia
Heinrich Albert Wieschhoff	Anthropology	Germany
Rupert Wildt	Astronomy	Germany
Ernest Witebsky	Bacteriology, Immunology	Germany
František Wolf	Mathematics	Czechoslovakia
Werner Wolff	Psychology	Germany
Bohdan Zawadzki	Psychology	Poland
Antoni Zygmund	Mathematics	Poland

* Listed also in *Who's Who in America*

INDEX

Abraham & Straus, Inc., 374
Accent, foreign, 90, 225, 226, 306
Actors, 90, 351–354; number of, 352
Adjustment, 53; age factor in, 143, 168; economic, 91, 119–142, 170; emotional, 85–86, 101; occupational, 128–142, 235; social and cultural, 47, 86, 91–92, 116–117, 143–170, 174, 183, 223–225, 229–232, 312, 387, 395–396; time factor in, 158, 160, 168–169, 170, 283
Advisory Committee on Uranium, 203
Affiants, 18, 81, 99
Age, 37, 38–39, 43–44, 119, 231–232; as a factor in adjustment, 143, 168
Aged, the, 100, 143, 149–151, 167–168, 173
Agencies cooperating in the Study, xi–xvi, xix, xx, xxi, 405–412
Albania, 22
Albany, New York, 80
Albers, Josef, 367
Alien Enemy Control Unit, 193–194
Alien Property Custodian, 377–378
Alien Registration Act, xiv–xv, 193; Division, xiv–xv, 81
Alien status, 122, 123
Aliens: debarred from certain occupations, 122, 123; departing from U.S., 20–21; liability of, for military service, 196–197
America First party, 371
America, notions about, before arrival, 48–50
American Academy of Arts, 343
American Artists Professional League, 328
American Association of Former European Jurists, 112
American Association of University Women, 301, 302
American Christian Committee for Refugees, xii, 97, 98, 105, 107, 108, 110, 115, 151, 304, 329, 339, 401, 408
American Committee for Emigre Scholars, Writers, and Artists, 110, 339
American Committee for the Guidance of Professional Personnel, xiv, 111–112, 288, 289–290
American Committee for Protection of the Foreign Born, 109
American Committee to Save Refugees, 113
American Council on Education, 272
American Federation of International Institutes, xii, 408

American Federation of Jews from Central Europe, Inc., xiii, 180, 235, 240, 246, 408
American Federation of Musicians, 348
American Friends Service Committee, 13, 97–98, 105, 106–107, 110, 111, 115, 180, 304–305, 314, 319, 331, 350, 352, 354, 405, 406, 409, 411, 412; see also Quakers
American Immigration Conference Board, 372
American Institute of Architects, 366
American Jewish Committee, 11, 109
American Jewish congregations, 355–356
American Jewish Congress, 107
American Jewish Joint Distribution Committee, 4, 13, 70
American Library Association, 112, 362
American life, aspects found most satisfying, 51, 62; aspects viewed unfavorably, 62–69; impressions of, 50–69
American Medical Association, 267, 269
American Medical Directory, 258
American Nationalist party, 371
American ORT Federation, 103–104
American Protective Association, 370
American Red Cross, 199, 200
American Section of the International Society for Contemporary Music, 346
Americans, friendliness and helpfulness of, 56–58, 109, 253, 369, 390; informality of, 54–55, 57, 58; other traits, 50, 51, 57, 58, 59–60, 62, 67; role of men, 61; women, 53–54, 61
Amsterdam, Netherlands, 241, 244
Angell, Sir Norman, 272, 399
Angold, Edith, 352
Anti-Defamation League of B'nai B'rith, 109
Anti-immigrant sentiment, 103, 369–371
Anti-refugee sentiment, 88, 292, 311, 372
Anti-Semitism: in the United States, xi, 63–69, 88, 89, 92, 116, 117, 177, 188, 216, 311, 371, 374, 388, 389; in other countries, 11, 71, 73, 74, 75, 206–208, 243
Antwerp, Belgium, 241
Architects, 134, 345, 366–368
Argentina, 11, 400, 401
Armed forces, refugees in the American, 177, 195–199, 200, 228–229; special services, 197–199
Armenian refugees, 3
Army Medical Corps, 273, 284
Army Specialized Training Program, 313, 315, 343

Arno, Sig, 352
Arrival, problems on, 84–92
Arrogance, 262, 383–384, 387
Art Digest, 328, 332, 367
Artists, 134, 136, 324–333; guest, 346
"Aryans," 7, 8, 97
Asch, Sholem, 50
Asheville, North Carolina, 246, 387
Assimilation, 46, 47, 77, 81; desire for, 156, 160–164, 185, 187; factors in, 156, 158, 164; pressure toward, 397
Assisting the refugee, 93–118, 139, 140
Associated Dry Goods Corporation, 373
Assyrian refugees, 3
Atlanta, Georgia, 80, 386
Atomic bomb research, 201, 203, 315, 322–323
Attitude: of Americans toward refugees, xi, 92, 117, 133, 162–163, 365, 367, 369–390; of refugees toward Americans, 47–69, 126, 133, 140, 215–216, 229, 383–386, 396
Aufbau, xv, 70, 125, 176, 178, 182, 183, 184, 199, 217, 243, 244, 352, 353
Austin, Texas, 237, 387
Australia, 11, 404
Austria, 9, 23, 25, 26, 27, 29, 30, 35, 73, 176, 201, 204, 207, 209, 210, 231
Austria, 182
Austrian Labor Information, 182
Austrian Labor News, 182
Austrian refugees, xvi, 9, 32, 36, 37, 43, 69, 73, 78, 128, 129, 130, 145, 158, 161, 172, 177, 178, 179, 192, 195, 231, 242, 243, 259–260, 284, 301, 331, 341, 343
Austro-American Tribune, 182
Austro-American Youth Council, 177
Automobiles, 51, 169
Axis-occupied or dominated countries, 22, 27
Aydelotte, Frank, 318

Baal kore, 356
Baltimore, Maryland, 80, 381, 386
Bankers, 134, 178
Bar examination requirements, 294–295
Baron de Hirsch Fund, 251
Barschak, Erna, 307
Barter, 382
Bassermann, Albert and Else, 352
Bat'a, Jan, 376
Bauhaus, 327, 367
Beer-Hoffmann, Richard, 343, 344
Behrendt, Walter Curt, 367, 432
"Bei-uns," 384
Belgian Embassy and Information Center, 243
Belgian refugees, 36, 37, 75–76, 177, 242, 244, 389
Belgium, 14, 23, 25, 29, 30, 35, 75–76, 210, 241, 243, 301, 304
Berl, Ernst, 322, 432, 435
Bernstein, Henry, 344
Bethe, Hans, 322–323, 432, 435
Billigmeier, Robert H., 9

Binghamton, New York, 252
Black Mountain College, 367
Blood donations, 199–200
Bloomingdale's, 373, 374
Bloomington, Indiana, 386
Blue Card, 176, 180
B'nai B'rith, 109, 115, 171
Board of Appeals on Visa Cases, 18, 391
Board of Economic Warfare, 201
Board of Missions of the Presbyterian Church, 98
Bohr, Neils, 203
Bolivia, 11, 401
Bolles, Blair, 12
Boston, Massachusetts, 80, 172, 192, 236, 237
Bound Brook, New Jersey, 251
Brancusi, 324
Brazil, 11, 401
Breton, André, 324, 333, 341
Breuer, Marcel, 367, 432
Bridgeport, Connecticut, 80, 386
British child evacuees, 115, 204, 205, 210
British Inter-Aid Committee for the Care of Children Coming from Germany, 209
British Medical Association, 272
Broch, Hermann, 343, 344
Brookings Institution, 400
Brooklyn, Connecticut, 252
Brooklyn Museum, 332
Brown, Richard H., 374
Brunswick, Mark, 113, 346, 347
Buffalo, New York, 80, 192, 237, 381, 386
Bulgaria, 23, 25, 29
Bulgarian refugees, 36
Bureau of War Records of the Jewish Welfare Board, 196, 197
Burial societies, 177
Burnstein, Rabbi Alexander J., 355
Businessmen and manufacturers, 39, 40, 41, 42, 69, 79, 86–87, 89, 94, 121, 128, 129, 131, 132, 133, 134, 135, 136, 137, 138, 139, 157, 158, 161, 168, 169, 201, 233–251; wealthy, 376–377
Business enterprises, 236–251

Café society, 375–376
California, 77, 78, 81, 93, 252, 253, 259, 278, 279, 324
Camden, New Jersey, 80
Camp de Gurs, 213
Canada, 14, 26, 30, 35, 399, 404
Canadian National Committee on Refugees, 399
Canadian Wartime Information Board, 399
Canby, Henry Seidel, 340
Cannon, Walter B., 322
Canton, Ohio, 387
Cantors, 350–351, 356, 359
Capital brought in by refugees, 87, 377, 394
Capital gains tax exemption, 378–380
Carl Schurz Memorial Foundation, 303
Carnegie Corporation, 304
Carpenter, Niles, 164
Carusi, Ugo, 194

Casa de España, 399
Castiglioni, Dr. Arturo, 120, 436
Catholic Committee for Refugees, 97, 105, 304, 409
Catholic refugees, xvii, 5, 36, 69, 145, 186, 193, 260
Catholics, prejudice against, 370, 371
Central America, 35, 404
Central Conference of American Rabbis, 355
Central Index of Refugee Physicians, Dentists, and Medical Scientists, xx, 258
Central Loan Trust, 235
Central Location Index, 108–109
Chagall, Marc, 324
Chain, Ernst B., 398
Chemists, 134, 136, 137, 138
Chermayeff, Serge, 367
Chicago, Illinois, xvi, 80, 157, 172, 192, 237, 381, 386, 388
Chicago Art Institute, 332
Child-caring organizations, 205, 208, 219–220, 223
Children, 30–31, 69, 72, 73, 74, 115, 147–148, 153–155, 187, 204–232, 395; emotional problems in adjustment, 215–216, 217–219, 220, 221–223, 231; experiences in Europe, 206–208; in school, 223–228; number of, 204; outstanding, 226–228; separation from parents, 204–205, 212, 213–214, 215–216, 217–219, 223; social and cultural adjustment, 143, 147–148, 167, 223–225, 229–230, 230–232
Chile, 400, 401
Chinese immigration, 16, 28
Chomski, I., 213
Christian refugees, 42, 43, 44, 68, 69, 78, 128–129, 130, 145, 158, 161, 168, 170, 192, 233–234, 259, 260, 261, 278, 301, 331, 333, 343, 388
Christians, Mady, 351
Churches, American, 56, 66–67, 357–358
C.I.O. National Committee to Abolish Racial Discrimination, 371
Cincinnati, Ohio, 38, 80, 387
Citizenship, 189–192, 278, 284, 299, 331, 343; attitude of refugees toward, 189–190; loss of, 285; required for bar examination, 294–295; for medical licensing examination, 267–268, 271, 278, for professional practice, 364, 366, 394; see also Naturalization
Civilian defense program, 175, 193, 200
Clair, René, 353
Clergymen, 134, 345, 354–360
Clerical and kindred workers, 128, 129, 131, 132, 133, 134, 135, 136, 137, 138, 139, 158, 161, 168, 169
Cleveland, Ohio, 80, 381, 387
Coates, Robert, 325, 326
Coffin, Patricia, 376
Cohen, Israel, 399
Cohn, Alfred E., 268

College fraternities, transplanted, 173, 179, 181
Colleges and universities, American, 109, 110, 301–304, 306–311, 312
Collier's, 325
Colorado Springs, Colorado, 387
Columbia University, 317; School of Library Service, 363
Columbus, Ohio, 80, 387
Committee for Refugee Education, Inc., 107–108, 189, 409
Committee for the Re-education of Refugee Lawyers, 290, 291, 292
Committee on Displaced Social Workers, 112, 361
Committee on Refugee Librarians, xiv, 362
Common Council for American Unity, xv, 26, 27, 32, 33, 109, 194
Community, size of, as a factor in adjustment, 68–69, 78–79, 158, 159, 160, 161, 168–169, 186, 283, 284
Community backgrounds and attitudes, reports on, xx–xxi, 206, 223, 230; schedule, 422–423
Concentration camps, 9, 13, 14, 74, 84, 146, 204, 207, 208, 213
Conference of Jewish Immigrant Congregations, 180
Confiscation of property in Germany, 7, 8, 120, 234, 235, 393
Congregational Christian Committee for War Victims and Services, 98, 114
Congress House, 107
Connecticut, 251, 278, 279
Connecticut Department of Labor, 373
Conspicuous consumption, 376
Contributions by refugees, 298–299, 343, 344, 349, 351, 367–368, 390, 391, 396–397
Cook, Walter W. S., 318
Cooley, Thomas M., II, 194
Cooperative College Workshop, 106, 319
Corporate affidavit, 30, 115, 205, 208
Council on Books under OWI, 343
Countries of refugee emigration, 11, 14, 22–23, 25, 27, 28, 34
Craener, Vera, 125
Cuba, 26, 30, 241
Culp, Eugene M., 194
Cultural adjustment, 47, 86, 91, 156, 166–168, 174, 183, 229–230, 312, 395–396; see also Social adjustment
Cultural conflict, 372, 383, 384; between parents and children, 147–148, 221, 222–223, 229–230
Customs and institutions, European contrasted with American, 51–52, 53, 59–62, 126, 147, 162, 168–170, 174, 234, 280, 282–283, 292–293, 306–308, 309–310, 327, 328, 338, 351–352, 355–356, 360, 361, 363, 380, 383
Czechoslovakia, 23, 25, 27, 29, 35, 73, 204, 327
Czechoslovakian refugees, 36, 37, 69, 73, 78,

158, 161, 203, 242, 244, 259–260, 284, 327, 331, 343, 389
Czinner, Paul, 352

Dallas, Texas, 80, 387
Dammann, Marjorie S., 296
Dancers, 354
Danish refugees, 37
Davidson, Gabriel, 252
Davis, John W., 290
Dayton, Ohio, 387
Delaware, 93
Denationalization, 2, 3, 4, 18; see also Statelessness
Denaturalization, 4, 7
Denmark, 14, 23, 25, 29, 35, 76, 203, 304
Dentists, 261, 271–272, 278, 279
Denver, Colorado, 80
Department stores, 373–374
Dependency, 148–155
Deportation as a public charge, 99, 100, 118
"Deportation delirium of 1920," 193
Derain, André, 325
Detroit, Michigan, 80, 192, 381, 387, 388
Detroit Council of Social Agencies, xiii, 407
Diamond Center, Inc., 243
Diamond Dealers' Club, 243
Diamond industry, 178, 241–243, 249, 376
Diamond Workers Union, 243
Diplomates, medical, 278
Discrimination, 63, 65, 67–69, 177, 181, 188, 267–273
Displaced persons, 2, 401–402, 403, 404
Distinguished refugees, 432–440
Doeblin, Alfred, 342
Domestic service, 123, 134, 137
Dominican Republic, 400, 401; Settlement Association, 400
Dos Passos, John, 50
Drachsler, Julius, 164
Drury, Betty, 313
Duchamp, Marcel, 324
Duggan, Stephen, 303, 313
Duluth, Minnesota, 386
Dutch, see Netherlands
Duvivier, Julien, 353

East Africa, 11, 14
Ecole Libre des Hautes Etudes, 304
Economic absorption, 393–395
Economic adjustment, 91, 119–127, 140–142, 170
Economic competition, 120, 140, 239–241, 245–246, 372–375; fear of, 257, 263, 268, 271, 272, 365, 367, 375, 388, 394
Economic depression of the 1930's, 1, 11, 17, 20, 69, 102, 122, 302, 373, 388, 393, 394
Edsall, David L., 268
Educational Alliance, 115
Einstein, Albert, 120, 203, 318, 323, 432, 433, 436
Einstein, Karl, 334
Eire, 22, 35
Eliasberg, W., 201–202

El Libro Libre, 342
Elizabeth, New Jersey, 80, 386
Elmira, New York, 386
Emergency Committee in Aid of Displaced Foreign Medical Scientists, 111, 276
Emergency Committee in Aid of Displaced Foreign Physicians, 97, 111
Emergency Committee in Aid of Displaced Foreign Scholars, xiii, xiv, 110, 303, 304, 312, 314, 329, 331, 339, 350, 352
Emergency Rescue Committee, 113, 339, 341, 344
Employment opportunities created by refugees, 239–241, 394, 398, 399
Endorsement, licensing by, 364, 366, 367
Enemy agents, see Foreign Agents
"Enemy aliens," 18, 20, 108, 123, 180, 192–194, 196, 394
Engineers, 134, 137, 138, 345, 364–366
England, 203, 209, 241, 273; see also Great Britain
English and citizenship classes, 91, 107–108, 175, 189, 265
English language, refugee knowledge of, xvi, 45, 46, 88–91, 116, 117, 125, 166–168, 225–226, 395
Episcopal Committee for European Refugees, 98, 114
Ernst, Max, 333
España Libre, 182
Estonia, 23, 25, 29
Estonian displaced persons, 402
Estorick, Eric, 348
Ethical Culture Society, 107
European-Jewish Children's Aid, Inc., xiii, 30, 97, 115, 208, 210, 409
Evian Conference, 11, 12, 400, 402
Exiled Writers Committee, 113
Exit permit, 20
Experiments in International Living, 111
Exploitation, 120
Exodus, from Germany, 8–11; conditions causing, 1–14

Fair employment practice laws, 123, 371
Falk, Louis A., 196
Family, 125, 145–148, 162, 221–223, 229–230; separation through persecution, 1, 39, 84, 85–86, 94, 101, 145–147, 163, 175–176, 204–205, 212, 213–214, 215–216, 217–219, 223, 293
Family service agencies, 94, 99, 100, 101
Farmers, 128, 129, 251–256
Farmingdale, New Jersey, 252
Fascism, 4, 22, 44
Fear, xvi, 51, 53, 55, 59, 85
Federal Bureau of Investigation, 17, 193, 194
Federal Council of the Churches of Christ in America, 98
Federal Register, 19
Federal Reserve Bank, 378
Feininger, Lyonel, 367
Fermi, Enrico, 120, 203, 323, 432, 433, 436
Feuchtwanger, Lion, 334, 344, 433

Field, Richard M., 322
Fields, Harold, 122
Fields of study, refugee scholars, 315–316; refugee scientists, 320, 321
Financiers, 234, 244
Financial assistance to refugees, 139–140, 276, 280
Finland, 22, 23, 25, 29, 35
Finnish refugees, 37
Fireside Group for New Americans, 107
First names, free use of by Americans, 57, 58
Fisher, Dorothy Canfield, 340
Fles, Barthold, 342
Flesch, Rudolph, 166
Flexner, Abraham, 318
Floersheimer, Walter, 244
Florida, 251, 252
Foreign agents, 17, 18, 194
Foreign Agents Registration Act, 371
Foreign assets frozen, 377, 378
Foreign born, 77, 78; in the armed forces, 195–197
Foreign Broadcast Intelligence Service, 202
Foreign Economic Administration, 298
Foreign Funds Control, 377
Foreign-language press, xiv, xv, 168, 181–182
Foreign trade promoted by refugees, 234, 240, 245–246, 249–251
Fort Ontario, see Oswego
Fortune, 375, 376, 377, 378
Foster home adjustment, 205, 208, 219–221
France, 4, 13, 14, 23, 25, 29, 30, 31, 180, 207, 210, 301, 342; refugees in, 207, 209, 213, 214
France-Amérique, 182
Franck, James, 323, 432, 433, 436
Franco, Francisco, 23, 44, 75
Frank, Bruno, 342
Frank, Leonhard, 342
Fredman, J. George, 196
Free Press, 182
French refugees, xvi, 36, 37, 43, 69, 75, 78, 177, 195, 242, 243, 244, 259–260, 324–326, 331, 341, 343, 399
Freund, Robert, 246
Friedrich, C. J., 201, 290
Friendship House, 107
Frisch, O., 203
Fry, Varian, 333, 334, 336, 341, 344

Garris, John, 346
German-American Jews, 389
German Christian refugees, 5–6, 8, 9, 13
German education, 55, 61
German immigrants, 36, 369, 370, 388
German Jews, 6–7, 389; persecution of, 4–10, 13–14, 206–208
German language, 167
German medical schools, 260, 262, 269
German propaganda, xi, 48, 50, 88, 371
German refugees, xvii, 36, 37, 43, 44, 50, 69, 70–72, 78, 128, 129, 145, 158, 161, 172, 177,
179, 192, 195, 231, 242, 244, 259–260, 284, 298, 301, 331, 343, 389, 402
German universities, 300
Germany, 22, 23, 25, 26, 27, 28, 29, 30, 31, 35, 47, 53, 60, 70, 71, 72, 170, 176, 201, 203, 204, 206–208, 209, 210, 300, 327, 360
Gessner, Adrienne, 352
Gestapo, 51
Giedion, Siegfried, 367
Gimbel's, 373
Ginsberg, Marie, 287, 335
Gleit, Maria, 336
Goddard College, 111
Goldscheider-Everlast Ceramics Works, 245
Goldschmidt, Jacob, 376
Good Neighbor Committee, 107
Gould, Leslie, 379
Government officials, 52
Graf, Herbert, 352
Great Britain, 12, 14, 22, 30, 35, 69, 301, 304, 322, 398–399
Great Falls, Montana, 387
Greater New York Federation of Churches, 98, 107
Greece, 3, 23, 25, 29, 30, 35
Greek Catholics, 186, 193
Greek refugees, 36, 37, 399
Greenleigh, Arthur, 118
Gropius, Ise, 59
Gropius, Walter, 367, 368, 433
Grossmann, Kurt R., 32
Guide to Interviewers and Suggested Topics for the Interview, xx, 420–421
Gumpert, Martin, 86, 147, 386

Haber, Fritz, 301
Hadassah, 13
Hahn, Otto, 202, 203
Hakoah, 179
Hanson, Earl P., 400
Harc, 182
Harrisburg, Pennsylvania, 387
Harrison, Earl G., 27, 70
Hartford, Connecticut, 80, 381, 386
Hartshorne, Edward Yarnall, Jr., 300
Harvard Committee to Aid Refugees, 31, 114–115
Harvard Law Review, 268, 294, 364, 366
Harvard University, 201
Hasenclever, Walter, 333
Haverford, Pennsylvania, 319
Health insurance, 63, 282
Hearn's, 373
Hebrew Sheltering and Immigrant Aid Society, xii, 13, 94, 99, 399
"Hebrew" immigrants, 33, 34
Hegemann, Werner, 367
Heiden, Konrad, 344
Heilberg, Freda, 125
Heinemann, D. N., 376
Hellin, F. P., 201
Hellmer, Kurt, 352
Help and Reconstruction, 179–180
Hemingway, Ernest, 50

Henderson, Harry, 325
Henry Street Settlement, 362
"Hidden money," 378, 381, 382
Hidden Valley Ranch, California, 111
High Commissioner of the League of Nations, 4, 36, 44
Hillel Foundation, 115
Hitler, Adolf, 1, 22, 44, 62, 203
Hoehler, Fred K., 402
Hollywood, 338, 342, 353, 374
Home ownership, 158, 160, 283, 380
Homolka, Oskar, 351
Hoover, John Edgar, 194
Hospites, 112
Hostovsky, Egon, 344
Housewives, 130, 133–134, 135, 137, 160, 169
Houston, Texas, 80, 387
Hudson, Mrs. Jane, 339
Huguenots, 1
Hull, Cordell, 334
Hungarian refugees, 36, 37, 69, 74, 78, 145, 158, 161, 177, 242, 259, 260, 284, 331, 343
Hungary, 13, 23, 25, 29, 35, 74
Hutchinson, E. P., 81

Ignotus, Hugo, 343
Illinois, 77, 78, 251, 259, 278, 279
Immigrant colonies, 157
Immigrant dossier, 17, 31
Immigrants, 2; characteristics of, 37–46; total number admitted, 20–21; intellectual type, 119, 120, 395–396; prejudice against, 369–371
Immigrants' Victory Council, 175, 180
Immigration Act of 1917, 15, 17
Immigration Act of 1924, 15–17, 21, 37, 39
Immigration, amount of, 20; economic gains of, 394–395; graph, 19; net, 20, 21; wartime regulation of, 17–20
Immigration laws and procedure, 15–21, 28, 30–32, 209
Immigration quota, 30; admissions, 204, 205, 208–209, 210; fulfillment, 20, 21, 29; regulations, 15–17, 30, 31; unblocked, 31–32, 114; unused, 20, 21, 28
Immigration restriction, 15–16, 404; attitude toward, 388, 396, 404
Immigration statistics by Europe as last place of permanent residence, 38, 39, 40, 257, 352, by "races or peoples," 33–34, 38, 39, 40, 257, 352
Immigration visas, 16–18, 26, 27, 28, 30, 31, 261
Income, source of, 137–140
Indiana, 251
Indianapolis, Indiana, 80, 237, 381, 386
Individual, respect for the, in the U.S., 54, 61–62
Institut de Droit International, 2
Institute for Advanced Study, 318
Institute of Fine Arts of New York University, 318
Institute of International Education, 110, 114, 303, 329, 339

Institute of Social Research, 317
Intention to return, 69–76, 189, 326, 327, 393, 396, 397
Intercollegiate Committee to Aid Student Refugees, 115
Interdepartmental Visa Committee, 17–18
Intergovernmental Committee on Refugees, 4, 11, 12, 403
Intermarriage, 164–166, 187, 283
Internal migration, 79–80, 81
Internal Revenue Code Act of 1936, 378, 379
International banking, 378
International Institutes, xiii, xv, 108
International Jewelry Workers' Union, 243
International Migration Service, 32, 108
International Red Cross, 12, 145
International Refugee Organization, 403
International Relief Association, 113
International Rescue and Relief Committee, Inc., 13, 32, 113–114, 409
International Student Service, 31, 114, 115
Internship, 269
Interviews, xx, xxi
Iranian Institute and School of Asiatic Studies, 318
Irish immigrants, 36, 369, 370
Italian immigrants, 36, 193, 389
Italian Jewish Club, 176
Italian refugees, xvi, 36, 37, 50, 69, 74–75, 78, 158, 161, 172, 177, 192, 242, 259–260, 331, 341, 343
Italy, 14, 22, 23, 25, 29, 35, 74–75, 203, 204, 301; religious tolerance in, 64, 74

Jackson, Justice Robert H., 298
Jacob, Rabbi Ernest I., 73
Janiszewski, T., 202
Jersey City, New Jersey, 80
Jewelers, 243–244, 249
Jewish Agricultural Society, xii, 112–113, 251, 252, 409
Jewish Club of 1933, 176
Jewish Colonization Association, 251
Jewish community, 56, 171, 178
Jewish congregation, 173, 177–178, 179, 181, 355–356
Jewish Family Welfare Society of Brooklyn, 97
Jewish Labor Committee, 13, 113, 409
Jewish organizations, 171, 172, 173, 176, 177
Jewish philanthropy, 95, 96
Jewish refugees, xi, xvi, 33–37, 42, 43, 44, 68, 69, 70, 74, 78, 128–129, 130, 145, 158, 161, 170, 171, 177, 186, 192, 193, 233–234, 251, 259, 260, 261, 278, 301, 331, 333, 343, 388, 389, 393, 398, 399, 401, 402
Jewish Social Service Association of New York, 97
Jewish Theological Seminary, 355
Jewish Way, 70, 182, 184
Jews, American, 188, 196, 197, 389–390
Job-finding, 68, 69, 102–103, 117, 121–122
Johnson, Alvin, 109, 303, 317
Joint Anti-Fascist Refugee Committee, 113

Joint Consultative Council, 208
Josephs, Ray, 400, 401

Kafka, Hans, 353
Kahler, Erich, 344
Kalamazoo, Michigan, 386
Kansas City, 80, 386
Karlweiss, Oscar, 351
Karski, Jan, 73
Kempner, Robert M. W., 32, 298
Kesser, Hermann, 341
Keun, Irmgard, 333
Kirchwey, Freda, 371
Kisling, Moise, 324, 325, 333
Knickerbocker, Cholly, 376
Know-Nothing Movement, 370
Kober, Adolf, 178
Kohs, Samuel C., 196, 197
Kolb, Annette, 336
Kotschnig, Walter M., 257, 288, 307
Kozmian, Henryk K., 365
Kracauer, Siegfried, 333
Krautheimer, Richard, 307
Krenek, Ernst, 346
Ku-Klux Klan, 370, 371
Kulischer, Eugene M., 402
Kulukundis, Nikolas, 376
Kummer, Gertrude, 1

Lamm, Hans, 194
Landowska, Wanda, 346
Landsmannschaften, 173, 176, 181, 187
Language, 345, 351; difficulty, 88–91, 265,
    306; spoken in the home, 167; see also
    English language
Lania, Leo, 341
Larned, Ruth, 32
Latin America, 14, 399–401
Latvia, 23, 25, 29
Latvian displaced persons, 402
Lawrence, Massachusetts, 386
Lawyers, 134, 136, 178, 287–299; organiza-
    tions of, 178, 299; services for, 111–112,
    291
Lawyer Retraining Program, xiv
Lebanon, Connecticut, 252
Legal absorption of refugees, 392
League of Nations, 3–4, 11, 36, 44
League of Women Voters, 61
Léger, Fernand, 324
Lehmann, Lotte, 346, 433
Leiper, Henry Smith, 75, 76, 374
Lestchinsky, Jacob, 37
Levin, Meyer, 241
Lewis, Sinclair, 46, 50
Lewisohn, Ludwig, 342
Liberty, 241
Librarians, 112, 345, 362–364
Libraries, American, 55
Life, 372, 376
Life stories, xx, 420–421
Likely-to-become-a-public-charge clause, 17
Lindsay, Denver, 336
Lipchitz, Jacques, 324, 333

L'Italia Libera, 182
Lithuania, 23, 25, 29, 35
Lithuanian refugees, 36, 37, 195, 402
Living conditions here compared to Europe,
    87–88, 168–170
Loans to refugees, 103, 104, 235, 361
Location bureaus, 145, 181, 183
Locum tenens, 273, 280
London, England, 244, 353
London, Jack, 50
London Spectator, 399
Long, Breckinridge, 28
Look, 372
Lord & Taylor, 339, 373
Los Angeles, California, 80, 172, 176, 192,
    381, 386
Louisville, Kentucky, 80
Lowe, Adolf, 48
Loyalty of refugees, 189, 195, 383, 393
Ludwig, Emil, 344, 433
Lussu, Emilio, 341
Luxembourg Jewish Information Office, 176
Luxembourgeois, 177

Maccabees, 179
Macy, R. H. & Co., 373
Madison, Wisconsin, 387
Maeterlinck, Maurice, 60, 339, 344, 432, 433
Maillol, Aristide, 324
Maladjustment, refugee, 101, 148–155, 221,
    222, 310
Malin, Patrick M., 2
Malnutrition, 215, 216, 275–276
Mankato, Minnesota, 387
Mann, Erika, 348, 434
Mann, Heinrich, 334, 342, 434
Mann, Ruth Z., 147
Mann, Thomas, 5, 335, 344, 432, 434
Manufacturers, see Businessmen
Marcu, Valeriu, 342
Marion, Indiana, 386
Maritain, Jacques, 54, 64, 120, 434
Massachusetts, 77, 78, 93, 251, 252, 259, 267,
    271, 278, 279
Massachusetts Medical Society, 271
Mashgihim, 356, 359–360
Masonic Order, 171
Masson, André, 324, 326, 333
Mathematical Reviews, 322
Mathis, Emile, 377
Matisee, Henri, 324, 326
Maurois, André, 344, 434
McDonald, James G., 9, 36, 44
McNutt, Paul V., 120–121, 272
Medical Economics, 257
Medical licensing, by endorsement, 278; ex-
    amination, 265–266
Medical society membership, 271
Medical practice, European vs. American,
    280, 282–283
Medical scientists, 262, 276
Mehring, Walter, 341, 344
Meitner, Luise, 203
Memphis, Tennessee, 80

Mendelsohn, Eric, 367
Mendizabal, Alfredo, 400
Menial jobs, 123–126, 277, 288, 296
Method of Study, xiv–xxi
Metropolitan Museum, 332
Mexico, 4, 35, 113, 342, 399–400; College of, 399–400
Meyer, André, 377
Meyer, Dr. Heinz C., 274–276
Michigan, 77, 78, 251
Middletown, New York, 252
Mies van der Rohe, Ludwig, 367, 434
Migration services, 108–109
Milhaud, Darius, 346, 434
Military service, 177, 196–197, 228–229
Military Intelligence, 17
Milwaukee, Wisconsin, 80, 237, 374, 381, 387, 388
Minneapolis, Minnesota, 80
Missouri, 251
Mobility, xx; of Americans, 58, 63
Mohel, 356
Moholy-Nagy, L., 367
Molnar, Ferenc, 344, 434
Mondrian, Piet, 324
Morse, S. F. B., 370
Motion pictures, 91; ideas about America derived from, 48–49, 56; refugees in, 353
Muller, Henry E., 32
Museum of Modern Art, 324, 326, 330
Music and fine arts in America, 48, 55–56, 349, 350
Music publishers, 348
Musicians, 134, 136, 137, 138, 330, 346–351
Musicians Emergency Fund, Inc., 113, 348
Mussolini, Benito, 4, 44, 74, 203
Mutual aid organizations, 172, 173, 175, 179–180

Nansen passport, 3, 31
Nashville, Tennessee, 80
Nasza Trybuna, 182
National Board of Medical Examiners, 267, 269, 278
National Catholic Welfare Conference, 13
National Committee for Refugee Musicians, xiv, 113, 346, 347, 348, 350
National Committee for Resettlement of Foreign Physicians, xiii–xiv, xix, xx, 111, 258, 274, 276–277, 279, 409
National Committee on Refugee Jewish Ministers, xiv, 113, 354–355
National Conference of Christians and Jews, 109, 343, 371
National Conference of Jewish Social Welfare, 208
National Co-ordinating Committee, xx, 96–97, 110, 240
National Council of Jewish Women, xii, 94, 99, 107, 108, 180, 208, 409
National Federation of Settlements, 112
National Lutheran Council, 98
National Non-Sectarian Committee, 115, 209, 210

National Organization of Polish Jews, 172, 176, 409
National Planning Association, 400, 402
National Refugee Service, xii, xx, 13, 27, 96, 97, 98, 99–100, 104, 105, 106, 108, 109, 110, 111, 112, 113, 148, 180, 208, 235, 252, 258, 276, 296, 297, 348, 350, 354, 355, 357, 359, 361, 387
National Research Council, 272
Nationalism, 1, 392, 393; American, 370–371
Native Americanism, 370–371
Natonek, Hans, 102, 336
Naturalization, 156, 192, 285, 392; of aliens in the armed forces, 191; of refugees, 192, 193; statistics, 190–191; see also Citizenship
Naval Intelligence, 17
Navy Medical Corps, 273
Navy Ordnance Department, 322
Navy V-12 program, 313
Nazism, xvi, 1, 4–8, 22, 44, 61, 68, 71, 88, 206, 391
Negroes, 63, 216, 370, 371
Netherlands, 14, 23, 25, 29, 30, 35, 75, 241, 243, 301, 304, 342; religious tolerance in, 64, 65–67, 75–76
Netherlands Jewish Society, 176, 409
Netherlands refugees, 36, 37, 69, 75–76, 78, 145, 161, 192, 242, 244, 327, 331, 341
Neugebauer, Otto, 322, 434, 439
New Hampshire, 251
New Haven, Connecticut, 80, 381
New Haven Council of Social Agencies, xiii, 406
New Jersey, 77, 78, 251, 252, 278
New Orleans, Louisiana, 80
New products and processes introduced by refugees, 241, 246–248, 398, 399
New School for Social Research, 48, 109, 110, 303, 304, 317, 409
New World Club, 112, 171, 172, 173, 176, 180, 410
New York Adult Education Council, 108
New York Bureau of Labor Statistics, 370
New York City, xiii, xvi, 50, 77, 78, 79, 80, 81, 82, 89, 94, 96, 104, 106, 107, 156, 157, 169, 172, 173, 175, 176, 177, 179, 192, 215, 236, 237, 241, 242, 243, 244, 259, 283, 328, 331, 343, 348, 362, 381–382, 386, 387, 388; Port of, 50, 78; real estate business in, 381–382; schools of, 206, 226, 227
New York Journal-American, 379
New York Post, 33, 377
New York School of Social Work, 112
New York State, 77, 78, 251, 252, 259, 267, 268, 274, 278, 279, 324; Board of Medical Examiners, 278; Department of Health, 164
New York Times, 33, 70, 145, 272, 273, 351, 380, 381
New York University, 339; Institute of Fine Arts, 318
New York World-Telegram, 379
Newark, New Jersey, 80, 381

News of the YIVO, 317
New Yorker, 125, 325, 326
Newspapers, American, 59, 62–63, 91, 168, 356
Niles' Weekly Register, 370
Nobel Prize winners, 6–7, 44, 322, 432
"Non-Aryans," xi, 5–6, 7, 202–203
Nonimmigrants, 2, 16, 24–27
Nonquota immigrants, 16
Nonresident aliens, 378–380
North Carolina, 251
Norway, 12, 23, 25, 29, 35, 76, 304
Norwegian refugees, 36, 37, 69
Notgemeinschaft Deutscher Wissenschaftler im Ausland, 305
Novotna, Jarmila, 347, 434
Nuremberg laws, 7, 9, 203
Nurses, 136, 137
Nussbaum, Dr. Schymen, 274
Nye, Senator, 375

Oakland, California, 80, 386
Oberlaender Trust, 110, 303, 304, 329
Occupational adjustment, 128–142, 235
Occupational progression, 129–130
Occupations, change of, 120–121, 125; distribution of, 39–42, 128, 140; in Europe compared to the United States, 131–136
O'Connor, Tom, 371
Odell, Clarence B., 9
Office of Censorship, 298
Office of Price Administration, 298
Office of Procurement and Assignment Service of the War Manpower Commission, 258, 273–274, 279
Office of Strategic Services, 201, 298, 343
Office of War Information, 202, 298, 341, 343
Ogden, Rollo, 370
Ohio, 77, 78, 259, 270–271, 278, 279
Oklahoma City, Oklahoma, 387
Old, *see* Aged
Olson, Charles, 371
Omaha, Nebraska, 80
Opera, 56, 346, 347
Organization for Protection of the Health of the Jews, 213
Oswego Emergency Shelter, 12, 27, 32–33, 108

Palestine, 9, 11, 12, 14, 37, 70, 241, 251, 389, 392, 404
Parent-teacher associations, 107
Paris, France, 324, 325, 326, 353
Participant observation, xxi
Passaic, New Jersey, 80
Paterson, New Jersey, 80, 386
Pauli, Hertha, 336
Peierls, Rudulf, 203
Pelc, Anton, 327
P.E.N., American Center of, 110, 339
Pennsylvania, 77, 78, 251, 279
Pennsylvania Academy of Fine Arts, 332
Peoria, Illinois, 223, 237, 386
Perry, Donald R., 81

Persecution, 1, 2, 34, 39, 145, 147, 188, 206–207, 212–214, 222; effects of, 84, 85; migration to escape, 43, 261
Petschek, Hans, 376
Philadelphia, Pennsylvania, xii, xvi, 80, 81, 167, 236, 237, 381, 387
Philippine Islands, 15–16, 28
Philips, Anton, 376
Physicians, xix–xx, 78, 79, 134, 136, 178, 257–286, 374–375, 388; attitude of American, 257, 262–264, 265, 271, 276, 394; attitude of refugee, 262, 263–265; characteristics of, 259–262; committees assisting, 111, 276–277; complaints against, 262–263; difficulties of, 261–273; discrimination against, 267–273; earnings of, 280–281; in private practice, 261, 280, 285; in rural communities, 274–276, 277; number of, 257–258; nationality background of, 259–260; occupational adjustment of, 277–283; restrictive measures against, 267–273; scientific contributions of, 285–286; shortage of American, 272–273; social adjustment of, 283–286; specialists among, 261, 278, 279
Physicians' questionnaire, xi, xix–xx, 258, 425–429; returns by states and number of communities, 413
Picasso, Pablo Ruiz, 324
Pick, Robert, 336
Piscator, Erwin, 351, 352, 434
Pitigliani, Fausto R., 201
Pittsburgh, Pennsylvania, 80, 237, 381, 387
Pittsburgh Better Business Bureau, 374
PM, 33, 371, 376
Poland, 13–14, 23, 25, 29, 35, 73, 204, 210, 285
Poland Fights, 182
Polgar, Alfred, 344
Polish immigrants, 64, 388, 389
Polish refugees, xvi, 36, 37, 43, 69, 73–74, 78, 129, 145, 149, 158, 161, 172, 177, 178, 195, 231, 242, 259–260, 284–285, 298, 325, 327, 331, 341, 343, 355, 365–366, 389, 399, 402
Political absorption of refugees, 392–393
Political activities and views of refugees, 179, 182, 183, 184–185, 393
Political refugees, 1, 5, 31–32, 43, 95, 113–114, 195
Polonia Technica, 365
Populations, exchange of, 3
Porter, Sylvia F., 243, 376, 377
Portland, Oregon, 80, 381
Portugal, 22, 35
Post, Emily, 376
Pour la Victoire, 182
Pratt Institute, 363
Preminger, Otto, 352
Prescott, Orville, 336
President's Advisory Committee on Political Refugees, 31–32, 114
Pringle, Henry F., 377

Professional organizations among refugees, 172, 173, 178, 181
Professional workers, 39, 40, 41, 42, 69, 78, 79, 86–87, 89, 92, 94, 98, 121, 122, 128, 129, 131, 132, 133, 134, 135, 137, 138, 139, 155, 157, 158, 161, 168, 169, 289, 360, 361, 363; services for, 109–113
Professors and teachers, 134, 136, 300–320
Protestant refugees, xvii, 5, 36, 186, 193, 260
Providence, Rhode Island, 80, 381
Psychological warfare, 201–202, 343
Puritans, 1
Putnam, Tracy J., 268
Puttkammer, Ernest W., 268

Quaker hostels and seminars, 105, 106, 111
Quaker refugee camps, 213, 214
Quakers, 1, 95, 97–98, 118; see also American Friends Service Committee
Questionnaire forms, 414–417, 422–423, 424–431
Questionnaire returns, xi, xiv, xvi, 77–78; by states and number of communities, 413
Questionnaires, xiii, xx, 47, 53; distribution of, xv–xvi
Quota rule of colleges, 65
Quotas, see Immigration quotas

Rabbinical Assembly of America, 355
Rabbis, 354, 355, 356, 358
Race persecution, 1, 2, 4
Race prejudice, 63–64, 370, 371
Racism, 202, 203
Radio, 91, 348, 383
Railroad securities, 378
Rauschning, Hermann, 5
Ready, John C., 373
Real estate speculation, 244, 380–383
Refugee, defined, 2–3
Refugee camps, 213–214, 216
"Refugee mentality," 393
Refugee movement, xi, 1, 8–14; effects of, in the United States, 391–396, in other countries, 397–401
Refugee organizations, xiii, xv, xxi, 171–181, 185, 186, 187–188, 195
Refugee press, xiv, 181–185
Refugee problem, international aspects of, 401–404; solution of, 391–397
Refugee Relief Trustees, Inc., 27, 151
Refugee Scholar Fund, 110, 115, 329, 339
Refugee-service organizations, xi, xiii, xv, 118, 140, 162, 175, 179–180, 235, 329, 330, 336, 390, 393; appraisal of program, 117–118; general, 95–98; opinions of refugees regarding, 115–117; special, 95, 109–115; types of service, 98–109
Refugee veterans' organizations, 176–177
Refugees: admission of, facilitated, 30–32; as citizens, 189–203; barriers to admission of, 11; characteristics of, xi, xvi, 37–46; complaints and allegations against, 371–386; compared with earlier immigrants, 2–3, 39–42, 45–46, 84, 156–157, 160, 164,

166, 170, 176, 181, 283, 385; compared with refugees in other countries, 392–401; contributions by, 298–299, 343, 344, 349, 351, 367–368, 390, 391, 396–397; departing, 23–24, 26; desire to become assimilated, 161–163, 185, 187; difficulties or problems of, 88–89, 120, 121, 171; discrimination against, 67–69; distinguished, 432–440; educational background of, 44, 45, 166; employment status, 128, 133, 134, 136–137; estimated number of, in the United States, xvi, 21–27, 28, in other countries, 4, 14, 398, 399, 400, 401; geographic distribution of, xv, xix, 77–83, 331, 343, 387; gratefulness of, 56, 69, 72, 73, 75, 116, 384–385; intention to remain, 69–76, 189, 326, 327, 393, 396, 397; language facility of, 166; listed in American Men of Science, 45, 435–440; listed in Who's Who in America, 45, 432–435; lists of, xv; loyalty of, 189, 195, 383, 393; maladjustment of, 101, 148–155, 221, 222, 310; marital status of, 38, 39, 160–161; membership in American organizations, 185–188, 284; middle-aged, 143–144, 168, 173; nationality background of, xvii, xviii, 22, 23, 30, 37, 242, 244; nonimmigrant, 24–27; occupational distribution of, xvii, xviii, 39–42; old, 100, 143, 149–151, 167–168, 173; participation in community life, 185–188; political, 1, 5, 31–32, 43, 95, 113–114, 195; proportion of, in the population, 387; psychological problem of, 170; recreation of, 173, 174, 179; religious affiliations of, xvii; sex distribution of, xviii, xix; urban background of, 45, 157, 171; wages received, 137–139; wealthy, 157, 375–380; with whom they associate, 160–164, 283; where they live, 156–160, 169; young, 30–31, 43–44, 69, 72, 73, 74, 91, 108, 115, 147–148, 153–155, 187, 204–232, 395; see also Cultural, Economic, Occupational, and Social Adjustment
Reinhardt, Max, 352, 434
Relatives of refugees, assistance by, 87, 91, 99, 139, 140, 393
Religious functionaries, 354–360
Religious segregation, 63–69
Remarque, Erich Maria, 336, 344, 434
Renoir, Jean, 353
République Française, 54, 182, 341
Rescue and relief efforts, 11–13, 108, 113, 211
Resettlement, 80, 81–83, 96, 104–105, 116, 117, 355, 388, 403–404
Rethymnis, Constantin, 376
Retraining, 103–104, 112, 116, 117, 166, 240, 272, 288, 290, 291, 292, 293, 296, 360, 361, 362
Richmond, Virginia, 80
Riesman, David, Jr., 290
Robison, Sophia M., 234, 240
Rochester, New York, 80, 223, 381, 386
Rockefeller Foundation, 304
Romains, Jules, 339, 344, 434

"Roof organizations" or federations, 173, 179, 180
Roosevelt, Eleanor, 61, 210
Roosevelt, Franklin D., 8, 12, 114, 123, 203, 400
Rosen, Joseph A., 400
Rosenwald Fellowships, 339
Roster of Alien Specialized Personnel, 201
Rothschild, Baron Edouard de, 377
Royal College of Physicians in the British Empire, 269
Rubin, Ernest, 38
Rubin, Laura G., 355
Rules for refugees, 385–386
Rumania, 23, 25, 29, 35
Rumanian refugees, 36, 37, 69, 145, 192, 327, 342
Rural communities, 78, 79, 251, 252, 253, 274–276, 277
Russia, Soviet, 2, 22, 23, 25, 29, 35, 73, 74, 251, 402
Russian refugees, 3, 37, 43, 69, 75, 78, 158, 161, 172, 177, 178, 192, 242, 244, 259–260, 298, 325, 331, 355, 389, 402
Ruthenian displaced persons, 402

Saarlander refugees, 3
Saenger, Gerhart, 126
Saint Exupéry, Antoine de, 342, 433
Saint Louis, Missouri, 80, 237, 381, 386
Saint Paul, Minnesota, 80, 386
Saint Petersburg, Florida, 386
Salganik, Morris, 355
Salonika, Greece, 244
Sample, Study, xvii–xix
San Antonio, Texas, 80, 387
San Francisco, California, 80, 192, 381
San Francisco Argonaut, 332
Santa Barbara, California, 386
Saturday Review of Literature, 346
Scandinavian immigrants, 369, 370
Schawinsky, Alexander, 367
Schochtim, 356, 359
Scholars, 300–318, 398–399; assistance to, 109–111, 301–305
School of Applied Social Sciences of Western Reserve University, 112
School of Social Administration of University of Chicago, 112
Schools, American, 55, 66, 67, 166, 167
Schnabel, Artur, 346, 434
Schrecker, Paul, 344
Schwarz, Alfred, 203
Scientists, 320–323; aid in the war effort, 201–203
Scotch-Irish, 1
Scranton, Pennsylvania, 80, 387
Scribes, 356
Seattle, Washington, 80, 381, 387
Second War Powers Act, 191
Secondary school teachers, 316, 318–320
Selective Service, 284; Report of the Director of, 196–197
Selective Training and Service Act, 196

Selfhelp of Emigres from Central Europe, Inc., xiii, 175, 179–180, 305, 410
Selver-Fraenkel Report, 297
Semiskilled workers, 128, 129, 131, 132, 133, 134, 135, 136, 137, 138, 139, 158, 161, 168, 170
Separation of families, see Family
Serkin, Rudolf, 346, 434
Settlement houses, 362
Sex ratio, 37, 38
Shamus, 356
Shanghai, China, 11, 14, 180
Shaw, Art, 325
Shelton, Connecticut, 373
Shepherd, Russell M., 202
Sickness, 151–153; insurance, 63, 282
Siebold, Janet, 401
Siegel, Mary, 99
Simon, Franz Eugen, 203
Simpson, Sir John Hope, 392, 399
Sinclair, Upton, 49–50
Skill, transferability of, 131, 133, 134, 234–235, 257, 266, 287–288, 315, 321, 330, 331, 335, 345, 360, 362, 394
Skilled workers, 40, 41–42, 128, 129, 131, 132, 133, 134, 136, 137, 138, 139, 161, 168, 169
Slang, American, 90, 167
Smyth, Henry DeWolf, 323
Social adjustment, 91–92, 116–117, 156–170, 387, 395–396; factors in, 143–155; services promoting, 105–108; see also Cultural adjustment
Social and cultural absorption, 395–397
Social case work, 94, 101, 102
Social classes, 54–55
Social insurance, 63, 101–102
Social and cultural organizations, 172, 173, 174
Social status, 126, 168–170, 395; compensation for loss of, 384
Social workers, 101–102, 112, 296, 345, 360–362
Socio-economic ranking of occupations, 129–130
Sollner, Karl, 202
Sorrell, Walter, 336
Sosua, Dominican Republic, 400
South America, 35, 113, 250–251, 404
South Bend, Indiana, 80
Spain, 4, 14, 22, 23, 25, 29, 30, 35, 113, 180, 214
Spanish-Portuguese Jews, 1
Spanish refugees, 4, 36, 75, 113, 210, 214, 244, 341, 399, 400, 402
Speier, Hans, 202
Speiser, Reuben, 38
Spiro, Eugen, 327
Sponsors Committee, vii–viii
Sports organizations, 179
Springfield, Illinois, 386
Springfield, Massachusetts, 80
SS St. Louis, 10, 11
State medical board examination, 265–266

State medical examining boards, 267–271, 272
Statelessness, 1, 2, 3–4, 190, 402
Stereotype thinking, 372
Stern Brothers, 373
Stewart, Marianne, 352
Stillwater, Minnesota, 111
Stock market speculation, 244, 377–380
Stockton, California, 386
Strunsky, Sheba, 32
Stuart, Graham, 18
Student Service of America, 114
Students, 16, 31, 58, 114–115, 130, 132, 135, 161, 169
Studies in Philosophy and Social Science, 317
Study Committee, vi, xii, xiii, xiv, xx, xxi, 36
Study forms, 414–431
Study staff, vi
Sudetenland, 9
Sully, Michael, 400
Survey of Foreign Experts, 201
Sweden, 12, 14, 22, 35, 203, 342, 403
Swiss, 242, 244
Switzerland, 12, 13, 14, 22, 30, 35, 70, 180, 260, 301, 342, 403
Syracuse, New York, 80
Szilard, L., 323
Szyk, Arthur, 327

Tacoma, Washington, 387
Talmudist, 356
Tanguy, Ives, 324, 326
Tartakower, Arieh, 32
Taylor, Henry J., 379
Tchelitchew, 326
Teller, E., 323
T. G. Masaryk Society, 176, 410
Thomas, Wilbur K., 303
Thompson, Dorothy, 61
Thompson, Joseph P., 370
Toledo, Ohio, 80
Toms River, New Jersey, 252
Toscanini, Arturo, 346, 435
Tourists, American, 48, 49
Trading Estates, 398
Translations, 335–336
Trenton, New Jersey, 80, 237, 245
Truman, Harry S., 33, 210, 404
Tulsa, Oklahoma, 387
Turkey, 3, 12
Turnbull, R. H., 332
Twin Editions, 246
Tygodnik Polski, 182

Ukrainian displaced persons, 402
Ukrainian nationalists, 195
Unaccompanied children, 205, 208–221, 224, 226, 230
Unblocking the quotas, 31–32, 114
Undset, Sigrid, 344, 432, 435
Unemployment, 136–137
Union of Orthodox Rabbis, 355
Unions, labor, 122, 237, 348

Unitarian Service Committee, 13, 32, 95, 98, 114
United Diamond Manufacturers Association, 243
United Nations, 403
United Nations Relief and Rehabilitation Administration, 298, 402–403
United Service for New Americans, Inc., xii
United States Bureau of Internal Revenue, 379
United States Bureau of the Census, 40, 42, 79, 128, 129
United States Chemical Warfare Service, 322
United States Committee for the Care of European Children, xiii, 30, 115, 209–210, 410
United States Committee of the International Student Service, 114
United States Department of Justice, 17, 28, 81, 114, 194, 371
United States Department of Labor, 139
United States Department of State, 17, 28, 30, 31, 32, 114
United States Employment Service, 122
United States Explosives Advisory Committee, 323
United States Government Survey of Foreign Experts, 201
United States Immigration and Naturalization Service, xiv, xvii, 17, 20, 21, 22, 24, 26, 27, 28, 30, 33, 37, 38, 40, 41, 81, 93, 190, 193, 194, 273
United States Immigration Commission, xi
United States Treasury Department, 298, 377–378, 382
University in Exile, 109–110, 337
University of Chicago, Graduate Library School, 363; School of Social Administration, 112
University of Kansas City, 344
University of Minnesota, 202
Unrepatriables, 402
Unskilled workers, 119, 128, 129, 131, 132, 133, 134, 135, 136, 137, 138, 139, 161, 168, 170
Uruguay, 400, 401
Utica, New York, 386

Vancouver Sun, 399
Vatican, 12
Verich, 351
Vichy government, 207
Vicksburg, Mississippi, 386
Viertel, Berthold, 344, 352
Vinalhaven, Maine, 274
Vineland, New Jersey, 80, 252
Virgin Islands, 259
Virginia, 251, 274
Visa, *see* Immigration visas
Vocational guidance, 117
Vocational Service for Juniors, 115
von Opel, Fritz, 376
von Unruh, Fritz, 333, 344
Voskovec, 351

Wagner, Martin, 367
Wagner-Rogers Bill, 30, 209
Waldrop, Frank C., 375
Walker, Delos, 373
Walter, Bruno, 346
War bonds, purchase of, 199, 200
War criminals excluded, 19
War effort, contributions to the, 175, 195, 199–203, 244, 248–249, 284, 313, 322–323, 343
War industries, 122–123, 193, 388, 394
War Refugee Board, 12–13, 32–33
War Relocation Authority, 32
Warren, George L., 32
Warsaw, Poland, 14
Washington, D.C., 80, 381, 387
Washington Times-Herald, 375
Waverly, Iowa, 240
Weinberger, Jaromil, 346
Weinreich, Max, 34, 317
Weiss, Ernst, 333
Weisskopf, V. F., 323
Werfel, Franz, 334, 342, 343, 344, 435
Wertheimer, Pierre, 377
Wessel, Bessie B., 164
West Indies, 35
Westchester County, New York, 381, 386
Westgate, Elizabeth, 374
Wheeler, Monroe, 326
Whitney Museum, 328, 330
Whyte, John, 308
Wigner, E., 323
Wilmington, Delaware, 80

Winchell, Walter, 376
Winona, Minnesota, 386
Wittlin, Josef, 343, 344
Wolfe, Thomas, 50
Women, 124–125, 133–136, 137–139, 144–145, 153–154, 160, 162, 168, 173, 192, 193, 280, 281, 283, 331, 364
World Jewish Congress, 13
World War I, 2, 3–4
World War II, 1, 17, 20
World's Fair, 26
Writers, 134, 136, 137, 178, 330, 333–344; American, 48, 49–50, 339–340

Year of arrival, xvii, 185, 186, 231, 261
Yiddish, 37, 341, 356
Yiddish Scientific Institute—YIVO, 317
Yidische Shprakh, 317
Yivo Bleter, 317
Young refugees, *see* Refugees
Young Women's Christian Association, National Board, xii, 108, 109, 209, 374, 410; International Center, 107, 410
Youngstown, Ohio, 387
Youth organizations, 173, 177–178, 179
Yugoslav refugees, 32, 33, 36, 37, 43, 78, 177, 192, 195, 327, 343, 402
Yugoslavia, 23, 25, 29, 35

Zadkine, Ossip, 324, 327
Zionist organizations, 179
Zucker, Paul, 367
Zweig, Stefan, 342, 344, 435

3782

27881

D
809
.U5
C6
1947

Committee for the
Study of Recent
Immigration from
Europe.
Refugees in
America.

DATE DUE

MAR 12 2001

FERNALD LIBRARY
COLBY-SAWYER COLLEGE
NEW LONDON, N.H. 03257

GAYLORD   PRINTED IN U.S.A.

may have looked to genre fiction as the safest bet for a best seller. At any rate, it seems to be more than a chance occurrence. Genre books retain their popularity among the most recent books, as will be seen in chapter 6.

There are also curious sales trends that occur from time to time. Why, for example, were six mysteries at the top of the best-seller list in 1981? Or six books about glamour in 1976 and none in 1977? Almost all of the top-selling science-fiction books were published in 1982, the same year as *E. T.*'s box-office success. Is all this chance, or does one good book lead to another, for the publisher or the reader? The answer is not known. People are asked why they buy particular detergents or vote for particular presidential candidates, but not why they read one book rather than another.

But look also at the *diversity* of best sellers that is shown in the table. Even the most popular genre, historical fiction, is represented by only a small proportion of the books overall, and the other categories account for even less. The books are scattered among many genres and topics, with no one type dominating. The authors, too, show more variety in the subjects they choose than people might think. It is true that some authors write all of their books in the same category. John MacDonald writes mysteries primarily, MacInnes writes spy stories, and Stone and Renault write historical novels. Drury and Knebel stay with American politics. Yet almost as many authors cross categories. Mary Stewart and Michael Crichton write suspense as well as historical fiction. Styron, Fowles, and Jong write historical novels and contemporary dramas; Fowles, in fact, consciously varies his style from one book to the next. Asimov shows he can write a mystery as well as science fiction, and King writes science fiction as well as horror.[4] Even L'Amour abandoned his tales of the Sackett family to write a 12th-century historical adventure. The winner, however, in the Most Varied category is probably Leon Uris with stories of war, spies, and international intrigue, a saga, and a contemporary drama.

An Ocean of Difference

It is interesting that very different books are published depending on which side of the Atlantic the author is from. The British-born authors specialize in historical novels, mysteries, and spy stories, whereas the American authors specialize in historical novels and books about sex:

The Most Frequent Best Sellers

AMERICAN MALE AUTHORS	AMERICAN FEMALE AUTHORS	BRITISH MALE AUTHORS	BRITISH FEMALE AUTHORS
Historical Novels	Sex	Spies	Historical Novels
Sex	Historical Novels and Glamour	War	Mysteries

This means that the categories would be ranked somewhat differently if we look only at the American-born authors. Nevertheless, the books remain fragmented, with each of the categories making up a small portion of the whole. (See table 5.)

There is another difference among the authors, however: American women have no mysteries, spy stories, or tales of horror among the top sellers. The only best-selling science-fiction book by a woman is the novelization of the film *Return of the Jedi* by Joan Vinge. British women write books about war and *American* politics, but American women do not. Their books are drawn largely from five categories: dramas (not included in the table), historical novels, sagas, and books on glamour and sex.

We know that American women also write books in the other genres,[5] but only the British women find theirs becoming best sellers. The problem does not seem to lie with the authors or the readers. Perhaps there are publishing stereotypes about who is expected to write what kind of book: so British women (following in the footsteps of Agatha Christie) are expected to write mysteries, and American women (following Jacqueline Susann) are expected to write about glamour and sex. The British men can follow Ian Fleming. One British mystery writer was advertised as "following in Agatha Christie's English brogues"! Whatever the answer, the problem deserves to be noticed and talked about more. If Caldwell, MacInnes, Holt, and James can make their respective genres into best-selling fiction, then American women writers can, too.

TABLE 5
Books by American-Born Authors[a]

Genre and Topic	PERCENTAGE OF ALL BOOKS IN EACH CATEGORY	
	All American Authors	American Women Authors
Historical Novels	14	21
Sagas	10	19
Mysteries	8	—
Science Fiction	5	2
Horror	4	—
Spy Stories	4	—
International Intrigue	4	—
Books about		
Sex	15	33
American Politics	9	—
Glamour	8	21
Religion	7	7
War	5	—
NUMBER OF BOOKS:	(304)	(58)

[a]Following table 4, books are counted more than once if they fall into more than one category. Drama, suspense, and adventure are excluded. Also excluded are the least frequently occurring categories of short stories, westerns, and books for young readers. The total number of books published by American-born authors is 304, including the books (drama, suspense, etc.) not listed in the table.

Overall, the most popular categories are historical novels; tales of spies and international intrigue; mysteries; sagas; and, books about war, politics, religion, glamour, and sex. These are described more fully in the pages that follow.

Historical Novels

Leading the best sellers in popularity are the historical novels, holding top place from the 1960s to the present. Notice, however, that the accent is on the familiar rather than the distant and exotic. Most of the books are set in England or America during the last 100 years. The time line touches prehistory and the classical era and, with only brief interruptions, settles into the recent past. The "history" between the 1st and the 19th centuries consists largely of the legendary tales of King Arthur. Only two books tell of the 12th century, two of the 14th, and one includes action from the 16th. Michener, of course, is the exception. Michener has his own time lines: five centuries for South Africa, eight for Poland, 12,000 years for Palestine, and even more for Centennial, Colorado. The town's history begins with the formation of the rocks and streams and proceeds through the dinosaurs, age by age, to the present day.

The books are different, nonetheless, in the amount of historical research they offer. Renault is a serious classical scholar and Stone an accredited biographer. In *The French Lieutenant's Woman*, Fowles captures the spirit and thinking of life in Victorian England. In the quotations beginning each chapter and the words of the characters themselves, he shows the clash of the new science with older values and the shifting codes and mores of the time. Vidal supplies a wealth of authentic detail in his historical novels. In *1876* he goes so far as to point out which buildings are under construction in New York and to show the goats grazing in Central Park. In contrast, *Calico Palace* tells little beyond the facts that people hunted for gold in 1849 and that wooden buildings were easily burned down. So, too, the tale of suffering and betrayal in *The Lost Queen* could be set in any century or royal court.

The writers' attitudes toward history are different as well, as the quotations at the end of Chapter 2 show clearly. Renault takes pride in the fact that she has "never knowingly falsified" the historical facts, Styron that he can mix facts and imagination, and Doctorow that he can create the facts that he needs for the novel. Did J. P. Morgan and Henry Ford really meet? "They have now," says Doctorow, pointing to his book. "They have . . . met now."

So let the readers beware if they seek their history from historical novels. Was Lucy Walter secretly married to the king of England? Did Thomas Jefferson really live beyond his means? Is that what Saint Paul was like as a boy? Did all those things really happen? Since each book gives a different mix of fact and fiction, all we can say, echoing Doctorow, is that they have all happened now.

The books are different, too, in their subject matter. Some recount the lives of famous personages: Cicero, Saint Paul, Marie Antoinette, Freud, and Lincoln, to mention a few. Others give a look at little-known people or events: the American slave Nat Turner, the Indian Sepoy Rebellion, the unhappy fate of the sister of King George III. Still others, and the large majority, use characters of the author's own creation to tell the story of a different place and time.

The following list shows the top-selling historical novels, along with the century and locale of their setting.

TOP-SELLING HISTORICAL NOVELS

AUTHOR	TITLE	CENTURY AND LOCALE
Adams, R.	Shardik	Prehistoric times
Auel	The Valley of Horses	Prehistoric times
Bristow	Calico Palace	19th, U.S.
Caldwell	Answer as a Man	Early 20th, U.S.
————	Captains and the Kings	Early 20th, U.S.
————	Ceremony of the Innocent	Early 20th, U.S.
————	Great Lion of God	1st A.D., Rome
————	A Pillar of Iron	1st B.C., Rome
————	Testimony of Two Men	19th–20th, U.S.
Clavell	Shōgun	17th, Japan
————	Tai-Pan	19th, Hong Kong
Crichton, M.	The Great Train Robbery	19th, England
Crichton, R.	The Camerons	20th, Scotland
Delderfield	God Is an Englishman	19th, England
————	Theirs Was the Kingdom	19th, England
Doctorow	Ragtime	Early 20th, U.S.
du Maurier	The House on the Strand	14th/20th, England
Eco	The Name of the Rose	14th, Italy
Eden	The Vines of Yarrabee	19th–20th, Australia
Fast	The Immigrants	Early 20th, U.S.
Follett	The Man from St. Petersburg	20th, England
Fowles	The French Lieutenant's Woman	19th, England
Gann	The Antagonists	1st A.D., Palestine
Goudge	The Child from the Sea	17th, England
Hayden	Voyage: A Novel of 1896	19th–20th, U.S. and at sea
Hill	Hanta Yo	18th–19th, U.S.
Holt	The Queen's Confession	18th, France
Howatch	Cashelmara	19th–20th, Ireland
————	Penmarric	19th–20th, England
Jakes	Love and War	U.S. Civil War
————	North and South	Pre–Civil War
Jong	Fanny	18th, England
Kaye	The Far Pavilions	19th, India
————	Shadow of the Moon	19th, India
Keyes	I, the King	17th, Spain
L'Amour	The Lonesome Gods	19th, U.S.
————	The Walking Drum	12th, Europe/Asia
Lofts	The Lost Queen	18th, England/Denmark

TOP-SELLING HISTORICAL NOVELS—*continued*

AUTHOR	TITLE	CENTURY AND LOCALE
Lord	*Spring Moon*	19th, China
Malamud	*The Fixer*	Early 20th, Russia
Marshall	*Christy*	Early 20th, U.S.
Meyer	*The Seven-Per-Cent Solution*	Early 20th, England and Vienna
————	*The West End Horror*	Early 20th, England
Michener	*Centennial*	Prehistoric times to the present, U.S.
————	*Chesapeake*	16th–20th, U.S.
————	*The Covenant*	15th–20th, S. Africa
————	*Poland*	12th–20th, Poland
————	*The Source*	Prehistoric times to the present, Palestine
Mydans	*Thomas*	12th, England
Portis	*True Grit*	19th, U.S.
Price	*New Moon Rising*	19th, U.S.
Renault	*Fire From Heaven*	4th, B.C., Greece
————	*The Mask of Apollo*	4th, B.C., Greece
————	*The Persian Boy*	4th, B.C., Greece
Santmyer	*". . . And Ladies of the Club"*	19th, U.S.
Seton	*Green Darkness*	16th–20th, England
Solomon	*The Candlesticks and the Cross*	19th–20th, Russia
Stewart, F.	*Century*	19th–20th, Sicily and U.S.
Stewart, M.	*The Crystal Cave*	5th–6th, Legendary England
————	*The Hollow Hills*	5th–6th, Legendary England
————	*The Last Enchantment*	5th–6th, Legendary England
————	*The Wicked Day*	5th–6th, Legendary England
Stone	*The Greek Treasure*	19th, Greece
————	*The Origin*	19th, England
————	*The Passions of the Mind*	19th–20th, Vienna
————	*Those Who Love*	18th, U.S.
Styron	*The Confessions of Nat Turner*	19th, U.S.
Trevanian	*The Summer of Katya*	Early 20th, Spain
Uris	*Trinity*	19th–20th, Ireland
Vidal	*1876*	19th, U.S.
————	*Burr*	18th, U.S.
————	*Creation*	5th B.C., Persia
————	*Julian*	4th A.D., Rome
————	*Lincoln*	19th, U.S.
West, J.	*Except for Me and Thee*	19th, U.S.
————	*The Massacre at Fall Creek*	19th, U.S.
White	*The Book of Merlyn*	5th–6th, Legendary England
Wilder, T.	*The Eighth Day*	Early 20th, U.S.

Stories of Spies and International Intrigue

A spy story is a novel of suspense or adventure which happens to involve espionage between nations, whether between the governments themselves or subgovernment groups. The stakes are high, engaging the fate of entire peoples. The scale is global. The resources are vast—with currency, jewels, military forces, and the latest technology crossing and recrossing national boundaries. It is no wonder, then, that authors deciding to write a thriller might cast their characters as spies. Readers, for their part, can enjoy the grand-scale adventure while they deal with their fears about world events. The Russians or Neo-Nazis or international conspiracies can be safely faced within the boundaries of the story.

The spy story of today had some illustrious forerunners. James Fenimore Cooper contributed one of the earliest examples in *The Spy*, published in 1821, and Joseph Conrad published *The Secret Agent* in 1907. The British spy stories of World War I included *The Thirty-nine Steps*, which would become the Alfred Hitchcock movie classic. Eric Ambler began writing his stories in the 1930s, and so did Graham Greene, terming them his "entertainments." Both Ambler and Greene have books among the contemporary best sellers.

Perhaps the most common kind of spy story is the "us-versus-them" thriller, with the villains represented by the national enemy of the time. Heroic British agents fought the Germans and then the Russians, while American agents have concentrated on the Russians from the 1950s to the present day. The Russians have returned the favor. The KGB evidently took James Bond so seriously that they commissioned the Bulgarian novelist Andrei Gulyashki to create a Communist hero who could liquidate Bond. And so *Avakum Zhakov versus 07* [*sic*] was published in 1966.[6]

Another kind of story focuses more on character than on nationalistic good-and-evil extremes. Beginning in the 1960s, le Carre created Alexander Leamas and George Smiley. Deighton, le Carre, and others began to show spies that had more in common with their opposite numbers than their governments might like to admit. In *The Fourth Protocol*, fully drawn characters are found on both sides of the Iron Curtain, and the petty bureaucrats and selfish politicians are, too. At the same time, a new cynicism and realism were introduced. The heroic adventure gave way to a more complex tale where the threats might come from within one's own government rather than from outside and where heroism and villainy were mixed. Spying was dirty, unglamorous, and unrewarding. In many books there were no heroes or villains but only survivors—and not too many of them. In *A Small Town in Germany*, le Carre shows how spying must be seen in its bureaucratic context. It is not heroism that determines the fate of nations, but detail, boredom, and breaks in routine. In some books, in fact—such as *The Man from St. Petersburg* and *The Human Factor*—the development of theme and character is clearly more important than the tale of espionage. Spying is only something that the very interesting characters do.

Examples of these different forms are found among the contemporary best sellers and continue to be produced in the 1980s. Daring CIA operatives still fight for the government, while other heroes fight against the government (including the CIA). And le Carre suggests in *The Little Drummer Girl* that the business of spying has nothing to do with heroism. Each of these forms has its loyal fans and very prolific writers. Four authors alone—Ludlum, Buckley, le Carre, and MacInnes—account for more than one-half of the top-selling spy novels.

The "major combatants" included in the following list help to show the world view of these stories. With Buckley and MacInnes, for example, the free world fights the Communists; Americans fight Russians. To increase the villainy in *The Double Image*, MacInnes does some political acrobatics and makes her Communists into Nazis too. With Ludlum, however, evil crosses national boundaries. Americans, Russians, and other powerful individuals join together to take over the world. And in the novels of Forsyth and le Carre, the greatest threat comes from people very close to home.

When the novels about spies and international intrigue are combined, the Russians lead as the enemy in 18 best sellers, followed closely by 15 world plots. Germany and the Nazis run a weak third. While isolated terrorists and Third World nations occasionally cause trouble, they are unimportant overall. The contemporary best sellers are not attempting to follow the headlines, it seems. Rather, they supply very old and familiar enemies to let their game of espionage proceed.

Only a thin and wavering line separates the spy story from other novels of international intrigue. In the famous introduction to *To Catch a Spy*, Eric Ambler tried a definition similar to the one we propose. "A spy story," wrote Ambler, "is a story in which the central character is a secret intelligence agent of one sort or another."[7] He then wondered if by his own definition he had ever written a spy story in his life! Conflict and conspiracy between nations can embroil the characters without involving intelligence agencies. The suspense can be as real and the stakes as high. Maybe there should be only one category, except it might be awkward to call a book a spy story if it does not include any spies.

Both kinds of stories are listed below. Ambler's book, by the way, is listed as a tale of international intrigue.

	SPY STORIES	
Author	Title	The Major Combatants[a]
Behn	*The Kremlin Letter*	U.S.
Buckley	*Marco Polo, if You Can*	U.S.-Russia
———	*Saving the Queen*	U.S.-Russia
———	*Stained Glass*	Germany
———	*The Story of Henri Tod*	U.S.-Russia
———	*Who's on First*	U.S.-Russia
Christie	*Postern of Fate*	World plot
Clavell	*Noble House*	Individuals and corporate rivals
Deighton	*Berlin Game*	Britain-Russia
———	*The Billion Dollar Brain*	Britain
———	*Funeral in Berlin*	Britain-Russia
———	*SS-GB*	Britain-Germany
Fleming	*The Man With the Golden Gun*	Britain
———	*You Only Live Twice*	Britain
Follett	*Eye of the Needle*	Britain-Germany

SPY STORIES—*continued*

Author	Title	The Major Combatants[a]
———	*The Key to Rebecca*	Britain-Germany
———	*The Man from St. Petersburg*	Britain
———	*Triple*	Israel-Egypt
Forsyth	*The Devil's Alternative*	U.S.-Russia
———	*The Fourth Protocol*	Britain-Russia
———	*The Odessa File*	Neo-Nazi plot
Gardner	*For Special Services*	World plot
Greene	*The Human Factor*	Britain-South Africa
le Carre	*The Honourable Schoolboy*	Southeast Asia
———	*The Little Drummer Girl*	Israel-Palestine
———	*The Looking Glass War*	Britain-Germany
———	*A Small Town in Germany*	Britain-Russia
———	*Smiley's People*	Britain
———	*The Spy Who Came in from the Cold*	Britain-Russia
———	*Tinker, Tailor, Soldier, Spy*	Britain-Russia
Ludlum	*The Bourne Identity*	World plot
———	*The Matarese Circle*	World plot
———	*The Parsifal Mosaic*	World plot
———	*The Rhinemann Exchange*	World plot
MacInnes	*Agent in Place*	Britain-Russia
———	*The Double Image*	Communist Nazi(!) plot
———	*Message from Malaga*	U.S.-Russia
———	*Prelude to Terror*	U.S.-Communists
———	*The Salzburg Connection*	Nazi plot
MacLean	*Caravan to Vaccares*	World plot
———	*Circus*	World plot
Trevanian	*Shibumi*	World plot
Uris	*Topaz*	U.S.-Russia
M. West	*The Salamander*	Italy
———	*The Tower of Babel*	Middle East
R. West	*The Birds Fall Down*	Czarist Russia

INTERNATIONAL INTRIGUE

Ambler	*The Levanter*	Middle East
Clancy	*The Hunt for Red October*	U.S.-Russia
L. Collins	*The Fifth Horseman*	U.S.-Iranian terrorists
Cussler	*Deep Six*	U.S.-Asians and Russians
de Borchgrave	*The Spike*	U.S.-Russia
Erdman	*The Billion Dollar Sure Thing*	Governments and banks
———	*The Crash of '79*	U.S.-Saudi Arabia
———	*The Last Days of America*	Governments and banks
Forsyth	*The Day of the Jackal*	France
———	*The Dogs of War*	Britain-Africa
Greene	*The Honorary Consul*	Latin America
Harris	*Black Sunday*	U.S.-Palestinian terrorists
Levin	*The Boys from Brazil*	Nazi plot
Ludlum	*The Aquitaine Progression*	World plot
———	*The Gemini Contenders*	World plot
———	*The Holcroft Covenant*	Nazi plot
MacInnes	*The Snare of the Hunter*	U.S.-Russia
Robbins	*The Adventurers*	Latin America

Author	Title	The Major Combatants[a]
————	*The Pirate*	Saudi Arabia
Salinger	*On Instructions of My Government*	U.S.-China; Latin America
Uris	*The Haj*	Israel-Arabs
Wallace	*The Plot*	World plot
M. West	*Harlequin*	World plot
————	*Proteus*	World plot

[a]When only one country is listed, the conflict usually involves individuals or groups within a country, such as terrorists or assassins, or else a plot within the government itself. World plot refers to conspiracies that cross national boundaries. They need not be worldwide.

Mysteries

Mystery stories have long been one of the most popular kinds of fiction, dating from the works of Edgar Allan Poe and others in the 19th century to the best sellers of the present. Abraham Lincoln was a fan of Poe, and Woodrow Wilson read the tales of J. S. Fletcher, a little known Yorkshire detective writer. Pulp magazine mysteries flourished in the early years of this century, and Sherlock Holmes clubs held meetings and produced a quarterly magazine. Hercule Poirot became so world-renowned that upon his death in Agatha Christie's 1975 best seller *Curtain*, he was given an obituary in the *New York Times*.

Mysteries usually involve the commission of a crime, often murder, directly challenging society and individual life. The crime is then solved and the criminal brought to justice by human processes of detection. Thus mysteries give people the chance to play both criminal and detective: readers can thrill to a crime they would not actually commit and then turn around and help the detective solve the puzzle. By the end of the book, order and justice are restored, bringing further satisfaction.

The basic plot may be similar, but variety is found in the character of the detective and the means by which the crime is solved. There are today three main kinds of mystery stories, which developed at different times.[8] The first, appearing in the mid-19th century, is the classic mystery story, or "whodunit." The world at the time was seen to be structured as tightly as the story. It was a world of rules, fair play, and clear social division; there was no room for accidents or chance. The detectives needed only their superior minds and powers of observation to solve the crime and bring order again.[9] Some of the modern novels still follow this classic model with detectives like Miss Jane Marple, Sherlock Holmes, and Rabbi David Small.

A different kind of mystery developed with the American pulp magazines of the 1920s. The detective changed to the hard-boiled private eye. It was a time of Prohibition, when gangsters were celebrities. People had read Freud: they knew that the mind could not be relied on and that violence was very real. The world was no longer as neat as an English country manor or bound by the same rules of rationality and fair play. So, while the detectives still operated alone and were morally superior to the criminals they were chasing, they needed less thought and more action. They had to be as tough as those they pursued. The heroes were men like Sam Spade and Philip Marlowe; their counterparts today can be found in Lew Archer and Travis McGee.

More recently, a third kind of mystery developed with the police procedural. The hero was no longer an amateur or loner but a skilled professional, a worker in a large police bureaucracy. A new realism entered the mystery genre. The cooperation of many people was necessary to find and capture a criminal. The detectives had human weaknesses and problems at home; bashes in the head resulted in concussions. So, also, the moral distinctions between police and criminal became hazy. Cops often had to make compromises with corruption and found themselves at times very much like the criminals they were chasing. The crimes seemed harder to solve and did not always have neat solutions. Justice was imperfect or incomplete.

These types of mysteries developed at different points in time; nevertheless, all continue in popularity. Some readers want the mental effort of solving the crime along with the detective, others want the action of their favorite private eye, and still others want the realism of an inside look at a big-city police department. So Hercule Poirot and Rabbi Small continue to use their wits; Archer and McGee take off on their own; and Wambaugh's blue knights adjust their car visors, ironically aware of their more heroic counterparts.

MYSTERIES

Author	Title	Popular Detective
Adler	Who Killed the Robins Family?	
Asimov	The Robots of Dawn	
Christie	Nemesis	Miss Jane Marple
———	Postern of Fate	T. and T. Beresford
———	Curtain	Hercule Poirot
———	Sleeping Murder	Miss Jane Marple
Cook	Coma	
———	Brain	
———	Godplayer	
Deighton	SS-GB	
du Maurier	The Flight of the Falcon	
Eco	The Name of the Rose	
Francis	Reflex	
Holt	On the Night of the Seventh Moon	
———	The Shivering Sands	
Kemelman	Saturday the Rabbi Went Hungry	Rabbi David Small
———	Sunday the Rabbi Stayed Home	Rabbi David Small

MYSTERIES—*continued*

Author	Title	Popular Detective
Lustbader, van	*The Ninja*	
MacDonald, J.	*The Dreadful Lemon Sky*	Travis McGee
———	*The Empty Copper Sea*	Travis McGee
———	*The Green Ripper*	Travis McGee
———	*Free Fall in Crimson*	Travis McGee
———	*Cinnamon Skin*	Travis McGee
Macdonald, R.	*The Goodbye Look*	Lew Archer
———	*The Underground Man*	Lew Archer
MacLean	*Bear Island*	
Meyer	*The Seven-Per-Cent Solution*	Sherlock Holmes
———	*The West End Horror*	Sherlock Holmes
Sanders	*The First Deadly Sin*	Edward X. Delaney
———	*The Second Deadly Sin*	Edward X. Delaney
———	*The Third Deadly Sin*	Edward X. Delaney
———	*The Sixth Commandment*	
Smith	*Gorky Park*	
Thorp	*The Detective*	
Wambaugh	*The Glitter Dome*	
———	*The Delta Star*	
———	*The Black Marble*	
Whitney	*Spindrift*	

Sagas

For centuries storytellers have spun sagas to recount the adventures of a family or group, from the Old English tales of journey and discovery to the Norse sagas of men at sea. Modern storytellers, too, have used sagas to show the adventures of immigrants in the New World; the founding of dynasties; or the struggle for fortune, fame, and revenge. According to the *Oxford English Dictionary*, any long, detailed narrative can be called a saga—and many of the best sellers are so called in their promotions and sales. But such a broad definition includes too many diverse books to be useful: most best sellers, after all, are long; they are narratives; and they have details of one kind or another. A narrower definition—the account of a family over more than one generation—has the virtue of showing what the best-selling sagas are like.

These books have several features in common. Most are chronological and simple in structure: the story moves from one birth, childhood, and marriage to the next. Most of the books focus on more than one central character and span the years of the 20th century. And most rely for the action of the story on the recounting of births and deaths, marriages and scandals, family trials and tragedies as viewed daily in the television soaps. In fact, the books appear to have paralleled television programming in their increasing frequency in the 1970s and 1980s. The few books listed for the 1960s are much less like the others and are unique in themselves.

The Ordways and *The Lockwood Concern* are original accounts of two unique families, while *Fathers* and *The Eighth Day* are concerned less with the telling of a saga than with statements about the continuities that cross generations.

The books are arranged by date of publication to show this growing popularity and similarity in the past years.

SAGAS

Author	Title	Year of Publication
Humphrey	*The Ordways*	1965
O'Hara	*The Lockwood Concern*	1965
Gold	*Fathers*	1966
Solomon	*The Candlesticks and the Cross*	1967
Wilder	*The Eighth Day*	1967
Delderfield	*God Is an Englishman*	1970
Shaw	*Rich Man, Poor Man*	1970
Delderfield	*Theirs Was the Kingdom*	1971
Howatch	*Penmarric*	1971
Wouk	*The Winds of War*	1971
Caldwell	*Captains and the Kings*	1972
Uhnak	*Law and Order*	1973
Howatch	*Cashelmara*	1974
Uris	*Trinity*	1976
Elegant	*Dynasty*	1977
Fast	*The Immigrants*	1977
Howatch	*The Rich Are Different*	1977
McCullough	*The Thorn Birds*	1977
Shaw	*Beggarman, Thief*	1977
Fast	*Second Generation*	1978
Michener	*Chesapeake*	1978
Plain	*Evergreen*	1978
Wouk	*War and Remembrance*	1978
Fast	*The Establishment*	1979
Freeman	*Portraits*	1979
Hill	*Hanta Yo*	1979
Howatch	*Sins of the Father*	1980
Michener	*The Covenant*	1980
Plain	*Random Winds*	1980
Van Slyke	*No Love Lost*	1980
Fast	*The Legacy*	1981
Freeman	*No Time for Tears*	1981
Steel	*Remembrance*	1981
Stewart, F.	*Century*	1981
Plain	*Eden Burning*	1982
Krantz	*Mistral's Daughter*	1983
Michener	*Poland*	1983
Santmyer	*"... And Ladies of the Club"*	1984

American Politics

Another popular subject for best-selling books is American politics and government. The primary setting is Washington, D.C. Characters are presidents, FBI chiefs, and candidates for Congress. The books sell "inside information." What kind of picture of government do the readers receive? What kind of information are they getting?

One picture of government is remarkably clear and consistent. Government is corrupt, and the city of Washington is the heart of this corruption. Members of Congress follow the stereotype of the dishonest politician. In *The Senator*, title character Benjamin Hannaford is shown handing out cash and taking it in throughout the novel. He even tries to bribe the president, with some prize frozen bull semen, at $1,000 a shot. In *Deep Six,* the Speaker of the House wants to be president and bribes and betrays everyone who gets in his way. In case we miss the point that he is a villain, he saves himself first in a shipwreck, letting others drown. The corruption is not limited to Congress. It is found in government agencies (*Vanished; The R Document*), the vice-presidency (*The President's Plane Is Missing*), and even the cabinet (*The Man; Full Disclosure*). Presidents are nominated in smoke-filled rooms and regularly assassinated. Allen Drury's novels feature one, and sometimes two, assassinations a year.

The presidency is less corrupt than chaotic. At times presidents are merely victims of the power-hungry people around them. They are fooled by unscrupulous journalists, blackmailed by secretaries, kidnapped and brainwashed by the Russians. At other times they single-handedly undertake actions that even their aides do not know about. They engineer their own disappearances and conduct negotiations on their own. One president, after suffering from a Russian brainwashing, even closes down Congress and the Supreme Court.

These are unconstitutional actions, and bizarre to say the least. But they are also impossible for any one person to carry out without the help of many other people. Although the books are advertised as authentic and "chillingly real," realism does not seem to be an important plot requirement.

Other countries have their problems, too. British heroes face dishonesty and treason within their own ranks in the spy stories of John le Carre and Graham Greene. Unscrupulous officials in both England and Russia complicate the plot in *The Fourth Protocol*. Political corruption was found in ancient Rome, say Caldwell and Vidal, and in other countries and other times. It is a favorite stereotype of the best sellers, and a stock picture of government that is not limited to contemporary America.

In fact, the stereotype is so strong that even when books do not show corruption, the promotional description says that they do. *Facing the Lions* is said to be about a candidate who sold out and sacrificed his ideals. In the actual story, however, the candidate does not sell out, although there is a big mystery surrounding what actually occurred. An investigative reporter, and friend of the candidate, tries to find out what happened, using his own professional skills to solve the mystery. It is a story not of corruption but of the reporter's trail back through the events of the convention. People would not guess this unless they had read the book.

These pictures of government are not entirely the same, however. They are colored by the author's own politics and point of view. Conservative champion Allen Drury argues for a stronger defense and shows a labor leader who is a Communist in disguise. He has his villain pressure the president into appointing a black astronaut to the space program, even though the black is not as well qualified as others. Liberal Irving Wallace chooses an FBI director as a villain who works to undermine civil liberties. Wallace's villains oppose blacks, whereas Drury's villains support them. Other books, too, take political positions. Writing before the Watergate scandal, Philip Roth gives a biting critique of the Nixon presidency (*Our Gang*). The book features Trick E. Dixon, a totally amoral opportunist who wants only to win elections. John Kenneth Galbraith, a liberal economist and Kennedy ambassador, satirizes the hard-line anti-Communists in the State Department who are supporting a corrupt Latin American dictatorship (*The Triumph*). Drury's heroes are the subjects of Galbraith's critique.

In some cases it is hard to say where the fiction ends and propaganda begins. In *The Hunt for Red October* (1984), a Russian captain defects and races to America with his submarine and crew. He leaves a Russia reminiscent of the Stalin era, with daily executions, required propaganda meetings, and political officers who tell him and his men what to think. His wife has died because of the low standard of Russian medical care. When he and his sub are rescued by the Americans, the U.S. Navy captain explains what freedom means. Someone may talk to them "for about two hours" about how the country works. The CIA will give them money and leave them alone. The men marvel. They marvel also at cable television and the huge navy breakfast they are given. They learn about supermarkets and shopping malls and the cars and computers they will be able to buy. The book was published by the U.S. Naval Institute.

On the liberal side, books by Wallace, Roth, and Galbraith total five, none published later than 1976. The conservatives are represented by Drury, Clancy, Cussler, and de Borchgrave and Moss with eight books, three published in the 1980s. New books by Cussler, Clancy, and Drury appeared in 1986. By this rough count, the conservatives not only have the edge; they are gaining.

The books are arranged by date of publication. Most were published before 1972, and few, except for historical accounts, after 1981. It appears that the widespread political interest of the 1960s brought forth a market for best sellers. Ten years later the interest, and the market, had disappeared. And perhaps, too, the Watergate crisis of the middle 1970s suggested that fact was stranger and more interesting than fiction. With most of the Watergate conspirators writing their memoirs, readers could get their political tales from the nonfiction best sellers.

POLITICAL NOVELS

Author	Title	Year of Publication
Wallace	*The Man*	1964
Knebel	*Night of Camp David*	1965

POLITICAL NOVELS—*continued*

Author	Title	Year of Publication
Drury	*Capable of Honor*	1966
O'Connor	*All in the Family*	1966
Serling	*The President's Plane Is Missing*	1967
Vidal	*Washington, D.C.*	1967
Wallace	*The Plot*	1967
Drury	*Preserve and Protect*	1968
Galbraith	*The Triumph*	1968
Knebel	*Vanished*	1968
Pearson	*The Senator*	1968
Drury	*The Throne of Saturn*	1971
Roth	*Our Gang*	1971
Salinger	*On Instructions of My Government*	1971
Caldwell	*Captains and the Kings*	1972
Knebel	*Dark Horse*	1972
Drury	*Come Nineveh, Come Tyre*	1973
Vidal	*Burr*	1973
Wicker	*Facing the Lions*	1973
Drury	*Promise of Joy*	1975
Agnew	*The Canfield Decision*	1976
Caldwell	*Ceremony of the Innocent*	1976
Vidal	*1876*	1976
Wallace	*The R Document*	1976
Safire	*Full Disclosure*	1977
Heller	*Good as Gold*	1978
Vonnegut	*Jailbird*	1979
Archer	*The Prodigal Daughter*	1982
Greeley	*Thy Brother's Wife*	1982
Michener	*Space*	1982
Cussler	*Deep Six*	1984
Vidal	*Lincoln*	1984

War Novels

Stories of war are the preferred choice of many readers, and their popularity has remained fairly consistent over time. One war, however, dominates the imagination of these writers. Most of the best-selling war novels are set in World War II. Only *August 1914* is directly about World War I, although Trevanian's *The Summer of Katya* and Caldwell's *Ceremony of the Innocent* convey the spirit of the times before the war. Jakes is the only author to write about the American Civil War, and only two best sellers are about Vietnam. Oddly enough, with all the increased social awareness of the Vietnam experience in the 1980s, the two novels were written in the 1960s, at the height of American involvement in the area. Two books, by Kazan and Seuss, are about war in general, both critical of the kind of thinking that leads to wars. Two books tell of non-American wars, and another one projects the course of World War III. The other 21 books are set in World War II.

In a film review in the *Village Voice*, Leo Cawley points out "how trapped we are in the perceptions of World War II. We liked that war too much and are reluctant to surrender the sense of unity and righteousness it brought. We liked the way we felt about ourselves during it."[10] Americans could feel virtuous fighting a war with clear good and evil sides, and so they could enjoy watching movies about it. The same point applies to the best-selling books.

While World War II is far and away the most popular setting, the authors' approach to the war varies greatly. MacLean and Patterson show the heroism and patriotism of Americans, while Crichton and Gainham tell of European civilians trying to maintain their way of life during wartime. In *The Eagle Has Landed*, Patterson, writing as Jack Higgins, uses ordinary German soldiers as protagonists, showing that the Germans were human, too. Hemingway conveys the life and tragedy of one character, while Wouk covers every aspect of the war, from Pearl Harbor to the home front to the Battle of Midway. Then there is Vonnegut, who portrays a grim and satirical picture of warfare in *Slaughterhouse-Five*, and Styron, who in *Sophie's Choice* shows that suffering and horror continue even when the war is over. Vonnegut's descriptions of the bombing of Dresden contain some of the strongest antiwar writing of the two decades.

The dates of publication show a brief moratorium for books on war in the early 1970s, corresponding to public attitudes at the time that supported an end to the unpopular Vietnam War and an end to the draft. When the books picked up again in the middle 1970s, they returned full-force to World War II!

WAR NOVELS

Year and War		Title	Author
1964	WWII	*Armageddon*	Uris
1965	Vietnam	*The Green Berets*	Moore
1965	Vietnam	*The Ambassador*	West, M.
1966	WWII	*The Secret of Santa Vittoria*	Crichton, R.
1966	WWII	*The Captain*	de Hartog
1967	WWII	*A Night of Watching*	Arnold
1967	WWII	*Night Falls on the City*	Gainham
1967	WWII	*An Operational Necessity*	Griffin
1967	WWII	*Where Eagles Dare*	MacLean
1968	WWII	*Force 10 from Navarone*	MacLean
1968	The Six-Day War	*The Tower of Babel*	West, M.
1969	WWII	*A Place in the Country*	Gainham
1969	WWII	*Slaughterhouse-Five*	Vonnegut
1970	The Roman Conquest	*The Antagonists*	Gann
1970	WWII	*Islands in the Stream*	Hemingway
1971	WWII	*The Winds of War*	Wouk
1972	War in general	*The Assassins*	Kazan
1972	WWI	*August 1914*	Solzhenitsyn

WAR NOVELS—*continued*

Year and War		Title	Author
1975	WWII	*The Eagle Has Landed*	Higgins
1976	WWII	*Storm Warning*	Patterson
1976	WWII	*The Valhalla Exchange*	Patterson
1977	War in general	*The Book of Merlyn*	White
1978	WWII	*Eye of the Needle*	Follett
1978	WWIII	*The Third World War: August 1985*	Hackett
1978	WWII	*Whistle*	Jones
1978	WWII	*War and Remembrance*	Wouk
1979	WWII	*SS-GB*	Deighton
1980	WWII	*The Key to Rebecca*	Follett
1980	WWII	*Sophie's Choice*	Styron
1981	WWII	*An Indecent Obsession*	McCullough
1982	Civil War	*North and South*	Jakes
1984	Civil War	*Love and War*	Jakes
1984	War in general	*The Butter Battle Book*	Seuss

Religion

Religious figures are familiar characters in American fiction. There are best sellers about priests (three), rabbis (four), ministers (three), a nun, a monk, and a pope. There are also books about missionaries and biblical scholars and the historical figures Thomas à Becket and Saint Paul. By and large the best sellers show a nice ecumenical balance across the major religions. Both rabbis and ministers have trouble coping with their congregations. Priests, ministers, and rabbis all suffer crises of faith (*The Exorcist; A Month of Sundays; The Rabbi*).

In only a few books, however, is the religious message the primary one. See, in particular, the novels by Godden and St. Johns. Many books combine a religious theme with other subjects: *The Exorcist*, with horror; *The Honorary Consul*, with international intrigue; *Love in the Ruins*, with science fiction and satire. Updike and Greeley combine religion and sex, while Kemelman and Eco bring together religion and mystery stories. Eco's Brother William and Kemelman's Rabbi Small join a long line of religious detectives in fiction, including Father Brown, Sister Mary Ursula, Father Bredder, Father Shanley, and Reverend Buell.

A good example of this combination is found in the book *The Exorcist*. There is taut suspense and graphic terror, well known to those who saw the film. But the book, unlike the film, is titled correctly: it is a full portrait of a priest who is caught in forces he did not even believe in. From the quotations at the beginning of the book to the final battle, it is also a study in the nature of evil and the power of faith. The author drew on his Jesuit training, church documents, and case studies of possession in writing the book. According to one reviewer, it is "a horror story for all midnights . . . taut, screaming with agony." It is also, in the words of another reviewer, "a deeply religious book."[11]

Religion is treated for the most part positively in these novels. In contrast to the books about war and politics, there is little in the way of criticism, satire, or stereotyped villains. The church fares better than the state in the American best sellers. Wallace's *The Word* shows that religious characters can lie, cheat, and be as self-serving as any others; but even here, compared to two of his political books—*The R Document* and *The Man*—the criticism is a mild one. Whereas the heroes in the political books fight against government corruption, the religious heroes typically use their faith to fight against an enemy outside. Rabbi Small, Father Karras, and Thomas à Becket, saint and archbishop, are good examples. Thomas, in fact, becomes a figure for a historical novel because he has held to his religion against the power of the king.

These books, however, are mainly a product of the past. Since 1980, only the two books by Greeley, Eco's *The Name of the Rose*, and Morris West's *The Clowns of God* have appeared among the top sellers. Greeley's books are contemporary dramas of sex, corruption, and conflict within a family. Eco's book is a mystery and a richly detailed historical novel. They do not need religion for their top sales.

RELIGIOUS NOVELS

Year	Title	Author
1965	*The Rabbi*	Gordon
1965	*The Source*	Michener
1965	*Thomas*	Mydans
1966	*Saturday the Rabbi Went Hungry*	Kemelman
1966	*The Fixer*	Malamud
1966	*Tell No Man*	St. Johns
1967	*Christy*	Marshall
1967	*The Chosen*	Potok
1968	*Heaven Help Us!*	Tarr
1969	*In This House of Brede*	Godden
1969	*Sunday the Rabbi Stayed Home*	Kemelman
1969	*The Promise*	Potok
1970	*Great Lion of God*	Caldwell
1970	*A Beggar in Jerusalem*	Wiesel
1971	*The Exorcist*	Blatty
1971	*Love in the Ruins*	Percy
1972	*I Heard the Owl Call My Name*	Craven
1972	*The Word*	Wallace
1973	*The Honorary Consul*	Greene, Graham
1975	*In the Beginning*	Potok
1975	*A Month of Sundays*	Updike
1977	*Illusions: The Adventures of a Reluctant Messiah*	Bach
1980	*Answer as a Man*	Caldwell

RELIGIOUS NOVELS—*continued*

Year	Title	Author
1981	*The Clowns of God*	West, M.
1982	*Thy Brother's Wife*	Greeley
1983	*The Name of the Rose*	Eco
1984	*Lord of the Dance*	Greeley

Glamour

Books about glamour, like so many of the best sellers, offer authentic "inside" accounts. Readers are shown the secrets beneath the surface: the drugs, alcoholism, and extramarital affairs. However, like the other books, too, these vary widely in their inside information, as the authors' backgrounds show. Haber was a Hollywood columnist, Tryon an actor, and Shaw a playwright and scriptwriter. Collins writes as an actress and the sister of an actress. Susann knew celebrities and acted in minor roles. Other authors, however, show little first-hand experience, while some major figures in entertainment turn from the subject completely for their best-selling books. Ludlum's career on Broadway is kept separate from his career as a novelist, and the same is true for Thornton Wilder and Elia Kazan. Actor Sterling Hayden wrote a novel about the year 1896 and the conditions of men at sea.

The books on glamour deal with the personalities and places of the entertainment industry. We thus include all novels about film and theatre people, models and media celebrities, and cult figures. Excluded are political celebrities, dealt with under the heading of American Politics, and a few characters who do not lead lives of celebrities. The heroine of *Heartburn* says she is a best-selling cookbook writer, but the story tells about her problems with her marriage and family. She might as well have been a secretary or a lawyer.

The definition is broad enough to include even the marginal cases— books about glamour do not need to be set in Hollywood. The point is important to show just how many—or how few—of the stories fit within this category. While glamour is a popular subject, it is no more popular overall than religion, politics, or war.

The word *glamour* suggests a romantic, often illusionary, attraction—it was originally used to mean a kind of magic spell. The books emphasize both the romance and the illusion. Many of the titles announce that something is wrong. There are pretenders, users, exhibitionists, love machines, strangers, and lonely ladies. Other words—"evening," "goodbye," "Dolores," "valley," "not enough"—add to the negative effect. However, the books themselves give more of a mixed message than their titles do. They show the problems beneath the surface of celebrities' lives, even while they use the glamour for all it is worth in the story. *Valley of the Dolls* and *Hollywood Wives* are cases in point. Drugs and alcohol mix with glittering dinner parties and trips to Spain and Italy. The illusion is maintained even while it is supposedly being dispelled.

The books, in fact, have become less critical, and more frequent, in recent years. As the number of religious books has decreased from the 1960s to the 1980s, the number of novels about glamour has increased. The strongest criticisms of this glamorous world (*The Pretenders*; *Evening in Byzantium*) were published no later than 1973. In contrast, the books since 1983 have returned to the surface. There is magic enough for happy endings and Academy Awards.

Novels about Glamour

Year	Title	Author
1966	*The Adventurers*	Robbins
1966	*Valley of the Dolls*	Susann
1967	*The Exhibitionist*	Sutton
1969	*The Pretenders*	Davis
1969	*The Inheritors*	Robbins
1969	*The Love Machine*	Susann
1973	*Evening in Byzantium*	Shaw
1973	*Once Is Not Enough*	Susann
1974	*The Fan Club*	Wallace
1976	*Blue Skies, No Candy*	Greene, Gael
1976	*The Users*	Haber
1976	*The Lonely Lady*	Robbins
1976	*A Stranger in the Mirror*	Sheldon
1976	*Dolores*	Susann
1976	*Crowned Heads*	Tryon
1978	*Scruples*	Krantz
1980	*Princess Daisy*	Krantz
1981	*Goodbye, Janette*	Robbins
1981	*The Glitter Dome*	Wambaugh
1982	*Mistral's Daughter*	Krantz
1982	*Celebrity*	Thompson
1983	*Voice of the Heart*	Bradford, B.
1983	*Hollywood Wives*	Collins, J.
1983	*Changes*	Steel
1985	*Family Album*	Steel

Books about Sex

Sex, like romance, is a staple of contemporary fiction. Books are included here, however, only when the sex is (1) explicit and (2) more than incidental to the story. The topic—whether an activity, a preoccupation, or a problem—forms a major theme or is described frequently enough to be important to the book, not merely to its cover or promotion. The topic, therefore, should be comparable with the other topics: one scene of battle does not make a war novel, and one scene of sex sufficient for an R movie rating does not make a book about sex.

It will surprise no one that the subject is indeed very popular—books about sex are second in frequency only to historical novels and are about as frequent as tales of spies and intrigue. But the comparison helps put these books in perspective. Best sellers are not only and automatically books about sex. In fact, the large majority are not.

The books range from serious novels of self-discovery to satires about attitudes toward sex to the more obviously sensational—all the way from Nin's classic *Delta of Venus* (worth an X rating) or Updike's powerful *A Month of Sundays* to the adventures of incestuous screen stars or Hollywood wives. These books appeared for the first time in the 1960s, benefiting from the new relaxed rules on censorship making their way through the courts. They continued, with at least one top best seller a year, and increased in frequency by the early 1980s.

During the debates on pornography in the 1960s, a Supreme Court justice was quoted as saying he knew it when he saw it. This led to cartoons showing the justice pointing at something and crying, "That's it! That's it!" In fact, books about sex are no more difficult to classify than those on any other topic. Readers can disagree about why a particular book was omitted or included, but the proportions overall would be the same. Andrew Greeley, for example, says that his book *Thy Brother's Wife* is a very religious book. He goes on to explain that "the gold cross in the mouth of the red-haired woman on the cover represents the oral incorporation of God in the Eucharist."[12] We classify it as a book on religion because one of the major characters is a priest. But we also call it a book about sex.

Novels about Sex

Year	Title	Author
1964	*Candy*	Southern and Hoffenberg
1965	*The Honey Badger*	Ruark
1966	*The Adventurers*	Robbins
1966	*Valley of the Dolls*	Susann
1967	*A Second Hand Life*	Jackson
1967	*Go to the Widow-Maker*	Jones
1967	*The Exhibitionist*	Sutton
1968	*Couples*	Updike
1968	*Myra Breckinridge*	Vidal
1969	*Naked Came the Stranger*	"Ashe"
1969	*The Pretenders*	Davis
1969	*Ada or Ardor*	Nabokov
1969	*The Inheritors*	Robbins
1969	*Portnoy's Complaint*	Roth
1969	*The Love Machine*	Susann
1970	*Doctor Cobb's Game*	Cassill
1970	*Such Good Friends*	Gould
1970	*The Lord Won't Mind*	Merrick
1971	*The Betsy*	Robbins
1972	*Semi-Tough*	Jenkins
1973	*Once Is Not Enough*	Susann
1974	*The Pirate*	Robbins

NOVELS ABOUT SEX—*continued*

Year	Title	Author
1974	*A Month of Sundays*	Updike
1974	*The Fan Club*	Wallace
1975	*Looking for Mr. Goodbar*	Rossner
1976	*Blue Skies, No Candy*	Greene, Gael
1976	*The Users*	Haber
1976	*The Lonely Lady*	Robbins
1976	*A Stranger in the Mirror*	Sheldon
1976	*Dolores*	Susann
1977	*The Women's Room*	French
1977	*How to Save Your Own Life*	Jong
1977	*Delta of Venus: Erotica*	Nin
1977	*Dreams Die First*	Robbins
1978	*Scruples*	Krantz
1979	*Class Reunion*	Jaffe
1979	*The Top of the Hill*	Shaw
1980	*The Bleeding Heart*	French
1980	*Fanny*	Jong
1980	*Princess Daisy*	Krantz
1980	*The Ninja*	van Lustbader
1980	*Rage of Angels*	Sheldon
1981	*Goodbye, Janette*	Robbins
1981	*The Third Deadly Sin*	Sanders
1981	*The Glitter Dome*	Wambaugh
1982	*Thy Brother's Wife*	Greeley
1982	*The Case of Lucy Bending*	Sanders
1982	*Master of the Game*	Sheldon
1983	*Hollywood Wives*	Collins, J.
1983	*Mistral's Daughter*	Krantz
1983	*The Seduction of Peter S.*	Sanders
1984	*Lord of the Dance*	Greeley
1984	*The Life and Hard Times of Heidi Abromowitz*	Rivers
1985	*Glitz*	Leonard

NOTES

1. General sources include the *Oxford English Dictionary*; *Literary Terms*, by Karl Beckson and Arthur Banz; and *A Dictionary of Literary Terms*, rev. ed., by J. A. Cudden. Sources for mysteries, spy stories, and science fiction are listed in Section II of the bibliography at the end of the book. Few guidelines exist for the other categories, as noted in Betty Rosenberg, *Genreflecting*, 2d ed. (Littleton, Colo.: Libraries Unlimited, 1986). We assigned categories to books when each of us independently made the classification and no reader of the manuscript strenuously objected.

2. Howard Phillips Lovecraft, the classic horror writer, has a good description. It is fear of the unknown that includes the "hint" of a "malign defeat of those fixed laws of Nature which are our only safeguard against the assaults of chaos and the

daemons of unplumbed space." *Supernatural Horror in Literature* (Dover, 1973), p. 15.

3. See James Monaco, *American Film Now* (New York: New American Library, 1979), pp. 54–68. Monaco finds eight dominant genres in Hollywood films: comedies, mysteries (including stories of gangsters and spies), horror, science fiction, war stories, westerns, romantic historical adventures, and musicals.

4. King admits this himself about *The Dead Zone* and *Firestarter*, among other stories. See the interview in Tim Underwood et al., *Stephen King Goes to Hollywood* (New York: New American Library, 1987), p. 58. And see Isaac Asimov on the difficulties of combining mysteries with science fiction: *Asimov on Science Fiction* (London: Granada, 1981), p. 33.

5. For example, Ursula Leguin writes science fiction and Amanda Cross and Jane Langton write mysteries. Langton has won American Book Award nominations and awards from the Mystery Writers of America. The Christie-like name Amanda Cross is a pseudonym for Carolyn Heilbrun.

6. Cudden, p. 656.

7. Eric Ambler, ed., *To Catch a Spy* (New York: Atheneum, 1965), p. 21.

8. More detail on these types is found in John Ball, ed., *The Mystery Story* (San Diego: University of California Press, 1976).

9. See, for example, David Willis McCullough, *Great Detectives* (New York: Pantheon, 1984), p. x, who says that the great detectives "cut through confusion and chaos, solve puzzles, and set things right to make the world seem quite a logical place after all."

10. Leo Cawley, "Refighting the War: Why the Movies are in Vietnam," *Village Voice*, September 8, 1987, p. 18.

11. The reviewers are quoted in the front pages of the paperback edition, *The Exorcist* (New York: Bantam, 1972).

12. Andrew Greeley, *Confessions of a Parish Priest* (New York: Pocket Books, 1987), p. 491.

F O U R

Characters—The Good, the Bad, and the Ordinary

BOOKS CAN BE KNOWN by their memorable characters. Brave and indestructible heroes and heroines are brought to life against fearsome villains
and enemies, while ordinary people and entire generations are shown gaining and losing in their everyday lives. Good characters are important elements in any story. They not only present the conflict and keep the plot
moving forward, but they can reach out and appeal directly to readers'
emotions. When it seemed that Little Nell was about to die in one of Charles
Dickens's next serial installments of the story, 19th-century readers be-
sieged the author with letters imploring mercy for Nell. In fact, when
authors have produced popular characters, they will use them over again
in several books, or in the continuation of the original one. A character
once established makes the next best-selling book. Blackford Oakes keeps
facing impossible assignments, and Rabbi David Small goes through the
days of the week solving mysteries. Author Jean Auel continues the adventures of Ayla, and John Updike's Rabbit runs on through middle age.

Characters do more than catch the reader's attention. They supply pictures of the world and the people in it. They say what is heroic and vil-
lainous, good and bad. They show who succeeds or fails and what kind of
success is possible. They provide models to live by, and they reinforce
clichés. We therefore turn to the characters first to see what the best sellers

are like. We look at the range of major characters and ask who are the heroes, heroines, and villains, as well as the champions of ordinary life. While these are by no means the only characters featured, they show who receives star billing and what traits are deemed the most important.

With so many books to choose from, it is easy to be too selective—to choose examples to make different arguments. Look, someone could say, at how stereotyped the best-selling characters are, selecting examples that vividly make the point. Or look at the traits that distinguish heroes, again carefully selecting the evidence. Instead, we have tried to give a more accurate account of the characters that do appear, indicating major types and selecting representative examples. We thus work from the books themselves to see what conclusions can be drawn about the role and variety of the characters.

One fact should be made clear at the beginning. Books do not need single leading characters to become best sellers. Only about 230, or around one-half, of the books feature a single leading character. These include heroes, a few heroines, and ordinary people pursuing goals, no matter how grand or small. About 170 of the books, or a little more than one-third, tell of multiple characters, with no one individual featured throughout the story. These include families chronicled over several generations, a cluster of film stars and Hollywood wives, partners in a law firm, college graduates at a reunion, and soldiers at war, among others. They range from books such as *Mistral's Daughter*, showing three characters (all red-haired models in the same family who love the same man), to Tom Clancy's *The Hunt for Red October*, which shows dozens of American and Russian military personnel in pursuit of a submarine. Clancy focuses on each "character" for a page or two before turning to the next. The remaining books show pairs, whether as couples (*Except for Me and Thee*) or antagonists (*The Third Deadly Sin*; *The Antagonists*); or they offer a commentary on events with or without a fictional narrator (*Centennial*; *The Third World War*; *Masquerade*); or they present short stories. We can look first at some individual characters and then at the remarkable, and growing, number of multicharacter stories.

Heroes

Throughout the ages, heroes have been one of the most enjoyable parts of literature. We have seen them as kings or knights errant, doing good deeds and defeating evil wherever it lurked. Although there are no dragons left to kill today, heroes still have found their way into best sellers. There are different evils now, and weapons other than swords. But fictional heroes still do battle, winning their readers' admiration. The classic heroes were admired for their great abilities and achievements, measured by the cultural values of the time. They functioned as defenders of society, or at least helped others beyond themselves.[1] Using this definition, we can look to see who the heroes are in the contemporary best sellers and what they are like.

By this definition, the chief protagonists of a story are not automatically heroes or heroines, as they are sometimes loosely called. Think of the man who builds a great financial empire, the woman who stumbles onto a mystery and must be rescued, the people who call on great inner resources to save their own lives. These are popular characters in the best sellers, but they are not heroic in the stricter sense of the term. Using the stricter definition, we ask who the heroes and heroines are and what contemporary heroism is said to be.

The male heroes can be divided into two basic groups. The first group are the modern knights—the heroes by occupation. They can be soldiers, policemen, government agents, private detectives. But when they risk their lives for someone else or for the good of society, they are basically only doing their job. The second group are heroes by circumstance. They can be anyone, of any occupation, who happens to be at a particular place and time. They stumble across a conspiracy, are required to save a friend or loved one, or find a stranger dying in their arms, whispering an urgent secret message. Forced into being heroes, they become as effective as the modern knights.

Heroes by Occupation—
The Modern Knights

One form of the modern knight can be found in the government agent who works in defense of his country or its allies. Two of the most popular examples are James Bond, of Ian Fleming's creation, and William Buckley's Blackford Oakes. James Bond is a commander in the British Secret Service, with an "oo" ranking giving him license to kill. We may think we know what he looks like, envisioning Sean Connery or Roger Moore from the movies, but Fleming tells us little about his appearance. He seems to be good looking, somewhere in his thirties, physically fit, with a scar on his face. We know more about his personality and job qualifications. He is an individual who is often in conflict with authority, but who is basically the best at his job. He is modest, too. Happy with his position in the service, he seeks no promotion and refuses to be knighted by the queen because he says he would laugh at himself being called "Sir."

Both of Fleming's best sellers begin with Bond in disgrace and not looking very heroic. In *The Man with the Golden Gun*, he tries to assassinate M., his superior, after being brainwashed by the KGB; in *You Only Live Twice*, he is deteriorating from grief and depression after the death of his new wife. In both cases, M. sends him on "impossible" missions: in one, so that he can "fall on the battlefield" rather than being court-martialed; and in the other, because M. hopes to snap Bond out of his depression. The villains that he confronts in these novels are some of the most dreadful but skilled individuals a man could go against, but Bond himself is also skilled. He has great cunning, always thinks quickly, and is an expert at many physical skills. He has honor even in the face of the enemy. At one point in *The Man with the Golden Gun,* Bond could shoot Scaramanga in the back and achieve quick success, but he would probably also have to kill the driver, with whom he has no quarrel. So he does not do it, although he thinks himself foolish not to. It is imperative that he achieve success against his foes, and although he suffers some personal loss and problems, he always completes his missions.

Similar to Bond is William Buckley's hero Blackford Oakes, a CIA agent recruited right out of Yale. He is young, only 25 in *Saving the Queen,* and ages only slightly in the subsequent books. We know that he is charming and attractive; however, once again we are not given much of a description. Blackie is not perfect. While he likes to make his own decisions, they are not always the right ones. In *Marco Polo, if You Can* he is fired, but only briefly. His physical courage is great, and his life is always in danger. But he is always able to defend his country successfully, sometimes even in spite of himself.

Other men who are heroes to their countries and its allies are the soldiers. In *Force 10 from Navarone* Alistair MacLean presents a group of men who must function together to be heroic. Three special Allied agents and three Marine commandos are sent to Yugoslavia to help free thousands of partisans who are trapped in the mountains by the Nazis. It is called an "impossible" mission, and the men attempting it are called "insane." But MacLean shows how only a few special men are able to defeat thousands of the enemy. There is Mallory, the brains of the operation, whose ability to observe the unusual and try the impossible helps the mission to succeed; Miller, who complains about everything he has to do, but who is able to perform splendidly; and Andrea, a Greek, who is an expert at hand-to-hand combat and pretty clever himself. Along with them are the Marine commandos, "the most highly trained combat troops . . . [with a] remarkable variety of skills." These heroes must work together in order to achieve victory, and must realize that their individual lives cannot weigh against the lives of thousands of their allies.

Some heroes work on a smaller scale, defending the inhabitants of a neighborhood. Bumper Morgan, of Joseph Wambaugh's *The Blue Knight,* is one such hero. He is a cop who patrols a small section of Los Angeles. Like Bond and Blackie, he makes his own rules but is excellent at his job. He loves his beat and his badge, and the neighborhood loves him, too. But Bumper is big and fat. He accepts free food from his beat and will even allow a suspect to "fall" from a fire escape to be sure that justice is done. Still, he is willing to risk his life to see that law and order are maintained. Although Bumper is unattractive physically and in some ways morally, he is still a hero to the neighborhood he defends.

As the title of the book makes clear, Bumper is the realistic modern knight. He has to laugh at the "grotesque fat policeman who held the four-inch glittering shield in front of him as he lumbered to his car . . . settled in his saddle seat, flipped down his visor and drove west to the Pink Dragon. 'Now I'll kill the dragon and drink its blood!' said the comic blue policeman."

Travis McGee, the hero of many John MacDonald novels, is another modern knight who works on a small scale. While he does not have a regular job, he is in effect a private detective, supporting himself from a share of the goods and money he retrieves for others. He dislikes most forms of authority and has his own code to live by. He has a strong sense of morality and set opinions on a wide range of social questions such as ecology and real-estate development. He is gallant, and risks his life for others. Like Bumper, Travis describes himself in *Free Fall in Crimson* as a kind of comic knight: "I ride around the sawdust trail in my own clown suit, from L. L. Bean's end-of-season sale: marked-down armor, wrong size helmet, sway-backed steed, mended lance, and rusty sword. And sometimes with milady's scarf tied to the helmet, whoever milady might be at the time of trial."

Helping even one person is enough to make a character a hero. In his job as a priest, Father Karras in *The Exorcist* can help people, although he is not too successful in this regard. Suffering from great personal problems (guilt about his mother and her death, and his own doubt of God), he sees drunks begging for help as a nuisance, and does not feel that he can give the guidance that he should. However, when a woman tells him about the demonic possession of her little girl, he tries to help. Trained as a psychiatrist, he tries to attribute the daughter's behavior to psychological causes, but soon comes to realize that it is a case of actual possession. He must fight to make the church believe him, and use all of his physical and spiritual strength in the exorcism. When the other father dies of a heart attack, Father Karras must complete the exorcism alone. He makes the ultimate sacrifice that a hero can, at the same time saving the girl's life, and renewing his own faith.

Some of the modern knights are very unusual. Take, for example, Yakov Lieberman of the novel *The Boys from Brazil*. He is in his seventies and in ill health. Once head of the world-famous War Crimes Information Center, he now works alone from an apartment with the ceiling cracking. When he hears from a student that the Nazi war criminal Josef Mengele is alive and involved in a plot, he takes it upon himself to investigate. He risks his life and physical health and finally confronts Mengele. Then he must wrestle with a great moral decision that could affect the future of the world.

These characters are representative of the many detectives, secret agents, and others who sally forth each year to see that justice is done. They can be old or young, romantic, quietly married, or celibate. They can serve their country or their neighborhood. Lieberman saves the world from a Nazi conspiracy, while Father Karras saves one little girl. In spite of this variety, they have important traits in common. They are all individuals somehow set apart from their society or in conflict with superiors. But *they conflict only up to a point:* they are the best at their job and seem to love to do it. George Smiley and Edward X. Delaney like it so much that they keep coming back from retirement for one more assignment. Lieberman, Bumper, and Poirot will work until they die. While they are all asked to risk their lives and use physical and mental skills, their main admirable trait appears to be the ability to do their job well—and keep doing it.

One of the best examples of this workmanlike hero is George Smiley, in le Carre's *Smiley's People*. Smiley is brought back from retirement after the killing of a close friend and former fellow worker. He soon finds a pattern of clues that revive the pain of his own broken marriage and suggest that the master Soviet agent Karla has a great emotional weak point, too. Nevertheless, all the while he is mourning his friend, suffering his own pain, and knowing what he will be doing to Karla, Smiley leads the investigation to a successful conclusion. He conducts his own field work: he develops film, wheedles information from witnesses, and pores over old files until midnight. He carries out the masterful interrogation of Grigoriev (shown detail by detail for 27 book pages) that forces the Soviet official to defect. And he then sets up the trap and orchestrates the final capture of Karla. At this point, a coworker summarizes his accomplishment:

> He had done everything he had set out to do, and more. . . . He had done it alone; and today as the record would show, he had broken and turned Karla's hand-picked agent in the space of a couple of hours. . . . He was in late age, yet his tradecraft had never been better. (p. 351)

The novel balances Smiley's "tradecraft" against his great emotional pain, a pain also reflected in the lives of other characters. We see Smiley's emotions from the inside, through his own thoughts and memories, and the tradecraft from the observations of others. His long silences, used by le Carre throughout the novel, reinforce both effects. People talk to Smiley and around him, but he says little in reply, at most murmuring a few polite words. The silences remind us of the pain he is feeling while, at the same time, they set him above those around him as he carries on his job.

Like Travis McGee mourning Gretel in *The Green Ripper*, George Smiley succeeds at what he sets out to do. Neither hero lets his emotions interfere with the quality of his work. Yet the books allow their heroes to have it both ways. Although they have given priority to the job at hand, their feelings allow them little joy or pride in its successful accomplishment. Travis goes fishing, to let time heal his wounds if it can. Smiley is absent-mindedly polishing his spectacles. "George, you won," a friend tells him as they walk away. "Did I?" said Smiley. "Yes. Yes, well I suppose I did."

Heroes by Circumstance—
The Reluctant Heroes

Some people are forced into being heroes. Given the means and the motivation, anyone can perform heroic acts—even rabbits! In *Watership Down*, Richard Adams shows a group of rabbits who must work together to save each other and establish a new warren. Nearly everyone is their enemy. They must avoid humans and other animals, and try to defeat the evil rabbits who would destroy them. Their lives are in constant danger, and they all are willing to sacrifice for their comrades. They call on their great historical legends to give them strength for their exploits, and they learn new ways of thinking and new technologies. By the end of the book, they have journeyed to a new land, gained victory in a deadly combat, and seen the birth of the second and third generations.

While the rabbits' success is a team effort, Hazel is singled out as the main hero and successful leader. Smaller than the typical rabbit leader, Hazel grows into his heroism in the course of the story. At the conclusion, Adams uses a quote from Shakespeare to honor him: "He did look far / Into the service of the time, and was / Discipled of the bravest: he lasted long. . . . " The threats of tragedy (with quotes from *Agamemnon*) have been dispersed, and all is well in the rabbits' kingdom. Just as Wambaugh and MacDonald place their heroes in a larger historical tradition, so Adams makes it clear that he is writing an epic of heroism.

In *The Talisman*, 12-year-old Jack also comes to be a hero. His mother is dying, and Jack is told by an old man that in order to save her, he, the boy, must travel into a parallel world to find a talisman. Jack does not have great physical strength, and his evil Uncle Sloat will stop at nothing to destroy him. Nevertheless, Jack is smart and determined to save his mother, and he has some allies to help him on his quest.

Jockeys can be heroes, too. In Dick Francis's novel *Reflex*, Philip Nore is a steeplechase jockey and amateur photographer who keeps mostly to himself. But when he is suddenly plunged into a mystery, he uses his wits and photography skills to unravel it, risking his own life along the way. When he figures out what has been going on, he decides for himself how justice should best be meted out.

All of Robert Ludlum's heroes are forced into their situations. In *The Aquitaine Progression*, Joel Converse is an attorney quietly pursuing his business in Geneva. He is also an ex–military pilot and prisoner of war who wants nothing more than to forget the past. But when he meets an old school friend, who later that day is shot and dies bleeding in his arms, he is caught up in a maze of intrigue. Joel uses his legal training to bluff opponents, gain information from people, and sort out the guilty from the innocent. However, he must use his past military training, too, and the memories he wished to forget. "In the jungles he had rested," he remembers, "knowing that rest was as much a weapon as a gun. . . . " He must trust his instincts and sense of direction as he hides and runs and tracks down the enemy. Joel has helped to save the world; yet when the novel concludes, we find him living quietly in Geneva, a normal citizen again.

Even the spy story can use ordinary people as heroes. According to one authority, the "typical" hero of Eric Ambler and Graham Greene "was neither a gentleman amateur nor a professional agent":

> Instead, he was usually a quite ordinary person caught up against his will in a web of espionage. This hero's adventures took place not on a frontier or in

enemy territory, but in the heart of what he had assumed was safe and friendly country. . . . The Ambler-Greene protagonist rarely brought a mission to a triumphant conclusion, saving the homeland from enemy threats. On the contrary, his greatest achievement was to narrowly escape with his life from the conspiracy into which he had been unwittingly and unwillingly implicated.[2]

No one wants to be more normal than John Smith in Stephen King's novel *The Dead Zone*. Smith has the ability to see the future of people he touches. He hates his power, seeing it as a curse and very frightening. Almost against his will, he begins to use it for good things, saving lives and helping the police. Then he is called on for an even greater heroic act and sacrifice. Yes, the best sellers say, kids and jockeys and all the John Smiths can be heroes too.

The reluctant heroes and modern knights share a common trait: modesty. They do not seek power for themselves, nor are they unduly impressed with it in others. Most of the occupational heroes are not looking for honor or promotion; they simply are doing their job. The reluctant heroes are even less eager for glory. John Smith does not want to save the world—he wants to get married. Thus a portrait begins to emerge from these books of a Democratic Hero: a strong individual with a highly developed work ethic; practical, skilled, and unassuming; willing to stand up against authority and be successful. He is almost like everyone else except better—better able to save the world or do whatever needs to be done.

We are not told very much about some of these characters, because *who* they are is not important. They could be anyone. Nor, as we will see later, are we told much about the enemy they are fighting against. Large global conspiracies and malign bureaucrats lie in wait to pounce on unwary individuals. Ordinary people face a society over which they have little control. Heroism is forced from this unequal encounter; and the reader's real fears about such a situation can be exorcised in the course of the novel.

Unusual Heroes

A few heroes do not fit into either group discussed to this point. David Champlin in Ann Fairbairn's *Five Smooth Stones* is a black hero—a rarity in a collection of books that produced few black characters. A smart and very successful man, he accomplishes everything he sets out to do. David goes to a white school, becomes a lawyer, and rises to be a leader in the civil-rights movement. Even his marriage, to a white woman, is successful. He selects himself for his heroic role. Throughout the book he struggles against the various kinds of prejudice, including patronizing friendships, and finally gives his life for his people. He is like the biblical David with a slingshot (and five smooth stones) against the Goliath of racial prejudice.

The Confessions of Nat Turner tells of the leader of a slave uprising in Virginia in 1831. Nat is a prodigy, educated beyond other blacks of his time, and an acknowledged leader. But his clear vision allows him to see

the evil around him too clearly and his powerful emotions lead to an unbearable torment. Like the classical tragic hero, Nat is taken too far by his
aspirations when both his patron and his Bible do not keep their promises.
Fortune and the gods betray him, bringing death and disgrace. Only his
testament survives.

Nat and David are exceptional not only for being heroes, but for appearing in these books as characters at all. Altogether, five books feature
black main characters and deal with the race issue as the central subject of
the story: In addition to *Confessions* and *Five Smooth Stones*, we find *The Man*;
Hurry Sundown; and *Tell Me How Long the Train's Been Gone*. Only the last
was written by a black author. In *The Man*, a black senator is suddenly
thrust into the presidency by the laws of succession. *Hurry Sundown* shows
the changes coming to the South after World War II, bringing conflict to
the town and strain between two soldiers, one black and one white, who
had been childhood friends. In *Tell Me How Long*, James Baldwin draws
on his own life to tell the story of a fictional black actor.

It is striking that all of these books were published between 1964 and
1968! The Civil Rights Act was passed by Congress in 1964, suggesting that
some issues of race were visible and acceptable to a majority of Americans
at that time. The books appeared as part of that climate of opinion—and
then were followed by no more. Doctorow's *Ragtime*, published in 1975,
shows the trials of a black musician, but he is not the only subject of the
author's satire. A few other books use blacks as minor characters. They are
strong and admirable figures in Knebel's *Vanished* (1968) and Caldwell's
Answer as a Man (1980). They are ineffectual protesters in Hailey's *Hotel*
(1965) and Drury's *Capable of Honor* (1966). And they are villains in Drury's
The Throne of Saturn (1971). *Throne* is the only best seller to take a position
against blacks. The astronaut Jayvee, according to Drury, "like so many of
his race," did not appreciate all the progress that had been made.[3] Jayvee's
anger leads to violence on the spaceship and almost destroys the mission.
Most of the other authors deal with race by not including any black characters. After 1975, blacks virtually disappeared from these novels.

Gore Vidal creates unique heroes by casting through history to show
traditional villains in a new and favorable light. In the novel *Julian*, Vidal
takes the title character, whom history has shown as the enemy of Christianity, and presents him as a hero. Instead of Julian the Apostate, he
becomes Julian the military genius, social reformer, and emperor of Rome.
He drives the barbarians back farther than anyone has since Julius Caesar
and suffers a hero's death on the battlefield. A villain of American history
books, Aaron Burr, also becomes a hero in Vidal's novel *Burr*. The story
is told from Burr's point of view, through his memoirs, and shows him as
a brave, intelligent man. At the same time, the historical heroes, the founding fathers, are not shown in a very favorable light. Washington did not
read books and was merely "an excellent politician who had no gift for
warfare." Jefferson was a hypocrite who lived beyond his means. It wasn't
principle that made him free his slaves; he needed them to *buy* their freedom.

Burr and Julian lose because the tide of history turns against them. Christianity wins out in Rome. Burr's enemies become the fathers of the new nation. It is Vidal's contribution to show these characters' heroic traits while taking some shots at the traditional heroes. Sophocles is honored today as a famous Greek playwright and author of *Oedipus Rex*. But when Sophocles came to dinner, a character points out in *Creation*, people had to tell their sons to hide.

The heroic legends of King Arthur are retold in four books by Mary Stewart and one by T. H. White. Shelley Mydans's *Thomas* tells of the life of Thomas à Becket, a 12th-century British commoner who rose to become chancellor and archbishop. Forced to choose between the two parts of his life that he had balanced so long, he died a martyr's death and was canonized as a saint. These extraordinary figures, however, are the exceptions among the best sellers. The kings and saints and classic heroes are outnumbered by the reluctant heroes and the modern knights.

Heroines

It is not only the men who perform heroic deeds. Some women, too, fight for justice, risk their lives, and defeat enemies. In this case, however, we do not need to select representative examples. The heroines are so few in number that each can speak for herself.

Miss Jane Marple, of Agatha Christie's creation, possesses the traits of a heroine, and has a few unique traits of her own. She is an elderly woman, with rheumatism in her back, who has been forbidden by her doctor even to work in her garden. But her physical limitations do not keep her from tracking down murderers. She can be "ruthless . . . in the cause of justice," and has a "natural genius . . . for investigation." Thus, she uses her intellect and reasoning powers as her weapons. In the novel *Nemesis*, Miss Marple inherits a crime to solve, but the man's will includes no clue as to what the crime is about. When she does get on the track and begins her investigation, she uses her age to her benefit. Elderly ladies are supposed to gossip, so she is able to get information from people without their suspecting anything. She takes her time, noticing little things and juxtaposing them with others to solve the mystery. Since her intellect is her main weapon, she falls into great physical danger at the climax, but two other heroines are supplied for her protection.

Medical student Susan Wheeler also helps solve a mystery in *Coma* and risks her career and life in the process. While the mystery is not solved until Susan becomes a patient in her own hospital, and in need of some rescue, she has helped provoke the criminal into revealing himself.

Christy Moreland, of *Spindrift*, also insists that justice will be served. When we first see her, she is in a hospital recovering from her father's tragic death, but she is in full possession of her senses. She knows that her father did not commit suicide, as everyone claims, and insists on discovering the real truth. Christy must also get her young son away from her mother-in-law, who is trying to turn him against her. She knows that neither task will be easy, but her determination is strong; her father had taught her to be a fighter and to stand up against her mother-in-law. When she returns to Spindrift, the house where her father died, no one appears to be on her side. She soon realizes that her life is in danger, but she is too stubborn to give up. When she finally does figure out what has happened, she is almost murdered because she makes one serious mistake in judgment. But she does accomplish what she sets out to do, and is able to right some wrongs of the past.

Another heroine who wants justice for her dead father is 14-year-old Mattie Ross from the novel *True Grit*. She hires Rooster Cogburn to help her track down the murderer, and although she is told that it would be too dangerous to go along, she does anyway. Her true grit helps her to stay alive and finally get her revenge. If Miss Marple is the oldest heroic character (people in the story guess that she must be close to 80), Mattie is almost the youngest, sharing the honors with Jack in *The Talisman*.

Ayla, in *The Valley of Horses*, is a classic heroic figure, setting forth on a quest that will determine the fate of the human race. She appears to have magical healing power, but her success is due mainly to her superior physical and mental skills. She survives on her own after being exiled and left to die. Ayla thinks for herself, rejects the traditional customs for women, and travels across an alien and forbidding land. The heroine of *The Candlesticks and the Cross* is another strong and determined woman who works for her own family and for all Jews in the upheaval of turn-of-the-century Russia. Ronya conducts diplomacy with heads of state, nurses soldiers through a cholera epidemic, and in the face of impending disaster engineers an escape, with some of her family, to America.

Linden Avery, in *The One Tree* and *White Gold Wielder*, also has special healing powers among other skills. She saves the lives of her companions more often than hero Thomas Covenant does, and she makes fewer mistakes than he does. For author Samuel Donaldson, heroism is a quality shared by both sexes. The chief warrior among the Giants in these stories is also a woman.

There are not many heroines in the best sellers, however, *if we apply the same standards to the women as to the men*. We ask that they be major characters and use their admirable abilities to fight for others beyond themselves. This excludes the women, described later in the chapter, who must undertake heroic efforts to put their own lives in order. And it excludes protagonists that we might sympathize with but not admire. The romantic Charlie in *The Little Drummer Girl* is less a heroine than a tool of both sides in the Middle East conflict. According to le Carré, the dirty business of international intrigue has no place for romanticism. It is not an admirable trait.

By this definition, there are fewer than 10 heroines in over 400 books. They include one very young girl; one elderly eccentric; one doctor-patient;[4] two other healers (Ayla and Linden), both of whom inhabit strange worlds far from contemporary America; and Ronya and Christy. Ronya engages in healing, and Christy has been in a hospital.

Doctor Celia Jordan in *Strong Medicine* might be called a heroine, and so might teenager Noele in *Lord of the Dance*. Each, however, is one of several main characters in the story. Noele, in fact, is more a symbol of goodness and innocence than a living character. Except for her slang, which matches neither her age nor her generation, she is given few identifying characteristics. Noele says things like "Geek," "Barf city," "Bad vibes," and "No way, Jose." After she has been raped, beaten, and sodomized by three thugs, she wakes to see a hospital psychiatrist at her bedside. She says to herself, "The yukky hospital smell made her want to throw up, hopefully all over this geek." This is probably not the typical reaction of a 17-year-old to the experience.

Readers might want to nominate one or two other heroines, but the grand total would stay very small. Even in this select group, only two— Susan Wheeler and Christy—are American women, and only Miss Marple stays out of the hospital.

Sometimes authors begin with women who seem to be heroic. In later chapters, however, they do not succeed, are killed, or have to wait for the dashing young hero to rescue them. In *Cujo*, a woman and her little boy are trapped inside a car by a rabid dog. The boy desperately needs water and medical attention, and the woman knows that she must get out and face the dog. She battles him to the death, defeating him totally, but not everything else turns out as well; so her fight becomes meaningless.

In *Rage of Angels*, Jennifer Parker gets to be a heroine in only half of the story. Jennifer is an attorney who has overcome adversity and is on her way to a brilliant career. She looks like a heroine, with "an intelligent, mobile face, and green, thoughtful eyes . . . a face that reflected pride and courage and sensitivity." Jennifer loves the law. She is very concerned about justice, and tries to take only clients she feels are innocent or deserving. She has rejected the advances, both professional and personal, of Mafia boss Michael Moretti. But when her son is kidnapped, she calls Moretti as the only one who can help. So far so good at the end of Part I.

Part II, however, tells a different story. Jennifer is Moretti's mistress, so physically caught up with him that she does not want to get away. We do not see any more brilliant courtroom strategies or victories. In fact, by the end of the novel, she has lost almost everything she has worked for, and is back in Kelso, Washington, where she came from.

Villains

Protagonists can be opposed by different kinds of characters. They can be enemies—people who wish the protagonist and others harm—or the faceless members of a nation or class. Or they may be nothing less than villains. The *Oxford English Dictionary* defines a villain as "an unprincipled or depraved scoundrel; a man naturally disposed to base or criminal actions, or deeply involved in the commission of disgraceful crimes; . . . that character . . . whose evil motives or actions form an important element in the plot." Villains, in short, are individual characters who become a major force in the story. They are often as powerful as the hero or even more powerful, but they are marked by evil. They lie, cheat, kill, maim, torture, destroy. They are "base," "depraved," "criminal." No run-of-the-mill enemy can compete with that.

It is often said that Satan was Milton's favorite character in *Paradise Lost*. The poet described him more fully and sympathetically than he did Adam or Eve. Villains have held a fascination for people of all ages. We secretly envy their power and freedom from conscience, but we hold our breath until the villains are defeated and the evil is destroyed. Just as there are few full-fledged villains in real life, there are not that many in the best sellers. Nevertheless, those that exist are memorable. We will look first at these individuals and then at the opponents who appear more frequently— the faceless enemies.

Unique Villains

Ian Fleming portrays powerful villains for his hero to defeat. In the novel *You Only Live Twice*, he created the villain Dr. Shatterhand. A morbid but brilliant man, Shatterhand has designed a garden filled with some of the most deadly plants, insects, and reptiles to be found. "He collects death," enticing the suicide-prone Japanese to enter this place and die a fascinating death. The government cannot touch him, for his gardens are walled, and inside the most deadly things are marked clearly so no one will stumble into them "accidentally." What he has actually done, however, is to show the Japanese where the best places are to end their lives. Even his guards do not try to keep people out; they are mostly around for the removal of bodies and his personal protection. Shatterhand plans to set up similar establishments in other countries, where, although there would not be as many suicides as in Japan—nearly 500 people there have already taken advantage of his service—he would be happy with whatever the country would provide. His genius and botanical protection make him a formidable foe for Bond to face.

Scaramanga, the villain of *The Man with the Golden Gun*, is more selective about the men he kills, with only 49 deaths to his credit. He is ruthless and heartless, and has been responsible for the deaths of several agents and the horrible maiming of another, who was shot in both kneecaps. A freelance assassin who also moves narcotics, he is feared and admired in his territory of the Caribbean and Central America. This man uses a "gold-plated, long-barrelled, single-action Colt .45" with special bullets that he makes himself for "maximum wounding effect." Scaramanga is a self-educated genius who is supposed to be impossible to assassinate because of his skill with his golden gun. Even Bond wonders if he can take him.

Similar in some ways to Scaramanga is Cloche, the villain of *The Deep*. He, too, has created a territory, in Bermuda, where he is feared and admired. He is a politician and a businessman, and the real government will not go near him; so he makes his own rules, scaring the inhabitants with the threat of magic and voodoo. When David and Gail Sanders stumble onto a huge sunken shipload of morphine, he wants it for himself. He forces them to dive for it, telling them there will be no place on earth that they would ever be safe from him. When the protagonists do not cooperate with him, Cloche starts getting his revenge.

"Rainbird was a troll, an orc, a balrog of a man. . . . His countenance was a horrorshow of scar tissue with runneled flesh. His left eye was gone." This villain of Stephen King's *Firestarter* is an awful man to look at, but his mind is even more terrible. He, too, is extremely smart, particularly when it comes to the psychological games he plays and his analysis of situations. He works for the Shop, a government agency like the CIA, and while the other members are enemies to the protagonists, John Rainbird is set apart by his total villainy. He works as an assassin, a job which suits him fine. "Dealing death had always been his business and was the only trade he had ever excelled at. . . . Death interested him." When he killed people he always searched their faces for a sign of what it was like, trying to see the moment of the soul's exit from the body. His current assignment is to end with the death of a child (he has never killed a child before that he knows of), and he wonders if the expression will be different from an adult's at the time of death. But he does not merely walk up and kill her—he makes her trust him first, feeling quite pleased with himself when she confides in him.

Power-Hungry Politicians

Villains are often so powerful that the government cannot touch them. At other times they are part of the government itself. Many of the books on American politics feature a power-hungry villain who will stop at nothing to become a dictator. (These villains differ in their jobs and philosophies depending on their authors' political beliefs. Some are liberal newsmen, others are pacifist vice-presidents, and others are conservative secret service heads.) FBI Director Vernon T. Tynan in *The R Document* is described as a large and scowling man who swears constantly and keeps thuglike bodyguards in constant attendance. Unmarried, he brings his mother his secret files so that she can read about the juiciest scandals. Tynan is trying to get the 35th Amendment passed, which will essentially wipe out the Bill of Rights and put into effect the infamous R Document, making him a virtual dictator. He and his men blackmail, slander, threaten, and murder. He is planning to have the president assassinated and to kill everyone else who stands in his way. In many ways Tynan looks like a stereotyped crime boss, but we do remember him while we forget the name of the nice young attorney general who finally defeats him.

Knife-Wielding Women

There are women villains, too. Portnoy's mother is not alone to blame for his problems as an adult, but she qualifies as a bona fide villain in the story *Portnoy's Complaint*. She dominates her household and appears to have supernatural powers. She can materialize in the form of his kindergarten teacher and then fly back in the window, becoming his mother at home. She can make peaches *hang* suspended in jello, and she uses a form of radar before it has been invented. When Portnoy hides under a bed, she attacks him with a broom and she holds a knife in front of his face to make him eat his supper. "Doctor, why oh why," the adult Portnoy asks, "would a mother hold a knife before her son's face?" It was a breadknife, Portnoy remembers, with little sawlike teeth.

Another female villain also wields a knife—Zoe Kohler, who is known as the Hotel Ripper Killer in *The Third Deadly Sin*. Most of the time Zoe is nondescript and mousy, excessively preoccupied with her body and illnesses. She visits her doctor regularly, has few friends, and works as a record clerk in a hotel. Once a month, however, she dresses up in her "secret clothes"—gowns, wigs, makeup—and lures men to hotel rooms, where she kills and castrates them. The story is as much about Zoe as about Edward X. Delaney, who finally figures out the kind of killer this must be. Although Zoe is sick, her disguise and skills are such that they have terrorized the city. Here we have the prototypical female villain whose embrace brings men to their destruction.[5]

Faceless Enemies

All these villains, however, must share evil honors with the faceless representatives of a nation or class. Evil appears all the more powerful when it is hidden and undefined—infesting a vast bureaucracy, hidden behind the walls of a foreign government, spreading from one world capital to another. Indeed, it is interesting how few individual villains there are compared to the collective enemies. In the books about spies and international intrigue, brave secret agents face collective enemies about one-third of the time. Russians and international conspirators are the favorite enemies, followed by Neo-Nazi groups. Asians and Third World peoples are apparently not as popular in the role of enemies, or as easy to write about, as Europeans.

One use of Asians as faceless enemies is found in Clive Cussler's *Deep Six*. At times they appear to be Korean and at other times Chinese; elsewhere in the book they are simply called "Asians." The enemies are seen spying through expensive binoculars, speaking in rapid Chinese, or peering through "half-slit eyes." They seem to be everywhere, Cussler is telling us, a formidable threat to the Americans and to hero Dirk Pitt.

Individual heroes face a large collective evil. "The final enemy," a character tells the hero in *Shibumi*, "is not chaos, but organizations . . . similarity . . . progress." It is hard to identify who this enemy is when it takes on these qualities, and harder still to know how to defeat it. The contest is unequal, terrifying, and unfair. That makes it all the more enjoyable to the readers of best sellers when the hero gets to win anyway. Terrors can be quieted for a time until the next faceless enemy appears.

Ordinary People

Ordinary life can have its own heroes and heroines, too. The conflicts are fought in suburb or supermarket, and the largest victories and defeats are internal ones. These people are not defending society, bringing about justice, or saving others. All their courage and strength are needed to save their own lives. While they vary in age, situation, and degree of success, a large majority of their crises are marital ones, and the most fearsome dragon is the midlife crisis. A pilgrimage, carried on by flashbacks and the chronological structure of the story, takes them back in time to come to terms with their lives at present. What separates these characters from other protagonists is their response to the crisis. Indeed, given the number of best sellers devoted to the subject, saving one's own life is a task of the utmost difficulty, requiring heroic efforts and skill.

A new kind of character arose from the women's movement of the late 1960s. She was an ordinary woman, usually married with children, struggling to find her own life and give voice to her own experience. In *How to Save Your Own Life*, Isadora Wing leaves her husband on Thanksgiving Day. The book recounts her life to that point, shows her process of self-discovery, and helps her gather the courage to leave. In *The War between the Tates*, Erica's discovery of her husband's affair impels her to take a new look at her own situation and to see the current state of the war between the sexes. Similar crises lead to new insights and decisions in *Such Good Friends* and *The Women's Room*.

The books focus on the details of ordinary life. We see the hospital rooms for childbirth and abortion, the kitchens for meal preparation, and conflict with children. We are told about the unromantic details of the first affair, and the inconveniences of contraception. Rachel Samstat in *Heartburn* finds out who the other woman is in her husband's life and thinks about a carrot cake with crushed pineapple. Erica Tate ponders justice as she watches her husband carry the garbage to the street. In *The Women's Room* Mira Ward's moment of decision and major battle occur in a restroom as she reads the graffiti on the wall. The details, often biological and unpleasant, are deliberate. They show the heightened perception of the narrator and the kind of experiences the women must work through to win whatever victory they can.

Many of the books also take a deliberately comic tone. The narrators use wry humor as they observe, with an uncompromising eye, the absurdities of their own and others' behavior. In fact, the narrators in three of the books—Gould's *Such Good Friends*, Ephron's *Heartburn*, and Lurie's *The War between the Tates*—could be used to comment on each other's experience. Lurie's Erica is the most intelligent of the three, and Ephron's Rachel tells the same joke too many times. Nevertheless, all have unfaithful husbands. They are all very angry and frank about sex. Finally, all respond to their situation with a kind of detached humor. In *The Women's Room* a character describes the conversations the women are having: "The catastrophes were always comic, even when in fact they were not. . . . The catastrophes were comic, the men were inadequate, and the women functioned against overwhelming odds, defeated before they began." One reviewer calls this "clown face of pain" the most original contribution of the feminist novels.[6] Since the heroines face the same pain, they look to the same black humor as the only lifesaving response.

Nevertheless, it is ironic that these feminist authors celebrate the very images of women they would like to shatter.[7] Their heroines are defined by biology and preoccupied with it. They are immersed in detail and largely indifferent to the world beyond their immediate circle. It is true that many of the women have successful careers—as a famous author, a professor, a writer of cookbooks, an illustrator of children's books. Their work, however, is only incidental to the action of the story. Their lives revolve around relationships with men.

Compare, for example, Mira cowering in the ladies' room or Rachel with her carrot cake with a more traditional heroine. A young woman by the name of Dallas Lawson sets off alone, with very little money, for a foreign country. Her father has just died, before he could accept a commission as a restorer of paintings. But Dallas needs a job and knows she is a better restorer of paintings than her father was. "You mustn't think of me as a young lady," she reminds people sharply. "I'm a restorer of pictures." Dallas fights against prejudice to get the job and in the process solves a mystery and finds a romance she was not looking for (*The King of the Castle*). People might not think of Victoria Holt as a feminist writer, but her androgynous character Dallas (named for her father Daniel and mother Alice) has the traits of courage, independence, and determination that are usually admired by society. And she even gets to win.

Still, these books do manage to show the lives of their women characters with realism and depth. In *The Women's Room*, author Marilyn French has her narrator admit, "Sometimes I get as sick of writing this as you may be of reading it. . . . I get sick because, you see, it's all true, it happened, and it was boring and painful and full of despair." The same circles, traps, and suffering are repeated until the sheer weight of the detail adds up to a picture that is more than the accumulation of its parts. Then, too, most of the characters take some action or make a discovery in the course of the novel to break out of the circles. Isadora leaves her husband. Mira emerges from the ladies' room with a new resolve. Rachel cannot go back to the kind of thinking she did before. All the memories recaptured, in all their boring and painful detail, have brought her to a new level of consciousness. Given the harsh reality presented in these novels, "winning" is irrelevant. The heroines succeed when they try to find—and save—their own lives.

Male characters also must do battle against the traps of day-to-day living. For all the novels about women's rise in consciousness (perhaps a dozen among the top best sellers), there are at least as many about middle-aged men. Moses Herzog, a respected professor and scholar, faces a breakdown when his second wife leaves him for another man. Herzog lives at a pitch of highest intensity. He feels passionately, thinks constantly, travels from one place to another. The crisis sends him into even more frenetic activity. He writes letters compulsively: "Dear Mama, As to why I haven't visited your grave in so long. . . . Dear Professor Hoyle, I don't think I understand just how the Gold-Pore Theory works. . . . Dear Herr Nietzsche. . . ." He makes plans, recalls bits and pieces of his past life, develops theories. He is constantly in motion throughout the story. He decides to confront his wife and her new lover, traveling to Chicago with a loaded gun that he knows he will not use. By the end of the novel all this wild energy has subsided somewhat. There is a last spate of letter writing and some work restoring his house in the Berkshires. He brings in wine and flowers and continues an old affair. Herzog has not changed his life—he has kept it. He has survived.

Prizewinning biographer William Dubin must decide whether or not to leave his marriage, and so must high-powered advertising executive and magazine writer Eddie Anderson (*Dubin's Lives*; *The Arrangement*). Like Herzog, Eddie undergoes a process of breakdown and survival; and like the narrators in the women's novels, he feels that things can never go back to what they were before. Herzog, Dubin, and Eddie are unique characters, drawn by the serious novelists Bellow, Malamud, and Kazan. Nevertheless, they show definite similarities to each other and to the many other best-selling domestic heroes. They are all middle-aged. They are very successful in their careers, and they are all sexually active. Dubin is comic as he runs back and forth between his wife and mistress. He is an expert on other people's lives with his own wildly out of control. Still, his career and romantic abilities are never in question. Even Eddie, who has changed his life drastically, continues to write magazine articles and remains with a woman he loves.

Not all of the conflicts are marital and domestic. Rabbi Michael Kind undergoes a crisis of faith at age 45 in which he questions his work and the value of his religion (*The Rabbi*). His wife, a convert to Judaism, has been hospitalized with a mental breakdown. He is filled with doubt and bitterness. However, as he reviews his life and the congregations he has served, some pieces begin to come together. The novel tells the story of a life, and, like the book about women, the story leads the character to a new

Saving One's Own Life: Some Examples		
The Book	*Age of the Character*	*The Problem*
THE MEN:		
Go to the Widow-Maker	36	Marriage and affair
A Month of Sundays	41	Religion and affairs
The Honey Badger	42	Health and affairs
An American Dream	43	Marriage and affair
The Arrangement	40s	Marriage and career
The Hurricane Years	44	Health, marriage, and career
The Rabbi	45	Religion and career
Herzog	40s	Marriage
Dubin's Lives	40s	Marriage and affair
Rabbit Is Rich	46	Marriage and family
Evening in Byzantium	48	Marriage and career
Bright Flows the River	55	Marriage and family
THE WOMEN:		
How to Save Your Own Life	32	Marriage
Heartburn	38	Marriage
The War between the Tates	39	Marriage and family
In This House of Brede	40	Religion
Blue Skies, No Candy	40	Affair
Class Reunion	40s	Marriage and affairs
Come Pour the Wine	45	Affair
The Bleeding Heart	45	Affair

resolution and confidence. By the end of the novel Michael, like Moses Herzog and Mira Ward, has worked through to a point of view that he did not have before.

Even more exceptional is Ezekiel Farragut, John Cheever's hero of *Falconer*. Ezekiel, once a college professor, has been imprisoned for murder after striking his brother once in anger. His wife is unkind, his father never liked him, and he has a drug habit from medication received when he was wounded in war. If the past has been hard, the present is even grimmer, filled with the brutality and ugliness of prison life. Nevertheless, Ezekiel retains a capacity for thought and feeling. He develops friendships in prison, thinks about religion, finds love with a fellow inmate. His spiritual triumph is paralleled by the physical one when he escapes, literally in the face of death, by hiding in a dead friend's burial sack.

Ordinary heroes, the best sellers make clear, must not only survive—they must continue. And while things may not be much better, or have changed that much at all, the characters must go on with their lives. They can change mates and careers; in fact, they may be encouraged to do so. But most will have a mate and a well-respected career at the end of the novel as at the beginning. They must gain self-knowledge, often by a painful review of the past, that will allow them confidence in the future. While not all characters would fit these conclusions, the number that do fit is striking.

Multiple Characters

One important kind of character remains to be looked at. Many of the best-selling books use multiple characters rather than a single protagonist. Typically, several different people are introduced in each of the first several chapters, with their fortunes followed in turn throughout the novel. In the first four chapters of *Class Reunion* we meet four women as they enter college: Emily Applebaum, Annabel Jones, Christine Spark, and Daphne Leeds. We learn about their college romances in chapters 6–9 and 11–16, with each character in turn given her own brief chapter. Part II follows the same order for the marriages and divorces of the 1960s, and Part III for the 1970s. Emily has had a breakdown, Chris has married a homosexual, Daphne remains married with four growing children. Annabel is divorced, has taken a job as a buyer at Bloomingdale's, and is engaged in a series of affairs. A short epilogue brings them together for their 20th reunion, and the novel concludes. Emily is distinguished among the four by being Jewish and a perfectionist, while Daphne is a debutante and beautiful. But the various romances, marriages, and divorces in the novel could be switched from one character to another with no difference in the story.

Jeffrey Archer introduces us to three young men in *First among Equals*: the aristocratic Charles Hampton, middle-class Simon Kerslake, and working-class member Raymond Gould. We follow the political careers of each in turn as they win seats in Parliament, gain power and recognition, and attempt to become prime minister. When one is finally chosen, the novel concludes. But we could not help advise the Crown on who should be selected. Apart from the class differences, the three men are the same.

The choice of multiple characters is often ideally suited to a particular story. Auchincloss, for example, creates a family portrait in *A World of Profit*, with each member of the Shallcross family fully and carefully drawn. Solzhenitsyn shows the spirit and suffering of very diverse political prisoners in *The First Circle*. Multiple characters help Michener convey the size and scope of the space program and let Hailey show the complex workings of various industries. At times, however, the device can allow an author to avoid developing any characters. At the extreme, if enough characters are introduced—each with his or her own childhood traumas, adult drives, and fortunes briefly chronicled—600 pages can be covered easily with no plot or character developed at all.

The use of multiple characters is found throughout the best sellers—in tales of glamour (*Hollywood Wives*), adventure (*Storm Warning*), horror (*Ghost Story*), and police procedure (*The New Centurions*). The sagas, of course, show many characters through several generations. Altogether, about 170 of the top sellers use the multiple-character device, or a little more than one in every three stories.

It is often said that it is difficult to write about heroes in modern society. The new stars are ordinary people like Harry (Rabbit) Angstrom or Erica Tate. But it looks as though even the ordinary folks must share star billing with another kind of character. The real protagonist of many of the best-selling stories is not the individual but the group. Even the villains are usually in groups, the faceless representatives of a nation or class.

What explains the choice and popularity of this kind of character? It may save authors the work of characterization, but this is not a good enough reason in itself. In many cases, a society is the real subject of the story, and so the more characters, the more parts of society can be written about. It takes multiple characters to show America in the 1920s or the Hollywood drug culture or the spirit of a police department or the exploits of men at war. There may be promotional considerations also. Books are advertised as "giants" and "sweeping sagas." They are called broad in vista and large in scope. It follows that multiple characters are well suited to this wide-angled fiction where sales are seen as proportionate to the number of pages and a giant subject predicts a giant success.

This trend, however, leads to the disturbing question of whether characters are necessary for a best-selling novel. The answer evidently is no. Authors can introduce many characters, saying little about them, oppose them with faceless enemies, and let events carry the story. The books tell about the California Gold Rush or a 17th-century court without saying what the characters are like. Even many of the heroes are less than full-dimensional. What if some detectives and secret agents switched assignments? Jack Higgins's heroes went on Green Beret missions? Mary Stewart's heroines wandered into Robin Cook's hospitals? The books would have the same action and outcome even though the characters were changed.

There are books for those who like original and fully drawn characters. Forsyth and Follett bring a host of intriguing characters to their spy novels, as do Greene in *The Human Factor* and Griffin in his story of war. Griffin shows how the mistakes and weaknesses found throughout a ship's crew lead to the "operational necessity" of gunning down a lifeboat with its survivors. In Follett's *The Man from St. Petersburg*, all four members of a family are portrayed fully. The fate of nations on the eve of World War I depends on how each character interacts with the others. Even the minor characters are interesting in some of these novels. Look at the variety of Russian bureaucrats shown in Forsyth's *The Fourth Protocol*, and the investigator in *The Human Factor* who is sympathetic to the other side. Those who like complex studies of character should see the books by Louis Auchincloss and P. D. James. Auchincloss builds his characters slowly and carefully, crafting them from several different points of view. In *Innocent Blood*, James looks beyond a terrible crime that was committed, to the relations between a mother and daughter and the tangled emotions of guilt, horror, and love. Renault's characters and Styron's Nat Turner are much richer than the historical record. O'Hara's Yank Lucas (*The Instrument*) is memorable, and so are Herzog and Dubin and Hercule Poirot. Readers could probably find another half-dozen examples, but the point remains. Best sellers can indulge in characterization, although they need not do so. And the majority do not.

Summary

If we ask who the best-selling characters are, the answers are surprising. No one stereotyped hero exists. The heroes differ greatly in age, physical characteristics, and circumstances. At the same time, many of the ordinary people, who are supposed to be unique, show a number of common traits. They face similar situations and hold on to the same things. They see the same kind of details and share the same memories. Some even have the same sense of humor.

However, the modern heroes do possess important traits in common. They are skilled at their work and devoted to it. They return from retirement for one more assignment just as the alienated executives save their own lives and go back to work. The heroes are similar, too, in their modesty and attitude toward authority. Unlike the power-hungry politicians, the heroes do not seek power for themselves or defer to it in others. Bond, Blackie, Smiley, Arkady Renko—all chafe against their bureaucratic hierarchies and get in trouble for doing so. Young Julian will not curry favor with the Emperor Constantine. Yet they are at the same time *part* of the hierarchy they are reacting against; they risk their lives for it and receive honor from it. The heroes, and the suicidal executives as well, challenge authority only to a point—far enough to be unusual, but not too far to jeopardize their status in the story.

Then, too, some kinds of characters appear much more frequently than others. That heroines are so scarce should not be surprising. If heroism is defined by the values of society, strong and successful women challenge these traditional values. In any case, readers too old for Mattie and too young for Miss Marple will find few models for heroism in the best sellers. If the readers are not lucky enough to find a mansion with a mystery or willing to be placed in hospitals, their options are reduced even further. It may be hard to identify with prehistoric Ayla—and even Ayla, basically, is searching for a mate. The books span two decades from before the women's movement in the late 1960s to the present day. While the changing attitudes are seen in the stories of ordinary women, the plight of the heroine has not improved with the years. *True Grit* appeared in 1968, *Sleeping Murder* in 1976, and *The Valley of Horses* in 1982.

Perhaps more surprising, villains are also scarce. There are familiar types: a few exotic foreigners and knife-wielding women and many power-hungry politicians. But beyond these cases we find few powerful individuals committed to evil acts. It seems that no one is creating good villains anymore.[8] Much more commonly, evil is shown as a collective force. The enemy is a nation, an international conglomerate, a bureaucracy. Evil is all the more terrifying, and the challenge to the hero all the greater, for being faceless, nonhuman, undefined.

Finally, we see that many of the books feature no individuals at all. The group or society is the real protagonist, with multiple characters used to tell the story. About one in three best sellers uses the multiple-character device, and more than one in three in recent years. Halfway through the 1980s, the top-selling books continued to show some individuals: King's story of Jack in *The Talisman*, Vidal's tale of Lincoln, Leonard's conflict between a detective and a psychopathic enemy. But they also told the collective stories of families during the Civil War, ladies in a book club, people who worked in a drug company, various Americans and Russians chasing a defecting Soviet submarine, and candidates struggling to be the next British prime minister. If villains have turned into faceless enemies, the protagonists also have dispersed and multiplied, becoming rather faceless themselves.

NOTES

1. See Karl Beckson and Arthur Ganz, *Literary Terms* (New York: Farrar, Straus, Giroux, 1975), p. 94.

2. John Cawelti and Bruce Rosenberg, *The Spy Story* (Chicago: University of Chicago Press, 1987), p. 46.

3. Page 99. Drury continues: "During the middle years of the century, the government of his [the black's] country and the great majority of its white citizens tumbled over themselves in their haste to pass laws, improve conditions, right old wrongs. To an amazing extent, they succeeded. . . . But by all too many vocal and vindictive blacks their achievements were greeted with jeers and contempt and shrill, childish demands for more."

4. Unlike Susan Wheeler, medical student Cassandra Kingsley in Robin Cook's *Godplayer* is not a heroine. While someone (again) is killing the patients in a large metropolitan hospital, Cassi, a diabetic, is preoccupied with her personal health and her husband's moods through most of the story. When the murderer finally confronts her, it is not because of her own doing; nor is she instrumental in bringing him to justice.

5. Audrey Rogers looks at the stereotypes of women in fiction in " 'Portrait of a Lady': Images of Women in Twentieth Century American Literature," in *The Study of Women* (New York: Harper, 1979), pp. 228–61. See also Susan Cornillon, ed., *Images of Women in Fiction* (Bowling Green, Ohio: Bowling Green University Press, 1972), esp. Joanna Russ, "What Can a Heroine Do?" pp. 3–20; and Sandra Gilbert and Susan Gubar, eds., *The Norton Anthology of Literature by Women* (New York: Norton, 1985), pp. 1230–33.

6. Nora Johnson, "Housewives and Prom Queens Twenty Five Years Later," *New York Times Book Review*, March 20, 1988, p. 1.

7. See the literature cited in note 5 above.

8. *The Great Book of Movie Villains*, by Jan Stacy and Ryder Syversten (Chicago: Contemporary Books, 1984), lists only 46 for the same years 1965–1985 that would meet our definition of powerful evil individuals. (The book also includes other characters distinguished only by the fact that they oppose the leading characters.) This total of 46 makes only about two villains a year for all the major movies released. Of course, even one villain can do a lot of harm.

Themes—American Dreams and Nightmares

ONE THEME STANDS OUT among the best sellers, dominating the others and persisting across the years. That is the American Dream: the pursuit of freedom, wealth, and success in a land of opportunity. In the New World, people not only have the right to life, liberty, and happiness, in the words of the Declaration of Independence, they have the chance for success. But the success has to be earned: the pursuit takes self-reliance and hard work. The dream thus includes the goals and the means of achieving them. Philosopher John Locke originally used the phrase "life, liberty, and the pursuit of property." The writers of the Declaration, drawing on Locke, changed "property" to "happiness" for a broader, less materialistic term. So one can pursue property and claim to be holding to the spirit of the American Dream. Individuals can seek their own success and fortune and be patriotic at the same time. They are demonstrating the opportunities of American society, giving proof that the dream can work.

The dream is found in the classic rags-to-riches story, in the chronicles of individual lives, and in all kinds of settings. Sagas show the dream at work across several generations. Immigrants come to America, rise from poverty to attain great wealth, and survive the ups and downs of the stock market, social change, and wars. Their children grow up and pursue personal dreams of their own. Other books criticize the effects of the dream, showing the emptiness and false values of an affluent society. The books of the 1980s embrace the dream again. Once more the Statue of Liberty beckons and the immigrants return. While the theme takes different forms across the years, the continuities are stronger than the differences.

Rags to Riches

The rise from rags to riches, first seen in the Horatio Alger tales of the 19th century, is a standard theme of the best sellers. But instead of merely showing a poor boy's rise to fortune, the stories now tell of immigrants from diverse countries struggling in the alien world of America. Where Alger's heroes spoke the same language and knew how their society operated, the immigrants are left without these small advantages. Faced with hardship and despair, they become vivid examples of how people can start at the bottom and work their way up. The immigrants are at the heart of the American Dream. The country was founded by them and continues to be inhabited by them. Therefore, the use of immigrants as characters is perhaps the clearest way for an author to show the American Dream at work.

In 1888, immigrants were arriving in the United States from all over the world. "The great lady of hope welcomed them. . . . The Eighth Wonder of the World." So writes Howard Fast in his book *The Immigrants*. However, only a few lines further Fast writes, "Lady Liberty was laughing at them." Ellis Island was a mystery to these people. They were herded around like sheep and given health checks and shots. Many had their names changed to fit in better in their new society. Then they were on their own. "There were Turks, and no one spoke Turkish; there were Greeks, and no one spoke Greek." Joseph and Anna Lavette, from France and Italy, thought they were lucky to meet a man who spoke Italian. He helped them cash their money in for American currency; yet it was some time later that Joseph realized that he had cheated them. Joseph quickly "learned that the process of being cheated, put upon, robbed, bamboozled was an intricate part of the existence in America of two immigrants who spoke no English." But the Lavettes had come to America to give their son, not yet born, a better chance in life. Finally reaching San Francisco, Joseph saves all his money to buy his boy a fishing boat. This is the beginning of the Lavettes' rise from rags to riches. With the small boat and the pennies saved, son Daniel can pursue the American Dream.

Although he stresses the terrible conditions that the immigrants were subject to, Fast follows only the lives of characters who achieve money and power. While he never lets his characters forget that they were once poor, he makes it look as though anyone can achieve riches given even the smallest opportunity.

Daniel Lavette's chance comes with the San Francisco Earthquake. With his parents lying dead in the rubble, Daniel sits in the small fishing boat, his heart filled with grief. But in a matter of several days, his pockets are filled with over $4,000. People are so desperate to get out of the city that they give huge sums of money to Daniel to ferry them over to Oakland. He goes on to buy more fishing boats, hire workers, and form a partnership with Mark Levy, a second-generation American. This is only the beginning, however. In World War I they get rich by shipping weapons and ammunition to the Allies, go on to become the owners of a huge department store, a passenger shipline, a hotel in Hawaii, and an airline. Although Daniel's fortune was lost with the stock market crash, he knows he can build it again if he wants to. The dream can be endlessly pursued.

Western writer Louis L'Amour also tells rags-to-riches stories. *The Lonesome Gods* is a tale of the American West in the mid-19th century, particularly the Los Angeles area. The main character grows from a boy to a man in the course of the novel, learning about the American Dream in the process. However, a secondary character, Miss Nesselrode, gives an even clearer example of the dream at work.

Throughout most of the story no one knows who she is, where she came from, or what interest Los Angeles holds for her. They do realize, however, that she is a lady in the best sense of the word, and one of education, intelligence, and courage. Later in the novel, the explanation for Miss Nesselrode's situation is given. She is an immigrant who has escaped from Russia for the freedom of America. In Russia she and her family had been persecuted and then exiled because her brothers spoke out against the government; and if she were to return she would be arrested. But she is not in America only for refuge. She is here because she seeks the opportunity to lead a successful life. In contrast to other books about American immigrants, here the fact that she is one is kept hidden. She fits in quite well with American society, and no one is the wiser to her heritage.

Through her own success, Miss Nesselrode shows the opportunities that Los Angeles has to offer. The climate is great for growing, and the ocean provides access to trade with China and other countries. She has very little money, so when she first starts out in business it is a big gamble. She buys skins at a low price which she in turn ships to China, knowing that her profits could be very large. However, with the dangers that plague ships at the time, she has no guarantee that her investment will be returned. At the same time she buys land and plants it in oranges and grapes, and is left with only a few dollars. Miss Nesselrode is a careful planner, however. She listens at every opportunity and is determined to succeed. At one point she says to Johannes, "I have been poor, Hannes, and I do not wish to be poor again. I work, I plan, I save." With three words she invokes the dream that could be hers only in America.

Taylor Caldwell's *Captains and the Kings* tells another tale of rags to riches. Joseph, a young Irish immigrant, comes to America steerage-class; his mother dies on the ship, and his brother and sister are placed in an orphanage. But Joseph is tough, hard-working, and bright. He saved his money, owes no one, and wins the trust of the powerful Mr. Healey, who

THE IMMIGRANTS COME TO AMERICA

Book	Publication Date
Fathers	1966
Rich Man, Poor Man	1970
Captains and the Kings	1972
Ragtime	1975
Ceremony of the Innocent	1976
The Immigrants	1977
Chesapeake	1978
Evergreen	1978
Kane and Abel	1979
Portraits	1979
Century	1981
Goodbye, Janette	1981
No Time for Tears	1981
Remembrance	1981
The Lonesome Gods	1983

works on both sides of the law. Joseph runs guns and liquor, studies law, and patents an invention that makes him rich. Then, on Mr. Healey's death and the reading of the will, Joseph becomes an even richer man.

While Caldwell tells a classic Horatio Alger tale, she gives no credit to society for Joseph's rise to fortune. Life is hard, and society is biased against the Irish. Senators are corrupt, and the law and Constitution are for sale to the highest bidder. Conspirators and conspiracies exist. What Joseph has won he has won by his own efforts, in spite of the injustice and bigotry around him. He prospers also because he is willing to go outside his religion and outside the law. While Joseph's story is an example of the American Dream, Caldwell would say that it is Joseph, not America, that made it possible.

Joseph goes on to amass even greater wealth and power. He founds a dynasty and dreams of his son becoming president. Although one son is killed in the war, his son Rory enters politics and soon is elected to the Senate. The country has not changed much across the years. While the dream is achieved with the immigrant's son on his way to the White House, conspiracies and lawlessness still exist and must be reckoned with.

Caldwell says in the Preface that she knows of no real family like her fictional creation: "There is not, to my knowledge, any family like the 'Armagh Family' in America, nor has there ever been, and all characters, except those obviously historical, are my own invention." If what she says is true, she must be the only one who does not know of such a family.

In many of these books the American Dream becomes merely a formula and substitute for a plot. An immigrant family comes to America. Characters whose personalities are not revealed to us rise from rags to riches, bearing children who face their own problems of success, and so on for the succeeding generations. The stock market crash, World War II, and the Nazi concentration camps tie the formula to events of the century and help the characters through a few more chapters. Many of the sagas, in fact, are really restatements of the same story. The names and circumstances of the characters could be interchanged, as well as the particular ways their fortunes are achieved.

In Belva Plain's *Evergreen*, for example, Anna, a poor Polish Jewish immigrant, comes to America, lives in a tenement, and works as a servant in a wealthy house. After a romance with the son of the house, she marries another poor immigrant; they have children and begin to make money in real estate. Their fortunes fall with the stock market crash and must be built again. This action takes about one-third of the book. The second part of the novel recounts the lives of their children, one of whom marries a survivor of the Nazi concentration camps. The final portion of the book tells about the grandchildren. Altogether, about 10 characters are focused on briefly.

The same formula is used in the multibook sagas, with the generations divided between the books. Howard Fast's *The Immigrants* is followed by *Second Generation*. The third book in the series traces the family through the 1950s and the fourth through the 1970s, for a total of about 90 years. Fast supplies more details of action than Plain does, as would be expected in a four-volume work, and he has room to stray from the theme and plot at times. In *The Immigrants* we learn the art of winemaking and the special conditions that apply to wine made for Jewish ceremonies as we watch two minor characters pursue their dream. We are also instructed on things such as the history of Hawaiian luaus and the diversities of the tongues of China. So although the amount of detail is greater than that of a single-volume saga, the restatement of the formula is the same.

Authors can show *two* characters in conflict: one rising from poverty, and the other a child of wealth and privilege. As the Horatio Alger hero surpasses the other character on his way to success, the story celebrates the American Dream. Jeffrey Archer's *Kane and Abel* contrasts the lives of William Kane and Abel Rosnovski, a Polish-born orphan who immigrates to the United States. While William goes to Harvard and is elected to the most exclusive clubs, Abel goes to night school, graduates from hotel waiter to assistant manager, and goes on to own the entire hotel chain. In Anton Myrer's *A Green Desire*, two brothers take very different paths in childhood: Chapin chooses to live in luxury, while Tip stays with his mother and remains poor. Tip makes all the right ethical choices, and Chapin makes all the wrong ones. Tip, the salesman, is the hero of the story, actually called by one of the characters "the absolute epitome of the American Dream."

While these characters pursue wealth, many others have already achieved it. Auchincloss wrote five best sellers about people in New York's financial world, while Erdman wrote three about international finance. One can read more about banks in Hailey's *The Money-Changers*. Krantz, Howatch, Robbins, and Sheldon feature characters who are wealthy. Other books show entrepreneurs in South Africa, Australia, and Hong Kong at work building their fortunes. Fortunes are made in diamonds, furs, shipping, hotels, fashion, and real estate. Altogether, about 50 books present main characters who are very rich or who become so in the course of the story. This count excludes the film stars and other celebrities. It also excludes those, we will see in the following section, who pursue other kinds of success.

The Pursuit of Happiness

Characters can pursue private goals and still carry on the dream. Once they have food on the table and decent clothes to wear, they turn to all the things that money cannot buy. They seek fame or pleasure or other kinds of self-fulfillment. They embark on a course of self-discovery or question the direction of their lives. Since readers concerned with these same pursuits will be keenly interested in the characters' experiences, it is not surprising how many examples of the theme we find.

Asher Lev, son of an Orthodox Jewish family, is born with a genius and passion for painting (*My Name Is Asher Lev*). The book recounts his childhood and upbringing, the increasing conflict with his family, and his single-minded pursuit of an artistic career:

> I drew endlessly all those weeks after my father's departure. I drew while I walked; I drew while I ate; I drew while I sat in class; I drew in Yudel Krinsky's store; I drew in the museum. . . .

The narrative goes on to show the detailed development of his lessons and his growing skill, his trip to Europe, and the paintings he completes. He becomes increasingly engrossed in painting crucifixions, and his first great success—and final break with his family—comes with his *Brooklyn Crucifixion*, a work that stuns the art world and assures his reputation.

Asher Lev is combining a social tradition with his own personal vision; his mother becomes a subject in the crucifixion painting. Nevertheless, his career requires an emphasis on the personal and the selfish, an emphasis shown in the title of the book and throughout the narrative. (There must be as many sentences beginning with "I" here as in any book in contemporary fiction.) He hurts his family badly—and knows he is doing so—as he pursues his need for happiness.

The Reverend Thomas Marshfield in *A Month of Sundays* engages in a series of liaisons with members of his own congregation as he tries to revitalize his religious faith. The sex he is so vigorously pursuing becomes part of the physical energy he seeks in God and in the forms of organized religion. Prayers become mixed together with masturbatory fantasies, and his counseling necessarily combines with his affairs. Calls on the Lord and Ms. Prynne are part of the same jumble of emotions. "Then don't come, you bitch," he cries, and then, "I have wasted the morning listening for you." And then again, "Even so, come." Like Asher Lev, the Reverend Marshfield hurts his family and separates himself from society in pursuing his own goals.

Jonathan Livingston Seagull finds self-fulfillment by improving his flying skill. For most seagulls, flight is important only as a means to catch food, and this accomplished, they fly right back to shore. But Jonathan and a few others find happiness and freedom in the skill; so they practice one technique or another until they can do it perfectly. It brings a purpose to their otherwise boring lives, and releases them from the routine of eating and flocking on the shores.

The story of *Jonathan Livingston Seagull* captures the purest ideals of the American Dream. Obviously, seagulls do not care about money; so instead they are shown pursuing freedom, success, and happiness. But this dream has its own problems, and only those with extra courage dare to pursue it. In their fast and fancy flight, the gulls could easily lose control and fall to their deaths or crash into something and be injured. But for the most part, this is a slight and acceptable risk. Worse is the certainty that the gull would be labeled as an Outcast by the Flock and forced to leave. Their laws say that this was the way that it had to be. To Jonathan and his friends, this alienation from the rest of their society was not as important as being true to themselves. So as Jonathan reaches new levels, he teaches other gulls like himself that the "only true law is that which leads to freedom."

Back down on Earth, but almost as fantastic as talking seagulls, is the story of the Thayer family of Hollywood. In *Family Album* Danielle Steel shows Faye and Ward Thayer and their five children pursuing happiness and success in a world full of changes. Faye has found the American Dream as she moved from the poverty of her childhood to become a very successful and beautiful movie star. She then falls in love with Ward Thayer, a "playboy millionaire," but is faced with a big decision. She can continue with her career that she has worked so hard at, and that has rewarded her with an Oscar, or she can have a place to really belong, with a husband and children. Faye realizes that the second choice would be the "fulfilling" one for her, so she and Ward marry, to be supported by his fortunes.

They start out very happy with their life together, having babies and vacationing, while all the time Ward enjoys his champagne and lavishes expensive gifts on Faye. Money is not that important to Faye's happiness, but Ward cannot imagine life without it. And when his wild spending gets out of control, the Thayers lose their fortune and Ward cannot handle the change. He tries to cope by deserting his family and having an affair with a rich young actress. But Faye hangs on to reality and soon is directing movies, a long-standing goal of hers, to keep the family going. Ward finally comes back, a much-matured person, and the Thayers have another chance at happiness. Together, she as director and he as producer, they are able to climb back to the top of Hollywood society.

In the meantime, their children grow up and try to pursue happiness, too. The oldest son finds out that he is gay and can be happy only loving another man. The other son goes to college to play football but cannot keep his grades up and is drafted. One of the twin girls is insanely jealous of Faye and makes a fool of herself as she starts off on an acting career. The other twin goes away to college to pursue a career in writing. And the youngest girl, neglected during the turbulent years, runs away to Haight-Ashbury and falls victim to drugs and pregnancy at the age of 14. Some of these choices result in isolation from the other family members, and yet they are a necessary part of the characters' self-fulfillment. Throughout these trials, Faye and Ward make their own decisions for the children's happiness and the good of the family, but their actions serve only to bring more misery. So after Ward runs away again, one son faces immeasurable grief, the other dies in Vietnam, and a daughter carries on a strange affair, it would hardly seem possible that they could be happy again.

But bad things happen in fairy tales, too, and they still have happy endings. So before the family album can be closed and put back on the shelf, we see that everyone gets what he or she wants, and we know that they will live happily ever after. Except, of course, the son who dies and Faye, but she does die happily.

These are only a few of the many books telling about the pursuit of happiness. They range from serious works to the most superficial fantasies. The theme is found in feminist novels and in the search for masculinity, through shark fishing and skydiving, seen in *Go to the Widow-Maker* and *The Top of the Hill*. It is found in Harold Robbins's *The Lonely Lady*, in the prodigal daughter's attempt to become president, and in Myra Breckinridge's struggle to define his or her correct sex. The theme is found in other books, too, as we will see in the following section, when self-fulfillment becomes self-indulgence and the pursuit of happiness is carried too far.

The emphasis throughout is on the individual, on the personal and private. It is the *individual's* story that is taken to be important and worth sharing with the world at large. This emphasis is carried through in the structure of the story and the kind of details included. The books typically take the form of a chronicle, with the life of a character retold from childhood to adulthood. Narrators recount their memories, emotions, and subjective experience. It is the smell of the cookies burning that tells Erica Tate that a domestic war has been declared. Asher Lev recalls a day of fog and rain with his father singing. Isadora Wing remembers the Thanksgiving Day parades. Several of the books consist almost entirely of memories: for example, *Heartburn*; *The Honey Badger*; *How to Save Your Own Life*. The prologue and epilogue explain what is happening in the present; the rest of the book tells of the narrator's earlier life.

The individuals are seen as separate from their family and often in conflict with it. We learn of their parents' lives, often back to the parents' own childhoods and immigration to America. However, the accounts are used to explain the narrator's own perceptions: parents are important only as they affect the individual's life. *Family Album*, to take an extreme case, is not about a family but about a collection of individuals who are each pursuing happiness. The same emphasis is seen in the immigrant sagas. The Lavettes, like the Thayers of *Family Album*, are each pursuing a separate American dream.

Like the heroes of the previous chapter, the characters rebel against authority up to a point. They separate themselves from a family or break out of marriages, at the very least. They thus follow the immigrants in declaring their own independence. The immigrants have left a homeland: these characters, too, set off on their own.

The Dream Gone Wrong

Dreams once obtained can bring disillusionment, and the pursuit of private happiness can lead to indulgence and despair. The American Dream contains its own pitfalls and problems, and many of the best-selling authors have written about them.

John Cheever shows the loneliness and agony that dwell just beneath the surface of nice suburban lives, where "the schools were excellent, the roads were smooth, the drains and other services were ideal" ("The Scarlet Moving Van"). In one story, Jim and Irene Westcott are living the American Dream: "They were the parents of two young children, they had been married nine years . . . they went to the theatre on an average of 10.3 times a year, and they hoped someday to live in Westchester." But a new radio they buy begins to tell them what is really going on in their neighbors' lives and leads them to see some not-so-pleasant secrets about themselves ("The Enormous Radio"). In another story, a man sees "that string of swimming pools" curving across the county. As he works his way home by swimming through his neighbors' pools, he finds that his beautiful life has disappeared ("The Swimmer").

Cheever ends many of his stories on the same ironic note. "Everyone is well," one character says; and another, "He appeared to be very happy." Another story ends, "They got richer and richer and richer and lived happily, happily, happily, happily." Beneath the surface, it seems, the people pursuing happiness are not really happy at all.

The same theme appears in Cheever's longer best seller, *Bullet Park*. The Nailles family has moved to a very pleasant suburb, where father Eliot commutes to the city and adolescent son Tony helps direct traffic at cocktail parties. The surface details of well-ordered lives—real-estate prices, dinner tables, a deepfreeze—are set off against the ever-present threat of violence and death. A man is burned to death at a barbecue; another falls off a commuter train. There is fighting in Vietnam and race riots close to home. The split between the orderly surface and the underlying terrors exacts its psychic costs. Tony takes to his bed and refuses to get up. Nailles increasingly needs drugs to get on the train to go to work: he meets his pusher at the supermarket parking lot. Neighbor Paul Hammer, too, fights the pressure until he decides to kidnap Tony, with the idea of crucifying him on the church altar. At the conclusion of the story, the father rescues his son. But Nailles, still drugged, will continue to go to work, and the book concludes, "Everything was as wonderful, wonderful, wonderful as it had been."

A classic statement of the dream gone wrong is provided in Joseph Heller's *Something Happened*. Bob Slocum is a successful corporate executive, married with three children, in line to be a company vice-president. But from the beginning of the novel we see his deep depression. He is unhappy with his marriage, his children, and his work, and beset by constant vague anxieties. His wife and children, he tells us, are unhappy, too. Suicides and breakdowns are common at work, although, of course "The company is benevolent. The people for the most part, are nice, and the atmosphere, for the most part, is convivial. . . . There are lots of office parties." Something has happened along the way toward achieving the American Dream to produce this emptiness and despair. His own depersonalization is a mirror of the society he sees around him. Moreover, he has lost the energy to rebel and knows that rebellion would be futile. He would simply be fired and filed away. When something finally does happen to him in the course of the story, his life continues on as before. The novel concludes with irony like Cheever's: "Everyone seems pleased with the way I've taken command."

Bob Slocum has a severe case of a malaise found among many of the best-selling protagonists. Jessie Craig, in *Evening in Byzantium*, is a successful film producer who questions his life and work. Eddie Anderson, the successful advertising executive in *The Arrangement*, does the same, and so does the established Rabbi Michael Kind. Harry Angstrom, achieving a more modest middle-class success, is aware that the dream is not all it should be. Even Arthur Hailey's executives, in *Wheels* and *The Money-Changers*, find that a disillusionment with life is one of the crises they must face in the course of the story. In *Bright Flows the River*, Guy Jerald, like Anderson, attempts suicide and will not speak to anyone for weeks afterward. Why would he do it, his wife asks, when he had "a wonderful family which is devoted to him, wonderful grandchildren, security, wealth, health, this lovely house, his business, his banks—?" Perhaps, her brother says, echoing Cheever in *Bullet Park*, "he couldn't stand all that 'wonderfulness' any longer."

It is important to see, however, that *all of these disillusioned and suicidal characters continue with their work*. They change wives and mistresses but keep their jobs. Anderson keeps writing, the rabbi stays with his congregation, and Craig writes a play that brings him new money and success. Jerald gets a divorce and gives up his banks, although he keeps his other businesses. Even Bob Slocum returns to work and is promoted at the end of the story. The dream is questioned, but it is not abandoned.

At times the theme becomes a simple formula. A book offers a glamorous, successful character who questions his life and thinks back on his past romances. He works out his conflict by breaking those romantic attachments and going back to work. Readers are given glamour, romance, conflict, and a solution—and a potential best seller. Neither Heller nor Cheever, of course, is offering any neat solutions. Indeed, *Something Happened* and *Bullet Park* make it very clear that the problem continues beyond the conclusion of the story. Still, all of these characters who question the dream end by reaffirming it. It may lead to emptiness and despair, but it is the only one available.

A few of the characters try more desperate solutions. Merlyn, Mario Puzo's protagonist in *Fools Die*, is a successful writer, married with three children and a home on Long Island. Yet, like his legendary namesake, he is seeking magic in life, and he finds it only in crime and gambling. The story moves between his life on the East Coast and his adventures in Las Vegas with a gambler and a hooker. Merlyn does not choose either life exclusively, although by the end of the story he has settled for less than he had hoped. "Oh Merlin," he invokes the great wizard. "Do you have one last magic spell that can work? A terrible long shot, but what's that to a gambler? I still have a stack of black chips and an itch for terror."

An even more radical solution is taken by Stephen Rojack, Norman Mailer's protagonist in *An American Dream*. After murdering his wife in a fit of rage, he finds himself, like Puzo's Merlyn, plunged into a world of magic, crime, and violence. He is a knight who, literally, must journey through the underworld. He must show courage, keep certain vows, and try to defend his new lady, a nightclub singer and Mafia mistress. Unlike Merlyn, however, and many of the other best-selling protagonists, Rojack does not make compromises for a safe existence. At the end of the novel, he, too, sets off for Las Vegas, but it is clear that he will not return.

The dream can also go wrong when the pursuit of happiness is carried too far, whether in the name of career, sex, or reputation. In *The Instrument*, John O'Hara skillfully draws a character so caught up in a career that he is capable of no human relationships. Gifted playwright Yank Lucas, like Asher Lev, is a man wholly dedicated to his art. But he carries it to the extent that others become simply the means to help his talent. After the success of his first play he leaves New York, and the leading actress who loves him, to work on another script in a small New England town. There he meets people with their own problems and emotions who try to help him and make him feel at home. Several of these will become characters in his plays. In the course of the book, a man saves Yank's life, and he himself is responsible for the deaths of two other people. As the story concludes, Yank finishes his second play and is ready to move on.

In *Couples*, John Updike gives a satirical picture of suburban life in an upper-middle-class community. Sex is the only pursuit of happiness left, and even it has lost its meaning. Four married couples interchange partners throughout the story, proceeding from barbecue to cocktail party and from affair to affair. At one point, a character, Piet, has to ask his wife to sleep with one of the men, whom she hates, because the man can help arrange an abortion for the woman Piet is sleeping with. Jobs, children, and their own marriages have lost meaning for these people, and nothing touches them from the world outside. They briefly consider canceling a party when President Kennedy is assassinated, but decide to go ahead with it anyway. What to do after the American Dream has been achieved? Updike's characters have not found the answer.

Another satire, *The Pretenders* by Gwen Davis, shows characters that confuse happiness with money. In the circle of Beautiful People of the 1960s, only the surface counts. Those who are rich, like Harry or Maggie, are courted and deferred to and those who are not rich pay much too high a price to join their circle. A party game called "Lifeboat" is played in which the group decides which people are the most superfluous and can be tossed overboard. As a matter of fact, Harry, whose funeral is being attended at the beginning of the story, did not have much to recommend him, and Maggie is so rich that people are afraid to point out that she is insane.

Other books, too, show that money or fame or sex cannot buy happiness. Nevertheless, these books reveal a curious double standard whereby the values supposedly called into question are celebrated throughout the story. We are shown the sexual adventures, the Hollywood glamour, and all the things that money and fame can buy. Then we are told, after everyone has bought the book and enjoyed the adventures, that the pursuit of these things can lead to a bad end. *The Users* shows a Hollywood society where everyone uses each other in the search for status and success. *Hollywood Wives* tells the same story, following the lives and careers of four couples dedicated to the pursuit of fame, sex, and money, and to keeping up appearances. What Gwen Davis satirized in 1969, *Hollywood Wives* was taking seriously in 1983! . The all-time top seller, *Valley of the Dolls*, traces the lives of three Hollywood stars, all of whom end up taking drugs. The promotion blurb announces, "Each of them learned about making love, making money, and making believe. Each of them rode the crest of the wave. And each of them came finally to the Valley of the Dolls." Drugs are bad, author Jacqueline Susann tells us seriously. But the book has told us about the love, money, and make-believe.

In his novel *Ragtime*, E. L. Doctorow shows the problems that arise with living the American Dream. The book is a critical look at American life in the early 20th century, showing the immigrants and the wealthy, their fears, successes, goals, and problems as they try to live the good life. Rather than just showing individuals in conflict, Doctorow conveys the point that American society itself compromises the dream. He says, "The immigrant population set great store by the American flag." But as soon as they got off the boat they were humiliated and scorned, particularly by the second-generation Americans. The rich company owners had no respect for the immigrants, because they "worked for next to nothing." When workers did strike, it usually ended in bloodshed. In the children's crusade, families agreed to care for the children of the striking workers until things were better, but the mill owners stopped them from leaving town. They resolved that "for the good of the country and the American democratic system . . . there would be no more children's crusade."

While this was happening to the immigrants, the rich were having their own problems. One wealthy man was in prison for murder, although his cell was decorated with a Tiffany lampshade and a bottle of champagne was near at hand. Other rich people were looking for ways to alleviate their boredom. A Mrs. Fish threw some good parties. At one, everyone had to talk baby talk throughout it all. And "it became fashionable to honor the poor." Balls were held where everyone came dressed in rags, or else the place was decorated like a stockyard with beef carcasses hanging around. They had a good time, and the proceeds went to help the poor.

Harry Houdini could not get any respect for what he did. He held the ideals of perfection, courage, and athletic form, but it all meant nothing to the wealthy. He hoped for a better response in Europe. When Freud visited America and had problems finding a public restroom, visited amusement parks, and saw the decorating mistakes Americans made, he declared "America is a mistake, a gigantic mistake." The rich grew fat. "The consumption of food was a sacrament of success. . . . America was a great farting country." J. P. Morgan, one of the most powerful men in the country, threw a dinner party where he invited others of the powerful elite. "Rockefeller startled him with the news that he was chronically constipated and did a lot of his thinking on the toilet. Carnegie dozed over his brandy. Harriman uttered inanities. . . . Without exception the dozen most powerful men in America looked like horses' asses."

Even the great American pastime of baseball does not escape Doctorow's satire. The Giants and the Braves met for a game, so Father took the little boy there to see them. He even bought box seats behind first base. They were perfect seats to hear all the obscenities and see the fighting and the blood, while chewing tobacco filled the players' cheeks and spittle littered the playing field. "The sky smelled like the backroom of a saloon." Father read the program and saw the names of the players and knew that "professional baseball was played by immigrants."

And still Lady Liberty beckons. Poor boys strive for success and finally come to America to play in the big leagues and make millions and achieve fame. The characters in *Ragtime* pursue the dream even as they are satirized for it.

Nightmares

CONSPIRACIES

"Walter did not smile. He nodded his head. 'They are about to instigate a world war in the near future. . . . They'll succeed, too, through their chaps in London, Paris, Berlin, Rome, St. Petersburg, Washington, Tokyo—Everywhere . . .' " (*Ceremony of the Innocent*).

Empty lives and suburban traps are not the only nightmares haunting the characters in best sellers. Secret conspiracies exist—in American government and the major capitals of the world. The conspirators, according to Caldwell and Ludlum, decide when wars will be waged and help to keep them going. In Erdman's books they make financial deals that cause the rise and fall of nations. In Drury's thrillers they nominate presidential candidates and assassinate them, and in *The Spike* they take over the White House and the American news media. "They have no brain," a character in *Shibumi* says, "but they have a thousand arms to grasp and clutch at you, drag you down."

These are the faceless enemies found in the preceding chapter, all the more fitting subjects of nightmare for being so shadowy and unknown. We see their effects in assassinations, riots, individuals driven insane. We see a few officials and the computer rooms where the terrible decisions are made. But the forces themselves remain undescribed. In *The Matlock Paper* Ludlum writes of a conspiracy taking over American universities: "Nimrod was an unseen master puppeteer. Faceless, formless, but with a frightening, viable authority. It wasn't a *he* or a *they*—it was a *force*." In *Captains and the Kings*, Caldwell describes a plot taking place before the Civil War: "The hours went by and Joseph was witness to incredible conspiracies against mankind, all discussed in voices like the grating of bloodless metal." Even Agatha Christie writes of conspiracies in *Passenger to Frankfurt* and *Postern of Fate*:

> Fear is awakening—fear of what may be.
> Not so much because of actual happenings
> but because of the possible causes behind
> them. Some known, some unknown, but *felt*. . . .
> Riots.
> Hate.
> Anarchy—all growing stronger.
>   (Introduction, *Passenger to Frankfurt*)

The thousand-armed monster of *Shibumi* is simply called the "Mother Company." As in all good nightmares, the details are best left to the reader's imagination.

Conspiracies dwell in science and medicine, too, as well as in government. Robin Cook warns us that the simple operation we are planning may lead to a brain transplant, and Michael Crichton says that even now science may be wiring a Terminal Man or wiping out whole communities with deadly germs. Notice that the American Dream is for individuals—it does not extend to the government or institutions of society. These make up the opposite side, or the nighttime side, of the individual's success story. While people pursue happiness and success, somewhere out there are nightmarish forces over which the individual has no control.

Stephen King's *Firestarter* shows the terror that his protagonists face when *both* science and government are out of control. It begins when two college students, Andy and Vicky, participate in a psychology experiment conducted by the university and are given a drug which affects them like LSD. When the experiment is over, one of them has the ability to put thoughts into other people's minds, and the other has telekinesis. They are surprised by the results, but not worried about them. What was terrifying was the experiment itself. It was conducted by a man that the students referred to as the "Mad Doctor," who gave a speech saying, "Do not fear. You are wrapped snugly in the arms of Modern Science." But while Andy and Vicky were under the drug, they saw one boy claw out his eyes and another die from a heart attack. Later we are told that other subjects either committed suicide or went insane.

They eventually are able to put this terror behind them, get married, and have a baby girl. But when they see her start fires in her crib, they become frightened. Things get even worse when they hear that the secret agency, the Shop, wants them for more experiments, and particularly the little girl, Charlie. When the Shop does catch up with them, Vicky is tortured and killed, and Andy and Charlie flee. There is no place to run to and no one to help them; even the police have become pawns of this powerful agency. Although the reader is shown the different individuals within the Shop in some detail, Andy and Charlie see them as a huge mass that they cannot fully understand. They are pursued by a green car and men who all look the same in their fine suits. Even the minor characters, the townspeople, are terrified of these men when they are questioned about the whereabouts of Andy and Charlie.

Although Andy and Charlie begin to see the members of the agency more as individuals when they are eventually captured, the terror is not lessened. Science and the government still are running their lives, and there is little hope left to them. We do see Andy and Charlie fight back at the end of the novel, and King leaves us with a possible solution to the problem. Still, we know that the solution will not necessarily work. A group as powerful as the Shop, which makes the FBI and the CIA look like Cub Scouts, cannot be exposed and terminated that easily.

Other Nightmares

Secret conspiracies are not the only nightmares that the characters suffer. A few tales of supernatural terror and other bizarre evils are also found in these books. *The Exorcist* and *Rosemary's Baby* deal with the Devil himself as he preys upon the most innocent of characters, a young girl and a woman who wants to have a baby. The presence of the Devil is one of the oldest nightmares in Christian history, but one does not need to be religious to be terrified by these tales. Stephen King succeeds as a best-selling author because he captures in fictional form the nightmares—lying just beneath the surface or around the corner—that haunt us all. If you are overweight, are moving into a new home, have a pet (particularly a St. Bernard), or even own a car or have a father, King has a tale to frighten you. Peter Straub provides a convincing haunting in *Ghost Story*, and Tryon sets an eerie atmosphere in *The Other* and *Harvest Home*.

It is the ordinary details the authors provide that make the unseen terror so effective and real. In *Pet Sematary*, King goes on for pages, as a father buries and unburies a body, showing each rope that must be tied and each ladder to be climbed along the way. In *Harvest Home*, since we see, hear, and smell everything that Ned Constantine does, his slowly encircling nightmare becomes ours. Readers are not asked to suspend disbelief, but to *believe*—in the height of the ladder and the smell of the soup and the terrible thing that lies just beyond them. The Devil comes to Manhattan and Georgetown, breaking into secure and modern lives. Rosemary and her husband are looking for a brownstone. Ned Constantine wants a nice home in the country and feels he deserves it. Vacationers throng a beach, and a teenager buys an old car. These characters, too, are pursuing the American Dream, but then Something gets in their way.

If the reader is the type to question these supernatural nightmares, there is no lack of human terrors. James Dickey's *Deliverance* strikes terror as it shows four ordinary men out for a canoe trip who are suddenly attacked and stalked by very real would-be murderers. Wambaugh shows the nightmares that lurk in everyday life in a big city. History gives us perhaps the most uncompromising look at evils that plague mankind. The Holocaust is the central nightmare in *Sophie's Choice*, seen as an unending torment in one individual's life. A city is destroyed by bombs in *Slaughterhouse-Five*. The science fiction in *Slaughterhouse* actually adds to the horror of the historical facts. Billy Pilgrim is so tortured by his memories of the Dresden bombing raid, of the schoolgirls boiled alive, and of the horses with their broken hooves, that it is no wonder he must escape to the planet of the Tralfamadorians to seek relief.

"We make up horrors," Stephen King remarks, "to help us cope with the real ones. With the endless inventiveness of humankind, we grasp the very elements which are so destructive and try to turn them into tools—to dismantle themselves."[1] Why is it, then, that many of the best-selling nightmares are so literal and pedestrian—tales more for the morning newspaper than the midnight campfire? King is the exception among these writers: without him there would be few stories of supernatural horror among the best sellers. But if vampires really did exist, science would take care of them. The president would appoint a commission. Ah, so it is science and government that people have to fear. What are the nightmares doing, then? *They are reflecting what we believe the real terrors to be.* Large social forces can overpower a nice American family: The Russians, as Communists, say that you cannot go from poverty to riches, you cannot accumulate wealth. The most frightening thing the best sellers imagine is a threat to the American Dream.

Three Decades of the American Dream

Times have changed during the years in which these best sellers were published, from the social ferment of the 1960s, to the "me decade" of the 1970s, to the mixture of very different styles of the 1980s. Have the books changed along with these attitudes and fashions? Has the treatment of the American Dream changed, and if so, what particular changes do we see?

One writer suggests that the dream has changed in popular novels across the years. Elizabeth Long argues that in the years after World War II, books dealt with the themes of rags to riches and entrepreneurial success. Then from 1956 to 1968 they turned to themes of self-fulfillment and the individual pursuit of happiness; and, finally, from 1969 to 1975, they became more critical of society and its struggles for success.[2] We can look to see just how many of the best sellers do emphasize one of these themes, turning first to Long's time period of 1969–1975 and then to the more recent years.

Long is correct that few books from 1969 to 1975 deal with the theme of rags to riches. Shaw wrote *Rich Man, Poor Man* during this time, and Caldwell wrote *Captains and the Kings*. Caldwell's book, however, attacks society while it shows young Joseph's rise to fortune. Joseph himself, with his gun running and other shady activities, is not a typical hero. Shaw, too, is cynical about society and human nature. The German immigrant father in the story is able to get to America because he has murdered a man for the passage money. Throughout the novel, money makes the difference between justice and injustice and life and death.

In the same period, it is true that we find many examples of the dream gone wrong: *Something Happened*; *Rabbit Redux*; *Bullet Park*; *Evening in Byzantium*. (Long includes Hailey's *Wheels* and *The Money-Changers* and Robbins's *The Inheritors* in the same category.) But we find at least as many books about individualism and self-fulfillment: *My Name Is Asher Lev*; *Jonathan Livingston Seagull*; *Theophilus North*; *A Month of Sundays*. The women in *Such Good Friends* and *The Bell Jar* are facing basic issues of identity and self-fulfillment, as are the homosexuals in *The Lord Won't Mind*. If there are seven showing examples of books criticizing the dream, there are at least seven showing the pursuit of happiness. We could add less obvious cases to each group without changing the overall proportions. So while the books of the early 1970s do downplay the theme of rags to riches, they continue to deal with the pursuit of happiness that Long associates with the earlier years.

Turning to the most recently published books, from 1976 to 1985, we see a clear shift in emphasis. The individual pursuit of happiness continues and becomes the dominant theme, with more than a dozen examples among the best sellers. The second and third generations pursue their individual lives and fortunes (*The Establishment, The Legacy; The Prodigal Daughter*). Characters are involved in problems of love (*Oliver's Story; Class Reunion; Heartburn; Come Pour the Wine*); identity (*August; How to Save Your Own Life; The Women's Room; The Top of the Hill*), or spiritual growth (*Illusions: Adventures of a Reluctant Messiah*). At the same time, the rags to riches stories return! *The Immigrants; Second Generation; Kane and Abel; Evergreen;* and *A Green Desire* have already been discussed in this chapter; add to these Michener's *Chesapeake*, Stewart's *Century*, and Freeman's *No Time for Tears*. The theme Long associates with the years following World War II reappears in the 1970s and 1980s. In contrast, books criticizing the dream are few in number—*Rabbit Is Rich; Fools Die;* and *Bright Flows the River*, as well as *The Stories of John Cheever*. Cheever's stories, however, with their classic description of the dream gone wrong, were all originally published earlier. According to Long, this theme followed the others in historical sequence; but from the standpoint of the 1980s, it seems the most dated.

Even Harold Robbins's protagonists have changed across the years. In *The Inheritors* (1969) Steven Gaunt is an alienated executive, while in *Dreams Die First* (1977) Gareth Brendan is a rising entrepreneur. An out-of-work writer and Vietnam veteran, Brendan is in debt to the mob. He takes on a pornographic newspaper to help launder the mob's money, and soon expands on his own to a chain of magazines and "Lifestyle" hotels. By the end of the book he has status on Wall Street and a net worth of millions. Business, of course, is not the major activity in a Harold Robbins story. While Brendan is hardly your typical Horatio Alger hero, he, too, rises from poverty to wealth.

Summary

The American Dream is a meta-theme, or dominant motif, embracing several themes found in these novels: the tales of immigrants who must make their way in a strange land; the climb from poverty to riches; the pursuit of individual success and happiness; and the critique of these pursuits. Individuals claim the right to life and happiness. They work hard, take risks, and set off on their own to seek their fortunes. The dream can go wrong or be threatened by large forces over which individuals have no control. Nevertheless, it is the only one available. There are many books, of course, that do not fit these descriptions: historical novels set in the distant past, British mysteries, and science-fiction stories, to name a few examples. However, these books do not combine into any alternative theme.

Novels do not need to be written by Americans to carry on the dream. We still find immigrants, workaholic detectives, and rising entrepreneurs. Ian Dunross builds his empire in a trading company in Hong Kong, while Adam Swann builds his in Victorian England (Clavell's *Noble House*; the books by Delderfield). In *The Thorn Birds* and *The Vines of Yarrabee* settlers face the harsh Australian frontier. The most heroic epic, however, must be *Watership Down*. A band of rabbits set off on their own to find a new world. Relying on their courage and great ingenuity, they make their way across a hostile environment. Finally, they must fight a war against the Nazi rabbits before they can live in peace in their new home.

So in the 1980s the immigrants return to America. Suicidal executives divorce their wives and go back to work. But where better to find the dream carried forward than among the best sellers? They are themselves examples of the dream's success.

N O T E S

1. Stephen King, *Danse Macabre* (New York: Berkeley, 1983), p. 13.
2. Elizabeth Long, *The American Dream and the Popular Novel* (Boston:. Routledge & Kegan Paul, 1985). Long's definition of *best seller* is similar to the one we use, although she does not show the full list from which her examples are drawn.

The Trends Today

THIS REVIEW of best sellers has shown several things, some more surprising than others. Most striking is the variety among the books and their authors—from formula fiction to Pulitzer Prize-winners, and from memorable individuals to stock characters. Contrary to the stereotypes, the books are not all sex and Hollywood glamour. The most prolific authors, in fact—Holt, King, and Ludlum—keep their characters remarkably celibate through the stories. While about two dozen books feature glamorous lives, more than two dozen respectively tell about religion, politics, or war. Even the most popular category, historical novels, accounts for only 15% of the books, with all the others—mysteries, spy novels, and so forth—accounting for less than 10% each. In other words, there is no one "type" of best seller or dominant category. In the total picture, each makes up a very small part.

Variety is seen among the authors as well. The group portrait shows a highly educated, decidedly middle-aged elite; nevertheless, there are many exceptional cases. While the average decade of birth is the 1920s, best sellers are published by authors as young as 27 and as old as 89. Almost one-third of the writers are women. In this profession there are no age or educational requirements: one can stay at home, be expelled from school, or earn an M.D.

Yet, several trends and patterns do emerge clearly. Some fictional types are more popular than others. Leading the genres are the historical novels, followed by spy stories and mysteries. Until recently, westerns and tales of horror and science fiction have been rare. Even King, who virtually makes up the horror genre by himself, writes other kinds of novels. Books on war, religion, and politics have declined in the 1980s, while tales of glamour have increased, and sagas have become a standard form. The sagas are as clear in their structure and conventions as any genre. Families, typically immigrants, make their way across the generations. They face births, marriages, and deaths, the stock market crash, the Depression, and the two world wars.

Among the characters, we find few heroines, many power-hungry politicians, and even more faceless enemies, villains who are uncharacterized members of a nation or class. We also find novels with no one leading character. The multicharacter device, a favorite with the sagas, is seen increasingly in other books. These are not stories about a character told from several points of view, but books about several characters. The characters are introduced briefly, with information on their childhood, parents, and key personality traits. The numbers speak for themselves. One in three best sellers uses the multicharacter form, and more than one in three in the 1980s. We can all name books that are exceptions, with their unique detectives or complex personality studies. But it is hard to avoid the conclusion that one does not need good characters to persuade publishers or readers to buy the book.

At first glance, the heroes appear undistinguished. They can be anyone—from jockeys to aging detectives to young Americans vacationing in Europe. On a closer look they reveal several features in common. Typically they do not seek to be heroic: heroism is forced on them by circumstances or comes as part of the job. Also typically, they operate alone. They live on houseboats, get in scrapes with their own bureaucracies, or find their friends and their government working against them. John Smith is set apart by his terrible psychic power, Thomas à Becket by his background and conflicting ambitions, the black heroes by their actions in a white world. Finally, they are alike in their skill at their job and devotion to it. Smiley, Delaney, Lieberman keep returning from retirement for one more mission; others suffer personal tragedy and go on with their work. Yet, apart from their modesty, individualism, and devotion to work, we are told little about many of these characters. Anyone can be heroic; thus the particular traits are not important.

Well, almost anyone. The heroine's plight has not changed across the years, if we apply the same standards to the women as to the men. Fewer than a dozen women protagonists undertake heroic action to fight for others or a cause beyond themselves. These are scattered from the 1960s to the 1980s, before and after the rise of the women's movement. A few mothers defend their families. Doctors solve mysteries, although they spend more time as patients in their own hospitals. Beyond these examples, people seeking models for their own heroic acts would find a very young girl, an aging and eccentric spinster, a prehistoric nomad, a character in science fiction, and very few others to choose from.

The clearest pattern among the best sellers is the dominance of one theme: the American Dream—the pursuit of life, liberty, and happiness, in the words of the Declaration of Independence (or life, liberty, and property, in the words of John Locke). The dream has four components or subthemes. We see the immigrants' arrival and their climb to fortune; their children's pursuit of happiness and self-identity; and the point in time when the characters discover that something has gone wrong. Here the women characters must spend their heroic efforts: breaking out of marriages, winning success on their own, achieving a new awareness. The men, too, come to face the traps that their own pursuit of the dream has built around them. The greatest challenge for many of the best-selling characters is how to save their own lives.

The theme stands out in the number of books devoted to it and its continuity across the years. It is interesting that books critical of the dream have dropped sharply in the past decade, while tales of rags to riches have returned. Nevertheless, the dream itself continues, with much the same story line in the 1980s as in the 1960s. Even the books that criticize the dream go only so far and no farther. Alienated characters somehow maintain their status and careers. After breakdowns and suicide attempts they take new wives and go back to work.

The immigrants work hard for survival; their children keep working, too. Aging detectives and secret agents return to work: they are heroes because they are the best at their job. Elsewhere in the best sellers, painters and playwrights are working furiously. Reporters track down conspiracies. In police departments, hotels, and airports, all of the characters are hard at work. Readers are given a day-by-day account of their jobs. It might seem curious that books for leisure reading would place such an emphasis on work. However, it takes work to climb from rags to riches. Work is a key component of the American Dream.

It is not surprising, then, that the most frequent nightmares are those that challenge the dream or oppose it. For real terror, see Elliot's nice suburban home being overrun by swarms of faceless scientists, or Charlie and her father fleeing from government agents (*E.T.*; *Firestarter*). The traditional monsters—creatures of the deep, rabid dogs, demons from hell—become the exception. They can do great damage, but unlike KGB agents, suburban traps, or global conspiracies, they do not directly oppose the American Dream.

We call this book *American Best Sellers* because it is based on American hardcover sales. But many of the best sellers are American in another way, too, in relying on national myths and values. Look at the immigrant story told again and again, and the emphasis on the individual's pursuit of happiness. The heroes are democratic, modest, and ordinary; after saving the world, they become private citizens again. They rebel against authority up to a point; nevertheless, they love their work and are very skillful at it. The chief enemies are those that oppose the dream, whether global conspirators, Communists opposing the free-enterprise system, or power-hungry politicians within the American government itself. With American practicality, we take our monsters from the newspapers and choose fiction that can claim to be fact.

There are many exceptions, of course. More than half of the historical novels have non-American settings. Books tell of Europe in World War II, colonial life in India, murders in British country houses and London's West End. Still, it is remarkable how many best sellers project an "American" image in the stories they tell and the values they affirm.

The Latest Books

We should now ask what is happening in the present, looking at the newest books immediately following those reviewed. Which of the patterns appear to be changing or continuing? What are the trends today?

The most recent best sellers are listed at the end of the chapter.[1] Sixteen of the authors have published top-selling books before, while six are new. Sanders follows his three deadly sins with a fourth, bringing Detective Delaney once more out of retirement. Ayla continues her adventures in a prehistoric time, and Cussler hero Dirk Pitt continues his. Ludlum literally resurrects Jason Bourne, transforming *The Bourne Identity* (1980) into *The Bourne Supremacy*. King publishes short stories written over the past 15 years, many of which appeared in print previously. Collins, Vonnegut, Steel, le Carre—all have written another book in the style that their fans have come to like and expect. L'Amour and Francis have, too.

Not only are many of the authors making a repeat appearance on the list, but the treatments and themes are familiar, also. Books continue to be found in almost all of the categories, led by historical novels and tales of intrigue. Of the stories of villainy, Cussler, Hyde, and Ludlum give us faceless enemies, while the murderer in *The Fourth Deadly Sin* is familiar enough to be recognized shortly into the story. The treatment of sex also continues to vary depending on the book one is reading. Sex is a major part of the action in the novels of Collins and Krantz; however, Steel wrote an entire romance with almost no reference to sex. There is a romance in L'Amour's *Last of the Breed* as well. While escaping from Siberia, the American hero meets a young Russian dissident. They fall so much in love that he asks her to come to America with him. She will leave her home and meet him later on. But as far as we can tell by the story, they have not touched each other once in their time together. She *has* knit him a sweater.

Other features found in the earlier books become even more striking. Almost half of the books use multiple leading characters, even discounting Vonnegut's satire and the short stories by King. Three countries are the real characters in *Red Storm Rising*. The war is recounted from the points of view of American, West German, and Russian military personnel. In other books we get to see the people involved in a western roundup, a prime-time television series, and a murder and scandal. We also meet their relatives and acquaintances. There are three main characters in *Lie Down with Lions*, and at least seven in *It*.

In the earlier novels of spies and intrigue, the Russians were the favorite enemy. But now they are everywhere. There are Russians in *Cyclops*; *Red Storm Rising*; *Last of the Breed*; and *The Red Fox*. In the background of *Lie Down with Lions*, the Russians fight Afghan guerrillas. While *Wanderlust* looks back at World War II enemies, the Chinese orphans must be saved from the Communists as well as the Japanese. Good and evil are no longer found on both sides of the Iron Curtain, as in some of the earlier stories (*The Fourth Protocol* or *Gorky Park*, for example). The Russians can be thug-like agents, sadists like Yakut, or power-hungry officials who betray each other. Often they are left uncharacterized. But there is no mistaking the enemy here.

The emphasis is all the more striking when seen against the news of the time. In the same years, the Americans and Russians negotiated a historic arms-limitation treaty. The Soviets were following a new policy of *glasnost*, an openness to the West. Russians appeared on American talk shows, while the U.S. visit of Mikhail and Raisa Gorbachev, the Soviet leader and his wife, became a major publicity event. The best sellers, however, do not follow the headlines, despite what the promotional material might say. James Clavell's *Whirlwind* is an exception in showing a Third World nation. More typically, the newest books about intrigue have European settings, while those about war refight World War II.

Although the list of latest books evokes a strong sense of déjà vu, a few changes are apparent. Two of the new authors, Anthony Hyde and Garrison Keillor, have written first novels. The style of *Lake Wobegon Days*, with its loose vignettes and low-key nostalgia, is new for a best seller. Three science-fiction stories and two westerns make the list, the two westerns equaling the number of these books in all of the preceding years.

And there are even some heroines! Carl Sagan introduces Eleanor Arroway, the pioneering scientist of *Contact*. As director of Project Argus, she is the one responsible for the earth-shaking discovery and its ultimate success. In *The Mammoth Hunters* Ayla continues her quest. Even Audrey Driscoll in *Wanderlust* gets the chance to play a heroic role. Traveling on her own through Europe in World War II, she manages to interview Rommel and bring critical information to the British. Steel's *Wanderlust*, by the way, contains the first description of war among the books by American women writers. The woman in *Lie Down with Lions* is also heroic, although she is only one of three characters followed in the novel.

Earlier we saw the curious trends in books that would continue for a time. One subject would dominate for a year or two and then disappear. It will be worth watching to see whether the westerns and the science-fiction tales, the heroines and the nostalgia continue in the future. Multiple characters and the Russians are probably here to stay.

A Trip to the Bookstore

Another way to gain perspective on the present is to ask how many of the past books continue to sell today. Are they buried on library shelves, the dinosaurs of the book-selling trade, or are they alive and well and still enjoying royalties? A trip to the bookstore to see what people were buying in the summer of 1987[2] gives a very clear answer.

Readers of this book could not get much past the door without seeing a number of old friends. King and Vidal would greet you on entering (with *Empire* and *Misery*, King's newest for the week). Immediately beyond them, on the New Fiction shelf, are Dickey, Wallace, Kotzwinkle, and two more Kings. If you turned to the right, to the *New York Times* best-seller rack, you would find nine familiar authors among the 16 books displayed: Sanders, Steel, Clancy, Bellow, L'Amour, Michael Crichton, and Douglas Adams, in addition to Vidal and the Kings. P. D. James is nearby. If you turned left at the door, you would face the new arrivals in paperback: Archer, Updike, Barbara Bradford, John MacDonald, and Michael Cruz Smith.

Inside, around the paperback shelves, more familiar faces are seen. A total of 115 of our authors had fiction books for sale. Among the 468 best sellers we reviewed, 114 books, or about one-fourth, were on the shelves. You could get most of the Micheners, the Ludlums, and the le Carres, a good choice of the novels by Stone, Mary Stewart, and Sanders, along with the shelf or two of Kings. A new book by an author inspires new printings of older books: thus Michael Crichton's *The Andromeda Strain* and *The Great Train Robbery* stand beside his new book *Sphere*; P. D. James's *Innocent Blood* reappears beside *A Taste for Death*; and Howard Fast's earlier sagas return to accompany *The Dinner Party*.

But many of these authors are *dead*. Does best-sellerhood continue beyond the grave? The answer appears to be a qualified yes: of the authors who had died as of 1987, almost as many had books for sale (20) as did not have books for sale (25). It helps to be alive: more than one-half of the living authors had books for sale, compared to less than one-half of the dead authors.[3] Nevertheless, death does not seem to be a serious obstacle. It is not surprising that Christie and Ian Fleming enjoy a kind of immortality. But there were books on the shelves by Delderfield, Plath, and Charles Jackson. Jackson died in 1968 and Delderfield in 1972. Santmyer's *Herbs and Apples*, first published in 1924, was reissued to stand beside ". . . *And Ladies of the Club*." Rebecca West's *Sunflower*, an unpublished novel from the 1920s, appeared in print for the first time in 1987.

Of course, this is only one limited view at the height of the paperback-reading season. There were new authors, too, on the *New York Times* rack, emerging among the new paperbacks and finding their own niche on the shelves. Still, the amount of continuity is striking, if not surprising. If people buy books because of the author's name, the best bet for tomorrow's sales is the best-selling author today. Or so the publishers figure. But this means that the bookstores will continue to show many of the same familiar faces, and that the trends across time will exhibit more stability than change.

Best sellers are an important part of the popular culture. They entertain and divert us, share our vacations, and help through delays at the airport. They also shape taste, set values, and construct pictures of the world and the men and women in it. They create heroes, repaint history, channel our dreams and nightmares, and pick out our enemies. Yet the book buyers, it seems clear, are not making these choices alone. Many decisions are made prior to a book's publication. "Best seller," then, becomes a self-fulfilling prophecy. It does not mean that thousands of happy readers are "recommending" the book. It means only that thousands of copies were expected to be sold. Perhaps no one liked the book at all.

What if the readers were asked what kind of books they like? Would there be more books bought and more readers? Would there be younger readers, those who now do not care for the recycling of their grandparents' favorite authors? The book buyers themselves might wish they had a better selection to choose from. It would be useful to ask the following questions, using the books listed in this volume:

Which authors would you most recommend to friends, and which would you warn friends away from?

What do you particularly like or dislike about these books?

What kind of books would you like to see more of?

This book can only say what the best sellers are like. But armed with this information, people can begin to think about the kind of entertainment they are getting and what they would like the future best sellers to be.

The Latest Books

Continuing Authors
(With best sellers between 1965 and 1985)

AUEL, JEAN
The Mammoth Hunters   CROWN, 1985

Adventure–Historical Novel. A sequel to *The Valley of Horses*, although there is more romance and less adventure here. Ayla continues her journey, along with her mate, Jondalar, into the land of the Mammoth Hunters. When she is drawn to Ranec, the carver of ivory tusks, Ayla must decide whether to stay with him or go on with Jondalar into the unknown.

CLANCY, TOM
Red Storm Rising
PUTNAM, 1986

War. When the Soviet oil supply is destroyed, Russia attacks the West with conventional weapons. What follows are short descriptions of the war, in the air and at sea, seen from the standpoints of the Americans, Russians, and West Germans.

Clancy says the book developed from the computer war game "Harpoon," in collaboration with the war game's author, Larry Bond.

CLAVELL, JAMES
Whirlwind
MORROW, 1986

International Intrigue. A close-up look at Iran in 1979, with its internal conflicts of religion and politics, ancient traditions and modern influences. With the country on the edge of revolution, Andrew Gavallan, head of a helicopter company, must get his planes and his pilots out of the country at once. The task is complicated by his feud with the company's owner, now Tai-Pan of the Noble House of Hong Kong. We see very different worlds here, from Iran, to the world of oil and international finance, to the lives of the commercial pilots and their families. The pilots' escape—Operation Whirlwind—begins late in this novel of 1,147 pages.

COLLINS, JACKIE
Lucky
SIMON & SCHUSTER, 1985

Glamour–Sex. Lucky Santangelo is the daughter of a top syndicate night club owner in Las Vegas. She sets out to win romance, her own gambling casino, and a fair share of her father's business. The stakes are life and death, but neither violence, betrayal, nor organized crime can stop the beautiful and determined Lucky.

CUSSLER, CLIVE
Cyclops
SIMON & SCHUSTER, 1986

International Intrigue. Hero Dirk Pitt seeks a sunken treasure off the Cuban coast along with a missing millionaire. The search soon leads to the White House, a Soviet plot against Castro, and a battle between the United States and Russia for a base on the moon.

FOLLETT, KEN
Lie Down with Lions
MORROW, 1986

Spy. A cold-war triangle between an American secret agent, a French doctor, and a courageous Englishwoman, set in the harsh and violent land of Afghanistan. As natives wage a guerrilla war against the Russians, each of the three main characters must fight for survival and face a terrible moment of decision.

FRANCIS, DICK
Break In PUTNAM, 1986

Suspense. A successful steeplechase jockey must save his brother from slander, forced bankruptcy, and the breakup of a marriage. As he tries to see that justice is done, he is kidnapped and threatened with death.

IRVING, JOHN
The Cider House Rules MORROW, 1985

Drama. This story portrays a doctor who performs abortions, an orphan, a war casualty, and others, all of whom are visited by hardship and affliction. But it also shows love, the ties between an "adopted" father and his son, and the rules people make in order to go on living.

KING, STEPHEN
Skeleton Crew PUTNAM, 1985

Short Stories–Horror–Science Fiction. A wide range of tales, 22 in all, combining horror with contemporary American life. A supermarket becomes the last refuge against annihilation, a milkman makes some unusual deliveries, a writer's typewriter breeds fornits.

It VIKING, 1986

Horror. "It" (a creature from the drains? a werewolf? a clown?) likes to feed on the children of Derry, Maine. Seven childhood friends witness this horror, which will come back to haunt them many years later. One by one they are called on the telephone and asked to make one final heroic stand.

KRANTZ, JUDITH
I'll Take Manhattan CROWN, 1986

Saga–Sex.The story spans two generations and a host of characters, all of whom are introduced briefly. Everyone is "very very rich." At the center is gorgeous Maxi Amberville, who must fight against the scheming of her mother's second husband to make her new magazine a success.

L'AMOUR, LOUIS
Jubal Sackett BANTAM, 1985

Western–Saga–Historical Novel. This is number 18 in the Sackett series, about an illustrious ancestor who combines the best of the white and Indian worlds. Jubal Sackett sets off across the North American continent in the 1600s. His battles, skill as a medicine man, and marriage to an Indian princess make him a legend in his own time.

Last of the Breed BANTAM, 1986

International Intrigue–Adventure. An American flyer must escape from the Russians, following the path of his Indian ancestors from Siberia across the Bering Strait. His enemies are the killing cold of winter, powerful KGB agents, and the evil Yakut.

LE CARRE, JOHN
A Perfect Spy
KNOPF, 1986

Spy. Magnus Pym, the perfect spy, is also a double agent who has learned from childhood that betrayal equals love. As Pym becomes the target for a worldwide manhunt, we see how he has come to serve two masters. Le Carre provides insight into the psychology of spying in this tight and suspenseful story.

LUDLUM, ROBERT
The Bourne Supremacy
RANDOM HOUSE, 1986

Spy. American agent David Webb must find out who is using his cover name, Jason Bourne, and spreading terror throughout the world. So he must become Bourne again and relive all the old nightmares if both Bournes are finally to be laid to rest. The character first appeared in *The Bourne Identity* (1980).

SANDERS, LAWRENCE
The Fourth Deadly Sin
PUTNAM, 1985

Mystery. Ex-detective Delaney returns from retirement once more when a psychiatrist is murdered and six patients are the likely suspects. When policemen are assigned to work with each of the suspects, we see the idiosyncracies and weaknesses of both the patients and the police.

The fourth deadly sin is anger.

STEEL, DANIELLE
Secrets
DELACORTE, 1985

Glamour. Behind the scenes of a prime-time television series, all of the characters have their own secrets. One by one they are revealed in the course of the production.

Wanderlust
DELACORTE, 1986

Drama—War. The story of a woman torn between her duty at home and her wanderlust and love for a handsome travel photographer. Audrey Driscoll cares for her grandfather and spoiled helpless sister and tries to forget her dreams of travel. When the chance comes, however, she travels through Europe in World War II, befriends Chinese orphans against the oncoming Japanese, and even interviews Rommel and brings key information back to the British. All the while, she is continually called back to her obligations at home.

VONNEGUT, KURT
Galápagos
DELACORTE, 1985

Science Fiction. From the viewpoint of one million years in the future, Vonnegut looks back at humanity as it existed in 1986. A group of people are taking the Nature Cruise of the Century to the Galápagos Islands. In contrast to these 20th-century humans, the new breed is *less* intelligent. They have flippers and small brains and seem to survive very well. Again, Vonnegut uses science fiction to satirize 20th-century ills.

New Authors
(Not previously listed with top best sellers)

DUNNE, DOMINICK

Born in Connecticut, 1925; educated at Williams College. He is known as a film producer (*The Panic in Needle Park; The Boys in the Band*) and is a contributing editor to *Vanity Fair*. He has also written the novels *The Winners* and *People like Us*.

The Two Mrs. Grenvilles CROWN, 1985

Glamour-Mystery. Conflict, scandal, and murder in the aristocratic Grenville clan as showgirl Ann Arden marries young navy ensign Billy Grenville. The novel is loosely based on a sensational murder that occurred in 1955. (The murder was also the subject of a book by Truman Capote.)

HYDE, ANTHONY

Born in Canada, 1946(?). *The Red Fox* is his first novel. He has also collaborated on stories with his brother Christopher Hyde, using the joint pseudonym Nicholas Chase.

The Red Fox RANDOM HOUSE, 1985

International Intrigue. Still haunted by his father's death, Robert Thorne helps a friend with her father's mysterious disappearance. The trail leads through murder and Russian agents to a 50-year-old conspiracy, while each step into his friend's past brings Thorne closer to his own.

KEILLOR, GARRISON

Born in Minnesota, 1942; educated at the University of Minnesota. As a disc jockey, Keillor starred in the popular radio series "A Prairie Home Companion." *Lake Wobegon* is a collection of monologues from that series. He has also written *Happy to Be Here*, a collection of satirical stories. Keillor has since left Wobegon for Manhattan, where he has joined the staff of the *New Yorker*.

Lake Wobegon Days VIKING, 1985

Drama. A story of the fictional town of Lake Wobegon, Minnesota (population 942), with its history, traditions, and local personalities. Keillor blends humor with nostalgia in this portrait of small-town American life.

McMURTRY, LARRY

Born in Texas, 1936, the son of a rancher; educated at North Texas State College and Rice University. He taught English and became co-owner of the Booked Up Book Store in Washington, D. C. He won an Oscar for the screenplay from his own novel *The Last Picture Show*, and he also wrote the screenplay for the award-winning *Terms of Endearment*. *Lonesome Dove* won the Pulitzer Prize for Fiction in 1986. Other novels are *The Desert Rose; Texasville;* and *Cadillac Jack.*

Lonesome Dove   SIMON & SCHUSTER, 1985

Western-Historical Novel. A cattle drive from Mexico to Montana in the 1870s gives a realistic view of life on the frontier. Western fans will recognize familiar types: the cowboys, the gambler, the sweetheart, the prostitute with the heart of gold. But the characters are so full-dimensional that we care about them and want to join in their grand adventure.

SAGAN, CARL

Born in New York City, 1934; educated at the University of Chicago, with a Ph.D. in astronomy and astrophysics. He has been a Cornell University professor, a lecturer, and a popular science writer. Sagan has won many scientific awards as well as a Pulitzer Prize for *The Dragons of Eden* and an Emmy award for the television series of his book *Cosmos*. *Cosmos* is said to be the best-selling science book ever published in the English language.

Contact   SIMON & SCHUSTER, 1985

Science Fiction. We are not alone. A communication comes to Project Argus from intelligent life somewhere beyond Earth. Eleanor Arroway, director of the project, must decode the message and persuade world leaders not to take it as a threat.

Sagan supplies a great deal of scientific fact along with the story.

TYLER, ANNE

Born in Minnesota, 1941, although she grew up in North Carolina and considers herself a southerner. She was educated at Duke University and Columbia University. Tyler has been writing novels since 1964, including *Earthly Possessions* and *Dinner at the Homesick Restaurant*. *Dinner* was nominated for several awards, and *The Accidental Tourist* won the National Book Critics Circle Award for fiction in 1986.

The Accidental Tourist   KNOPF, 1985

Drama. Macon writes travel books for people who want to stay home. But after suffering a broken marriage following the death of his child, he drifts further from life into his own eccentric routines. Then he meets Muriel, a dog-obedience trainer at the Meow-Bow. In this novel an assortment of unique characters wrestle with their habits, longings, troubles, and love.

N O T E S

1. The best-selling books of 1986–1987 as listed in the *World Almanac* of 1987 and 1988.

2. A medium-size bookstore in Madison, Wisconsin, in the first week of July.

3. Of the 163 living authors at the time, 96 had fiction books for sale and 67 did not. Of the 45 dead authors, 20 had fiction books for sale and 25 did not. Three authors are not included in the totals: K. B. Gilden, Southern and Hoffenberg, and the multiple authors going by the name of Penelope Ashe. Bert Gilden and Mason Hoffenberg are dead. Deaths were taken from the 1987 Cumulative Index to the *Contemporary Authors* series.

Appendix A

AWARDS AND DISTINCTIONS

Number of Best Sellers by Author, 1965–1985

10	Holt
9	King (Bachman)[a]
	Ludlum
8	Robbins
7	Caldwell
	le Carre
	Michener
	M. Stewart
	Vidal
6	Hailey
	J. MacDonald
	MacInnes
	MacLean
	Sanders
	Updike
	Wallace
	Wambaugh
	M. West
5	8 authors
4	13 authors
3	18 authors
2	44 authors[a]
1	115 authors

Almost half of the 216 authors and coauthors have more than one best seller in the time period; 26% have three or more.

Major Literary Awards

I. *Nobel Prize Winners—Literature*
   Pearl Buck 1938
   Ernest Hemingway 1954

---

[a]Includes the coauthored book by King and Straub.

Alexander Solzhenitsyn 1970
Saul Bellow 1976

II. *Pulitzer Prize Winners—Fiction*

Best Sellers 1965–85
Bernard Malamud *The Fixer* 1967
William Styron *The Confessions of Nat Turner* 1968
Saul Bellow *Humboldt's Gift* 1976
John Cheever *The Stories of John Cheever* 1979
Norman Mailer *The Executioner's Song* 1980
John Updike *Rabbit Is Rich* 1982

Other Books
Thornton Wilder *The Bridge of San Luis Rey* 1928
Pearl Buck *The Good Earth* 1932
John Hersey *A Bell for Adano* 1945
James Michener *Tales of the South Pacific* 1948
Herman Wouk *The Caine Mutiny* 1952
Ernest Hemingway *The Old Man and the Sea* 1953
Allen Drury *Advise and Consent* 1960
Edwin O'Connor *The Edge of Sadness* 1962
Wallace Stegner *Angle of Repose* 1972
Eudora Welty *The Optimist's Daughter* 1973
Alison Lurie *Foreign Affairs* 1985

Best Sellers since 1985
Larry McMurtry *Lonesome Dove* 1986

III. *Pulitzer Prize Winners—Other Categories*

Poetry
Sylvia Plath *The Collected Poems* 1982

General Nonfiction
Norman Mailer *The Armies of the Night* 1969

Drama
Thornton Wilder *Our Town* 1938; *The Skin of Our Teeth* 1943

Distinguished Commentary
William Safire 1978

Special Citation
Theodore Geisel (Dr. Seuss) 1984

IV. *National Book Award Winners-Fiction*[a]

Best Sellers 1965–85
Saul Bellow *Herzog* 1965
Bernard Malamud *The Fixer* 1967
Thornton Wilder *The Eighth Day* 1968
Saul Bellow *Mr. Sammler's Planet* 1971
William Styron *Sophie's Choice* 1980
John Updike *Rabbit Is Rich* 1982

---

[a]Amid controversy, the Association of American Publishers changed the name of the awards after 1979 to the American Book Awards, using a different kind of selection committee.

Other Books

James Jones *From Here to Eternity* 1952
Saul Bellow *The Adventures of Augie March* 1954
John O'Hara *Ten North Frederick* 1956
John Cheever *The Wapshot Chronicle* 1958
Bernard Malamud *The Magic Barrel* 1959
Philip Roth *Goodbye, Columbus* 1960
Walker Percy *The Moviegoer* 1962
John Updike *The Centaur* 1964
John Barth *Chimera* 1973
Wallace Stegner *The Spectator Bird* 1977
E. L. Doctorow *World's Fair* 1986

Other Major Awards and Recognitions

Nobel Peace Prize Elie Wiesel 1986
National Medal for Literature Thornton Wilder 1965
Congressional Medal of Honor for Literature Louis L'Amour
Presidential Medal of Freedom Thornton Wilder (1963—Kennedy);
James Michener (1977—Ford); Eudora Welty (1980—Carter);
Louis L'Amour (1984—Reagan)
Dame of the British Empire Agatha Christie; Daphne du Maurier

Entertainment Awards

Several best-selling authors have received major awards for their work in show business. A (+) after an author's name indicates more than one award in that category.

Academy Awards	*Emmy Awards*
Blatty	Clavell
Kazan (+)	Midler
Puzo (+)	Seuss (+)
Seuss (+)	
Sheldon	

Tony Awards	*Grammy Awards*
de Hartog	Midler (+)
Kazan (+)	
Sheldon	

The Theatre Hall of Fame
Kazan
T. Wilder

Major American Novelists
(ACCORDING TO TWO SOURCES[a])

Prizes are not the only form of literary recognition. Writers seek the regard of critics and peers about the quality of their work. The *Dictionary of Literary*

[a]"American Novelists, 1910–1945." *Dictionary of Literary Biography*, vol. 9; Matthew Bruccoli, ed., *American Novelists since World War II*, vols. 2 and 6 (Detroit: Gale Research, 1981, 1978); and James Hart, ed., *The Oxford Companion to American Literature*, 5th ed. (New York: Oxford University Press, 1983).

Biography lists the major American novelists from 1910 to 1980, summarizing their work and the reactions to it. While the criticism is not always positive, it is a mark of distinction to be included at all. A total of 43, or about one-third, of the American writers who wrote best sellers are cited. *The Oxford Companion to American Literature* also cites contemporary writers as part of its survey of the field, giving the author's major work and contribution. *Oxford* includes 52 of the best-selling writers.

The experts agree by and large about who the major American novelists are. Altogether, 38 of the authors are on *both* lists, with an additional 19 on one or the other. The volumes were published in the early 1980s, and so the newest authors would be omitted. All non-American authors are also omitted. Writers such as Greene, Fowles, and Solzhenitsyn must get their recognition elsewhere.

These 38 novelists are included in both sources:

Auchincloss	Hemingway	O'Hara
Baldwin	Hersey	Percy
Barth	Humphrey	Plath
Bellow	Irving	Roth
Buck	Jones	Shaw
Cassill	Jong	Stegner
Cheever	Lurie	Styron
Didion	Macdonald, R.	Updike
Doctorow	Mailer	Vidal
Fast	Malamud	Vonnegut
Gardner, J. C.	Michener	West, J.
Gold	Nabokov	Wilder, T.
Heller	Nin	

Writers in Show Business

The following authors have worked in show business beyond the experience of producing a screenplay for their own books. The list is based on *Variety's Who's Who in Show Business*, supplemented where possible from other sources.

Adams, D.	TV and radio writer; radio producer; script editor
Ambler	Screenwriter
Behn	Off-Broadway producer; founded the Musical and Dramatic Theatre Academy
Blatty	Film producer; screenwriter
Bradford, R.	Screenwriter for Universal Pictures
Buckley	Hosted "Firing Line" on TV
Christie	Her play *The Mousetrap* ran for 30 years in London
Clavell	TV producer; screenwriter
Collins, J.	Screen actress
Crichton, M.	Film director
Davis	Screenwriter
de Hartog	Screenwriter

Fast	Writer of plays and TV scripts
Gainham	Broadcaster for BBC and for West German and Austrian TV
Gann	Screenwriter
Gardner, J. E.	Theatre critic
Gilden, K. and B.	Screenwriters
Greene, Graham	Film critic
Hailey	TV writer
Hawley	Screenwriter for film, radio, and TV
Hayden	Film and TV actor
Isaacs	Screenwriter
Jackson	Screenwriter for film, radio, and TV
Kazan	Film director; film and stage actor
King	Screenwriter
Leonard	Screenwriter; TV pilots
Levin	Screenwriter
Ludlum	TV and stage actor; stage producer
Merrick	Actor; TV writer
Meyer	Film director: screenwriter
Michener	TV narration
Midler	Broadway and film actress; singer; dancer
Puzo	Screenwriter
Raucher	Screenwriter
Rivers	Film actress, writer, director; TV personality; nightclubs
Robbins	Executive at Universal Pictures
Safire	Radio, TV producer
St. Johns	Screenwriter
Segal	Screenwriter; TV commentator for the Olympics
Seuss	Film producer
Shaw	Screenwriter
Sheldon	Screenwriter; playwright; creator of TV shows
Southern	Screenwriter
Susann	Broadway and TV actress
Thompson	TV writer
Tryon	Film and TV actor
Uris	Screenwriter
Vidal	Screenwriter
Vonnegut	TV writer and host; cameo appearance in film *Back to School*
Wallace	Screenwriter
West, R.	Cameo appearance in film *Reds*
Wilder, R.	Screenwriter
Wilder, T.	Playwright
Wouk	Playwright

Appendix B

LIST OF PSEUDONYMS

"What's the use of their having names," the
Gnat said, "if they won't answer to them?"
"No use to *them*," said Alice; "but it's useful
to the people that name them, I suppose."

(Lewis Carroll, *Through the Looking Glass*)

Names can be useful to readers, too, in tracing the facts of an author's life or seeing behind the many masks that a single writer is at work. In the list below, the first column gives the real names of the authors, and the second column shows the pen names used. The names actually appearing on the best sellers are printed in boldface type.

We exclude the cases where only a first name was changed; where women, after marriage, retained their original name; or where a birth name was legally changed. The list is compiled from books on individual authors and collections of genre fiction; from the *Contemporary Authors* series; and from Frank Atkinson, ed., *Dictionary of Literary Pseudonyms* (Chicago: American Library Association, 1987).

REAL NAMES	PEN NAMES
Adler, Bill	Jay David
Ames, Rachel	**Sarah Gainham**
Andrews, Cicely Isabel, née Fairfield	**Rebecca West**
Asimov, Isaac	Paul French; Dr. A
Auchincloss, Louis	Andrew Lee
Buck, Pearl	John Sedges
Cassill, R. V.	Owen Aherne
Challans, Mary	**Mary Renault**
Christie, Agatha	Mary Westmacott; Agatha Mallowen
Cornwell, David	**John le Carre**
Crichton, Michael	Jeffrey Hudson; John Lange
de Hartog, Ian	F. R. Eckmar
Durrell, Lawrence	Charles Norden
Fast, Howard	E. V. Cunningham; Walter Ericson
Feinberg, Bea	**Cynthia Freeman**
Freedgood, Morton	**John Godey**

REAL NAMES	PEN NAMES
Galbraith, John Kenneth	Mark Epernay
Geisel, Theodore Seuss	**Dr. Seuss**
Hibbert, Eleanor Burford	**Victoria Holt**; Jean Plaidy; Philippa Carr; Elbur Ford; Eleanor Burford; Kathleen Kellow; Ellalice Tate
Jakes, John	Alan Payne; Jay Scotland
King, Stephen	**Richard Bachman**
L'Amour, Louis	Tex Burns
Lofts, Norah	Peter Curtis; Juliet Astley
Ludlum, Robert	Jonathan Ryder; Michael Shepherd
Millar, Kenneth	**Ross Macdonald**; John Ross Macdonald; John Macdonald[a]
Molinsky, Joan	**Joan Rivers**
Patterson, Harry	**Jack Higgins**; Martin Fallon; Hugh Marlowe; James Graham
Puzo, Mario	Mario Cleri
Slavitt, David	**Henry Sutton**
Smith, Martin Cruz	Jake Logan, Martin Quinn, Simon Quinn, Nick Carter
Southern, Terry, and Mason Hoffenberg	Maxwell Kenton
Tait, Dorothy	**Ann Fairbairn**
25 reporters who collaborated on *Naked Came the Stranger*	**Penelope Ashe**
Vidal, Gore	Edgar Box
West, Morris	Michael East; Julian Morris
Whitaker, Rodney	**Trevanian**[b]; J. L. Moran; Nicholas Seare; Benat le Cagat
Wicker, Tom	Paul Connolly

---

[a]Not to be confused with the other mystery writer, John D. MacDonald. See main entries.
[b]See *Contemporary Literary Criticism*, ed. Jean Stine and Daniel Marowski (Detroit: Gale Research, 1984), 29: 429. Note that *Contemporary Authors*, vol. 108, also published by Gale, reports that Trevanian's real name is not known.

Appendix C

BOOKS THAT BECAME MOVIES

Books are listed by title, along with the release date of the film. Unless otherwise indicated, the book title is the same as the movie title. *TV* indicates an original television production. As of this listing, more than one-third of the books have been produced for the movies or television. Movies of the latest books, reported in chapter 6, are not included.[a]

The Adventurers (1968)
Airport (1966)
An American Dream (1966)
The Andromeda Strain (1971)
The Antagonists (*Masada*, 1980)
The Arrangement (1969)
Bear Island (1979)
Beggarman, Thief (TV, 1979)
The Bell Jar (1978)
The Betsy (1978)
The Billion Dollar Brain (1967)
The Black Marble (1980)
Black Sunday (1977)
Bloodline (*Sidney Sheldon's Bloodline*, 1979)
The Blue Knight (TV, 1975)
The Bourne Identity (TV, 1988)
The Boys from Brazil (1978)
Candy (1968)
Captains and Kings (TV, 1976)
Caravan to Vaccares (1974)
Celebrity (1985)
Centennial (TV, 1979)
The Choirboys (1977)
The Chosen (1981)
Christine (1983)
Coma (1978)
The Comedians (1967)
Condominium (1984)
The Confessions of Nat Turner (1969)
A Covenant with Death (1966)

Crowned Heads: "Fedora" (*Fedora*, 1979)
Cujo (1982)
The Day of the Jackal (1972)
The Dead Zone (1983)
The Deep (1977)
Deliverance (1972)
The Detective (1968)
Different Seasons: "The Body" (*Stand by Me*, 1986)
The Dogs of War (1980)
A Dream of Kings (1969)
E.T.: The Extraterrestrial (1982) (movie became book)
Evening in Byzantium (1978)
Evergreen (TV, 1985)
Except for Me and Thee (TV)
The Executioner's Song (1982)
The Exorcist (1973)
Eye of the Needle (1981)
The Far Pavilions (1983)
Firestarter (1984)
The First Deadly Sin (1981)
The Fixer (1969)
Force 10 from Navarone (1978)
The Fourth Protocol (1987)
The French Lieutenant's Woman (1981)
Funeral in Berlin (1966)
The Gang That Couldn't Shoot Straight (1972)
The Gemini Contenders (1978)

---

[a]Complete through 1984 and updated, where possible, through 1988. Derived from A. G. S. Enser, ed., *Filmed Books and Plays, 1928–1983* (Lexington, 1985); Leslie Halliwell, *Halliwell's Film Guide*, 6th ed. (Charles Scribner's Sons, 1988); Alvin Marill, *Movies Made for Television* (New York Zoetrope, 1987); and other film and television listings.

Ghost Story (1981)
The Glitter Dome (1984)
Glitz (TV, 1988)
The Godfather (1971)
Gorky Park (1983)
The Great Train Robbery (1979)
The Green Berets (1968)
Harvest Home (The Dark Secret of Harvest Home, 1978)
Heartburn (1986)
The Holcroft Covenant (1985)
Hollywood Wives (TV, 1985)
The Honorary Consul (Beyond the Limit, 1983)
Hotel (1966)
The Hotel New Hampshire (1984)
The Human Factor (1980)
Hurry Sundown (1967)
If Tomorrow Comes (TV, 1986)
I Heard the Owl Call My Name (TV, 1973)
The Immigrants (1978)
In This House of Brede (1975)
An Indecent Obsession (1983)
Islands in the Stream (1977)
Jaws (1975)
Jonathan Livingston Seagull (1974)
Kane and Abel (TV, 1985)
The Key to Rebecca (TV, 1985)
The Kremlin Letter (1970)
Law and Order (1976)
Lincoln (TV, 1988)
The Little Drummer Girl (1984)
The Lonely Lady (1983)
Looking for Mr. Goodbar (1978)
The Looking Glass War (1969)
Love and War (TV)
The Love Machine (1971)
Love Story (1970)
The Man (1972)
The Man with the Golden Gun (1974)
Master of the Game (TV, 1984)
Mistral's Daughter (TV, 1984)
The Money-Changers (TV, 1976)
Myra Breckinridge (1969)
The Name of the Rose (1986)
Nemesis (TV, 1988)
The New Centurions (1972)
Nickel Mountain (1985)
Noble House (TV, 1988)
North and South (TV, 1985)
The Odessa File (1974)
Oliver's Story (1979)
Once Is Not Enough (1975)
The Other (1972)

The Pirate (Harold Robbins's The Pirate, TV, 1978)
Portnoy's Complaint (1972)
Postern of Fate (TV, 1988)
The President's Plane Is Missing (1971)
Princess Daisy (1983)
Puppet on a Chain (1971)
QB VII (TV, 1974)
Rage of Angels (1982)
Ragtime (1981)
Red Sky at Morning (1970)
Return of the Jedi (1983) (movie became book)
The Rhinemann Exchange (TV, 1977)
Rich Man, Poor Man (TV, 1976)
Rosemary's Baby (1968)
The Salzburg Connection (1972)
Scruples (TV, 1981)
The Secret of Santa Vittoria (1969)
Semi-Tough (1977)
The Seven Minutes (1971)
The Seven-Per-Cent Solution (1976)
The Shining (1982)
Shōgun (1981)
The Sicilian (1987)
Sins of the Father (1985)
Slapstick (1981)
Slaughterhouse-Five (1972)
Sleeping Murder (TV, 1988)
Smiley's People (TV, 1982)
Sophie's Choice (1982)
Space (TV, 1985)
The Spy Who Came in from the Cold (1966)
Strong Medicine (TV, 1986)
Such Good Friends (1972)
Summer of '42 (1971)
Tai-Pan (1986)
The Taking of Pelham One Two Three (1974)
The Terminal Man (1974)
Testimony of Two Men (TV, 1977)
The Thorn Birds (1979)
Tinker, Tailor, Soldier, Spy (TV, 1988)
To Serve Them All My Days (TV)
The Top of the Hill (1980)
Topaz (1968)
Travels with My Aunt (1972)
True Grit (1969)
2010: Odyssey Two (1984)
The Underground Man (1974)
Up the Down Staircase (1966)
The Users (TV, 1978)
Valley of the Dolls (1968)
Vanished (1971)

War and Remembrance (TV, 1988)
The War between the Tates (1977)
Watership Down (1978)
The West End Horror (1977)
Wheels (TV, 1978)

Where Eagles Dare (1969)
The Winds of War (TV, 1983)
The Women's Room (1980)
The World According to Garp (1982)
You Only Live Twice (1966)

Appendix D

Books by Year of Publication: The 468 Best Sellers
(Based on the copyright date, not the year of top sales.)

1964

Auchincloss	*The Rector of Justin*	Drama
Bellow	*Herzog*	Drama
Fleming	*You Only Live Twice*	Spy
Gilden	*Hurry Sundown*	Drama
Kaufman	*Up the Down Staircase*	Drama
Keyes	*The Explorer*	Drama
le Carre	*The Spy Who Came in from the Cold*	Spy
O'Hara	*The Horse Knows the Way*	Short Stories
Southern and Hoffenberg	*Candy*	Sex
Stewart, M.	*This Rough Magic*	Suspense
Uris	*Armageddon*	War
Vidal	*Julian*	Historical Novel
Wallace	*The Man*	American Politics

1965

Becker	*A Covenant with Death*	Drama
Caldwell	*A Pillar of Iron*	Historical Novel
Deighton	*Funeral in Berlin*	Spy
du Maurier	*The Flight of the Falcon*	Mystery
Fleming	*The Man with the Golden Gun*	Spy
Gordon	*The Rabbi*	Religion
Hailey	*Hotel*	Drama
Holt	*The Legend of the Seventh Virgin*	Suspense
Humphrey	*The Ordways*	Saga
Knebel	*Night of Camp David*	Suspense–American Politics
le Carre	*The Looking Glass War*	Spy
Mailer	*An American Dream*	Drama
Michener	*The Source*	Religion–Historical Novel
Moore	*The Green Berets*	War
Mydans	*Thomas*	Religion–Historical Novel
O'Hara	*The Lockwood Concern*	Saga
Ruark	*The Honey Badger*	Drama–Sex
Stewart, M.	*Airs above the Ground*	Suspense
Stone	*Those Who Love*	Historical Novel
West, M.	*The Ambassador*	Drama–War
Wouk	*Don't Stop the Carnival*	Drama

1966

Auchincloss	*The Embezzler*	Drama
Barth	*Giles Goat-Boy*	Science Fiction
Behn	*The Kremlin Letter*	Spy
Buck	*The Time is Noon*	Drama
Clavell	*Tai-Pan*	Adventure–Historical Novel
Crichton, R.	*The Secret of Santa Vittoria*	War
de Hartog	*The Captain*	War
Deighton	*The Billion Dollar Brain*	Spy
Drury	*Capable of Honor*	American Politics
Fairbairn	*Five Smooth Stones*	Drama
Gold	*Fathers*	Saga
Greene	*The Comedians*	Drama
Holt	*Menfreya in the Morning*	Suspense
Kemelman	*Saturday the Rabbi Went Hungry*	Religion–Mystery
Keyes	*I, the King*	Historical Novel
MacInnes	*The Double Image*	Spy
Malamud	*The Fixer*	Religion–Historical Novel
O'Connor	*All in the Family*	American Politics
O'Hara	*Waiting for Winter*	Short Stories
Petrakis	*A Dream of Kings*	Drama
Renault	*The Mask of Apollo*	Historical Novel
Robbins	*The Adventurers*	Glamour–International Intrigue–Sex
St. Johns	*Tell No Man*	Religion
Susann	*Valley of the Dolls*	Glamour–Sex
Thorp	*The Detective*	Mystery
West, R.	*The Birds Fall Down*	Drama–Spy
Whitney	*Columbella*	Suspense

1967

Arnold	*A Night of Watching*	War
Auchincloss	*Tales of Manhattan*	Short Stories
Gainham	*Night Falls on the City*	War
Griffin	*An Operational Necessity*	War
Hersey	*Under the Eye of the Storm*	Drama
Holt	*The King of the Castle*	Suspense
Jackson	*A Second-Hand Life*	Drama–Sex
Jones	*Go to the Widow-Maker*	Drama–Sex
Kazan	*The Arrangement*	Drama
Levin	*Rosemary's Baby*	Horror
MacLean	*Where Eagles Dare*	War
Marshall	*Christy*	Religion–Historical Novel
O'Hara	*The Instrument*	Drama
Potok	*The Chosen*	Drama–Religion
Roth	*When She Was Good*	Drama
Serling	*The President's Plane Is Missing*	American Politics
Solomon	*The Candlesticks and the Cross*	Saga–Historical Novel
Stegner	*All the Little Live Things*	Drama
Stewart, M.	*The Gabriel Hounds*	Suspense

Styron	*The Confessions of Nat Turner*	Historical Novel
Sutton	*The Exhibitionist*	Glamour–Sex
Uris	*Topaz*	Spy
Vidal	*Washington, D.C.*	American Politics
Wallace	*The Plot*	American Politics–International Intrigue
Wilder	*The Eighth Day*	Saga–Historical Novel

1968

Auchincloss	*A World of Profit*	Drama
Baldwin	*Tell Me How Long the Train's Been Gone*	Drama
Bradford, R.	*Red Sky at Morning*	Drama
Caldwell	*Testimony of Two Men*	Historical Novel
Drury	*Preserve and Protect*	American Politics
Durrell	*Tunc*	Drama–Science Fiction
Galbraith	*The Triumph*	American Politics
Hailey	*Airport*	Suspense
Hawley	*The Hurricane Years*	Drama
Holt	*The Queen's Confession*	Historical Novel
Knebel	*Vanished*	Suspense–American Politics
le Carre	*A Small Town in Germany*	Spy
MacInnes	*The Salzburg Connection*	Spy
MacLean	*Force 10 from Navarone*	War
O'Hara	*And Other Stories*	Short Stories
Pearson	*The Senator*	American Politics
Portis	*True Grit*	Western–Historical Novel
Solzhenitsyn	*The First Circle*	Drama
Tarr	*Heaven Help Us!*	Religion
Updike	*Couples*	Drama–Sex
Vidal	*Myra Breckinridge*	Sex
West, M.	*The Tower of Babel*	Spy–War

1969

"Ashe"	*Naked Came the Stranger*	Sex
Breslin	*The Gang That Couldn't Shoot Straight*	Drama
Buck	*The Three Daughters of Madame Liang*	Drama
Cheever	*Bullet Park*	Drama
Crichton, M.	*The Andromeda Strain*	Suspense
Davis	*The Pretenders*	Drama–Glamour–Sex
du Maurier	*The House on the Strand*	Historical Novel
Eden	*The Vines of Yarrabee*	Historical Novel
Fowles	*The French Lieutenant's Woman*	Historical Novel
Gainham	*A Place in the Country*	War
Godden	*In This House of Brede*	Religion
Greene	*Travels with My Aunt*	Drama
Holt	*The Shivering Sands*	Mystery
Kemelman	*Sunday the Rabbi Stayed Home*	Religion–Mystery
Lofts	*The Lost Queen*	Historical Novel

Macdonald, R.	*The Goodbye Look*	Mystery
MacLean	*Puppet on a Chain*	Suspense
Nabokov	*Ada or Ardor*	Drama–Sex
Petrakis	*The Waves of Night and Other Stories*	Short Stories
Potok	*The Promise*	Drama–Religion
Price	*New Moon Rising*	Historical Novel
Puzo	*The Godfather*	Drama
Renault	*Fire from Heaven*	Historical Novel
Robbins	*The Inheritors*	Glamour–Sex
Roth	*Portnoy's Complaint*	Drama–Sex
Susann	*The Love Machine*	Glamour–Sex
Vonnegut	*Slaughterhouse-Five*	Science Fiction–War
Wallace	*The Seven Minutes*	Drama
West, J.	*Except for Me and Thee*	Historical Novel
Wilder, R.	*An Affair of Honor*	Drama

1970

Bach	*Jonathan Livingston Seagull*	Drama
Bellow	*Mr. Sammler's Planet*	Drama
Bristow	*Calico Palace*	Historical Novel
Caldwell	*Great Lion of God*	Religion–Historical Novel
Cassill	*Doctor Cobb's Game*	Drama–Sex
Christie	*Passenger to Frankfurt*	Suspense
Delderfield	*God Is an Englishman*	Saga–Historical Novel
Dickey	*Deliverance*	Adventure
Gann	*The Antagonists*	War–Historical Novel
Goudge	*The Child from the Sea*	Historical Novel
Gould	*Such Good Friends*	Drama–Sex
Hemingway	*Islands in the Stream*	War
Holt	*The Secret Woman*	Suspense
MacLean	*Caravan to Vaccares*	Spy
Merrick	*The Lord Won't Mind*	Drama–Sex
Segal	*Love Story*	Drama
Shaw	*Rich Man, Poor Man*	Saga
Stewart, M.	*The Crystal Cave*	Adventure–Historical Novel
Updike	*Bech: A Book*	Drama
Uris	*QB VII*	Drama
Wambaugh	*The New Centurions*	Drama
Welty	*Losing Battles*	Drama
Wiesel	*A Beggar in Jerusalem*	Drama–Religion

1971

Blatty	*The Exorcist*	Horror–Religion
Christie	*Nemesis*	Mystery
Delderfield	*Theirs Was the Kingdom*	Saga–Historical Novel
Drury	*The Throne of Saturn*	American Politics
Forsyth	*The Day of the Jackal*	International Intrigue
Hailey	*Wheels*	Drama
Holt	*The Shadow of the Lynx*	Suspense
Howatch	*Penmarric*	Saga–Historical Novel

Macdonald, R.	*The Underground Man*	Mystery
MacInnes	*Message from Malaga*	Spy
MacLean	*Bear Island*	Mystery
Michener	*The Drifters*	Drama
Percy	*Love in the Ruins*	Science Fiction–Religion
Plath	*The Bell Jar*	Drama
Raucher	*Summer of '42*	Drama
Robbins	*The Betsy*	Drama–Sex
Roth	*Our Gang*	American Politics
Salinger	*On Instructions of My Government*	American Politics– International Intrigue
Stone	*The Passions of the Mind*	Historical Novel
Tryon	*The Other*	Horror
Updike	*Rabbit Redux*	Drama
Wouk	*The Winds of War*	Saga–War

1972

Ambler	*The Levanter*	International Intrigue
Caldwell	*Captains and the Kings*	Saga–American Politics– Historical Novel
Crichton, M.	*The Terminal Man*	Suspense
Crichton, R.	*The Camerons*	Historical Novel
Delderfield	*To Serve Them All My Days*	Drama
Forsyth	*The Odessa File*	Spy
Gardner	*The Sunlight Dialogues*	Drama
Holt	*On the Night of the Seventh Moon*	Mystery
Jenkins	*Semi-Tough*	Drama–Sex
Kazan	*The Assassins*	Drama–War
Knebel	*Dark Horse*	American Politics
McClary	*A Portion for Foxes*	Drama
Potok	*My Name Is Asher Lev*	Drama
Renault	*The Persian Boy*	Historical Novel
Seton	*Green Darkness*	Historical Novel
Solzhenitsyn	*August 1914*	War
Wallace	*The Word*	Religion
Wambaugh	*The Blue Knight*	Drama

1973

Breslin	*World without End, Amen*	Drama
Christie	*Postern of Fate*	Mystery–Spy
Craven	*I Heard the Owl Call My Name*	Drama–Religion
Drury	*Come Nineveh, Come Tyre*	American Politics
Erdman	*The Billion Dollar Sure Thing*	International Intrigue
Gardner	*Nickel Mountain*	Drama
Godey	*The Taking of Pelham One Two Three*	Suspense
Greene	*The Honorary Consul*	Religion–International Intrigue
Ludlum	*The Matlock Paper*	Suspense
Sanders	*The First Deadly Sin*	Mystery
Shaw	*Evening in Byzantium*	Drama–Glamour

Stewart, M.	*The Hollow Hills*	Adventure–Historical Novel
Susann	*Once Is Not Enough*	Glamour–Sex
Tryon	*Harvest Home*	Horror
Uhnak	*Law and Order*	Drama–Saga
Vidal	*Burr*	American Politics— Historical Novel
Vonnegut	*Breakfast of Champions; or, Goodbye Blue Monday!*	Drama
West, M.	*The Salamander*	Spy
Wicker	*Facing the Lions*	American Politics
Wilder, T.	*Theophilus North*	Drama

1974

Adams	*Shardik*	Adventure–Historical Novel
Adams	*Watership Down*	Adventure
Auchincloss	*The Partners*	Drama
Benchley	*Jaws*	Adventure-Horror
Forsyth	*The Dogs of War*	International Intrigue
Fowles	*The Ebony Tower*	Short Stories
Heller	*Something Happened*	Drama
Holt	*The House of a Thousand Lanterns*	Suspense
Howatch	*Cashelmara*	Saga–Historical Novel
le Carre	*Tinker, Tailor, Soldier, Spy*	Spy
Ludlum	*The Rhinemann Exchange*	Spy
Lurie	*The War between the Tates*	Drama
MacInnes	*The Snare of the Hunter*	International Intrigue
Meyer	*The Seven-Per-Cent Solution*	Mystery–Historical Novel
Michener	*Centennial*	Historical Novel
Robbins	*The Pirate*	International Intrigue–Sex
Tryon	*Lady*	Drama
Wallace	*The Fan Club*	Drama–Glamour–Sex
West, M.	*Harlequin*	International Intrigue

1975

Bellow	*Humboldt's Gift*	Drama
Christie	*Curtain*	Mystery
Clavell	*Shōgun*	Adventure–Historical Novel
Crichton, M.	*The Great Train Robbery*	Historical Novel
Doctorow	*Ragtime*	Historical Novel
Drury	*Promise of Joy*	American Politics
Hailey	*The Money-Changers*	Drama
Harris	*Black Sunday*	International Intrigue
Higgins (Patterson)	*The Eagle Has Landed*	War
MacDonald, J.	*The Dreadful Lemon Sky*	Mystery
MacLean	*Circus*	Spy
Potok	*In the Beginning*	Drama–Religion
Rossner	*Looking for Mr. Goodbar*	Drama–Sex
Stone	*The Greek Treasure*	Historical Novel
Updike	*A Month of Sundays*	Religion–Sex

Wambaugh	*The Choirboys*	Drama
West, J.	*The Massacre at Fall Creek*	Historical Novel
Whitney	*Spindrift*	Mystery

1976

Agnew	*The Canfield Decision*	American Politics
Benchley	*The Deep*	Adventure
Buckley	*Saving the Queen*	Spy
Caldwell	*Ceremony of the Innocent*	American Politics–Historical Novel
Christie	*Sleeping Murder*	Mystery
Erdman	*The Crash of '79*	International Intrigue
Gardner	*October Light*	Drama
Greene, Gael	*Blue Skies, No Candy*	Glamour–Sex
Haber	*The Users*	Glamour–Sex
Hayden	*Voyage: A Novel of 1896*	Historical Novel
Holt	*The Pride of the Peacock*	Suspense
Levin	*The Boys from Brazil*	International Intrigue
Ludlum	*The Gemini Contenders*	International Intrigue
MacInnes	*Agent in Place*	Spy
Meyer	*The West End Horror*	Mystery–Historical Novel
Patterson (Higgins)	*Storm Warning*	War
Patterson	*The Valhalla Exchange*	War
Robbins	*The Lonely Lady*	Glamour–Sex
Sheldon	*A Stranger in the Mirror*	Glamour–Sex
Susann	*Dolores*	Glamour–Sex
Tryon	*Crowned Heads*	Short Stories–Glamour
Uris	*Trinity*	Saga–Historical Novel
Vidal	*1876*	American Politics–Historical Novel
Vonnegut	*Slapstick; or, Lonesome No More!*	Science Fiction
Wallace	*The R Document*	American Politics

1977

Bach	*Illusions: The Adventures of a Reluctant Messiah*	Religion
Cheever	*Falconer*	Drama
Cook	*Coma*	Mystery
Didion	*A Book of Common Prayer*	Drama
Elegant	*Dynasty*	Saga
Fast	*The Immigrants*	Saga–Historical Novel
Fowles	*Daniel Martin*	Drama
French	*The Women's Room*	Drama–Sex
Howatch	*The Rich Are Different*	Saga
Jong	*How to Save Your Own Life*	Drama–Sex
King	*The Shining*	Horror
le Carre	*The Honourable Schoolboy*	Spy
Ludlum	*The Chancellor Manuscript*	Suspense
McCullough	*The Thorn Birds*	Saga
MacDonald, J.	*Condominium*	Suspense

Nin	*Delta of Venus: Erotica*	Short Stories–Sex
Robbins	*Dreams Die First*	Drama–Sex
Safire	*Full Disclosure*	American Politics
Sanders	*The Second Deadly Sin*	Mystery
Segal	*Oliver's Story*	Drama
Shaw	*Beggarman, Thief*	Saga
Tolkien	*The Silmarillion*	Science Fiction–Short Stories
White	*The Book of Merlyn*	War–Historical Novel

1978

Buckley	*Stained Glass*	Spy
Caldwell	*Bright Flows the River*	Drama
Cheever	*The Stories of John Cheever*	Short Stories
Fast	*Second Generation*	Saga
Follett	*Eye of the Needle*	War–Spy
Greene	*The Human Factor*	Drama–Spy
Hackett et al.	*The Third World War: August 1985*	War
Irving	*The World According to Garp*	Drama
Jones	*Whistle*	War
Kaye	*The Far Pavilions*	Historical Novel
Krantz	*Scruples*	Glamour–Sex
Ludlum	*The Holcroft Covenant*	International Intrigue
MacDonald, J.	*The Empty Copper Sea*	Mystery
MacInnes	*Prelude to Terror*	Spy
Michener	*Chesapeake*	Saga–Historical Novel
Plain	*Evergreen*	Saga
Puzo	*Fools Die*	Drama
Sheldon	*Bloodline*	Suspense
Updike	*The Coup*	Drama
Wambaugh	*The Black Marble*	Suspense
Wouk	*War and Remembrance*	Saga–War

1979

Archer	*Kane and Abel*	Drama
Deighton	*SS-GB*	Mystery–Spy–War
Fast	*The Establishment*	Saga
Follett	*Triple*	Spy
Forsyth	*The Devil's Alternative*	Spy
Freeman	*Portraits*	Saga
Hailey	*Overload*	Drama
Heller	*Good as Gold*	American Politics
Hill	*Hanta Yo*	Saga–Historical Novel
Jaffe	*Class Reunion*	Drama–Sex
Kaye	*Shadow of the Moon*	Historical Novel
King	*The Dead Zone*	Suspense–Science Fiction
Ludlum	*The Matarese Circle*	Spy
MacDonald, J.	*The Green Ripper*	Mystery
Mailer	*The Executioner's Song*	Drama
Malamud	*Dubin's Lives*	Drama
Robbins	*Memories of Another Day*	Drama

Sanders	*The Sixth Commandment*	Mystery
Shaw	*The Top of the Hill*	Drama–Sex
Stewart, M.	*The Last Enchantment*	Adventure–Historical Novel
Straub	*Ghost Story*	Horror
Styron	*Sophie's Choice*	Drama–War
Trevanian	*Shibumi*	Spy
Van Slyke	*A Necessary Woman*	Drama
Vonnegut	*Jailbird*	Drama–American Politics
West, M.	*Proteus*	International Intrigue

1980

Buckley	*Who's on First*	Spy
Caldwell	*Answer as a Man*	Religion–Historical Novel
Collins and Lapierre	*The Fifth Horseman*	International Intrigue
de Borch- grave and Moss	*The Spike*	International Intrigue
Doctorow	*Loon Lake*	Drama
Follett	*The Key to Rebecca*	War–Spy
Freeman	*Come Pour the Wine*	Drama
French	*The Bleeding Heart*	Drama–Sex
Howatch	*Sins of the Father*	Saga
James	*Innocent Blood*	Suspense
Jong	*Fanny*	Sex–Historical Novel
King	*Firestarter*	Suspense–Science Fiction
Krantz	*Princess Daisy*	Glamour–Sex
le Carre	*Smiley's People*	Spy
Ludlum	*The Bourne Identity*	Spy
Lustbader, van	*The Ninja*	Mystery–Sex
Michener	*The Covenant*	Saga–Historical Novel
Plain	*Random Winds*	Saga
Sheldon	*Rage of Angels*	Drama–Sex
Stone	*The Origin*	Historical Novel
Tolkien	*Unfinished Tales*	Short Stories–Science Fiction
Van Slyke	*No Love Lost*	Saga
Williams	*Masquerade*	Mystery

1981

Clavell	*Noble House*	Drama–Spy
Cook	*Brain*	Mystery
Erdman	*The Last Days of America*	International Intrigue
Fast	*The Legacy*	Saga
Francis	*Reflex*	Mystery
Freeman	*No Time for Tears*	Saga
Herbert	*God Emperor of Dune*	Science Fiction
Irving	*The Hotel New Hampshire*	Drama
King	*Cujo*	Horror
Lord	*Spring Moon*	Historical Novel

McCullough	*An Indecent Obsession*	Drama–War
MacDonald, J.	*Free Fall in Crimson*	Mystery
Robbins	*Goodbye, Janette*	Drama–Glamour–Sex
Sanders	*The Third Deadly Sin*	Mystery–Sex
Smith	*Gorky Park*	Mystery
Steel	*Remembrance*	Saga
Stewart, F.	*Century*	Saga–Historical Novel
Updike	*Rabbit Is Rich*	Drama
Vidal	*Creation*	Historical Novel
Wambaugh	*The Glitter Dome*	Mystery–Glamour–Sex
West, M.	*The Clowns of God*	Religion

1982

Archer	*The Prodigal Daughter*	American Politics
Asimov	*Foundation's Edge*	Science Fiction
Auel	*The Valley of Horses*	Adventure–Historical Novel
Bellow	*The Dean's December*	Drama
Buckley	*Marco Polo, if You Can*	Spy
Clarke	*2010: Odyssey Two*	Science Fiction
Donaldson	*The One Tree*	Science Fiction
Follett	*The Man from St. Petersburg*	Spy–Historical Novel
Francis	*Twice Shy*	Suspense
Gardner, J. E.	*For Special Services*	Spy
Greeley	*Thy Brother's Wife*	Religion–American Politics– Sex
Jakes	*North and South*	War–Historical Novel
King	*Different Seasons*	Short Stories–Horror– Science Fiction
Kotzwinkle	*E.T.: The Extraterrestrial*	Science Fiction
Krantz	*Mistral's Daughter*	Saga–Glamour–Sex
Ludlum	*The Parsifal Mosaic*	Spy
MacDonald, J.	*Cinnamon Skin*	Mystery
Michener	*Space*	Drama–American Politics
Myrer	*A Green Desire*	Drama
Plain	*Eden Burning*	Saga
Sanders	*The Case of Lucy Bending*	Drama–Sex
Sheldon	*Master of the Game*	Drama–Sex
Thompson	*Celebrity*	Drama–Glamour

1983

Adler and Chastain	*Who Killed the Robins Family?*	Mystery
Asimov	*The Robots of Dawn*	Science Fiction Mystery
Bradford, B.	*Voice of the Heart*	Glamour
Collins, J.	*Hollywood Wives*	Glamour–Sex
Cook	*Godplayer*	Mystery
Donaldson	*White Gold Wielder*	Science Fiction
Eco	*The Name of the Rose*	Religion–Mystery–Historical Novel
Ephron	*Heartburn*	Drama

King	*Christine*	Horror
King	*Pet Sematary*	Horror
L'Amour	*The Lonesome Gods*	Western–Historical Novel
le Carre	*The Little Drummer Girl*	Spy
Michener	*Poland*	Saga–Historical Novel
Rossner	*August*	Drama
Sanders	*The Seduction of Peter S.*	Drama–Sex
Steel	*Changes*	Glamour
Stewart, M.	*The Wicked Day*	Adventure–Historical Novel
Trevanian	*The Summer of Katya*	Historical Novel
Vinge	*Return of the Jedi*	Juvenile–Science Fiction
Wambaugh	*The Delta Star*	Mystery

1984

Adams, D.	*So Long, and Thanks for All the Fish*	Science Fiction
Archer	*First among Equals*	Drama
Buckley	*The Story of Henri Tod*	Spy
Clancy	*The Hunt for Red October*	International Intrigue
Cussler	*Deep Six*	American Politics–International Intrigue
Deighton	*Berlin Game*	Spy
Forsyth	*The Fourth Protocol*	Spy
Greeley	*Lord of the Dance*	Religion–Sex
Hailey	*Strong Medicine*	Drama
Herbert	*Heretics of Dune*	Science Fiction
Hoffman	*Nutcracker*	Juvenile
Isaacs	*Almost Paradise*	Drama
Jakes	*Love and War*	War–Historical Novel
King (Bachman)	*Thinner*	Horror
King and Straub	*The Talisman*	Horror–Science Fiction
L'Amour	*The Walking Drum*	Adventure–Historical Novel
Ludlum	*The Aquitaine Progression*	International Intrigue
Puzo	*The Sicilian*	Adventure
Rivers	*The Life and Hard Times of Heidi Abromowitz*	Drama–Sex
Santmyer	*"... And Ladies of the Club"*	Saga–Historical Novel
Seuss	*The Butter Battle Book*	War–Juvenile
Steel	*Full Circle*	Drama
Uris	*The Haj*	International Intrigue
Vidal	*Lincoln*	American Politics–Historical Novel

1985

Leonard	*Glitz*	Suspense–Sex
Sheldon	*If Tomorrow Comes*	Drama
Steel	*Family Album*	Drama–Glamour

Latest Books

These books were published after the 468 previously listed (see chapter 6).

1985

Auel	*The Mammoth Hunters*	Adventure–Historical Novel
Collins, J.	*Lucky*	Glamour–Sex
Dunne	*The Two Mrs. Grenvilles*	Glamour–Mystery
Hyde	*The Red Fox*	International Intrigue
Irving	*The Cider House Rules*	Drama
Keillor	*Lake Wobegon Days*	Drama
King	*Skeleton Crew*	Short Stories–Horror– Science Fiction
L'Amour	*Jubal Sackett*	Western–Saga–Historical Novel
McMurtry	*Lonesome Dove*	Western–Historical Novel
Sagan	*Contact*	Science Fiction
Sanders	*The Fourth Deadly Sin*	Mystery
Steel	*Secrets*	Glamour
Tyler	*The Accidental Tourist*	Drama
Vonnegut	*Galápagos*	Science Fiction

1986

Clancy	*Red Storm Rising*	War
Clavell	*Whirlwind*	International Intrigue
Cussler	*Cyclops*	International Intrigue
Follett	*Lie Down with Lions*	Spy
Francis	*Break In*	Suspense
King	*It*	Horror
Krantz	*I'll Take Manhattan*	Saga–Sex
L'Amour	*Last of the Breed*	International Intrigue– Adventure
le Carré	*A Perfect Spy*	Spy
Ludlum	*The Bourne Supremacy*	Spy
Steel	*Wanderlust*	Drama–War

A NOTE ON SOURCES

The main source for this book is the best sellers themselves, as listed each year in the *World Almanac* from the top hardcover sales. Many of the books are still on the bookstore shelves in paperback form, and the rest are easily found in libraries. We have used the hardcover edition (the first U.S. edition) as the source for publication information and the spelling of the author's name. Where the spelling is inconsistent across several books, we have followed the *Contemporary Authors* series listing. Where two publishers are listed on the copyright page, we have taken the more inclusive of the two: i.e., the parent firm and not the division.

The *World Almanac* takes its list from the *Publishers Weekly* annual report of the top fiction hardcovers in U.S. sales in bookstores. Book-club sales are not included. *Publishers Weekly* lists the books that cluster together within clear groupings (such as 150,000 or 200,000 copies sold); thus the number of books listed will vary slightly from year to year.

Information about the authors has been gained from a number of sources: chiefly, the *Contemporary Authors* series (Detroit: Gale Research, various years); *World Authors* (New York: H. Wilson, various years); *Who's Who in America* (Wilmette, Ill.: Macmillan); *The Oxford Companion to American Literature*, ed. James Hart, 5th ed. (New York: Oxford University Press, 1983); and, where appropriate, *Variety's Who's Who in Show Business*, ed. Mike Kaplan (New York: Garland, 1983). *Contemporary Authors* is the most inclusive of the sources and provides a cumulative index to all the authors, with dates of birth and death, and the volume number where the entry can be found.

No standard source exists for classifications by genre and category, as one library scholar notes with dismay (see Betty Rosenberg, *Genreflecting*, 2d ed., Littleton, Colo.: Libraries Unlimited, 1986). Bookstores might place their mysteries under Fiction or under Mysteries, or even under Romance. One major chain includes the very unromantic books by Caldwell and Robbins under Romance, too. The authors themselves disagree as to where the boundaries should be drawn. Isaac Asimov and Brian Aldiss define science fiction differently, and Eric Ambler found, by his own definition, that he had never written a spy story in his life. We have, therefore, developed our own definitions, drawing on our reading in section II of the bibliography below, standard dictionaries, and books on literary terms.

The greatest difficulty of a book of this kind is keeping it up to date. A new book by an author is quickly supplanted by a newer one; authors die; and books turn into movies at a magical rate. We found ourselves developing a morbid interest in the health of some authors born around the turn of the century—in case one died and we had him living with his wife in London! Deaths are up to date through 1988, as of the *Contemporary Authors* listing, volume 122. Books that became movies are current through 1988. Sources are A. G. S. Enser, ed., *Filmed Books and Plays, 1928–1983* (Lexington, 1985), Alvin Marill, *Movies for Television* (New York, 1987) and Leslie Halliwell, *Halliwell's Film Guide*, 6th ed. (Charles Scribner's Sons, 1988), updated from other film and television listings. But since even as we write there are new miniseries in the making, "Books That Became Movies" must be considered a partial list.

Other useful sources will be found in the following bibliography. The books included meet two standards. They are worth reading and they are widely available, either currently in print or at most libraries. Part I lists general books about popular fiction; part II points to books on special categories and genres; and part III lists autobiographies and other writings by the authors.

Readers who want more on the authors should look to the *Contemporary Authors* series, found in the reference rooms of most major libraries. More about the books can be found in the *Book Review Digest* (New York: H. W. Wilson), usually for the year following the book's publication, also in the library reference section. The *Dictionary of Literary Biography* (Detroit: Gale Research, 1978, 1981), vols. 2, 6, and 9, includes both biography and criticism for the most highly regarded American authors.

BIBLIOGRAPHY

I. GENERAL

Aldridge, John. *The American Novel and the Way We Live Now* (New York: Oxford University Press, 1983).
    Literary criticism, with comments on a few of the best-selling authors: Heller, Styron, Lurie, Baldwin, Mailer, Barth, and others.
Boswell, John. *The Awful Truth about Publishing* (New York: Warner, 1986).
    On the difficulties of publishing books and selling them.
Elson, Ruth. *Myths and Mores in American Best Sellers, 1865–1965* (New York: Garland, 1985).
Hackett, Alice. *Eighty Years of Best Sellers* (R. R. Bowker, 1977).
    Lists the books through the mid-1970s, but supplies little other information.
Hart, James, ed. *The Oxford Companion to American Literature*, 5th ed. (New York: Oxford University Press, 1983).
    A standard reference for books of American literature; includes biographies and comments on some of the best-selling authors.
Karl, Frederick. *American Fictions, 1940–1980* (New York: Harper & Row, 1983).
    Literary criticism, with comments on a few of the best-selling authors: Doctorow, Roth, Mailer, Styron, feminist writers, others.
Kelley, Karol. *Models for the Multitudes* (Westport, Conn.: Greenwood Press, 1987).
Long, Elizabeth. *The American Dream and the Popular Novel* (Boston: Routledge & Kegan Paul, 1985).
    An excellent analysis of the American Dream in best sellers from the 1950s to the 1970s.
Polak, Maralyn. *The Writer as Celebrity: Intimate Interviews* (New York: M. Evans, 1986).
    Less here than meets the eye, although a few interesting facts are included.
Prescott, Peter. *Never in Doubt* (New York: Arbor House, 1986).
    One of the few collections of reviews of current popular fiction. Prescott is a book reviewer for *Newsweek*.
Silverman, Al, ed. *The Book of the Month* (Boston: Little, Brown, 1986).
    Includes good interviews with a few of the best-selling authors: Mailer, Puzo, Vonnegut, Vidal, Solzhenitsyn, Doctorow, Percy, Michener, others.
Somer, John, and Barbara Eck Cooper. *American and British Literature, 1945–1975: An Annotated Bibliography* (Lawrence, Kans.: Regents Press of Kansas, 1980).
    For further reading.
Sutherland, John. *Bestsellers: Popular Fiction of the 1970s* (London: Routledge & Kegan Paul, 1981).
    An excellent review of books of the 1970s.
Whiteside, Thomas. *The Blockbuster Complex* (Middleton: Wesleyan University Press, 1980).

Uses examples from only a few best sellers to show how books are promoted and sold.

II. SPECIAL CATEGORIES AND GENRES

Aldiss, Brian. *Trillion Year Spree: The History of Science Fiction* (New York: Atheneum, 1986).
> Comprehensive, through writers of the 1980s.

Asimov, Isaac, ed. *Asimov on Science Fiction* (London: Granada, 1981).
> The author's views on science fiction.

Ball, John, ed. *The Mystery Story* (San Diego: University of California Press, 1976).
> One of the most useful volumes of many on the subject; essays on the amateur detective, the private eye, Gothic mysteries, the great crooks, and much more.

Beckson, Karl, and Arthur Ganz, eds. *Literary Terms* (New York: Farrar, Straus, & Giroux, 1975), rev. ed.
> A standard short reference, alphabetized in dictionary form.

Bourgeau, Art. *The Mystery Lover's Companion* (New York: Crown, 1986).
> A list of 2,500 mysteries alphabetized by author with summaries and ratings.

Cawelti, John. *Adventure, Mystery, and Romance: Formula Stories as Art and Popular Culture* (Chicago: University of Chicago Press, 1976).
> Literary formulas—what they are and how they develop.

———. *The Six-Gun Mystique* (Bowling Green, Ohio: Bowling Green University Press, 1971).
> The western novel; analysis and bibliography.

Cawelti, John, and Bruce Rosenberg. *The Spy Story* (Chicago: University of Chicago Press, 1987).
> Excellent bibliography, including studies of real-life espionage, a listing of major films, and landmarks in the history of the spy story. Also chapters on Ambler, Greene, Fleming, le Carre.

Cornillon, Susan, ed. *Images of Women in Fiction* (Bowling Green, Ohio: Bowling Green University Press, 1972).
> Essays by feminist writers. See especially the introductory essay by Joanna Russ.

Cudden, J. A. *A Dictionary of Literary Terms*, rev. ed. (New York: Penguin, 1982).
> A standard short reference, alphabetized in dictionary form.

Dove, George. *The Police Procedural* (Bowling Green, Ohio: Bowling Green University Press, 1982).
> A short overview of the major types and formulas.

Dulles, Allen, ed. *Great Spy Stories* (Secaucus, N.J.: Castle, 1969).
> Commentary and choices by the former director of the Central Intelligence Agency.

Folsom, James. *The American Western Novel* (New Haven: College & University Press, 1966).

Gilbert, Michael. "The Spy in Fact and Fiction." In Ball, *The Mystery Story*, cited above.
> Worth citing separately.

Harper, Ralph. *The World of the Thriller* (Baltimore: Johns Hopkins University Press, 1974).

Jones, Peter. *War and the Novelist* (Columbia: University of Missouri Press, 1976).
> Vonnegut, Jones, Mailer.

Keating, H. R. F. *Crime and Mystery: The 100 Best Books* (New York: Carroll & Graf, 1987).
> Christie, James, John MacDonald, Ross Macdonald, Uhnak, and Wambaugh make the list.

King, Stephen. *Danse Macabre* (New York: Everest House, 1981).
King is better at writing horror stories than writing about them.

Lovecraft, Howard Phillips. *Supernatural Horror in Literature* (New York: Dover, 1973).
Observations by a classic horror-story writer.

Masters, Anthony. *Literary Agents: The Novelist as Spy* (New York: Basil Blackwell, 1987).
Fleming, le Carre, Deighton.

Merry, Bruce. *Anatomy of the Spy Thriller* (Montreal: Queen's University Press, 1977).
An analysis of the various kinds of spy stories.

Panichas, George, ed. *The Politics of Twentieth-Century Novelists* (New York: Hawthorn, 1971).
Baldwin, Greene, Mailer, Styron.

Pratt, Annis. *Archetypal Patterns in Women's Fiction* (Bloomington: Indiana University Press, 1981).

Roller, Judi. *The Politics of the Feminist Novel* (Westport, Conn.: Greenwood Press, 1986).
French, Jong, Rossner.

Rosenberg, Betty. *Genreflecting: A Guide to Reading Interests in Genre Fiction*, 2d ed. (Littleton, Colo.: Libraries Unlimited, 1986).
Suggested categories and topics for library use.

Ross, Mitchell. *The Literary Politicians* (New York: Doubleday, 1978).
Opinions on Galbraith, Vidal, Mailer, Buckley.

Smith, Myron, Jr. *Cloak and Dagger Fiction: An Annotated Guide to Spy Thrillers*, 2d ed. (Santa Barbara: ABC-Clio, 1982).
Indexes by title and author, guides to pseudonyms, major characters, and espionage organizations, bibliography.

Symons, Julian. *Bloody Murder: A History from the Detective Story to the Crime Novel* (New York: Penguin, 1985).
A very good short overview.

Walsh, Jeffrey. *American War Literature, 1914 to Vietnam* (New York: St. Martins, 1982).

Yanarella, Ernest, and Lee Sigelman, eds. *Political Mythology and Popular Fiction* (Westport, Conn.: Greenwood Press, 1988).
Includes essays on war novels, historical novels, westerns, and children's books. See especially the studies of " . . . *And Ladies of the Club*" and *Watership Down*.

III. The Authors—Autobiographies and Essays

Unless otherwise indicated, the books are autobiographies.

Agnew, Spiro. *Go Quietly . . . Or Else* (New York: Morrow, 1980).
The former vice-president's account of his resignation from office.

Ambler, Eric. *Here Lies Eric Ambler* (New York: Farrar, Straus, and Giroux, 1985).

Asimov, Isaac. *In Memory Yet Green* (New York: Doubleday, 1979).
———. *In Joy Still Felt* (New York: Doubleday, 1980).

Auchincloss, Louis. *A Writer's Capital* (Minneapolis: University of Minnesota Press, 1974).

Baldwin, James, *Notes from a Native Son* (New York: Beacon, 1955).
Essays.
———. *The Fire Next Time* (New York: Dial, 1963).
Essays.

Buck, Pearl. *My Several Worlds* (New York: John Day, 1954).
———. *A Bridge for Passing* (New York: Day, 1962).

Christie, Agatha. *An Autobiography* (New York: Ballantine, 1978).

Crichton, Michael. *Travels* (New York: Knopf, 1988).
du Maurier, Daphne. *Myself When Young: The Shaping of a Writer* (New York: Double-day, 1977).
———. *The "Rebecca" Notebook and Other Memories* (New York: Doubleday, 1980).
Fast, Howard. *The Naked God* (New York: Praeger, 1957).
  His experience with the Communist party.
Fowles, John. *The Aristos: A Self-portrait in Ideas* (Boston: Little, Brown, 1964).
  The author's philosophy.
Francis, Dick. *The Sport of Queens*. Orig. published 1957; reissued.
  All about the jockey, not the writer.
Galbraith, John Kenneth. *The Scotch* (New York: Houghton Mifflin, 1964).
———. *Ambassador's Journal: A Personal Account of the Kennedy Years* (New York: Houghton Mifflin, 1969).
Gann, Ernest. *A Hostage to Fortune* (New York: Knopf, 1978).
Gold, Herbert. *My Last Two Thousand Years* (New York: Random House, 1972).
  An autobiography in the form of a novel.
Goudge, Elizabeth. *Joy of the Snow* (New York: Coward, 1974).
Greeley, Andrew. *Confessions of a Parish Priest* (New York: Pocket, 1987).
Greene, Graham. *A Sort of Life* (New York: Simon & Schuster, 1971).
———. *Ways of Escape* (London: Bodley Head, 1980).
Hayden, Sterling. *The Wanderer* (New York: Knopf, 1963).
Hemingway, Ernest. *A Moveable Feast* (New York: Scribners, 1964).
———. *By-line Ernest Hemingway: Selected Articles and Dispatches of Four Decades*, ed. William White (New York: Scribners, 1967).
Humphrey, William. *Farther Off from Heaven* (New York: Knopf, 1977).
  The first 13 years of the author's life.
Kazan, Elia. *America, America* (New York: Stein & Day, 1962).
———. *Elia Kazan: A Life* (New York: Knopf, 1988).
Keyes, Francis Parkinson. *All Flags Flying* (New York: McGraw, 1972).
McCormack, Thomas, ed. *Afterwords: Novelists on Their Novels* (New York: St. Martins, 1988).
  Auchincloss, Renault, Fowles, Robert Crichton, Ross Macdonald, Mailer.
Nabokov, Vladimir. *Speak Memory* (New York: Putnam, 1966).
Nin, Anaïs. *The Diaries of Anaïs Nin*, 6 vols. (New York: Harcourt, 1966–1981).
O'Hara, John. *An Artist Is His Own Fault*, ed. Matthew Bruccoli (Carbondale: Southern Illinois University Press, 1977).
  Essays and other writings.
Plath, Sylvia. *Letters Home: Correspondence, 1950–63*, ed. Aurelia Schober Plath.
  Edited by her mother. Most biographers say that *The Bell Jar* is a more accurate autobiography.
Puzo, Mario. *The Godfather Papers and Other Confessions* (New York: Putnam, 1972).
  Essays.
Roth, Philip. *Reading Myself and Others* (New York: Farrar, Straus, & Giroux, 1975).
  Essays and criticism.
St. Johns, Adela. *Final Verdict* (New York: Doubleday, 1962).
———. *The Honeycomb* (New York: Doubleday, 1969).
Styron, William. *Conversations with William Styron* (Jackson University Press of Mississippi, 1985), ed. James West III.
  Interviews with the author and others.
Uhnak, Dorothy. *Policewoman: A Young Woman's Initiation into the Realities of Justice* (New York: Simon & Schuster, 1964).
Vidal, Gore. *Matters of Fact and Fiction: Essays, 1973–76* (New York: Random House, 1977).
  Collected essays.

Vidal, Gore. *Views from a Window: Conversations with Gore Vidal* (New York: Lyle Stuart, 1980).
  Comments by the author on diverse subjects.
West, Jessamyn. *To See the Dream* (New York: Harcourt, 1957). *Hide and Seek* (New York: Harcourt, 1973). *The Woman Said Yes* (New York: Harcourt, 1976).
Wiesel, Elie. *Night*.
  The author as a young boy during the Holocaust.

INDEX *

Academy Awards, 224
The Accidental Tourist, 220
Adams, Douglas, *14*, 125, 130, 214, 225
Adams, Richard, *15*, 146, 171–72
Ada or Ardor, 84, 163
Adler, Bill, *15*, 152, 227
Adventure, 138, 147, 185; defined, 140
The Adventurers, 92, 150, 162, 163
An Affair of Honor, 122
Agent in Place, 78, 150
Agnew, Spiro, 8, *16*, 128, 130, 132, 133, 157
Airport, 54
Airs Above the Ground, 103
Alger, Horatio, 128, 191, 193, 194, 207. *See also* Immigrants; Rags to Riches
All in the Family, 10, *85*, 157
All the Little Live Things, 102
Almost Paradise, 61
The Ambassador, 119, 158
Ambler, Eric, *16*, 124, 129, 148, 149, 150, 172, 174, 225
American Book Award. *See* National Book Award
An American Dream, 79, 132, 184, 200
American Indians, 4, 32, 58, 70, 88, 118
American politics, 6, 8, 10, 133, 138, 141, 142, 143, 144, 160, 179, 209, 210; defined, 140, 154–57; novels listed, 156–57
"... *And Ladies of the Club,*" 97, 126, 147, 154, 214
And Other Stories, 5, 86
The Andromeda Strain, 32, 214
Answer as a Man, 27, 146, 160, 174
The Antagonists, 48, 146, 158, 167
The Aquitaine Progression, 9, *74*, 150, 172
Archer, Jeffrey, 8, *16*, 130, 133, 157, 186, 194, 214
Armageddon, 111, 158
Arnold, Elliot, *17*, 158
The Arrangement, 65, 129, 132, 183, 184, 199
Arthurian legend, 48, 103, 104, 120, 139, 145, 175
Ashe, Penelope, *17*, 163

Asimov, Isaac, 4, *18*, 127, 128, 135, 141, 143, 152, 227
The Assassins, 65, 158
Auchincloss, Louis, 4, 10, *18*, 128, 130, 186, 194, 225, 227
Auel, Jean, *19*, 146, 166, 215
August, 93, 207
August 1914, 4, *101*, 157, 158
Authors: diversity, 4, 130, 209; women, 4, 130, 143, 144, 209; attitudes, 5, 6; research by, 7; black, 20, 130; age, 125–26, 209; birthplaces, 126–27; as elite, 126, 130, 209; education and experience, 127–30, 131, 209; as celebrities, 129–31, 133, 161; autobiography in novels, 131–33; British, 131, 143, 144; on writing, 134–36, 145; major American novelists, 224–25; in show business, 255–56

Bach, Richard, *19*, 130, 132, 141, 160
Bachman, Richard. *See* King, Stephen
Baldwin, James, *20*, 128, 130, 132, 174, 225
Barth, John, *20*, 131, 224, 225
Bear Island, 79, 153
Bech: A Book, 110
Becker, Stephen, *21*, 133
A Beggar in Jerusalem, 121, 160
Beggarman, Thief, 99, 154
Behn, Noel, *21*, 133, 149, 225
The Bell Jar, 88, 131, 206
Bellow, Saul, 3, *21*, 183, 214, 223, 224, 225
Benchley, Peter, *22*, 132
Berlin Game, 35, 149
The Betsy, 92, 163
The Billion Dollar Brain, 35, 149
The Billion Dollar Sure Thing, 41, 131, 150
The Birds Fall Down, 120, 150
The Black Marble, 117, 153
Blacks: as authors, 20, 130; as heroes, 173–74; as other characters, 174. *See also* Baldwin, James
Black Sunday, 55, 150
Blatty, William, *22*, 160, 224, 225

---

*The main listings for authors and books are printed in italic type.

The Bleeding Heart, 47, 164, 184
Bloodline, 99
The Blue Knight, 117, 169
Blue Skies, No Candy, 52, 162, 164, 184
Bond, James, 39, 42, 43, 133, 148, 168, 169, 178, 187. *See also* Fleming, Ian; Gardner, J. E.; Heroes; Spy Novels
A Book of Common Prayer, 36
The Book of Merlin, 120, 147, 159
Bookstores, 2, 11, 13, 214–15, 245
The Bourne Identity, 74, 150, 212
The Bourne Supremacy, 212, *218*
The Boys from Brazil, 72, 150, 170
Bradford, Barbara, *23,* 128, 162, 214
Bradford, Richard, *23,* 225
Brain, 9, 31, 152
Breakfast of Champions, 115
Break In, 217
Breslin, Jimmy, *23*
Bright Flows the River, 26, 184, 199, 207
Bristow, Gwen, *24,* 146
Buck, Pearl, *24,* 131, 222, 223, 225, 227
Buckley, William F., Jr., *9, 25,* 124, 133 149, 168, 169, 225
Bullet Park, 27, 198, 199, 200, 206
Burr, 6, *113,* 147, 157, 174
The Butter Battle Book, 7, *98,* 159

Caldwell, (Janet) Taylor, *25,* 133, 144, 146, 154, 155, 157, 160, 174, 192, 193, 203, 206, 222
Calico Palace, 24, 145, 146
The Camerons, 33, 146
The Candlesticks and the Cross, 100, 147, 154, 176
Candy, 102, 163
The Canfield Decision, 8, *16,* 157
Capable of Honor, 38, 157, 174
The Captain, 34, 158
Captains and the Kings, 10, *26,* 146, 154, 157, 192, 193, 203, 206
Caravan to Vaccares, 79, 150
The Case of Lucy Bending, 96, 164
Cashelmara, 60, 146, 154
Cassill, R. V. (Ronald Verlin), *27,* 163, 225, 227
Categories. *See* Genres, Topics
Celebrity, 107, 162
Centennial, 82, 147, 167
Century, 103, 147, 154, 193, 207
Ceremony of the Innocent, 26, 146, 157, 193, 203
The Chancellor Manuscript, 73
Changes, 102, 162
Characters, 2, 3, 6, 9, 211; multiple, 153, 167, 185–87, 188, 210, 212, 213; ordinary people, 181–85, 186. *See also* Heroes; Heroines; Enemies; Villains
Chastain, Thomas, *15,* 158
Cheever, John, *27,* 124, 128, 129, 141, 184, 198, 199, 200, 207, 223, 224, 225

Chesapeake, 82, 147, 154, 193, 207
The Child from the Sea, 51, 146
Children's books (juvenile), 7, *58, 98,* 114, 138, 140, 141, 142
The Choirboys, 117
The Chosen, 89, 160
Christie, Agatha, 1, 9, *28,* 128, 130, 133, 134, 144, 149, 151, 152, 175, 203, 214, 224, 225, 227
Christine, 67
Christy, 80, 147, 160
The Cider House Rules, 217
Cinnamon Skin, 77, 153
Circus, 79, 150
Clancy, Tom, *29,* 131, 150, 156, 167, 214, 216
Clarke, Arthur Charles, *29,* 141
Class Reunion, 62, 164, 184, 185, 207
Clavell, James, *29,* 146, 149, 207, 213, 216, 224, 225
Cleland, John, 4
The Clowns of God, 119, 160, 161
Collins, Jackie, 9, *30,* 161, 162, 164, 212, 216, 225
Collins, Larry, *31,* 150
Columbella, 121
Coma, 9, *31,* 152, 175
The Comedians, 52
Come Nineveh Come Tyre, 38, 157
Come Pour the Wine, 46, 184, 207
Condominium, 76
The Confessions of Nat Turner, 3, *106,* 147, 173, 223. *See also* Blacks
Congressional Medal of Honor, 224
Contact, 213, *220*
Cook, Robin, 9, *31,* 128, 129, 131, 132, 152, 186, 203
The Coup, 111
Couples, 110, 163, 200
The Covenant, 82, 147, 154
A Covenant with Death, 21
The Crash of '79, 41, 150
Craven, Margaret, *32,* 160
Creation, 114, 147
Crichton, Michael, 7 *32,* 124, 125, 128, 143, 146, 203, 214, 225, 227
Crichton, Robert, *33,* 146, 158
Critics, 2, 11, 28, 76, 105. *See also* Reviewers
Crowned Heads, 110, 162
The Crystal Cave, 104, 147
Cujo, 67, 177
Curtain, 28, 151, 152
Cussler, Clive, *99,* 131, 132, 150, 156, 157, 180, 212, 216
Cyclops, 213, *216*

Daniel Martin, 45
Dark Horse, 8, *68,* 157
Davis, Gwen, *33,* 162, 163, 201, 225
The Day of the Jackal, 8, *44,* 150
The Dead Zone, 67, 173

The Dean's December, 22
de Borchgrave, Arnaud, *34*, 150, 156
The Deep, 22, 179
Deep Six, 33, 150, 155, 180
de Hartog, Ian, *34*, 127, 132, 158, 224, 225, 227
Deighton, Len, *34*, 148, 149, 152, 157
Delderfield, R. F., *35*, 146, 154, 208, 214
Deliverance, 36, 205
Delta of Venus: Erotica, 84, 164
The Delta Star, 118, 153
The Detective, 108, 153
The Devil's Alternative, 44, 150
Dickey, James, *36*, 205, 214
Didion, Joan, *36*, 225
Different Seasons, 67
Doctor Cobb's Game, 27, 163
Doctorow, E. L., *36*, 136, 145, 146, 174, 201–202, 224, 225
The Dogs of War, 44, 150
Dolores, 107, 162, 164
Donaldson, Stephen, *37*, 130, 176
Don't Stop the Carnival, 123
The Double Image, 77, 149, 150
Drama, 138, 142–44; defined, 140
The Dreadful Lemon Sky, 76, 153
A Dream of Kings, 87
Dreams Die First, 93, 164, 207
The Drifters, 82
Drury, Allen, *3, 5, 6, 8, 37*, 143, 155, 156, 157, 174, 203, 223
Dubin's Lives, 80, 183, 184
du Maurier, Daphne, *38*, 146, 152, 224
Dunne, Dominick, *219*
Durrell, Lawrence, *39*, 131, 227
Dynasty, 40, 154

The Eagle Has Landed, 86, 158, 159
The Ebony Tower, 45
Eco, Umberto, *1, 39*, 128, 134, 146, 152, 159, 160, 161
Eden, Dorothy, *40*, 146
Eden Burning, 88, 154
1876, 114, 145, 147, 157
The Eighth Day, 122, 132, 147, 154, 223
Elegant, Robert, *40*, 154
The Embezzler, 2, 19
Emmy Awards, 224
The Empty Copper Sea, 76, 153
Enemies, 13, 166, 167, 171, 173, 180–81, 188, 203, 210, 212, 213, 215; as spies, 148–50. *See also* Villains; Heroes; Heroines
Ephron, Nora, *40*, 182
Erdman, Paul, 10, *41*, 128, 131, 150, 194, 203
The Establishment, 42, 140, 154, 207
E.T.: The Extraterrestrial, 6, 7, 69, 211
Evening in Byzantium, 99, 162, 184, 199, 206
Evergreen, 88, 154, 193, 194, 207
Except for Me and Thee, 118, 147, 167
The Executioner's Song, 3, 80, 223

The Exhibitionist, 107, 162, 163
The Exorcist, 23, 159, 160, 170, 204
The Explorer, 66
Eye of the Needle, 43, 149, 159

Facing the Lions, 121, 155, 157
Fairbairn, Ann, *41*, 173, 228
Falconer, 27, 184
Family Album, 102, 162, 196–97, 198
The Fan Club, 116, 162, 164
Fanny, 4, 64, 146, 164
The Far Pavilions, 65, 146
Fast, Howard, 10, *41*, 139, 146, 154, 191, 194, 214, 225, 226, 227
Fathers, 50, 131, 154, 193
Feminism in Novels, 4, 46, 47, 120, 182, 197. *See also* Women's movement
The Fifth Horseman, 31, 150
Fire from Heaven, 91, 147
Firestarter, 67, 177, 204, 211
First among Equals, 8, 17, 185
The First Circle, 101, 132, 141, 185
The First Deadly Sin, 96, 153
Five Smooth Stones, 41, 173. *See also* Blacks as Heroes
The Fixer, 3, 80, 147, 160, 223
Fleming, Ian, *42*, 131, 133, 144, 149, 168, 178, 214. *See also* Bond, James
The Flight of the Falcon, 38, 152
Follett, Ken, *43*, 133, 146, 149, 159, 186, 216
Fools Die, 90, 200, 207
Force 10 from Navarone, 79, 158, 169
For Special Services, 49, 150
Forsyth, Frederick, *44*, 150, 186
Foundation's Edge, 18
The Fourth Deadly Sin, 212, 218
The Fourth Protocol, 45, 148, 150, 155, 186, 213
Fowles, John, *2, 45*, 143, 145, 146
Francis, Dick, *45*, 128, 131, 132, 152, 172, 212, 217
Free Fall in Crimson, 76, 153, 170
Freeman, Cynthia, *46*, 154, 207, 227
French, Marilyn, *46*, 128, 164, 182
The French Lieutenant's Woman, 45, 145, 146
Full Circle, 102
Full Disclosure, 8, 95, 155, 157
Funeral in Berlin, 35, 149

The Gabriel Hounds, 103
Gainham, Sarah, *47*, 158, 226, 227
Galápagos, 218
Galbraith, John Kenneth, *8, 47*, 128, 131 132, 156, 157, 228
The Gang That Couldn't Shoot Straight, 23
Gann, Ernest, *48*, 131, 146, 158, 226
Gardner, John Champlin, *48*, 126, 128, 141, 142, 225
Gardner, John Edmund, *49*, 131, 133, 150, 226. *See also* Bond, James

The Gemini Contenders, 73, 150
Genres, 12, 141–43, 210, 245; defined, 138–40. *See also* Topics
Ghost Story, 105, 185, 205
Gilden, K. B. (Katya and Bert), *49,* 226
Giles Goat-Boy, 20, 140
Glamour, 7, 9, 138, 141, 142, 143, 144, 185, 201, 209; defined, 140, 161–62; novels listed, 162
The Glitter Dome, 118, 153, 162, 164
Glitz, 4, 71, 164
Godden, Rumer, *49,* 159
God Emperor of Dune, 57
Godey, John, *50,* 227
The Godfather, 90
God Is an Englishman, 35, 146, 154
Godplayer, 9, 32, 152
Gold, Herbert, *50,* 131, 154, 225
Good as Gold, 56, 157
Goodbye, Janette, 93, 162, 164, 193
The Goodbye Look, 11, 77, 153
Gordon, Noah, *50,* 160
Gorky Park, 4, 100, 153, 213
Go to the Widow-Maker, 63, 163, 184, 197
Goudge, Elizabeth, *50,* 146
Gould, Lois, *51,* 163, 182
Grammy Award, 224
Great Lion of God, 26, 146, 160
The Great Train Robbery, 32, 146, 214
The Greek Treasure, 105, 147
Greeley, Andrew, 4, 5, *51,* 131, 132, 134, 157, 159, 160, 161, 163, 164
The Green Berets, 83, 158
Green Darkness, 98, 147
A Green Desire, 84, 194, 207
Greene, Gael, *52,* 162, 164
Greene, Graham, 4, 6, *52,* 140, 141, 148, 150, 156, 160, 172, 186, 226
The Green Ripper, 76, 153, 171
Griffin, Gwyn, *53,* 131, 158, 186

Haber, Joyce, *53,* 161, 162, 164
Hackett, General John, *53,* 131, 159
Hailey, Arthur, 7, 9, *54,* 141, 174, 194, 199, 206, 222, 226
The Haj, 112, 151
Hanta Yo, 4, 58, 146, 154
Harlequin, 119, 151
Harris, Thomas, *55,* 150
Harvest Home, 2, 109, 205
Hawley, Cameron, *55,* 226
Hayden, Sterling, *55,* 146, 161, 226
Heartburn, 40, 161, 181, 182, 184, 197, 207
Heaven Help Us!, 107, 160
Heller, Joseph, *56,* 131, 157, 199, 200, 225
Hemingway, Ernest, *56,* 158, 222, 223, 225
Herbert, Frank, *57,* 141
Heretics of Dune, 57
Heroes, 8, 10, 13, 148, 166, 167–75, 184, 186, 187, 198, 210–212, 215; in mysteries, 152;

in American politics, 155, 156; in religion, 160; black characters, 173–74, 210; in history, 174–75
Heroines, 3, 4, 13, 161, 166, 167, 175–77, 186, 187, 210, 213; as ordinary people, 182, 183
Hersey, John, *57,* 131, 223, 225
Herzog, 21, 183, 184
Higgins, Jack. *See* Patterson, Harry
Hill, Ruth Beebe, 4, *58,* 146, 154
Historical Novels, 4, 7, 11, 12, 138, 139, 141–44, 160, 207, 209, 210, 212; defined, 6, 139, 145–47; listed, 146–47
Hoffenberg, Mason, *101,* 163
Hoffman, E.T.A., *58,* 125
The Holcroft Covenant, 5, 9, 73, 150
The Hollow Hills, 104, 147
Hollywood Wives, 31, 161, 162, 164, 185, 201
Holmes, Sherlock, 81, 151, 153
Holt, Victoria, 3, *58,* 128, 144, 146, 152, 182, 207, 222, 228
The Honey Badger, 94, 163, 184, 197
The Honorary Consul, 52, 150, 159, 160
The Honourable Schoolboy, 71, 150
Horror, 3, 6, 10, 138, 141–44, 159, 185, 202–206; defined, 139, 211
The Horse Knows the Way, 85
Hotel, 54, 174
The Hotel New Hampshire, 61
The House of a Thousand Lanterns, 60
The House on the Strand, 39, 146
Howatch, Susan, *60,* 146, 154, 194
How to Save Your Own Life, 64, 164, 181, 184, 197, 207
The Human Factor, 52, 140, 148, 150, 186
Humboldt's Gift, 3, 22, 223
Humphrey, William, *61,* 126, 154, 225
The Hunt for Red October, 29, 150, 156, 167
The Hurricane Years, 55, 184
Hurry Sundown, 49, 140, 174. *See also* Blacks
Hyde, Anthony, 212, 213, *219*

I Heard the Owl Call My Name, 32, 160
If Tomorrow Comes, 100
I'll Take Manhattan, 217
Illusions: The Adventures of a Reluctant Messiah, 20, 160, 207
The Immigrants, 42, 146, 154, 191, 193, 194, 207
Immigrants, 10, 153, 190–94, 197, 198, 201, 206, 208, 210, 211; novels listed, 193. *See also* Rags to Riches; Sagas
An Indecent Obsession, 75, 159
Indians. *See* American Indians
The Inheritors, 92, 162, 163, 206, 207
Innocent Blood, 63, 186, 214
The Instrument, 85, 187, 200
International Conspiracies, 3, 9
International Intrigue (novels of), 6, 138, 141–44, 159, 212, 213; defined, 140, 147–

International Intrigue—*continued*
51; listed, 150–51. *See also* International
Conspiracies; Spy Novels
In the Beginning, 89, 160
In This House of Brede, 50, 160, 184
Irving, John (Winslow), 61, 128, 217, 225
Isaacs, Susan, 61, 226
Islands in the Stream, 56, 158
It, 213, 217
I, the King, 66, 146

Jackson, Charles, 62, 163, 214, 226
Jaffe, Rona, 62, 135
Jailbird, 115, 157
Jakes, John, 62, 146, 157, 159, 228
James, P. D. (Phyllis Dorothy), 63, 128, 131,
134, 144, 186, 214
Jaws, 22
Jenkins, Dan, 63, 163
Jonathan Livingston Seagull, 6, 20, 141, 196,
206
Jones, James, 63, 124, 133, 159, 163, 224, 225
Jong, Erica, 4, 64, 143, 146, 164, 225
Jubal Sackett, 217
Julian, 113, 147, 174

Kane and Abel, 10, 17, 193, 194, 207
Kaufman, Bel, 64
Kaye, M. M. (Mary Margaret), 64, 146
Kazan, Elia, 65, 124, 127, 129, 132, 157, 158,
161, 183, 224, 226
Keillor, Garrison, 213, 219
Kemelman, Harry, 65, 152, 159, 160
Keyes, Francis Parkinson, 66, 146
The Key to Rebecca, 43, 150, 159
King, Stephen, 1, 3, 66, 125, 129, 136, 143,
173, 179, 188, 204, 205, 209, 210, 212, 213,
214, 217, 222, 226, 228
The King of the Castle, 59, 182
Knebel, Fletcher, 8, 68, 134, 143, 156, 157,
174
Kotzwinkle, William, 69, 130, 214
Krantz, Judith, 69, 130, 154, 162, 164, 194,
212, 217
The Kremlin Letter, 21, 149

Lady, 109
Lake Wobegon Days, 213, 219
L'Amour, Louis, 11, 69, 125, 128, 130, 131,
143, 146, 192, 212, 214, 217, 224, 228
Lapierre, Dominique, 31
The Last Days of America, 8, 41, 150
The Last Enchantment, 104, 147
Last of the Breed, 212, 213, 217
Law and Order, 110, 154
le Carre, John, 70, 131, 133, 148, 149, 150,
155, 171, 176, 212, 214, 218, 222
The Legacy, 42, 154, 207
The Legend of the Seventh Virgin, 59
Leonard, Elmore, 4, 5, 71, 164, 188, 226
The Levanter, 16, 150

Levin, Ira, 71, 150, 226
Lie Down with Lions, 213, 216
The Life and Hard Times of Heidi Abronowitz,
92, 164
Lincoln, 114, 147, 157, 188
The Little Drummer Girl, 71, 148, 150, 176
The Lockwood Concern, 85, 154
Lofts, Norah, 72, 146, 228
The Lonely Lady, 93, 162, 164, 197
Long, Elizabeth, 206–207
Lonesome Dove, 220
The Lonesome Gods, 11, 70, 146, 192, 193
Looking for Mr. Goodbar, 93, 164
The Looking Glass War, 70, 150
Loon Lake, 37
Lord, Bette Bao, 72, 127, 132, 147
Lord of the Dance, 51, 161, 164, 177
The Lord Won't Mind, 81, 163, 206
Losing Battles, 118
The Lost Queen, 72, 145, 146
Love and War, 62, 146, 159
Love in the Ruins, 87, 159, 160
The Love Machine, 106, 162, 163
Love Story, 97, 141
Lucky, 216
Ludlum, Robert, 3, 5, 9, 72, 133, 149, 150,
161, 172, 203, 209, 212, 214, 218, 222,
226, 228
Lurie, Alison, 74, 182, 223, 225
Lustbader, Eric van, 74, 153, 164

McClary, Jane, 75, 128
McCullough, Colleen, 4, 75, 131, 154, 159
MacDonald, John D., 9, 76, 135, 143, 153,
170, 172, 214, 222
Macdonald, Ross, 11, 77, 129, 153, 225, 228
MacInnes, Helen, 77, 133, 143, 144, 149, 150,
222
MacLean, Alistair, 78, 131, 150, 153, 158,
169, 222
McMurtry, Larry, 220, 223
Mailer, Norman, 3, 79, 124, 132, 200, 223,
225
Malamud, Bernard, 3, 80, 147, 160, 183, 223,
224, 225
The Mammoth Hunters, 213, 215
The Man, 116, 133, 155, 156, 160, 174
The Man from St. Petersburg, 44, 146, 148, 150,
186
The Man with the Golden Gun, 43, 149, 168,
169, 178
Marco Polo, if You Can, 25, 149, 169
Marple, Miss Jane (character), 28, 29, 133,
151, 152, 175, 176, 177, 187. *See also* Her-
oines; Mysteries
Marshall, Catherine, 80, 147, 160
The Mask of Apollo, 91, 147
Masquerade, 123, 129, 167
The Massacre at Fall Creek, 118, 147
Master of the Game, 100, 164
The Matarese Circle, 5, 73, 150

The Matlock Paper, 73, 203
Memories of Another Day, 93
Menfreya in the Morning, 59
Merrick, Gordon, *81,* 163, 226
Message from Málaga, 78, 150
Meyer, Nicholas, *81,* 147, 153, 226
Michener, James, 4, 6, *81,* 124, 128, 145, 147, 154, 157, 160, 207, 214, 222, 223, 224, 225, 226
Midler, Bette, *83,* 129, 224, 226
Mr. Sammler's Planet, 21, 223
Mistral's Daughter, 69, 154, 162, 164, 167
The Money-Changers, 54, 138, 194, 199, 206
A Month of Sundays, 111, 159, 160, 164, 184, 195, 206
Moore, Robin, *83,* 133, 158
Moss, Robert, *34,* 156
Mydans, Shelley, *83,* 147, 160, 175
My Name Is Asher Lev, 89, 195, 206
Myra Breckinridge, 3, 113, 163, 197
Myrer, Anton, *84,* 194
Mysteries, 9, 11, 12, 131, 138, 141–44, 159, 160, 172, 175, 207, 209, 210; defined, 139, 151–53; listed, 152–53

Nabokov, Vladimir, *84,* 127, 163, 225
Naked Came the Stranger, 17, 163
The Name of the Rose, 1, 39, 134, 146, 152, 160, 161
National Book Award, 223–24
National Medal for Literature, 224
A Necessary Woman, 112
Nemesis, 28, 152, 175
The New Centurions, 117, 185
New Moon Rising, 90, 147
Nickel Mountain, 48
Nightmares, 7, 10, 202–206, 211, 215. *See also* Horror; Enemies
Night of Camp David, 68, 156
A Night of Watching, 17, 158
Nin, Anaïs, *84,* 127, 128, 163, 164, 225
The Ninja, 74, 153, 164
Nobel Prize, 222–23, 224
Noble House, 30, 149, 207
No Love Lost, 112, 154
North and South, 62, 146, 159
No Time for Tears, 46, 154, 193, 207
Nutcracker, 7, 58, 125

O'Connor, Edwin, *2, 85,* 157, 223
October Light, 48
The Odessa File, 44, 150
O'Hara, John, *5, 85,* 135, 154, 187, 200, 224, 225
Oliver's Story, 97, 207
Once Is Not Enough, 106, 132, 162, 163
The One Tree, 37, 176
On Instructions of My Government, 95, 151, 157
On the Night of the Seventh Moon, 59, 152
An Operational Necessity, 53, 158

The Ordways, 61, 126, 154
The Origin, 105, 147
The Other, 2, 109, 205
Our Gang, 94, 156, 157
Overload, 7, 54

The Parsifal Mosaic, 9, 74, 150
The Partners, 19
Passenger to Frankfurt, 28, 203
The Passions of the Mind, 105, 147
Patterson, Harry, *58, 86,* 133, 158, 159, 186, 228
Pearson, Drew, *3, 86,* 157
Penmarric, 60, 146, 154
Percy, Walker, *87,* 160, 224, 225
A Perfect Spy, 218
The Persian Boy, 91, 147
Petrakis, Harry, *87*
Pet Sematary, 67, 205
A Pillar of Iron, 26, 146
The Pirate, 92, 151, 163
A Place in the Country, 47, 158
Plain, Belva, *88,* 154, 194
Plath, Sylvia, *88,* 131, 214, 223, 225
The Plot, 116, 151, 157
Poirot, Hercule (character), 9, 28, 151, 152. *See also* Heroes; Mysteries
Poland, 82, 147, 154
Politics. *See* American Politics
A Portion for Foxes, 75
Portis, Charles, *88,* 147
Portnoy's Complaint, 94, 163, 180
Portraits, 46, 154, 193
Postern of Fate, 28, 149, 203
Potok, Chaim, *7, 89,* 131, 135, 160
Prelude to Terror, 78, 150
Preserve and Protect, 3, 5, 38, 157
Presidential Medal of Freedom, 11, 224
The President's Plane Is Missing, 98, 155, 157
The Pretenders, 33, 162, 163, 201
Price, Eugenia, *89,* 147
The Pride of the Peacock, 60
Princess Daisy, 69, 162, 164
The Prodigal Daughter, 10, 17, 157, 207
The Promise, 89, 160
Promise of Joy, 38, 157
Promotion, *2, 8, 11, 106,* 153, 155, 162, 201, 213
Proteus, 119, 151
Publishers, *2, 11,* 142, 210
Pulitzer Prize, 3, 209, 223
Puppet on a Chain, 79
Puzo, Mario, *90,* 200, 224, 226, 228

QB VII, 111, 132
The Queen's Confession, 59, 146

The Rabbi, 50, 159, 160, 183, 184
Rabbit Is Rich, 3, 111, 184, 207, 223
Rabbit Redux, 110, 206
Rage of Angels, 100, 164, 177

Rags to Riches, 6, 10, 128, 190–193, 206, 207,
    211. *See also* Sagas; Immigrants
Ragtime, 37, 136, 146, 174, 193, 201–202
Random Winds, 88, 154
Raucher, Herman, *90,* 226
The R Document, 117, 155, 157, 160, 179
The Rector of Justin, 2, 19
The Red Fox, 213, 219
Red Sky at Morning, 23
Red Storm Rising, 212, 213, *216*
Reflex, 46, 152, 172
Religion (in novels), 138, 141–42, 144, 162,
    183, 195, 209, 210; defined, 140, 159–61;
    listed, 160–61
Remembrance, 102, 154, 193
Renault, Mary, *91,* 136, 143, 145, 147, 186,
    227
Return of the Jedi, 6, 114, 144
Reviewers, 2, 6, 159, 182. *See also* Critics
The Rhinemann Exchange, 5, 73, 150
The Rich Are Different, 60, 154
Rich Man, Poor Man, 99, 154, 193, 206
Rivers, Joan, *92,* 129, 164, 226, 228
Robbins, Harold, 2, 9, *92,* 128, 131, 133, 150,
    162, 163, 164, 194, 197, 206, 207, 222, 226
The Robots of Dawn, 18, 152
Rosemary's Baby, 71, 204
Rossner, Judith, *93,* 164
Roth, Philip, *94,* 124, 156, 157, 163, 224, 225
Ruark, Robert, *94,* 163

Safire, William, 7, 8, *95,* 131, 132, 133, 157,
    223, 226
Sagan, Carl, 213, *220*
The Saga of Baby Divine, 83, 141
Sagas defined, 6, 139, 153–54; mentioned,
    10, 138, 141–44, 185, 210; novels listed,
    154; American dream in, 190, 194, 198. *See
    also* Immigrants; Rags to Riches
St. Johns, Adela, *95,* 159, 160, 226
The Salamander, 119, 150
Sales: in defining bestsellers, 1, 3, 245; high-
    est, 3; mentioned, 11, 106, 133, 143, 153,
    160, 186, 211, 214; highest for paperback
    rights, 75
Salinger, Pierre, 7, *95,* 131, 132, 133, 151, 157
The Salzburg Connection, 78, 150
Sanders, Lawrence, 5, 6, 9, *96,* 134, 153, 164,
    212, 214, 218, 222
Santmyer, Helen Hooven, *97,* 125, 126, 130,
    147, 154, 214
Satire, 7, 102, 113, 141, 200–201, 202, 212
Saturday the Rabbi Went Hungry, 66, 152, 160
Saving the Queen, 25, 149
Schorr, Todd (illustrator), 83
Science Fiction, 6, 138, 141–44, 159, 207,
    210, 213, 245; defined, 139
Scruples, 69, 162, 164
The Second Deadly Sin, 96, 153
Second Generation, 42, 154, 194, 207
A Second-Hand Life, 62, 163

The Secret of Santa Vittoria, 33, 158
Secrets, 218
The Secret Woman, 59
The Seduction of Peter S., 96, 164
Segal, Erich, *97,* 226
Semi-Tough, 63, 163
The Senator, 3, 87, 155, 157
Sendak, Maurice, *58,* 126
Serling, Robert, *97,* 132, 157
Seton, Anya, *98,* 147
Seuss, Dr. (Theodore Seuss Geisel), *98,* 125,
    157, 159
The Seven Minutes, 116
The Seven-Per-Cent Solution, 81, 147, 153
Sex, 2, 9, 182, 183, 212; stereotyping of best-
    sellers, 3, 209; as topic, 7, 138, 140, 142,
    144; American authors' use of, 131; topic
    defined, 140, 162–64; and religion, 159,
    160; novels listed, 163–64; and American
    dream, 195, 200, 201
The Shadow of the Lynx, 59
Shadow of the Moon, 65, 146
Shardik, 15, 146
Shaw, Irwin, *98,* 154, 161, 162, 206, 225, 226
Sheldon, Sidney, *99,* 133, 162, 164, 194, 224,
    226
Shibumi, 109, 150, 203
The Shining, 67
The Shivering Sands, 59, 152
Shogun, 30, 146
Short Stories, 7, 138, 140, 167, 198, 212; cited
    19, 28, 45, 67, 84–87, 108, 110, 217
The Sicilian, 90
The Silmarillion, 108
Sins of the Father, 60, 154
The Sixth Commandment, 96, 153
Skeleton Crew, 217
Slapstick; or, Lonesome No More!, 115
Slaughterhouse-Five, 115, 140, 158, 205
Sleeping Murder, 29, 152, 187
A Small Town in Germany, 70, 148, 150
Smiley's People, 71, 150, 171
Smith, Martin Cruz, 4, *100,* 153, 214, 228
The Snare of the Hunter, 78, 150
Solomon, Ruth, *100,* 127, 147, 154
So Long, and Thanks for All the Fish, 15
Solzhenitsyn, Alexander, 4, *101,* 132, 141,
    158, 223
Something Happened, 56, 199, 200, 206
Sophie's Choice, 106, 158, 159, 205, 223
The Source, 82, 147, 160
Southern, Terry, *101,* 163, 226, 228
Space, 82, 157
The Spike, 8, 34, 150, 203
Spindrift, 121, 153, 175
Spring Moon, 72, 132, 147
Spy Novels, 6, 8, 9, 11, 131, 138, 141–44, 155,
    172, 209, 210, 213, 243; defined, 147–51;
    listed, 149–50. *See also* International In-
    trigue
The Spy Who Came in from the Cold, 70, 150

SS-GB, 35, 149, 152, 159
Stained Glass, 25, 149
Steel, Danielle, *102*, 131, 142, 154, 162, 196, 212, 213, 214, 218
Stegner, Wallace, *102*, 223, 224, 225
Stewart, Fred Mustard, *103*, 147, 154, 207
Stewart, Mary, *103*, 143, 147, 175, 186, 214, 222
Stone, Irving, 4, *104*, 125, 143, 147, 214
The Stories of John Cheever, 3, 28, 207, 223
Storm Warning, 86, 159, 185
The Story of Henri Tod, 25, 149
A Stranger in the Mirror, 99, 162, 164
Straub, Peter, *105*, 205
Strong Medicine, 55, 141, 177
Styron, William, 3, *105*, 136, 143, 145, 147, 158, 159, 186, 222, 223, 225
Such Good Friends, 2, *51*, 163, 181, 182, 206
Summer of '42, 91, 141
The Summer of Katya, *109*, 147, 157
Sunday the Rabbi Stayed Home, 66, 152, 160
The Sunlight Dialogues, 48, 126
Susann, Jacqueline, 2, 3, 9, 11, *106*, 124, 132, 144, 161, 162, 163, 164, 201, 226
Suspense, 138, 147; defined, 140, 143
Sutton, Henry, *107*, 162, 163, 228

Tai-Pan, 30, 146
The Taking of Pelham One Two Three, 50
Tales of Manhattan, 19
The Talisman, 68, 172, 176, 188
Tarr, Herbert, *107*, 131
Tell Me How Long the Train's Been Gone, 20, 132, 174
Tell No Man, 95, 160
The Terminal Man, 32
Terror. *See* Horror
Testimony of Two Men, 26, 146
Theatre Hall of Fame, 224
Theirs Was the Kingdom, 35, 146, 154
Theophilus North, 122, 132, 206
Thinner, 68
The Third Deadly Sin, 96, 153, 164, 167, 180
The Third World War: August, 1985, 53, 159, 167
This Rough Magic, 103
Thomas, 84, 147, 160, 175
Thompson, Thomas, *107*, 162, 226
The Thorn Birds, 4, 75, 154, 208
Thorp, Roderick, *108*, 153
Those Who Love, 104, 147
The Three Daughters of Madame Liang, 24
The Throne of Saturn, 38, 157, 174
Thy Brother's Wife, 51, 157, 161, 164
The Time Is Noon, 24
Tinker, Tailor, Soldier, Spy, 71, 150
Tolkien, J.R.R., *108*
Tony Awards, 224
Topaz, *111*, 150
Topics: defined, 138–40, 141–43. *See also* Genres

The Top of the Hill, 99, 164, 197, 207
To Serve Them All My Days, 36
The Tower of Babel, *119*, 150, 158
Travels with My Aunt, 52, 138
Trevanian, *109*, 133, 147, 150, 157, 228
Trinity, *112*, 147, 154
Triple, 43, 150
The Triumph, 8, 47, 156, 157
True Grit, 88, 138, 147, 176, 187
Tryon, Thomas, 2, *109*, 161, 162, 205, 226
Tunc, 39
Twice Shy, 46
The Two Mrs. Grenvilles, *219*
2010: Odyssey Two, 29
Tyler, Anne, *220*

Uhnak, Dorothy, *110*, 129, 131, 132, 154
The Underground Man, 77, 153
Under the Eye of the Storm, 57
Unfinished Tales, 108
Updike, John, 3, 5, 6, *110*, 142, 159, 160, 163, 164, 166, 200, 214, 222, 223, 224, 225
Up the Down Staircase, 64
Uris, Leon, 4, *111*, 132, 135, 143, 147, 150, 151, 154, 158, 226
The Users, 53, 162, 164, 201

The Valhalla Exchange, 86, 159
The Valley of Horses, 19, 146, 176, 187
Valley of the Dolls, 3, 11, *106*, 132, 161, 162, 163, 201
Vanished, 68, 155, 157, 174
Van Slyke, Helen, *112*, 154
Vidal, Gore, 3, 6, *113*, 145, 147, 155, 157, 163, 174–75, 188, 213, 214, 222, 225, 226, 228
Villains, 13, 155, 156, 166, 167, 168, 174, 177–81, 187, 210; as spies, 148–50. *See also* Enemies; Heroes; Heroines
The Vines of Yarrabee, 40, 146, 208
Vinge, Joan, *114*, 131, 144
Voice of the Heart, 23, 162
Vonnegut, Kurt, Jr., *115*, 133, 157, 158, 212, 218, 225, 226
Voyage: A Novel of 1896, 56, 146

Waiting for Winter, 85
The Walking Drum, 70, 146
Wallace, Irving, *116*, 133, 151, 156, 157, 160, 162, 164, 214, 222, 226
Wambaugh, Joseph, 4, 7, *117*, 131, 132, 153, 162, 164, 169, 172, 205, 222
Wanderlust, 213, *218*
War (novels of), 6, 7, 133, 138, 141–44, 209, 210, 212, 213; defined, 140, 157–59; listed, 158–59
War and Remembrance, *123*, 154, 159
The War between the Tates, 74, 181, 182, 184
Washington, D.C., *113*, 157
Watership Down, 15, 171–72, 208
The Waves of Night and Other Stories, 87

Welty, Eudora, 5, *118*, 223, 224
West, Jessamyn, *118*, 147, 225
West, Morris, *119*, 133, 150, 151, 158, 160, 161, 222, 228
West, Rebecca, *120*, 150, 214, 226, 227
The West End Horror, *81*, 147, 153
Westerns, 6, 11, 70, 88, 138, 140, 192, 210, 213, 217, 220
Wheels, *54*, 199, 206
When She Was Good, *94*
Where Eagles Dare, *78*, 158
Whirlwind, 213, *216*
Whistle, *63*, 159
White, Terence Hanbury, *120*, 129, 147, 159, 175
White Gold Wielder, *37*, 176
Whitney, Phyllis, *120*, 153
Who Killed the Robins Family?, *15*, 152
Who's on First, *25*, 149

The Wicked Day, *104*, 147
Wicker, Tom, *121*, 157, 228
Wiesel, Elie, *121*, 160, 224
Wilder, Robert, *122*, 226
Wilder, Thornton, *122*, 132, 147, 154, 161, 223, 224, 225, 226
Williams, Kit, *122*, 129
The Winds of War, *123*, 154, 158
Women's movement, 181, 187, 210. *See also* Feminism in Novels
The Women's Room, *46*, 164, 181, 182, 207
The Word, *116*, 160
The World According to Garp, *61*
A World of Profit, *19*, 185
World without End, Amen, *24*
Wouk, Herman, *123*, 133, 154, 158, 159, 223, 226

You Only Live Twice, *43*, 149, 168, 178